APPALACHIAN TRAIL

Thru-Hikers' Companion 2025

APPALACHIAN TRAIL

Thru-Hikers' Companion 2025

The Appalachian Long Distance Hikers Association
Robert "Sparky" Palermo, Editor
John "Dice" LaManna, Assistant Editor
Robert "Sly" Sylvester, Editor Emeritus (2014-2023)

MOUNTAINEERS BOOKS

Dedicated to all the volunteers who make thru-hiking possible

 MOUNTAINEERS BOOKS is dedicated to the exploration, preservation, and enjoyment of outdoor and wilderness areas.

1001 SW Klickitat Way, Suite 201, Seattle, WA 98134
800-553-4453, www.mountaineersbooks.org

Printed in the United States of America
Thirty-second edition, 2025

Design and layout: Mountaineers Books
Cartographer: Robert Sylvester; revisions by Robert "Sparky" Palermo
Cover photograph: *Appalachian Trail, Albert Mountain, North Carolina* (Photo by Janet "Miss Jane" Hensley)
Elevation profiles: Derived from the 2025 Appalachian Trail Data Book and other ATC sources and produced by Mapping Specialists, Fitchburg, WI.

Mountaineers Books titles may be purchased for corporate, educational, or other promotional sales, and our authors are available for a wide range of events. For information on special discounts or booking an author, contact our customer service at 800-553-4453 or mbooks@mountaineersbooks.org.

Join the Appalachian Long Distance Hikers Association to receive a membership copy or PDF of this edition, www.aldha.org.

Printed on FSC®-certified materials

MIX
Paper | Supporting
responsible forestry
FSC
www.fsc.org   FSC® C008955

ISBN (paperback): 978-1-68051-800-9

An independent nonprofit publisher since 1960

Contents

Foreword

Welcome to the thirty-second edition of the *Appalachian Trail Thru-Hikers' Companion*. The 2025 *Companion* is a meticulously compiled collection of trail information gathered by volunteer field editors and ATC staff members who have worked to make this guide accurate and up-to-date. The *Companion* can help you plan your hike and help you navigate the Trail while hiking. While our modern world has embraced technology, this book provides a simpler and more reliable way to navigate. It doesn't need to be recharged, nor will it suddenly fail, leaving one stranded in the middle of the forest.

The tables in this guide include more than 2,080 waypoints that are keyed to the ATC and club maps, as well as the AMC White Mountain trail system. Separate columns show northbound and southbound mileage, distance to the next waypoint, elevation, and a features column that shows towns, road crossings, water sources, and distances to the next shelter.

This book was published shortly after Hurricane Helene inflicted extensive damage to the Trail and towns and roads surrounding it. The region between Davenport Gap, Tennessee, and Southern Virginia experienced the greatest impacts, along with the the trail towns of Hot Springs, North Carolina; Erwin, Tennessee; and Damascus, Virginia. Roads that access the Trail have been closed, and repairs are not scheduled to be completed until 2025 or perhaps beyond. The Trail has significant damage in this region, with significant blowdowns, washouts, and bridge issues.

When planning your hike for 2025, keep this in mind: The Trail will be difficult to hike, and parts may not be open in the spring. Because land management agencies have not fully been able to assess damage, a timeline for repair is unknown. What's more, resupply and town access will likely be limited until roads and damage to the communities are restored. A flip-flop or southbound hike may be the best choice for 2025.

For those who wish to help, please consider volunteering and/or donating to efforts to repair the Trail. Opportunities abound for doing trail work in the impacted areas. Several ATC clubs would love your help, including The Smoky Mountain Hiking Club (smhclub.org), Carolina Mountain Club (carolinamountainclub.org), Tennessee Eastman Hiking & Canoeing Club (tehcc.org) and the Mount Rogers Appalachian Trail Club (mratc.pbworks.com/w/page/8862374/FrontPage). Contact these clubs via their website to find out when and where their trail work will be done.

Hurricane Helene demonstrates that conditions change on the Trail after publication. There also may be something new that has not been pointed out before. The ALDHA welcomes your comments, as well as corrections to maps, trail, shelter, or town descriptions. Please email these to companion@aldha.org.

And to everyone who contributed in some way to the publication of this book, many heartfelt thanks!

 —Robert J "Sparky" Palermo
  AT11, AT17, PCT18, CDT22, 12,000–miler
  Editor

Introduction

The *Thru-Hikers' Companion* is compiled, written, and edited by volunteers of the Appalachian Long Distance Hikers Association (ALDHA) and published by Mountaineers Books, a nonprofit publisher, as a service to those seeking to explore the Trail. It is intended as a logistical guide for those making thru hikes but is also valuable for those taking shorter section-hikes or overnight backpacking trips. The Companion provides details on shelters, water sources, post offices, hostels, campgrounds, lodging, groceries, restaurants, outfitters, and other related services along the Trail. In addition, the Companion offers information of historical significance about places you pass through while hiking the A.T. Unlike commercial guidebooks, this book benefits from the latest information from volunteers who measure, maintain, and manage the Trail and those who hike it regularly. Consider it the "local gossip" from those who live there.

Due to publication deadlines, we cannot guarantee that the information in this book will not change by the time you arrive in an area, despite the efforts of volunteers to acquire the most up-to-date information. Businesses close or change hours, hostels change rates and policies, and the Trail itself is subject to relocation. This edition was produced in the fall of 2024, before the impacts of Hurricane Helene were known.

As you walk, talk to other hikers and read shelter registers. ALDHA's website periodically posts updates at aldha.org/companion-updates. Updates can also be found at appalachiantrail .org/trail-updates.

Inclusion in this book is not an endorsement by ALDHA, but rather a listing of services available and contacted by field editors. Likewise, the businesses listed do not pay for inclusion but are listed because of their proximity to the Trail. Editors are volunteers and members of ALDHA.

Additional copies of the 2025 *Appalachian Trail Thru-Hikers' Companion* are online at aldha.org/companion/online. Members of the Appalachian Long Distance Hikers Association may download a PDF of the entire book for free. Information includes periodic updates, waypoints, and maps to Trailhead parking. It also includes maps to post offices, hostels, and other lodging, the A.T. mailing-label maker, and much more.

On the Trail

REGISTERING FOR YOUR HIKE
The ATC strongly encourages would-be northbound thru-hikers to use its voluntary, online registration system at atcamp.org to help determine your starting date. This site is not a reservation system but it enables you to see how many other hikers are registered for specific start dates and assists in spreading out start times.

GETTING TO THE TRAIL
Section-hikers looking for shuttle services should check the business and individual listings for the area in which they plan to hike. (See the Getting to the Termini chapter for an important note on shuttles.) The public transportation section of the ATC website provides links to information on Trailhead parking.

SAFETY
An important part of your planning is preparation for making your hike safe. Lack of preparation can turn an otherwise enjoyable time into a nightmare. Take the time to study precautions, such as handling adverse weather and preventing injuries. There are many resources available online as well as at ALDHA rucks that are held in January and February every year.

While bear encounters might seem like your main safety concern, less dramatic threats to safety, such as contaminated water, dehydration, and hypothermia, afflict far more hikers—particularly those who are unprepared.

If you are unfamiliar with backcountry travel, ask questions and read and learn about backpacking safely. Learn about dehydration, heat exhaustion, and hypothermia; learn safe ways of fording rivers and purifying water; and learn how to avoid lightning, rabies, and Lyme disease. Before starting an end-to-end hike, take shorter backpacking trips until you feel confident in the backcountry. Finally, information and experience are useless if you forget one thing—common sense. Information on many of these topics can be found on the ALDHA website aldha.org/education, as well as many other websites.

Crime on the A.T.
If you tell friends you are planning a long-distance hike on the A.T., one of the first questions is likely to be, "Aren't you afraid? What will you do to protect yourself?" There are natural dangers in the backcountry, but because of media coverage of rare incidents on the Trail, the first concern is often about the dangers posed by other humans. However, of the three to four million people who use the the Trail annually, violent crimes have occurred at a rate of fewer than two every ten years. Statistically, it is one of the safest areas in the country.

The difference on the A.T. and in any wilderness setting—other than people's expectations—is that you only have yourself and your instincts for protection. That means you must use common sense and your training to avoid potential dangers. There are a few tips you should always keep in mind:

- Eliminate opportunities for theft. Don't bring jewelry. Keep wallets and money on your person rather than in your pack or tent. Leaving a pack unattended at trailheads or shelters is risky, even when it is hidden.
- Leave an itinerary of your trip with family or friends.
- If you use a Trail name, make sure the folks back home know what it is.
- Even with a partner, don't be lulled into a false sense of security. Two or more can also be vulnerable.

It is best not to hike alone but if you choose to, a few additional precautions can help keep you safe:

- Don't tell strangers where you are headed or plan to camp for the night and don't post plans in real time on online journals or blogs.
- If you encounter a suspicious person in camp, consider moving on to another location.
- Avoid camping or staying at shelters that are within a mile of a road crossing.
- Trust your gut. Always.

Note that the ATC and most long-distance hikers strongly discourage the carrying of a gun on the Trail. Guns are restricted (you can carry with all the proper permits but not legally discharge) on national park lands (40 percent of the route) and in many other jurisdictions through which the Trail passes.

Report any crime or harassment immediately to the local police (911) and ask the dispatcher to contact the National Park Service 24-hour communications center at (866) 677-6677. Report incidents using the ATC's incident report form but note that submitting an incident report does not trigger an immediate law enforcement response (appalachiantrail.org/incident). Remember: Facebook, Instagram, and other social media are not 911.

Bears

Black bears live in each of the fourteen Trail states and are particularly common in Georgia, Shenandoah and Great Smoky Mountains National Parks, and north of Shenandoah on into New York. While attacks on humans are rare, a startled bear or a bear that's been conditioned to human food may react aggressively. The best way to avoid an encounter while you are hiking is to make noise by whistling, talking, etc., to give the bear a chance to move away before you get close enough to make it feel threatened. If you encounter a black bear and it does not move away, you should back off and avoid making eye contact. Do not run or "play dead," even if the bear makes a bluff charge. If attacked, fight for all you are worth with anything at hand—rocks, sticks, fists.

The ATC tracks bear encounters along the A.T. to assist partners in the management of the Trail and inform hiker education. Please report bear encounters using the ATC's Bear Encounter Report form at appalachiantrail.org/bears.

Food Storage

Proper food storage is imperative to keep wildlife from becoming attuned. Protecting food from bears is tantamount, but smaller critters, such as squirrels, chipmunks, raccoons, and mice, can easily raid an unprotected food stash and become annoying pests.

New food storage regulations were issued by the US Forest Service (USFS) in 2023 and apply to virtually the whole Trail south of Shenandoah National Park, as well as on the A.T. on national forest lands in Vermont and New Hampshire. Under the new rules A.T. visitors must properly store food, refuse, and scented items. This means storing those items in solid, nonpliable, bear-resistant canisters; in USFS-provided food-storage devices such as lockers, cables, poles, etc.; or properly hanging your food. A.T. visitors must store bear canisters at least 70 adult paces (about 200 feet) from campsites.

Soft-sided food bags like Ursacks or stuff sacks must be hung at least 70 adult paces (about 200 feet) from campsites. Food must be hung a minimum of 6 feet from the tree trunk, 6 feet below the branch, and 12 feet from the ground to the bottom of the food bag. Please note that it may be difficult to find suitable places to hang food on many sections of the Trail.

Do not hang a bear canister except in the Great Smoky Mountains National Park, where hanging food and scented items from the provided cable system is required. There, hang your canister in your pack. Never tie ropes to your canister as this can allow a bear to carry it away.

Never leave food unattended. Your bear canister must always be closed and locked except when you add or remove food and scented items. Storing food in tents and shelters is NOT permitted.

Food-storage regulations are also in place on the A.T. for non-USFS land as well, including in Great Smoky Mountains National Park, Shenandoah National Park, and Appalachian National Scenic Trail National Park Service lands. Visit the ATC website (appalachiantrail.org) for a complete list of food-storage regulations.

The ATC strongly recommends bear canisters as the surest and most flexible way to store your food, cookware, toothpaste, personal-hygiene items, water bottles with drink mixes, and trash along the entire Trail. See Interagency Grizzly Bear Committee–approved storage devices at igbconline. org/programs/bear-resistant-products. If you aren't planning on carrying your own canister, each shelter entry in this guide indicates whether a bear box is available.

A few other tips can reduce your chances of a bear encounter:
- Cook and eat meals at least 70 adult paces (200 feet) away from your tent or shelter so food odors do not linger.
- Never feed bears or leave food behind for them.
- Do not burn food waste or trash; pack out all of these items.
- A bear entering a campsite should be considered predatory. Yelling, making loud noises, and throwing rocks may frighten it away, but be prepared to fight back.

Lyme Disease
In the Northeast, there is a heightened risk for Lyme disease (LD) from April to July and October to November, which coincides with the time frame thru-hikers pass through the states with the highest reported cases of the disease. Cases have been reported in all fourteen Trail states.

LD is a bacterial infection transmitted to humans by the bite of infected blacklegged ticks (formerly called deer ticks). Hikers should watch carefully for flu-like symptoms of LD, which may include fever, headache, chills, and fatigue and a characteristic bulls-eye skin rash—called erythema migrans—at the site of the tick attachment. Hikers showing these symptoms should seek immediate medical attention for treatment. This disease can become more severe if it progresses undetected and undiagnosed.

Steps you can take to prevent LD include using insect repellent with DEET on exposed skin; spraying clothing items with the insecticide permethrin; removing ticks promptly; conducting a daily full-body tick check, including the head, underarms, and groin area; minimizing contact with high grass, brush, and woody shrubs; wearing long pants tucked into your socks; and wearing long sleeves, tucking your shirt into your pants to keep ticks off your torso. "Buddy checks" are often the safest way to find hard-to-detect ticks.

Hunting Seasons
Hunters are rarely an issue for northbound thru-hikers, but southbounders need to be aware of the hunting seasons, which may begin as early as mid-October, as you progress south toward Springer Mountain. Hunting is legal along many parts of the Trail, and ATC's website lists local hunting seasons. Wearing bright ("blaze") orange is a necessity in fall, winter, and spring.

Hitchhiking
Hitchhiking is illegal in certain states. It is your responsibility to know the motor-vehicle law as it applies to hitchhiking where you are hiking to avoid being fined or hitching into worse trouble. Hitchhiking poses the risk of being picked up by an unsafe driver or someone who is personally dangerous. Hitchhiking is prohibited on interstate highways, the Blue Ridge Parkway, and Skyline Drive in Shenandoah National Park. Shuttles are a safer way to travel.

Water
Adequate hydration on the trail is imperative. Dehydration can create many problems for the hiker, including fatigue, headache, disorientation, and poor decision-making. These can lead to poor decisions that can further jeopardize the health of the hiker. Water is readily available on the A.T., but it can require careful planning in drier regions. Be ready to carry two liters of water in

Between Springer Mountain and the entrance to Shenandoah National Park above Waynesboro, VA, and again from the Massachusetts–Vermont line to the New Hampshire–Maine line, the A.T. runs mostly through national forest lands. The U.S. Forest Service offers digital maps of the whole forests for iPhone and Android devices at iTunes and the Android Play Store. Prices range from $1 to $5.

the heat of the summer, and more if you camp where there isn't a nearby water source. Be sure to filter all water found on the trail. Contamination can occur in many ways. Digestive issues caused by parasites in untreated water can easily derail one's hike.

Weather

Weather on trail can change drastically, especially in the springtime, and hikers must be prepared. The Great Smoky Mountains National Park is known as the "Great Soaky Mountains" because of the rainfall in the spring, and getting wet can lead to a significant risk of hypothermia. Like dehydration, hypothermia can also cause a loss of mental awareness that leads to poor decision-making as well as serious health risks. Avoid this situation by having base layers and good rain gear, as well as a set of dry clothes specifically for camp.

Equally dangerous is the hot weather during the heat of summer. Be prepared to take breaks in the shade to wait for the hot afternoon heat to subside. Learn to recognize heat exhaustion and take action immediately. Hydration and electrolytes are your friend in the heat. Also, avoid being on a mountain top during a thunderstorm, especially where there is no tree cover.

TRAIL ETIQUETTE

While hiking may be a freeing experience in that there are not a lot of rules, one does need to consider others while hiking. It is about respect–respect the trail, respect other hikers, respect hostels and lodging facilities, respect shuttle drivers, respect businesses and respect towns. Hiking with this ethos will improve the trail experience for everybody involved. For further information, please go to the Hike in Harmony website at hikeinharmony.com.

THE TEN ESSENTIALS

The Ten Essentials, created by The Mountaineers, strives to answer two basic questions: Can you prevent emergencies and respond positively should one occur (items 1–5)? And can you safely spend a night—or more—outside (items 6–10)? Use this list as a guide and tailor it to the needs of your outing.

1. **Navigation:** The five fundamentals are a map, altimeter, compass, GPS device, and a personal locator beacon or other device to contact emergency first responders.
2. **Headlamp:** Include spare batteries.
3. **Sun protection:** Wear sunglasses, sun-protective clothes, and broad-spectrum sunscreen rated at least SPF 30.
4. **First aid:** Basics include bandages; skin closures; gauze pads and dressings; roller bandage or wrap; tape; antiseptic; blister prevention and treatment supplies; nitrile gloves; tweezers; needle; nonprescription painkillers; anti-inflammatory, anti-diarrheal, and antihistamine tablets; topical antibiotic; and any important personal prescriptions, including an EpiPen if you are allergic to bee or hornet venom.
5. **Knife:** Also consider a multitool, strong tape, some cordage, and gear repair supplies.
6. **Fire:** Carry at least one butane lighter (or waterproof matches) and firestarter, such as chemical heat tabs, cotton balls soaked in petroleum jelly, or commercially–prepared firestarter.
7. **Shelter:** In addition to a rain shell, carry a single-use bivy sack, plastic tube tent, or jumbo plastic trash bag.
8. **Extra food:** For shorter trips a one-day supply is reasonable.
9. **Extra water:** Carry sufficient water and have the skills and tools required to obtain and purify additional water.
10. **Extra clothes:** Pack additional layers needed to survive the night in the worst conditions that your party may realistically encounter.

A NOTE ABOUT SAFETY

Safety is an important concern in all outdoor activities. No guidebook can alert you to every hazard or anticipate the limitations of every reader. Therefore, the descriptions of roads, trails, routes, and natural features in this book are not representations that a particular place or excursion will be safe for your party. When you follow any of the routes described in this book, you assume responsibility for your own safety. Under normal conditions, such excursions require the usual attention to traffic, road and trail conditions, weather, terrain, the capabilities of your party, and other factors. Keeping informed on current conditions and exercising common sense are the keys to a safe, enjoyable outing.   —*Mountaineers Books*

LEAVE NO TRACE

With the millions who enjoy this place each year, the chances are great that any of us may inadvertently damage the natural environment along the Trail and mar the experience for others. Those negative effects can be minimized by adopting the sound hiking and camping techniques of Leave No Trace™ (LNT), which, while simple to learn, requires some committed effort. Think of LNT, wholly endorsed by the ATC and ALDHA, as an educational and ethical program for responsible enjoyment of the outdoors, not a set of rules. If we are successful, the Trail will retain its essential natural qualities and continue to be a place where an extraordinary outdoor experience is available. Everyone's help is important. Please do your part by committing to these practices and encourage others to learn about techniques that "Leave No Trace" on the Appalachian Trail. More information can be found at LNT.org and appalachiantrail.org/lnt.

Here are the seven principles of Leave No Trace™ and the ways you can implement them while on the Trail:

PLAN AHEAD AND PREPARE

- Check Appalachian Trail guidebooks and maps for guidance and note that camping regulations vary considerably along the Trail. Travel in groups of ten or fewer to reduce impact on the Trail. If in a group of more than five, leave shelters for lone hikers and smaller groups.
- Bring a lightweight trowel or wide tent stake to dig a hole for burying human waste.
- Pack a piece of screening to filter food scraps from your dishwater and pack them out.
- If you're planning to hang food and scented articles, bring a waterproof bag and at least 50 feet of rope.
- Repackage food in resealable bags to minimize waste.
- Prepare for extreme weather, hazards, and emergencies—especially the cold—to avoid impacts from searches, rescues, and campfires.
- Try to avoid areas when they are most crowded. If you are planning a northbound thru hike, avoid starting on March 1, March 15, the first day of spring, or April 1.

TRAVEL AND CAMP ON DURABLE SURFACES

- Stay on the Trail; never shortcut switchbacks. Take breaks off-trail on durable surfaces, such as rocks or grass; restrict activities to areas where vegetation is already absent.
- Avoid expanding existing trails and campsites by walking in the middle of the trail and using the already-impacted core areas of campsites.
- If branches block the trail, move them if possible, rather than going around and creating new trails.
- Wear gaiters and waterproof boots, so you can walk through puddles instead of walking around them and creating a wide spot in the trail.
- Camping at designated sites is required in many areas of the A.T., including (but not limited to) the Smokies, some areas in Virginia, and much of the A.T. from Harpers Ferry, West Virginia, north to Katahdin. Even where dispersed camping (sometimes called "stealth camping") is allowed, camping at designated sites helps conserve the Trail.

- A list of camping and campfire regulations can be found at appalachiantrail.org/explore/hike-the-a-t/thru-hiking/camping-regulations.
- Planning your hike to avoid the most popular times, such as the southern end of the A.T. in March and April, will allow you to stay at designated sites and still avoid crowded conditions.

DISPOSE OF WASTE PROPERLY
- "Pack it in, pack it out." Don't burn, bury, or leave litter or extra food. That includes cigarette butts, fruit peels, and hygiene articles. Keep your trash bag handy, so you can pick up litter left by others.
- Use the privy for human waste only (feces). Do not add trash. If there is no privy, dispose of human waste by burying it in a cathole, a hole 6–8 inches deep, 4–6 inches wide, at least 200 feet (80 steps) from campsites, water sources, and shelters, and well away from trails. Add dirt to the hole and stir with a stick to promote decomposition. Push toilet paper to the bottom of the hole and leave your stick in the hole. Don't hide your waste under a rock; this slows decomposition.
- Note that most "disposable wipes" are made from nonbiodegradable material that must be carried out rather than buried, burned, or left in privies. For those willing to go the extra mile, consider packing out your toilet paper, too. Animals' curiosity often brings toilet paper and other trash to the surface.
- Wash dishes, bodies, and clothing 200 feet away from water sources. Use biodegradable soap sparingly, or not at all. Avoid polluting the water by rinsing off at a distance to remove your excess sunscreen, bug repellent, etc., before swimming in a lake or stream.
- Disperse dishwater and toothpaste and urinate well away (at least 100 feet) from shelters and popular campsites to avoid attracting wildlife close to camp. Animals sometimes defoliate plants to consume the salt in urine, so urinate on rocks or bare ground rather than on vegetation. Where water is plentiful, consider diluting the urine by adding water to the site.
- If you wish to donate items to other hikers (food, extra gear, clothing, books, etc.), don't leave them at shelters—use the hiker boxes at motels and hostels.

LEAVE WHAT YOU FIND
- Leave plants, artifacts, and natural objects where you found them for others to enjoy.
- Don't build structures or dig trenches around tents.
- Do not damage live trees or plants; green wood burns poorly. Collect only firewood that is dead, down, and no larger than your wrist. Leave dead standing trees and dead limbs on standing trees for wildlife.
- Consider using rubber tips on the bottom of your trekking poles to avoid scratch marks on rocks, "clicking" sounds, and holes along the Trail.
- Do not tag or graffiti shelters, signs, or other trail structures. Leave your mark in the shelter logbook instead.

MINIMIZE CAMPFIRE IMPACTS
- Use stoves for cooking—if you need a fire, build one only where it's legal and in an existing fire ring. Leave hatchets and saws at home. Burn all wood to ash.
- Do not try to burn trash, including foil, plastic, glass, cans, tea bags, food, or anything with food on it. These items do not burn thoroughly. They create noxious fumes, attract wildlife like skunks and bears, and make the area unsightly.
- Where campfires are permitted, leave the fire ring clean by removing others' trash and scattering unused wood, cold coals, and ashes 200 feet away from camp after the fire is cold and completely out. Check for local and seasonal burn bans and forgo having a fire during periods of dry and/or windy weather.

RESPECT WILDLIFE
- Bears live or travel through nearly every part of the A.T., and sightings have increased at shelters and campsites. Even small food rewards teach bears to associate humans with food. When that happens, they often must be killed to protect human safety. Dropped, spilled, or

improperly stored food also attracts rodents. Clean up spills completely and pack out all food scraps. Even a few noodles are a large meal for mice.
- Store your food according to local regulations. Store all food, trash, and scented articles (toothpaste, sunscreen, insect repellent, water-purification chemicals, balm, etc.) out of reach of bears and other animals. See the Bears section above for information on safe food storage.
- Keep a respectful distance. If hiking with a dog, keep it on a short leash. Do not follow or approach wild animals. Particularly avoid wildlife during sensitive times, i.e., when they are mating, nesting, or raising young.

BE CONSIDERATE OF OTHER VISITORS
- Let nature's sounds prevail. Respect others by keeping loud voices and noise to a minimum. Do not use cell phones or audio equipment within sight or sound of other hikers and turn ringers off.
- A.T. shelter space is available on a first-come, first-served basis in most (but not all) areas, regardless of the type of hiker or length of their hike.
- Limit-of-stay is generally two nights at any one shelter or campsite.

Hiking with Dogs
If you choose to hike with your canine companion, treat your dog as another backpacker and be aware of its potential impact on animals and other hikers. You are responsible for your dog, and you will be held accountable if it decides to steal another hiker's food or flop its wet body on another hiker's equipment. It is best to always keep your dog on a leash and under control; regulations require dogs to be leashed on national park lands (40 percent of the Trail). Dogs are prohibited in the Great Smoky Mountains National Park, the zoo area of Bear Mountain State Park in New York, and Maine's Baxter State Park. (For information on kennels near GSMNP and BSP, see entries for those sections.)

Ask permission before bringing your dog into a shelter. If you find the shelter is crowded, be considerate and tent with your dog. Keep your pet under control in camp, on the Trail, and in towns. Many hostels and other accommodations don't allow dogs, and in those that do, a dog does not belong in the communal kitchen and sleeping areas. Most post offices allow only guide dogs inside.

Bury your dog's waste as you would your own and carry a water bowl so your dog won't drink directly from Trailside water sources. Please keep your dog from swimming in water sources, as dogs can be a vector for transmitting Giardia.

Closely monitor your pet's feet for torn flesh, bleeding, and other sores especially in areas where there are many rocks. After the weather warms up, check for ticks; dogs can catch Lyme and other diseases, too. Carry current rabies vaccine certification papers in addition to a tag on the dog's collar. At all times both you and your dog should respect the experience of everyone you're sharing the trails with.

Town Conduct
As a result of tension between hikers and some communities along the Trail, ALDHA started an "Endangered Services Campaign" now known as "Hike in Harmony" to educate hikers to be responsible for their actions. In town, consider yourself a walking, talking billboard for all backpackers and the Trail. Your actions have a direct impact on the businesses that provide services for the long-distance hiking community.

The success of a thru-hiker's journey depends on Trail towns and the services they provide. Remember that you are a guest of the community, no matter how large or small, even though you may be pumping money into the local economy. Be courteous to those who earn their livelihood there and remember that your conduct will have a bearing on how well—or badly—the next hiker is treated. As with so many other things in life, we are never truly alone. You are an ambassador for all those who follow you on the Trail. Nothing can turn a person or town against backpacking and the Trail quicker than an arrogant, smelly, and ill-behaved hiker.

Some business owners have reduced services or closed their doors to hikers simply because some hikers wouldn't respect their rules. Be a part of a movement that will reverse this practice and ensure that no one closes another door because of bad hiker behavior.

Hike in Harmony

This effort was created to encourage all hikers to follow a set of best practices that ensure everyone associated with the Trail has the best possible experience. Hike in Harmony asks that hikers:

1. **Respect the Trail.** Most trails are maintained by trail clubs, whose members volunteer countless hours of their time, blood, sweat, and tears building, rerouting, and maintaining these pathways through our wild areas. We ask hikers to be mindful of this on their walks. Learn and follow the seven principles of Leave No Trace (see above).

2. **Respect other hikers.** Whether it's thru-hikers, section-hikers, weekenders, or day-hikers, we're all out there to enjoy the natural world. A little common courtesy goes a long way. If you're not sure who has the right of way, be the first to yield. Keep noise to a minimum; not everybody wants to hear your music. When camping with others at established sites, try to camp away from others whenever possible to give them some personal space. Be helpful if asked, but don't offer unsolicited advice. If you smoke, whether it's tobacco or cannabis, do it well away from others. Be discreet as well with alcohol, particularly if families with children are camped nearby. Hikers generally go to sleep early to get an early start the next day so respect "hiker midnight" and keep noise and talk to a minimum after dark. Really, it just comes down to practicing the Golden Rule—treat others the way you would like to be treated. Let your interactions with other hikers be a good example.

3. **Respect hostels and other lodging.** For many hostel owners, running a hostel is a labor of love. While some hostels run a year-round business, for others, it is highly seasonal.

   Some hostel rates are expensive and may include such amenities as showers, laundry, Wi-Fi, meals, shuttles to town for resupply, shuttles to and from the trailhead, etc. While tipping a hostel owner isn't mandatory, it is the right thing to do if an owner or staff member went above and beyond to provide a service they normally don't.

   Some hostels may be "donation based." This doesn't mean "free." Although it's not mandatory, please be generous whenever possible.

   Hostel owners always are greatly appreciative to those who pitch in with cleaning the dishes, sweeping out common areas, and helping clean up.

   Many hostels are private homes in residential neighborhoods. Please respect the rules of the hostel, especially regarding the use of alcohol, tobacco, and drugs, including cannabis. If you smoke, ask the owner if there is a permissible area to do so, and always respect the neighbors. Long after you're gone, the hostel owner stays. Don't give the neighbors a reason to shut the hostel down.

   The same principles apply to hotels, motels, and other lodging. And remember to leave a tip for housekeeping. They are generally paid minimum wage or less and rely on tips for the bulk of their income.

4. **Respect shuttle drivers.** Shuttle drivers may be independent owner-operators, employees of hostels or lodging facilities, or hostel owners themselves. An owner-operator may set a fee for your ride, while others get paid by the establishment they work for. For many, the work is seasonal and tipping is encouraged, particularly for those who have gone out of their way for you. And while not mandatory for owner-operators, they also appreciate tips.

   Many have very busy seasons, so it's important to be on time for your pick-up. If you're running late or your plans change and you no longer need a ride, please let the shuttle driver know so that he or she can adjust their schedule. There is nothing worse for a shuttle driver to get to a pick-up point only to find his fare accepted a free ride instead and left the driver hanging. Some shuttle drivers may now request a deposit. If possible, let the shuttle driver know ahead of time if you need to go into town for resupply. Most drivers will accommodate you when possible.

   Remember, for most, this is their livelihood. Don't forget to pay them!

5. **Respect all businesses.** Almost all hikers will need to resupply during their thru hikes and section-hikes. They will eat and drink at restaurants in town. To help ensure continued goodwill towards hikers, please adhere to any rules that may be posted, especially no bare feet and no backpacks allowed inside. Clean yourself up before visiting eating and drinking establishments. Hiker funk can be a turn-off to the locals, who frequent those businesses regularly. Remember to tip your servers, many of whom work for minimum wage. And if you choose to drink, do so responsibly.

6. **Respect the townspeople.** This really should go without saying. Our trail towns are a treasure. While you may only be there for a day or two, they will continue to see hikers day after day, year after year, long after you are gone. Obey the local laws, especially regarding alcohol and drugs. Be discreet with the use of tobacco and cannabis. Keep noise to a minimum, especially at night.

This is their home they have welcomed you into. Give them a good reason to continue to welcome all of the hikers that will come after you.

AFTER YOUR HIKE
Whether you're a thru-hiker who would like to make it official, offer feedback, or simply wants to give back to the A.T. in some way, there are a variety of resources available for you.

2,000-Miler Certificates
The ATC recognizes anyone who reports completion of the entire Trail as a "2,000-Miler" with a certificate. The term "2,000-Miler" is a matter of tradition and convenience, based upon the original estimated length of the Trail. The ATC operates on the honor system and assumes that those who apply for 2,000-Miler status have hiked all of the A.T. between Katahdin and Springer. In the event of an emergency, such as a flood, forest fire, or an impending storm on an exposed high-elevation stretch, blue-blazed trails or officially required roadwalks are considered viable substitutes for the white-blazed route. Issues of sequence, direction, speed, length of time, or whether one carries a pack or not (slack-packing) are not considered. The ATC assumes that those who apply have made an honest effort to walk the entire Trail. (P.S. The Shenandoah River (aqua-blazing) is not the official Trail route.)

Trail-Maintaining Clubs and Registers
Trail-maintaining clubs are listed throughout the book. You may use the addresses provided to contact the clubs with any comments, suggestions, or feedback. The official shelter registers are the property of the maintaining club and should not be removed by hikers. The register is a useful tool for information on Trail conditions and other things that are happening in its section of the A.T. It may also help locate a hiker in case of an emergency. If you wish to donate a register (assuming that one doesn't already exist), you should include a note asking the maintaining club to forward it to you when it's filled.

Giving Back
If you would like to give back what was freely given to you by those who maintain the Trail or while you stayed in Trail towns, volunteer your time, effort, or money to the services and people who supported you. Consider contacting a Trail-maintaining club and work with them to organize or participate in a work trip, a Trail construction project, or regular maintenance. Join ALDHA and stay connected to the trails (aldha.app.neoncrm.com/forms/8). Every year, ALDHA assists work trips to Trail establishments. The Konnarock and other ATC crews seek volunteers during the summer, and you often will pass a Trail club working busily as you head along the path. Be sure to acknowledge their work with your thanks and respect. Giving back to the Trail and community helps keep the Trail safe and services available.

APPALACHIAN TRAIL MUSEUM SOCIETY
The Appalachian Trail Museum opened in June 2010 in Pine Grove Furnace State Park near the Trail's midpoint after years of work by the Appalachian Trail Museum Society (ATMS), formed in 2002. The group includes representatives of the ATC and ALDHA and works with the National Park Service and the Pennsylvania Department of Conservation and Natural Resources. The Society is collecting items for eventual display in the museum and monetary donations. They are also in need of volunteers to help in many areas. Please contact ATMS and join, if you'd like to help, at atmuseum.org.

APPALACHIAN LONG DISTANCE HIKERS ASSOCIATION
The Appalachian Long Distance Hikers Association (ALDHA) is a nonprofit organization founded in 1983 to promote the welfare of the Appalachian Trail and the Trail community. ALDHA conducts

work weekends on the Trail, speaks out on issues concerning the A.T. and its environs, and collects the information for this book. It has worked with various clubs and hostels to maintain areas widely used by hikers. ALDHA is open to anyone. A membership form is included at the back of this book. Annual dues are $20 for one year, $35 for two years, and $45 for three years for an individual and family of up to four members. Benefits include the *Thru-Hikers' Companion* in PDF format, a membership directory, and a quarterly newsletter, as well as many opportunities to interface with other hikers who understand long-distance hiking. For more information, visit our website at aldha.org.

The Gathering

Hikers who want to learn what it takes to thru-hike the Appalachian Trail can find out everything they need to know at the annual fall Gathering. If you are already thru-hiking the Trail this year, the Gathering is also the place to receive an "ALDHA Way" certificate and patch for your accomplishment and to find out what's next for your worn-in hiking boots. More than fifty hours of slide shows and how–to workshops on how to hike, reviews of trails, and skills are offered during the weekend event. The 43rd Gathering will be Oct. 10–12, 2025, at the Southwest Virginia Higher Education Center, Abingdon, VA. For more information, visit aldha.org/gathering. Special notice to 2025 thru-hikers and 2000-Milers: Bring your Trail-worn *Thru-Hikers' Companion* (or the Maine section in its entirety) and a completed-trail form to the registration desk, and your Gathering fee is on ALDHA!

AN INVITATION

This is the thirty-second edition of the *Thru-Hikers' Companion*, and ALDHA will again depend on comments, suggestions, and volunteers to update it in the fall of 2025. If you see information that needs correcting or come across information that should be included, or you would like to be a volunteer field editor, please contact the editor at companion@aldha.org.

How to Use This Guide

The *Companion* is a comprehensive guide, but you may find you don't need all of the information or need it only in sections. So make your *Companion* your own. Highlight key sections, rip out pages you don't want, take it completely apart and send sections ahead to mail drops. As a backup, you can store the full PDF on your phone as well.

READING THE *COMPANION*

Study these terms and abbreviations so you can easily find the information you need throughout the guide.

In the body of the text:

Abbreviations:

M—Monday	W—Wednesday	F—Friday	Su—Sunday
Tu—Tuesday	Th—Thursday	Sa—Saturday	

FedEx—Federal Express	B/L/D—breakfast/lunch/dinner	d—double
USPS—U.S. Postal Service	CATV—cable television	s—single
UPS—United Parcel Service	pp—per person	t—triple
AYCE—all-you-can-eat	eap—each additional person	a/c—air conditioning

Appalachian Trail Communities™ are marked with the ⊕ icon. Towns and counties participating in this Appalachian Trail Conservancy program agree to help promote, preserve, and maintain the A.T. in various ways while the ATC helps them with economic development. (Note that several communities participate but are outside the distance scope of this book.)

East (E) and west (W) are used as they are in the *A.T. Data Book* and the series of ATC's 11 A.T. guides: "East" is always to the northbounder's right and the southbounder's left, when referring to the Trail.

Road crossings and trailheads with significant services nearby are marked with the ⍓ icon and are indicated in south-to-north order (NOBO).

Services are indicated with **bold italics** for major categories, specifically groceries, lodging, hostels, campgrounds, doctors or hospitals, restaurants, Internet access, laundries, veterinarians, and outfitters.

Towns and post offices (including P.O. hours) are printed in **bold type**. A listing of post offices can also be found on page 272.

Trail-maintaining club information is provided at the southern end of their sections and is offset by two rules.

Tables at beginning of each chapter:

MILES FROM SPRINGER AND MILES FROM KAHTADIN

These are the cumulative distances from the two endpoints on the Trail.

MILES TO NEXT POINT

This tells provides the distance to the next waypoint in the table.

FEATURES

Here you'll find detailed information on all waypoints, including trail junctions, road crossings, campgrounds and campsites, towns, water sources, and other landmarks and places of interest.

- Post offices (P.O.) are shown in bold with distance and direction off Trail.
- Services separated by parentheses are not all in the same location. For example, (E–0.2m C, S) (W–0.1m w) means that the campsite and shelter are east 0.2 mile, and the water source is west 0.1 mile from the Trail.
- Services separated by commas are in the same location. For example, "E–1.5m P.O., G" means that the post office and grocery store are both located 1.5 miles east.
- Shaded features are explored in more detail in the text.
- Shelters (may also be referred to as lean-tos) are shown in bold, with distance and direction off Trail, water-source location, and distance to the next shelter (in italics, both north and south). The distance to the next north and south shelter shown in the *Companion* includes side trail distance from one to the other, if the shelter is not located on the Trail.

SERVICES
Services are indicated with the following abbreviations:

B—bus	H—hostels	sh—shower
C—campground, campsites	L—lodging	T—train
Cl—coin laundry	M—meals; restaurants	nw—no potable water
D—doctor, medical	m—miles	V—veterinarian
f—fuel	O—outfitter	w—water
G—groceries, supplies	P—parking	
g—short-term resupply	R—road access	

ELEVATION
In this column you'll find the approximate elevation (in feet) of each landmark.

MAP
This column provides the name of the recommended map for each section.

Getting to the Termini

GETTING TO BAXTER STATE PARK, MAINE

No public transportation is available to or from Baxter State Park, but there are several private options so you can easily start or end your journey at the park. The nearest airport is in Bangor, though the Portland and Boston airports have more competitive rates. From any of these airports you'll need to reach Medway and then go on to Millinocket, which is still 20 miles southeast of the park.

Portland or Boston to Medway

There is bus transportation from Boston to Portland and from Portland to Medway. Concord Coach Lines, (800) 639-3317 and (603) 228-3300, concordcoachlines.com, provides bus service between both Logan Airport in Boston and Portland and Maine. Its schedule has several departures and arrivals, which makes catching the connecting bus straightforward. Those taking Amtrak to Portland can schedule the Concord Coach Line bus along with their train ticket purchase. (Note: Amtrak allows all gear, including lighters and fuel, on the train.)

Bangor to Medway

Cyr Bus Lines of Old Town, Maine, (800) 244-2335 and (207) 827-2335, cyrbustours.com, serves northern Maine. A bus leaves Bangor/Hermon Greyhound bus station at 6:00 p.m. and Concord–Trailways bus station at 6:30 p.m. and arrives at Medway at 7:40 p.m. Returning to Bangor, a bus leaves Medway at 9:30 a.m. and arrives at Concord-Trailways station at 10:50 a.m. and at Bangor/Hermon Greyhound station at 11:10 a.m. ($12 fare).

Medway to Millinocket and Baxter State Park

Today there are several transportation options between Medway and Baxter State Park. Maine Quest Adventures (mainequestadventures.com, 207-447-5011) offers a shuttle from the Medway bus stop to BSP or Abol Bridge, $75 for two people, $10 each additional. Bull Moose Taxi, (207) 447-8070, charges $55 to Katahdin Stream Campground or to the A.T. Hostel and Outfitters in Millinocket. The A.T. Hostel and Outfitters, (207) 723-4321 also offers a SOBO special: pick-up in Medway, bed in the bunkroom, breakfast at the A.T. Café, and shuttle to Katahdin Stream Campground, and a shuttle back to Medway.

Baxter State Park

The park, (207) 723-5140, baxterstatepark.org, has 10 campgrounds available May 15–Oct 22 by reservation, $30 per night per 4-person lean-to or 6-person-max tentsite, except at the Birches long-distance hiker site, where the fee is $10pp/night.

The Birches campsite, near Katahdin Stream Campground, is intended for northbound long-distance hikers who have hiked 100 miles or more contiguously within the park on their current trip. Hikers staying at the Birches must sign up at the information kiosk just north of Abol Bridge. Please see the entry for Baxter on page 265 for more information and details about camping and regulations near Katahdin.

Southbound hikers should reserve a regular lean-to or tentsite at Katahdin Stream or Abol campgrounds. Reservations for most sites may be made up to four months in advance online, but some reservations (backcountry, bunkhouse, group sites) need to be made by phone, mail, or in person. More information, and a chart outlining real-time availability of sites, is available at baxterstatepark.org. Inside the park, ranger stations do not accept credit cards. Every hiker must register with a ranger upon entering Baxter. Information kiosks are located at Abol Stream and Katahdin Stream campgrounds.

Pets: No dogs or other pets are allowed. Please see Medway and Millinocket entries for kennels.

Parking: No long-term parking is available, and parking at all trailheads and campgrounds is at a premium and is managed at the entrance gates. Check the park website for information on how to reserve a parking space. Reservations for day-use parking May 15–Oct 22 becomes available for Maine residents on April 1 and for nonresidents two weeks later. When the spaces for a particular day have been reserved, that specific parking lot is closed. Plan ahead!

Approach to Katahdin

A note for would-be southbounders: Katahdin is no stroll in the park. The profile and topo on the Maine ATC's maps only give you a hint of what to expect: the single greatest sustained climb on the A.T. Get yourself physically prepared before you start at Baxter State Park (you will be on your own once you get past the ranger station). Northbounders routinely leave their full packs on the ranger's porch and hike up with daypacks provided there for that purpose. Every year, several stubborn southbounders, invariably much less-conditioned than seasoned northbounders, insist on carrying their fully loaded packs up the A.T. beyond Katahdin Stream Campground. This results in knee injuries and aborted climbs or even entire A.T. hiking plans. Take a hint from the northbound veterans: Hike Katahdin with a day pack, and pick up your full pack on your way back through the campground; you will still be a thru-hiker, and you will enjoy your day, rather than suffer the entire time and predispose yourself to any number of injuries or the need for a rescue on your first Trail day.

The footpath below treeline is more rocks and roots than soil—no problem for the hikers who have been rock-hopping for 2,000 miles, but not a pleasant journey straight from the desk chair. Above treeline, you pull yourself over rocks in a few places and walk across slanted, roof-sized boulders in others. The climb is tough, even without a pack. In your day pack be sure to carry plenty of water, lots of snacks, sunscreen, a first-aid kit, gloves, hat, and extra layers of clothing. If you don't want to retrace your steps, you might consider going up the Abol Trail (part of which is referred to as the "Abol Slide," because of the loose rocks and steepness formed by a nineteenth century landslide) and down the Hunt Trail (A.T.). That requires a two-mile walk or ride from Katahdin Stream along the Perimeter Road to Abol Campground before starting your hike. The Abol Trail usually opens after the Hunt Trail; until the sandy, gravelly soils dry out, the trail is unstable, and boulders can become dislodged.

Weather permitting, you can begin a southbound hike as early as May 31. Before then, trails are so wet, even without snow and ice, that foot traffic would irreparably harm the alpine and subalpine areas. However, even for the following few weeks, the tiny, biting blackflies can drive you out of the woods in agony and frustration, leaving behind a contribution of your blood to the North Woods ecosystem. Overnight camping season in Baxter is May 15–Oct 22.

Baxter Park provides information on weather and conditions and recommendations regarding climbing, but it will remind hikers that your safety and good decision-making are your responsibility. The park is largely wilderness, and hikers should not expect timely rescue or assistance and should be prepared to self-rescue. Each morning, rangers at Chimney Pond (elev. 2,914 feet)

AN IMPORTANT NOTE ABOUT SHUTTLE SERVICES

Beginning in 1995, USDA Forest Service law enforcement rangers in the South (who report to the regional office rather than the supervisor of an individual forest) began enforcing agency regulations on "special-use permits." The regulations say anyone taking money for a service involving Forest Service lands (including roads) must obtain a permit to do so; profit is not a factor. Permit-holders must pay a fee (up to $75) and, more prohibitively, carry high-premium insurance. Some A.T. shuttlers have been fined. Responding to questions from the ATC and its Park Service partners, regional officials made it clear they will continue to enforce the policy and cited directives stating that it is to be enforced consistently and nationally. The A.T. crosses six national forests in the South and two in New England. Some state and local law-enforcement agencies also are regulating shuttle services that charge a fee.

observe conditions. At times, trails are closed for safety considerations and to protect the rare and endangered alpine plants, animals, and their habitat, as well as unstable soils. Weather reports, trail statuses, and alerts such as a high heat index, blowdowns, thunderstorms, high water, snow, ice, etc. are posted at campgrounds throughout the park and at trailheads at 7 a.m. to assist hikers in planning their day's hike. Be sure to check this information before embarking on your hike and be prepared to change plans if warranted.

Note: Hikers who hike closed trails are subject to a court summons and fine and having park visitation privileges revoked.

GETTING TO AMICALOLA FALLS STATE PARK, GEORGIA

No public transportation is available to or from Amicalola Falls State Park (AFSP), but hikers have several private transportation options from Atlanta, Gainesville (located 40 miles southeast of the park), and the mountain town of Dahlonega (located 16 miles east of Amicalola Falls). Shuttle services in the area cover all these locations. They will pick up at airports, Amtrak stations, and the MARTA station in the north except as noted. Those arriving into Harstfield-Jackson Airport in Atlanta, can book shuttle services directly. When arriving by Greyhound or Amtrak, it is better to book your bus to Gainsville instead of Atlanta. It's much easier to get around Gainesville, and the area near the stations is safer. It's an especially good idea if one is traveling from the north as the ticket price will be slightly less than to Atlanta and the shuttling costs are about the same.

Shuttle services to Amicalola State Park: The Grateful Hiker (gratefulhiker.com); Donald Ballard (772) 321-0905 and Mary Bastin (706) 400-9105); Ron Brown Shuttles (706) 669-0919; hikershuttles@outlook.com; Jeff Moon, Appalachian Trail Shuttles and Tours (706) 994-2307); Brett Eady (404) 569-8776, Beady2727@gmail.com); Michelle Coler (706) 300-8964)

Atlanta to Amicalola Falls State Park

If you are coming from Hartsfield-Jackson Airport in Atlanta, the most direct way to get to Amicalola Falls State Park and Lodge or a Springer Mountain trailhead is to contact a shuttle service and get picked up directly at the airport. The other option is to take the MARTA train to the North Springs Station; it is the last stop on the MARTA red line. The shuttle of your choice can pick you up there and take you to your destination. When arriving by plane, there is no need to travel to Gainsville as an intermediate step to reach Amicalola Falls State Park; it's best to plan to shuttle directly to the park from the Atlanta area.

Should you choose to spend the night in Atlanta or in Sandy Springs near the MARTA, your shuttle driver can also pick you up at any of the nearby hotels. Transportation also can be easily arranged if you are going into the Atlanta Greyhound or Atlanta Amtrak station.

Gainesville to Amicalola Falls State Park

Gainesville is a recommended option for those arriving via Greyhound or Amtrak. It is easier to get around, and the area near the bus and train stations is safer than Atlanta.

Lodging: Motel 6 (770) 532-7531, weekdays $75, weekends $85, $3eap, Wi-Fi, pet-friendly; Lanier Center Holiday Inn, (770) 531-0907, $85–$100, no dogs, hot B, Wi-Fi; Country Hearth and Suites, (770) 287-3205, $68.27–$72.99d weekdays, $69.57–$84d weekends, B buffet, pets $15; Hampton Inn, (770) 503-0300, $140–$160, Wi-Fi, no pets, hot B; Best Value Inn, (770) 534-0303, $65–$75d, Wi-Fi, no pets. All are within 4 miles of the bus and train stations.

Gainesville to Dahlonega

Some hikers choose to stay in Dahlonega rather than Gainesville. The site of the country's first gold rush, in the 1830s, Dahlonega sits 16 miles east of Amicalola Falls and offers all major services. Don Ballard offers service to Dahlonega.

Dahlonega—*Lodging:* Hotel rates in Dahlonega vary with the season. After May 1 and on weekends, expect listed rates to increase. Barefoot Hills, 7693 Hwy. 19N, Dahlonega, (770) 312-7342, barefoothills.com, bunk $42 plus tax; Comfort Inn & Suites, (706) 867-7777, $129–$329, $5eap, includes hot B, no pets or smoking allowed; Dahlonega Mountain Inn, (706) 864-4343, hiker rate Su–Th $65d, F–Sa $75, includes B, $20 for pets, Wi-Fi; Days Inn, (706) 864-2338, $70–$150, B, Wi-Fi; Quality Inn, (706) 864-6191, $70–$150, includes B, limited room for pets <20 pounds $25 fee, Internet access and Wi-Fi; Holiday Inn Express, 32 E. Main St., (706) 707-8000, $139–$339,

$5eap; Smith House, (706) 867-7000, smithhouse.com, $139–$209, no dogs, no smoking. The Smith House Restaurant, in operation since 1922, is famous for its family-style AYCE fare (beginning in April): closed M, Tu–Th 11–2:30, F–Sa 11–7:30, Su 11–4. Hours are seasonal and may vary. Call ahead. *Outfitter:* Woodlands Edge, 36 N. Park St., (706) 864-5358, woodlands.dahlonega@gmail.com, M–Su 10:30–5, boots and apparel, gear.

AMICALOLA FALLS APPROACH TRAIL

Miles from Springer	Miles to Next Point	Features	Services	Elev	Miles from Katahdin	M A P
8.8	0.5	Amicalola Falls State Park	R, P, C, sh, cl, w	1,700'	0.0	
		Visitor Center Archway AFSP "Max Epperson" Shelter, *0.0mS; 7.3mN* *East–20m to* **Dahlonega, GA, P.O. 30533** *West–25m to* East Ellijay, GA	S G, M, L, O, cl O			
8.3	0.6	Base of Amicalola Falls, *604 steps*		2,150'	0.5	
7.7	0.1	Wide Trail to Amicalola Lodge *(E–0.1m), restrooms*	P, L, M, w	2,540'	1.1	
7.6	0.2	Amicalola Lodge Road, *paved (E–0.1m lodge)*	R, P, L, M, w	2,550'	1.2	
7.4	0.1	+Len Foote Hike Inn Trail *(E–5m)*	L, M, w	2,600'	1.4	ATC: NC-GA Map 4
7.3	1.7	USFS-46, *log steps on north side*	R	2,580'	1.5	
5.6	1.6	High Shoals Road	R	2,800'	3.2	
4.0	0.3	Frosty Mountain: *former firetower site*	C, w	3,382'	4.8	
3.7	0.3	Frosty Mountain Road, USFS-46	R	3,192'	5.1	
3.4	0.3	+Len Foote Hike Inn Trail, *blazed lime-green (E–1m)*	L, M, w	3,310'	5.4	
3.1	0.3	Woody Knob		3,400'	5.7	
2.8	0.8	Nimblewill Gap, USFS-28	R	3,100'	6.0	
2.0	0.5	Black Mountain: *western shoulder*		3,600'	6.8	
1.5	1.5	**Black Gap Shelter**, *7.3mS; 1.9mN*	S, C, w	3,300'	7.3	
0.0		Springer Mountain: **Southern terminus**, *bronze plaque, register in rock*		3,782'	8.8	

+ Fee charged

Amicalola Falls State Park—Amicalola Falls State Park, nestled almost nine miles southwest of Springer Mountain, is the gateway to the southern terminus of the A.T. Scales to weigh packs and showers are located near the new visitor center entrance, as well as a restroom, snack machines, and water fountain. The visitor center, (706) 265-4703, sells guidebooks, maps, and gift items and is open 8:30 a.m.–5 p.m. daily. Sign in at the thru-hiker registration desk inside the visitor center.

The park holds UPS and USPS packages sent c/o Amicalola Falls State Park, 240 Amicalola Falls State Park Rd., Dawsonville, GA 30534. Indicate on the box to hold the package at either the visitor center or the lodge.

Lodging and Camping: The park offers campsites, cabins, Amicalola Lodge, and a shelter for thru-hikers. Campsites $30 with shower, coin laundry; 1- to 3-bedroom cabins (2-night minimum), call for pricing. Amicalola Lodge, (706) 265-8888, (800) 573-9656, gastateparks.org, desk is staffed around the clock; call for pricing on rooms, B included. Reservations suggested for cabins, campsites, and the lodge. *Max Epperson Shelter:* Located 50 yards behind the visitor center, the AFSP shelter sleeps 12 and is available to thru-hikers at no charge. A group of Trail backpacking enthusiasts—the "A.T. Gang"—from nearby Canton spent 800 hours constructing the facility in 1993 in memory of their friend, Max Epperson. Epperson hiked the Trail as far north as Connecticut before his health failed. Afterward, he continued to offer shuttles and support for his hiking friends. Water source and restroom 50 yards away at the visitor center. *Restaurant:* The lodge houses the Maple Restaurant, daily buffets, full-buffet B 7–10:30, L 11:30–3, D 5–8. *Pets:* Dogs must be on a leash within the park. *Parking:* A $5/day vehicle user fee is charged to all park visitors. Section-hikers

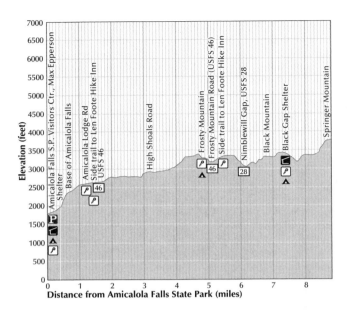

Distance from Amicalola Falls State Park (miles)

may want to use the long-term parking; an annual parking pass is also available. Long-distance hikers may leave vehicles only in the parking area opposite the visitor center for up to 14 days.

Approach Trail to Springer Mountain—From the park visitor center, it is an 8.8-mile trek to the first white blaze, most of it uphill. To cut off the steep, one-mile ascent of the falls, catch a ride to the top of the falls, and pick up the blue blazes there. Construction on the new visitor's center is now complete. The archway is open once again for those wanting to start at the center. While there, do take the time to look around the new center as it is very well done. "Zeno," an ALDHA member, supervises the maintenance of this section.

Approach Trail via Nimblewill Gap and Cooper Gap—This alternative puts you 2.2 miles south of Springer Mountain on the Approach Trail but requires a bumpy, muddy drive up Forest Service roads. From the park entrance, go east 9.5 miles on GA-52 to the abandoned Grizzles Store. Turn left on Nimblewill Road and continue past Nimblewill Church at 6.6 miles. Just beyond the church, pass a road on the left where the pavement ends. Continue to the right on the unpaved road and reach Nimblewill Gap at 14 miles. Turn left on FS Road 42. This is a very rough road and probably should not be attempted unless you have 4WD or high clearance. FS Road 42 may be accessed by traveling out of Dahlonega on Camp Wahsega Road to Camp Merrill. At the gate, look to the right and take the dirt road, Cooper Gap Road, for 3 miles. Turn left onto FS Road 42 toward Big Stamp Gap Parking.

From Amicalola Falls to Springer Mountain via Forest Service roads—The easiest route for 2WD and low-clearance vehicles takes you within one mile of the Springer summit; it is clearly outlined on ATC's map #4 for the area (North Carolina–Georgia Maps at mountaineersbooks.org). From the park, go west on GA-52 for 13.6 miles to Roy Road, at Cartecay Church and Stanley's Store. Turn right and proceed 9.5 miles to the second stop sign at the junction with Doublehead Gap Road. At the stop sign, bear right, and go 2.3 miles to Mt. Pleasant Church on the left. Across from the church, turn right onto unpaved Forest Service Road 42. This well-graded gravel road, suitable for all vehicles, winds 6.6 miles to the A.T. crossing at Big Stamp on the north side of the road. To reach the summit of Springer Mountain, walk 0.9 mile south. If you don't want to retrace your steps on the A.T., an alternative is to continue 1.7 miles past the A.T. crossing to USFS 42's intersection with the Benton MacKaye Trail (BMT). The BMT leads 1.5 miles up Springer and joins the A.T. just north of the southern terminus.

Len Foote Hike Inn—(800) 581-8032, hike-inn.com. This $1-million lodge is similar to huts in New Hampshire's White Mountains. The 40-bed, 20-room inn is approximately 5.0 miles north of Amicalola Falls State Park facilities and 4.5 miles south of the Springer Mountain summit. The yellow-blazed Hike Inn Trail creates a loop with the blue-blazed Approach Trail that leads from the park to Springer. Overnight stays, which include family-style B/D, are $117S, $170D, rates subject to change; no dogs allowed. Amenities include linens, hot showers, composting toilets, and electricity (outlets in bath house only). Owned by the Georgia Department of Natural Resources, the inn is operated by the Appalachian Education and Recreation Services, Inc., a nonprofit corporation affiliated with the Georgia Appalachian Trail Club. Walk-ins are allowed, subject to availability. Registration is at the Amicalola Falls State Park Visitor Center, where you can check on room availability. Open year-round, guest rooms in the bunkhouse are heated. Sleeping bags recommended Nov–Mar.

Black Gap Shelter (1953/1995)—Sleeps 8. Privy. Once the Springer Mountain Shelter, dismantled and moved to this location in 1995. This shelter is 1.5 miles south of the summit of Springer Mountain on the Approach Trail. Water is located 300 yards downhill to the right of the shelter.

REGISTER YOUR HIKE

ATC strongly encourages would-be northbound thru-hikers to use its voluntary, online registration system to help determine their starting date. This system lets you see how many are planning to start on a given date. This allows hikers to spread out their start dates, which relieves pressure on themselves and the Trail's resources. Please go to atcamp.org to register.

Flip flopping: Increasingly, hikers choose to start somewhere in the middle of the Trail. These alternative itineraries offer a gradual progression from easier to more difficult terrain and more frequent resupplies. You can also avoid crowds and the party atmosphere, follow favorable weather conditions, reduce shelter overflow, and minimize damage to the Trail. More details can be found at appalachiantrail.org/explore/hike-the-a-t/thru-hiking/flip-flop.

Georgia

Miles from Springer	Miles to Next Point	Features	Services	Elev	Miles from Katahdin	M A P
0.0	0.2	Springer Mountain: *bronze plaque, register in rock*	southern terminus	3,782'	2,197.4	
0.2	0.1	**Springer Mountain Shelter** *(E–0.2m), 1.9mS; 3mN*	S, C, w	3,730'	2,197.2	
0.3	0.7	Benton MacKaye Trail *(southern terminus)*		3,710'	2,197.1	
1.0	0.3	USFS-42, Big Stamp Gap	R, P	3,350'	2,196.4	
1.3	0.3	Benton MacKaye Trail		3,370'	2,196.1	
1.6	0.3	Davis Creek	w	3,220'	2,195.8	
1.9	0.7	Rich Mountain, Benton MacKaye Trail		3,430'	2,195.5	
2.6	0.2	Stover Creek	w	2,850'	2,194.8	
2.8	0.1	**Stover Creek Shelter** *(E–0.2m), 3mS; 5.7mN*	S, C, w	2,870'	2,194.6	
2.9	0.9	Stover Creek	w	2,850'	2,194.5	
3.8	0.4	Stover Creek	w	2,660'	2,193.6	
4.2	0.1	Benton MacKaye Trail		2,580'	2,193.2	
4.3	0.9	USFS-58, Three Forks	R, P, C, w	2,530'	2,193.1	
5.2	1.0	Side trail to Long Creek Falls: *waterfalls (W–0.1m)* Benton MacKaye and Duncan Ridge Trails Jct.	w	2,800'	2,192.2	
6.2	1.2	USFS-251, Hickory Flats: *picnic pavilion, cemetery*	R	3,000'	2,191.2	
7.4	0.6	Hawk Mountain Campsite *(W–0.2m)*	C, w	3,250'	2,190.0	ATC: NC-GA Map 4
8.0	0.1	Stream	w	3,225'	2,189.4	
8.1	0.5	**Hawk Mountain Shelter** *(W–0.2m S; 0.4m stream), 5.7mS; 7.9mN*	S, C, w	3,200'	2,189.3	
8.6	1.9	Hightower Gap, USFS-42/69	R, P	2,854'	2,188.8	
10.5	1.0	Horse Gap	R, P	2,673'	2,186.9	
11.5	0.7	Sassafras Mountain		3,336'	2,185.9	
12.2	0.6	Cooper Gap, USFS-42/80	R, P	2,828'	2,185.2	
12.8	0.3	Justus Mountain		3,224'	2,184.6	
13.1	0.5	Brookshire Gap		2,936'	2,184.3	
13.6	0.6	Old logging road		2,920'	2,183.8	
14.2	0.1	Justus Creek	C, w	2,564'	2,183.2	
14.3	0.9	Justus Creek tentpads	C	2,590'	2,183.1	
15.2	0.5	Blackwell Creek	w	2,600'	2,182.2	
15.7	0.9	**Gooch Mountain Shelter** *(W–0.1m), 7.9mS; 12.5mN*	S, C, w	2,778'	2,181.7	
16.6	0.3	Spring	w	2,850'	2,180.8	
16.9	0.1	Gooch Gap, USFS-42 *(E–0.1m campsite)* West–3.3m to **Suches, GA, P.O. 30572**	R, P, C, w g,f	2,821'	2,180.5	
17.0	0.9	Marked trail to water (E–230 yds.)	w	2,815'	2,180.4	
17.9	0.3	Cross abandoned old road		3,000'	2,179.5	
18.2	0.6	Liss Gap: *poplar tree stand*		3,028'	2,179.2	
18.8	0.2	Jacks Gap		3,000'	2,178.6	

Miles from Springer	Miles to Next Point	Features	Services	Elev	Miles from Katahdin	M A P
19.0	0.5	Ramrock Mountain: *views south*		3,260'	2,178.4	
19.5	1.0	Tritt Gap		3,050'	2,177.9	
20.5	1.2	Woody Gap, GA-60: *picnic area, privy, spring (W–0.1m)* West–2m to **Suches, GA, P.O. 30572** East–7m to Barefoot Hills East–15m to **Dahlonega, GA P.O. 30533**	R, P, C, w H, g, f, D L G, M, L, O, cl	3,173'	2,176.9	
21.7	0.2	"Preaching Rock": *views east and south*		3,700'	2,175.7	
21.9	0.5	Big Cedar Mountain: *rock ledges*		3,737'	2,175.5	
22.4	0.4	Augerhole Gap: *spring*	w	3,560'	2,175.0	
22.8	0.1	Small stream	w	3,120'	2,174.6	
22.9	0.8	Dan Gap		3,261'	2,174.5	
23.7	0.3	Miller Gap, Dockery Lake Trail: *spring (E–100 yds.)*	w	2,995'	2,173.7	
24.0	0.8	Lance Creek Campsite: *tentpads*	C, w	2,880'	2,173.4	
24.8	0.9	Henry Gap		3,100'	2,172.6	
25.7	0.6	Burnett Field Mountain		3,480'	2,171.7	ATC: NC-GA Map 4
26.3	0.4	Jarrard Gap: *unpaved private road (W–0.3m stream)* West–1m to USFS Lake Winfield Scott Recreation Area	w C, sh	3,250'	2,171.1	
		Bear Canisters required if camping from here to Neel Gap				
26.7	0.7	Gaddis Mountain		3,410'	2,170.7	
27.4	0.3	Turkey Stamp Mountain		3,740'	2,170.0	
27.7	0.3	Bird Gap, **Woods Hole Shelter** (W–0.4m), 12.5mS; 1.6mN Freeman Trail (1.8m) rejoins A.T. north	S, C, w	3,650'	2,169.7	
28.0	0.1	Slaughter Creek Trail at Slaughter Creek Gap: *spring*	w	3,790'	2,169.4	
28.1	0.8	Blood Mountain Campsites: *tentpads*	C	3,800'	2,169.3	
28.9	1.4	Blood Mountain: *views* **Blood Mountain Shelter**, 1.6mS; 10.3mN	S	4,461'	2,168.5	
30.3	0.1	Flatrock Gap; Freeman Trail (1.8m) rejoins A.T. south West–0.2m to spring; 1m to Byron Reece Memorial picnic area	P, w	3,420'	2,167.1	
30.4	0.9	Balance Rock		3,410'	2,167.0	
31.3	1.1	Neel Gap, US-19 & 129 *On A.T.–Mountain Crossings at Walasi-Yi Center* East–0.3m to Blood Mountain Cabins East–14m to Barefoot Hills East–22m to **Dahlonega, GA, P.O. 30533** West–3m to Vogel State Park West–13m to **Blairsville, GA, P.O. 30512**	R, P O, H, cl, sh, f L, g L G, L, M, cl C, G, cl, sh G, L, M, cl	3,125'	2,166.1	ATC: NC-GA Map 3
		Bear Canisters required if camping from here to Jarrad Gap				
32.4	0.4	Bull Gap	C, w	3,644'	2,165.0	
32.8	0.7	Levelland Mountain: *open rocky area*		3,942'	2,164.6	
33.5	0.8	Swaim Gap		3,450'	2,163.9	
34.3	0.7	Rock Spring Top: *west to spring*	w	3,526'	2,163.1	
35.0	0.5	Wolf Laurel Top: *views*		3,766'	2,162.4	
35.5	0.8	Baggs Creek Gap: *west to spring*	C, w	3,591'	2,161.9	

Miles from Springer	Miles to Next Point	Features	Services	Elev	Miles from Katahdin	M A P
36.3	1.0	Cowrock Mountain: *views*		3,842'	2,161.1	
37.3	0.7	Tesnatee Gap, GA-348	R, P	3,138'	2,160.1	
38.0	0.2	Crest of Wildcat Mountain **Whitley Gap Shelter** *(E-1.2m S; 1.5m spring),* *10.3mS; 6.3mN*	S, w	3,600' 3,370'	2,159.4	
38.2	0.9	Hogpen Gap, GA-348: *A.T. plaque*	R, P, w	3,450'	2,159.2	
39.1	1.2	White Oak Stamp		3,470'	2,158.3	
40.3	0.7	Poor Mountain		3,650'	2,157.1	
41.0	1.2	Wide Gap		3,150'	2,156.4	
42.2	0.8	Sheep Rock Top		3,575'	2,155.2	
43.0	1.4	**Low Gap Shelter** *(E-0.1m), 6.3mS; 7.4mN*	S, C, w	3,050'	2,154.4	
44.4	2.4	Poplar Stamp Gap	C, w	3,350'	2,153.0	
46.8	1.2	Cold Springs Gap *SoBo cross several small streams*		3,450'	2,150.6	
48.0	0.7	Chattahoochee Gap: *spring (E-0.2m)* *West-2.4m on Jacks Knob Trail to GA-180*	w R	3,500'	2,149.4	
48.7	0.7	Red Clay Gap		3,450'	2,148.7	
49.4	0.2	Spaniards Knob Campsite	C	3,600'	2,148.0	
49.6	0.2	Spring	w	3,500'	2,147.8	
49.8	0.1	Rocky Knob	w	3,590'	2,147.6	
49.9	0.3	Henson Gap		3,550'	2,147.5	
50.2	0.1	Spring: *water for Blue Mountain Shelter*	w	3,890'	2,147.2	
50.3	0.9	**Blue Mountain Shelter,** *7.4mS; 8.3mN*	C, S, w	3,900'	2,147.1	
51.2	1.5	Blue Mountain		4,025'	2,146.2	
52.7	0.6	Unicoi Gap, GA-75: *A.T. plaque* *East-9m to* **Helen, GA, P.O. 30545** *East-17m to* Cleveland, GA *West-4.8m to* Enota Mountain Retreat *West-11m to* **Hiawassee, GA, P.O. 30546**	R, P G, L, M, cl O, D C, L, g, cl, f G, L, M, O, D, V, cl	2,949'	2,144.7	
53.3	0.3	Stream	w	3,300'	2,144.1	
53.6	0.5	Rocky Mountain Trail *(W-1m USFS-283)*		3,700'	2,143.8	
54.1	1.3	Rocky Mountain: *views*	C	4,017'	2,143.3	
55.4	0.7	Indian Grave Gap, USFS-283 *East-1.9m blue-blaze to* USFS Andrews Cove CG	R, P C, w	3,113'	2,142.0	
56.1	0.3	Tray Mountain Road, USFS-79	R	3,580'	2,141.3	
56.4	0.7	Cheese Factory Site: *campsites (W-0.1m spring)*	C, w	3,590'	2,141.0	
57.1	0.8	Tray Gap, Tray Mountain Road, USFS-79/698	R, P	3,847'	2,140.3	
57.9	0.5	Tray Mountain: *views*		4,430'	2,139.5	
58.4	1.2	**Tray Mountain Shelter** *(W-0.2m S; 0.3m spring),* *8.3mS; 7.9mN*	S, C, w	4,200'	2,139.0	
59.6	0.6	Wolfpen Gap		3,550'	2,137.8	
60.2	0.5	Steeltrap Gap		3,500'	2,137.2	
60.7	1.3	Younglick Knob		3,800'	2,136.7	
62.0	1.1	Swag of the Blue Ridge		3,400'	2,135.4	
63.1	0.9	Sassafras Gap *(E-190 yds. spring)*	w	3,500'	2,134.3	
64.0	1.0	Addis Gap *East-0.5m on old fire road to* USFS 26-2 and stream	C R, C, w	3,304'	2,133.4	

ATC: NC-GA Map 3

Miles from Springer	Miles to Next Point	Features	Services	Elev	Miles from Katahdin	M A P
65.0	0.8	Kelly Knob		4,085'	2,132.4	
65.8	1.0	**Deep Gap Shelter** (E–0.3m), 7.9mS; 8.6mN	S, C, w	3,550'	2,131.6	
66.8	0.2	Campsite: east on blue-blaze with view	C	3,625'	2,130.6	
67.0	0.2	McClure Gap	C	3,650'	2,130.4	
67.2	1.0	Powell Mountain		3,850'	2,130.2	
68.2	0.6	Moreland Gap		3,050'	2,129.2	
68.8	0.6	Snake Mountain: cross small streams	w	2,650'	2,128.6	
69.4	1.1	Dicks Creek Gap, US-76: picnic area, stream West–0.5m to Hostel Around the Bend West–11m to **Hiawassee, GA, P.O. 30546** East–15m to **Clayton, GA, P.O. 39525**	R, P, w H, f G, L, M, O, D, V, cl M, L, O	2,675'	2,128.0	ATC: NC-GA Map 3
70.5	0.7	Little Bald Knob Campsite	C, w	3,160'	2,126.9	
71.2	1.1	Cowart Gap		2,920'	2,126.2	
72.3	0.4	Buzzard Knob		3,680'	2,125.1	
72.7	1.2	Bull Gap		3,550'	2,124.7	
73.9	0.7	**Plumorchard Gap Shelter** (E–0.2m), 8.6mS; 7.5mN	S, C, w	3,050'	2,123.5	
74.6	0.6	As Knob		3,460'	2,122.8	
75.2	1.0	Blue Ridge Gap, USFS-72: dirt road	R, P	3,020'	2,122.2	
76.2	0.2	Wheeler Knob: campsite, spring	C, w	3,560'	2,121.2	
76.4	1.9	Rich Cove Gap		3,400'	2,121.0	
78.3	0.1	Georgia–North Carolina State Line: tree register		3,825'	2,119.1	

The Appalachian Trail begins at Springer Mountain and follows a rugged, often rocky terrain, reaching a height of more than 4,461 feet and never dipping below 2,500 feet. It passes through five major gaps and more than 25 smaller ones. Thru-hikers starting their journey in March or April will probably see snow, which can add to the difficulty. Spring melts give way to many of the wildflowers common throughout the mountains, including bloodroot, trillium, and azalea. Forests are mostly second-growth hardwoods of hickory, oak, and poplar. Half of the Trail lies within five designated wilderness areas in the forest.

Georgia Appalachian Trail Club—GATC maintains the 78.3 miles from Springer Mountain to the North Carolina line. Correspondence should be sent to GATC, P.O. Box 654, Atlanta, GA 30301; (404) 494-0968; georgia-atclub.org; trails_supervisor@georgia-atclub.org.

Chattahoochee National Forest—The Trail in Georgia winds through the Chattahoochee National Forest, created by Congress in 1936. By that time, much of the land had been laid bare from intensive timber harvesting. Today, little virgin timber remains, but the hardwoods have reestablished themselves with the help of 89 years of management and protection.

Note: With the loss of habitat from development in the mountains, black bears are roaming farther in search of food. To combat this problem, the GATC and the USFS are placing bear boxes and/or bear cables for hanging food at the shelters most affected. If bear cables are not available, secure food using bear-proof techniques. See page 9.
   The U.S. Forest Service rules require using a bear canister while camping overnight between Jarrard and Neel gaps, a five-mile stretch that includes Woods Hole and Blood Mountain shelters and Slaughter Gap Campsite. Plan accordingly.

Springer Mountain—Springer has served as the A.T.'s southern terminus since 1958. Before that, Mt. Oglethorpe, to the southwest, was the terminus. In 1993, GATC members and the Forest

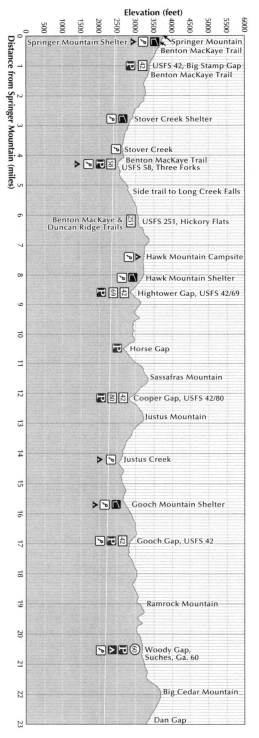

Elevation (feet) — Distance from Springer Mountain (miles)

- Springer Mountain Shelter
- Springer Mountain / Benton MacKaye Trail
- USFS 42, Big Stamp Gap / Benton MacKaye Trail
- Stover Creek Shelter
- Stover Creek
- Benton MacKaye Trail / USFS 58, Three Forks
- Side trail to Long Creek Falls
- Benton MacKaye & Duncan Ridge Trails / USFS 251, Hickory Flats
- Hawk Mountain Campsite
- Hawk Mountain Shelter
- Hightower Gap, USFS 42/69
- Horse Gap
- Sassafras Mountain
- Cooper Gap, USFS 42/80
- Justus Mountain
- Justus Creek
- Gooch Mountain Shelter
- Gooch Gap, USFS 42
- Ramrock Mountain
- Woody Gap, Suches, Ga. 60
- Big Cedar Mountain
- Dan Gap

Service installed a new plaque marking the Trail's southernmost blaze. The hiker register is located within the boulder on which the plaque is mounted. The original bronze plaque marking the southern terminus, one of three intended for road crossings, was created in 1934 by GATC member and amateur sculptor George Noble at a cost of $20—a hefty amount in those days. Warner Hall, the club's second president, served as Noble's model and coined the phrase, "A footpath for those who seek fellowship with the wilderness." That plaque was moved to the mountain in May 1959; keep an eye out for the other two at road crossings along the Trail in Georgia. The overlook at the 3,782-foot summit provides views to the west—a nice sunset spot.

Springer Mountain Shelter (1993)—Sleeps 12. Privy. Tentpads. Bear boxes. Near the summit, 250 yards north of the bronze plaque, then east 200 yards on a blue-blazed side trail. Water source is a spring 80 yards on a blue-blazed trail in front of the shelter; spring may go dry in times of drought.

Stover Creek Shelter (2006)—Sleeps 16. Privy. Tentpads. Bear box and cables. Water source is the creek. No tenting near water.

Hawk Mountain Campsite (2016)—30 tentpads, 3 bear boxes, privy, water.

Hawk Mountain Shelter (1993)—Sleeps 12. Limited camping. Privy. Bear boxes and cables. Army Rangers from nearby Camp Frank D. Merrill use the area for training exercises and have been spotted all times of the day and night. Water source is 300 yards on a blue-blazed trail behind the shelter.

Gooch Mountain Shelter (2001)—Sleeps 14. Privy. Bear boxes and cables. Additional tenting space 1.6 miles farther north at Gooch Gap, near the old shelter site. Excellent water source is 100 yards behind the shelter.

GA-60/Woody Gap/Suches—Parking area, picnic tables, and chemical toilets. A spring is on a poorly marked side trail 0.1 mile west of the A.T. on northern side of the gap. *Shuttles servicing Amicalola to Fontana:* White Blaze Shuttle (706)-300-8964, Grateful Hiker Shuttle (772)321-0905, Ron's Appalachian Trail Shuttle (706-669-0919),

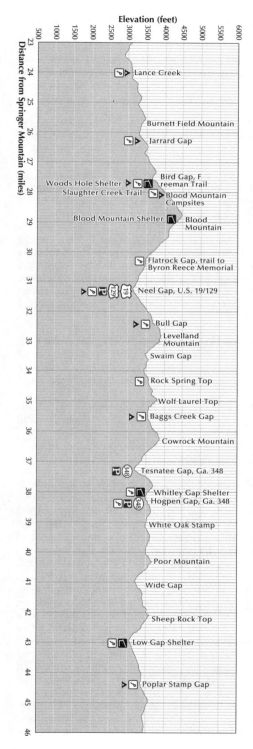

Bret Eady AT Hiker Shuttle (404) 569-8776, Richard Anderson (404) 408-2524, Jeff (706) 994-2307. Text is preferred for all shuttlers!

West 1.3 miles to *Hostel:* Above the Clouds Hostel; 1487 State Hwy 60, Suches, GA, 30572; (706) 747-1022, (678) 983-0954; abovethecloudshostel.com; hostel, shuttles, slackpacking, call for rates.

East 7 miles to *Lodging:* Barefoot Hills, 7693 Hwy 19N, Dahlonega, GA, (770) 312-7342, barefoothills.com, Private bunk rooms $95/night, beer, wine, to-go charcuterie trays, Door Dash available.

⛺ **West** 2.4 miles to *Hostel:* Hidden Pond Hostel, 191 Holly Hill Rd., Suches, GA 30572, (706) 747-3736, text (919) 920-0990, Shuttles, resupply, laundry, Wi-Fi. Reservations required. M–F 12:15–4:15 p.m., closed Sa. Suches Wilderness Ranch, (407) 271-9493, Wi-Fi, Outdoor Shower, campers available across road from Hidden Pond. *Groceries:* Wolfpen Gap Country Store (short-term resupply), 41 Wolf Pen Gap Rd., **Suches, GA [P.O. ZIP 30572; M–F 12:15–4:15 p.m., closed Sa; (706) 747-2271]**, fuel, pizza, wings, premade subs, Wi-Fi. Store open M–Sat 7 a.m.–10p.m., Su 8 a.m.–9 p.m. *Other services:* Medical: Union General Hospital Suches Clinic, 56 Firewater Ln., Suches, GA 30572, (706) 747-1036; Jim Ann Miner, (706) 747-5434, lives in town and is available if you need help. *Shuttles:* A.T. Hiker Shuttle, (404) 569-8776, beady2727@gmail.com, owner, Brett "Suches" Eady (SOBO A.T. 2017, SOBO BMT 2019), based out of Suches, pet-friendly, insured, 365 days, 24/7, some holidays. S to Atlanta/Springer Mountain, N to Fontana Dam; airport, bus, and train terminals; slackpacking; offers Georgia section-hiker package. Also covers the Benton MacKaye Trail.

Gooch Lance Creek—Campsite with 4 tent platforms, built by the ATC Konnarock crew. Bear cables. Good water.

Gooch Jarrard Gap—West 1 mile on blue-blazed trail to USFS Lake Winfield Scott Recreation Area; tentsites, showers, $15; dogs must be leashed. **Bear canisters for food storage are required if you plan to camp between here and Neel Gap.**

Gooch Woods Hole Shelter (1998)—Sleeps 7. Privy. Bear box. Located 0.4 mile west on a blue-blazed side trail, this "Nantahala design" shelter is named in honor of the late Tillie and

Roy Wood, original owners of the Woodshole Hostel near Pearisburg, Virginia. Water source is an unreliable spring along the trail to the shelter.

Gooch Bird Gap—From here, the Freeman Trail leads 1.7 miles around the south slope of Blood Mountain and rejoins the A.T. 1.1 miles from Neel Gap. Those who choose this blue-blazed route miss the climb to the Trail's high point in Georgia; it serves as a foul-weather route around Blood Mountain.

Gooch Slaughter Gap—Slaughter Creek Trail leads to tentsites near Slaughter Creek that ease the load on Blood Mountain. Note: To counter visitor impact, fires have been banned along a 3.3-mile section between Slaughter Gap and Neel Gap.

Gooch Blood Mountain—According to tales of the Creek and Cherokee, a battle here between the two nations left so many dead and wounded that the ground ran red with blood. Blood Mountain is the most-visited spot on the A.T. south of Clingmans Dome, and the impact of more than 40,000 visitors a year has taken its toll. Vandalism in and around the shelter is a chronic problem.

Gooch Blood Mountain Shelter (1934)—Sleeps 8. Privy. Food canisters required Mar 1–Jun 1. Located atop the highest peak on the A.T. in Georgia (4,461 feet), this historic two-room stone structure was last refurbished in 2012. No water or firewood available; no fires permitted. Northbounders can get water from a stream 0.3 mile north of Bird Gap or on a blue-blazed side trail at Slaughter Gap, 0.9 mile from the shelter. Southbounders can get water at Neel Gap or at a spring located on the blue-blazed trail to Byron Reece Memorial, 0.2 mile from where the trail joins the A.T., 2.4 miles south of Neel Gap.

US-19 & 129/Neel Gap—Mountain Crossings at Walasi-Yi Center, 12471 Gainesville Hwy, Blairsville, GA 30512; (706) 745-6095, mountaincrossings.com. A full-service **Outfitter** with all stove fuels and gift shop (short-term resupply). Expert footwear and pack fitters also offer free pack shakedown service. UPS, FedEx, and USPS packages held, $10 donation. **Hostel** is open $35pp first-come/first-served.
    East 0.3 mile to **Lodging:** Blood Mountain Cabins (706) 745-9454, bloodmountain.com, recently updated cabins, 1br+loft (sleeps 4), bathroom, kitchen, fireplace, Wi-Fi, laundry, short path to trail and Mountain Outfitters. Book online or call for info.
    West 3 miles to **Camping:** Vogel State Park, (800) 864-7275, gastateparks.org. Tentsites with shower $25–$30, showers only $2. Camp store (limited resupply) has snacks; coin laundry (detergent $1); and cabins, reservations suggested. Leash dogs inside the park.
    West 13 miles to **Blairsville, GA [P.O. ZIP 345 Young Harris St, 30512: M-F 8:309–54:30, Sa 8:309–12; (706) 745-4123].** The Grateful Hiker (hiker lounge) has closed but still operates the shuttle; Donald Ballard, (772) 321-0905, and Mary Bastin, (706) 400-9105. **Lodging:** Seasons Inn, 94 Town Sq. (706) 745-1631 , ask for hiker discount; Best Western, 201 Hwy 515W, (706) 745-6995, ask for hiker discount; Comfort Inn, 90 Fisher St., (706) 745-6844, prices may vary. Laundry on-site, indoor heated pool. **Groceries:** Ingles Market, Walmart, Dollar General, Family Dollar. **Restaurants:** Numerous restaurants and fast food. **Shuttles:** The Further Shuttle and The Grateful Hiker, Donald Ballard, (772) 321-0905, and Mary Bastin, (706) 400-9105, cover from Atlanta airport to Davenport Gap, call for pricing, dogs welcome, booster/baby seats available, resupply drops with numerous drivers, accept mailings of backpack and other resupply items to bring on the day of hiker pick-up; will pick up at Gainesville bus/train stations and any airport within 200 miles of Blairesville. Jeff's Appalachian Trail Shuttles and Tours, (706) 994-2307, please call or text, owner Jeff Moon, based out of Blairsville, pet-friendly, insured, 365 days/24/7/holidays, North Springs MARTA to Fontana Dam, , slackpacking, free parking; Ron's Appalachian Trail Shuttle, (706) 669-0919, Texting is preferred, hikershuttles@outlook.com (Ron's Appalachian Trail Shuttle-Facebook), based out of Ellijay, Springer Mountain, pet-friendly, insured, 365 days/24/7/holidays, can accommodate early starts, Atlanta to Fontana Dam, airport, bus, and train terminals, slackpacking, please leave a message or text with your phone number if you get voice mail, flat rate for shuttles to, or from any part of the A.T. and nearby towns as well as Amicalola Falls State Park, Atlanta airport ,and Gainesville, extra stops OK, fuel on request; Richard Anderson, (404) 408-2524 texts preferred, or

email richardjanderson@etcmail.com, based near Springer, covers AT, BMT, and Pinhoti in GA and NC up to Fontana, will pick up at Dalton, GA or Gainesville, GA bus station and Chattanooga airport, dogs ok, 17 years of experience reliable shuttling with fair fees.

Whitley Gap Shelter (1974)—Sleeps 6. Privy. Bear cables. This shelter is located 1.2 miles east of the A.T. down a steep side trail. Water source is a spring 0.3 mile beyond the shelter.

Low Gap Shelter (1953)—Sleeps 7. Privy. Bear cables. Water source is crossed at the shelter; a second source can be found 30 yards in front of the shelter.

Chattahoochee Gap—A blue-blazed side trail leads east to Chattahoochee Spring, source of the Chattahoochee River, which supplies drinking water to Atlanta and almost half of the state's population. Some 500 miles from this point, the river empties into the Gulf of Mexico.

Blue Mountain Shelter (1988)—Sleeps 7. Privy. Bear cables. Located on a short side trail. Water source is a spring on the A.T. 0.1 mile south of the shelter.

⚠ ⛺ **GA-75/Unicoi Gap–East** 9 miles to **Helen, GA [P.O. ZIP 7976 S. Main St., 30545: M–F 8:30–5, Sa 9–12; (706) 878-2422].** *Lodging:* Helendorf River Inn, (706) 878-2271, ask for hiker discount, coin laundry, pets $30 in designated rooms only, B, Wi-Fi, heated pool; Days Inn, newly remodeled (706) 878-8000, ask for hiker discount, Wi-Fi, B, $20/pets under 20 lbs. in selected rooms; Baymont Inn, (706) 878-2111 $40 pet fee; Amerivu Inn , (706) 878-4079, pets ($20) under 30 lbs., Wi-Fi, B, outdoor seasonal pool; Quality Inn, (706) 878-2268 call for hiker discount, B, $40/pet up to 40 lbs., Wi-Fi; RiverBend, (706) 878-2155, call for hiker rate, , rooms and cabins up to 4-8 people, no smoking, Wi-Fi, B, pets $30 ea.; Alpine Valley Inn, (706) 878-2141, call for hiker discount, B, guest laundry, shuttle to/from Unicoi Gap $5 per person; Red Roof Inn, (706) 878-8888, call for hiker discount B, Wi-Fi. *Groceries:* Betty's Country Store and Deli (long-term resupply), ATC books, open daily 7–9. *Restaurants:* Wendy's, Huddle House, and numerous others. *Internet access:* White County Library, Helen Branch. *Other services:* bicycle rentals available at Woody's Mountain Bikes, (706) 878-3715, woodysmtb.com; pharmacy.

East 17 miles to **Cleveland, GA** *Outfitter:* Smoky Mountain Trader, 18 W. Jarrard St., (706) 865-7296, smokymountaintrader.com, open M–F 10–5,closed Wednesdays/Sundays , full-service outfitter/resupply, canister fuels(butane/isopro). *Medical:* Northeast Georgia Physicians Group, (706) 348-4280, Guilford Immediate Care, M–F 8–7, Sa/Su 8–2.

West 2.3 miles, then left 2.5 miles on GA-180 to *Lodging:* Enota Mountain Retreat (also known as Camp Pioneer), 1000 Hwy 180, Hiawassee, GA 30546; (706) 896-9966, enota.com; waterfalls, organic gardens, and an animal sanctuary; $15 membership per visit and $5 campfire fee; tent-sites available with access to bathhouse, cabins available, bunkhouses, RV sites, dogs $5. Free

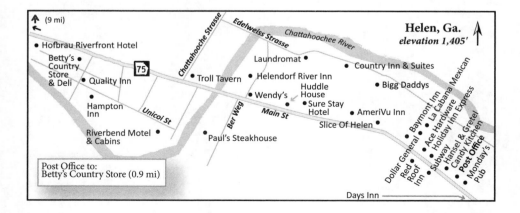

Helen, Ga.
elevation 1,405'

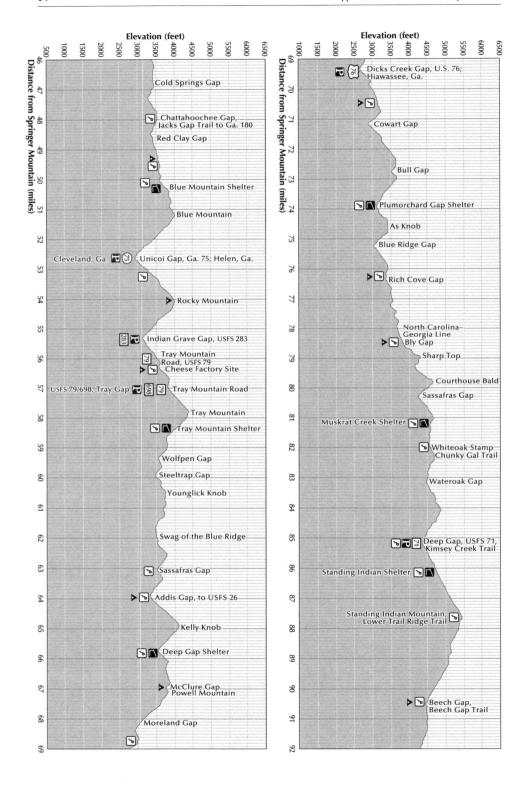

Left panel (Distance from Springer Mountain, miles 46–69; Elevation in feet):

- Cold Springs Gap
- Chattahoochee Gap, Jacks Gap Trail to Ga. 180
- Red Clay Gap
- Blue Mountain Shelter
- Blue Mountain
- Cleveland, Ga.
- Unicoi Gap, Ga. 75; Helen, Ga.
- Rocky Mountain
- Indian Grave Gap, USFS 283
- Tray Mountain Road, USFS 79
- Cheese Factory Site
- USFS 79/698, Tray Gap
- Tray Mountain Road
- Tray Mountain
- Tray Mountain Shelter
- Wolfpen Gap
- Steeltrap Gap
- Younglick Knob
- Swag of the Blue Ridge
- Sassafras Gap
- Addis Gap, to USFS 26
- Kelly Knob
- Deep Gap Shelter
- McClure Gap
- Powell Mountain
- Moreland Gap

Right panel (Distance from Springer Mountain, miles 69–92; Elevation in feet):

- Dicks Creek Gap, U.S. 76; Hiawassee, Ga.
- Cowart Gap
- Bull Gap
- Plumorchard Gap Shelter
- As Knob
- Blue Ridge Gap
- Rich Cove Gap
- North Carolina–Georgia Line
- Bly Gap
- Sharp Top
- Courthouse Bald
- Sassafras Gap
- Muskrat Creek Shelter
- Whiteoak Stamp Chunky Gal Trail
- Wateroak Gap
- Deep Gap, USFS 71, Kimsey Creek Trail
- Standing Indian Shelter
- Standing Indian Mountain, Lower Trail Ridge Trail
- Beech Gap, Beech Gap Trail

long-distance phone, coin laundry with soap, video library. Holds packages for guests only.

West 7.5 miles to Green Dragon Hostel (see below).

West 11 miles to **Hiawassee, GA** (see below).

⚠ USFS 283, Indian Grave Gap— USFS Andrews Cove Campground, open seasonally, $12.

Cheese Factory Site—In the mid-1800s, a New Englander established a dairy near Tray Mountain, about 15 miles from the nearest farmhouse. Other Georgians, who received parcels in the mountains after a government survey of former Indian lands in the 1830s, opted to sell their land to speculators rather than tame the untamable. For years, the man reportedly produced a superior cheese that won several awards. Little evidence of the dairy remains today, although the spot is a designated campsite with a spring.

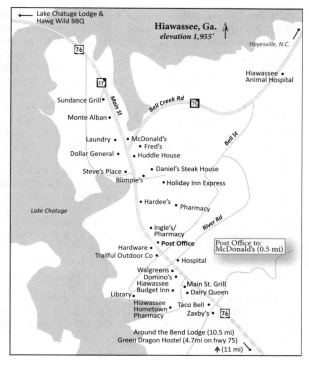

Hiawassee, Ga.
elevation 1,955'

Tray Mountain—Spectacular views from the 4,430-foot summit and probably the southernmost breeding area in the United States for Canada warblers. These small, active songbirds may be spotted in the rhododendron thickets along the southern approach to the summit. Males are blue-gray above and yellow throughout the chest. Look for the distinctive "necklace" on both the males' and females' chests. The Canada warbler's song is an irregular burst of beautiful notes.

Tray Mountain Shelter (1971)—Sleeps 7. Privy. Bear cables. Excellent spot for taking in the sunset and sunrise from the summit or from viewpoints along the 0.2-mile trail to the shelter. Water source is a spring located 260 yards behind the shelter.

Addis Gap—East 0.5 mile to stream at USFS 26.

Deep Gap Shelter (1983)—Sleeps 12. Privy. Bear box. On a 0.3-mile side trail to the east. Water source is on the blue-blazed trail to the shelter.

⚠ US-76/Dicks Creek Gap/Hiawassee—Parking lot, picnic tables, and small creek.

West 0.5 mile to *Hostel:* Around the Bend Lodge (no longer a hostel), 7675 Hwy 76 E, Hiawasee, GA 30546, Reservations required. Contact at placestostayinnorthga.com

West 7.7 miles on Hwy 76 then 1.3miles after left on Hwy 75 to *Hostel:* Green Dragon Hostel, (407) 435-0294 thegreendragonhostel@gmail.com , texting is preferred, full service hostel. Included with bunk is free 10-minute shuttle to and from Unicoi and/or Dick's Creek, free shuttle into town for resupply, fresh linens, hot showers and toiletries, laundry done for you, loaner clothes, Wi-Fi, printing services, indoor/outdoor community spaces. Breakfast included with stay. Longer shuttles available for fee. Slackpacking services for guests from Neel Gap to Winding Stair with shuttle fees. Use USPS or FedEx for mail drops and include name, ETA, and phone number.

⚠ **West** 11 miles to **Hiawassee, GA [P.O. ZIP 110 N. Main St., 30546: M–F 8:30–5, Sa 8:30–12; (706) 896-3632].** *Lodging:* Hiawassee Budget Inn, 193 S. Main St., (706) 896-4121, Internet/Wi-Fi access, holds packages only for guests. Holiday Inn Express, 300 Big Sky Dr., (706) 896-8884, ihg.com, ask for hiker discount, no pets, coin laundry indoor pool, Wi-Fi/Internet access, will hold UPS packages. *Groceries:* Ingles (ATM), both long-term resupply, Dollar General, Walgreens. *Restaurants:* Huddle House, Domino's, Marco's Pizza (both deliver to Green Dragon) Main Street Grill, B/L; Monte Alban Mexican, L/D; Tilted Café, Hiawasse Brew (closed M & Th); various fast-food places. *Outfitter:* Trailful Outdoor Co., 15 North Main St., trailful.com, hello@trailful.com, full-service outfitter, mail drops accepted, provides 'safe place' for pack while in Hiawassee. *Internet access:* Towns County Public Library. *Other services:* Western Union; coin laundry; Chatugue Regional Hospital, (706) 896-2222, known for treatment of blisters and ER; dentist; banks with ATM; hardware store; Hiawassee Animal Hospital, (706) 896-4173.

East 16 miles to **Clayton, GA [P.O. ZIP 30525: M–F 8:30–5, Sa 8:30–12; (706) 782-5795].** On US 441 and on Main St. *Restaurants:* La Pachanga Mexican Restaurant, U-Joint Restaurant: outdoor seating and pet friendly, Burger King, Dairy Queen, Chick-fil-a. *Lodging:* Days Inn, Mountainaire Cottages & Inn (706) 782-9568, Bridgecreek Inn (706) 960-4300. *Outfitter:* Outdoor 76, short-term resupply, hiking gear and beer on tap,hiker lounge, laundry and showers available. *Other services:* Currahee Brewing Company. Ingles with Starbucks. Most locations are close to town center. *Shuttle:* Free shuttle from Dick's Creek Gap to Clayton starting March thru April; leaves Outdoor 76 at 10am arrives at Dick's Creek Gap at 10:30 then again at Outdoor 76 at 3 p.m. and at Dick's Creek Gap at 3:30. Call (828) 349-7676.

Plumorchard Gap Shelter (1993)—Sleeps 14. Privy. Bear box and cables. The stump in front has been home to copperheads. Water source is a creek that crosses the trail to the shelter or a spring located 200 yards west of the A.T., opposite the shelter trail. Food-hoisting cables.

North Carolina

Miles from Springer	Miles to Next Point	Features	Services	Elev	Miles from Katahdin	M A P
78.3	0.1	Georgia–North Carolina State Line: *tree register*		3,825'	2,119.1	
78.4	0.7	Bly Gap: *gnarly oak tree (spring 250 ft. south and east)*	C, w	3,840'	2,119.0	
79.1	0.7	Sharp Top: *vista*		4,338'	2,118.3	
79.8	0.5	Courthouse Bald		4,690'	2,117.6	
80.3	0.6	Sassafras Gap		4,300'	2,117.1	
80.9	0.3	Stream	w	4,625'	2,116.5	
81.2	0.8	**Muskrat Creek Shelter**, *7.5mS; 4.9mN*	S, C, w	4,600'	2,116.2	
82.0	0.2	Whiteoak Stamp	C, w	4,620'	2,115.4	
82.2	0.9	Chunky Gal Trail (W–5.5m to US-64)		4,700'	2,115.2	
83.1	2.1	Wateroak Gap		4,460'	2,114.3	
85.2	0.9	Deep Gap, USFS-71: *campsite (W–0.1m)* *West–3.7m on Kimsey Creek Trail to USFS Standing Indian Campground*	R, P, C, w C, g, sh	4,341'	2,112.2	
86.1	1.5	**Standing Indian Shelter**, *4.9mS; 7.6mN*	S, C, w	4,760'	2,111.3	
87.6	2.9	Lower Ridge Trail; Standing Indian Mountain (5,498') *South–100ft. of jct.–unmarked spring trail (W–0.2m)* *East–to campsite; 0.2m to summit* *West–4.2m to USFS Standing Indian Campground*	 w C C, g, sh	5,410'	2,109.8	ATC: NC-GA Map 2
90.5	1.8	Beech Gap, Beech Gap Trail	C, w	4,460'	2,106.9	
92.3	1.0	Coleman Gap		4,220'	2,105.1	
93.3	0.4	Timber Ridge Trail		4,700'	2,104.1	
93.7	1.4	**Carter Gap Shelter**, *7.6mS; 8.7mN*	S, C, w	4,540'	2,103.7	
95.1	0.3	Ridgepole Mountain		4,990'	2,102.3	
95.4	2.3	Little Ridgepole Vista		4,800'	2,102.0	
97.7	0.6	Betty Creek Gap, Betty Creek Trail	C, w	4,300'	2,099.7	
98.3	0.3	Mooney Gap, USFS-83	R, P	4,400'	2,099.1	
98.6	0.6	Log steps: *spring*	w	4,500'	2,098.8	
99.2	0.4	Bearpen Gap: *USFS-67 nearby*		4,700'	2,098.2	
99.6	0.3	Bearpen Trail, USFS-67, Albert Mtn Bad Weather Bypass	R	4,790'	2,097.8	
99.9	0.2	Albert Mountain: *firetower*	P	5,250'	2,097.5	
100.1	0.4	Albert Mountain bad-weather bypass trail		5,020'	2,097.3	
100.5	1.9	Big Spring Gap		4,940'	2,096.9	
102.4	0.9	**Long Branch Shelter**, *8.7mS; 3.4mN*	S, C, w	4,503'	2,095.0	
103.3	2.5	Glassmine Gap, Long Branch Trail		4,400'	2,094.1	
105.8	0.1	**Rock Gap Shelter**, *3.4mS; 8mN*	S, C, w	3,760'	2,091.6	
105.9	0.6	Rock Gap, USFS-67 *West–1.5m to USFS Standing Indian Campground*	R, P C, g, sh	3,750'	2,091.5	

Miles from Springer	Miles to Next Point	Features	Services	Elev	Miles from Katahdin	M A P
106.5	3.1	Wallace Gap, "Old US-64, Old Murphy Road", SR-1448	R	3,738'	2,090.9	
		West–1.5m to USFS Standing Indian Campground	C, g, sh			
109.6	0.2	Winding Stair Gap, US-64: *piped spring*	R, P, w	3,770'	2,087.8	
		East–10m to **Franklin, NC, P.O. 28734**	H, all			
109.8	0.7	East Fork Moore Creek: *bridge, waterfall*	w	3,780'	2,087.6	
110.5	0.2	Moore Creek Campsite	C, w	3,970'	2,086.9	
110.7	0.9	Swinging Lick Gap		4,100'	2,086.7	
111.6	1.7	Panther Gap		4,480'	2,085.8	
113.3	0.5	**Siler Bald Shelter** (E–0.5m on loop trail), 8mS; 7.8mN	S, C, w	4,700'	2,084.1	
113.8	1.7	Snowbird Gap, **Siler Bald Shelter** (E–0.6m)	S, C, w	4,980'	2,083.6	
		West–0.2m to Siler Bald summit (5,216')				
115.5	1.3	Wayah Gap, SR-1310: *picnic area*	R, P	4,180'	2,081.9	
116.8	0.5	Wilson Lick Ranger Station: *historic site*		4,650'	2,080.6	
117.3	0.5	USFS-69: *log steps, piped spring*	R, w	4,900'	2,080.1	
117.8	1.8	Wine Spring, Bartram Trail (E–campsite; W–water)	C, w	5,360'	2,079.6	
119.6	0.1	Latrines, USFS-69 parking area	R, P	5,320'	2,077.8	
119.7	0.4	Wayah Bald: *stone observation tower*		5,342'	2,077.7	ATC: NC-GA Map 2
120.1	0.1	Spring *(west)*	w	5,250'	2,077.3	
120.2	0.4	Bartram Trail: *campsite, spring (E–200 yds.)*	C, w	5,200'	2,077.2	
120.6	1.3	**Wayah Shelter**, 7.8mS; 4.8mN	S, C, w	4,480'	2,076.8	
121.9	2.3	Licklog Gap: *logging road (W–0.1m C; 0.5m stream)*	C, w	4,440'	2,075.5	
124.2	1.2	Burningtown Gap, SR-1397	R, P	4,236'	2,073.2	
125.4	0.7	**Cold Spring Shelter**, 4.8mS; 5.8mN	S, C, w	4,920'	2,072.0	
126.1	1.2	Copper Ridge Bald Lookout		5,080'	2,071.3	
127.3	0.3	Rocky Bald Lookout side trail *(E–0.2m)*		5,030'	2,070.1	
127.6	1.4	Big Branch Campsite	C, w	4,900'	2,069.8	
129.0	1.4	Tellico Gap, Otter Creek Road, S.R. 1365: *powerline*	R, P	3,850'	2,068.4	
130.4	-9.3	Wesser Bald Observation Tower *(E–100 feet)*		4,627'	2,067.0	
121.1	10.1	Spring: *water for Wesser Bald Shelter (east)*	w	4,100'	2,076.3	
131.2	1.8	**Wesser Bald Shelter**, Wesser Creek Trail, 5.8mS; 4.9mN	S, C, w	4,115'	2,066.2	
133.0	3.1	Jump-up Lookout		4,000'	2,064.4	
136.1	0.8	**A. Rufus Morgan Shelter**, 4.9mS; 7.9mN	S, C, w	2,300'	2,061.3	
136.9	0.1	US-19, US-74, Nantahala River, N.O.C., Wesser, NC	R, P, H, G, L, M, O, cl, sh, f	1,723'	2,060.5	
		East–1m to Nantahala Food Mart	G			
		East–13m to **Bryson City, NC, P.O. 28713**	G, L, M, D, cl			ATC: NC-GA Map 1
137.0	1.2	Railroad tracks		1,795'	2,060.4	
138.2	0.3	Powerline		2,030'	2,059.2	
138.5	0.7	Wright Gap: *dirt road*	R	2,390'	2,058.9	
139.2	0.4	Tyre Knob: *skirt southeast side*		2,760'	2,058.2	
139.6	0.4	Campsite and spring	C, w	2,940'	2,057.8	
140.0	0.4	Grassy Gap		3,050'	2,057.4	
140.4	1.4	Grassy Top		3,290'	2,057.0	

Miles from Springer	Miles to Next Point	Features	Services	Elev	Miles from Katahdin	MAP
141.8	0.6	Spring: *at trail switchback*	w	3,690'	2,055.6	
142.4	0.7	The Jump-up: *trail switchback*		3,780'	2,055.0	
143.1	0.9	Swim Bald: *views of the Smokies*		4,720'	2,054.3	
144.0	1.2	**Sassafras Gap Shelter**, *7.9mS; 9.1mN*	S, C, w	4,330'	2,053.4	
145.2	0.4	Cheoah Bald: *vistas, Bartram Trail northern terminus*	C	5,062'	2,052.2	
145.6	2.0	Bartram Trail		4,830'	2,051.8	
147.6	1.0	Locust Cove Gap: *spring (west)*	C, w	3,690'	2,049.8	
148.6	1.4	Simp Gap		3,700'	2,048.8	
150.0	0.7	Ridge High Point *(W-0.1m to spring on logging road)*	w	3,520'	2,047.4	
150.7	1.0	Stecoah Gap, NC-143, Sweetwater Creek Road: *table* West-2m to Cabin in the Woods West-9m to **Robbinsville, NC, P.O. 28771**	R, P, w L G, L, M	3,165'	2,046.7	
151.7	1.4	Sweetwater Gap		3,220'	2,045.7	
153.1	0.4	**Brown Fork Gap Shelter**, *9.1mS; 6.3mN*	S, C, w	3,800'	2,044.3	
153.5	1.8	Brown Fork Gap *(E-35 yds. spring)*	w	3,580'	2,043.9	
155.3	0.8	Hogback Gap		3,500'	2,042.1	
156.1	2.0	Cody Gap	C, w	3,600'	2,041.3	
158.1	0.4	Stream	w	3,560'	2,039.3	
158.5	0.9	Yellow Creek Gap, NC-1242, Yellow Creek Mountain Road	R, P	2,980'	2,038.9	
159.4	1.4	**Cable Gap Shelter**, *6.3mS; 6.8mN*	S, C, w	2,880'	2,038.0	
160.8	1.4	Black Gum Gap		3,400'	2,036.6	
162.2	0.4	Walker Gap, Yellow Creek Trail West-2.8m to Fontana Village	PO, G, L, M, O, cl, f	3,450'	2,035.2	
162.6	0.1	Campsite: *stream*	C, w	3,200'	2,034.8	
162.7	1.5	Crest of Bee Cove Lead		2,620'	2,034.7	
164.2	0.4	Spring	w	2,470'	2,033.2	
164.6	0.3	Benton Mackaye Trail West-3m to Fontana Village	PO, G, L, M, O, cl, f	2,070'	2,032.8	
164.9	0.1	NC-28: *stone steps* East-6m to The Hike Inn West-2m to **Fontana Dam, NC, P.O. 28733**	R, P L, f G, L, M, O, cl, f	1,810'	2,032.5	
165.0	1.2	S.R 1245, Fontana Lake Marina: *restrooms*	P	1,170'	2,032.4	
166.2	0.3	**"Fontana Hilton" Shelter**, *6.8mS; 11.8mN*	R, P, S, C, sh, w	1,775'	2,031.2	
166.5	0.1	Fontana Dam bypass trail: *TVA maintenance area*		1,725'	2,030.9	
166.6	0.4	Fontana Dam Visitors Center: *showers*	R, P, sh, w	1,821'	2,030.8	

(side text: ATC: NC-GA Map 1)

At Bly Gap, northbounders enter the Nantahala National Forest with 4,000-foot gaps and 5,000-foot peaks. Nantahala is Cherokee for "land of the noonday sun." Long climbs between the Stecoah–Cheoah Mountain area and Cheoah Bald offer panoramic views of western North Carolina. Don't rush; enjoy the landscape from an observation tower or two.

Nantahala Hiking Club—NHC maintains the 58.6 miles between the Georgia line and the Nantahala River. Correspondence should be sent to NHC, 173 Carl Slagle Rd., Franklin, NC 28734; nantahalahikingclub.org.

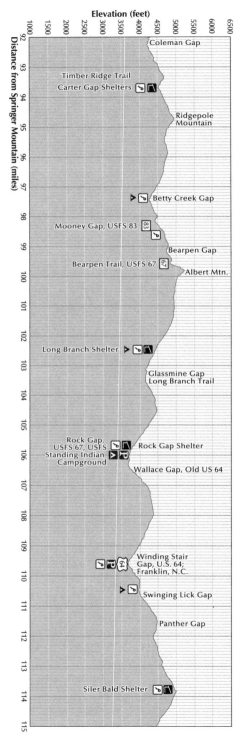

(see next page)

Note: No road access to the A.T. is available between Bly Gap and Rock Gap during Jan, Feb, and part of Mar. The Forest Service closes USFS 71 to all vehicular traffic until Mar 1 and USFS 67 until Mar 15. Frequently used trailheads at Deep Gap and others are inaccessible.

Bly Gap—If you are thru-hiking, it is time to celebrate your first (or last) state line. When you see the gnarled oak in a clearing, you're officially in North Carolina. The gap, with its grassy area and views to the northwest, makes a good campsite. Water from a spring about 100 yards south on the A.T.

Muskrat Creek Shelter (rebuilt 1995)—Sleeps 8. Moldering privy. This shelter uses the "Nantahala design." Water source is just south and visible from the shelter.

Deep Gap—From here, the Kimsey Creek Trail leads 3.7 miles west to the Forest Service's Standing Indian Campground (see next page).

Standing Indian Shelter (1996)—Sleeps 8. Privy. "Nantahala design" shelter. Water source is a stream opposite the side trail to the shelter. Recent bear sightings—use bear-proofing techniques.

Standing Indian Mountain—The 5,498-foot summit of the mountain 0.2 mile east is reached via a blue-blazed side trail. Cliff-top views to the south gave it the nickname, "Grandstand of the Southern Appalachians." At the top are flat areas for camping and views south toward Blood Mountain. A spring is located 0.2 mile downhill on an unmarked trail near the A.T. junction with Lower Ridge Trail. Please tread lightly if you choose to camp here; the area receives tremendous use.

Carter Gap Shelter (1998)—Shelter sleeps 8. Privy. Water source is a spring located downhill on the west side of the Trail.

Mooney Gap—This gap has been identified as among the wettest places in the eastern U.S., with an estimated annual precipitation of 93.5 inches.

Long Branch Shelter (2012)—Timber frame, sleeps 8. Privy. Water is on right of side trail to shelter.

Rock Gap Shelter (1965/2023)—Sleeps 8+. Privy, tentsites. Bear cables. Located only 0.1 mile from the road. Water source is a spring to the left and behind the shelter.

Rock Gap/Standing Indian Campground—West 1.5 miles on a paved road to the Forest Service campground with tentsites $20, restroom, warm showers ($2 shower only); small camp store with snacks open M–Sa 10–5, Su 1–4 Apr–Nov; will hold packages shipped UPS to 2037 Standing Indian Campground Rd., Franklin, NC 28734. **Shuttles:** Macon County Transit, (828) 349-2222, $5pp from Rock Gap to Franklin, M–F 9:45 a.m., 12:45 p.m., and 3:45 p.m. in season (Feb–May).

US-64/Winding Stair Gap—East 10 miles to **Franklin, NC [P.O. ZIP 28734: M-F 8:30-5, Sa 9-12; (828) 524-3219].** Although a bit spread out, most major services are within walking distance along Business US-441. The town runs several Trail-related events in Mar and Apr. **Hostels:** The Grove Hostel, 130 Hayes Circle, (828) 346-7657, contact@grovehostel. com, thru-hiker owned and operated. Amenities available: private rooms, semiprivate rooms, bunks. Lodging includes shower, laundry, Wi-Fi, kitchenette. Text for

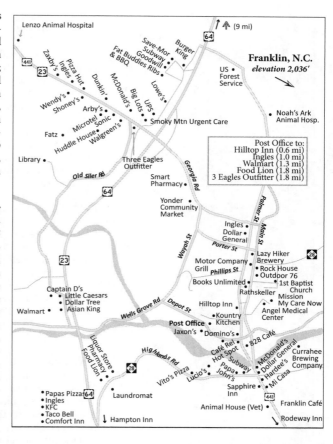

Franklin, N.C.
elevation 2,036'

Post Office to:
Hilltop Inn (0.6 mi)
Ingles (1.0 mi)
Walmart (1.3 mi)
Food Lion (1.8 mi)
3 Eagles Outfitter (1.8 mi)

p/u from either Rock or Winding Stair Gap; other shuttles and slackpacking opportunities available upon request. In-town shuttles, re-supply shuttles, and parking for section hikers available. The Barn AT Hiker Hostel (252) 646-3580 call or text to ensure availability Chica & Sunsets Place: (715) 315-0876 Rent whole place via AirBnB.com for 1–4 people; Private apartment has 2 bedrooms, 4 twin beds, bathroom, washer/dryer, full kitchen/living room. **Lodging:** Hilltop Inn, 433 E. Palmer St., (828) 524-4403, $67d, no pets, microwave, refrigerator, Internet, Wi-Fi, guest laundry, will hold packages for guests only; The Sapphire Inn, 761 E. Main St., (828) 524-4406, (ask for hiker rate), microwave, refrigerator, Internet, Wi-Fi, pets up to 50 lbs. $10, will hold packages for guests only; Quality Inn, (828) 369-9200, 313 Cunningham Rd., starting at $103 including B, dogs only $25 each, pool, Wi-Fi, coin laundry; Microtel Inn & Suites, (828) 349-9000, 81 Allman Dr., pets $45 up to 35 lbs., B, Wi-Fi. **Groceries**: Ingles Supermarket, Food Lion, Sav-Mor, and Walmart (long-term resupply). **Restaurants:** Kountry Kitchen, B/L; Shoney's, AYCE; Sunset Restaurant, (828) 524-4842, M–F, 6 a.m.–8 p.m., Sa 7–2:30, B/L/D, daily specials, 10% hiker discount; Rock House Lodge, (828) 349-7676, M–Sa 10–6, quality craft beers on tap, Internet access, located inside Outdoor 76. **Outfitters:** Three Eagles Outfitters, 78 Siler Rd. (main location), (828) 524-9061, open M–Sa 10–6, Su 12–4, full-service outfitter with 30 years A.T. experience and on-site trained footwear specialists, Wi-Fi and Internet kiosk, Coleman and alcohol fuel by the ounce, Esbit and canisters, will ship and hold packages; Outdoor 76, 35 East Main St., (828) 349-7676, outdoor76. com, full-service outfitter, lightweight gear, food, fuel, footwear experts with trained staff, M–Sa 10–6, 10% thru-hiker discount on one item, Internet access, mail drops accepted (include hiker's name on packages), laundry available including soap/dryer sheet. **Internet access:** Macon County Library, open M–Th 9–6, F–Sa 10–5. **Other services:** Franklin First Baptist Church, free B daily

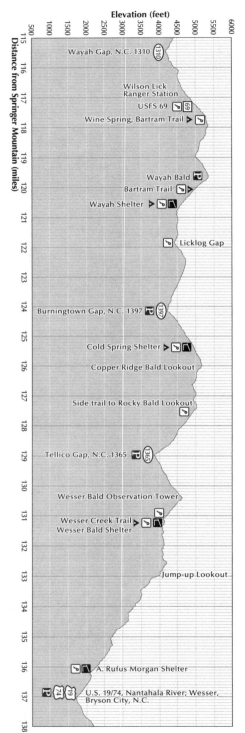

Elevation (feet)

Distance from Springer Mountain (miles)

Wayah Gap, N.C. 1310

Wilson Lick
Ranger Station

USFS 69

Wine Spring, Bartram Trail

Wayah Bald

Bartram Trail

Wayah Shelter

Licklog Gap

Burningtown Gap, N.C. 1397

Cold Spring Shelter

Copper Ridge Bald Lookout

Side trail to Rocky Bald Lookout

Tellico Gap, N.C. 1365

Wesser Bald Observation Tower

Wesser Creek Trail
Wesser Bald Shelter

Jump-up Lookout

A. Rufus Morgan Shelter

U.S. 19/74, Nantahala River; Wesser,
Bryson City, N.C.

Mar 14–Apr 14; UPS Store, (828) 524-9800; coin laundry; Mission My Care Now Health clinic, (828) 369-4427, 190 Riverview St., M–F 8–6, Sa 9–4; Franklin Health & Fitness, (828) 369-5608, yoga, massage therapy, pool, hiker discount; Currahee Brewery, open daily, Wi-Fi, printer, charging outlets, library, food cart; Lazy Hiker brewery, food truck; pharmacy; veterinarian. Lotus Massage-Hiker Special, schedule online mysite.vagaro.com/lotusevolutionmassage. **Shuttles:** Macon County Transit, (828) 349-2222, $5pp, town shuttle leaves from Winding Stair Gap at 9:30, 12:30 and 3:30; Sunset Shuttles (715) 315-0849, text preferred, based in Franklin, provides shuttles from Amicalola to Fontana Dam. Asheville airport pickup/drop off, slackpacking available.

Siler Bald Shelter (1959)—Sleeps 8. Privy. Bear cables. Located 0.5 mile on a blue-blazed loop. Water source is 80 yards down a blue-blazed trail from the shelter.

Wayah Bald—The stone observation tower at the summit of Wayah Bald (5,342 ft.) was built in 1937 by the CCC and renovated in 1983. Wayah is Cherokee for "wolf."

Wayah Shelter (2007)—Sleeps 8. Privy. Five tentsites. Nantahala-style. Water source is Little Laurel Creek, 600 feet west of A.T. on blue-blazed trail. This shelter was built by the NHC in memory of Ann and Larry McDuff, thru-hikers and ALDHA members who were killed about a year apart in eerily similar accidents, hit by vehicles while riding bikes near home.

Cold Spring Shelter (1933)—Sleeps 6. Privy. Food canisters required Mar 1–Jun 1. Shelter built by the CCC. Tentsites on the east side of the Trail 200 yards north on A.T. Water source is 5 yards in front of the shelter.

Wesser Bald—Formerly a firetower, the structure atop Wesser Bald is now an observation deck offering panoramic views. The Great Smoky Mountains and Fontana Lake dominate to the north.

Wesser Bald Shelter (1994)—Sleeps 8. Privy. Bear cables. This was the first of the "Nantahala design" shelters. Tentsites in clearing where the blue-blaze leads to the shelter. Water source is a spring 0.1 mile south on the A.T., then 75 yards on a blue-blazed trail.

Rufus Morgan Shelter (rebuilt 1989)—Sleeps 6. Privy. Located in a small cove, this shelter is named

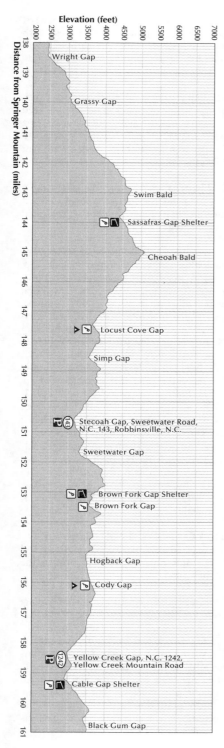

Elevation (feet)

Distance from Springer Mountain (miles)

Wright Gap

Grassy Gap

Swim Bald

Sassafras Gap Shelter

Cheoah Bald

Locust Cove Gap

Simp Gap

Stecoah Gap, Sweetwater Road, N.C. 143, Robbinsville, N.C.

Sweetwater Gap

Brown Fork Gap Shelter
Brown Fork Gap

Hogback Gap

Cody Gap

Yellow Creek Gap, N.C. 1242, Yellow Creek Mountain Road

Cable Gap Shelter

Black Gum Gap

after the Nantahala club's founder. The water source is a stream across the A.T. from the shelter.

Smoky Mountains Hiking Club—SMHC maintains the 102.5 miles between the Nantahala River and Davenport Gap. Correspondence should be sent to the SMHC, P.O. Box 51592, Knoxville, TN 37950; smhclub.org.

US-19/Nantahala River/Nantahala Outdoor Center— At US-19, the A.T. passes through the Nantahala Outdoor Center (NOC), (800) 232-7238, noc.com, an outdoor-adventure center with many services for back-packers; call ahead for shuttles. Between the outfitter and River's End Restaurant, the A.T. crosses a pedes-trian bridge over the Nantahala River. Note: NOC could be closed during inclement weather in Feb and Mar. *Lodging:* NOC call ahead for reservations; check in at the general store; hostel $30 based on availability, no pets allowed in hostel; basecamp lodging $50–$200 (2–8); motel room, $75-$200D; NOC cabins $250 and up with cleaning fee; Reservations recommended. *Groceries:* NOC General Store (short-term resupply), open 9–5 *Restaurants:* River's End Restaurant, open 11–7 L/D, Wi-Fi; Big Wesser Riverside Bar, open May 1, 10 a.m.–11 p.m., snacks, light meals, drinks, open seasonally. *Outfitter:* NOC Outfitters (short-term resupply), 9–5 (varies with season), offers backpacking gear, ability to print your GSMNP permit, Coleman and alcohol fuel by the ounce, Isopro canisters, ATM, stamps, ATC publications, Wi-Fi. Restroom and coin showers are located on the southern side of US-19. NOC accepts USPS, UPS, and FedEx packages sent to 13077 Hwy 19W, Bryson City, NC 28713. Check with the front desk; packages must be marked "Hold for A.T. Hiker." NOC can ship packages via UPS.

East 1 mile to *Groceries:* Nantahala Food Mart (medi-um-term resupply), daily 6am-9pm, biscuits, pizza.

East 2 miles to Gorgeous Stays, bunkhouse and cabin lodging for solo and group hikers (bedding pro-vided), Licensed Chiropractor on site, shuttle provided to and from the NOC, showers, bathhouse, towels, soap, Wi-Fi, lodge, laundry service available, some food and snacks available for sale.

East 13 miles on US-19 to **Bryson City, NC [P.O. ZIP 28713: M-F 9-4:30, Sa 10-12; (828) 488-3481]**. Bryson City is a large town with many services, including Ingles Supermarket (long-term resupply), pharmacy, coin laundry, several restaurants, banks with ATM, Western Union, hospital, and several hotels.

Whitewater Rafting—The Nantahala marks the north-bounder's first chance at Trail-side whitewater rafting. The French Broad River in Hot Springs, NC, and the Nolichucky River in Erwin, TN, are also whitewater hot spots. Guided tours on the Nantahala are available

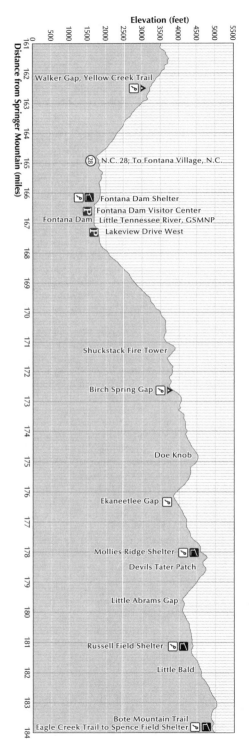

through NOC for about $25 on nonpeak days, but you can rent a raft or "ducky" for less, with shuttles to the put-in point upstream included. Mountain biking, zipline, and horseback riding also available.

Sassafras Gap Shelter (2002)—Sleeps 14. Privy. Located in a ravine 100 yards in on a blue-blazed side trail, this wood-framed shelter features a covered porch and benches. Water source is a reliable spring in front of the shelter. Nice tent sites down the hill.

⚠ **NC-143/Stecoah Gap**—A good spring can be found by following the paved road west 200 feet to an overgrown logging road. Spring is located down the logging road on the left.

East 2 miles to Cabins in the Woods, 386 W. Stecoah Heights, Robbinsville, NC 28771; call or text (980) 406-6446. Free pickup at Stecoah Gap, other shuttles fee based, thecabinsinthewoods.com; Hawks Hiker Haven (3 beds) has TV, Wi-Fi, shower, pets allowed, laundry, breakfast options, shuttles and slackpacking, mail drops accepted for guests, larger cabins subject to availability.

East 3.4 miles to *Hostel:* Stecoah Wolfcreek Hostel, (828) 735-0768, $40pp, a full house with soft beds, full kitchen, laundry included, shuttle to Ingles, free pickup and dropoff at Stecoah Gap.

West 9 miles to **Robbinsville, NC [P.O. ZIP 28771: M–F 9–4:30** closed Sa; (828) 479-3397]. *Groceries*: Ingles Market. *Restaurants*: Wendy's; McDonald's; Subway; Pop & Nana's Kitchen and The Scoop, B all day; various other restaurants. *Lodging*: Quality Inn, (828) 479-6772, 111 Rodney Orr Bypass, B, Wi-Fi; San Ran Motel, (828) 479-3256, 253 Rodney Orr Bypass, hiker-friendly with reasonable rates, A/C, Wi-Fi. *Other services:* Walgreens, Family Dollar, Dollar General, Ace Hardware.

Brown Fork Gap Shelter (1996)—Sleeps 6. Privy. Constructed by the SMHC, Konnarock Crew, and the USFS. Water source is a reliable spring to the right of the shelter.

⚠ **Yellow Creek Road**—**West** 2.2 miles to *Lodging:* Creekside Paradise B&B, 259 Upper Cove Rd., Robbinsville, NC 28771, (828) 346-1076 no texts, $70s, $100d, $40pp for 3 or more, includes B, Wi-Fi, resupply trip & amenities (shower, laundry, hot tub). Camping $20pp includes Wi-Fi & amenities. Breakfast $10. Resupply trip $10. All stays include p/u & d/o at Yellow Creek Gap. Fees apply for p/u & d/o at Stecoah, Fontana, and NOC. Shuttles & slackpacking available. Costs based on distance and # of passengers.

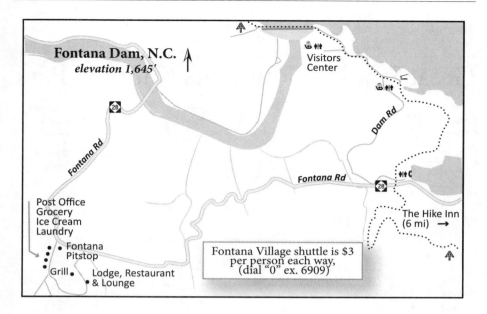

Fontana Dam, N.C. ↑
elevation 1,645'

Visitors Center

Dam Rd

Fontana Rd

Fontana Rd

The Hike Inn (6 mi) →

Post Office
Grocery
Ice Cream
Laundry

• Fontana
  Pitstop

Grill •   Lodge, Restaurant
        • & Lounge

Fontana Village shuttle is $3
per person each way,
(dial "0" ex. 6909)

Cable Gap Shelter (1939/1988)—Sleeps 6. Privy. Shelter originally built by the CCC. The water source is a reliable spring in front of the shelter. Roof leaks.

Walker Gap—The Yellow Creek Trail leads 2.5 miles west to Fontana Village. However, it is a poorly marked, difficult shortcut to the resort.

NC-28/Fontana Dam—East 6 miles to *Lodging:* The Hike Inn, 3204 Fontana Rd. Fontana Dam, NC 28733, (828) 479-3677, hikeinn@graham.main.nc.us,. Welcoming foot travelers for 30 years. A hikers-only lodging and shuttle service run by Nancy "Coffee Break" Hoch. Reservations requested. Thru-hiker packages available. Free slackpacking between Stecoah Gap, Yellow Creek Gap, and Fontana Dam with 2-night stay; free printing of Smokies permit; and mail drops held free for guests only. Prices vary for section-hikers with vehicles. Shuttles available between Atlanta and Damascus.

West 2 miles to **Fontana Dam, NC [P.O. ZIP 28733; M-F 11:45-3:45, closed Sa; (828) 498-2315]**, which is located 2 miles from Fontana Dam within the Fontana Village Resort. Note: Some services may close or be under reduced hours during off-season, and supplies are limited; most services available by late Mar. *Lodging:* Fontana Lodge, Fontana Village, 300 Woods Rd., Fontana Dam, NC 28733; (800) 849-2258, fontanavillage.com; cabins (2-night minimum) or lodge rooms; tentsites available, reservations recommended; will hold packages at Check-in. *Groceries:* Fontana General Store and The Pit Stop with outfitter supplies (both short-term resupply). *Other services:* restaurant, coin laundry, ice cream/soda fountain (open in May) with Internet access, disc golf, mountain bike rentals, and fitness center. *Shuttle:* Seasonal shuttle available between Fontana Village Resort and Fontana Dam/Hilton, $5 per person either way.

Fontana Dam Shelter (1982)—Sleeps 24. Restroom with water, showers, USB chargers at shelter. Known as the "Fontana Hilton," this spacious shelter is located 0.3 mile south of the dam on TVA land. Shower facilities also are located at the dam; see below.

Fontana Dam—At 480 feet, Fontana Dam is the highest dam in the eastern United States, built during World War II as part of the Manhattan Project. This TVA facility offers a visitor center with restrooms and shower that is normally open 9-7 Apr–Aug and 9-6 Sep–Oct (last Su). Wi-Fi available with passcode from Visitor center. Overnight parking available. Small gift shop at visitor center with snack/drinks.

Great Smoky Mountains National Park

Miles from Springer	Miles to Next Point	Features	Services	Elev	Miles from Katahdin	M A P
166.6	0.4	Fontana Dam Visitors Center: *showers*	R, P, sh, w	1,821'	2,030.8	
167.0	0.1	Little Tennessee River, Fontana Dam; southern boundary, **Great Smoky Mountains National Park**	R	1,821'	2,030.4	
167.1	0.6	Fontana Dam bypass trail		1,755'	2,030.3	
167.7	3.6	Lakeview Drive West, Benton MacKaye Trail, Lakeshore Trail	R, P	1,800'	2,029.7	
171.3	0.3	Shuckstack Firetower *(E-0.1m): on old road*		3,800'	2,026.1	
171.6	1.0	Sassafras Gap, Lost Cove Trail, Twentymile Trail Jct.		3,653'	2,025.8	
172.6	2.2	Birch Spring Gap, Campsite #113: *tentpads, spring*	C, w	3,834'	2,024.8	
174.8	0.5	Doe Knob, Gregory Bald Trail		4,520'	2,022.6	
175.3	1.0	Mud Gap		4,260'	2,022.1	
176.3	1.7	Ekaneetlee Gap: *spring (west 300 ft.)*	w	3,842'	2,021.1	
178.0	0.5	Gant Lot (Rich Gap) **Mollies Ridge Shelter**, *11.8mS; 3.1mN*	S, w	4,570'	2,019.4	
178.5	1.1	Devils Tater Patch		4,775'	2,018.9	
179.6	0.3	Little Abrams Gap		4,120'	2,017.8	
179.9	1.2	Big Abrams Gap		4,080'	2,017.5	
181.1	0.3	Russell Field Trail Jct. **Russell Field Shelter** *(W-150 yds. stream), 3.1mS; 3.1mN*	S, w	4,360'	2,016.3	
181.4	2.6	McCampbell Gap		4,328'	2,016.0	
184.0	0.4	Eagle Creek Trail to **Spence Field Shelter** *(E-0.2m), 3.1mS; 6.3mN* Bote Mountain Trail *(W-0.2m spring)*	S, w w	4,915'	2,013.4	
184.4	0.7	Jenkins Ridge Trail		4,950'	2,013.0	
185.1	0.6	Rocky Top: *vista*		5,441'	2,012.3	
185.7	1.1	Thunderhead *(east peak):* vista		5,527'	2,011.7	
186.8	0.6	Beechnut Gap *(W-75 yds.):* spring	w	4,920'	2,010.6	
187.4	0.3	Mineral Gap		5,030'	2,010.0	
187.7	0.6	Brier Knob: *vista*		5,215'	2,009.7	
188.3	0.8	Starkey Gap		4,500'	2,009.1	
189.1	1.0	Sugar Tree Gap		4,435'	2,008.3	
190.1	0.3	**Derrick Knob Shelter**, *6.3mS; 5.7mN*	S, w	4,880'	2,007.3	
190.4	2.1	Sams Gap, Greenbrier Ridge Trail *(W-100 yds.): spring*	w	4,840'	2,007.0	
192.5	0.3	Cold Spring Knob		5,240'	2,004.9	
192.8	3.0	Buckeye Gap, Miry Ridge Trail *(E-200 yds.): spring*	w	4,817'	2,004.6	
195.8	0.2	**Silers Bald Shelter**, *5.7mS; 1.7mN*	S, w	5,460'	2,001.6	
196.0	0.2	Silers Bald: *vistas*		5,607'	2,001.4	
196.2	0.8	Welch Ridge Trail		5,430'	2,001.2	
197.0	0.5	Jenkins Knob		5,550'	2,000.4	
197.5	0.6	**Double Spring Gap Shelter**, *1.7mS; 6.1mN*	S, w	5,507'	1,999.9	

National Geographic: Smokies Park Map

Miles from Springer	Miles to Next Point	Features	Services	Elev	Miles from Katahdin	M A P
198.1	1.8	Goshen Prong Trail		5,750'	1,999.3	
199.9	0.1	Mt. Buckley: *vista*		6,582'	1,997.5	
200.0	0.3	Kuwohi Bypass Trail		6,550'	1,997.4	
200.3	0.5	Kuwohi (Clingmans Dome) *(E–0.5m): observation deck*	R, P, w	6,643'	1,997.1	
200.8	0.2	Mt. Love		6,446'	1,996.6	
201.0	1.7	Collins Gap		5,886'	1,996.4	
202.7	0.4	Mt. Collins		6,188'	1,994.7	
203.1	0.2	Sugarland Mountain Trail **Mt. Collins Shelter** *(W–0.5m), 6.1mS; 8.5mN*	S, w	5,900'	1,994.3	
203.3	3.0	Fork Ridge Trail, Mountains to the Sea Trail *(E–35 yds.)*	R	5,890'	1,994.1	
206.3	0.4	Indian Gap, Road Prong Trail	R, P	5,317'	1,991.1	
206.7	1.3	Mt. Mingus Lead: *feral hog barrier*		5,460'	1,990.7	
208.0	1.7	Newfound Gap, US-441, TN-71 Rockefeller Memorial: *restrooms* *East–18m to* **Cherokee, NC, P.O. 28719** *West–15 m to* **Gatlinburg, TN, P.O. 37738**	R, P, w all all	5,045'	1,989.4	
209.7	0.8	Sweat Heifer Trail		5,820'	1,987.7	
210.5	0.3	Mt. Ambler		6,000'	1,986.9	
210.8	0.3	Boulevard Trail to Mt. LeConte *(W–5.3m L, M)*		5,695'	1,986.6	
211.1	0.1	**Icewater Spring Shelter**, *8.5mS; 7.8mN*	S, w	5,920'	1,986.3	
211.2	0.7	Spring	w	5,900'	1,986.2	
211.9	0.1	Charlies Bunion: *southern loop trail jct to view from Fodder Stack*		5,500'	1,985.5	
212.0	0.4	Charlies Bunion: *northern loop trail jct to view from Fodder Stack*		5,500'	1,985.4	
212.4	0.1	Dry Sluice Gap		5,375'	1,985.0	
212.5	0.9	Dry Sluice Gap Trail		5,310'	1,984.9	
213.4	1.3	Porters Gap, the Sawteeth		5,500'	1,984.0	
214.7	1.8	False Gap		5,400'	1,982.7	
216.5	2.0	Bradley's View: *vistas*		5,200'	1,980.9	
218.5	1.7	Hughes Ridge Trail to **Peck's Corner Shelter** *(E–0.4m), 7.8mS; 5.6mN* *Intermittent spring 100 feet north on A.T.*	S, w w	5,280'	1,978.9	
220.2	0.7	Copper Gap		5,478'	1,977.2	
220.9	1.0	Mt. Sequoyah		6,003'	1,976.5	
221.9	0.7	Chapman Gap		5,801'	1,975.5	
222.6	1.1	High Point on Mt. Chapman		6,218'	1,974.8	
223.7	0.3	**Tri-Corner Knob Shelter**, *5.6mS; 7.7mN*	S, w	5,920'	1,973.7	
224.0	1.1	Balsam Mountain Trail		6,000'	1,973.4	
225.1	0.6	Guyot Spur		6,360'	1,972.3	
225.7	0.1	Guyot Spring: *on A.T.*	w	6,150'	1,971.7	
225.8	0.4	Mt. Guyot side trail		6,395'	1,971.6	
226.2	0.5	Cross Pinnacle Lead: *NoBo enter "Hell Ridge"*		6,260'	1,971.2	
226.7	0.7	Deer Creek Gap		6,020'	1,970.7	
227.4	0.3	Yellow Creek Gap		5,900'	1,970.0	
227.7	1.3	Snake Den Ridge Trail, Inadu Knob		5,491'	1,969.7	

National Geographic: Smokies Park Map

Miles from Springer	Miles to Next Point	Features	Services	Elev	Miles from Katahdin	M A P
229.0	0.9	Camel Hump Knob		5,250'	1,968.4	
229.9	1.1	Camel Gap, Camel Gap Trail		4,645'	1,967.5	
231.0	0.4	Cosby Knob, State-Line Ridgecrest, *SoBo enter "Hell Ridge"*		5,150'	1,966.4	
231.4	0.7	**Cosby Knob Shelter**, *7.7mS; 6.9mN*	S, w	4,700'	1,966.0	
232.1	2.1	Low Gap, Low Gap Trail *West–2.5m to NPS Cosby Campground*	C, w	4,242'	1,965.3	
234.2	0.4	Mt. Cammerer side trail to firetower (W–0.6m)		5,000'	1,963.2	
234.6	1.5	Spring *(west)*	w	4,300'	1,962.8	
236.1	0.2	Spring *(E–50 yds.)*	w	3,700'	1,961.3	
236.3	1.0	Lower Mt. Cammerer Trail *West–7.8m to NPS Cosby Campground*	C, w	3,465'	1,961.1	
237.3	1.0	Chestnut Branch Trail *East–2m to Big Creek Ranger Station* *East–2.3m to Big Creek Country Store* *East–2.5m to NPS Big Creek Campground*	G P, C, w	2,900'	1,960.1	
238.3	1.1	**Davenport Gap Shelter**, *6.9mS; 10.9mN*	S, w	2,600'	1,959.1	
239.4	0.7	Davenport Gap, TN-32, SR-1397 (Old NC-284/Cove Creek Road) Eastern boundary, **Great Smoky Mountains National Park** *East–1.3m to Big Creek Ranger Station* *East–2.3m to NPS Big Creek Campground*	R, P C, w	1,975'	1,958.0	

National Geographic: Smokies Park Map

Established in 1934, the Great Smoky Mountains National Park (GSMNP) is the most visited of the traditional national parks. For that reason, it is especially important to practice Leave No Trace here. The highest elevation on the A.T. is here at Kuwohi at 6,643 feet. GSMNP also has the most rainfall and snowfall on the A.T. in the South, and many hikers are caught off-guard by the snow and cold temperatures at these high elevations, especially in the spring.

Note: Park regulations require you to hang food sacks or packs from provided cables at all overnight sites.

Great Smoky Mountains National Park—The Trail through the park officially begins for northbound-ers on the northern side of Fontana Dam; for southbounders, Davenport Gap is the beginning. In recent years, the park has hosted more than 12 million visitors annually. Home to the most diverse forest in North America, the park includes more than 100 species of trees, 1600 species of flowering plants, 65 species of mammals, more than 30 different salamanders, and 2,000 varieties of mush-rooms. Park information, as well as seasonal and temporary closures, can be found at nps.gov/grsm.

Backcountry Permits—**Backcountry permits must be obtained before entering the park**. The thru-hiker fee is $40 for a seven-night permit, as of March 1, 2023. Purchase permits online up to 30 days before your planned entry of the park at smokiespermits.nps.gov or by phone at (865) 436-1297; good for 8 days and 7 nights in the park. You will need a paper copy. Fontana Lodge has a work station for printing permits, and other options are available either side of the park. Anyone caught without a permit may be issued a fine! Plan ahead and print the permit as soon as you can. Addi-tional rangers are being deployed in the backcountry to enforce this fee.

Human Waste and Privies—In past years, the park's administration shunned privies at backcountry facilities. Instead, "toilet areas" were designated where backpackers are supposed to dig cat holes and bury their waste. A privy-building campaign, underwritten by ATC and SMHC, resulted in privies at 7 of the 12 shelters. If there is no privy, the best decision is to do your business away from the shelter area before you get to camp or after you leave. Pick a spot far from any trails and 200 feet or more from any water, and practice Leave No Trace methods.

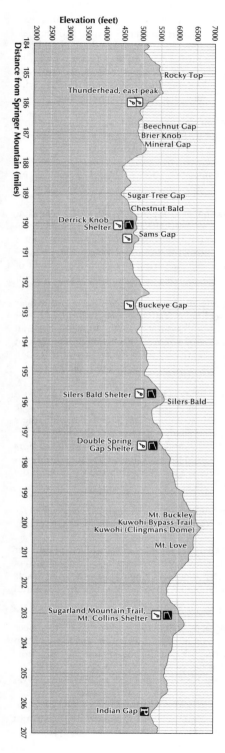

Elevation (feet)

Distance from Springer Mountain (miles)

Rocky Top

Thunderhead, east peak

Beechnut Gap
Brier Knob
Mineral Gap

Sugar Tree Gap
Chestnut Bald

Derrick Knob Shelter
Sams Gap

Buckeye Gap

Silers Bald Shelter
Silers Bald

Double Spring Gap Shelter

Mt. Buckley
Kuwohi Bypass Trail
Kuwohi (Clingmans Dome)

Mt. Love

Sugarland Mountain Trail,
Mt. Collins Shelter

Indian Gap

Horses—Within the park, half of the A.T. is open to horseback riding; horse users may also share A.T. shelters. SMHC and ATC have made a concerted effort to resolve issues with the horse users, who have helped with major rehabilitation and other projects along the Trail in that half.

Bears—Roughly 1,900 bears reside in the park. They become more active in the early spring and remain active through the fall. Following a few simple guidelines can help keep bears and other animals away from people and safe within the park. **Be sure to hang food on the provided bear-bag system, and do not feed or leave food for these wild creatures to eat.** Except for Davenport Gap, shelters no longer have chain-link fences to keep bears out. Whenever possible, keep food away from the shelter sleeping areas.

Dogs—Dogs are not permitted on trails in the park. Hikers violating this rule will be fined up to $5,000. Those hiking with dogs should arrange to board their pets. Several kennels provide this service: Standing Bear Farm Hiker Hostel, call or text (423) 608-0149; contact for details. Loving Care Kennels, (865) 453-2028, lovingcarekennels.net, in Pigeon Forge, TN; owner Lida O'Neill will pick up and/or drop off your dog at Fontana Dam and Davenport Gap for $425 for one dog, discount for two dogs; also holds mail drops.

Pests and Disease—At Kuwohi and throughout the park, you will witness changes in the Smokies' ecosystem. The most obvious has been the death of conifers at higher elevations. Atmospheric pollution weakens the trees, which makes it easier for the balsam woolly adelgid to attack and eventually kill the park's Fraser firs. Other pests and diseases affecting the park's ecosystem include chestnut blight, southern pine beetle, hemlock woolly adelgid, and dogwood anthracnose.

Air Pollution—This is one of the Smokies' most conspicuous problems. Pollution can drop visibility from 93 to 22 miles on an otherwise clear day. Ozone can make breathing difficult and causes visible damage to black cherry, milkweed, and thirty other species of plants in the park. The park's ozone, nitrogen, and sulfur levels are among the nation's highest and often remain high longer than in nearby urban communities. The Park service has implemented propane mowers, electric vehicles in campgrounds, and charging stations in recent years.

Shelter Policy—Park regulations require that you stay in a shelter or Birch Spring Campsite. While other backpackers must make reservations to use back-

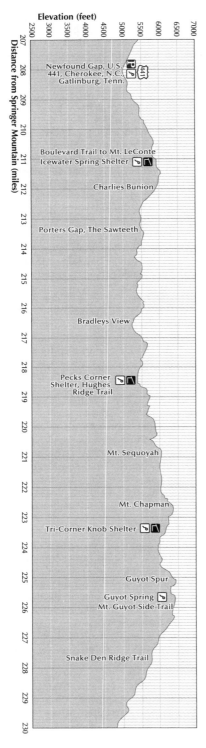

country shelters, thru-hikers are exempt from this shelter-specific regulation from Mar 15 to Jun 15. If the shelter is occupied by reservation, thru-hikers should tent close by and use the bear cables. Because only thru-hikers are permitted to tent-camp at shelters, the burden is on them to make room inside shelters for others who have reserved space; that is also the regulation.

Shelters South of Newfound Gap—Seven shelters and a campsite are located between the Little Tennessee River (Fontana Dam) and Newfound Gap.

Birch Spring Campsite—Spring water, bear cables, and tent pads.

Mollies Ridge Shelter (1961/2003)—Sleeps 12. No privy. Bear cables. Legend says the area was named for a Cherokee maiden who froze to death looking for a lost hunter and that her ghost still haunts the ridge. Water source is a somewhat reliable spring 200 yards to the right of the shelter.

Russell Field Shelter (1961)—Sleeps 14. No privy. Bear cables. This section of Trail is popular with riders. Water source is a spring 150 yards down the Russell Field Trail toward Cades Cove. A short walk beyond the spring is an open, grassy area with views of Cades Cove; the Russell Gregory family grazed stock here in the 1800s.

Spence Field Shelter (1963/2005)—Sleeps 12. Privy. Bear cables. Shelter is located 0.2 mile east on the Eagle Creek Trail. This section of Trail is popular with riders and bears. Spence Field, to the north of the shelter, offers azaleas, blueberries, and open views into North Carolina and Tennessee from the largest grassy bald in the Smokies. Water source is a reliable spring 150 yards down the Eagle Creek Trail.

Derrick Knob Shelter (1961)—Sleeps 12. No privy. Bear cables. Water source is a reliable spring near the shelter.

Silers Bald Shelter (1961/2001)—Sleeps 12. No privy. Bear cables. The increasingly overgrown bald 0.3 mile north of the shelter offers views of Clingmans Dome and sunsets over Cove Mountain. Water source is to the right; a trail leads 75 yards to a reliable spring.

Double Spring Gap Shelter (1963)—Sleeps 12. Privy. Bear cables. Gap was named to indicate the existence of two springs, one on each side of the state line and both now unreliable. The better water source is on the North Carolina side, 15 yards from the crest; second source is on the Tennessee side, 35 yards from the crest.

Kuwohi—Formerly known as Clingmans Dome, Kuwohi is the highest point on the A.T. at 6,643 feet. There are

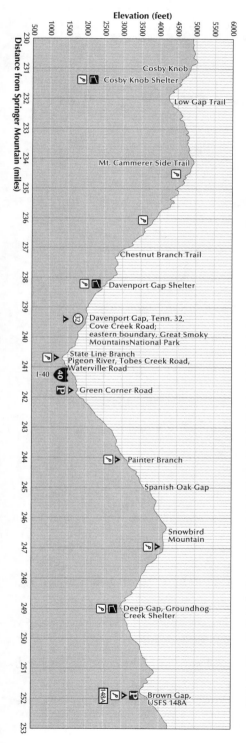

Elevation (feet)

Distance from Springer Mountain (miles)

Cosby Knob
Cosby Knob Shelter
Low Gap Trail
Mt. Cammerer Side Trail
Chestnut Branch Trail
Davenport Gap Shelter
Davenport Gap, Tenn. 32, Cove Creek Road; eastern boundary, Great Smoky Mountains National Park
State Line Branch
Pigeon River, Tobes Creek Road, Waterville Road
I-40
Green Corner Road
Painter Branch
Spanish Oak Gap
Snowbird Mountain
Deep Gap, Groundhog Creek Shelter
Brown Gap, USFS 148A

no feet-on-the-ground views from the tree-clad summit, but the observation tower provides 360-degree views. The summit is usually busy; a park road leads to within 0.5 mile of the tower. From here to the northern end of the park, Fraser firs and red spruce are now dying en masse—a dramatic change from the southernmost 30 miles of the park.

Mt. Collins Shelter (1960)—Sleeps 12. Privy. Bear cables. Nestled in spruce thicket. Water source is a small spring 200 yards beyond the shelter on the Sugarland Mountain Trail.

US-441/Newfound Gap—The only road crossing along the Trail in the Smokies. Plenty of traffic goes through the gap with its large parking lot and scenic overlook; usually an easy hitch into Gatlinburg.

East 18 miles to **Cherokee, NC [P.O. ZIP 28719: M-F 9-4:30, closed Sa; (828) 497-3891]**, visitcherokeenc.com, home of the Eastern Band of the Cherokee, with more than 24 motels and most major services. Attractions include the Museum of the Cherokee Indian, Unto These Hills Mountainside Theatre, Qualia Arts & Crafts center, and Harrah's Hotel & Casino. *Lodging:* Microtel Inn & Suites (828) 497-7800, contact for rates; Wi-Fi, B, pool; coin laundry.

West 15 miles to the resort town of **Gatlinburg, TN [P.O. ZIP 37738: M-F 9-5, Sa 9-11; (865) 436-3229]**. *Lodging:* Motel 6, (865) 436-7813, near edge of town closest to the park, hiker rate, Wi-Fi. Nearly 100 other hotels and motels, including the A.T.-centric Appy Lodge, an ATC partner, 168 Parkway, (865) 430-3659, theappylodge.com; Econo Lodge on the River for Chalet Inn, etc. *Restaurants:* More than 70, including Shoney's, with AYCE B and soup/salad bar. *Groceries:* Food City, etc. (see map). *Outfitter:* NOC's Great Outpost, 1138 Parkway, (865) 277-8209; full-service outfitter west of downtown on US-441, ask about discount lodging until May 1 (A.T. hikers only), Internet access, white gas, canister gas, and alcohol fuel by the ounce. Mail drops accepted; may ship as well. *Other services:* Banks with ATM; doctor; A Walk in the Woods, awalkinthewoods.com, (865) 436-8283 for hiker shuttles.

Boulevard Trail—This side trail, located 2.7 miles north of Newfound Gap, leads 5 miles to the summit of Mt. LeConte. A shelter and LeConte Lodge, (865) 429-5704, lecontelodge.com, are

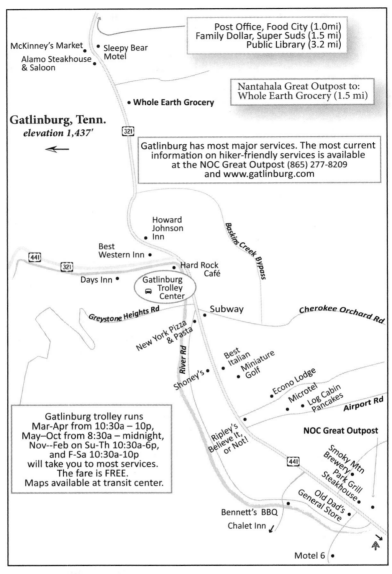

McKinney's Market
Alamo Steakhouse
& Saloon

Sleepy Bear
Motel

Post Office, Food City (1.0mi)
Family Dollar, Super Suds (1.5 mi)
Public Library (3.2 mi)

Nantahala Great Outpost to:
Whole Earth Grocery (1.5 mi)

Whole Earth Grocery

Gatlinburg, Tenn.
elevation 1,437'
321

Gatlinburg has most major services. The most current
information on hiker-friendly services is available
at the NOC Great Outpost (865) 277-8209
and www.gatlinburg.com

Howard
Johnson
Inn

Baskins Creek Bypass

Best
Western Inn
441
321
Days Inn
Gatlinburg
Trolley
Center

Hard Rock
Café

Greystone Heights Rd

Subway

Cherokee Orchard Rd

New York Pizza
& Pasta

River Rd

Shoney's

Best
Italian
Miniature
Golf

Econo Lodge
Microtel
Log Cabin
Pancakes

Airport Rd

Gatlinburg trolley runs
Mar-Apr from 10:30a – 10p,
May–Oct from 8:30a – midnight,
Nov--Feb on Su-Th 10:30a-6p,
and F-Sa 10:30a-10p
will take you to most services.
The fare is FREE.
Maps available at transit center.

Ripley's
Believe It,
or Not!

NOC Great Outpost

441

Smoky Mtn
Brewery
Park Grill
Steakhouse
Old Dad's
General Store

Bennett's BBQ
Chalet Inn

Motel 6

located at the top (reservations required; $184pp includes B/D). The round-trip to this spectacular peak is worth it, if you have the time.

Shelters North of Newfound Gap—GSMNP has five shelters between Newfound Gap and Davenport Gap.

Icewater Spring Shelter (1963/1999)—Sleeps 12. Privy. Bear cables. Water source for this heavily used shelter is 50 yards north on the A.T.

Charlies Bunion—Views of Mt. LeConte to the west. It got its name on a hike in 1929, when Charlie Conner and Horace Kephart, an A.T. pioneer and famed writer/conservationist of the period, discovered this feature, created by a landslide after a disastrous rain that year. The two decided the rocky outcropping stuck out like a bunion on Charlie's foot. The narrow path was blasted out by the Park Service.

Pecks Corner Shelter (1958/2000)—Sleeps 12. Privy. Bear cables. Follow the Hughes Ridge Trail 0.4 mile to a junction with the 0.1m side trail to the shelter. Water source is in front of the shelter 50 yards.

Tri-Corner Knob Shelter (1961/2004)—Sleeps 12. Privy. Located on the North Carolina side of the A.T., this is the most remote shelter in the GSMNP. The water source for this shelter is a reliable spring 10 yards in front of the shelter.

Cosby Knob Shelter (1959)—Sleeps 12. Privy. Bear cables. Shelter is located 100 yards east down a side trail. Water source is a reliable spring 35 yards downhill and in front of the shelter.

Mt. Cammerer Side Trail—This trail to the west leads 0.6 mile to the Mt. Cammerer firetower, a historic stone-and-timber structure originally built in 1939 by the CCC and rebuilt in 1994. Panoramic views from its octagonal platform with sides facing N, NE, E, SE, S, SW, W and NW for ease of reporting fire locations in the past.

Davenport Gap Shelter (1961/1998)—Sleeps 12. No privy. Your last, or first, GSMNP A.T. shelter, dubbed the "Smokies Sheraton." Water source is a spring in front of the shelter. Still has the old chain-link bear fence across the opening. No bear cables.

⋔ TN 32, Cove Creek Rd. (Old NC-284)/Davenport Gap—East 1.3 miles to Big Creek Ranger Station, (828) 486-5910; 1 mile farther to the station's seasonal campsites, $30/site, no showers. The Chestnut Branch Trail leads out from the ranger station and, in two miles, meets the A.T. one mile south of Davenport Gap Shelter.

North Carolina & Tennessee Border

Miles from Springer	Miles to Next Point	Features	Services	Elev	Miles from Katahdin	MAP
239.4	0.7	Davenport Gap, TN-32, SR-1397 (Old NC-284/Cove Creek Road) Eastern boundary, **Great Smoky Mountains National Park** *East–1.3m to* Big Creek Ranger Station *East–2.3m to* NPS Big Creek Campground	R C, w	1,975'	1,958.0	
240.1	0.6	Powerline		1,840'	1,957.3	
240.7	0.2	State Line Branch: *blue-blaze to spring (W–60 yds.)*	C, w	1,600'	1,956.7	
240.9	0.4	Pigeon River; Tobes Creek Road, Waterville Road	R	1,400'	1,956.5	
241.3	0.5	I-40: *underpass and 150 yds. north to* Green Corner Road, steps in rock cut *West–7.6m to* Discerning Hiker Hostel *West–16.1m to* The Hikers Rest at Hickory Hollow Hostel *West–16.8m to* Newport, TN	R H H all	1,500'	1,956.1	
241.8	2.3	Green Corner Road *West 0.11m to* Standing Bear Farm Hiker Hostel	R, P H, g, cl, sh, f	1,800'	1,955.6	
244.1	0.9	Painter Branch Campsite: *blue-blaze*	C, w	3,100'	1,953.3	
245.0	1.5	Spanish Oak Gap: *sharp switchback*		3,730'	1,952.4	
246.5	0.5	Snowbird Mountain: *FAA tower*		4,263'	1,950.9	
247.0	0.2	Campsite: *spring*	C, w	4,100'	1,950.4	
247.2	1.8	Wildcat Spring	w	4,000'	1,950.2	
249.0	2.3	Deep Gap **Groundhog Creek Shelter** *(E-0.2m), 10.9mS; 8.5mN*	S, C, w	2,900'	1,948.4	
251.3	0.1	Harmon Den Mountain, Rube Rock Trail		3,800'	1,946.1	
251.4	0.5	Hawk's Roost	C	3,800'	1,946.0	
251.9	0.6	Brown Gap, USFS-148A	R, P, w	3,500'	1,945.5	
252.5	1.9	Spring: *steep ravine (W–100 yds.)*	w	4,320'	1,944.9	
254.4	0.2	Cherry Creek Trail		4,250'	1,943.0	
254.6	0.8	Max Patch Road, S.R. 1182: *stile*	R, P	4,280'	1,942.8	
255.4	1.4	Max Patch Summit: *1933 benchmark*		4,629'	1,942.0	
256.8	0.5	Stream: *dense rhododendron*	w	4,050'	1,940.6	
257.3	0.3	**Roaring Fork Shelter**, *8.5mS; 4.8mN*	S, C, w	3,950'	1,940.1	
257.6	0.7	Footbridge		3,940'	1,939.8	
258.3	2.3	Footbridge over creek, cross road		3,840'	1,939.1	
260.6	0.2	Stream, campsite, and woods road	C, w	3,590'	1,936.8	
260.8	0.7	Lemon Gap, SR-1182, TN-107, USFS-3505	R, P	3,550'	1,936.6	
261.5	0.6	Stream(s)	w	3,940'	1,935.9	
262.1	0.8	**Walnut Mountain Shelter** *(W–0.1m), 4.8mS; 9.9mN*	S, w	4,260'	1,935.3	
262.9	0.7	Kale Gap: *woods road*		3,700'	1,934.5	
263.6	0.2	Catpen Gap: *views*		4,130'	1,933.8	

ATC: TN-NC Map 4

Miles from Springer	Miles to Next Point	Features	Services	Elev	Miles from Katahdin	MAP
263.8	0.7	Brooks	w	4,160'	1,933.6	
264.5	0.8	Bluff Mountain		4,686'	1,932.9	ATC: TN-NC Map 4
265.3	0.8	Spring: *blue-blaze (W–50 yds.)*	w	4,360'	1,932.1	
266.1	0.3	Big Rock Spring: *base of log steps (E–50 yds.)*	w	3,730'	1,931.3	
266.4	0.9	Cross old road		3,360'	1,931.0	
267.3	0.8	Small brook: *cascades*	C, w	2,520'	1,930.1	
268.1	0.5	Vista *(E–0.1m): blue-blaze*		2,640'	1,929.3	
268.6	1.8	Garenflo Gap, Garenflo Gap Road	R, H, P	2,500'	1,928.8	
270.4	0.3	Lamb Knob		2,880'	1,927.0	
270.7	1.3	Little Bottom Branch Gap		2,700'	1,926.7	
272.0	2.8	Gragg Gap, **Deer Park Mountain Shelter**, *9.9mS; 14.2mN*	S, C, w	2,330'	1,925.4	
274.8	0.1	Serpentine Street: *kiosk*	R, P, H	1,408'	1,922.6	
274.9	0.3	NC-209	R	1,340'	1,922.5	
275.2	0.4	US-25 & 70, NC-209 **Hot Springs, NC, P.O. 28743**	R, P G, L, H, M, O, cl, f	1,326'	1,922.2	
275.6	0.5	Highway bridge, French Broad River, Spring Creek, Hot Springs Spa	R, C, g, sh	1,320'	1,921.8	
276.1	0.5	Bank of French Broad River		1,320'	1,921.3	
276.6	1.9	Lovers Leap Rock		1,820'	1,920.8	
278.5	1.6	Pump Gap		2,100'	1,918.9	
280.1	0.2	Campsite near pond dam: *boxed spring*	C, w	2,490'	1,917.3	
280.3	0.8	Mill Ridge: *piped spring on gated USFS Road (W–50 ft.)*	P, w	2,800'	1,917.1	
281.1	1.4	Tanyard Gap, US-25 & 70 overpass, Lookout Mountain Road	R, P	2,278'	1,916.3	ATC: TN-NC Map 3
282.5	0.5	Cross foot log: *below is a good spring*	w	3,020'	1,914.9	
283.0	0.4	Roundtop Ridge Trail		3,250'	1,914.4	
283.4	0.1	Rich Mountain Firetower side trail *(W–0.1m)*		3,600'	1,914.0	
283.5	0.5	Campsite and spring	C, w	3,550'	1,913.9	
284.0	0.3	Spring	w	3,380'	1,913.4	
284.3	0.2	Gated USFS-3514	R	3,160'	1,913.1	
284.5	1.7	Hurricane Gap, USFS-467	R, P	2,900'	1,912.9	
286.2	1.5	**Spring Mountain Shelter**, *14.2mS; 8.6mN*	S, C, w	3,300'	1,911.2	
287.7	0.2	Spring *(west)*	w	3,190'	1,909.7	
287.9	2.0	Deep Gap, Little Paint Creek Trail		2,930'	1,909.5	
289.9	1.6	Allen Gap, NC-208, TN-70, Paint Creek: *spring (E–200 ft.)*	R, P, w	2,234'	1,907.5	
291.5	3.3	Log Cabin Drive *West–0.7m to* Hemlock Hollow Hostel	R C, G, H, M, sh, f	2,560'	1,905.9	
294.8	1.8	**Little Laurel Shelter**, *8.6mS; 7.3mN*	S, C, w	3,300'	1,902.6	
296.6	1.7	Bald Mountain Road, Camp Creek Bald Firetower trail (W–0.2m)	R	4,844'	1,900.8	
298.3	0.1	Spring, creek: *blue-blaze trails both sides of A.T.*	w	4,390'	1,899.1	
298.4	0.2	White Rock Cliffs *(E–0.1m)*		4,450'	1,899.0	
298.6	0.2	Blackstack Cliffs *(W–0.1m)*		4,420'	1,898.8	

Miles from Springer	Miles to Next Point	Features	Services	Elev	Miles from Katahdin	M A P
298.8	0.8	Bad-weather trail *(1.5m), rejoins A.T. north*		4,425'	1,898.6	
299.6	0.8	Big Firescald Knob	w	4,360'	1,897.8	
300.4	0.6	Bad-weather trail *(1.5m), rejoins A.T. south*		4,280'	1,897.0	
301.0	0.9	Round Knob Trail		4,200'	1,896.4	
301.9	0.2	USFS Fork Ridge Trail		4,210'	1,895.5	
302.1	1.6	**Jerry Cabin Shelter**, *7.3mS; 6.7mN*	S, C, w	4,150'	1,895.3	
303.7	0.3	Dirt road		4,690'	1,893.7	
304.0	1.1	Big Butt; Squibb Creek Trail	C	4,750'	1,893.4	
305.1	0.5	Spring: *seasonal*	w	4,480'	1,892.3	
305.6	1.1	Shelton graves *(E–80 yds.)*		4,500'	1,891.8	
306.7	0.5	Snake Den ridgecrest: *old logging road*		4,520'	1,890.7	
307.2	0.8	Seasonal water source	w	4,240'	1,890.2	
308.0	0.8	Flint Gap: *old logging railroad grade*		3,425'	1,889.4	
308.8	0.9	**Flint Mountain Shelter**, *6.7mS; 8.9mN*	S, C, w	3,570'	1,888.6	
309.7	1.8	Campsite: *water west in ravine*	C, w	3,400'	1,887.7	
311.5	0.5	Devil Fork Gap, TN-352/NC-212	R, P	3,107'	1,885.9	
312.0	0.3	Rector Laurel Road	H, R, w	2,960'	1,885.4	
312.3	0.3	Pass small cemetery, cross stream	w	3,060'	1,885.1	
312.6	0.3	Cross stream and woods road	w	3,210'	1,884.8	
312.9	0.4	Cross stream at waterfall	w	3,990'	1,884.5	
313.3	0.4	Sugarloaf Gap		4,000'	1,884.1	
313.7	0.8	Spring: *big rocks*	w	4,280'	1,883.7	
314.5	0.3	Cross summit of Frozen Knob		4,570'	1,882.9	
314.8	0.6	Lick Rock		4,579'	1,882.6	
315.4	1.0	Big Flat	C	4,160'	1,882.0	
316.4	1.2	Rice Gap: *rough gravel road impassable by car*		3,800'	1,881.0	
317.6	0.6	**Hogback Ridge Shelter** *(E–0.1m S; 0.3m spring)*, *8.9mS; 10.3mN*	S, C, w	4,255'	1,879.8	
318.2	1.8	High Rock *(E–150 ft.)*		4,460'	1,879.2	
320.0	0.7	Sams Gap, US-23, I-26, Flag Pond Road *West–2.5m to Nature's Inn Hostel & Cabins*	R, P H	3,760'	1,877.4	
320.7	1.6	Springs	w	4,000'	1,876.7	
322.3	0.1	Street Gap Road, Street Gap	R, P	4,100'	1,875.1	
322.4	1.1	Powerline		4,180'	1,875.0	
323.5	0.2	Spring: *blue-blaze (E–20 yds.)*	w	4,240'	1,873.9	
323.7	0.6	Low Gap: *campsite, spring*	C, w	4,300'	1,873.7	
324.3	1.4	Spring	w	4,660'	1,873.1	
325.7	0.1	Spring *(W–100 yds.)*	w	4,850'	1,871.7	
325.8	0.4	Blue-blazed bypass trail southern jct.		5,001'	1,871.6	
326.2	0.3	Slipper Spur		5,160'	1,871.2	
326.5	0.3	Big Bald		5,516'	1,870.9	
326.8	0.9	Big Stamp, bypass trail northern jct., spring *(W–0.3m)*	C, w	5,298'	1,870.6	
327.7	0.2	**Bald Mountain Shelter** *(W–0.1m): no tent camping, 10.3mS; 10.7mN*	S, w	5,100'	1,869.7	
327.9	0.2	Spring and stream	w	5,000'	1,869.5	

ATC: TN-NC Map 3

Miles from Springer	Miles to Next Point	Features	Services	Elev	Miles from Katahdin	M A P
328.1	1.0	Blue-blaze to campsite (W–0.2m spring)	C, w	4,890'	1,869.3	
329.1	2.0	Little Bald: wooded summit		5,185'	1,868.3	
331.1	0.3	Whistling Gap: small clearing, campsite, spring (W–0.1m)	C, w	3,650'	1,866.3	
331.4	1.5	Blue-blazed trail to High Rocks: east to views		4,280'	1,866.0	
332.9	0.5	Campsite and stream	C, w	3,490'	1,864.5	
333.4	0.6	Spivey Gap, US-19W	R, P, w	3,200'	1,864.0	
334.0	0.7	Oglesby Branch: plank bridge	w	3,800'	1,863.4	
334.7	0.2	Stream	w	3,815'	1,862.7	
334.9	0.8	USFS-278	R	3,770'	1,862.5	
335.7	2.4	Devils Creek Gap: overgrown logging road		3,400'	1,861.7	
338.1	0.2	Spring: hemlock grove, water for No Business Knob Shelter (west)	w	3,300'	1,859.3	
338.3	2.4	**No Business Knob Shelter**, 10.7mS; 10.5mN	S, C	3,251'	1,859.1	
340.7	0.7	Temple Hill Gap: old logging road		2,850'	1,856.7	
341.4	3.2	Access road, to former Temple Hill Firetower	R	3,250'	1,856.0	
344.6	0.1	River Road, Chestoa Bridge, Nolichucky River West–1.3m to Mountain Inn & Suites West–3.8m to **Erwin, TN, P.O. 37650**	R, P, H, C, sh, cl, f L G, L, M, D, V, cl, f	1,700'	1,852.8	
344.7	0.1	Chestoa Pike: East 1.2m to NOC and Nolichucky Gorge Campground	C, L, g	1,700'	1,852.7	ATC: TN-NC Map 3
344.8	0.8	CSX Railroad track: caution		1,715'	1,852.6	
345.6	0.3	Nolichucky River Gorge view		1,760'	1,851.8	
345.9	0.7	Nolichucky River Valley: side trail to private Nolichucky Gorge Campground	C, L, g	1,760'	1,851.5	
346.6	0.7	Two bridges over Jones Branch	w	1,720'	1,850.8	
347.3	0.2	Bridge over Jones Branch	w	1,780'	1,850.1	
347.5	0.2	Bridge over Jones Branch: hemlock tree stand	w	1,810'	1,849.9	
347.7	0.9	Jones Branch	w	2,480'	1,849.7	
348.6	0.2	Jones Branch	w	2,280'	1,848.8	
348.8	0.1	**Curley Maple Gap Shelter**, 10.5mS; 12.9mN	C, S, w	3,070'	1,848.6	
348.9	1.0	Curley Maple Gap: abandoned USFS road		3,080'	1,848.5	
349.9	0.2	Small stream	w	3,280'	1,847.5	
350.1	2.8	Spring	w	3,280'	1,847.3	
352.9	0.7	Indian Grave Gap, TN-395, NC-197 West–7m to **Erwin, TN, P.O. 37650**	R, P, C G, L, M, D, V, cl, f	3,360'	1,844.5	
353.6	0.4	Powerline		3,760'	1,843.8	
354.0	1.2	Cross USFS-230, Beauty Spot Gap Road	R	3,770'	1,843.4	
355.2	0.3	Beauty Spot: grassy bald	R, C	4,437'	1,842.2	
355.5	1.3	Spring	R, w		1,841.9	
356.8	0.2	USFS-230, Beauty Spot Gap: spring	R, C, w	4,300'	1,840.6	
357.0	0.4	Campsite: spring across road at gate	C, w	4,100'	1,840.4	
357.4	1.0	USFS-230, Unaka Mountain Road	R	4,660'	1,840.0	
358.4	2.2	Unaka Mountain		5,180'	1,839.0	
360.6	1.1	Low Gap	w	3,900'	1,836.8	

Miles from Springer	Miles to Next Point	Features	Services	Elev	Miles from Katahdin	M A P
361.7	0.4	**Cherry Gap Shelter**, *12.9mS; 9.2mN*	C, S, w	3,900'	1,835.7	
362.1	2.7	Cherry Gap		3,900'	1,835.3	
364.8	1.2	Iron Mountain Gap, TN-107, NC-226 *East–3m to* convenience store *West–10.3m to* **Unicoi, TN, P.O. 37692**	R, P G, f M, D, g	3,723'	1,832.6	
366.0	0.2	Campsite: *northern end of orchard*	C, w	3,950'	1,831.4	
366.2	1.0	Weedy Gap		4,000'	1,831.2	
367.2	1.0	Large rock formation: *granite gneiss and schist*		4,426'	1,830.2	
368.2	0.7	High point near summit of knob		4,332'	1,829.2	
368.9	0.8	Greasy Creek Gap: *old roadbed to Greasy Creek Road (W-0.2m spring)*	C, R, w	4,034'	1,828.5	
369.7	1.1	Campsite, spring: *in row of gnarled maple trees*	C, w	4,110'	1,827.7	
370.8	1.2	**Clyde Smith Shelter** *(W-0.1m), 9.2mS; 13.7mN*	S, C, w	4,400'	1,826.6	
372.0	2.2	Little Rock Knob	C	4,918'	1,825.4	
374.2	0.4	Hughes Gap, Hughes Gap Road, NC-1330	R, P, C	4,040'	1,823.2	
374.6	2.1	Spring: *piped (W-65 yds.)*	w	4,440'	1,822.8	
376.7	0.5	Beartown Mountain		5,481'	1,820.7	
377.2	1.4	Ash Gap: spring (E-0.1m)	C, w	5,340'	1,820.2	
378.6	0.2	Trail to Roan High Bluff USFS Cloudland Rhododendron Garden Road Parking Area: *former Cloudland Hotel Site*	R, P, w	6,200'	1,818.8	
378.8	1.6	Pass old chimney		6,220'	1,818.6	
380.4	0.3	Hack Line Road: *old carriage route*		5,640'	1,817.0	
380.7	0.1	Northernmost board bridge: *piped spring*	w	5,560'	1,816.7	
380.8	0.7	Carvers Gap, TN-143, NC-261: *picnic area, spring*	R, P, w	5,512'	1,816.6	
381.5	0.3	Skirt west side of Round Bald		5,826'	1,815.9	
381.8	0.4	Engine Gap		5,640'	1,815.6	
382.2	0.5	Jane Bald		5,807'	1,815.2	
382.7	0.1	Side trail to Grassy Ridge		5,770'	1,814.7	
382.8	1.7	Springs	w	5,800'	1,814.6	
384.5	0.4	Low Gap; **Stan Murray Shelter**, *13.7mS; 19.9mN*	S, C, w	5,050'	1,812.9	
384.9	0.7	Elk Hollow Ridge		5,180'	1,812.5	
385.6	0.8	Buckeye Gap		4,730'	1,811.8	
386.4	1.2	Yellow Mountain Gap *(E-0.2m spring; 0.3m C)*	C, w	4,682'	1,811.0	
387.6	0.4	Saddle in open field: *spring (E-100 yds.)*	w	5,180'	1,809.8	
388.0	1.3	Little Hump Mountain: *exposed campsites*	C	5,459'	1,809.4	
389.3	0.9	Bradley Gap: *campsites and springs*	C, w	4,960'	1,808.1	
390.2	2.4	Hump Mountain: *Stan Murray plaque*		5,587'	1,807.2	
392.6	0.4	Doll Flats northern end; North Carolina-Tennessee State Line	C, w	4,600'	1,804.8	
393.0	0.1	Crest of Rocky Spur: *overlook to east*		4,400'	1,804.4	
393.1	1.8	Overhanging rock above the Trail: *cliff*		4,820'	1,804.3	
394.9	0.1	Wilder Mine Hollow Group Campsite			1,802.5	
395.0	0.4	Apple House campsite and spring *(west)*	C, w	3,060'	1,802.4	
395.4	0.2	Old Mine Road in Wilder Mine Hollow		2,860'	1,802.0	

ATC: TN-NC Map 2

Miles from Springer	Miles to Next Point	Features	Services	Elev	Miles from Katahdin	M A P

395.6	0.2	US-19E, Buck Creek
		  East–2.5m to **Elk Park, NC, P.O. 28622**
		  West–0.3m to Mountain Harbour B&B and Hostel
		  West–2m to restaurant (pizza/subs)
		  West–2.5m to Dollar General
		  West–3.4m to **Roan Mountain, TN, P.O. 37687**
		  West–7.5m to Roan Mountain State Park
			R, P
			G, M
			H, C, L, sh, f
			M
			G
			G, M, D, V
			C, L, sh
				2,880'	1,801.8	ATC: TN-NC Map 2

This section has plentiful 360-degree views and ever-changing scenery flowing from rich mountain coves, boreal forests, and heath balds. Highlights are Max Patch, Big Bald, Beauty Spot, Unaka Mountain, Roan Mountain at 6,285 feet, and the open, grassy bald of Hump Mountain.

Carolina Mountain Club—CMC maintains the 94 miles between Davenport Gap and Spivey Gap. Send correspondence to CMC, P.O. Box 68, Asheville, NC 28802; carolinamountainclub.org.

Note: At the time of printing, the impacts of Hurricane Helene to the Trail and nearby towns were not fully known. Thru-hikers in 2025 may encounter adverse trail conditions, damaged shelters, and reduced access to and services in nearby towns. Hot Springs and Erwin were heavily impacted, and some services there may not be available this year. It's important to check with businesses in the affected areas before planning a hike. Find the latest trail conditions ATC's website at appalachiantrail.org/trail-updates. In addition, due to trailhead vandalism, the supervisor of trails for the Carolina Mountain Club does not advise leaving cars at trailheads for anything longer than a day trip and to take all valuables with you.

⚠ I-40 at Waterville Road
West 7.5 miles to *Hostel:* The Discerning Hiker Hostel, 4319 Groundhog Rd, Cosby, TN 37722, (423) 721-5278, text is best, March through October, starting at $75 per person, includes laundry, pick up and drop off at the I-40 on the Trail, ride to Walmart, morning coffee. Frozen pizza and other food available; space for 4 hikers, call ahead for mail drops, reservations strongly recommended, hot showers, 2 bathrooms, limited Wi-Fi, hiker box.

West 16.1 miles to the Hikers Rest at Hickory Hollow hostel, 2721 Autumn Woods Dr, Cosby, TN 37722, (317) 417-5351, $30 for a bunk, $20 for tenting, includes pick up and drop off at the trail at I-40, ride to Walmart, hot water outdoor shower, clean port-a-potty, pets ok at tent sites, Wi-Fi, mail drops ok. Laundry is $5; other shuttles for a fee; can hold 6 hikers in the bunk house and 8 tenting.

West 16.8 miles to Newport, TN, **[P.O. ZIP 37821: M–F 8:30–4:30 & Sa 9:30–12; (423) 623-6136]**. *Lodging:* Best Western, Hampton Inn, Holiday Inn Express. *Other services:* Walmart Supercenter, restaurants.

⚠ Green Corner Road—West 0.15 mile to *Hostel:* Standing Bear Farm Hiker Hostel, 4255 Green Corner Rd., Hartford, TN 37753; (423) 487-0014 (preferred) or call/text (423) 608-0149; standingbearfarmhostel.com; owner Maria Guzman; bunkhouse $25pp, tenting or hammock $20pp, creek cabin or tree house $50s, $80d, 4-bed cabin $35pp (do a chore, save $5; see staff), showers for non-guests $5; free Wi-Fi, camp store with pizza, beer, trail food, fuel; overnight parking $5; leashed dogs $5pn, kennel services (shuttle and boarding during GSMNP traverse) $280 or $25/day. Holds packages (free for guests, $5 for non-guests). Cash or Venmo only. *Directions:* Beginning at the I-40 overpass, continue about 30 yards to where the rock steps go up steeply on the left, continue north on the A.T. about 1.0 mile to the first gravel road (Green Corner Rd.), turn left, walk 200 yards to hostel on right.

Groundhog Creek Shelter (1939)—Sleeps 6. Tiny privy. Bear box and cables. Stone shelter located 0.2 mile on a blue-blazed side trail. Water source is a reliable spring to the left of the shelter.

Max Patch—The site of an old homestead and logging camp, Max Patch was originally forested, but early inhabitants cleared the mountaintop to graze sheep and cattle. The summit also has been used as a landing strip for small planes. In 1982, the USFS purchased the 392-acre grassy-top mountain for the A.T. and now uses mowing and controlled burns to maintain its bald appearance. The wide grassy summit, at 4,629 feet, offers panoramic views of the Smokies to the south and a glimpse east to Mt. Mitchell (at 6,684 feet, the highest peak east of the Mississippi). *Note: Due to chronic overuse and littering, the USFS has ordered that the area closes 1 hour after sundown and reopens 1 hour before sunrise. Visitors prohibited during closed hours; camping, fires, and fireworks are prohibited. Group size limit is 10. Dogs must be kept on a leash shorter than 6'.*

Roaring Fork Shelter (2005)—Sleeps 8. Privy. Bear cables. Two water sources, both located on the A.T., 800 ft. north and south of side trail to shelter.

Walnut Mountain Shelter (1938)—Sleeps 6. Privy. Bear cables. An old shelter, with a water source located down the blue-blazed trail to the left of Rattlesnake Trail; may be seasonal. The neighborhood bears show no fear of hikers.

Map of Hot Springs, N.C. elevation 1,330'. Features: Laughing Heart Lodge, Hostel at Laughing Heart Lodge, Little Bird Cabins, The Appalachian Trail-er (hostel), Newport, Tenn., Mountain Diner, Dollar General, Hillbilly Market, Sunnybank Inn (Elmer's), Tobacco Road, Mountain Magnolia Inn, Walnut St, Bridge St, Surpentine Ave, Post Office, Creekwater Inn, Welcome Center, Spring Creek Tavern, Gentry Hardware, Mosiac Gourmet, Bluff Mountain Outfitter, Spring St, Library, Iron Horse Station, ArtiSun Gallery, S. Andrews Ave, Springbrook Cottages, Hot Springs Resort & Campground, French Broad River, Weaverville & Asheville. Post Office to: Hostel at Laughing Heart Lodge (0.4 mi)

Deer Park Mountain Shelter (1938)—Sleeps 5. Privy. Bear cables. A former farmstead; the water source is located on the trail to the shelter. Multiple tent sites here across from the side trail to the shelter.

⚠🅰 NC-209/Hot Springs, NC. [P.O. ZIP 28743: M-F 9–11:30 & 1–4, Sa 9–10:30; (828) 622-3242]. The A.T., now marked by special A.T. diamonds in the sidewalk, passes through the center of Hot Springs on Bridge Street, and most services are located on the Trail. ***Hostels:*** The Hostel at Laughing Heart Lodge, 289 NW US-Hwy 25/70, (828) 206-8487, a stone's throw from the A.T. as you exit the woods at south Trailhead parking lot. Open year-round. Prices include tax: $30 bunks, $40 semiprivate, $50s private, $70d private (one full bed). All rooms include shower & towel, movies, hiker kitchen, morning coffee service, Wi-Fi. Pet-friendly but no pets in bunk rooms. Tenting with shower $15 one person/one tent, $20 two/one tent. Shower only, $5; laundry, $5 includes wash/dry/soap. Quiet time 10 p.m.–7 a.m. Blue Ridge Hiking Co., Appalachian Trail-er bunkhouse, 200 Lance Ave., Hot Springs, NC 28743, (828) 622-3319 or (828) 713-5451, bunkhouse, cottage, gear sales and rentals, shuttles, guided backpacking trips. ***Lodging:*** The Sunnybank Inn, 26 Walnut St. (P.O. Box 233), (828) 622-7206, sunnybankretreatassociation.org, managed by Elmer Hall, located at the white Victorian house across the street from the Dollar Store; private rooms available, call for rates, pillows and linens; hot showers (towel, soap, shampoo), all with shared bath; work exchange is possible; 10 p.m. quiet hours; no pets, no smoking, no tents; holds packages for guests,

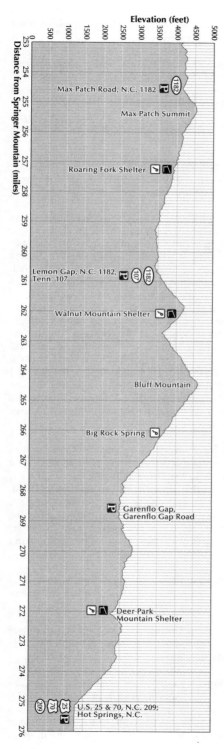

Elevation (feet)

Distance from Springer Mountain (miles)

Max Patch Road, N.C. 1182

Max Patch Summit

Roaring Fork Shelter

Lemon Gap, N.C. 1182, Tenn. 107

Walnut Mountain Shelter

Bluff Mountain

Big Rock Spring

Garenflo Gap, Garenflo Gap Road

Deer Park Mountain Shelter

U.S. 25 & 70, N.C. 209; Hot Springs, N.C.

Internet available. Creekwater Inn, (828) 206-5212, creekwaterinn.com, clean, book through AIRBNB, nightly rentals, call for rates. Hot Springs Resort and Spa, (828) 622-7676, nchotsprings.com, thru-hiker cabin rate $75–$90, up to 5; $45 for 4 with 2-night min stay at primitive tentsites. Iron Horse Station, (828) 622-0022, theironhorsestation.com, bunkroom with special hiker rate $85d weekdays, $95d weekends. The restaurant is open F–M, 11:30 to 8, Th 4–8 and closed M,Tu. Little Bird Cabins, 49 S. Serpentine Ave. on the A.T., (828) 206-1487, littlebirdcabinrentals.com, owner Natalie Hesed, two cabins each with an efficiency kitchen, usually a 2 night minimum; one cabin sleeps 4, one cabin sleeps up to seven $95d Su–Th, $115d F–Sa $5eap; Wi-Fi; pet-friendly with $30 fee. Springbrook Cottages, (828) 622-7385, 94 S. Andrews St., springbrookcottages.com, springbrookcottages1@gmail.com, owner Carolyn Ammons; call for cabin rates ($90-$110). Spring Creek Tavern, 145 Bridge St., (828) 622-0187, no pets, call for room rates above tavern. *Groceries:* Dollar General and Hillbilly Market (both long-term resupply). *Restaurants:* Smoky Mountain Diner, B/L/D, closed Su, M, Tu, Th, F 6–7, W 6–2, Sa 7–2; Mountain Magnolia Inn, D Th–M; Spring Creek Tavern; Ironhorse Station, open F–M, 11:30–8, Th 4–8 and closed M, Tu., occasional live music; Mosaic Gourmet; ArtiSun Gallery, (828) 539-0030, open 8–8 daily, espresso/coffee bar, Ultimate ice cream, wine bar, free Wi-Fi. *Outfitter:* Bluff Mountain Outfitters, 152 Bridge St. (P.O. Box 114), (828) 622-7162, bluffmountain.com; owner Wayne Crosby; a full-service outfitter including full resupply, ATM, SoBo GSMNP permits and printing; mail drops accepted. *Internet access:* Library, 170 Bridge St., (828) 622-3584, 10–6 M–F, 10–2 Sa, $1 computer fee. *Other services:* ATM; Dollar General; Gentry Hardware.

Southbound permits for Smokies—*Southbounders must have a backcountry permit before entering Great Smoky Mountains National Park (see page 48 for details). Permits can be obtained at Bluff Mountain Outfitters, (828) 622-7162, open daily 9:30–5:30, Su 10–5.*

Whitewater Rafting—Rafting companies offer guided trips on the French Broad River: Nantahala Outdoor Center, (800) 232-7238; Hot Springs Rafting Co., (877) 530-7238.

Hot Springs Spa—(828) 622-7676. At the northern end of town, on the southern bank of the French Broad River, the spa offers baths and massages at the famous therapeutic mineral baths for which the town was named.

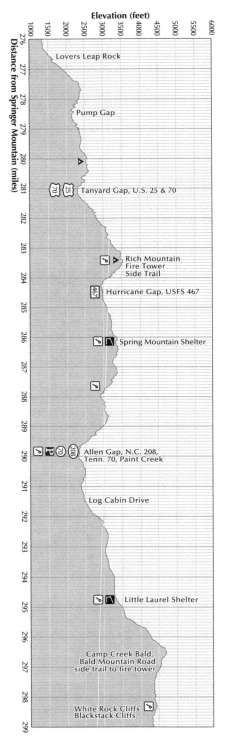

Rich Mountain—The firetower has been rehabilitated and is open for viewing.

Spring Mountain Shelter (1938)—Sleeps 5. Privy. Bear cables. The shelter is on the west side of the Trail. Water source is 75 yards down a blue-blazed trail on the east side of the A.T.

Allen Gap—Paint Creek is 350 yards west, but water quality is questionable.

Little Laurel Shelter (1967)—Sleeps 5. Privy. Bear cables. Water source is 100 yards down a blue-blazed trail behind the shelter.

Jerry Cabin Shelter (1968)—Sleeps 6. Privy. Bear cables. Water source is on a small knoll, up a path found on the opposite side of the A.T. CMC member and honorary ALDHA life member Sam Waddle was the caretaker of this shelter and 2.9 miles of the Trail, from Round Knob to Big Butt, for 26 years until his death February 1, 2005. Sam had a good sense of humor and was responsible for a light bulb and telephone installed on the shelter wall. Sam's volunteer efforts transformed this shelter from "the dirtiest shelter on the entire Trail to one of the cleanest," according to Ed Garvey, by hauling out an estimated 20 bushels of litter. He was devoted to the A.T. and an inspiration to all volunteers who share the commitment it takes to make a difference. The electric outlet and telephone may be gone, but Sam's legacy will live forever.

Shelton Grave—North of Big Butt on a short side trail is the resting place of deserters William and David Shelton, who lived in Madison County, NC, but enlisted in the Union Army during the Civil War. While returning to a family gathering during the war in July 1864, the uncle and nephew and nine others were ambushed near here; five were killed by Confederates. It's a single grave for the Sheltons and a 13-year-old.

Flint Mountain Shelter (1988)—Sleeps 8. Privy. Bear cables. Water source is on the A.T. north of the shelter.

Hogback Ridge Shelter (1986)—Sleeps 6. Privy. Bear cables. Water source is a spring 0.3 mile on a side trail near the shelter.

Sams Gap—*Hostel:* Nature's Inn Hostel and Cabins, 4872 Old Asheville Hwy, Flag Pond, TN 37657, (828) 216-1611 or (423) 270-9171 to speak with owner Taft Ring; pet-friendly with dogs leashed at all times; 2 bunkhouses, one sleeps 8, one sleeps 5;

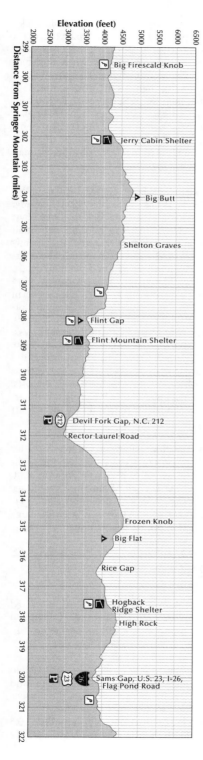

Elevation (feet)

Distance from Springer Mountain (miles)

Big Firescald Knob

Jerry Cabin Shelter

Big Butt

Shelton Graves

Flint Gap

Flint Mountain Shelter

Devil Fork Gap, N.C. 212

Rector Laurel Road

Frozen Knob

Big Flat

Rice Gap

Hogback Ridge Shelter

High Rock

Sams Gap, U.S. 23, I-26, Flag Pond Road

creekside cabins, each with 1 queen and 1 twin bunk; private rooms in main hostel, 2 queen rooms, 1 king room; hilltop cabin available; tenting; hammock lodge; tiled bath house; common area with hot food available; short-term resupply; laundry service; call for details and pricing (best after 3 p.m.); Venmo, credit cards accepted; free shuttle to and from Sam's Gap; quiet time 10 p.m. –7 a.m.; mail drops accepted, pet friendly, moderately priced.

Big Bald—Big Bald offers 360-degree views at an elevation of 5,516 feet. From 1802 to 1834, the bald was inhabited by a cantankerous hermit named David Greer. Spurned by a woman, he retreated to the mountaintop where he lived in a small, cave-like structure (no longer visible). He declared himself sovereign of the mountain and eventually killed a man, only to be acquitted on grounds of insanity. The life of "Hog Greer," called so by the neighbors because he lived like one, ended when a local blacksmith shot him in the back (but was never charged). Greer Bald eventually became known as Big Bald. A golf and ski resort, Wolf Laurel, is clearly visible from the summit. A spring and campsite can be found by following the A.T. 0.2 mile north of the summit to a dirt road and then walking west 0.3 mile down the dirt road.

Bald Mountain Shelter (1988)—Sleeps 10. Privy. Bear cables. One of the highest on the A.T. (5,100 feet). The surrounding area is too fragile for tenting. Water source is a spring on the side trail to the shelter.

Tennessee Eastman Hiking & Canoeing Club—TEHC maintains the 133.9 miles between Spivey Gap and the Tennessee–Virginia line. Correspondence should be sent to TEHC, P.O. Box 511, Kingsport, TN 37662; tehcc.org.

No Business Knob Shelter (1963)—Sleeps 6. No privy or cables. Surrounded by large Fraser magnolias and mammoth hemlocks, this concrete-block shelter was built by the Forest Service. Reliable water is found 0.2 mile south of the shelter on the A.T.

River Road/Chestoa Bridge/Nolichucky River/Erwin, TN. *Hostel:* Nolichucky Hostel and Outfitters (Uncle Johnny's); 151 River Rd.; (423) 735-0548, ATunclejohnnys .com; hostel $30/night; climate-controlled private cabins $70–$120, camping $20pp; hammock space $20, showers and towel free with stay, shower without stay $5; laundry $5 load; dog-friendly; Wi-Fi; free town shuttles for guests for B/L/D; section-hike and slackpacking shuttles; bicycles available for $2 fee (free for guests), fully equipped outfitter store; mail drops accepted.

West 1 mile to Unicoi County Memorial Hospital, 2030 Temple Hill Rd., (423) 735-4700, balladhealth.org, full-service 10-bed medical facility with 24/7 emergency department.

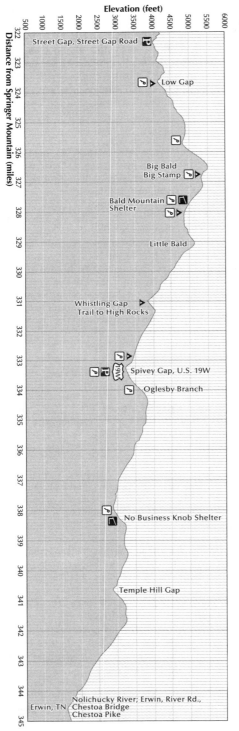

Elevation (feet)

Street Gap, Street Gap Road
Low Gap
Big Bald
Big Stamp
Bald Mountain Shelter
Little Bald
Whistling Gap
Trail to High Rocks
Spivey Gap, U.S. 19W
Oglesby Branch
No Business Knob Shelter
Temple Hill Gap
Nolichucky River; Erwin, River Rd.,
Erwin, TN Chestoa Bridge
Chestoa Pike

Distance from Springer Mountain (miles)

West 1.3 miles to *Camping:* Nolichucky Gorge Campground, 101 Jones Branch Rd., (423) 743-8876, nolichucky.com, day use $5, campsites $20pp, cabins starting at $60-75 when available.

West 1.3 miles to *Lodging:* 0.5 mile on River Rd. (best hitch), then 0.8 mile on Temple Hill Rd. to Mountain Inn & Suites, 2002 Temple Hill Rd.; (423) 743-4100; $90d per night ($10eap, 4 max), no pets, hot B buffet, Internet in lobby, guest coin laundry, hot tub and swimming pool (both seasonal), parking for section-hikers, mail drops accepted.

⌂ **West 3.8 miles to Erwin, TN [P.O. ZIP 37650: M–F 8:30–4:45; Sa 10–12; (423) 743-9422].** *Lodging:* Best Southern Motel, 1315 Jackson Love Hwy, (423) 743-6438, contact for rates, no pets, mail drops accepted; Super 8 Motel, 1101 N. Buffalo St., (423) 743-0200, $70s includes B, Internet, no pets, coin laundry, accepts mail drops. *Restaurants:* Many; see map. *Groceries:* Food Lion, Food City, Price Less Foods (all long-term resupply); Dollar General, Dollar General, Dollar Tree. *Outfitter:* Mahoney's, (423) 282-8889, in Johnson City, 13 miles north. *Internet access:* library; Chamber of Commerce, (423) 743-3000, M–F 9–5, Sa& Su closed, also has information on shuttles. *Other services:* banks; ATM; barber; coin laundries; thrift stores; hardware; dentists; 24-hour emergency center; Walgreens; Walmart (4.5 mi. off I-26); shoe repair; movie theater; art gallery; veterinarian.

Whitewater Rafting—Rafting companies offer guided trips on the scenic, free-flowing Nolichucky River: NOC, (800) 232-7238; USA Raft, (800) USA-RAFT; High Mountain Expeditions, (800) 262-9036; Wahoo's Adventures, (800) 444-RAFT, which also provides rafting on Watauga River near Hampton–Elizabethton.

Curley Maple Gap Shelter (1961/2010)—Sleeps 12. No privy or cables. Water source is a spring south on the A.T.

Unaka Mountain—With a large stand of red spruce atop its 5,180-foot summit, Unaka will remind southbounders of the Maine woods. Unaka is the Cherokee word for "white."

Cherry Gap Shelter (1962, 2021)—Sleeps 14. No privy or cables. Water source is a spring found 80 yards on a blue-blazed trail from the shelter.

⚠ **TN-107, NC-226/Iron Mountain Gap—West** 10.3 miles to **Unicoi, TN. [P.O. ZIP 37692: M–F 8:45–12**

& 1–3:45 Sa 8:30–10:30; (423) 743-4945], with Clarence's Restaurant B/L/D, Maple Grove Restaurant, minimarts, and a doctor.

Greasy Creek Gap—East 0.6 mile to Former *Hostel:* Greasy Creek Friendly, 1827 Greasy Creek Rd., Bakerville, NC 28705; (828) 688-9948; parking available and possible help obtaining shuttles, all with proof of vaccination. Directions: At gap, opposite blue-blaze, go through campsite "down" old dirt road past old barns through service gate to first house on right.

Clyde Smith Shelter (1976)—Sleeps 10. No privy or cables. Water source is a spring 100 yards behind the shelter on a blue-blaze.

Roan Mountain—For northbounders, this will be the last time the A.T. climbs above 6,000 feet until Mt. Washington in New Hampshire. At the top is a parking area, with restroom and running water (May–Oct). Roan Mountain is arguably the coldest spot, year-round, on the southern A.T. Upon reaching the top of the main climb (for northbounders), enter a clearing, and pass the foundation of the former Cloud-

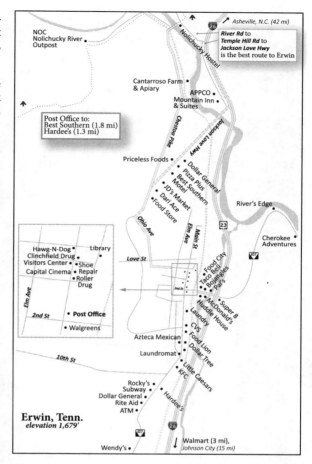

land Hotel. The state line ran through the center of the hotel's ballroom when Cloudland was a thriving resort in the late 1800s and early 1900s. It was demolished in 1915, after loggers harvested the fir and spruce on the mountaintop. Much of the Catawba rhododendron was dug up and sold to ornamental nurseries. The remaining rhododendron covered the slopes of Roan, hence the famous gardens. The peak blooming time is usually around Jun 20. The gardens can be reached by taking the USFS road (visible from the hotel foundation) west, uphill, along the top of the mountain, where an information station is located.

Roan High Knob Shelter (1980)—*Closed for renovation in 2025.* Sleeps 15. No privy or cables. Highest shelter on the A.T. (6,275 feet). Originally a firewarden's cabin; loft is known to leak. Unreliable water source can be found on a 100-yard blue-blaze near the shelter. More reliable sources are south on the A.T. at Roan Mountain restroom, when open, or spring at Carvers Gap picnic area, 1.3 miles north.

Gray's lily—A protected, red, nodding lily can be seen blooming on the slopes of Round Bald, Grassy Ridge, and Hump Mountain in Jun–early Jul. Named for botanist Asa Gray, who found it in the 1840s.

Roan Mountain to Hump Mountain—Between Roan Mountain and Hump Mountain, the Trail crosses several balds. Round Bald (5,826 feet) is the site of a USFS experiment in which goats were used

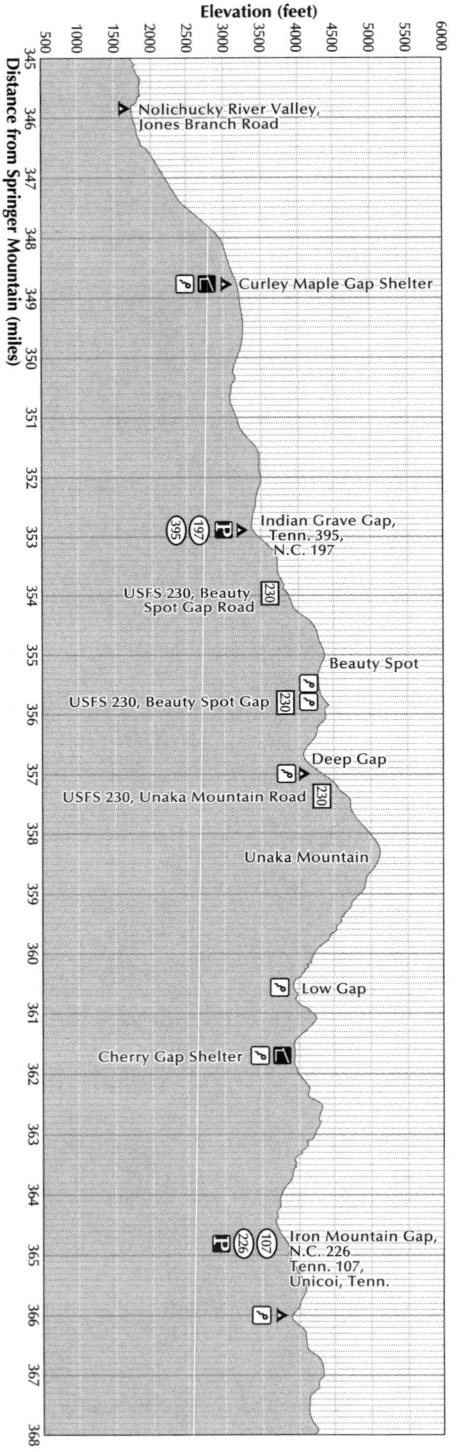
Elevation (feet)
Distance from Springer Mountain (miles)
Nolichucky River Valley, Jones Branch Road
Curley Maple Gap Shelter
Indian Grave Gap, Tenn. 395, N.C. 197
USFS 230, Beauty Spot Gap Road
Beauty Spot
USFS 230, Beauty Spot Gap
Deep Gap
USFS 230, Unaka Mountain Road
Unaka Mountain
Low Gap
Cherry Gap Shelter
Iron Mountain Gap, N.C. 226 Tenn. 107, Unicoi, Tenn.

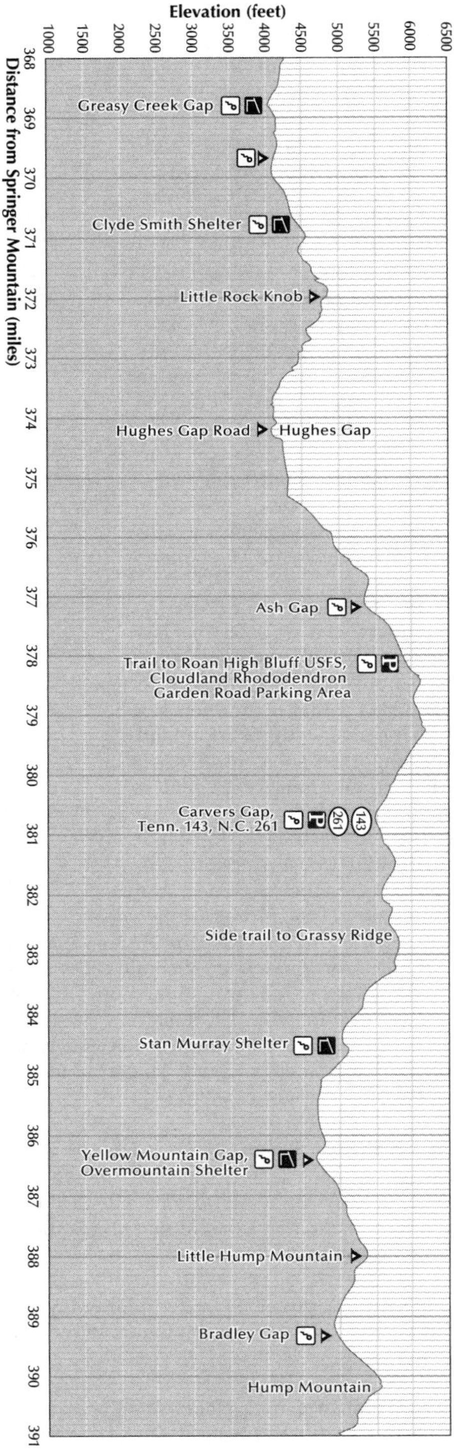
Elevation (feet)
Distance from Springer Mountain (miles)
Greasy Creek Gap
Clyde Smith Shelter
Little Rock Knob
Hughes Gap Road
Hughes Gap
Ash Gap
Trail to Roan High Bluff USFS, Cloudland Rhododendron Garden Road Parking Area
Carvers Gap, Tenn. 143, N.C. 261
Side trail to Grassy Ridge
Stan Murray Shelter
Yellow Mountain Gap, Overmountain Shelter
Little Hump Mountain
Bradley Gap
Hump Mountain

to keep briars and brambles from encroaching on the bald. Although the southern Appalachians do not rise above treeline, they have many balds, the origins of which remains a mystery. Some point to the harsh conditions at high elevations, while others claim Indians cleared the mountains for religious ceremonies. Many cite extensive grazing and cropping. The 6,189-foot summit of Grassy Ridge is reached by following a side trail east before the A.T. begins its descent off the ridge to Stan Murray Shelter. It is the only natural 360-degree viewpoint above 6,000 feet near the Trail. (Clingmans Dome has its observation tower, and Mt. Washington's summit in New Hampshire is covered with buildings.) To avoid potential damage to endangered species, please do not camp between the summit and the southern peak. For northbounders, the A.T. veers west from the state line into Tennessee at Doll Flats, where it remains until crossing into Virginia south of Damascus.

NC-261/TN-143/Carvers Gap—Picnic area and parking area with restrooms; piped spring beyond restrooms. North out of Carvers Gap, the Trail has been relocated with switchbacks to control erosion and heal the scar of the old treadway. Please stay off the treadway to allow this area time to recover.

Stan Murray Shelter (1977)—Sleeps 6. No privy. Formerly the Roan Highlands Shelter, this shelter was renamed for the former ATC chair and originator of the Appalachian Greenway concept. Water source is a spring on a blue-blazed trail opposite the shelter.

Overmountain Shelter—The shelter was dismantled in 2023. Camping is still allowed in the area. Privy. Water source is a spring found to the left once you reach the old road before the shelter.

Tennessee

Miles from Springer	Miles to Next Point	Features	Services	Elev	Miles from Katahdin	M A P
395.6	0.2	US-19E, Buck Creek *East–2.5m to* **Elk Park, NC, P.O. 28622** *West–0.3m to* Mountain Harbour B&B and Hostel *West 1.5m to* The Refuge Hostel *West–2m to* restaurant (pizza/subs) *West–2.5m to* Dollar General *West–3.4m to* **Roan Mountain, TN, P.O. 37687** *West–7.5m to* Roan Mountain State Park	R, P G, M H, sh, f H, C, L, sh, f M G G, M, D, V C, L, sh	2,880'	1,801.8	ATC: TN-NC Map 2
395.8	2.7	Bear Branch Road: *bridge*	R	2,900'	1,801.6	
398.5	0.4	Isaacs Cemetery		3,600'	1,798.9	
398.9	0.3	Buck Mountain Road	R	3,340'	1,798.5	
399.2	0.6	Campbell Hollow Road	R, P	3,393'	1,798.2	
399.8	1.1	Spring, campsite along Elk River	C, w	3,430'	1,797.6	
400.9	0.7	Side trail to Jones Falls *(E–0.1m)*	w	2,997'	1,796.5	
401.6	0.3	Elk River: *southern junction*	w	2,703'	1,795.8	
401.9	0.4	Sugar Hollow Stream Campsite	C, w	3,590'	1,795.5	
402.3	1.9	Elk River: *northern junction*	w	2,675'	1,795.1	
404.2	0.2	Mountaineer Falls Campsite: *west on blue-blaze*	C, w	3,137'	1,793.2	
404.4	0.8	**Mountaineer Falls Shelter,** *19.9mS; 9.6mN*	S, w	3,470'	1,793.0	
405.2	0.8	Campsite south of Slide Hollow: *east on blue-blaze*	C	3,260'	1,792.2	
406.0	1.2	Walnut Mountain Road: *gravel*	R, P	3,583'	1,791.4	
407.2	0.5	Stream	w	3,400'	1,790.2	
407.7	0.5	Viewpoint : *memorial bench*		3,350'	1,789.7	
408.2	1.0	Upper Laurel Fork: *footbridge*	w	3,290'	1,789.2	
409.2	0.8	USFS-293 at "Bitter End"		3,590'	1,788.2	
410.0	0.9	Stream	w	3,840'	1,787.4	
410.9	2.4	Hardcore Cascades: *100 yards south of large rock*	C, w	3,920'	1,786.5	
413.3	0.7	White Rocks Mountain		4,121'	1,784.1	
414.0	1.2	**Moreland Gap Shelter,** *9.6mS; 24mN*	S, C, w	3,813'	1,783.4	
415.2	0.9	Crest of White Rocks Mountain	R	4,206'	1,782.2	
416.1	0.3	Canute Place: *west on blue-blaze to water*	C, w	3,700'	1,781.3	
416.4	0.1	Forest Road to Lacy Trapp Trail/USFS-36 *(E–0.1m)*; *(W–4m to US-19E)*	R	3,800'	1,781.0	
416.5	2.1	Powerline		3,760'	1,780.9	
418.6	1.7	Trail to Coon Den Falls		2,660'	1,778.8	
420.3	0.1	Dennis Cove, USFS-50 *West–0.2m to* Kincora Hiking Hostel *East–0.4m to* Black Bear Resort	R, P, w H, C, G, L, cl, f H, C, G, L, cl, f	2,510'	1,777.1	ATC: TN-NC Map 1
420.4	0.2	Campsite near "Wye": *two small bridges*	C, w	2,510'	1,777.0	
420.6	0.5	Pond Mountain Wilderness boundary		2,440'	1,776.8	

Miles from Springer	Miles to Next Point	Features	Services	Elev	Miles from Katahdin	M A P
421.1	0.3	Koonford Bridge over Laurel Fork	w	2,420'	1,776.3	
421.4	0.1	High water bypass to site of former Laurel Fork Shelter: *southern junction*	S	2,200'	1,776.0	
421.5	0.7	Laurel Fork Falls, Laurel Fork Gorge	w	2,120'	1,775.9	
422.2	0.3	High water bypass to site of former Laurel Fork Shelter: *northern junction*	S, w	2,450'	1,775.2	
422.5	0.1	Waycaster Spring: *footbridge*	w	1,900'	1,774.9	
422.6	0.2	Footbridge over stream	w	1,900'	1,774.8	
422.8	0.2	Footbridge over stream	w	1,900'	1,774.6	
423.0	2.5	Hampton Blueline Trail to US-321 *West–0.8m to* **Hampton, TN, P.O. 37658**	w G, L, M, D, f	2,000'	1,774.4	
425.5	0.3	Spring	w	3,650'	1,771.9	
425.8	2.6	Pond Flats: *campsite, east to "pond"*	C, w	3,700'	1,771.6	
428.4	0.4	Pond Mountain Wilderness boundary: *campsite south of boundary*	C	2,200'	1,769.0	
428.8	0.1	Shook Branch Road: *gravel, campsite* *West 0.1m to Boots Off Hostel & CG*	R, C H	2,000'	1,768.6	
		BEAR CLOSURE AREA North to Wilbur Dam Road				
428.9	1.5	US-321, Shook Branch Picnic Area *West–1.2m to Dividing Ridge Hiker CG* *West–2m to* **Hampton, TN, P.O. 37658** *West–9m to Elizabethton, TN*	R, P, w C, sh G, L, M, D, f G, L, M, D, V, cl	1,990'	1,768.5	
430.4	0.4	Griffith Branch	w	2,100'	1,767.0	
430.8	1.0	Stream	w	2,091'	1,766.6	
431.8	0.2	Watauga Dam water inlet tower		2,000'	1,765.6	
432.0	0.3	Watauga Dam *(north end)*, Lookout Road		1,915'	1,765.4	
432.3	0.5	Side trail to Watauga Dam Visitors Center *(E–0.5m)*	w	2,100'	1,765.1	
432.8	0.5	Minor summit: *view of Watauga Lake*		2,480'	1,764.6	
433.3	1.0	Wilbur Dam Road *(E–0.9m to dam visitors center)* Big Laurel Branch Wilderness: *southern boundary*	R, P, w	2,240'	1,764.1	
434.3	2.0	Knob: *follow narrow crest of Iron Mtn.*		3,000'	1,763.1	
436.3	1.7	Spring	w	3,360'	1,761.1	
438.0	1.4	**Vandeventer Shelter** *(W–0.5m spring), 24mS; 6.8mN*	C, S, w	3,510'	1,759.4	
439.4	2.4	Big Laurel Branch Wilderness: *northern boundary*		3,600'	1,758.0	
441.8	1.4	Spring: *tentsites 175 yards north at boggy spring*	C, w	3,900'	1,755.6	
443.2	0.6	Turkeypen Gap		3,970'	1,754.2	
443.8	0.3	Iron Mountain Highpoint		4,190'	1,753.6	
444.1	0.5	Powerlines		4,100'	1,753.3	
444.6	0.2	Spring: *water for Iron Mountain Shelter*	w	4,000'	1,752.8	
444.8	1.3	**Iron Mountain Shelter**, *6.8mS; 7.7mN*	S, C	4,125'	1,752.6	
446.1	0.1	Nick Grindstaff Monument		4,090'	1,751.3	
446.2	0.4	Spring *(W–100 yds.)*	w	4,090'	1,751.2	
446.6	1.0	High Point		4,120'	1,750.8	
447.6	1.0	Top of rise in ridge		3,750'	1,749.8	
448.6	0.9	Cross two streams: *100 yards apart on bog bridges*	w	3,500'	1,748.8	
449.5	0.8	TN-91, Cross Mountain Road: *ridgecrest* *East–2.5m to* Switchback Creek Campground	R, P C, L, cl	3,450'	1,747.9	

ATC: TN-NC Map 1

Miles from Springer	Miles to Next Point	Features	Services	Elev	Miles from Katahdin	M A P
450.3	1.3	Edge of woods on old Osborne Farm		3,600'	1,747.1	
451.6	0.9	Campsite north of Osborne Farm: *spring*	C, w	3,990'	1,745.8	
452.5	0.5	**Double Springs Shelter**, *7.7mS; 8.3mN* Holston Mountain Trail Jct.	S, C, w	4,080'	1,744.9	
453.0	2.9	Locust Knob		4,020'	1,744.4	
455.9	0.1	Campsite: *near old homesite*	C	3,480'	1,741.5	
456.0	1.0	Low Gap, US-421: *picnic table, spring* *East–2.7m* to **Shady Valley, TN, P.O. 37688**	R, P, w G, M	3,384'	1,741.4	ATC: TN-NC Map 1
457.0	0.9	Minor summit	C, w	3,643'	1,740.4	
457.9	1.4	Double Spring Gap		3,650'	1,739.5	
459.3	0.1	McQueens Knob: *former firetower site*		3,885'	1,738.1	
459.4	0.3	McQueens Knob Shelter: *emergency use only*		3,900'	1,738.0	
459.7	1.1	McQueens Gap, USFS-69	R	3,653'	1,737.7	
460.8	5.4	**Abingdon Gap Shelter** *(E–0.2m spring): 8.3mS; 20mN*	S, C, w	3,773'	1,736.6	
466.2	1.1	Backbone Rock Trail *(E–3m to USFS Recreation Area)*		3,466'	1,731.2	
467.3	1.0	Tennessee–Virginia State Line: *Mt. Rogers N.R.A. sign*		3,300'	1,730.1	

Here, you will stroll along the Elk River, pass Jones and Mountaineer falls, see the impressive 50-foot Laurel Falls in the Pond Mountain Wilderness, look over the 16-mile-long Watauga Reservoir, and climb Iron Mountain. Water sources between Wilbur Dam Road and TN-91 often are unreliable in late summer.

Note: At the time of printing, the impacts of Hurricane Helene to the Trail and nearby towns were not fully known. Thru-hikers in 2025 may encounter adverse trail conditions, damaged shelters, and reduced access to and services in nearby towns. It's important to check with businesses in the affected areas before planning a hike. Find the latest trail conditions ATC's website at appalachiantrail.org/trail-updates.

⚠ US-19E—Numerous incidents of vandalism have been reported at this parking area. Overnight parking is not recommended.
    East 2.5 miles to **Elk Park, NC [P.O. ZIP 28622: M–F 9–12:30 & 1:30–4, Sa 8–11:30; (828) 733-5711].** *Other services:* Hardware store with Coleman fuel, fuel canisters, and denatured alcohol by the ounce; Dollar General; mini-mart.
    West 0.3 mile to *Lodging:* Mountain Harbour B&B and Hiker Hostel, 9151 Hwy 19E, Roan Mountain, TN 37687; (866) 772-9494; mountainharbour.net. Voted "Best Breakfast on Trail." Hostel with common area and Wi-Fi includes laundry; semiprivate king bed, treehouse, clean linens; tenting. Non-guest shower, laundry w/ soap, B when available. B&B rooms include B. Seasonal food trailer and general store on-site for full resupply. Slackpack/shuttles by arrangement. Secure parking w/shuttle. Mail drops (non-guests fee). View website for latest rates.
    West 1.5 miles to *Hostel:* The Refuge Hostel, 240 Roby Miller Rd., TN 37687; (423) 772-3125. At 0.4 mile from the A.T., at forestry gate, look for blue blazes and follow road to hostel. Open year-round. $20 bunk includes shower, laundry, linen, coffee, and tea; small resupply, snacks, canister/fuel by oz. available; slackpack options; 5 p.m. daily town ride; Wi-Fi; pet friendly; maildrops; non-guest fees, $5 ea. for shower, laundry, maildrops.
    West to *Restaurant:* 2.0 miles to Frank & Marty's, pizza/subs T–W Sa 4–9, Th–F 11–9, closed Su–M. *Other services:* 2.5 miles, Dollar General open 8-11 every day.
    ⌂ **West** 3.4 miles to **Roan Mountain, TN [P.O. ZIP 37687: M–F 8:00–12 & 1–4, Sa 7:30–9:30; (423) 772-3014].** *Restaurants:* Smoky Mountain Bakers Pizza, T–Sa 8–8; Highlander BBQ, W–Sa 11–7; Subway; Puerto Nuevo Mexican & Seafood; Americano Steak House. *Other services:* RediMart (long-term resupply); bank with ATM; pharmacy; medical center, open M–F 8–5; veterinarian closed W, Sa, Su.

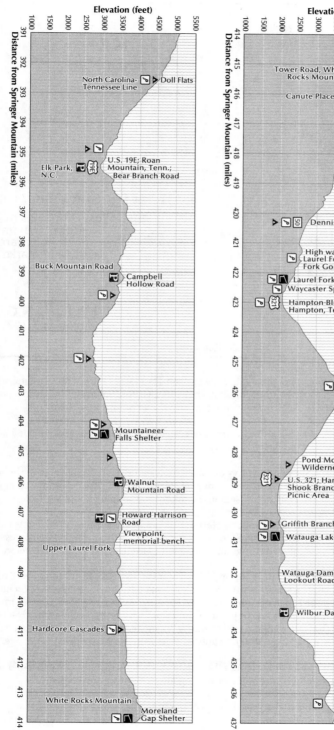

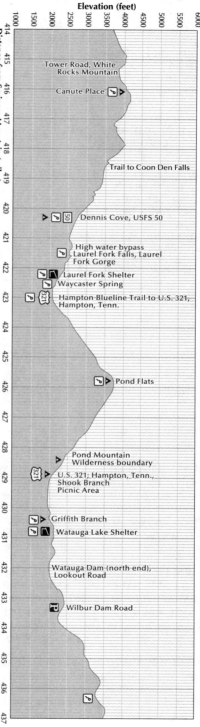

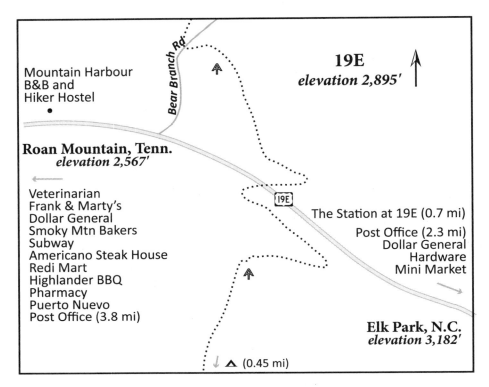

Mountain Harbour
B&B and
Hiker Hostel
  •

Bear Branch Rd.

19E
elevation 2,895'

Roan Mountain, Tenn.
elevation 2,567'

Veterinarian
Frank & Marty's
Dollar General
Smoky Mtn Bakers
Subway
Americano Steak House
Redi Mart
Highlander BBQ
Pharmacy
Puerto Nuevo
Post Office (3.8 mi)

19E

The Station at 19E (0.7 mi)
Post Office (2.3 mi)
Dollar General
Hardware
Mini Market

Elk Park, N.C.
elevation 3,182'

↓ ▲ (0.45 mi)

West 7.5 miles to *Camping:* Roan Mountain State Park on TN 143, (423) 547-3900; tnstateparks. com/parks/roan-mountain, campground with showers, cabins; visitor center, and swimming pool. Closed in 2024 for renovation, check for reopening in 2025. Reservations suggested.

Mountaineer Falls Shelter (2005)—Sleeps 14. No privy or cables. Water source 200 feet on blue-blaze. Tent camping 0.2 mile south of the shelter.

Moreland Gap Shelter (1960)—Sleeps 6. No privy or cables. Water source is 0.2 mile down the hollow across from the shelter. Northwest exposure; wet during storms. This shelter was damaged at the time of printing. Its availability for the 2025 seasons is unknown. Camping is still available.

Dennis Cove Road/USFS 50—West 0.2 mile to *Hostel:* Kincora Hiker Hostel, 1278 Dennis Cove Rd., Hampton, TN 37658; (423) 725-4409, $5/night donation; owner Bob Peoples welcomes old friends and guests. No dogs, alcohol, or drugs allowed. Shuttles available. Plan to arrive before 10 p.m.
    East 0.4 mile to *Lodging:* Black Bear Resort, 1511 Dennis Cove Rd., Hampton, TN 37658; (321) 271-5188, text or call, blackbearresortttn.com. Open Mar 21–Oct 31. Bunkroom includes laundry and a trip to town for $30; tent or hammock $15pp; rustic cabins $70+, $10eap (6 max). Courtesy phone and free morning coffee for guests. Camp store with resupply items, freeze-dried meals, snacks, pizza, beer, sodas, ice cream. Fuel by ounce & canister. Dogs $10. Laundry, showers, maildrops $5 for non-guests. Parking $3/night. Shuttles. Prices and services subject to change.

Laurel Fork Falls–The Trail passes within sight of this waterfall, under which two hikers, father and son, drowned in 2012. Be careful if swimming or wading; the undertows are dangerous.

Laurel Fork Shelter (1977)— This shelter was destroyed by a fire in 2024.

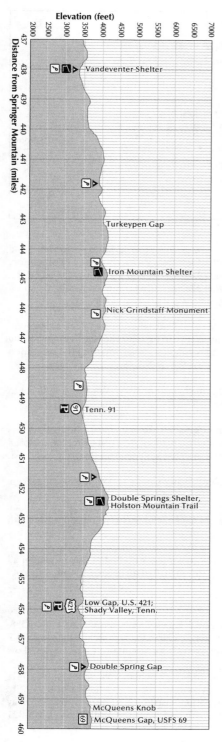

Elevation (feet)

Distance from Springer Mountain (miles)

Vandeventer Shelter

Turkeypen Gap

Iron Mountain Shelter

Nick Grindstaff Monument

Tenn. 91

Double Springs Shelter,
Holston Mountain Trail

Low Gap, U.S. 421;
Shady Valley, Tenn.

Double Spring Gap

McQueens Knob
McQueens Gap, USFS 69

Shook Branch Road—West 0.1 mi to *Hostel:* Boots Off Hostel & Campground, 142 Shook Branch Rd., Hampton, TN 37658, call or text (239) 218-3904, alt phone (423) 725-3094, owner Jim Gregory. Register on-line in advance, at bootsoff.camp. Bunkhouse $35+tax, tent/hammock $17.50+tax. Private Space Options, $70+tax for one, $17.50eap, 2-3 people max. All stays include AC/heat, continental B, shower ($5 w/o stay), kitchen, Wi-Fi, evening town shuttle ($5 w/o stay). See website for all our unique lodging spaces (Domes, Canvas Cabin Tents, Tiny Cabins). Shuttles from Devils Fork Gap to Damascus for a fee. Small store with hiker resupply on site including Peak Refuel meals and gas canisters. Pet-friendly; call ahead (before coming up the driveway with dogs). Mail drops accepted ($5 w/o stay). Lake recreational equipment available. Inquire about aqua-blaze. Closure Notice

Closure Notice: National forest lands around Watauga Lake are closed to most recreation from north of Shook Branch (US-321) to Wilbur Dam Rd., including former site of Watauga Lake Shelter. No picnicking, lingering, or overnight camping. Only hiking is allowed on this 4-mile section of Trail. Please use caution while hiking through and do not stop. This closure is effective until further notice. Bear canisters are highly recommended from here to Damascus and may be required. Check the ATC website for the latest information on this section.

US-321—West 2 miles to **Hampton, TN [P.O. ZIP 37658: M–F 7:30–11:30 & 12:30–4:00, Sa 8–10; (423) 725-2177]**. Best access to Hampton from the A.T. is the 0.8-mile blue-blaze in Laurel Gorge, 1.5 miles downstream from Laurel Falls. *Lodging:* Braemar Castle Hostel and Guest House, (423) 725-2411 or 725-2262. Sutton and Beverly Brown offer hiker bunk space ($20), kitchen, showers, Wi-Fi, laundry ($5), and private single rooms ($30), cash only, will pick up at trailhead. Iron Mountain Inn B&B, (423) 768-2446, ironmountaininn.com; private room and bath $155+D, includes B. Creekside Chalet, same phone as Iron Mountain Inn, creeksidechalet.net, $250 chalet with a 2-night min stay that can sleep 6 adults & 3 kids. *Restaurants:* Laurel Fork Restaurant, Tu-Su 7–4, closed M; Dunkin' Donuts, McDonald's; Subway. *Groceries:* Brown's Grocery, 613 US-321, (423) 725-2411, long-term resupply, closed Su; check with Sutton at the grocery store for accommodations; Coleman fuel, denatured alcohol, and gas canisters; holds USPS and UPS packages; Redi Mart. *Other services:* Dollar General, convenience stores, health clinic, banks, and ATM. *Shuttles:* Hampton Trails Bicycle Shop, (423) 725-5000 or (423) 957-9847, owner Brian White, hamptontrails .com, brian@hamptontrails.com.

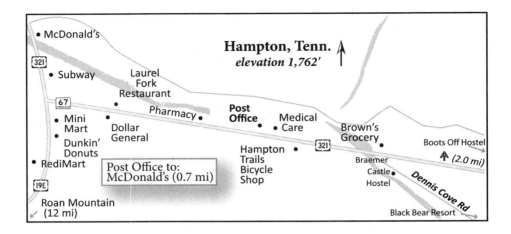

West 9 miles to **Elizabethton, TN.** *Lodging:* Hotels here receive poor reviews. *Groceries:* Food City, Walmart Supercenter, Ingles. *Outfitter:* Hellbender Outfitters, 547 E. Elk Ave., Elizabethton, TN 37643, (423) 430-9123, hellbenderoutfitterstn@gmail.com, new and used gear, closed Su, M, open T-W 11-6, Th-Sa 9-6. *Internet access:* library. *Other services:* restaurants, convenience stores, hospital, bank, veterinarian, laundry, and ATM.

Shook Branch Recreation Area—This developed area on Watauga Lake offers picnic tables, a restroom, and a beach for swimming. This is a fee area, and water is turned on after the last freeze of spring (usually by late Apr). Please be considerate of rules and regulations when entering the recreation area. Regulations are posted on the information board near the fee tube.

Watauga Lake Shelter (1980)—Dismantled and removed due to bear activity. Water is on A.T., south of the former shelter area (if dry, follow stream up to small pool). No camping.

Watauga Dam—The A.T. crosses the Watauga River on this dam at Watauga Lake. Hiking north, as the Trail leaves the road, a side trail leads 0.5 mile to a visitor center with restroom, often closed during cold-weather months. It also can be reached by following Wilbur Dam Road 0.9 mile east.

Vandeventer Shelter (1961)—Sleeps 6. No privy or cables. Water source is 0.3 mile down a steep, blue-blazed trail south of the shelter.

Iron Mountain Shelter (1960)—Sleeps 6. No privy or cables. Water source is a spring 500 yards south on A.T.

Nick Grindstaff Monument—Nick Grindstaff traveled west to win his fortune but was robbed of all his money during the journey. He then returned to Iron Mountain, where he lived for more than 40 years as one of the region's most famous hermits. He died in 1923, and the plaque on the chimney was erected in 1925.

TN-91/Cross Mountain Road—**East** 2.5 miles to Switchback Creek Campground, (407) 484-3388. Open Apr 1–Oct 31. Tenting $15, cabin $40d, $10 for 1 extra person. Shower included; laundry $5. Call for directions. Credit cards accepted. Can pick up from Cross Mountain Rd. or US-421/Low Gap or Shady Valley Country Store.
   East 11 miles on VA/TN-91 to Mountain City, TN, and Appalachian Folk School, (423) 341-1843, www.warrendoyle.com. Only for hikers who have a respectful appreciation of the entire white-blazed Trail. Open Mar 12–Nov 12. Lodging donation based or 2-3 hours of work-for-stay for each night. Kitchen privileges, shower, Wi-Fi. Rides to and from the Trail between US-321

(Watauga Lake) and VA-603 (Fox Creek). No smoking, alcohol, drugs, or pets. Will pay $50/day for manual labor May 1–26 and Sept 23–Oct. 31.

Double Springs Shelter (1960)—Sleeps 6. No privy or cables. Water source is a spring located 100 yards in the draw beyond the shelter.

Closure Notice: National forest lands from US-421 to the Virginia line (including Abingdon Gap Shelter) were closed to overnight camping at times in the fall of 2022 because of an "aggressive" bear. Please look for signs indicating a continued closure. Please use caution while hiking through and do not stop.

⚠ US-421/Low Gap—A piped spring is located in the gap, on the A.T. **East** 2.7 miles to **Shady Valley, TN [P.O. ZIP 37688: M-F 8–12, Sa 8–10; (423) 739-2173]**. *Groceries:* Shady Valley Country Store & Deli, (423) 739-2325, closed W, Th-Tu open 8-8, short-term resupply; Dollar General. *Restaurant:* Raceway, (423) 739-2499, closed Su.

⚠ McQueens Knob Shelter (1934)—Sleeps 2 (if that). No privy. This shelter is one of the A.T.'s oldest. Not up to current standards, it is intended *for emergency use only,* and, even then, the unchinked walls allow for the weather to easily enter. No water at this site.

Abingdon Gap Shelter (1959)—Sleeps 5. No privy or cables. Water source is a spring 0.2 mile east on a steep, blue-blazed side trail, downhill behind the shelter.

Tennessee/Virginia State Line—You're entering or leaving Virginia when you see the Mt. Rogers National Recreation Area sign, which is on the state line.

Virginia—Part 1 (Southwest)

Miles from Springer	Miles to Next Point	Features	Services	Elev	Miles from Katahdin	M A P
467.3	1.0	Tennessee–Virginia State Line: *Mt. Rogers N.R.A. sign*		3,300'	1,730.1	
468.3	0.6	Campsite	C		1,729.1	
468.9	1.6	Spring: *downhill (E–250 yds.)*	w	2,600'	1,728.5	
470.5	0.1	Mock Ave. and Water St.		1,975'	1,726.9	
470.6	0.3	Gravel path: *through town park*		1,960'	1,726.8	
470.9	0.1	Beaverdam Creek: *bridge*	P	1,928'	1,726.5	
471.0	1.0	US-58, Laurel Ave., Damascus Town Hall	R, P	1,928'	1,726.4	
		*On A.T.–***Damascus, VA, P.O. 24236** *East–10m on* VA/TN-91 *to Appalachian Folk School* *West–2m to veterinarian* *West–12m to Abingdon, VA*	H, G, L, M, O, D, cl, sh, f work for stay V all			
472.0	1.9	US-58/VA-91, Virginia Creeper Trail: *steps*	R	1,928'	1,725.4	
473.9	0.6	Cuckoo Knob		2,920'	1,723.5	
474.5	1.5	Iron Mountain Trail, Feathercamp Ridge		2,850'	1,722.9	
476.0	0.5	Beech Grove Trail		2,490'	1,721.4	
476.5	0.1	Feathercamp Trail, Feathercamp Branch	w	2,330'	1,720.9	
476.6	1.4	US-58 at Straight Branch Creek: *picnic area, privy*	R, P, w	2,310'	1,720.8	
478.0	0.6	Creek: *log bridge above small falls*	w	2,490'	1,719.4	
478.6	1.4	Taylors Valley side trail *East–0.7m on* Virginia Creeper Trail	M, w	2,400'	1,718.8	
480.0	0.2	South side trail to **Saunders Shelter** *(W–0.3m)*, 20mS; 0.8mN	S, w	3,310'	1,717.4	
480.2	0.3	Straight Mountain		3,440'	1,717.2	
480.5	2.3	North side trail to **Saunders Shelter** *(W–300 yds.)*, 0.8mS; 6.5mN	S, w	3,310'	1,716.9	

482.8	1.5	Beartree Gap Trail: *to USFS Beartree Recreation Area*
		   West–0.6m to bathouse, lake, swimming area
		   West–3.6m to campground
			P, w, sh
			C, w, sh
				3,050'	1,714.6	

484.3	0.3	Junction with Virginia Creeper Trail		2,700'	1,713.1	
484.6	0.6	Creek Junction Station to VA-728: *old railroad bed (E–0.5m P, privy)*	R	2,720'	1,712.8	
485.2	0.6	Virginia Creeper Trail, Whitetop Laurel Creek: *Luther Hassinger Memorial Bridge*	R, P	2,690'	1,712.2	
485.8	0.2	VA-859, Grassy Ridge Road	R	2,900'	1,711.6	
486.0	0.6	Streams	w	3,040'	1,711.4	
486.6	0.4	Lost Mountain		3,400'	1,710.8	
487.0	1.1	**Lost Mountain Shelter**, *6.5mS; 12.4mN*	S, w	3,360'	1,710.4	
488.1	0.4	US-58; Summit Cut, VA	R	3,160'	1,709.3	
488.5	0.9	Campsites near stream	C, w	3,300'	1,708.9	
489.4	2.5	VA-601, Beech Mountain Road: *reliable boxed spring*	R, P, w	3,530'	1,708.0	

ACT: SW VA Map 4

Miles from Springer	Miles to Next Point	Features	Services	Elev	Miles from Katahdin	M A P
491.9	0.8	Buzzard Rock on Whitetop Mountain		5,080'	1,705.5	
492.7	0.1	Spring: *piped (east)*	w	5,100'	1,704.7	
492.8	2.4	Whitetop Mountain Road, USFS-89 to summit (5,520')	R, P, C	5,150'	1,704.6	
495.2	0.5	VA-600, Elk Garden, Whitetop, VA	R, P, privy	4,458'	1,702.2	
495.7	1.4	Lewis Fork Wilderness boundary		4,640'	1,701.7	
497.1	0.1	Campsite: *blue-blaze (east)*	C	4,850'	1,700.3	
497.2	0.1	Deep Gap: *no-camping zone, piped spring (E-0.2m)*	w	4,900'	1,700.2	
497.3	1.0	Mt. Rogers Trail *West-4m to USFS Grindstone Campground at VA-603*	R, C, w, sh	5,200'	1,700.1	
498.3	0.9	Brier Ridge Saddle: *views in meadow*		5,125'	1,699.1	
499.2	0.2	Spur Trail *West-0.5m to* summit of Mt. Rogers (5,729')		5,490'	1,698.2	
499.4	1.0	**Thomas Knob Shelter**, *12.4mS; 5.1mN*	S, w	5,400'	1,698.0	ACT: SW VA Map 4
500.4	0.5	Rhododendron Gap, Pine Mountain Trail	C	5,400'	1,697.0	
500.9	0.1	Wilburn Ridge Trail: *southern jct.*		5,440'	1,696.5	
501.0	0.6	Fatman Squeeze: *narrow rock tunnel*		5,300'	1,696.4	
501.6	0.3	Wilburn Ridge Trail: *northern jct.*		4,900'	1,695.8	
501.9	0.5	Grayson Highlands State Park: *cross fence*		4,880'	1,695.5	
502.4	0.7	Park service road to Massie Gap *East-0.5m to* Grayson Highlands State Park: *day parking* *East-2m to* campground	R, P C, g, sh	4,800'	1,695.0	
503.1	0.5	A.T. spur trail on Wilburn Ridge *(E-0.8m)*	R, P	4,920'	1,694.3	
503.6	0.9	Quebec Branch	w	4,200'	1,693.8	
504.5	0.1	**Wise Shelter**, *5.1mS; 6mN*	S, w	4,460'	1,692.9	
504.6	0.2	Big Wilson Creek: *footbridge*	C, w	4,300'	1,692.8	
504.8	0.1	Wilson Creek Trail: *footbridge (E-1.3m to CG)*	R, C, sh	4,300'	1,692.6	
504.9	1.0	Scales Trail junction		4,650'	1,692.5	
505.9	1.2	Spring: *unreliable*	w	4,610'	1,691.5	
507.1	0.4	Stone Mountain		4,800'	1,690.3	
507.5	0.7	The Scales, USFS-613: *livestock corral, privy*	P, R	4,620'	1,689.9	
508.2	0.7	Stream	w	4,700'	1,689.2	
508.9	1.6	Pine Mountain Trail		4,960'	1,688.5	
510.5	0.1	**Old Orchard Shelter**, *6mS; 4.9mN*	S, C, w	4,050'	1,686.9	
510.6	0.7	Upper Old Orchard Trail		4,020'	1,686.8	
511.3	0.9	Old Orchard Trail One		3,750'	1,686.1	
512.2	0.1	VA-603, Fairwood Road, Fox Creek: *Fox Creek Horse Camp* *East-4m to* **Troutdale, VA, P.O. 24378** *West-1.9m to* USFS Grindstone CG	R, P, C, w H C, w, sh	3,480'	1,685.2	ATC: SW VA Map 3
512.3	1.9	Fox Creek: *footbridge*		3,450'	1,685.1	
514.2	0.3	Hurricane Mountain; Tennessee–New River Divide		4,325'	1,683.2	
514.5	0.9	Iron Mountain Trail, Chestnut Flats		4,240'	1,682.9	
515.4	0.6	**Hurricane Mountain Shelter**, *4.9mS; 9.3mN*	S, w	3,850'	1,682.0	
516.0	0.8	Hurricane Creek Trail: *old logging road*		3,300'	1,681.4	
516.8	2.1	Stream	w	3,000'	1,680.6	

Miles from Springer	Miles to Next Point	Features	Services	Elev	Miles from Katahdin	M A P
518.9	0.4	Dickey Gap Trail *West–0.4m to* USFS Hurricane Campground	C, w, sh	3,090'	1,678.5	
519.3	1.2	Comers Creek Falls Trail, Comers Creek: *Follow marked 2.2-mile detour if water is high;* waterfalls	w	3,120'	1,678.1	
520.5	0.8	Dickey Gap, VA-650, Comers Creek Road *East 180 ft. to VA-16–from VA-16:* *East–2.6m to* **Troutdale, VA, P.O. 24378** *East–3.6m to* Fox Creek General Store *East–4.3m to* Grayson Highlands Clinic *West–5m to* **Sugar Grove, VA, P.O. 24374**	R, P H, L G, M, f D G, M, f	3,310'	1,676.9	
521.3	0.7	Virginia Highlands Horse Trail		3,480'	1,676.1	
522.0	0.5	Bobby's Trail to campsite and spring *(E–0.2m)* *East–3.3m to* USFS Raccoon Branch CG	C, w C, w, sh	3,570'	1,675.4	
522.5	2.1	High Point		4,040'	1,674.9	
524.6	1.2	Slabtown Trail Jct., **Trimpi Shelter** *(E–0.1m)*, 9.3mS; 9.9mN	S, w	2,900'	1,672.8	
525.8	0.7	VA-672, Slabtown Road: *gravel*	R	2,700'	1,671.6	
526.5	0.2	Slabtown Trail		2,600'	1,670.9	
526.7	1.5	VA-670, Teas Road, South Fork Holston River: *bridge*	R, P	2,470'	1,670.7	
528.2	0.1	Campsite	C	2,720'	1,669.2	
528.3	2.2	Stream: *intermittent*	w	2,780'	1,669.1	
530.5	1.6	VA-601, Pugh Mountain Road: *gravel*	R, P	3,250'	1,666.9	
532.1	0.9	Powerline		3,300'	1,665.3	
533.0	1.4	Creek: *footbridge*	w	3,010'	1,664.4	
534.4	0.2	**Partnership Shelter**, 9.9mS; 7mN	S, w, sh	3,360'	1,663.0	
534.6	0.7	VA-16, Mt. Rogers NRA Headquarters *East–3.2m to* **Sugar Grove, VA, P.O. 24375** *West–6m to* **Marion, VA, P.O. 24354**	R, P, w G, M, f G, H, L, M, O, D, cl, f	3,240'	1,662.8	
535.3	1.9	VA-622, Nick's Creek Road	R	3,250'	1,662.1	
537.2	1.0	Brushy Mountain: *northern end*		3,700'	1,660.2	
538.2	0.4	Locust Mountain		3,900'	1,659.2	
538.6	1.3	USFS-86, Glade Mountain Road: *campsite, spring*	C, w	3,530'	1,658.8	
539.9	1.5	Glade Mountain		4,093'	1,657.5	
541.4	0.3	**Chatfield Shelter**, 7mS; 19.3mN	S, w	3,150'	1,656.0	
541.7	1.5	USFS-644	R	3,100'	1,655.7	
543.2	0.5	VA-615, Rocky Hollow Road, Settlers Museum, Lindamood Schoolhouse	R, P	2,590'	1,654.2	
543.7	0.4	VA-729, Kegley Lane: *gravel*	R	2,540'	1,653.7	
544.1	1.0	Kegley Trail: *old road*	R	2,540'	1,653.3	
545.1	0.9	Middle Fork of Holston River Bridge: *active railroad tracks*	w	2,420'	1,652.3	
546.0	1.0	US-11, I-81 (exit 54), VA-683, Groseclose, VA *West–3.2m to* **Atkins, VA, P.O. 24311** *West–10.2m to* **Marion, VA, P.O. 24354**	R, P, G, L, M, B, sh, cl, f G, L, M, cl G, B, H, L, M, D, cl	2,420'	1,651.4	
547.0	0.7	VA-617, Davis Valley Road	R, P	2,580'	1,650.4	
547.7	1.1	Spring: *blue-blaze, 300 yards E*	w	2,610'	1,649.7	
548.8	2.8	Davis Path Campsite	C	2,840'	1,648.6	

ATC: SW VA Map 3

Miles from Springer	Miles to Next Point	Features	Services	Elev	Miles from Katahdin	MAP
551.6	1.1	Little Brushy Mountain, Crawfish (Channel Rock) Trail		3,300'	1,645.8	ATC: SW VA Map 3
552.7	0.1	Reed Creek, Crawfish Valley	w on A.T. (E–0.3m C, w)	2,600'	1,644.7	
552.8	1.8	Crawfish (Channel Rock) Trail		3,300'	1,644.6	
554.6	1.5	Tilson Gap, Big Walker Mountain		3,500'	1,642.8	
556.1	1.5	VA-610, Old Rich Valley Road *West–0.3m to Quarter Way Inn, Ceres, VA*	R H, C, g, sh	2,700'	1,641.3	
557.6	0.4	VA-742, Shady Grove Road, N. Fork of Holston River, Tilson's Mill: *low-water bridge*	R, w	2,460'	1,639.8	
558.0	0.6	Spring: *25 yds. downhill*	w	2,550'	1,639.4	
558.6	0.9	VA-42, Ceres, VA *(E–0.2m small creek)* *East–0.1m to Bear Garden Hiker Hostel* *West–2.5m to Appalachian Dreamer Hiker Hostel*	R, P, w H H, C, g, sh	2,500'	1,638.8	
559.5	1.2	Brushy Mountain		3,200'	1,637.9	
560.7	0.5	**Knot Maul Branch Shelter**, *19.3mS; 9.4mN*	S	2,800'	1,636.7	
561.2	0.6	Campsite and creek: *water for Knot Maul Branch Shelter*	C, w	2,810'	1,636.2	
561.8	1.1	Lynn Camp Creek: *footbridge*	w	2,400'	1,635.6	
562.9	1.2	Lynn Camp Mountain		3,000'	1,634.5	
564.1	1.4	Lick Creek: *ford*	C, w	2,250'	1,633.3	
565.5	2.8	USFS-222, VA-625: *dirt*	R, P	2,310'	1,631.9	
568.3	1.1	Spring-fed pond: *spring box NE end of pond, water for Chestnut Knob Shelter*	w	3,800'	1,629.1	
569.4	0.5	Chestnut Ridge: *views*		3,700'	1,628.0	
569.9	0.2	Spring: *intermittent on old jeep road (E–0.1m)*	w	4,300'	1,627.5	
570.1	1.4	**Chestnut Knob Shelter**, *9.4mS; 10.7mN* Burkes Garden overlook: *"God's Thumbprint" view*	S	4,409'	1,627.3	ATC: SW VA Map 2
571.5	4.8	Walker Gap: *water for Chestnut Knob Shelter, blue-blaze to spring (E–130 yds.)*	R, P, w	3,520'	1,625.9	
576.3	1.0	VA-623, Burkes Garden Road, Garden Mountain	R, P	3,880'	1,621.1	
577.3	2.6	Davis Farm Campsite	C	3,850'	1,620.1	
579.9	0.9	Stream	w	3,700'	1,617.5	
580.8	0.1	**Jenkins Shelter**, *10.7mS; 13.8mN*	S, w	2,470'	1,616.6	
580.9	3.3	Hunting Camp Creek	w	2,450'	1,616.5	
584.2	0.2	High-water trail		2,950'	1,613.2	
584.4	0.8	Brushy Mountain		3,080'	1,613.0	
585.2	2.1	VA-615, Suiter Road, Laurel Creek	R, P, C, w	2,450'	1,612.2	
587.3	4.3	Trail Boss Trail		3,100'	1,610.1	
591.6	0.5	USFS-282 (Wyrick Road): *gravel*	R	2,950'	1,605.8	
592.1	0.4	US-52 *East–2.7m to* **Bland, VA, P.O. 24315** *East–3.3m to services* *West–2.5m to* **Bastian, VA, P.O. 24314** *West–3.5m to services* *West–20m to Bluefield, WV*	R, P G, M, f G, L, M, D D, M, g B, all	2,910'	1,605.3	
592.5	0.4	VA-612, I-77 overpass	R	2,750'	1,604.9	
592.9	1.4	VA-612, Kimberling Creek	R, P, w	2,600'	1,604.5	
594.3	6.6	**Helveys Mill Shelter** *(E–0.3m), 13.8mS; 10mN*	S, w	3,090'	1,603.1	

Miles from Springer	Miles to Next Point	Features	Services	Elev	Miles from Katahdin	MAP
600.9	1.4	VA-611, Slide Mountain Road: *gravel*	R, P	2,720'	1,596.5	
602.3	1.7	Brushy Mountain		3,101'	1,595.1	
604.0	1.2	**Jenny Knob Shelter**, *10mS; 14.5mN*	S, w	2,800'	1,593.4	
605.2	3.4	VA-608, Lickskillet Hollow	R, P	2,200'	1,592.2	ATC: SW VA Map 2
608.6	1.8	Brushy Mountain		2,680'	1,588.8	
610.4	0.1	Kimberling Creek: *suspension bridge*	C, w	2,090'	1,587.0	
610.5	1.9	VA-606, Wilderness Road *West–0.5m to* Trent's Grocery	R, H C, G, L, M, cl, sh, f, w	2,040'	1,586.9	
612.4	1.1	Dismal Creek Falls Trail: *waterfalls (W–0.3m)*	w	2,320'	1,585.0	
613.5	0.8	Bridge: *over deep gully*		2,390'	1,583.9	
614.3	2.0	Bridge, trail to Walnut Flats Campground *(W–0.4m)*	C, w	2,400'	1,583.1	
616.3	0.1	Lion's Den Road		2,400'	1,581.1	
616.4	0.3	Ribble Trail south junction: *USFS White Cedar Horse Campground (W–0.5m)*	C, w	2,400'	1,581.0	
616.7	0.8	Creek: *bridge*	w	2,500'	1,580.7	
617.5	0.8	Creek: *two bridges*	w	2,550'	1,579.9	
618.3	0.2	Levee and pond		2,570'	1,579.1	
618.5	0.6	**Wapiti Shelter**, *14.5mS; 9.5mN*	S, w	2,600'	1,578.9	
619.1	2.0	Dismal Creek	w	2,700'	1,578.3	
621.1	2.9	Sugar Run Mountain: *rocky outcrop*		3,870'	1,576.3	ATC: SW VA Map 1
624.0	0.1	Ribble Trail north junction	w	3,800'	1,573.4	
624.1	1.2	Big Horse Gap, USFS-103	R	3,752'	1,573.3	
625.3	0.4	Nobusiness Creek Road: *closed road*		3,500'	1,572.1	
625.7	1.4	Sugar Run Gap, Sugar Run Gap Road, VA-663 *East–0.5m to* Woods Hole Hostel	R, P H	3,382'	1,571.7	
627.1	0.9	Rock Cliff Overlook: *blue-blaze (E–60 yds.)*		3,850'	1,570.3	
628.0	5.7	**Doc's Knob Shelter**, *9.5mS; 16.5mN*	S, w	3,555'	1,569.4	
633.7	0.2	Rock-ledge view on Pearis Mountain		3,770'	1,563.7	
633.9	0.5	Campsite and spring *(W–300 yds.)*	C, w	3,750'	1,563.5	
634.4	1.0	Angels Rest on Pearis Mountain: *vista*		3,550'	1,563.0	
635.4	1.0	Abandoned powerline tower		2,740'	1,562.0	
636.4	1.0	VA-634, Cross Ave. *(E–0.8m Pearisburg, VA)*	R, PO, all	2,200'	1,561.0	

The state's highest mountain, Mt. Rogers, an area of spectacular highland meadows, routinely receives snowfall from October to May, making it considerably colder, wetter, and snowier than other areas of Virginia. Northbounders may be tempted to mail home their cold-weather gear, only to see spring flavored by winter.

Note: At the time of printing, the impacts of Hurricane Helene to the Trail and nearby towns were not fully known. Thru-hikers in 2025 may encounter adverse trail conditions, damaged shelters, and reduced access to and services in nearby towns, including Damascus. It's important to check with businesses in the affected areas before arriving there. Find the latest trail conditions ATC's website at appalachiantrail.org/trail-updates.

Caution: According to Mt. Rogers National Recreation Area officials, hikers should use caution when leaving vehicles at any local trailhead. Safer hiker parking is available at some locations in Damascus, as well as the Mt. Rogers NRA headquarters.

Mt. Rogers Appalachian Trail Club—MRATC: Maintenance responsibility for the A.T. from the Tennessee line north to Teas Road/Rte. 670 (59.4 miles). Maintains trails in the Mt. Rogers NRA, Jefferson National Forest and Grayson Highlands State Park. Report trail problems on this section or ask questions by emailing mratcinfo@gmail.com. Website: mratc.org. Check the sidebar "Current Week's Information" for updates or for locations to join the club on weekly trail maintenance outings.

⚠ ⌂ US-58/Damascus, VA [P.O. ZIP 24236: M–F 8:30–1 & 2–4:30, Sa 9–11; (276) 475-3411]—Called "the friendliest town on the Trail" and the home of Trail Days (scheduled this year for May 16–18). First held in 1987 as a commemorative event for the 50th anniversary of the A.T., the festival's activities and crowds have grown each year since. Activities include a hiker reunion and talent show, hiking-related exhibits, arts-and-crafts exhibits, street dances, live music, and the popular hiker parade through downtown. If you are unable to walk into Damascus for the weekend, rides are easy to find from all points along the Trail. Be aware that state open-container laws that restrict drinking in public places are enforced. Hiker camping during Trail Days is at the south edge of town on Shady Avenue. Camping is prohibited everywhere else. Please keep quiet in the late evening and early

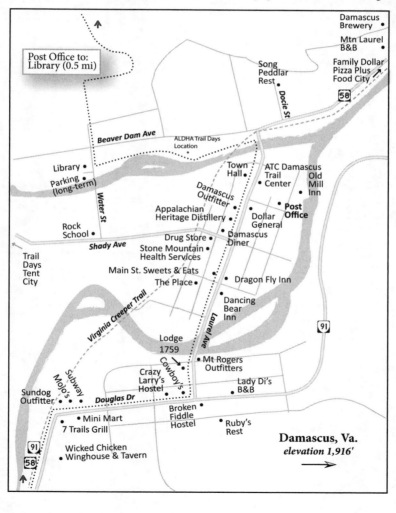

Damascus, Va.
elevation 1,916'

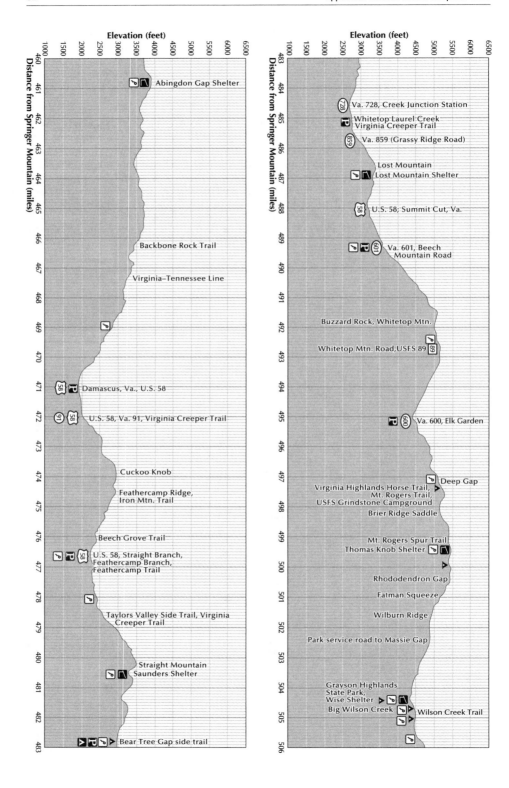

Elevation (feet)

Distance from Springer Mountain (miles)

Abingdon Gap Shelter

Backbone Rock Trail

Virginia–Tennessee Line

Damascus, Va., U.S. 58

U.S. 58, Va. 91, Virginia Creeper Trail

Cuckoo Knob

Feathercamp Ridge,
Iron Mtn. Trail

Beech Grove Trail

U.S. 58, Straight Branch,
Feathercamp Branch,
Feathercamp Trail

Taylors Valley Side Trail, Virginia
Creeper Trail

Straight Mountain
Saunders Shelter

Bear Tree Gap side trail

Elevation (feet)

Distance from Springer Mountain (miles)

Va. 728, Creek Junction Station

Whitetop Laurel Creek
Virginia Creeper Trail

Va. 859 (Grassy Ridge Road)

Lost Mountain
Lost Mountain Shelter

U.S. 58; Summit Cut, Va.

Va. 601, Beech
Mountain Road

Buzzard Rock, Whitetop Mtn.

Whitetop Mtn. Road, USFS 89

Va. 600, Elk Garden

Deep Gap
Virginia Highlands Horse Trail,
Mt. Rogers Trail,
USFS Grindstone Campground
Brier Ridge Saddle

Mt. Rogers Spur Trail
Thomas Knob Shelter

Rhododendron Gap

Fatman Squeeze

Wilburn Ridge

Park service road to Massie Gap

Grayson Highlands
State Park,
Wise Shelter
Big Wilson Creek   Wilson Creek Trail

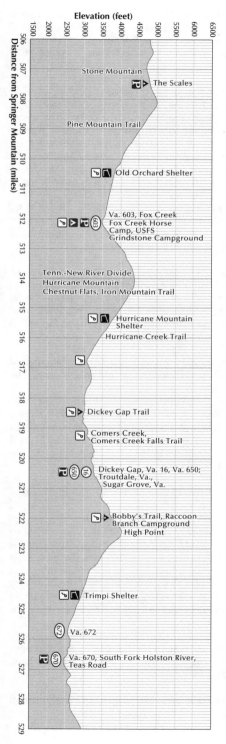

Elevation (feet)

Distance from Springer Mountain (miles)

Stone Mountain

The Scales

Pine Mountain Trail

Old Orchard Shelter

Va. 603, Fox Creek
Fox Creek Horse
Camp, USFS
Grindstone Campground

Tenn.-New River Divide
Hurricane Mountain
Chestnut Flats, Iron Mountain Trail

Hurricane Mountain
Shelter
Hurricane Creek Trail

Dickey Gap Trail

Comers Creek,
Comers Creek Falls Trail

Dickey Gap, Va. 16, Va. 650;
Troutdale, Va.,
Sugar Grove, Va.

Bobby's Trail, Raccoon
Branch Campground
High Point

Trimpi Shelter

Va. 672

Va. 670, South Fork Holston River,
Teas Road

morning, and, upon departure, leave your campsite clean. Leave No Trace camping principles apply in town as well as on the Trail. You'll find all major services, except veterinary, in Damascus. *Hostels:* The Place, First United Methodist Church, facebook.com/theplacehostel, open mid-Mar–mid-Jun, closed 'til Labor Day, closes early Nov or when the pipes are in danger of freezing. Check in 3–9 p.m., closed Su. Stays are limited to two days (unless sick or injured). A large house for hikers and TA cyclists only, with Wi-Fi, tents/hammocks, bunk space, showers (towels/soap), and pavilion/picnic tables. Ten-dollars-per-night donation is requested, but larger donations are appreciated in addition to cleaning chores. Seasonal caretaker. No vehicle-assisted hikers except during Trail Days. No dogs, drinking, or smoking are allowed on the church property, its parking lot, or pavilion. Crazy Larry's Hostel and Outdoors Inn, 209 Douglas Dr., facebook.com/crazy larryshostel, (276) 475-7130 or (276) 525-5138, $40, includes shower, B, laundry, Wi-Fi, will accept mail. Woodchuck Hostel & Song Peddlar Rest and Woodchuck Hostel, 533 Docie St., (276) 356-7286. Thru-hikers only; $45 per bunk, laundry included, new foam mattresses and sheets. Broken Fiddle Hostel, 104 Damascus Dr., (276) 608-1055; bunk $40, private room $85d $10eap; includes shower, laundry; non-guest shower $5/laundry $7; Wi-Fi and kitchen available; dog-friendly but must book a private room. *Lodging:* Mountain Laurel Inn, (276) 475-8822, 0.5 mile west of town on US-58; Ruby's Rest, 719 E. 2nd St., (276) 475-3914, text or call, $50, flat rate for 1 room cottage that can sleep 4 hikers, with a full-size bed and a bunkbed, laundry included, dogs free in fenced yard. Lady Di's B&B, 217 Damascus Dr., (612) 695-4738 (text preferred 1-2 days in advance), ladydibnb.com, 1 block off Trail, bed in shared hostel room $60 includes hot B, laundry, taxes, loaner clothes, and bikes; private room $135 and up; cash, Venmo, or PayPal; mail drops accepted. *Groceries:* Food City (long-term resupply). *Restaurants:* Subway; Cowboy's Deli and convenience store, with ATM; Wicked Chicken Winghouse; Damascus Diner; Main StreetSweets & Eats. *Outfitters:* Mt. Rogers Outfitters (MRO), 335 E. Laurel Ave. (P.O. Box 546), (276) 475-5416, owned and operated by Mike "Lumpy" Price, backpacking gear and supplies, stove fuel, shuttles, accepts mail drops, open M– F 9-6, Sa 9–5, Su 12–6; Damascus Outfitter, 128 W. Laurel Ave., (888) 595-2453, open 7 days/week, full line of backpacking gear and clothing, denatured alcohol and other fuels available, will hold UPS and USPS mail drops; Sundog Outfitter, 331 Douglas Dr., (276) 475-6252, sundogoutfitter. com, mostly a bike shop, limited supply of backpacking gear and clothing, hiker food, call ahead for bike shuttles, same owners as Damascus Outfitter. *Internet access:* Damascus Public Library & Visitor Center, Wi-Fi/Skype, closed Su–M; long-term parking available, inquire on-line at visitdamascus. org/parking. *Other services:* Damascus Brewery; Appalachian Distillery; town-wide Wi-Fi; clinic; pharmacy; Dollar General; two banks with ATM. *Shuttles:* David (Lonewolf) Blair, (276) 206-6078 (cell, texts ok), gypwolf@gmail.com.

ATC's Damascus Trail Center, 209 W. Laurel Ave., (276) 323-3046 or (304) 535-6331, ext 7, open every day except holidays, 10-5. Connects people to nature and acts as a hub uniting visitors and volunteers with a wide range of regional outdoor resources, including interpretive exhibits. The center caters to a broad community of people, from experienced outdoor enthusiasts to those who are at the very beginning of building a relationship with nature. All hikers can add the pet-friendly DTC as a destination along their journey. While visiting the center, they can expect to find current trail updates and historical exhibits, pick up thru-hiker hangtags, relax on the porch (or inside), and enjoy pop-up services geared for hikers and outdoor enthusiasts. Other amenities include water, restrooms, and free public Wi-Fi. For more info: appalachiantrail.org/dtc.

West 2 miles on US-58 to Fisher Hollow Veterinary Clinic, (276) 475-5397. M–Tu, Th–F 7:30–5, W & Sa 8–12.

⊕ **West** 12 miles on US-58 to Abingdon, VA, a large town near I-81 with all major services, including a Walmart, veterinarian, and movie theater

Virginia Creeper Trail—The Virginia Creeper stretches 33 miles along an old railroad bed from Abingdon to the North Carolina state line. It began as a native-American footpath. Later, it was used by pioneers, including Daniel Boone, and, beginning in the early 1900s, by a quintessential mountain railroad, its namesake, with 100 trestles and bridges, as well as many steep grades and sharp curves. The A.T. shares the Creeper route north of Damascus for 300 yards and again 10 miles north.

Saunders Shelter (1987)—Sleeps 8. Privy, 2 bear boxes. Shelter is located on a 0.2-mile blue-blazed trail. Water source is behind and to the right of the shelter, then down an old road to a reliable, seeping spring.

USFS Beartree Campground on Bear Tree Gap Trail **West** 3.6 miles. Part of Mt. Rogers National Recreation Area, (276) 783-5196, with a bathhouse, lake is drained, and former swimming area 0.6 mile from the A.T. Open May 25–Oct 31, open 9 a.m.–10 p.m.. Campground is 3 miles beyond swimming area, beach is closed to swimming, with tent sites $24 for 2 tents/8 people, and hot showers included with camping fee, shower only is $4. Parking $5/day. Cash or check only.

Lost Mountain Shelter (1994)—Sleeps 8. Privy. Bear boxes. Water source is on a trail to the left of the shelter.

Whitetop Mountain—At 5,520 feet, this is Virginia's second-highest peak, but the A.T. does not go to the top. The nearby town of Whitetop is home to a ramp festival the weekend after Memorial Day. The festival includes a ramp-eating contest thru-hikers have won in past years. Ramps emerge from the forest floor in early spring. The two-leafed greens sprout from an onion-like tuber that can be used to spice up meals. Other plants have a similar look; ramps are identified easily by their smell and taste, which are akin to onions and garlic. Harvesting ramps so that they survive is a delicate balance, try to leave the roots in the ground or take just the leaves, so the bulb can continue to produce.

🔺**VA-600, Elk Garden**—Elk Garden is named after the extinct eastern elk that once roamed throughout this area, along with timber wolves, mountain lions, and bison. Today, none of those exist here, but black bear, white-tailed deer, and wild turkey which are all are common.

Note: Since 2019, an active bear problem in the High Country led to bear-resistant storage boxes being installed at shelters and campsites. Pay attention to any informational signs and use the food boxes provided.

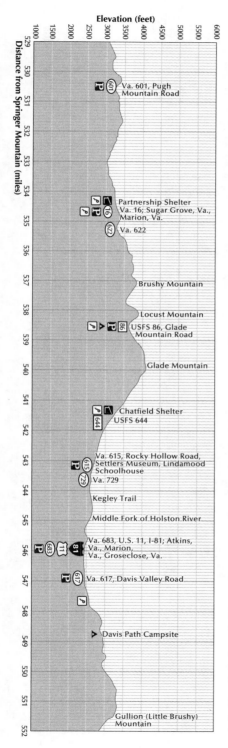

Elevation (feet)

Distance from Springer Mountain (miles)

Va. 601, Pugh Mountain Road

Partnership Shelter
Va. 16; Sugar Grove, Va.,
Marion, Va.

Va. 622

Brushy Mountain

Locust Mountain

USFS 86, Glade Mountain Road

Glade Mountain

Chatfield Shelter
USFS 644

Va. 615, Rocky Hollow Road,
Settlers Museum, Lindamood
Schoolhouse

Va. 729

Kegley Trail

Middle Fork of Holston River

Va. 683, U.S. 11, I-81; Atkins,
Va., Marion,
Va., Groseclose, Va.

Va. 617, Davis Valley Road

Davis Path Campsite

Gullion (Little Brushy)
Mountain

USFS Grindstone Campground—via Mt. Rogers Trail **west** 4 miles. Open April 1–Nov 30. Primitive tent-sites $24; parking $5/day. No reservations. Cash or check only.

Mt. Rogers—Virginia's highest peak, at 5,729 feet; the Trail does not go to the viewless summit, but it can be reached via a side trail, going west 0.5 mile. Camping is prohibited in the area from the A.T. to the summit due to fragile plant life and the endangered Wellers salamander. The Wellers, a dark blue-black salamander with gold splotches on its back, can be found only in coniferous forests above 5,000 feet. You may also see or hear northern birds, such as the hermit thrush and winter wren. Such species nest here because of the favorable altitude at the summit area.

Thomas Knob Shelter (1991)—Sleeps 16. Moldering privy. This two-level shelter was built by the MRATC and Konnarock Crew. Water source is in an enclosed area in a pasture behind the shelter; lock the gate leading to the water source to keep the feral ponies in the area from polluting the water. Be aware those ponies like to chew on packs, trekking pole grips and other salty items. No tenting near shelter. *Hikers are strongly encouraged to store all food in the metal bearbox located just past the shelter.*

Rhododendron Gap—Just below the highest point on the Virginia A.T. on Pine Mountain and Wilburn Ridge. Many large, established campsites are located between Thomas Knob and Rhododendron Gap, with a bear box just south of the gap. This section is extremely popular with weekend and day-hikers. In June, rhododendron blooms here in full force. Panoramic views of the rhododendron thickets can be seen from a rock outcropping. Watch your step from Thomas Knob through the Grayson Highlands State Park area; cattle and feral ponies roam the area. In the spring, you will see mares tending their foals.

Grayson Highlands State Park—(276) 579-7092. At Massie Gap, a blue-blaze leads **East** 0.5 mile to a parking area, then 1.5 miles farther on roads or horse trail to campground. Park is open year-round from dawn to 10 p.m. The camp store and showers are open May 1–Oct 31; tent site with water and electricity $45, shower only $5. Camp store is usually open on weekends during the season, but hours vary; call for details and hours. The park hosts Appalachian music festivals on summer weekends.

Wise Shelter (1996)—Sleeps 8. Privy. Bear box. Water source is a reliable spring south of the shelter on a trail east of the A.T. No tenting around the shelter or

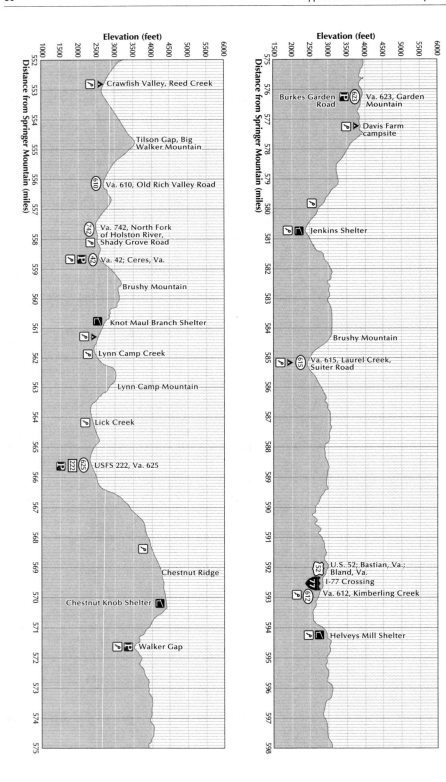

in the state park. Tent sites are in the Mt. Rogers NRA, across Wilson Creek, 0.3 mile north. Grayson Highlands State Park is accessible via the Seed Orchard Trail, 2 miles.

Old Orchard Shelter (1970)—Sleeps 6. Privy. Bear boxes. Water source is 100 yards on a blue-blazed trail to the right of the shelter.

⚠ **VA-603/Fox Creek**—Parking. **East** 100 yards to Fox Creek Horse Camp, $5/night, no water. Multiple bear incidents were reported in 2019, and bears were able to grab food hung in trees.
West 2.5 miles to USFS Grindstone Campground (see above).

Hurricane Mountain Shelter (2004)—Sleeps 8. Moldering privy. Bear boxes. Water source is a nearby stream.

USFS Hurricane Campground—**West** 0.5 mile via side trail to Hurricane Campground, (276) 783-5196, one of nine USFS campgrounds within the George Washington and Jefferson National Forests. The campground charges $20 per site; $2 shower; parking $3/day. Open Apr 15–Oct 31, depending on weather. Cash or check only.

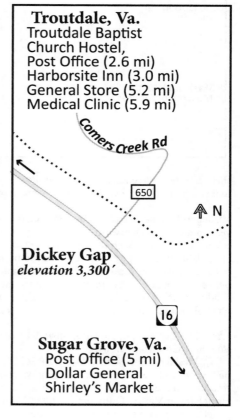

Troutdale, Va.
Troutdale Baptist
Church Hostel,
Post Office (2.6 mi)
Harborsite Inn (3.0 mi)
General Store (5.2 mi)
Medical Clinic (5.9 mi)

Comers Creek Rd

650

⚵ N

Dickey Gap
elevation 3,300´

16

Sugar Grove, Va.
Post Office (5 mi)
Dollar General
Shirley's Market

⚠ **VA-650, East 100 yards to VA-16/Dickey Gap**—Parking lot for 5 cars. Turn right **(compass south)** on VA-16, 2.6 miles to **Troutdale, VA [P.O. ZIP 24378: M–F 8-12, Sa 8:30-11:30; (276) 677-3221]**. *Hostels:* Troutdale Baptist Church, Pastor Ken Riggins, (276) 677-4092, located at 66 Sapphire Ln., offers a place to tent or use of a hiker bunkhouse, shower, pets welcome, donations accepted; Harborsite Inn, 67 High Country Ln., (276) 677-0195, is under new ownership. Veteran-owned/operated. Veterans get a 10% discount. They offer private hiker rooms from $60-$120, a bunk in a shared room $40, includes B, shower/towel/toiletries, laundry, accepts mail drops for guests, non-guests $10, parking for $7 per day, and shuttle service. Limited small store on site, enough to get you to the outfitters in Damascus and Marion. Pets welcome, but need to know in advance.
Continue on VA-16, 3.6 miles to Sarah's Fox Creek General Store & Restaurant (short-term resupply), 7116 Troutdale Hwy, (276) 579-6033, open Th–Sa 11–9, Su 11–3; canister and alcohol fuel, beer, wine, and BBQ.
From gap, left on VA-16, 5 miles to **Sugar Grove, VA [P.O. ZIP 24375: M–F 8:30-12:30 & 1:30-3:30, Sa 8:15-10:30; (276) 677-3200]**. *Groceries:* Shirley's Market (short-term resupply), open M–Sa 6 a.m.–11 p.m., Su 6 a.m.–10 p.m., snack bar, ice cream, ATM. Dollar General, (276) 521-2110, open daily 8-10.

Trimpi Shelter (1975)—Sleeps 8. Privy. Bear boxes. A reliable spring is in front of the shelter.

Partnership Shelter (1998)—Sleeps 16. Privy and cold-water shower (available during warmer months; single-use towel for sale in headquarters during operating hours). No tenting around the

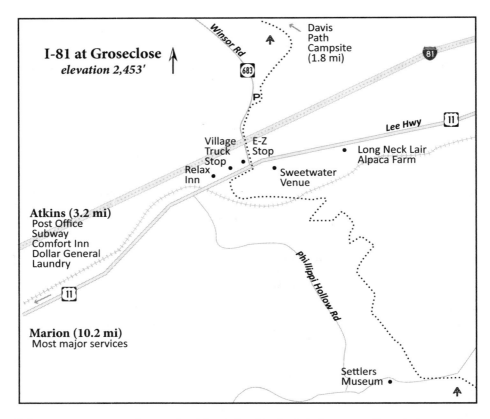

shelter. Water source is a faucet behind the shelter. No alcoholic beverages allowed. For a week or more after Trail Days, expect law-enforcement officers to be checking in.

Mt. Rogers National Recreation Area Headquarters—(276) 783-5196 or (800) 628-7202, M–F 8:30–4 year-round, May–Oct (weather permitting). Two hundred yards north of Partnership Shelter, the headquarters houses an interpretive center with information about the area's natural history. Water is available from a spigot outside. Restroom outside (closes 15 minutes before HQ). From the outside phone (free local calls), you may be able to order pizza from several area pizzerias, to be delivered to gate (subject to limited delivery hours and minimum orders). Do not sleep on the headquarters' covered porch. No overnight parking. Marion Transit Authority, (276) 782-9300, offers shuttles from HQ to Marion (call for ride).

VA-16—East 3.2 miles to **Sugar Grove, VA** (see above). The town is home to the ATC Konnarock Volunteer Crew (see below).
   West 6 miles to **Marion, VA [P.O. ZIP 24354: M–F 9–5 Sa 9:30–12; (276) 783-5051]**, a larger town on I-81 with all major services, including Walmart, Food Lion, and Ingles supermarkets (long-term resupply), restaurants, fast-food outlets, and a coin laundry. **Hostel & Outfitter:** Merry Inn Hiker Hostel above Marion Outdoors Outfitter, 208 E. Main St., (276) 706-8252, marionvaoutdoors@gmail.com, 13 bunks $35pp, 1 private room $70, and 1 private Apartment $100 (4 guests), Laundry, Loner clothes, Boot dryer, Free Wi-Fi, Pets welcome; Mail drops accepted by outfitter. Free pick up (please tip) from Partnership Shelter and Route 11 Exxon station near Atkins. Outfitter open all year M–Sa 10–6, Su 12–5; Apr and May, open M–Sa 9–6, Su 12–5. **Lodging:** Various motels, including the hiker-friendly Travel Inn, (276) 783-5112; Econo Lodge, (276) 783-6031; Red Roof Inn, (276) 378-0481. **Other services:** Historic downtown Marion offers several restaurants, including the Better Coffee Co, (276) 378-0071, open 7 days, 7-5; an Army Navy Store, 219 E. Main St.,

(276) 783-3832, open 9–5:30 M–F and 9–5 Sa (alcohol, white gas, canister fuel, outdoor clothing, shoes, hiker supplies, will accept mail drops, call first); and a hospital, (276) 378-1000.

Konnarock Crew—Based 1 mile from Sugar Grove post office at USFS facility. If you want part of your experience to be a week on the crew that builds and rehabilitates the Trail, call the Roanoke, VA, ATC regional office at (540) 904-4393 before your hike to arrange. Getting to base camp and back is your responsibility, but, once there, food and amenities are provided. Commitments include 5 days/4 nights along the Trail in the South. Be prepared to work and have a lot of fun.

Chatfield Shelter (1970s)—Sleeps 6. Privy. A creek is in front.

⚠ **VA-615, Settlers Museum**—On USFS lands adjacent to the Trail, the farmstead and visitor center include exhibits of rural life at the time the valley was settled. Admission free to hikers. Picnic pavilion. Closed M. No camping.

⚠ **VA-683, US-11, I-81**—At Groseclose, VA (no post office), this is the southernmost Trail crossing of I-81. See map. *Groceries:* Village Truck Stop (Sunoco station open 24 hours), (276) 783-5775, ATM, convenience store food, showers $10, Heet fuel (in season), and short-term resupply; E-Z Stop (Exxon), open 7–11 (short-term resupply, has Heet, Wi-Fi, ATM), Burrito Loco restaurant adjacent, Tu–Sa 11–9, Su 11:30–8. *Lodging:* The Relax Inn, 7253 Lee Hwy, Rural Retreat, VA 24368, (276) 783-5811; long-term hiker parking $3/day; coin laundry; call for rates and possible shuttle; free mail drop for guests, will hold 30 days max. Long Neck Lair Alpaca Farm, east 0.3 mile on US-11, 7530 Lee Hwy, Rural Retreat, VA 24368, (276) 698-2079 or (757) 871-9232, bunkhouse $38pp includes cold B, shower, and laundry, private room (up to 2) with bath $90/night, Wi-Fi, farm store w/ limited resupply, shuttle service, and mail drops. *Restaurant:* Sweetwater Venue, (276) 781-3071, open F–Sa 12–7:30, Su 12–4:30, for L/D. *Shuttles and area info:* Marion Transit Authority runs a bus from the Exxon station to Marion in season; call (276) 782-9300 for pick-up.
    West 10.2 miles (on US-11 south) to **Marion, VA** (see above), a larger town.

Davis Path Campsite—Tent platform, table, and privy. Water source is a spring 0.9 mile south of the campsite. Southbounders can carry water from Crawfish Valley, 3.5 miles north.

⚠ **VA-610, Old Rich Valley Road**—**West** 0.3 mile to *Hostel:* Quarter Way Inn, 4083 Old Rich Valley Rd., Ceres, VA, 24318, (276) 522-4603, quarterwayinn.com, open Apr 1–Jun 30, run by '09 thru-hiker Tina "Chunky" and husband Brett; all lodging includes shower, towel, laundry, loaner clothes, and morning coffee; $35pp bunk, $75s/$90d for private room or $18pp tenting. Snacks, canister fuel, mountain house, pasta sides, oatmeal, pizza, pop, and ice cream. Gourmet B at 7 a.m. $15 for hostel guests only. Slackpacking often available—call in advance. Parking $3/day. Credit cards accepted. No dogs. Outgoing mail and mail drops accepted for guests (ID required for guests and packages).

⚠ **VA-42**—**East** 0.1 mile to *Hostel:* Bear Garden Hiker Hostel, 306 W Blue Grass Trail, Ceres, VA 24318, (248) 249-1951, owned by Bob and Roberta 'Bertie' Lingham. Open year 'round. Bunkhouse sleeps 12, $25pp (Wi-Fi) or small house, sleeps up to 6, $150. Includes cold breakfast of cereal/toast/jelly/coffee/tea. Laundry $5, shuttles available. Small resupply. Accepts mail drops (within 30 days of ETA).
    East 2.5 mile to *Hostel:* Appalachian Dreamer Hiker Hostel, 502 Dotson Ridge Rd., Ceres, VA 24318, call or text Mack at (276) 970-2834, mspain7857@aol.com, 6 bunks in bunkroom, 2 in basement; 2 full bathrooms; call or text ahead for availability; suggested $25 donation, laundry and B included; working farm with firm rules; no pets, smoking, or alcohol/drugs; check appalachian dreamerhikerhostel.com for all of the hostel guidelines.

Knot Maul Branch Shelter (1980s)—Sleeps 8. Privy. Water source is 0.2 mile north on A.T.

Chestnut Knob Shelter (renovated 1994)—Sleeps 8. Privy. A former firewarden's cabin; plexiglass windows to let in some light. No water at this shelter, but water is sometimes found 0.2 mile

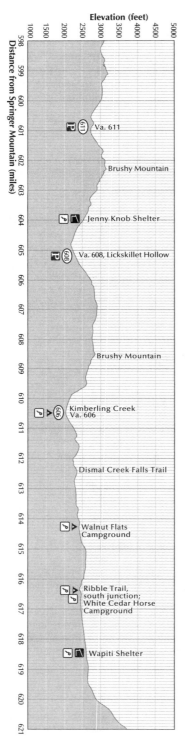

Elevation (feet)

Distance from Springer Mountain (miles)

Va. 611

Brushy Mountain

Jenny Knob Shelter

Va. 608, Lickskillet Hollow

Brushy Mountain

Kimberling Creek
Va. 606

Dismal Creek Falls Trail

Walnut Flats
Campground

Ribble Trail,
south junction;
White Cedar Horse
Campground

Wapiti Shelter

south on the A.T., then 50 yards east on an old jeep road. Otherwise, southbounders can find water 1.3 miles north in Walker Gap, and northbounders can find water at a spring-fed pond 1.8 miles south.

Burkes Garden—Chestnut Knob Shelter, elevation 4,410 feet, overlooks this unusual geologic feature. It is a large, crater-shaped depression surrounded on all sides by a high ridge that the A.T. follows for nearly 8 miles. From Chestnut Knob, you can see how it got its nickname, "God's Thumbprint."

VA-727, Walker Gap—West 0.7 mile downhill to Burkes Garden Hostel, 3713 West End Rd., Tazewell, VA 24651 (1st farm on right), (276) 722-2343, call or text, burkesgarden hostel.com. Renovated Amish pole barn, sleeps 12, 8 twin XL beds $35pp, 1 full XL bed $70s/d; private room with a full XL bed $90s, $105d, camping $20pp, bedroom in main house $125s, $150d. Wi-Fi, kitchen, showers, laundry, make your own waffles and coffee included for guests. Resupply includes dehydrated meals, gas canisters, fresh fruit, snacks, drinks, pizza, ice cream, and frozen food. Mail drops accepted for guests within 10 days of ETA. Small fee for non-guest showers, laundry & mail drops. Slackpacking, shuttles, and overnight parking available; call in advance. Free ride back to Walker Gap in the morning. Will pick up and return hikers to VA-623 for a small fee. Pets allowed, but must be kept on a leash in the hostel, private room, or camping. E-bike rentals for a zero day. Open mid-Mar–Oct. Other dates available with notice.

VA-623, Garden Mountain—West 3.7 miles to *Groceries:* Mattie's Place & Burke's Garden General Store (short-term resupply), (276) 472-2222, 920 Gose Mill Rd. Soups, sandwiches, pizza (Wednesdays), pastries, ice cream, deli. Sourdough bread is baked daily; cinnamon rolls, pies, cakes, and cookies. Camping $10 with water spigot and port-a-john, call for Trailhead shuttles (donations accepted). Open daily 10–5.

Jenkins Shelter (1960s)—Sleeps 8. Privy. Water source is stream 100 yards north on blue-blazed trail.

US-52—Brushy Mountain Outpost, (276) 266-0537, M–F 7–4, short-term resupply, sandwiches, burgers, breakfast, fuel.
    East 2.7 miles to **Bland, VA [P.O. ZIP 24315: M–F 8:30–11:30 & 12–4, Sa 9–11; (276) 688-3751].** *Groceries:* Grant's Grocery. *Restaurant:* Bland Square Grill (in Bland Square Citgo), 8870 S. Scenic Hwy, first block west of Main on US-52 in downtown, (276) 688-3851, B/L/D, 7 days, groceries, canister fuel. *Internet access:* townwide Wi-Fi; library, (276) 688-3737, M Th F 10–5, Tu–W 10–8. *Other services:* Napa Auto; banks, ATM.
    East 3.3 miles to *Lodging:* Big Walker Motel, 70 Skyview Ln., (276) 688-3331, $110.25S, $121.28D, $127.90T, pets OK,

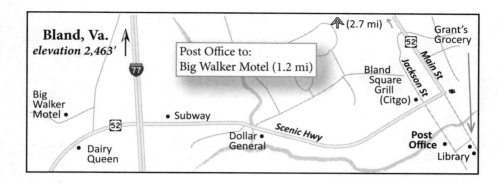

Wi-Fi, will hold packages for guests. Call motel or text Bubba, (276) 730-5869, for shuttle possibilities. *Other services:* Bland Family Clinic, (276) 688-0500, call to verify hours; Dairy Queen/gas station (short-term resupply) with ATM; Subway; Dollar General. *There is no place to camp in Bland.*

West 2.5 miles to **Bastian, VA [P.O. ZIP 24314: M-F 8-12, Sa 9:15-11:15; (276) 688-4631]**. P.O. is west 1.9 miles, left on Railroad Trail, right on Walnut Dr. Two miles farther down US-52 to *Other services:* medical clinic, after hours call (276) 688-4331, M 8–6, Tu Th 8–8, F 8:30–5; pharmacy next door, (276) 688-2424, M Th–F 9–5, Tu–W 9–6; Kangaroo Express, 24-hour ATM; Greyhound bus, (304) 325-9442, available for the I-77 corridor in Bluefield, WV, about 10 miles beyond Bastian on US-52 (closed Su, holidays); Pizza Plus, (276) 688-3332, will deliver to US-52 Trailhead and Bland.

Outdoor Club of Virginia Tech—OCVT maintains the 8.8 miles between US-52 and VA-611 and 19.2 miles in central Virginia between US-460 and Pine Swamp Branch Shelter. Correspondence should be sent to OCVT Box 538, Blacksburg, VA 24060; outdoor.org.vt.edu.

Helveys Mill Shelter (1960s)—Sleeps 6. Privy. Water source is down a switch-backed trail in front of the shelter.

Jenny Knob Shelter (1960s)—Sleeps 6. Privy. Water source (unreliable) is a seasonal spring near shelter.

Roanoke Appalachian Trail Club—RATC maintains the 36.9 miles between VA-611 and US-460 and 87.2 miles in the next section between Pine Swamp Branch Shelter and Black Horse Gap. Correspondence should be sent to RATC Box 12282, Roanoke, VA 24024; ratc.org.

VA-606—East 0.5 miles to *Hostel:* Weary Feet Hostel, 13152 E Bluegrass Trail, Bland, VA 24315, (276) 617-8434, wearyfeethostel@gmail.com, historic home with big porch, creek, and room for tenting. Check-in 2–9, check-out by 11 a.m. Bunk inside $25, private room $60, outdoor bunkhouse $15, tenting $10; includes shower; laundry $5. Home-cooked B $8, D $12, also burgers, dogs, and fries. Pet friendly. Free shuttle to trailhead on VA-606 or Trent's grocery, slackpacking available. Non-guest day pass $8, includes shower, laundry, and coffee. Mail drops accepted.

West 0.5 mile to *Groceries:* Trent's Grocery, 900 Wilderness Rd., Bland, VA 24315; (276) 928-1349; with ATM, deli, and pizza; possible shuttles. Open M–Sa 7–7, Su 9–5, Coleman and denatured alcohol by the ounce, canister fuel, and soda machines. Camping, shower, and laundry $6, or shower and laundry $3. Room with 2 beds, $40–$50, includes fridge, microwave, laundry. Accepts packages.

Wapiti Shelter (1980)—Sleeps 8. Privy. Water source is Dismal Creek, just south of the turn-off to the shelter.

Sugar Run Road/Sugar Run Gap—East 0.5 mile to *Hostel:* Woods Hole Hostel & B&B, 3696 Sugar Run Rd., Pearisburg, VA 24134; (540) 921-3444, woodsholehostel.com. Isolated 1880s chestnut-log cabin was discovered in 1940 by Roy & Tillie Wood, who opened the hostel in 1986. Their

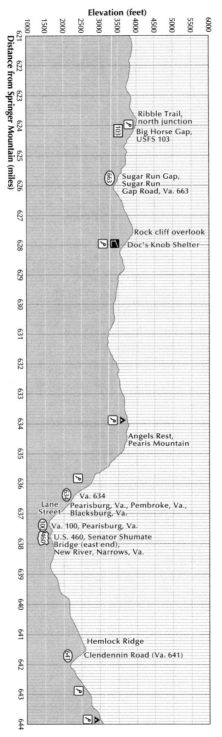

granddaughter, Neville, continues the legacy, with emphasis on sustainable living through organic gardening, yoga, and more. Heated bunkhouse $24pp; camping $15pp. Indoor rooms/safari tents, $37/$75. Farm-fresh communal meals B $11, D $16. Full resupply, home-baked goods, laundry, and shuttles. Pet-friendly, work-for-stay available. Mail drops for guests. *Directions:* Turn east at Sugar Run Gap/dirt road, left at fork.

Doc's Knob Shelter (1971)—Sleeps 8. Privy. A reliable spring is to the left of the shelter.

Virginia—Part 2 (Central)

Miles from Springer	Miles to Next Point	Features	Services	Elev	Miles from Katahdin	MAP
636.4	1.0	VA-634, Cross Ave. (E–0.8m Pearisburg, VA)	R, PO, all	2,200'	1,561.0	
637.4	0.4	VA-100, Narrows Road East–1m to **Pearisburg, VA, P.O. 24134** East–2.9m to Holy Family Church Hostel East–6m to Pembroke, VA West–3.9m to **Narrows, VA, P.O. 24124**	R H, G, L, M, D, V, cl, f H O C, G, L, M, cl		1,560.0	
637.8	3.4	US-460, Senator Shumate Bridge (east shore) over New River East–1.5m to **Pearisburg, VA, P.O. 24134** West–4.3m to **Narrows, VA, P.O. 24124**	R all C, G, L, M, cl	1,600'	1,559.6	
641.2	0.5	Hemlock Ridge		2,470'	1,556.2	
641.7	0.1	VA-641, Clendennin Road	R, P	2,220'	1,555.7	
641.8	1.1	Pocahontas Road: reenter woods	R, P	2,230'	1,555.6	
642.9	1.0	Stream	w	2,600'	1,554.5	
643.9	0.6	Campsite and springs	C, w	3,200'	1,553.5	
644.5	1.5	**Rice Field Shelter** (E–0.5m spring), 16.5mS; 12.5mN	S, C	3,400'	1,552.9	
646.0	3.5	Campsite (west) and spring (east)	C, w	3,450'	1,551.4	
649.5	1.0	Symms Gap meadow	C, w	3,480'	1,547.9	
650.5	1.6	Groundhog Trail, (W–1.9m to USFS parking area on WV-219/24)		3,400'	1,546.9	
652.1	2.2	Dickenson Gap		3,300'	1,545.3	
654.3	0.2	Peters Mountain ridgecrest (WV state line)		3,860'	1,543.1	
654.5	2.5	Allegheny Trail Junction		3,740'	1,542.9	
657.0	0.3	**Pine Swamp Branch Shelter**, 12.5mS; 3.9mN	S, C, w	2,530'	1,540.4	
657.3	1.1	VA-635, Big Stony Creek Road, Stony Creek Valley: USFS parking area (E–200 ft.)	R, P	2,370'	1,540.1	
658.4	1.0	Dismal Branch: bridge	w	2,480'	1,539.0	
659.4	1.1	VA-635, Big Stony Creek Road, Stony Creek	R, P, w	2,524'	1,538.0	
660.5	0.2	VA-734, Seven Mile Road: gravel fire road		3150'	1,536.9	
660.7	0.2	Spring: water for Bailey Gap Shelter (E–125 yds.)	w	3,490'	1,536.7	
660.9	3.7	**Bailey Gap Shelter**, 3.9mS; 8.8mN	S	3,525'	1,536.5	
664.6	0.2	VA-613, Mountain Lake Road, Salt Sulphur Turnpike East–5m to Mountain Lake Lodge and Conservancy	R, P L	3,950'	1,532.8	
664.8	1.2	Wind Rock: vista		4,121'	1,532.6	
666.0	3.7	Campsite and piped spring	C, w	4,000'	1,531.4	
669.7	0.8	**War Spur Shelter**, 8.8mS; 5.8mN	S, C, w	2,340'	1,527.7	
670.5	1.0	Johns Creek Valley, USFS-156, VA-632	R, P, w	2,102'	1,526.9	
671.5	1.0	Stream	w	2,700'	1,525.9	
672.5	0.5	VA-601, Rocky Gap	R, P	3,159'	1,524.9	
673.0	0.1	Johns Creek Mountain Trail			1,524.4	

ATC: Central VA Map 4

Miles from Springer	Miles to Next Point	Features	Services	Elev	Miles from Katahdin	M A P
673.1	1.2	Former firetower site		3,788'	1,524.3	
674.3	0.3	White Rock (E–100 yds.)			1,523.1	
674.6	0.9	Kelly Knob		3,742'	1,522.8	
675.5	0.1	**Laurel Creek Shelter** (E–100 ft.), 5.8mS; 7mN	S, w	2,720'	1,521.9	ATC: Central VA Map 4
675.6	1.1	Laurel Creek	w		1,521.8	
676.7	1.2	Spring	w	2,400'	1,520.7	
677.9	0.9	Sinking Creek Valley, VA-42	R	2,150'	1,519.5	
678.8	0.5	VA-630, Sinking Creek: road bridge	R, P, w	2,100'	1,518.6	
679.3	1.2	Keffer Oak		2,240'	1,518.1	
680.5	1.6	Sinking Creek Mountain (south)		3,490'	1,516.9	
682.1	3.6	Sarver Hollow Shelter (E–0.4m), 7mS; 6.4mN	S, w	3,000'	1,515.3	
685.7	2.4	Sinking Creek Mountain (north)		3,490'	1,511.7	
688.1	1.3	**Niday Shelter**, 6.4mS; 10.4mN	S, w	1,800'	1,509.3	
689.4	3.4	Craig Creek Valley, VA-621	R, P	1,560'	1,508.0	
692.8	0.4	Brushy Mountain		3,100'	1,504.6	
693.2	2.2	Audie Murphy Monument (W–50 yds.)		3,100'	1,504.2	
695.4	1.6	Brushy Mountain: vistas		2,600'	1,502.0	
697.0	1.2	VA-620, Miller Cove Road, Trout Creek	R, P, w	1,525'	1,500.4	
698.2	4.2	**Pickle Branch Shelter** (E–0.3m), 10.4mS; 13.9mN	S, w	1,845'	1,499.2	
702.4	1.0	Cove Mountain, Dragons Tooth (E–0.1m)		3,020'	1,495.0	
703.4	0.5	Lost Spectacles Gap (W–1.5m to VA-311)		2,550'	1,494.0	
703.9	0.6	Rawies Rest		2,350'	1,493.5	
704.5	0.4	Scout Trail			1,492.9	
		Camping Restrictions Northbound to US-220				
704.9	1.6	VA-624, Newport Road, North Mountain Trail East–0.4m to 4 Pines Hostel West–0.4m to Catawba Grocery	R, P H G, M	1,790'	1,492.5	ATC: Central VA Map 3
706.5	3.7	VA-785, Blacksburg Road: between two stiles West–1.5m to Solstice Farm Brewery	R C, M, sh	1,790'	1,490.9	
710.2	0.6	Catawba Greenway			1,487.2	
710.8	0.3	VA-311, Catawba Valley Drive West–1m to **Catawba, VA, P.O. 24070**	R, P G	1,980'	1,486.6	
711.1	0.7	Fire Road Connector Trail south junction			1,486.3	
711.8	1.0	**Johns Spring Shelter**, 13.9mS; 1mN	S, w	1,980'	1,485.6	
712.8	0.1	**Catawba Mountain Shelter**, 1mS; 2.4mN	S, w	2,580'	1,484.6	
712.9	0.3	Campsites (east)	C		1,484.5	
713.2	1.3	Fire Road Connector Trail north junction			1,484.2	
714.5	0.6	McAfee Knob: vista		3,199'	1,482.9	
715.1	0.1	Pig Farm Campsite: spring (E–0.1m)	C, w	3,000'	1,482.3	
715.2	1.9	**Campbell Shelter** (E–0.2m spring), 2.4mS; 6mN	S, w	2,580'	1,482.2	
717.1	1.2	Snack Bar Rock: two large rocks			1,480.3	
718.3	1.8	Brickey's Gap (Tinker Cliffs bypass E–1.7m to Lamberts Meadow Campsite)		2,250'	1,479.1	
720.1	0.5	Tinker Cliffs		3,000'	1,477.3	
720.6	0.6	Scorched Earth Gap, Andy Layne Trail (W–3.1m to VA-779)		2,360'	1,476.8	

Miles from Springer	Miles to Next Point	Features	Services	Elev	Miles from Katahdin	MAP
721.2	0.3	Lamberts Meadow Shelter, 6mS; 14.4mN	S, w	2,080'	1,476.2	
721.5	4.0	Lamberts Meadow Campsite, Sawmill Run (Tinker Cliffs bypass E–1.7m to Brickey's Gap)	C, w	2,000'	1,475.9	
725.5	1.1	Angels Gap: gas-line right of way		1,800'	1,471.9	
726.6	1.9	Hay Rock, Tinker Ridge: view of Carvins Cove Reservoir		1,900'	1,470.8	
728.5	1.0	Tinker Ridge: crest			1,468.9	
729.5	0.6	Trail Register: kiosk			1,467.9	
730.1	0.5	Tinker Creek: concrete bridge		1,165'	1,467.3	
		Camping Restrictions Southbound to VA-624				
730.6	1.2	US-220 East–0.8m to services near I-81 on US-11 East–12m to Roanoke, VA West–0.3m to Botetourt Commons Shopping Plaza West–1m to **Daleville, VA, P.O. 24083**	R, P, G, L, M G, L, M, cl, sh O, all G, M, O, f G, D, V	1,350'	1,466.8	
731.8	0.3	US-779, I-81 underpass	R, L	1,400'	1,465.6	
732.1	0.5	US-11, Norfolk Southern Railway West–0.8m to **Troutville, VA, P.O. 24175**	R, P H, C, G, M	1,300'	1,465.3	ATC: Central VA Map 3
732.6	1.6	VA-652, Mountain Pass Road	R	1,450'	1,464.8	
734.2	1.4	Tollhouse Gap			1,463.2	
735.6	2.8	Fullhardt Knob Shelter, 14.4mS; 6.2mN	S, w	2,676'	1,461.8	
738.4	0.8	USFS-191, Salt Pond Road	R, P	2,260'	1,459.0	
739.2	1.9	Curry Creek, Curry Creek Trail	w	1,680'	1,458.2	
741.1	0.7	Wilson Creek	w	1,690'	1,456.3	
741.8	0.4	Wilson Creek Shelter (W–150 ft.), 6.2mS; 7.5mN	S, w	1,830'	1,455.6	
742.2	2.0	Spring: unreliable	w	2,050'	1,455.2	
744.2	0.8	USFS-186/Old Fincastle Road at Black Horse Gap, BRP mp 97.7	R, H, P	2,402'	1,453.2	
745.0	1.1	Taylors Mountain Overlook; BRP mp 97.0	R, P	2,365'	1,452.4	
746.1	0.6	Montvale Overlook; BRP mp 95.9	R, P	2,456'	1,451.3	
746.7	1.6	Harveys Knob Overlook; BRP mp 95.3	R, P	2,540'	1,450.7	
748.3	0.8	Hammond Hollow Trail		2,300'	1,449.1	
749.1	0.7	Bobblets Gap Shelter (W–0.2m), 7.5mS; 6.7mN	S, w	1,920'	1,448.3	
749.8	0.7	Peaks of Otter Overlook; BRP mp 92.5	R, P	2,354'	1,447.6	
750.5	1.7	Mills Gap Overlook; BRP mp 91.8	R, P	2,448'	1,446.9	
752.2	1.6	Bearwallow Gap, VA-43; BRP mp 90.9 East–4.4m to Peaks of Otter Area West–5m to **Buchanan, VA, P.O. 24066**	R, P C, L, M H, G, M, L	2,228'	1,445.2	
753.8	0.4	Cove Mountain		2,707'	1,443.6	
754.2	1.4	Little Cove Mountain Trail (E–2.8m to VA-614)		2,563'	1,443.2	
755.6	1.7	Cove Mountain Shelter, 6.7mS; 7mN	S	1,996'	1,441.8	ATC: Central VA Map 2
757.3	1.5	Buchanan Trail (W–0.2m spring)	w	1,780'	1,440.1	
758.8	1.6	VA-614, Jennings Creek Road, Panther Ford Bridge, Jennings Creek East–1.4m to Middle Creek Campground	R, P, C, w G, C, cl, sh, f	987'	1,438.6	
760.4	2.2	Fork Mountain		2,042'	1,437.0	
762.6	1.4	Bryant Ridge Shelter, 7mS; 4.9mN	S, w	1,330'	1,434.8	
764.0	2.9	Bryant Ridge		2,394'	1,433.4	

Miles from Springer	Miles to Next Point	Features	Services	Elev	Miles from Katahdin	M A P
766.9	0.6	Floyd Mountain		3,560'	1,430.5	
767.5	0.9	**Cornelius Creek Shelter**, *4.9mS; 5.3mN*	S, w	3,145'	1,429.9	
768.4	0.6	Black Rock		3,420'	1,429.0	
769.0	1.1	Cornelius Creek Trail		3,179'	1,428.4	
770.1	0.1	Apple Orchard Falls Trail		3,364'	1,427.3	
770.2	1.4	Parkers Gap Rd., USFS-812; BRP mp 78.4	R, P	3,410'	1,427.2	
771.6	0.3	Apple Orchard Mountain: *FAA radar dome*		4,206'	1,425.8	
771.9	0.6	The Guillotine: *large boulder suspended overhead*		4,090'	1,425.5	
772.5	0.3	Upper BRP crossing mp 76.3	R	3,900'	1,424.9	
772.8	1.0	**Thunder Hill Shelter**, *5.3mS; 12.6mN*	S, w	3,960'	1,424.6	
773.8	0.6	Lower BRP crossing mp 74.9	R, P	3,650'	1,423.6	
774.4	1.7	Thunder Hill Overlook; BRP mp 74.7	R, P	3,525'	1,423.0	
776.1	1.4	Harrison Ground Spring	w	3,200'	1,421.3	
777.5	1.2	Petites Gap, USFS-35; BRP mp 71.0	R, P	2,369'	1,419.9	
778.7	1.2	Highcock Knob		3,054'	1,418.7	
779.9	0.5	Marble Spring *(W–330 ft. spring)*	C, w	2,300'	1,417.5	
780.4	1.8	Sulphur Spring Trail *(2.3m)* rejoins A.T.		2,415'	1,417.0	
782.2	0.5	Hickory Stand, Gunter Ridge Trail		2,650'	1,415.2	
782.7	0.8	Sulphur Spring Trail *(2.3m)* rejoins A.T.		2,588'	1,414.7	
783.5	1.9	Big Cove Branch	w	1,853'	1,413.9	
785.4	0.8	**Matts Creek Shelter**, *12.6mS; 3.9mN*	S, w	835'	1,412.0	
786.2	1.2	Campsites	C, w	700'	1,411.2	
787.4	0.2	James River Foot Bridge		678'	1,410.0	
787.6	0.1	US-501, VA-130: *jct. with USFS-36/VA-812 (Hercules Rd.)* *East–5.6m to* **Big Island, VA, P.O. 24526** *West–5.9m to* **Glasgow, VA, P.O. 24555**	R, P G, M, D S, H, G, M, D, cl	680'	1,409.8	
787.7	0.9	Lower Rocky Row Run Bridge	w	740'	1,409.7	
788.6	0.1	Rocky Row Run: *campsites along creek*	C, w	760'	1,408.8	
788.7	0.6	VA-812, USFS-36 (Hercules Rd.)	R, P	825'	1,408.7	
789.3	2.0	**Johns Hollow Shelter** *(E–400 ft.), 3.9mS; 9mN*	S, w	1,020'	1,408.1	
791.3	0.1	Rocky Row Trail *(W–2.8m to US-501)*		2,431'	1,406.1	
791.4	1.0	Fullers Rocks, Little Rocky Row		2,486'	1,406.0	
792.4	1.5	Big Rocky Row		2,974'	1,405.0	
793.9	1.1	Saddle Gap, Saddle Gap Trail *(E–2.5m to VA-812, USFS-36, Hercules Rd.)*		2,590'	1,403.5	
795.0	1.5	Saltlog Gap *(south)*		2,573'	1,402.4	
796.5	1.1	Bluff Mountain: *Ottie Cline Powell Memorial*		3,391'	1,400.9	
797.6	0.5	Punchbowl Mountain		2,841'	1,399.8	
798.1	0.4	**Punchbowl Shelter** *(W–0.2m), 9mS; 9.7mN*	S, w	2,500'	1,399.3	
798.5	0.1	Punchbowl Mountain crossing; BRP mp 51.7	R, P	2,170'	1,398.9	
798.6	0.2	Spring *(E–150 ft.): piped*	w		1,398.8	
798.8	1.9	VA-607, Robinson Gap Road: *jct. with Little Irish Creek Rd. (USFS-311)*	R	2,100'	1,398.6	
800.7	0.7	Rice Mountain		2,169'	1,396.7	
801.4	0.4	Spring *(west)*	w		1,396.0	
801.8	0.8	USFS-311A: *log steps both sides*	R		1,395.6	

ATC: Central VA Map 2

Miles from Springer	Miles to Next Point	Features	Services	Elev	Miles from Katahdin	M A P
802.6	0.1	USFS-39	R, P	990'	1,394.8	
802.7	2.5	Pedlar River Bridge	w	970'	1,394.7	
805.2	0.4	Swapping Camp Creek	w		1,392.2	
805.6	1.0	Swapping Camp Road, USFS-38	R, P	1,000'	1,391.8	
806.6	1.0	Brown Mountain Creek: *footbridge*	w		1,390.8	
807.6	0.2	**Brown Mountain Creek Shelter,** *9.7mS; 6.2mN*	S, w	1,395'	1,389.8	
807.8	1.6	Joseph Richeson Spring *(E–15 yds.): walled*	w		1,389.6	
809.4	0.9	US-60, Lexington Turnpike, Long Mountain Way-side: *picnic tables* *West–9.7m to* **Buena Vista, VA, P.O. 24416** *West–16.2m to* **Lexington, VA, P.O. 24450**	R, P, C C, G, L, M, D, V, sh, cl, f all	2,060'	1,388.0	ATC: Central VA Map 2
810.3	1.9	USFS-507: *campsite and spring (E–0.5m)*	C, w		1,387.1	
812.2	1.0	Bald Knob: *wooded summit*		4,059'	1,385.2	
813.2	1.2	Old Hotel Trail to **Cow Camp Gap Shelter** *(E–0.6m), 6.2mS; 10.8mN*	S, w	3,428'	1,384.2	
814.4	1.3	Cole Mountain		4,022'	1,383.0	
815.7	0.9	Hog Camp Gap, USFS-48, Wiggins Spring Rd.	R, P, C, w	3,522'	1,381.7	
816.6	1.3	Tar Jacket Ridge		3,840'	1,380.8	
817.9	1.2	Salt Log Gap *(north)*, USFS-63, VA-634	R, P	3,290'	1,379.5	
819.1	0.5	USFS-246	R	3,500'	1,378.3	
819.6	1.0	Greasy Spring Road, USFS-1176A	R	3,600'	1,377.8	
820.6	0.9	Wolf Rocks *(W–50 yds.)*		3,893'	1,376.8	
821.5	1.2	North Fork of Piney River	C, w	3,500'	1,375.9	
822.7	0.7	Elk Pond Branch	C, w	3,750'	1,374.7	
823.4	1.1	**Seeley–Woodworth Shelter** *(E–120 yds.), 10.8mS; 6.6mN*	S, w	3,770'	1,374.0	
824.5	1.7	Porters Field: *campsites, spring (W–100 ft. down old road)*	C, w	3,650'	1,372.9	
826.2	0.8	Spy Rock *(E–400 ft.): vista*		3,680'	1,371.2	
827.0	1.3	Cash Hollow Rock		3,556'	1,370.4	
828.3	0.8	Cash Hollow Road: *dirt* *West* via *VA-826–5.3m to* **Montebello, VA, P.O. 24464**	R C, G, L, cl, sh, f	3,280'	1,369.1	ATC: Central VA Map 1
829.1	0.9	Shoe Creek Gap, VA-826, Meadows Lane *West–0.5m to* Crabtree Meadows and Crabtree Falls Trail *East–4.1m to* campsite	R C, w C, L	3,319'	1,368.3	
830.0	0.5	**The Priest Shelter,** *6.6mS; 7.6mN*	S, w	3,840'	1,367.4	
830.5	3.0	The Priest		4,063'	1,366.9	
833.5	1.3	Cripple Creek	w	1,800'	1,363.9	
834.8	0.1	VA-56, Crabtree Falls Highway *West–4.1m to* Crabtree Falls Cmpgrnd *West–8m to* **Montebello, VA, P.O. 24464**	R, P C, G, sh C, G, L, cl, sh, f	997'	1,362.6	
834.9	1.8	Tye River, Three Ridges Wilderness: *suspension bridge*	C, w	970'	1,362.5	
836.7	0.9	Mau-Har Trail (3m) rejoins A.T. at Maupin Field Shelter		2,090'	1,360.7	
837.6	2.0	**Harpers Creek Shelter,** *7.6mS; 6.2mN*	S, w	1,800'	1,359.8	
839.6	1.7	Chimney Rocks		3,190'	1,357.8	

Miles from Springer	Miles to Next Point	Features	Services	Elev	Miles from Katahdin	M A P
841.3	0.5	Three Ridges		3,970'	1,356.1	
841.8	1.6	Hanging Rock: *vista*		3,750'	1,355.6	
843.4	0.4	Bee Mountain		3,034'	1,354.0	
843.8	1.7	**Maupin Field Shelter**, *6.2mS; 16mN* West-1.5m on fire road (USFS-306) to BRP at Love Gap	S, w R	2,720'	1,353.6	
845.5	0.5	Reids Gap, VA-664; BRP mp 13.6 *East 5.5m to Devil's Backbone Brewery*	R, P C, w, sh, M	2,645'	1,351.9	
846.0	3.8	Three Ridges Parking Overlook; BRP mp 13.1	R, P	2,700'	1,351.4	
849.8	0.5	Cedar Cliffs: *vista*		2,800'	1,347.6	
850.3	1.2	Dripping Rock Parking Area; BRP mp 9.6	R, P, w	2,950'	1,347.1	
851.5	1.6	Humpback Rocks Picnic Area *(W–0.3m)*	R, P, w	3,200'	1,345.9	
853.1	1.2	Humpback Mountain		3,606'	1,344.3	ATC: Central VA Map 1
854.3	0.6	Side trail to Humpback Rocks *(W–0.3 views; 1.3m VC)*	R, w	3,250'	1,343.1	
854.9	2.3	Bear Spring *(west)*	w	3,200'	1,342.5	
857.2	0.9	Side trail to Humpback Visitors Center *(W–2m BRP; 2.2m VC)*	R, w	2,150'	1,340.2	
858.1	0.4	Side trail to Glass Hollow Overlook *(E–0.2m)*		2,750'	1,339.3	
858.5	1.3	Jack Albright Trail	R, w	2280'	1,338.9	
859.8	1.7	Mill Creek, **Paul C. Wolfe Shelter**, *16mS; 12.8mN*	S, w	1,700'	1,337.6	
861.5	3.1	Former Mayo Cabin: *hearth, chimney*			1,335.9	
864.6	0.1	Rockfish Gap, US-250, I-64, Crozet Tunnel *West–500 yds. to Rockfish Gap Visitors Ctr.* *West–1m to Grey Pine Lodge* *West–4.5m to* **Waynesboro, VA, P.O. 22980**	R, P, L, M L all	1,902'	1,332.8	

BRP=Blue Ridge Parkway; mp=milepost

Central Virginia's treadway is well-graded and includes several 2,000- to 3,000-foot climbs. You will traverse some of the northernmost balds on the Trail. Unusual rock formations offer up views to the valley below from the peaks of Humpback Rocks, Three Ridges, The Priest, McAfee Knob, and Dragons Tooth. This section, more rugged and remote than Shenandoah to the north, parallels the Blue Ridge Parkway for 90 miles.

🔺 🏠 **VA-100/East** 1.0 miles to **Pearisburg, VA [P.O. ZIP 24134: M-F 9-11 & 12:15-4:30, Sa 10-12: (540) 921-1100].** *Lodging:* Plaza Motel, 415 N. Main St., (540) 921-2591, $55s, $5eap, Wi-Fi, laundry, no pets, will hold packages whether guest or not, e-mail available in office; Holiday Motor Lodge, 401 N. Main St., (540) 921-1551, $69d weekdays, $79.95 Sa-Su, $10eap; May 1–Sep 15 hostel $20 (shower, TV, fridge, microwave); Internet access, pet-friendly, accepts packages. *Hostel:* Angels Rest Hiker's Haven, 204 Douglas Lane, Pearisburg, VA 24134, call or text (540) 599-5717, angelsresthikershaven.com, open Mar 1–Nov 15. Bunks $25, private rooms $45-$70, tent/hammock $12pp. Military and first-responder discount. Leashed dogs $5 with stay, Wi-Fi, computer, printer, full kitchen; $7 day pass includes pick-up and return to local Trailhead, shower, laundry, and all amenities until 6 p.m. Cash or credit, limited work-for-stay. Responsible drinking, no drunks, no drugs, no drama. Accepts mail drops. Slackpacking and shuttles available. Chiropractic and acupuncture available by appointment. *Groceries:* Food Lion and Grant's Grocery (long-term resupply). *Restaurants:* Pizza Plus, buy one pizza, get one free, AYCE salad/pizza buffet, and free delivery; Pizza Hut with AYCE L buffet. Others, see map. *Internet access:* Pearisburg Public Library, (540) 921-2556. *Other services:* Pearis Mercantile, (540) 921-2260, large selection of hiking supplies, holds hiker packages, may shuttle; Community Health Center, (540) 921-3502, M-F 8–4:30 ($20 walk-ins without insurance); Rite Aid with one-hour photo service; automotive and hardware stores; Walmart; coin laundry; ATM; hospital; dentist; veterinarian; municipal swimming pool open to the public Memorial Day to Labor Day (fee). ***Shuttles:*** Tom Hoffman, (540) 921-1184, gopullman@aol.com; Don Raines, (540) 921-7433, ratface20724@aol.com.

East 2.9 miles, follow blue-blaze to ***Hostel:*** Holy Family Church Hostel is located in a peaceful setting on a hill, hidden by trees beyond the church parking lot. Refrigerator, microwave, and loft with sleeping pads, $10 suggested donation per night; additional donations and cleaning appreciated. Stays are limited to two nights. Open Mar–Nov. Alcoholic beverages and drugs are prohibited. Pets allowed if well taken care of. Calls only (540) 921-3547 or call or text (850) 346-8523.

East 6 miles on US-460 to ***Outfitter:*** Tangent Outfitters, 201 Cascade Dr., Pembroke, VA 24136.

West 4.3 miles via US-460 to VA-61 to **Narrows, VA [P.O. ZIP 24124: M-F 9:30-1:15 & 2-4:15, Sa 9-11, (540) 358-3010].** ***Lodging:*** MacArthur Inn, 117 MacArthur Ln., (540) 726-7510, macarthur-inn.com; renovated hotel, 22 rooms; call for rates; shower $8; laundry; no pets; Wi-Fi; fuel; shuttle to and from Trail $5 round-trip (call from Pearisburg); accepts mail drops; old-time music and country dinner Th. ***Other services:*** town campground on river $5; restaurant; deli; groceries; coin laundry.

Rice Field Shelter (1995)—Sleeps 7. Privy, bear box. Shelter has an excellent viewing area for sunsets and clouded valleys in the morning. Northbounders, pick up water at spring 0.5 mile before shelter; southbounders, water is on a steep, 0.5-mile downhill hike behind and to the left of the shelter.

Symms Gap Meadow—The traverse of Peters Mountain on the Virginia–West Virginia state line is a dry one. At this mountain meadow, with views into West Virginia, a small pond, which might be dry in summer and fall, is downhill from the A.T. on the West Virginia side, with camping nearby.

Allegheny Trail—2.5 miles south of Pine Swamp Branch Shelter is the A.T.'s junction with the southern end of the Allegheny Trail, which extends about 300 miles across West Virginia to Pennsylvania. The trail is maintained by the West Virginia Scenic Trails Association, wvscenictrails.org. Portions are being incorporated into the Great Eastern Trail, greateasterntrail.net.

Pine Swamp Branch Shelter (1980s)—Sleeps 8. Privy. Stone shelter. Water is from the stream 75 yards down a blue-blazed trail west of the side trail to the shelter.

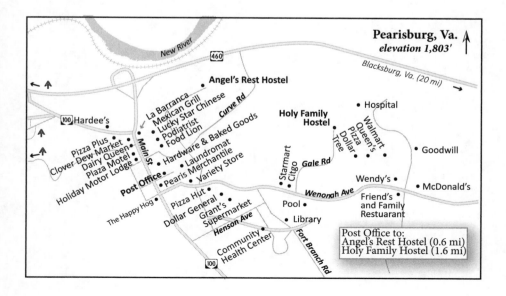

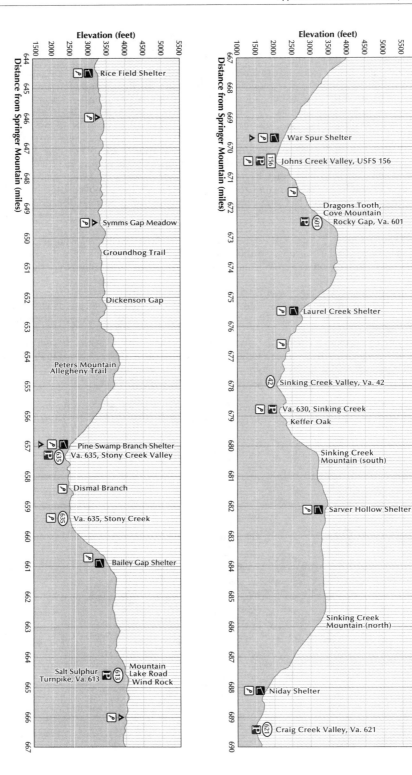

Elevation (feet)

Distance from Springer Mountain (miles)

Rice Field Shelter

Symms Gap Meadow

Groundhog Trail

Dickenson Gap

Peters Mountain
Allegheny Trail

Pine Swamp Branch Shelter
Va. 635, Stony Creek Valley

Dismal Branch

Va. 635, Stony Creek

Bailey Gap Shelter

Salt Sulphur
Turnpike, Va. 613

Mountain
Lake Road
Wind Rock

Elevation (feet)

Distance from Springer Mountain (miles)

War Spur Shelter

Johns Creek Valley, USFS 156

Dragons Tooth,
Cove Mountain
Rocky Gap, Va. 601

Laurel Creek Shelter

Sinking Creek Valley, Va. 42

Va. 630, Sinking Creek

Keffer Oak

Sinking Creek
Mountain (south)

Sarver Hollow Shelter

Sinking Creek
Mountain (north)

Niday Shelter

Craig Creek Valley, Va. 621

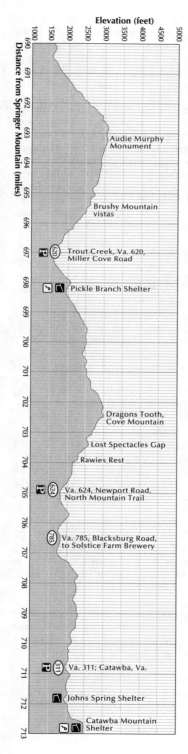

Bailey Gap Shelter (1960s)—Sleeps 6. Privy. Water is 0.2 mile south on the A.T., then east down a blue-blazed trail.

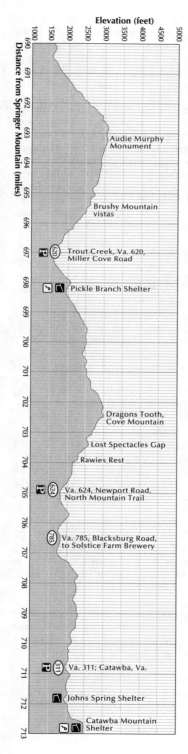 **VA-613, Salt Sulfur Turnpike—East** 5 miles to *Lodging:* Mountain Lake Lodge and Conservancy, 115 Hotel Circle, Pembroke, VA 24136; (540) 626-7121, mtnlakelodge.com; site of one of only two natural lakes in Virginia; reservations required; call for rates. Will hold packages for registered guests. One of the locations where the movie "Dirty Dancing" was filmed. The $1.2-million Giles County Trail Center here opened in 2023.

War Spur Shelter (1960s)—Sleeps 6. Privy. Water source is a stream 80 yards north of the shelter on the A.T.

Laurel Creek Shelter (1988)—Sleeps 6. Privy. Water is west on the A.T., 45 yards south of the shelter-trail junction.

Keffer Oak—Located about 0.2 mile north of VA-630, this is the largest oak tree on the A.T. in the South. Last measured, the girth was more than 19 feet; it is estimated to be 300 years old. The Dover Oak along the A.T. in New York is slightly larger.

Sarver Hollow Shelter (2001)—Sleeps 6. Privy. Water source is a spring located on a blue-blazed trail near the shelter.

Sinking Creek Mountain—The northernmost spot where the A.T. crosses a notable "continental divide." Waters flowing down the western side of the ridge drain into Sinking Creek Valley and the Mississippi River to the Gulf of Mexico. Waters flowing on the eastern side empty into Craig Creek Valley, the James River, and the Atlantic Ocean. Terrain can be difficult in this area.

Niday Shelter (1980)—Sleeps 6. Privy. Water source is 75 yards down a blue-blazed trail west of the A.T.

Craig Creek/VA-621—The unsafe bridge has been removed. The creek crossing may be impassable or unsafe during high water. During high water events, hikers should wait for water levels to recede or utilize the high-water route/road walk. Hikers should follow directions from posted signs.

Audie Murphy Monument—located on a blue-blazed trail to the west on Brushy Mountain. Murphy was the most decorated American soldier of World War II, and his single-handed capture of a large number of German soldiers made him a legend. After the war, he starred in many Hollywood war and B-grade western movies. He died in a 1971 plane crash near this site. A trail leads beyond the monument to a view from a rock outcropping.

Pickle Branch Shelter (1980)—Sleeps 6. Privy. Water from stream below the shelter.

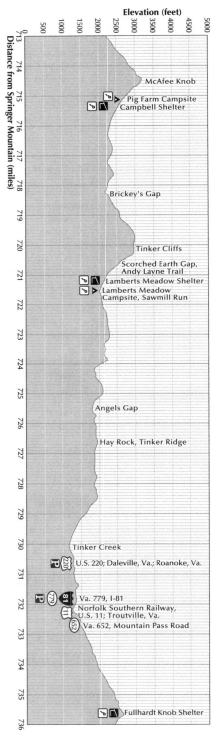

Elevation (feet)

Distance from Springer Mountain (miles)

McAfee Knob

Pig Farm Campsite
Campbell Shelter

Brickey's Gap

Tinker Cliffs

Scorched Earth Gap,
Andy Layne Trail
Lamberts Meadow Shelter
Lamberts Meadow
Campsite, Sawmill Run

Angels Gap

Hay Rock, Tinker Ridge

Tinker Creek

U.S. 220; Daleville, Va.; Roanoke, Va.

Va. 779, I-81
Norfolk Southern Railway,
U.S. 11; Troutville, Va.
Va. 652, Mountain Pass Road

Fullhardt Knob Shelter

Dragons Tooth—Named by Tom Campbell, an early RATC member and prime mover in the 1930s–1950s in locating the A.T. here. He also named Lost Spectacles Gap, north of Dragons Tooth, after his glasses disappeared on a scouting/work hike. *Pay special attention to roped-off resource-protecting areas.*

Camping Restrictions: Between VA-624 and US-220, camping and fires are allowed only at the following designated sites of this heavily used section: Johns Spring, Catawba Mountain, Campbell, and Lamberts Meadow shelters and Pig Farm and Lamberts Meadow campsites. Adherence to this regulation, as well as the one banning consumption of alcohol on this section of the Trail, is being vigorously monitored due to increased use and abuse. This is one the most heavily used areas of the A.T.; please honor these regulations so that all may continue to enjoy it.

VA-624/North Mountain Trail—West 0.3 mile to VA-311, then left 0.1 mile to Catawba Grocery, (540) 384-8050 (short-term resupply), open M–F 5:30–10, Sa 6–10, Su 6–9. Nearby North Mountain Trail was once the A.T. route. A 30-mile loop is possible.

East 0.4 mile to *Hostel:* 4 Pines Hostel, 6164 Newport Rd., Catawba, VA 24070; (540) 309-8615; large garage with bunks, kitchen, shower; donations accepted; tenting, washing machine; shuttles (fee); no pets. Will hold UPS and USPS packages.

VA-785—East 1.5 miles to Solstice Farm Brewery, (804) 712-3175, free camping, cold outdoor shower, bathroom, food truck, snacks, live music, craft beer.

Catawba Greenway—As you begin the final downhill on Sawtooth Ridge, the Catawba Greenway is on the left. It descends about a mile into Catawba near the PO and ascends about another 2 miles back to the Catawba Mountain Fire Road, close to the A.T. 0.4 mile north of VA-311.

VA-311—West 1 mile to **Catawba, VA [P.O. ZIP 24070: M–F 9–12 & 1–4, Sa 8–10:30; (540) 384-6011]**. *Groceries:* Catawba Valley Farmers Market, held at the Catawba Community Center in the village of Catawba; open Th, Jun–Sep, 10–1 p.m.

Johns Spring Shelter (2003)—Sleeps 6. Privy. Must camp at designated sites. Unreliable water in front of the shelter; follow blue-blazed trail 0.25 mile to a slightly more reliable spring.

Catawba Mountain Shelter (1984)—Sleeps 6. Privy. Bear box. Must camp at designated sites. Water is 50 yards south on the A.T. Tent sites north on the A.T.

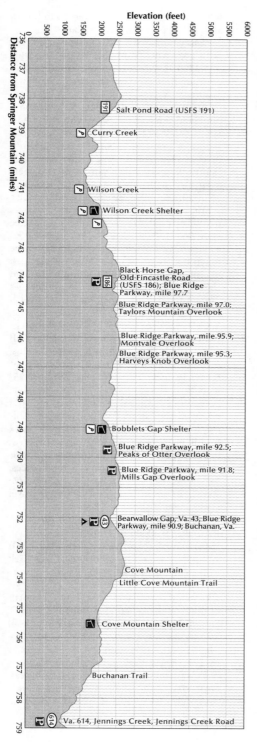

Elevation (feet)

Distance from Springer Mountain (miles)

- 738　191 Salt Pond Road (USFS 191)
- 739　Curry Creek
- 741　Wilson Creek
- 742　Wilson Creek Shelter
- 744　Black Horse Gap, Old Fincastle Road (USFS 186); Blue Ridge Parkway, mile 97.7
- 745　Blue Ridge Parkway, mile 97.0; Taylors Mountain Overlook
- 746　Blue Ridge Parkway, mile 95.9; Montvale Overlook
- 747　Blue Ridge Parkway, mile 95.3; Harveys Knob Overlook
- 749　Bobblets Gap Shelter
- 750　Blue Ridge Parkway, mile 92.5; Peaks of Otter Overlook
- 751　Blue Ridge Parkway, mile 91.8; Mills Gap Overlook
- 752　Bearwallow Gap, Va. 43; Blue Ridge Parkway, mile 90.9; Buchanan, Va.
- 754　Cove Mountain
- 754　Little Cove Mountain Trail
- 755　Cove Mountain Shelter
- 757　Buchanan Trail
- 759　Va. 614, Jennings Creek, Jennings Creek Road

McAfee Knob—Considered by many to have the best view in Virginia, McAfee Knob is a tempting campsite. *However, it is absolutely forbidden to camp here; the knob already sustains tremendous impact and campers' trash has attracted bears.*Campbell Shelter or Pig Farm Campsite are alternatives if you want to climb back up to catch the sunset or sunrise from the cliff.

Campbell Shelter (1989)—Sleeps 6. Privy. Bear box. Must camp at designated sites. Water can be found by following the blue-blazed trail left and behind the shelter. Follow the trail through the "electrified meadow" to the spring.

Tinker Cliffs—A 0.5-mile cliff-walk, with views back to McAfee Knob. Folklore says the name comes from Revolutionary War deserters who hid near here and repaired pots and pans ("tinkers"). *No camping here.*

Lamberts Meadow Shelter (1974)—Sleeps 6. Privy. Bear box. Must camp at designated sites. Tent sites are 0.3 mile farther north and also just past the water by the shelter. Water is 50 yards down the trail in front of the shelter; may run dry in drought years.

US-220/I-81 Interchange Area—The interchange area offers all the comforts of interstate travel, with most services near the A.T.

On US-220. *Lodging:* Super 8, (540) 992-3000, hiker rates subject to availability, Su–Th $70s/d, F–Sa $80s/d, $6eap, coffee and B item, coin laundry, no pets. *Other services:* Several convenience stores.

West 0.3 mile to Botetourt Commons Shopping Plaza. *Restaurants:* Mill Mountain Coffee House, 3 Little Pigs BBQ, Wendy's, Bojangles. *Groceries:* Kroger Super Store, with pharmacy (long-term resupply). *Outfitter:* Outdoor Trails, Botetourt Commons, 28 Kingston Dr., Daleville, VA 24083; (540) 992-5850; M–Sa 10–6, closed Su; a full-service outfitter, sells fuel by the ounce and accepts mail drops ($5 to hold commercial packages); make reservation for shuttle or slackpacking; free Wi-Fi. *Other services:* UPS Store, (540) 824-1088, M–Th 8–6:30, Sa 9–2:30, closed F and Su; bank with ATM.

West 1 mile to **Daleville, VA [P.O. ZIP 24083: M–F 8:30–5, Sa 8:30–12:30 (540) 992-4422]**. Convenience stores, Food Lion (long-term resupply), CVS, and bank are nearby.

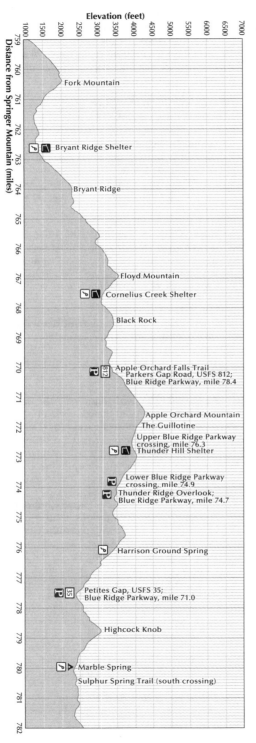

Elevation (feet)

Distance from Springer Mountain (miles)

Fork Mountain

Bryant Ridge Shelter

Bryant Ridge

Floyd Mountain

Cornelius Creek Shelter

Black Rock

Apple Orchard Falls Trail
Parkers Gap Road, USFS 812;
Blue Ridge Parkway, mile 78.4

Apple Orchard Mountain
The Guillotine
Upper Blue Ridge Parkway
crossing, mile 76.3
Thunder Hill Shelter

Lower Blue Ridge Parkway
crossing, mile 74.9
Thunder Ridge Overlook;
Blue Ridge Parkway, mile 74.7

Harrison Ground Spring

Petites Gap, USFS 35;
Blue Ridge Parkway, mile 71.0

Highcock Knob

Marble Spring
Sulphur Spring Trail (south crossing)

Other services: Medical center fits in hikers as schedule permits; veterinarian.

East 0.8 mile to US-11. *Lodging:* Motel 6, 2619 Lee Hwy., Troutville, VA 24175, (540) 992-6700, $72d, $5eap, coin laundry, pets permitted; Best Western, 2545 Lee Hwy, Troutville, VA 24175, (540) 992-5600, $114, includes continental B, pets $25, seasonal pool, and Internet access; Comfort Inn and Suites, (540) 992-5055, $89s/d, hot and cold B, indoor pool, guest laundry; Quality Inn, 3139 Lee Hwy. South, Troutville, VA 24175, (540) 992-5335, hiker rate of $69s/d, pets permitted with one-time $15 fee, hot and cold continental B, seasonal pool, exercise room, microwave and refrigerator, accepts mail drops; Holiday Inn Express, 3200 Lee Hwy. South, Troutville, VA 24175, (540) 966-4444, $150s/d, weekends are higher (may be much higher on "special event" weekends), microwave and refrigerator in rooms, hot and cold B, pool, holds UPS and USPS packages for registered guests. *Lodging/Hostel:* BeeCh Hill B&B/Hostel, 624 Valley Rd., Troutville, VA 24175, call or text (540) 462-7248, beech-hilltroutville@gmail.com, bunks $30, B&B $80s/$100d, tent/hammock $20pp; linens, shower, local shuttle for dinner/resupply, B, Wi-Fi included; self-serve laundry $5/load; cash or Venmo; limited work-for-stay; accepts mail drops; slackpacking (shuttle not provided), and limited vehicle parking available. A place for responsible hikers to relax & chill out. Property is adjacent to the A.T., just 200 steps down a maintenance access path. *Restaurants:* Several fast-food places; Italian Bella, closed Su; Best Wok, closed M; Angelle's Diner; Subway inside One 9 Travel Center, which also has $18 shower.

East 12 miles to **Roanoke**. *Outfitter:* In Roanoke, Walkabout Outfitter, downtown, (540) 777-2727, and Valley View Mall, (540) 777-0990, owned by 1999 thru-hiker Kirk Miller (Flying Monkey), open daily.

US-11—West 0.8 mile (1.5 miles north of the interchange area) to **Troutville, VA [P.O. ZIP 24175: M-F 9-12 & 1-5, Sa 9-11; (540) 992-1472]**. Town hall, (540) 992-4401, M–Th 8–12 & 1–4, sometimes allows hikers to camp at the city park and obtain free showers, but hikers must contact town hall for access. *Groceries:* Troutville Grocery and Goods (long-term resupply), M–Sa 8–7, closed Su.

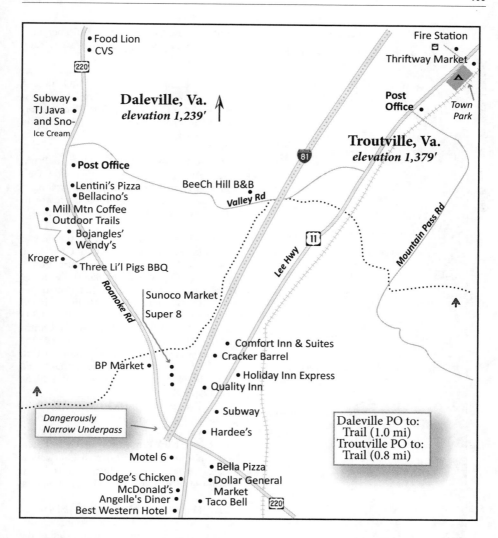

Daleville, Va.
elevation 1,239'

Troutville, Va.
elevation 1,379'

- Food Lion
- CVS

220

Subway •
TJ Java •
and Sno-
Ice Cream

- **Post Office**
- Lentini's Pizza
- Bellacino's
- Mill Mtn Coffee
- Outdoor Trails
- Bojangles'
- Wendy's

Kroger •
- Three Li'l Pigs BBQ

Roanoke Rd

Sunoco Market
Super 8

BP Market •

*Dangerously
Narrow Underpass*

Motel 6 •

Dodge's Chicken •
McDonald's •
Angelle's Diner •
Best Western Hotel •

BeeCh Hill B&B
Valley Rd

Lee Hwy

11

Mountain Pass Rd

81

Post
Office

Fire Station
Thriftway Market

Town
Park

- Comfort Inn & Suites
- Cracker Barrel
- Holiday Inn Express
- Quality Inn
- Subway
- Hardee's
- Bella Pizza
- Dollar General
  Market
- Taco Bell

220

Daleville PO to:
Trail (1.0 mi)
Troutville PO to:
Trail (0.8 mi)

Other services: Pomegranate Restaurant, (540) 966-6052, 106 Stoney Battery Rd., Tu–Sa open for D at 4 p.m., fine dining.

Fullhardt Knob Shelter (1960s)—Sleeps 6. Privy. The (not-always-reliable) water source for this shelter is a cistern system of run-off hooked to the shelter's roof. Give the water time to flow through the freeze-proof valve, which is a few feet up the pipe toward the cistern. Please make sure spigot is off when you have finished drawing water.

Wilson Creek Shelter (1986)—Sleeps 6. Privy. Water source is reliable stream 200 yards in front of the shelter.

Blue Ridge Parkway—Black Horse Gap is the A.T.'s southernmost encounter with the Blue Ridge Parkway (BRP). The A.T. parallels BRP, and later Skyline Drive, for approximately 200 miles. Much of the original A.T. route along the Blue Ridge south of Roanoke was displaced by the parkway when it was built. Hitchhiking is not permitted on the BRP. *Hostel:* Duck-N Hut Hiker's Hostel, 11597 Stewartsville Rd., Vinton, VA 24179, (540) 819-2164. Donation-based, free shuttle to and

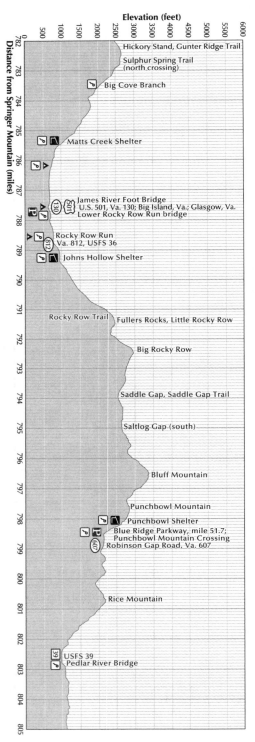

Elevation (feet)

Distance from Springer Mountain (miles)

Hickory Stand, Gunter Ridge Trail

Sulphur Spring Trail (north crossing)

Big Cove Branch

Matts Creek Shelter

James River Foot Bridge
U.S. 501, Va. 130; Big Island, Va.; Glasgow, Va.
Lower Rocky Row Run bridge

Rocky Row Run
Va. 812, USFS 36

Johns Hollow Shelter

Rocky Row Trail

Fullers Rocks, Little Rocky Row

Big Rocky Row

Saddle Gap, Saddle Gap Trail

Saltlog Gap (south)

Bluff Mountain

Punchbowl Mountain

Punchbowl Shelter
Blue Ridge Parkway, mile 51.7;
Punchbowl Mountain Crossing
Robinson Gap Road, Va. 607

Rice Mountain

USFS 39
Pedlar River Bridge

from the hostel, other shuttles $1.75 per mile. Short and long-term resupply nearby. Many animals on site and pet-friendly.

Natural Bridge Appalachian Trail Club— NBATC maintains the 90.7 miles between Black Horse Gap and the Tye River. Correspondence should be sent to NBATC Box 3012, Lynchburg, VA 24503; nbatc.org.

Bobblets Gap Shelter (1961)—Sleeps 6. Privy. Water source is a spring to the left of the shelter that is prone to go dry after prolonged rainless periods. Look farther downstream if the first source is dry. Limited tent spots.

⚠ VA-43/Bearwallow Gap—East, then north 4.4 miles on the BRP to Peaks of Otter Area, (540) 586-1081. Lodge and restaurant open daily May–Oct. Mail drops: 85554 Blue Ridge Pkwy., Bedford, VA 24523. Management has offered a discount on lodging to hikers, based on best available rates. B 7:30–10:30, L 11:30–3:30, D 4:30–9 daily; limited Wi-Fi. Campsites, (877) 444-6777, by reservation with the NPS at nps.gov/blri, open early May–late Oct.
West 5 miles on VA-43 to **Buchanan, VA** [P.O. ZIP 24066: M-F 8:30-1 & 1:30-4:30, Sa 10-12; (540) 254-2178].
Lodging: Anchorage House B&B, 19391 Main St. Buchanan, (540) 425-5239, private room with bath and B $149. Call to check if an RV out back is maybe available to hikers for $49/night. Shuttle to/from Bearwallow Gap. *Internet access:* Buchanan Library. *Other services:* bank with ATM, restaurants.

Cove Mountain Shelter (1981)—Sleeps 6. Privy. No convenient water source at this shelter. A steep, unmarked trail to left of the shelter leads 0.5 mile downhill to a stream.

⚠ VA-614/Jennings Creek—Jennings Creek is a popular swimming hole for both hikers and local residents.
East 0.2 mile to VA-618, then 0.1 mile to the USFS Middle Creek Picnic Area with covered picnic pavilions; 1.1 miles farther on VA-618 to *Camping:* Middle Creek Campground, 1164 Middle Creek Rd., Buchanan, VA 24066; (540) 254-2550, middlecreek campground.com, tentsites with shower start at $10pp; bunkhouse $25pp, private cabins start at $60 for 2; showers $5, leashed dogs allowed. Camp store (short-term resupply)

M-Su 8–7. Fuel canisters; coin laundry; mail drops accepted; when available, shuttle to Jennings Creek or the Blue Blaze to Bryant Ridge.

Bryant Ridge Shelter (1992)—Sleeps 20. Privy. This tri-level, timber-frame shelter is one of the largest. Water source is a stream 25 yards in front of the shelter, also crossed on the trail to the shelter. Limited tentsites.

Cornelius Creek Shelter (1960)—Sleeps 6. Privy. A blue-blazed trail leads to the shelter, but just north of the turn-off is a branch of Cornelius Creek where you can find water. Water can also be found on the trail to the shelter. An unmarked trail behind the shelter leads 0.1 mile to a fire road and then left 0.2 mile to the BRP, where it is then 6 miles south to the Peaks of Otter Area.

Apple Orchard Falls Trail—Located 2.6 miles north of Cornelius Creek Shelter. When the water is high, these falls are impressive, making the 3-mile round-trip worth the effort.

Apple Orchard Mountain—When you reach the top, you will be at 4,225 feet. Once an Air Force radar base, the meadows were covered with barracks and support-service buildings for 250 people. On the northern side of the mountain, the A.T. leads you under The Guillotine—an impressively large boulder stuck over the Trail between rock formations. No camping is permitted on top of the mountain, the highest point on the A.T. between Chestnut Knob and Mt. Moosilauke in New Hampshire.

Thunder Hill Shelter (1962)—Sleeps 6. Privy. Bear box. Water source is a walled-in spring south of the shelter, prone to go dry by late summer. A larger, reliable spring can be found by going south on the A.T. to the BRP. At the BRP, turn left, walk 0.3 mile to a gated road on the left; 500 feet down the gated road, where the road turns left, angle right to a spring basin.

Note: In May 2023, due to reports of aggressive bear activity, officials with the USFS closed the A.T. to camping between Petites Gap Road and the James River Foot Bridge. This includes Matts Creek Shelter and camping on the Matts Creek Trail. Check for signs. Also, be aware that an 11,000-acre wildfire here in November 2023 started near the A.T.

Matts Creek Shelter (1961)—**Survived the wildfire but may still be closed.**Sleeps 6. Privy. Several small swimming holes are nearby. The rocks you will find in this area are 500 million years old. Tentsites north 1.0 mile, where Matts Creek flows into the James River, with river views and the sound of trains across the river. Water source is Matts Creek, in front of the shelter.

James River Foot Bridge—This bridge, the longest foot-use-only bridge on the A.T., is dedicated to the memory of Bill Foot, a 1987 thru-hiker and ALDHA honorary life member (Trail-named "The Happy Feet" with his wife, Laurie) whose efforts in securing the existing piers, applying for grants, and gaining numerous agencies' cooperation made it a reality.

 US-501/James River—East 5.0 miles to **Big Island, VA [P.O. ZIP 24526: M-F 8:15-12 & 1-4, Sa 8-10; (434) 299-5072]**. *Groceries:* Exxon H&H Market, (434) 299-5153, open daily 5:30–9 (long-term resupply), short-order restaurant, B/L/D. *Other services:* bank with ATM and Big Island Family medical center, open M-F 9-5, (434) 299-5951.
 West 6.1 miles to **Glasgow, VA [P.O. ZIP 24555: M-F 8-11:30, 12:30-4:30, Sa 8:30-10:30; (540) 258-2852]**.
 Hostel: Stanimal's 328 Hostel and Shuttle, 1131 Rockbridge Rd., (540) 480-8325, $40pp includes pick-up at footbridge (call for pick-up from ridgetop; no service at bridge), a/c, Internet access, laundry, and showers; slackpacking; private-room options, tenting. *Shelter:* Glasgow Hiker's Shelter, 9th St., sleeps 12, camping, water, showers, electricity, microwave, fire pit, and Little Free Library. *Groceries:* Glasgow Grocery Express (long-term resupply), (540) 258-1818, open M–Sa 6 a.m.– 11:30 p.m., Su 8 a.m.–11:30 p.m., has Coleman fuel by the ounce, denatured alcohol, and Heet; Dollar General, (540) 572-0882, open daily 8–10. *Restaurants:* Scotto's, (540) 258-2500, Tu–Sa 11–9, Su 11–8, closed M; Petro's Stop & Go, (540) 258-2012, deli and convenience store. *Internet*

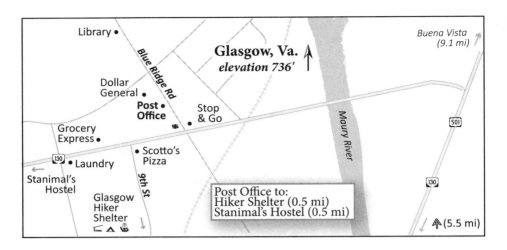

access: library, (540) 258-2509; M 10–6; T–Th 10–5, Sa 10–2. *Other services:* coin laundry, doctor. *Shuttles:* See Buena Vista below.

Johns Hollow Shelter (1961)—Sleeps 6. Privy. Water source is a spring to the left of the shelter or a stream to right 25 yards from the shelter.

Bluff Mountain—Site of a monument (with incorrect dates) to four-year-old Ottie Cline Powell. In the fall of 1891, Ottie went into the woods to gather firewood for his schoolhouse and never returned. His body was found five months later on top of this mountain. NBATC members erected a permanent gravestone for his final resting place, seven miles from the monument.

Punchbowl Shelter (1961)—Sleeps 6. Privy. Some believe this shelter is haunted by Little Ottie's ghost. Tent sites nearby if the shelter is full, which it often is. Water source is a spring by a tree next to the pond drainage in front and to the left of the shelter. An alternative water source is a spring in the ravine north 0.4 mile, shortly after crossing the BRP.

Brown Mountain Creek Valley—Community of freed slaves lived here from the Civil War until about 1918; remains of cabins and interpretive signs tell of life in the valley then.

Brown Mountain Creek Shelter (1961)—Sleeps 6. Privy. Water source is a spring in front of, and uphill from, the shelter. In dry conditions, get water from Brown Mountain Creek, crossed on the trail south of the shelter.

US-60—West 9.7 miles to **Buena Vista, VA [P.O. ZIP 24416: M-F 8:30-4:30, closed Sa; (540) 261-8959].** *Lodging:* Budget Inn, (540) 261-2156, call for rates, pets allowed in smoking rooms only, laundry, Wi-Fi. *Camping:* Glen Maury Campground, (540) 261-7321, hiker specials, tent sites with shower, $5 per tent, free shower without stay, laundromat is less than a mile away; pool fee is $4 in season. *Groceries:* Food Lion, Kroger, Walmart Supercenter and Family Dollar (long-term resupply); Coiner's Country Store (resupply and hiker services); Sheltman's Gas & Grocery (short-term resupply). *Restaurants:* Original Italian Pizza, Nick's Italian Kitchen may give discount to hikers, Five and Dime Pizza may give a discount to hikers; Mexican, BBQ, Chinese, seafood, ice cream, and fast-food choices. *Shuttles:* Rockbridge Taxi Service, (540) 261-7733. An hourly fixed-rate service (Maury Express) runs between Lexington and Buena Vista M–F 8–6 and Sa 10–4 for 50¢ each way. *Other services:* Buena Vista Visitor Center, (540) 261-8004, Th–M 10:30–3:30; library with Internet access; Michael Ohleger, (540) 460-0236, may be able to arrange shuttles and other support; Advanced Auto (Heet); coin laundry; banks with ATM; doctor; dentist; pharmacy; and veterinarian. *Other attractions:* The annual Maury River Fiddlers Convention, popular with hikers,

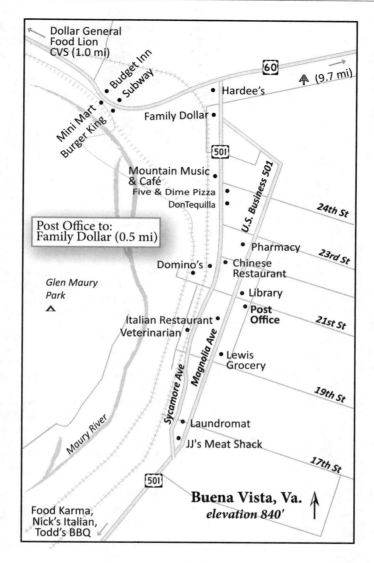

Dollar General
Food Lion
CVS (1.0 mi)

Budget Inn
Subway

60

🌲 (9.7 mi)

Hardee's

Family Dollar •

Mini Mart
Burger King

Family Dollar •

501

Mountain Music
& Café

Five & Dime Pizza •

DonTequilla •

U.S. Business 501

24th St

Post Office to:
Family Dollar (0.5 mi)

Pharmacy •   23rd St

Domino's •   • Chinese
                  Restaurant

Glen Maury
Park
⌃

• Library

•**Post**
  Office   21st St

Italian Restaurant •
Veterinarian •

Magnolia Ave

• Lewis
  Grocery

Sycamore Ave

19th St

Maury River

• Laundromat
  JJ's Meat Shack

17th St

501

Buena Vista, Va. ⬆
elevation 840'

Food Karma,
Nick's Italian,
Todd's BBQ

is held at Glen Maury Park, the second weekend in Jun; Beach Music Festival, last Sa in Jul; Nothin'
Fancy Bluegrass Festival, last weekend in Sep; annual Mountain Day street festival, second Sa in Oct.

    West 16.2 miles to **Lexington, VA [P.O. ZIP 24450: M-F 9-5, Sa 10-12; (540) 463-6449]**. A larger
town with groceries, motels, doctors, vets, and breweries. ***Outfitter:*** Walkabout Outfitter, (540)
464-4453, 21 S. Main St., M–Th 10–5:30, F–Sa 10–7, Su 10–5, owned by Kirk Miller (Flying Monkey '99), full-service outfitter, fuel canisters. ***Other services:*** Maury Express, from Buena Vista to
Lexington & back hourly, M–F 8–6, Sa 10–4, closed holidays, 50¢; Enterprise Car Rental, (540)
463-4679, 33 Quarry Ln.; Cassie's Cab, (540) 784-3785; Cobblestone Shoe & Leather Repair, 121
S. Main St., (540) 461-8248.

Cow Camp Gap Shelter (1986)—Sleeps 8. Privy. Water source is on blue-blazed trail to the left of the
shelter; if you have crossed a small stream, you missed the spring.

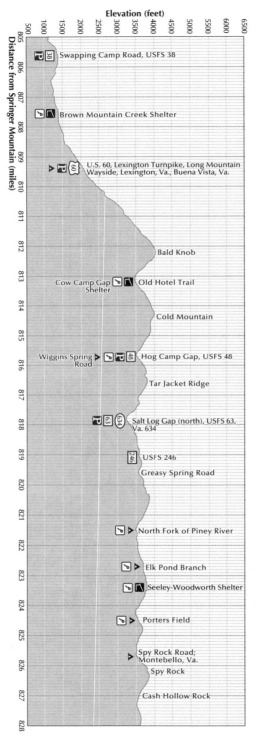

Elevation (feet)

Distance from Springer Mountain (miles)

- 805 — Swapping Camp Road, USFS 38
- 807 — Brown Mountain Creek Shelter
- 809 — U.S. 60, Lexington Turnpike, Long Mountain Wayside, Lexington, Va.; Buena Vista, Va.
- 812 — Bald Knob
- 813 — Cow Camp Gap Shelter / Old Hotel Trail
- 814 — Cold Mountain
- 815 — Wiggins Spring Road / Hog Camp Gap, USFS 48
- 816 — Tar Jacket Ridge
- 817 — Salt Log Gap (north), USFS 63, Va. 634
- 818 — USFS 246
- 819 — Greasy Spring Road
- 821 — North Fork of Piney River
- 822 — Elk Pond Branch
- 823 — Seeley-Woodworth Shelter
- 824 — Porters Field
- 825 — Spy Rock Road; Montebello, Va.
- 826 — Spy Rock
- 827 — Cash Hollow Rock

Cole Mountain—Bald Knob, south of Cole Mountain, isn't a bald, but Cole Mountain and Tar Jacket Ridge are. A mowing project was undertaken by NBATC and the Forest Service to preserve the open views and habitat for northern cottontail rabbits, various raptors, turkey, and grouse.

Seeley-Woodworth Shelter (1984)—Sleeps 8. Privy. A blue-blaze leads 100 yards to shelter and 0.1 mile beyond to piped spring.

Porters Field—West to a spring and campsite 300 feet down the second of two dirt roads.

Spy Rock Road—This "private road"—formerly known as Fish Hatchery Road—is closed.

West 5.3 miles to **Montebello, VA [P.O. ZIP 24464: M–F 10–2, Sa 10–1; (540) 377-9218]**, with post office, general store (open Su–Th, 9–5, F 9–6, Sa 8–6), and campground, can go down Cash Hollow Road until it ends at low-traffic Meadows Ln., then turn left/downhill and follow Meadows Ln. to VA-56, or continue on the Trail to VA-56, where likelihood of a ride is much higher. *Lodging:* Montebello Camping and Fishing, (540) 377-2650, montebellova.com, special thru-hiker-rate tent sites with shower, call for rates, they also have furnished efficiency cabins and bed-only camping cabins, shower, laundry, short-term resupply, leashed dogs allowed. Call from ridgetop before arrival.

Meadows Lane—West 0.5 mile to campsite and spring; 2 miles farther on the Crabtree Falls Trail to Crabtree Falls, one of the highest cascades in the East. High-clearance vehicle may be needed.

The Priest Shelter (1960)—Sleeps 8. Privy. Named for the massif dominating the area; near a busy access for backpackers and often full. Water source is a spring to left of the shelter.

Tidewater Appalachian Trail Club—TATC maintains the 10.6 miles between the Tye River and Reids Gap. Correspondence should be sent to P.O. Box 8246, Norfolk, VA 23503; president@tidewateratc.com; tidewateratc.com.

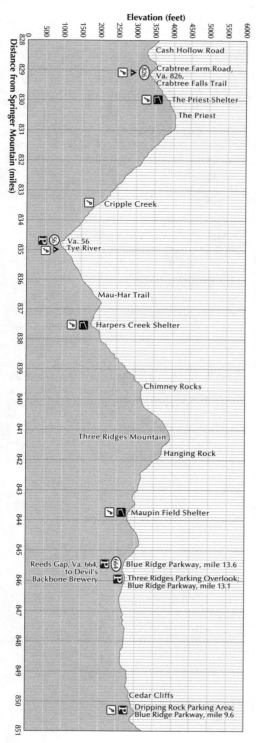

Elevation (feet)

Distance from Springer Mountain (miles)

Cash Hollow Road

Crabtree Farm Road,
Va. 826,
Crabtree Falls Trail

The Priest Shelter

The Priest

Cripple Creek

Va. 56
Tye River

Mau-Har Trail

Harpers Creek Shelter

Chimney Rocks

Three Ridges Mountain

Hanging Rock

Maupin Field Shelter

Reeds Gap, Va. 664,
to Devil's
Backbone Brewery

Blue Ridge Parkway, mile 13.6

Three Ridges Parking Overlook;
Blue Ridge Parkway, mile 13.1

Cedar Cliffs

Dripping Rock Parking Area;
Blue Ridge Parkway, mile 9.6

⛰ VA-56/Tye River—West 3.9 miles to *Camping:* Crabtree Falls Campground (short-term resupply), 11039 Crabtree Falls Hwy., Tyro, VA 22976; (540) 377-2066, crabtree fallscampground.com; reservations recommended, tent sites with shower weekdays $40d, cabins $85d; office open M–Th 10–2, F 10–9, Sa 10–8, Su 9–12. Accepts mail drops for guests. *Northbound directions:* Take Route 826 (Shoe Creek Rd.) west 0.5 mile to Crabtree Meadows parking lot, then down Crabtree Falls Trail 2.9 miles to VA-56, then east 0.5 mile to campground. *Southbound:* VA-56 west 2.5 miles to campground. Staffing is limited, but campground will shuttle hikers to the trailheads when possible.

Mau-Har Trail—Traversing an area with a waterfall, this 3-mile blue-blaze goes around Three Ridges and connects with the A.T. at Maupin Field Shelter.

Harpers Creek Shelter (1960)—Sleeps 6. Privy, food-bag pole. Designated low-impact tentsites, which campers are requested to use. Water source is Harpers Creek, in front of the shelter. In extreme droughts, go upstream, and find water in the spring-fed ponds.

Maupin Field Shelter (1960)—Sleeps 6. Privy, food-bag pole. Designated low-impact tent sites, which campers are requested to use. The Mau-Har Trail begins behind the shelter and rejoins the A.T. 3 miles south. Water source is a dependable spring behind the shelter.

Rusty's Hard Time Hollow Hostel—(Editor's note: This hostel may be closed in 2025 due to Rusty's health.) From Maupin Field Shelter, turn left on fire road (just north of shelter), 1.2 miles to BRP and south on BRP 1.3 miles to hostel. Rusty Nesbitt's gravel driveway with gray pipe gate is on the left at BRP mile 16.7. Section-hikers, thru-hikers, long-distance cyclists, and weekenders are welcome (no groups). The Hollow is a primitive, 19-acre, back-to-basics, Appalachian Mountain farm and includes bunkhouses, springhouse, outhouse, and hot shower. No illegal drugs or alcohol, and no tenting allowed during peak season. Limited stay; exceptions for medical conditions. Trips to nearby Sherando Lake for swimming on hot days. Rides to/from the Trail (no town shuttles). Keep in mind that the Hollow is Rusty's home. Donations are needed and appreciated, since Rusty has

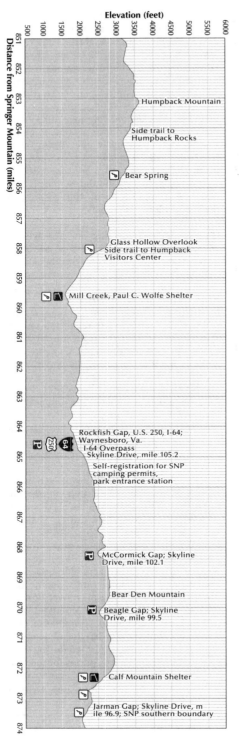

Elevation (feet)

Distance from Springer Mountain (miles)

Humpback Mountain

Side trail to
Humpback Rocks

Bear Spring

Glass Hollow Overlook
Side trail to Humpback
Visitors Center

Mill Creek, Paul C. Wolfe Shelter

Rockfish Gap, U.S. 250, I-64;
Waynesboro, Va.
I-64 Overpass
Skyline Drive, mile 105.2

Self-registration for SNP
camping permits,
park entrance station

McCormick Gap; Skyline
Drive, mile 102.1

Bear Den Mountain

Beagle Gap; Skyline
Drive, mile 99.5

Calf Mountain Shelter

Jarman Gap; Skyline Drive, m
ile 96.9; SNP southern boundary

no other means to keep the hostel going. Mail drops are not accepted.

Old Dominion Appalachian Trail Club—ODATC maintains the 19.1 miles between Reids Gap and Rockfish Gap. Correspondence should be sent to P.O. Box 25283, Richmond, VA 23260; odatc. president@gmail.com; odatc.net.

Reids Gap, VA-664—**East** 5.5 miles to Devil's Backbone Brewery, 200 Mosbys Run, Roseland, VA 22967, (434) 361-1001 (limited cell service at gap); open M-W 3-8, Th & Sun 11:30-8, F & Sa 11:30-10; craft beer and food, shuttle service is subject to availability, free tenting/showers for hikers.

Humpback Rocks—The Trail circumvents the rocks, but, if you are seeking a bouldering opportunity, they may still be reached by a short, blue-blazed side trail.

Paul C. Wolfe Shelter (1991)—Sleeps 10. Privy. Bear box and two poles. Tent sites. This shelter has windows and a porch cooking area. Water source is Mill Creek, located 50 yards in front of the shelter.

Paul Wolfe Shelter to Rockfish Gap—The Trail passes remnants of a cabin, cemetery, and rock piles, all evocative of settlement by early mountain folks.

Virginia—Part 3 (Shenandoah)

Miles from Springer	Miles to Next Point	Features	Services	Elev	Miles from Katahdin	M A P
864.6	0.1	Rockfish Gap, US-250, I-64, Crozet Tunnel *West–500 yds. to* Rockfish Gap Visitor Center *West–1m to* Grey Pine Lodge *West–4.5m to* **Waynesboro, VA, P.O. 22980**	R, P, L, H, M L all	1,902'	1,332.8	
864.7	0.2	I-64 overpass	R	1,902'	1,332.7	
864.9	0.5	Skyline Drive mp 105.2	R, P	1,902'	1,332.5	
865.4	2.9	Self-registration for SNP camping permits; park entrance station (W–0.2m R)	Kiosk on Trail	2,200'	1,332.0	
868.3	1.3	McCormick Gap; Skyline Drive mp 102.1	R, P	3,450'	1,329.1	
869.6	0.5	Bear Den Mountain: *old tractor seats, vista*		2,885'	1,327.8	
870.1	2.2	Beagle Gap; Skyline Drive mp 99.5	R, P	2,550'	1,327.3	
872.3	0.6	**Calf Mountain Shelter** (W–0.3m), 12.8mS; 13.5mN	S, w	2,700'	1,325.1	
872.9	0.4	Spring	w	2,200'	1,324.5	
873.3	0.2	Jarman Gap; Skyline Drive mp 96.9; SNP southern boundary	R	2,173'	1,324.1	
873.5	1.6	Spring	w	2,150'	1,323.9	
875.1	1.6	Sawmill Run Overlook; Skyline Drive mp 95.3	R, P	2,200'	1,322.3	
876.7	2.0	Turk Gap; Skyline Drive mp 94.1	R, P	2,600'	1,320.7	
878.7	4.1	Skyline Drive mp 92.4	R, P	3,100'	1,318.7	
882.8	1.8	Skyline Drive mp 88.9	R, P	2,350'	1,314.6	
884.6	0.2	Blackrock Gap; Skyline Drive mp 87.4	R, P	2,321'	1,312.8	
884.8	0.5	Skyline Drive mp 87.2	R	2,700'	1,312.6	
885.3	0.6	**Blackrock Hut** (E–0.2m), 13.5mS; 13.5mN	S, w	2,645'	1,312.1	
885.9	1.0	Blackrock: *open rocky summit*		3,100'	1,311.5	
886.9	1.3	Skyline Drive mp 84.3	R, P	2,800'	1,310.5	
888.2	0.2	Dundo Group Campground (W–0.1m)	w	2,700'	1,309.2	
888.4	0.9	Browns Gap; Skyline Drive mp 82.9	R, P	2,600'	1,309.0	
889.3	0.4	Skyline Drive mp 82.2	R	2,800'	1,308.1	
889.7	0.9	Doyles River Parking Overlook; Skyline Drive mp 81.9	R, P	2,800'	1,307.7	
890.6	2.1	Doyles River Cabin *(locked) (spring E–0.3m)*; Skyline Drive mp 81.1	R, P, w	2,900'	1,306.8	
892.7	1.1	+Loft Mountain Campground (W–0.2m) *West–1.2m to* Loft Mountain Wayside	C, G, cl R, M	3,300'	1,304.7	
893.8	0.7	Frazier Discovery Trail to Loft Mountain Wayside (W–0.6m)	R, M	2,950'	1,303.6	
894.5	0.3	Loft Mountain		3,200'	1,302.9	
894.8	2.1	Spring (W–0.1m)	w	2,950'	1,302.6	
896.9	1.6	Ivy Creek Overlook; Skyline Drive mp 77.5	R, P	2,800'	1,300.5	
898.5	0.2	**Pinefield Hut** (E–0.1m), 13.5mS; 8.4mN	S, C, w	2,430'	1,298.9	
898.7	1.9	Pinefield Gap; Skyline Drive mp 75.2	R	2,590'	1,298.7	

Miles from Springer	Miles to Next Point	Features	Services	Elev	Miles from Katahdin	M A P
900.6	3.3	Simmons Gap; Skyline Drive mp 73.2 *East–0.2m to* water pump at ranger station	R, P w	2,250'	1,296.8	
903.9	0.4	Powell Gap; Skyline Drive mp 69.9	R	2,294'	1,293.5	
904.3	1.2	Little Roundtop Mountain		2,700'	1,293.1	PATC: Map 11
905.5	1.2	Smith Roach Gap; Skyline Drive mp 68.6	R, P	2,600'	1,291.9	
906.7	0.5	**Hightop Hut** *(W–0.1m S; 0.2m spring), 8.4mS;* *12.6mN*	S, C, w	3,175'	1,290.7	
907.2	0.1	Spring	w	3,450'	1,290.2	
907.3	1.5	Hightop Mountain		3,587'	1,290.1	
908.8	1.3	Skyline Drive mp 66.7	R, P	2,650'	1,288.6	

910.1	3.0	Swift Run Gap; US-33; Skyline Drive mp 65.5;
		Spotswood Trail; self-registration kiosk for SNP
		camping permits
		   West–2.9m to Country View Motel
		   West–3.2m to Swift Run Camping; Store
		   West–7.5m to **Elkton, VA, P.O. 22827**
			R, w
			
			L
			C, G, M, cl
			G, M
				2,367'	1,287.3	

913.1	3.3	South River Picnic Grounds *(W–0.1m)*	P, w	3,200'	1,284.3	
916.4	0.3	Pocosin Cabin *(locked) (W–0.1m spring)*	w	3,150'	1,281.0	
916.7	1.7	Spring	w	3,100'	1,280.7	
918.4	0.7	+Lewis Mountain Campground and Cabins; Skyline Drive mp 57.6 (W–0.1m)	R, C, G, L, cl, sh	3,500'	1,279.0	
919.1	2.6	**Bearfence Mountain Hut** *(E–0.1m), 12.6mS;* *11.8mN*	R, P, S, C, w	3,110'	1,278.3	
921.7	0.9	Bootens Gap; Skyline Drive mp 55.1	R, P	3,243'	1,275.7	
922.6	1.9	Hazeltop		3,812'	1,274.8	
924.5	0.9	Milam Gap; Skyline Drive mp 52.8	R, P	3,300'	1,272.9	
925.4	0.8	Spring	w	3,380'	1,272.0	
926.2	0.9	Lewis Spring; Big Meadows Wayside; Harry F. Bird Sr. Visitors Center *(E–0.4m)*	R, P, G, M, w	3,390'	1,271.2	PATC: Map 10
927.1	0.6	Big Meadows Lodge *(E–0.1m)*; +Big Meadows Campground *East–0.9m to* Big Meadows Wayside	R, P, C, L, M, cl, sh G, M	3,490'	1,270.3	
927.7	1.0	David Spring *(W–50 ft.)*	w	3,490'	1,269.7	
928.7	1.9	Fishers Gap; Skyline Drive mp 49.3	R	3,050'	1,268.7	
930.6	0.3	**Rock Spring Hut** *(W–0.2m)* and *(locked) cabin,* *11.8mS; 11.1mN*	S, C, w	3,465'	1,266.8	
930.9	1.0	Trail to Hawksbill Mountain, Byrd's Nest #2 Picnic Shelter *(E–0.9m)*	R	3,600'	1,266.5	
931.9	0.4	Hawksbill Gap; Skyline Drive mp 45.6	R, P	3,361'	1,265.5	
932.3	2.1	Side trail to Crescent Rock Overlook; Skyline Drive mp 44.4		3,450'	1,265.1	
934.4	0.8	Skyland Service Road *(south)*: horse stables	R, P	3,550'	1,263.0	
935.2	0.4	Skyland Service Road *(north)*: *best access to Skyland* *Resort (W–0.2m)*	R, P, L, M	3,790'	1,262.2	
935.6	1.6	Side trail to Stony Man Mountain Summit	R, P	3,837'	1,261.8	
937.2	2.2	Hughes River Gap; Trail to Stony Man Mountain Overlook; Skyline Drive mp 38.6	R, P, w	3,097'	1,260.2	
939.4	0.1	Pinnacles Picnic Ground; Skyline Drive mp 36.7	R, w	3,390'	1,258.0	
939.5	1.0	Side trail to Jewell Hollow Overlook; Skyline Drive mp 36.4	R	3,350'	1,257.9	
940.5	1.0	The Pinnacle		3,730'	1,256.9	

Miles from Springer	Miles to Next Point	Features	Services	Elev	Miles from Katahdin	M A P
941.5	0.7	**Byrds Nest #3 Hut** *(E–0.3m spring), 11.1mS; 4.6mN*	S, C, w	3,290'	1,255.9	
942.2	0.6	Meadow Spring *(E–0.3m)*	w	3,100'	1,255.2	PATC: Map 10
942.8	1.9	Mary's Rock: *vista*		3,514'	1,254.6	
944.7	1.2	Thornton Gap, Panorama *(W–0.1m)*; US-211; Skyline Drive mp 31.5	R, P, w	2,307'	1,252.7	
		West–4.6m to Brookside Cabins	L, M			
		West–5.6m to motels and campground	C, G, L, cl			
		West–8m to **Luray, VA, P.O. 22835**	all			
945.9	0.8	**Pass Mountain Hut** *(E–0.2m), 4.6mS; 13.5mN*	S, w	2,690'	1,251.5	
946.7	1.1	Pass Mountain		3,052'	1,250.7	
947.8	0.3	Skyline Drive mp 28.6	R	2,490'	1,249.6	
948.1	0.1	Beahms Gap; Skyline Drive mp 28.5	R, P	2,490'	1,249.3	
948.2	4.6	Byrds Nest #4 Picnic Shelter *(E–0.5m)*	w	2,600'	1,249.2	
952.8	0.5	Spring	w	2,600'	1,244.6	
953.3	0.8	Elkwallow Gap; Elkwallow Wayside Skyline Drive mp 23.9 (E–0.1m)	R, P, G, M	2,480'	1,244.1	
954.1	0.7	Range View Cabin *(locked) (E–0.1m spring)*	w	2,950'	1,243.3	
954.8	0.6	Rattlesnake Point Overlook, Skyline Drive mp 21.9	R, P	3,100'	1,242.6	
955.4	0.4	Tuscarora Trail (southern terminus) to +Mathews Arm Campground *(W–0.9m)*	C, w	3,400'	1,242.0	
955.8	0.2	Skyline Drive mp 21.1	R, P	3,350'	1,241.6	
956.0	0.1	Hogback Third Peak		3,400'	1,241.4	
956.1	0.2	Skyline Drive mp 20.8	R, P	3,350'	1,241.3	
956.3	0.2	Hogback Second Peak		3,475'	1,241.1	
956.5	0.1	Spring (E–0.2m)	w	3,250'	1,240.9	
956.6	0.7	Hogback First Peak		3,390'	1,240.8	
957.3	0.1	Little Hogback Overlook; Skyline Drive mp 19.7	R, P	3,000'	1,240.1	PATC: Map 9
957.4	0.5	Little Hogback Mountain		3,050'	1,240.0	
957.9	1.1	Skyline Drive mp 18.9	R	2,850'	1,239.5	
959.0	0.2	**Gravel Springs Hut** *(E–0.2m), 13.5mS; 10.7mN*	S, C, w	2,480'	1,238.4	
959.2	1.1	Gravel Springs Gap; Skyline Drive mp 17.7	R, P	2,666'	1,238.2	
960.3	0.5	South Marshall Mountain		3,212'	1,237.1	
960.8	0.7	Skyline Drive mp 15.9	R, P	3,050'	1,236.6	
961.5	0.9	North Marshall Mountain		3,368'	1,235.9	
962.4	0.6	Hogwallow Spring	w	2,950'	1,235.0	
963.0	1.7	Hogwallow Gap; Skyline Drive mp 14.2	R	2,739'	1,234.4	
964.7	0.9	Jenkins Gap; Skyline Drive mp 12.3	R	2,400'	1,232.7	
965.6	0.4	Compton Springs	w	2,700'	1,231.8	
966.0	0.8	Compton Peak		2,909'	1,231.4	
966.8	0.3	Compton Gap; Skyline Drive mp 10.4	R, P	2,550'	1,230.6	
967.1	1.5	Indian Run Spring *(E–0.3m)*	w	2,350'	1,230.3	
968.6	0.2	Compton Gap Horse Trail; Trail to Chester Gap		2,350'	1,228.8	
968.8	0.7	Possums Rest Overlook; self-registration at kiosk for SNP camping permits; SNP northern boundary		2,300'	1,228.6	
969.5	1.0	**Tom Floyd Wayside Shelter**, *10.7mS; 8.1mN*	S, w	1,900'	1,227.9	
970.5	0.5	Northern Virginia 4-H Swimming Pool *(W–0.3m)*		1,350'	1,226.9	

Miles from Springer	Miles to Next Point	Features	Services	Elev	Miles from Katahdin	M A P
971.0	1.4	VA-602	R	1,150'	1,226.4	PATC: Map 9
972.4	3.3	US-522 *East-120 yds. to Mountain Home B&B* *West-3.2m to Front Royal, VA, P.O. 22630*	R, P L all	950'	1,225.0	

+Fee charged, mp=milepost

Shenandoah National Park, with 96 miles of well-graded Appalachian Trail, is memorable for its many vistas and abundant wildlife. Skyline Drive, which you will cross 28 times, has many waysides and concessions for resupply stops. Backcountry permits are required when camping in the park. Check the park's website, nps.gov/shen, for closures or reroutes.

⚑ **US-250, I-64/Rockfish Gap**—Information specifically for hikers notes area volunteers who provide free shuttles between Rockfish Gap and downtown. (See list at the visitor center, YMCA, and various other locations.) Download the Waynesboro Guide for AT Hikers at VisitWaynesboro.com; click on plan your visit, and then maps. *Lodging:* Yurt, (434) 882-1587, $50s/d, single bed/futon, wood stove, large deck on 70 acres, bath/shower in main house with private entrance; B available. Call Mary to arrange for pick-up, but must book through AirBnB, airbnb.com/rooms/17677894. No smoking, well-behaved-pet-friendly; some limitations; see website. *Food:* Kings Kettle Corn, snacks, drinks, info; open seasonally.

West 0.5 mile to *Lodging:* Grey Pine Lodge, 494 Three Notched Mtn. Hwy; for rates and booking, visit greypinelodgeva.com, dog-friendly, fire pits, gourmet retail shop, hiker rooms.

🚶 **West** 4.5 miles to **Waynesboro, VA [P.O. ZIP 22980: M–F 9–5, closed Sa, 200 S Wayne Ave. (540) 942-7320]**. There are 2 locations; hikers have gotten mail by knocking on the back door. A large, hiker-friendly town with most services. Third Annual Hiker Fest, Sa Jun 7th, a free community event downtown with live music all day, vendors, drinks, food, ice cream, yoga, activities. *Hostels:* Grace Evangelical Lutheran Church, 500 S. Wayne Ave., free and friendly open Jun 2–28, closed Sa and Su nights, check-in 5–9 p.m., check-out 9 a.m, but will store packs for those staying another night, lounge with big-screen TV, a/c, Internet, showers, cots, kitchen, snacks, and continental B, members of the congregation host a Wed-night supper for hikers (max. 10) followed by an optional vespers service, no pets, drugs, smoking, alcohol, firearms, foul language, max 10 hikers; 2-night limit, donations accepted; Stanimal's 328 Hostel, book online at stanimals328.com, (540) 290-4002, 1333 W. Main St., owner Adam Stanley AT'04, PCT'10, $40pp includes pick-up/return to Trail, bunk mattress with clean linens, shower with towel, soap and laundry, semi-private rooms for $45,private rooms starting at $90, large private area, sunroom, Wi-Fi, DVDs, full-sized fridge, microwave, hiker box, slackpacking discounts for multi-night guests. *Camping:* Waynesboro Parks and Recreation offers tent and hammock sites on a grassy area at the foot of 14th St. near the South River, the ALDHA Hiker Pavilion, free 3-day-max permits with restrictions, available at Y, tourist office, library, and outfitters, now required for this area; the YMCA, (540) 942-5107, on S. Wayne Ave., valid photo ID required, $2 shower, hours M–F 5:30 a.m.–7:30 p.m., Sa 7–4:30, Su 12–4:30 p.m., phone (540) 943-9622, check in at desk, donations appreciated. *Lodging:* Bowman House B&B, 11 Wayne Ave., (256) 347-2021, Facebook, @thebowmanhouseva, bed, B, laundry, and shuttle to the Trailhead and in town; Quality Inn, (540) 942-1171, hikers get 10% room discount, pets okay. *Groceries:* Walmart Neighborhood Market, Kroger (both long-term resupply). *Restaurants:* Ming Garden, AYCE L/D; Ciros Pizza; French Press; River Burger Bar; Sam's Hotdogs; Benny Stivales Pizza and Beer Garden; NY Flying Pizza; Delly Up; Stella, Bella & Lucy Café; Weasie's Kitchen, B/L/D with AYCE pancake B anytime; Greenleaf Grill; Basic City Beer Co., cold craft beer; and many fast-food outlets. *Internet access:* Waynesboro Public Library, M–F 10–9, Sa 10–2, Wi-Fi (24 hours) and the A.T. Hiker's Corner; Grace Church during times of hostel operation (see above). *Other services:* cobbler; pharmacy; ATM; doctor; dentist; veterinarian; River City Barber Shop ($10 hiker haircuts); massages; Western Union; one-hour photo service; South River Fly Shop, stove fuel.

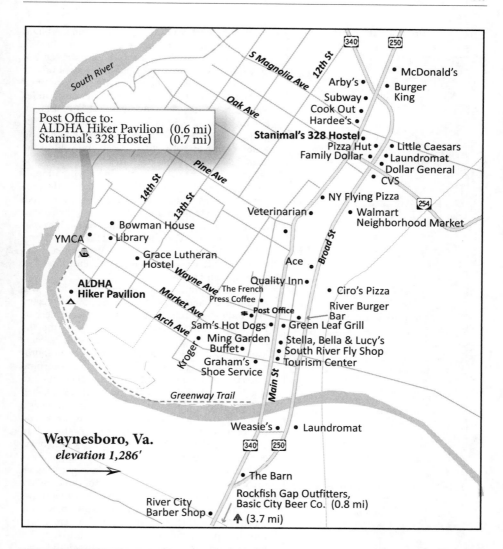

Post Office to:
ALDHA Hiker Pavilion   (0.6 mi)
Stanimal's 328 Hostel   (0.7 mi)

McDonald's
Burger King
Arby's
Subway
Cook Out
Hardee's
Stanimal's 328 Hostel
Pizza Hut
Little Caesars
Family Dollar
Laundromat
Dollar General
CVS
NY Flying Pizza
Veterinarian
Walmart Neighborhood Market
Bowman House
YMCA
Library
Grace Lutheran Hostel
Ace
ALDHA Hiker Pavilion
Quality Inn
The French Press Coffee
Ciro's Pizza
River Burger Bar
Post Office
Green Leaf Grill
Sam's Hot Dogs
Ming Garden Buffet
Stella, Bella & Lucy's
South River Fly Shop
Graham's Shoe Service
Tourism Center
Greenway Trail

Waynesboro, Va.
elevation 1,286'

Weasie's
Laundromat

The Barn
River City Barber Shop
Rockfish Gap Outfitters, Basic City Beer Co. (0.8 mi)
(3.7 mi)

Potomac Appalachian Trail Club—PATC maintains the 240.8 miles between Rockfish Gap and Pine Grove Furnace State Park in Pennsylvania. Send correspondence to PATC, 118 Park St. SE, Vienna, VA 22180; (703) 242-0693; patc.net; info@patc.net.

Shenandoah National Park—Although the SNP presents some significant ascents and descents, hikers generally will find the Trail within the park well-graded.

Park history—In 1926, Congress authorized the Shenandoah and Great Smoky Mountains national parks. Unlike western parks, most of today's Shenandoah land was privately owned; the Blue Ridge here had been dotted with communities and isolated groups of settlers since the 1750s. Areas had long been farmed and grazed. Out-of-state corporations had exploited some areas for timber and mineral ores. Three resorts provided Victorian-era vacationers with cool mountain breezes and recreation.

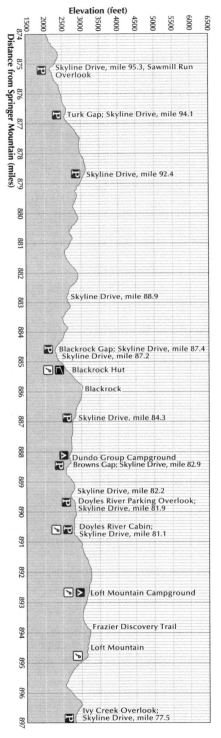

Elevation (feet)

Distance from Springer Mountain (miles)

Skyline Drive, mile 95.3, Sawmill Run Overlook

Turk Gap; Skyline Drive, mile 94.1

Skyline Drive, mile 92.4

Skyline Drive, mile 88.9

Blackrock Gap; Skyline Drive, mile 87.4
Skyline Drive, mile 87.2

Blackrock Hut

Blackrock

Skyline Drive, mile 84.3

Dundo Group Campground
Browns Gap; Skyline Drive, mile 82.9

Skyline Drive, mile 82.2
Doyles River Parking Overlook;
Skyline Drive, mile 81.9

Doyles River Cabin;
Skyline Drive, mile 81.1

Loft Mountain Campground

Frazier Discovery Trail

Loft Mountain

Ivy Creek Overlook;
Skyline Drive, mile 77.5

By the 1910s, conditions were changing. A blight killing American chestnut trees, some 30–40 percent of the Appalachian forest, had destroyed not only large swaths of the forest but a way of life for many. Those trees provided nuts that were shipped by railroad to cities, providing mountain families with cash income. The chestnut was strong, straight, and rot-resistant, and its wood was valuable for fence posts, railroad ties, roof shingles, siding boards, and general lumber that residents used and sold in the Shenandoah Valley and the Piedmont.

In 1927, Virginia authorized condemnation of all private property within the boundary of the proposed park. More than 4,000 tracts were surveyed, and 1,081 were purchased and given to the federal government, uprooting most of the 465 families who lived on the land. Virginia resettled the majority and evicted those unwilling to move. Approximately 45 elderly residents were allowed to spend their last years in their homes.

In 1931, four years before Shenandoah was established, construction of Skyline Drive began. First built as a second entrance to President Herbert Hoover's summer White House, Rapidan Camp, the road was only to go from the camp to Skyland. State leaders successfully lobbied for congressional appropriations to extend the highway north to Thornton Gap (US-211), on to Front Royal, and then south to Rockfish Gap. But, until the park was established in December 1935, Skyline Drive existed only as a 100-foot right-of-way within privately held land that basically coincided with the route of the A.T. In 1933, President Franklin D. Roosevelt's CCC "boys" established camps along the route and built many of the facilities, overlooks, rock walls, and gutters seen there today. They planted hundreds of thousands of trees and shrubs, creating the landscape that draws millions of visitors to the park, and built a new route for the A.T. ATC Chair Myron Avery's acceptance of this disruption, after years of simmering disagreements, produced an open schism between the organization's leadership and founder Benton MacKaye and his allies in New York and New England.

Today, 95 percent reforested, the park is home to wild turkey, white-tailed deer, black bears, and shelter mice. Hundreds of migrating birds and butterflies summer or stop over in this central Appalachian biome. Nearly one million visitors a year come to watch wildlife, get back to nature, view the Shenandoah Valley to the west and the foothills to the east, or visit land on which their ancestors lived.

Ranger Programs—From Memorial Day into Oct, rangers present a organized hikes, programs and events highlighting the natural and human history

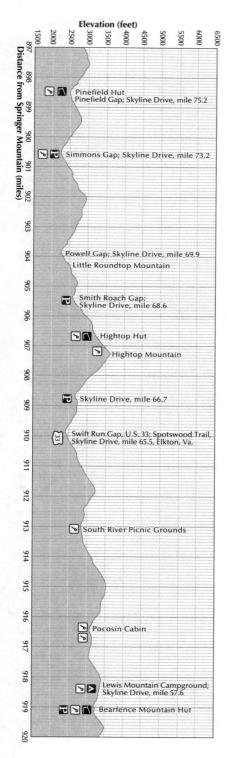

Elevation (feet)

Distance from Springer Mountain (miles)

Pinefield Hut
Pinefield Gap; Skyline Drive, mile 75.2

Simmons Gap; Skyline Drive, mile 73.2

Powell Gap; Skyline Drive, mile 69.9
Little Roundtop Mountain

Smith Roach Gap;
Skyline Drive, mile 68.6

Hightop Hut

Hightop Mountain

Skyline Drive, mile 66.7

Swift Run Gap, U.S. 33; Spotswood Trail,
Skyline Drive, mile 65.5, Elkton, Va.

South River Picnic Grounds

Pocosin Cabin

Lewis Mountain Campground;
Skyline Drive, mile 57.6

Bearfence Mountain Hut

of the park. The visitors' guide, available at entrances and visitor centers, has the schedule.

Forest Damage—Hurricane Isabel (2003) and fires before it damaged thousands of acres. Coupled with the floods, Tropical Storm Fran in 1996, a severe ice storm in 1998 and 2006, a 2012 derecho, and gypsy-moth and woolly adelgid infestations, the park has been hit hard in recent years. Be mindful of trees and branches that have been weakened by those events and could still fall.

Fee—Hikers entering the park via the A.T. are not charged a fee; hikers entering at other trailheads in SNP may incur a $15 fee. Entering by vehicle, the fee is $30/vehicle for a stay of 1-7 days. During the spring (mid-Feb to mid-Apr), the park occasionally conducts prescribed burns along the A.T. to manage vegetation. During burns, a hut may be closed up to 3 days. Check the ATC or park websites or ask at any NPS station for current information.

Backcountry Permits—Free permits are **required** of all thru-hikers and overnight backcountry travelers. Backcountry self-registration kiosks are located on the A.T. near the north and south boundaries of SNP. If you fail to register or can't show proof of registration when rangers ask for it, they may issue a citation or fine. Permits may also be obtained at Skyline Drive entrance stations and park visitor centers when they are open. A permit can be acquired in advance M–F 8–4. Be familiar with the regulations, have your exact itinerary ready. For all permit questions, contact the Park Permit Office at (540) 999-3500, ext. 3374, or e-mail shen_permits@nps.gov, or mail to Backcountry Camping Permit, 3655 US-Hwy 211 East, Luray, VA 22835.

Backcountry Accommodations—Two types of three-sided structures are near the A.T.—day-use (called "shelters") and overnight-use (called "huts"). Camping at or near the shelters is prohibited. Huts are available to long-distance hikers (those with an itinerary of at least three consecutive nights) on a first-come, first-served basis. Tenting at huts is permitted in designated campsites marked with a post and a tenting symbol; all huts within the park have campsites. The PATC also operates several locked cabins within the park that require advance reservations and other arrangements. Contact PATC for details.

Backcountry Regulations
- Campfires are prohibited in SNP, except at the commercial campgrounds and established fireplaces at shelters, huts, and cabins. Use a backpacking stove.

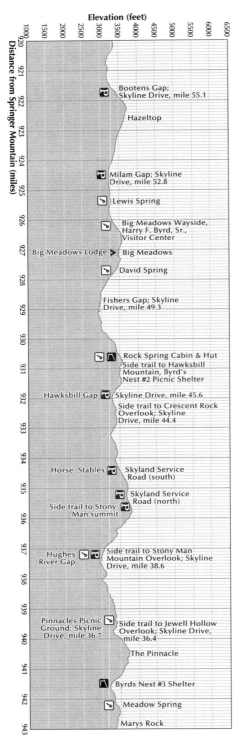

Elevation (feet)

Distance from Springer Mountain (miles)

Bootens Gap;
Skyline Drive, mile 55.1

Hazeltop

Milam Gap; Skyline
Drive, mile 52.8

Lewis Spring

Big Meadows Wayside,
Harry F. Byrd, Sr.,
Visitor Center

Big Meadows Lodge ▶ Big Meadows

David Spring

Fishers Gap; Skyline
Drive, mile 49.3

Rock Spring Cabin & Hut
Side trail to Hawksbill
Mountain, Byrd's
Nest #2 Picnic Shelter

Hawksbill Gap Skyline Drive, mile 45.6

Side trail to Crescent Rock
Overlook; Skyline
Drive, mile 44.4

Horse Stables Skyland Service
Road (south)

Skyland Service
Road (north)

Side trail to Stony
Man summit

Hughes Side trail to Stony Man
River Gap Mountain Overlook; Skyline
Drive, mile 38.6

Pinnacles Picnic Side trail to Jewell Hollow
Ground; Skyline Overlook; Skyline Drive,
Drive, mile 36.7 mile 36.4

The Pinnacle

Byrds Nest #3 Shelter

Meadow Spring

Marys Rock

- Camping is prohibited within 10 yards of a stream or other natural water source; within 20 yards of a park trail or unpaved fire road; within 50 yards of culturally historic sites, other campers, or no-camping signs; within 100 yards of a hut, cabin, or day-use shelter (except designated sites); within 0.25 mile of a paved road, park boundary, picnic area, visitor center, or commercial facility. Several zones have been designated "noncamping areas," including Limberlost, Hawksbill Summit, Whiteoak Canyon, Old Rag summit, Big Meadows clearing, and Rapidan Camp.
- Camping is permitted almost everywhere else. New regulations encourage hikers to seek "preexisting campsites" in legal locations that show signs of use and are not posted with no-camping signs. Camping at those sites is limited to two consecutive nights. If necessary, dispersed camping at undisturbed sites is permissible, but they must be left in pristine condition; use such sites only one night.
- Maximum group size is 10 people.
- Food must be stored so that wildlife cannot get it—hang food from a tree branch at least ten feet from the ground and four feet away from a tree's trunk. Alternatively, overnight huts feature food-storage poles or bear boxes, which are to be used instead of the familiar "mouse hangers." Park-approved, bear-resistant food-storage canisters are also permissible.
- Solid human waste should be buried in accordance with Leave No Trace ethics, under 6 inches of soil, more than 200 feet from trails, water sources, or roads. In moldering privies, add a small handful of wood chips.
- Carry out all trash from the backcountry, and dispose of it properly.
- Glass containers are discouraged.
- Pets must be leashed at all times and are prohibited on certain side trails.

Commercial Facilities—Campgrounds, restaurants, lodges, waysides, and small stores are normally open spring through fall and are located strategically near the A.T. and Skyline Drive. Long-distance hikers may be able to save pack weight by resupplying or taking meals at these facilities. Call the park for the precise dates and times of operation. More details can be found at nps.gov/shen. Site rate is $30 for up to 6 hikers.

Calf Mountain Shelter (1984)—Sleeps 6. Privy. Food-hanging pole. Featuring two skylights, this shelter is not a part of the hut system, so SNP rules don't apply here. Water source is a piped spring on the access trail. From here to Blackrock Hut, the A.T. usually is without reliable water sources; plan accordingly.

Blackrock Hut (1941)—Sleeps 6. Moldering privy. Food-hanging poles. Designated tentsites nearby. Water source is a piped spring 10 yards in front of the shelter.

Loft Mountain Campground—Open mid-May to late Oct. The A.T. skirts the campground, but several short side trails lead to campsites and the camp store (short-term resupply, canister fuel). Campsites $30, subject to change; coin laundry, restroom, and soda machine. Loft Mountain Wayside and Grill serves B/L/D, short-order menu, soda machine. From the camp store, follow the paved road 1.0 mile downhill to Skyline Drive or continue north on the A.T. 0.9 mile and take the Frazier Discovery Trail 0.5 mile west (steep descent) to Skyline Drive.

Pinefield Hut (1940)—Sleeps 6. Moldering privy. Food-hanging poles. Designated tentsites nearby. Water source is a spring behind the shelter 50 yards that tends to fail during dry seasons. Northbounders can get water from Ivy Creek or Loft Mountain Campground; southbounders, an outdoor spigot at the Simmons Gap ranger station.

Simmons Gap—Simmons Gap ranger station is down the paved road 0.2 mile east from where the A.T. crosses Skyline Drive. Frost-free pump.

Hightop Hut (1939)—Sleeps 6. Moldering privy. Food-hanging poles. Designated campsites nearby. Water source is a usually reliable piped spring 0.1 mile from the shelter on a side trail. An alternative water source is a boxed spring 0.5 mile north on the Trail.

⋔ US-33/Swift Run Gap/Spotswood Trail—West from Skyline Drive to water. Backcountry self-registration station located at SNP entrance station, north of US-33 bridge.
   On US-33—West 2.9 miles to *Lodging:* Country View Motel, 19974 Spotswood Trail, Elkton, VA 22827, (540) 298-0025, countryviewlodging.com, call for room or cabin rates, no pet fee, laundry, shuttle possible back to Trail and Elkton, mail drops accepted for guests.
   West 3.2 miles to *Camping:* Swift Run Camping, (540) 298-8086, $29 campsite with electrical outlet, laundry, pool, and snack bar. *Groceries:* Bear Mountain Grocery, with a deli, daily 6–9.
   ⊘ West 7.5 miles to **Elkton, VA [P.O. ZIP 22827: M–F 8:30–4:30, Sa 9–11; (540) 298-7772].** *Groceries:* Food Lion, O'Dell's Grocery (both long-term resupply). *Restaurants:* fast-food places. *Other services:* Appalachian Trail Outfitters, 311 West Spotswood Trail, Elkton, VA 22827, (540) 713-9015, open M–Sa 10–6, Su 1–5; pharmacy; bank; and ATM.

South River picnic area—Water, picnic benches, restrooms with sinks.

⋔ Lewis Mountain Campground and Cabins—Open early May to Nov; reservations, (540) 999-2255, goshenandoah.com/lodging. The A.T. passes in sight of the campground, and several short side trails lead to campsites and the camp store. Campsites $30; hiker special only for cabins available. Lewis Mountain Camp Store (short-term resupply), open 9–7 in summer. Showers $1, laundry, restroom, and soda machine.

Bearfence Mountain Hut (1940)—Sleeps 6. Privy. Food-hanging poles and bear box. Designated tentsites nearby. Located on a blue-blazed trail off a fire road. Water source is a piped spring in front of the shelter; prone to fail during even moderately dry spells.

⋔ Big Meadows Lodge, Campground, and Wayside—The A.T. passes within sight of the campground, and short side trails lead to the lodge, which also houses a restaurant and tap room and has Internet access. *Lodging:* hiker rates may be available, call (877) 847-1919; rooms available in main lodge; also cabins, suites, and motel-type accommodations. A few pet-friendly rooms. Reservations required. Lodging and restaurant open late May–late Oct. *Camping:* Open early Apr–late Nov,

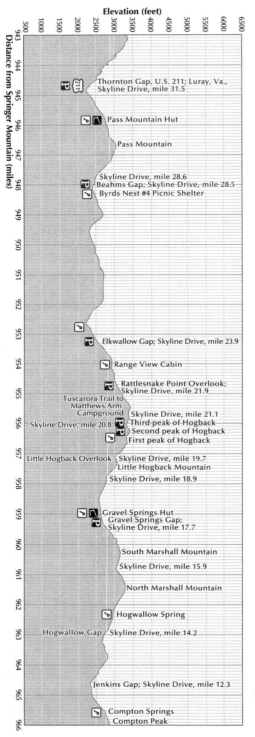

Elevation (feet)

Distance from Springer Mountain (miles)

Thornton Gap, U.S. 211; Luray, Va., Skyline Drive, mile 31.5

Pass Mountain Hut

Pass Mountain

Skyline Drive, mile 28.6
Beahms Gap; Skyline Drive, mile 28.5
Byrds Nest #4 Picnic Shelter

Elkwallow Gap; Skyline Drive, mile 23.9

Range View Cabin

Rattlesnake Point Overlook; Skyline Drive, mile 21.9
Tuscarora Trail to Matthews Arm Campground Skyline Drive, mile 21.1
Skyline Drive, mile 20.8 Third peak of Hogback
Second peak of Hogback
First peak of Hogback
Little Hogback Overlook Skyline Drive, mile 19.7
Little Hogback Mountain
Skyline Drive, mile 18.9

Gravel Springs Hut
Gravel Springs Gap;
Skyline Drive, mile 17.7

South Marshall Mountain
Skyline Drive, mile 15.9

North Marshall Mountain

Hogwallow Spring
Hogwallow Gap Skyline Drive, mile 14.2

Jenkins Gap; Skyline Drive, mile 12.3

Compton Springs
Compton Peak

campsites $30, reservations recommended. Walk-ins are possible, but the campground is often full; showers $1, laundry. *Restaurant:* Dining room open daily for L/D; tap room, with nightly entertainment and light fare, open daily from late afternoon to late evening. From the lodge, follow the paved entrance road 0.9 mile to Big Meadows Wayside and Grill, B/L/D, open late Mar–late Nov, with short-order menu. *Groceries:* Wayside has a good selection (short-term resupply) and camping supplies, and soda machine. Next door is the Harry F. Byrd, Sr., Visitor Center, with exhibits and videos on area history.

Rock Spring Hut (1940, updated 1980)—Sleeps 8. Privy. Food-hanging pole and bear box. Designated tentsites nearby. Located on 0.2-mile blue-blazed trail. Water source, down a steep trail in front of the hut, flows from beneath a rock.

⚑ Skyland Service Road/Skyland—Skyland was originally a 19th-century mountain summer resort owned by A.T. pioneer George Freeman Pollock, who pushed hard to evict surrounding small landholders and create a national park and then, ironically, was forced to sell and give up management of the resort. Cross the road at the stables, and follow the A.T. north, passing a water tank on your right and the junction marked by a post, which points to Skyland and dining room.

West 0.2 mile to *Lodging:* Skyland, (877) 847-1919, late Mar–late Nov; hiker special available; also motel-type accommodations and suites, reservations required. A few pet-friendly rooms. *Restaurant*: Pollock Dining Room serves B/L/D; limited hours. Tap room, light fare, nightly entertainment.

Pinnacles picnic area—Restrooms, covered area, picnic tables, fireplaces. Uphill from picnic pavilion is a frost-free pump for year-round water.

Byrds Nest #3 Hut—Sleeps 8. Moldering privy. Food-hanging poles. A picnic shelter converted to overnight use. A spring is 0.3 mile east, down the fire road.

⚑ US-211/Thornton Gap/Panorama—A short side trail, on the southern side of Thornton Gap, leads to Panorama area. The restaurant

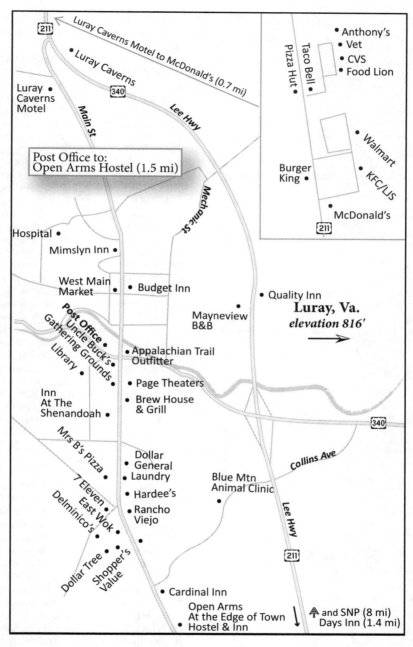

Map of Luray, Va. (elevation 816')

Locations shown on the map include:

211 Luray Caverns Motel to McDonald's (0.7 mi)

340 Luray Caverns — Lee Hwy — Main St — Mechanic St

Luray Caverns Motel

Post Office to: Open Arms Hostel (1.5 mi)

Hospital •
Mimslyn Inn •
West Main Market •
• Budget Inn
Post Office
Uncle Buck's
Gathering Grounds
Library
• Appalachian Trail Outfitter
Inn At The Shenandoah •
• Page Theaters
• Brew House & Grill
Mayneview B&B
• Quality Inn
Luray, Va.
elevation 816' →

Mrs B's Pizza
7 Eleven
East Wok
Delminico's
• Dollar General
• Laundry
• Hardee's
• Rancho Viejo
Blue Mtn Animal Clinic
Collins Ave
Lee Hwy
340
211
Dollar Tree
Shopper's Value
• Cardinal Inn
Open Arms At the Edge of Town
• Hostel & Inn
↓ ⚑ and SNP (8 mi)
Days Inn (1.4 mi)

Inset (upper right):
• Anthony's
• Vet
• CVS
• Food Lion
Taco Bell
Pizza Hut
• Walmart
Burger King •
• KFC/LJS
• McDonald's
211

and backcountry-permit office were torn down in 2008; new restrooms, water source, and a parking area have been installed at "east" end of lot. Park entrance station is north of US-211, east of where the Trail crosses Skyline Drive, with water. *Until further notice, treat or boil water from both those locations due to contamination.*

On US-211—West 4.6 miles to *Lodging:* Brookside Cabins, (540) 743-5698, brooksidecabins.com, luxury cabins $95–$210; full-menu restaurant featuring home-style foods and daily AYCE L/D buf-

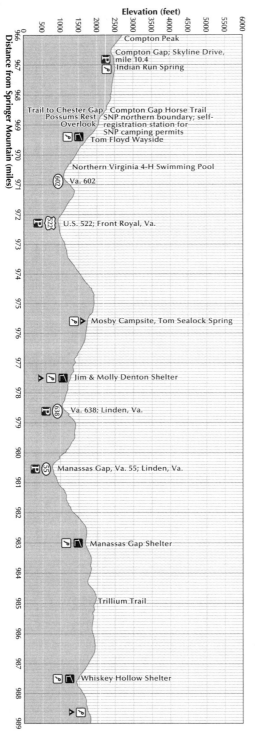

Elevation (feet)

Compton Peak

Compton Gap; Skyline Drive, mile 10.4
Indian Run Spring

Trail to Chester Gap / Compton Gap Horse Trail
Possums Rest / SNP northern boundary; self-
Overlook — registration station for
SNP camping permits
Tom Floyd Wayside

Northern Virginia 4-H Swimming Pool

Va. 602

U.S. 522; Front Royal, Va.

Mosby Campsite, Tom Sealock Spring

Jim & Molly Denton Shelter

Va. 638; Linden, Va.

Manassas Gap, Va. 55; Linden, Va.

Manassas Gap Shelter

Trillium Trail

Whiskey Hollow Shelter

fet, weekend B buffet, open W–Th 11:30–8, F 11:30–8:30, Sa 9-8:30, Su 9-8. Closed early Dec–Mar.

West 5.6 miles to **Lodging:** Days Inn, (540) 743-4521, $90–$250, pets $15/night, seasonal outdoor pool, B item and coffee, coin laundry. **Camping:** Yogi Bear's Jellystone Park, (540) 300-1697, campluray.com, tentsites 2-night minimum, cabins, 3-night minimum, call for rates; camp store (short-term resupply), seasonal outdoor pool, laundry, pets allowed (free) only at sites.

West 8.0 miles to the town of **Luray, VA [P.O. ZIP 22835: M–F 8:30–4:30, closed Sa; (540) 743-2100]**. Luray-Page County Chamber of Commerce, 18 Campbell St., (540) 743-3915, visitluraypage.com, daily 9–5. **Hostel:** Open Arms at the Edge of Town Hostel & Inn, 1260 East Main St., (540) 244-5652, owned by Alison Coltrane, openarmsluray.com; call or text for availability/pick-up from Thornton Gap; twin bed/linens/shower/kitchen access $35pp; tentsite/shower/kitchen access $20pp; B, soda, and snacks; Wi-Fi; laundry $5; light fee for cards/Venmo; pet-friendly; mail drops free to guests. **Lodging:** Cardinal Inn, (540) 743-5010, $75 and up, no pets; Mimslyn Inn, (540) 743-5105; Quality Inn, (540) 743-6511; Budget Inn, (540) 743-5176, call for rate, dogs $10/night; Luray Caverns Motels East and West, (540) 743-4531, 20% discount coupon for food/merchandise at Luray Caverns, no dogs; Inn of the Shenandoah, (540) 300-9777, 138 East Main St., B&B; Woodruff House B&B and Cabins, 330 Mechanic St., and Mayne View B&B, 439 Mechanic St., both (540) 843-3200, call for rates. **Groceries:** Shopper's Value, Food Lion, Walmart (all long-term resupply). **Restaurants:** Anthony's Pizza, L/D; East Wok, L/D and AYCE L; Gathering Grounds, espresso, sandwiches, meals; West Main Market & Deli, soups and sandwiches; The Speakeasy at the Mimslyn Inn, sandwiches and Th–Sa 5–10, Su–W 5–9, Su 2–10, full bar; Hawksbill Brewery; and several fast-food restaurants. **Internet access:** Page Public Library, no Wi-Fi, M–Th 10–6, F–Sa 11–2. **Outfitter:** Appalachian Outfitters, 2 W. Main St., (540) 743-7400, ato.luray@gmail.com, full-service outfitter, M–Sa 10–6, Su 1–5. **Other services:** veterinarian, Blue Mountain Animal Clinic, (540) 743-7298, M–F 8–6, closed weekends; laundromats; hospital; ATMs; and the 5-screen Page Theater.

Pass Mountain Hut (1939)—Sleeps 8. Privy. Food-hanging poles. Known for the "kissing trees," shelter is located on a blue-blazed trail. Designated campsites nearby. Water source is a piped spring 15 yards behind the shelter.

⚠ **Elkwallow Wayside and Grill**—Open 9–7 early Apr–early Oct. Visible from where the A.T. crosses Skyline Drive in Elkwallow Gap, the wayside includes a grill, gift shop, and restroom. Grill, B/L/D. Last chance in SNP for northbounders to get a blackberry milkshake. Gift shop offers limited groceries, camping supplies, soda machine outside. Frost-free pump at picnic area south of wayside.

Mathews Arm Campground—West 0.9 mile from the A.T., 0.3 mile south of the Hogback Parking Area via the Tuscarora and Traces trails. Signs lead to nearby primitive campground, open mid-May–late Oct, campsites $30/night, rate subject to change. This junction is the southern end of the 260-mile Tuscarora Trail; the northern is on the A.T. south of Darlington Shelter in Pennsylvania.

Gravel Springs Hut (1940)—Sleeps 8. Moldering privy. Food-hanging pole and bear box. Designated tentsites nearby on a blue-blazed trail. Water source is a boxed spring found on side trail near the shelter.

Southbound Registration Station– 0.7 mile south of Tom Floyd Wayside.

Tom Floyd (Wayside) Shelter (1980s)—Sleeps 6. Privy. Food-hanging pole and bear box. Tentsites. Shelter has an overhanging front deck with storage space above, a railed deck with benches. Outside the SNP boundary, so SNP rules don't apply. Water source 0.2 mile on a blue-blazed trail to the right of the shelter often stops flowing. Next closest water source is a stream crossing about 1.5 miles north on the A.T. near VA-602.

Northern Virginia 4-H swimming pool—Blue-blazed side trail 0.9 mile north of Tom Floyd Wayside leads 0.3 mile **West** to the swimming pool. It is open to the public, including hikers, hours vary (Memorial Day–Labor Day), $6 admission, swimsuits required. Concessions. Shower only, $1. Inquire at 4-H office, (540) 635-7171, about free 30-day parking availability (advance arrangements required).

Virginia—Part 4 (Northern Virginia)

Miles from Springer	Miles to Next Point	Features	Services	Elev	Miles from Katahdin	MAP
972.4	3.3	US-522 *East–120 yds.* to Mountain Home B&B *West–3.2m* to **Front Royal, VA, P.O. 22630**	R, P L all	950'	1,225.0	
975.7	1.9	Mosby Campsite, Tom Sealock Spring	C, w	1,800'	1,221.7	
977.6	1.1	**Jim and Molly Denton Shelter**, *8.1mS; 5.5mN*	S, C, w	1,310'	1,219.8	
978.7	1.9	VA-638 (Fiery Run Road) *West–1.1m* to **Linden, VA, P.O. 22642** *West–2.5m* to Apple House *West–7m* to **Front Royal, VA, P.O. 22630**	R, P H, g G, M all	1,150'	1,218.7	
980.6	2.5	VA-55 & Tucker Lane (VA-725), Manassas Gap *West–1.1m* to **Linden, VA, P.O. 22642**	R, P H, g	800'	1,216.8	
983.1	1.9	**Manassas Gap Shelter**, *5.5mS; 4.7mN*	S, C, w	1,655'	1,214.3	
985.0	2.6	Trillium Trail		1,900'	1,212.4	
987.6	1.0	**Whiskey Hollow Shelter** *(E–0.2m), 4.7mS; 8.8mN*	S, C, w	1,230'	1,209.8	
988.6	1.2	Campsite and spring	C, w	1850'	1,208.8	
989.8	0.8	+Sky Meadows State Park side trail *(E–1.7m)*	C, w	1,780'	1,207.6	PATC: Map 8
990.6	1.8	Ambassador Whitehouse Trail *(E–0.25m)* to lovely day/night view east			1,206.8	
992.4	3.3	Ashby Gap, US-50, US-17 *East–1.1m* to Paris, VA	R, P L, M	900'	1,205.0	
995.7	0.3	Fisher Loop Trail *(south junction)*			1,201.7	
996.0	0.3	**Rod Hollow Shelter** *(W–0.2m), 8.8mS; 7.1mN*	S, C, w	840'	1,201.4	
996.3	0.6	Fisher Loop Trail *(north junction)*			1,201.1	
996.9	2.7	Roller Coaster: *south end*		860'	1,200.5	
999.6	0.1	Morgans Mill Stream: *footbridge*	C, w	780'	1,197.8	
999.7	1.2	VA-605, Morgans Mill Road: *gravel*	R, P	1,140'	1,197.7	
1,000.9	0.5	Spring	w	1,150'	1,196.5	
1,001.4	1.5	Buzzard Hill: *view*		1260'	1,196.0	
1,002.9	1.3	**Sam Moore Shelter**; Sawmill Spring, *7.1mS; 11.2mN*	S, C, w	990'	1,194.5	
1,004.2	1.2	Stream		715'	1,193.2	
1,005.4	0.5	Stream and campsite: *footbridge*	C, w	800'	1,192.0	
1,005.9	0.6	Bears Den Rocks, Bears Den Hostel *(E–0.2m)*	P, H, L, C, g, cl, sh, f	1,350'	1,191.5	
1,006.5	2.2	Snickers Gap, VA-7, VA-679 *East–0.5m* to Nestle Inn B&B *East–1.6m* to Bluemont General Store *East–1.7m* to **Bluemont, VA, P.O. 20135** *West–0.3m* to Horseshoe Curve Restaurant *West–8.9m* to **Berryville, VA, P.O. 22611**	R, L, P L G L M G, L, M, cl	1,000'	1,190.9	PATC: Map 7
1,008.7	0.3	Spring	w	1,083'	1,188.7	
1,009.0	0.1	Virginia–West Virginia State Line		1,140'	1,188.4	
1,009.1	0.6	Crescent Rock		1,312'	1,188.3	
1,009.7	0.1	Sand Spring	w	1,150'	1,187.7	
1,009.8	0.5	Devils Racecourse: *boulder field*		1,200'	1,187.6	

Miles from Springer	Miles to Next Point	Features	Services	Elev	Miles from Katahdin	M A P
1,010.3	2.4	Roller Coaster: *north end*			1,187.1	
1,012.7	1.2	Wilson Gap		1,380'	1,184.7	
1,013.9	3.2	Trail(s) to **Blackburn Trail Center** *(E-0.2m), 11.2mS; 3.5mN*	R, P, C, S, w	1,650'	1,183.5	PATC Map: 7
1,017.1	3.0	**David Lesser Memorial Shelter** *(E-0.1m S; 0.3m spring), 3.5mS; 16.1mN*	S, C, w	1,430'	1,180.3	
1,020.1	1.5	Keys Gap, WV-9 *East-0.3m to* Sweet Springs Country Store *East-5.5m to* Stoney Brook Organic Farm & Hostle *West-0.3m to* Torlone Mini Mart and Restaurant	R, P, w G H, g, w G, M, w	935'	1,177.3	

+ Fee charged

Note: Higher rates of Lyme disease occur from northern Virginia into New England. Take precautions.

⚠ US-522—East 120 yards to Hostel and *Lodging:* Mountain Home B&B and Cabbin, (540) 692-6198, 3471 Remount Rd./US-522, Front Royal, VA 22630; first driveway on the left, 120 yards east of the Trail from the "Gate 7" sign; open year-round, owned by Scott "Possible" (AT '12) and Lisa "Anything" Jenkins, mountainhomeat@gmail.com. Reservations recommended, walk-ins welcome. Shared space in "Cabbin" (sleeps 6-8) or Rainbow Room (sleeps 3-4) in main house, $40pp cash, or $41pp card, includes bed with fresh linens, breakfast, shower, Wi-Fi, free shuttles to/from town, and mail drops. Private game room (sleeps 2) also includes private half-bath, shared bath with shower, foosball, $85/night. Nice, big private rooms with private bath (1-3 beds each), regular rate $175/nite, call for walk-in-weekday hiker and seasonal rates. Pizza, ice cream, snacks, and fuel available. Ask about free food. Laundry with loaner clothes ($5). Shower for non-guests ($5), parking for non-guests ($4 day). Dogs in Cabbin only ($5 dog/night). All welcome to lemonade/juice, tea and water, and relaxing on the patio.

⌂ West 3.2 miles to **Front Royal, VA [P.O. ZIP 22630: M-F 8:30-5, Sa 8:30-1; (540) 635-7983].** The post office is 1.0 mile farther. *Local transportation:* Four times a day M-F and twice a day Sa–Su, Apr–Oct, free Front Royal Trolley offers services from/to the US-522 Trailhead to/from town (check trailhead kiosk for map and schedule). It's also a fairly easy hitch. Uber is also available. Front Royal Taxi, (540) 313-5009 ($15 from/to trailhead). The large town offers all major services spread out over a wide area. Except for the post office, most services are located on South and Main Streets. *Lodging:* Front Royal is the gateway to Shenandoah National Park, with motel rates that vary considerably according to season; be sure to specify you are a hiker, as most have special rates. Mountain Home B&B is on the trail just east of the 522 crossing and provides free shuttles to Front Royal for guests (see US 522 above). Super 8 Motel, (540) 636-4888, best location/quality/price for hikers, $5 hiker discount, $100 deposit only when using cash or debit card–, free B, dogs $10 (based on availability), accepts mail drops; Twi-Lite Inn, (540) 635-4148, very clean, low price, OK location, outdoor pool, free Wi-Fi, no pets; Baymont Inn, (540) 635-3161, great location, low price, limited free B, laundry on site, outdoor pool, dogs $20; Woodward House B&B, (540) 635-7010, lovely B&B at South and Royal Streets, includes full B, no dogs, shuttle to/from nearby Trailheads; *Groceries:* Martin's (long-term resupply), Better Thymes natural foods, Big Lots, Dollar General, Rural King, Family Dollar, and, in north of town, Aldi and Walmart Supercenter (all long-term resupply). *Food and drink:* On Main Street—Vibrissa Microbrewery and Restaurant, Down Home Comfort Bakery, Garcia and Gavino Bakery, Catamount Lounge, Honey and Hops Meadery/Cidery, On Cue Restaurant with Pool and Darts, L'Dees Pancake House, Main Street Mill Restaurant, Cee and Cee Frozen Treats, Manor Line Market and Back 40 (gluten-free), Royal Zaika Indian Grill and Bar, Element Restaurant, Try Thai, Talk of the Mountain Seafood, Downtown Blends, Dynamic Life Coffee and Ice Cream; On Commerce Avenue—Hibachi Fresh, Thunwa Thai: On South Street; John Marshall Highway—Soul Mountain Restaurant and Bar, Castiglia's Family Italian, El Mague Mexican, B&L Custard Ice Cream, Spelunkers Burgers, Shenandoah Axe Throwing Bar and Restaurant, Foxes Pizza; On Chester Street—Chester Street Tavern, Virginia Beer Museum, Yamafuji

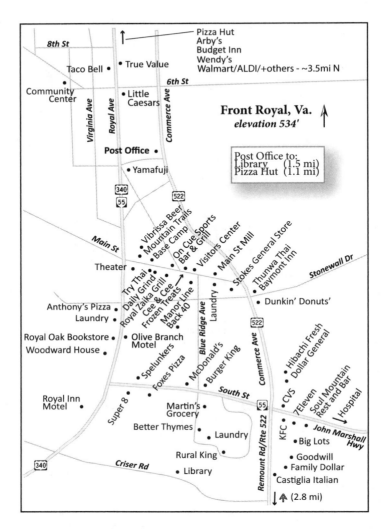

Front Royal, Va.
elevation 534'

Japanese; On Royal Avenue—Poppies Breakfast and Lunch, Melanias Bakery. **Outfitters:** Mountain Trails, 120 E. Main St. (540) 749-2470, hiker box, accepts mail drops. **Internet access:** Most retail and Samuels Public Library, M–Sa. **Other services and stores:** Base Camp, 122 E. Main St., (540) 631-0773, for hikers, includes free showers, lockers, laundry, and Wi-Fi; visitor center, 414 E. Main St., (800) 338-2576, open Th–M 9–4. Front Royal also has cell phone retail stores, Royal Cinemas movie theater, Royal Family Bowling Center, Play Favorites Game Store, arcade shops, Goodwill and Salvation Army, Family Dollar and Dollar General stores, Warren Heritage Society 101 Chester Street, Warren Rifles Museum, CVS, Valley Health Urgent Care (540) 635-0700 and Urgent Care Express (540) 636-0495, and Warren Memorial Hospital 351 Valley Health Way (540) 636-0300. Bus service: Virginia Breeze to/from Dulles Airport and Washington, DC. Arrives/leaves Front Royal each direction about noon daily. Bus continues to Blacksburg with stops along the way. About $20/person. **Shuttles:** Susan Tschirhart of Next Bend Adventures, (703) 907-9662; Bill Markunas, (540) 830-5778; Tony "Smooth" Smith, (703) 206-8490; Patricia "Blue Heron" Phair, (615) 806-9009; Scott Martin, (360) 513-4234; Nina/Janine Murphy's Shuttles, (703) 398-9164 or (703) 946-9404. For big groups, Mountain Trails 15-person van, (540) 749-2470, ask for Gary, Charlie, or Mike.

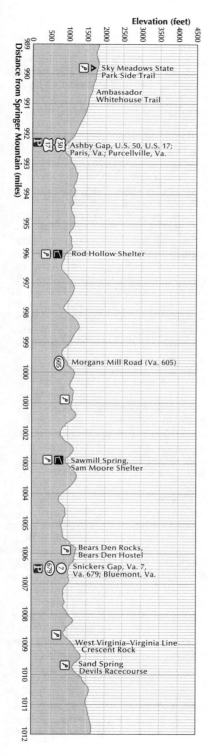

Elevation (feet)

Distance from Springer Mountain (miles)

Sky Meadows State Park Side Trail

Ambassador Whitehouse Trail

Ashby Gap, U.S. 50, U.S. 17; Paris, Va.; Purcellville, Va.

Rod Hollow Shelter

Morgans Mill Road (Va. 605)

Sawmill Spring, Sam Moore Shelter

Bears Den Rocks, Bears Den Hostel

Snickers Gap, Va. 7, Va. 679; Bluemont, Va.

West Virginia–Virginia Line Crescent Rock

Sand Spring Devils Racecourse

Smithsonian Conservation Biology Institute (SCBI)—Next to US-522, on the north side of the highway, the A.T. follows one of the fences of the SCBI, which plays a leading role in the Smithsonian's global efforts to save endangered wildlife species from extinction and train future generations of conservationists. Endangered animals are sometimes visible to hikers through the fence just north of 522. Not open to the public.

Mosby Campsite—Blue-blazed trail leads 0.1 mile **east** to primitive campground (no privy or bear pole) purportedly used by Confederate Col. John Mosby. Multiple tentsites and fire pit with benches. Follow blue-blaze to nearby Tom Sealock Spring.

Jim and Molly Denton Shelter (1991)—Sleeps 8. Privy. Bear pole. Enlarged front porch for extra sleepers. Water source is a spring on the A.T. near the sometimes-functional solar shower. Small picnic pavilion sits on a green area with several tentsites, horseshoe pit.

VA-638 (Fiery Run Rd.)—**West** 1.1 mile to **Linden, VA [P.O. ZIP 22642: M–F 8–12 & 1–5, Sa 8–12; (540) 636-9936].** A small outpost on VA-55, Linden has a post office, farm stand, and convenience store (540) 636-6791; an alternative to a hitch to Front Royal to get a mail drop. *Hostel:* Wonderland Hiker Refuge, 39 Parkside Rd., Linden, VA 22642, (571) 722-4842, donation-based, no pets; bunk room stay includes shower, free Wi-Fi, and laundry; shuttle to Trailhead and Front Royal. *Groceries:* Monterey Service Station, M–F 4–9, Sa 7–9, Su 8–8; Giving Tree, M–Sa 10–5; both short-term resupply, hiker-friendly, accept credit cards.

  West 2.5 miles to *Restaurant:* Apple House and Bushel Pub, (540) 636-6329, B, fresh-baked pies, doughnuts, sandwiches, BBQ, buffalo burgers, deli foods, soft-serve ice cream; M 7–5, Tu–Su 7–8; credit cards accepted, ATM. *Groceries:* 7-Eleven (short-term resupply), (540) 635-1899, open 24 hrs., ATM, deli sandwiches, ice cream; Apple Mountain Exxon, (540) 636-2960, large store, open 24 hrs., ATM, fresh pies, deli sandwiches.

  West 7 miles to Front Royal on VA-55 (see above).

VA-55 and Tucker Lane (VA-725), Manassas Gap—**West** 1.1 miles into Linden (see above). VA-55 is a busy road, parallel to I-66, which leads east to Washington.

Manassas Gap Shelter (1933/2002)—Sleeps 6. Privy. Bear pole. Picnic table and fire pit in front of shelter. Several tentsites in area. Water source is a reliable spring near the shelter on a side trail.

Whiskey Hollow Shelter (2016)—Bi-level, sleeps 8. Privy. Bear pole. Picnic tables and fire pit with benches. Wooden tent pad at old Dick's Dome location. Water

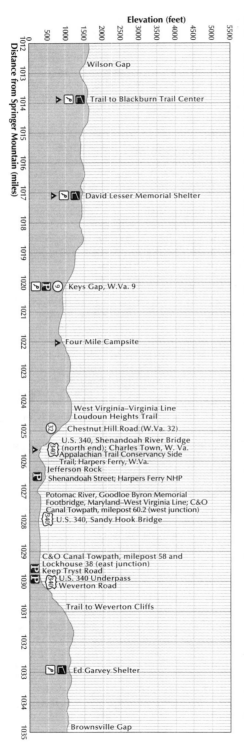

Elevation (feet)

Distance from Springer Mountain (miles)

Wilson Gap

Trail to Blackburn Trail Center

David Lesser Memorial Shelter

Keys Gap, W.Va. 9

Four Mile Campsite

West Virginia–Virginia Line
Loudoun Heights Trail
Chestnut Hill Road (W.Va. 32)
U.S. 340, Shenandoah River Bridge
(north end); Charles Town, W. Va.
Appalachian Trail Conservancy Side
Trail; Harpers Ferry, W.Va.
Jefferson Rock
Shenandoah Street; Harpers Ferry NHP

Potomac River, Goodloe Byron Memorial
Footbridge, Maryland–West Virginia Line; C&O
Canal Towpath, milepost 60.2 (west junction)
U.S. 340, Sandy Hook Bridge

C&O Canal Towpath, milepost 58 and
Lockhouse 38 (east junction)
Keep Tryst Road
U.S. 340 Underpass
Weverton Road

Trail to Weverton Cliffs

Ed Garvey Shelter

Brownsville Gap

source (unreliable) is Whiskey Hollow Creek in front of shelter; treat if flowing.

Sky Meadows State Park Side Trail—Sky Meadows State Park can be accessed from the A.T. by either North Ridge Trail or Ambassador Whitehouse Trail. Look for Virginia State Park junction posts with square signage. Look for the resting bench at path that leads **east** 1.7 miles to the visitor center, (540) 592-3556, built in the 1840s. Open M–Th 10–4, F–Su 10–5. Water fountain and rest rooms; drinks and snacks for sale when open. Park open daily from 8 until dusk. Year-round programs; schedule can be viewed on Virginiastateparks. gov. Gift shop open 10–4 M–Th and 10–5 F–Su. Each primitive campsite includes a 16'x16' tent pad, bear-proof locker, lantern hook, fire pit (firewood for sale at $6/10 sticks), nonpotable water spigot, pit privies. Cost is $20/night for VA residents and $25/night for non-residents. Reservations encouraged; space is limited. A.T. hikers with a reservation don't need to check-in at the visitor center but must be able to provide their reservation number, if asked by a ranger. Reservations are site-specific and can be made at online at reservevaparks.com or by phone (800) 933-7275 or (540) 592-3556.

US-50, US-17/Ashby Gap—**East** 0.8 mile on US-50/17, then 0.3 mile south past barrier on VA-759 to community of Paris. *Lodging:* The Ashby Inn, (540) 592-3900, restaurant serves L F–Su 11:30–2:30; D T–Su 5:00–8:30 (last seating); rooms are $200 and up and include B. Reservations recommended. Mail drops accepted. Snacks for sale in gift shop.

Rod Hollow Shelter (1986)—Sleeps 8. Privy. Bear pole. Tent pads. Located on a blue-blazed trail. Water source is a spring or the streams just south of the shelter. Dining pavilion rebuilt in 2010.

The "Roller Coaster"—Northbounders leaving the Rod Hollow Shelter will enter the "roller coaster," a 13.5-mile section with 10 ascents and descents (SOBOs will have just completed their ride.) When crews were challenged with designing a trail to avoid road-walking on VA-601, they had to work within a very narrow corridor, with little choice other than to route the path up and over each of these viewless and rocky ridges and hollows.

Sam Moore Shelter (1990)—Sleeps 6. Privy. Bear pole. Covered picnic table and fire ring. Named for maintainer Sam Moore, who gave 55 years of volunteer service to the A.T. Water source is Sawmill Spring in front of shelter or spring to left of shelter.

Bears Den— This historic stone mansion on 66 acres is 150 yards from the A.T. Bears Den Rocks provide a fine view of the Shenandoah Valley to the west. **East** 0.1 mile to Bears Den Hostel, owned by ATC, operated by PATC; 18393 Blue Ridge Mountain Rd., Bluemont, VA 20135; (540) 554-8708, bearsdencenter.org. Hiker special $40 includes bunk, shower; laundry available $3 a load detergent included; pizza, soda, and a pint of Ben & Jerry's ice cream; bunk & shower, $30 ($12 for children 12 and under); camping on lawn $15 (with shower and indoor-cooking privileges); shower only, $3. Private rooms and cottage available. Hiker room with phone, TV, Internet, and soda is accessible all day. Lodge, kitchen, store, and office open at 5 p.m. daily. Check out is at 9 a.m. Mail drops accepted. Shuttle and slackpacking available during peak thru-hiking season. Group rates available for lodge and/or camping. No pets in lodge or hostel. No alcohol or drugs. *Lodging and Restaurant:* Bear Chase Brewing Co., across Blue Ridge Mountain Rd. from Bears Den Road entrance, (540) 554-8210; taproom w/ food opens at 11 a.m. daily; first-come/first-served (no reservations). Several lodging options are available; call for lodging information.

⚠ **VA-7, VA-679/Snickers Gap—East** 1.6 miles to Bluemont General Store, 33715 Snickersville Turnpike, 6:30 a.m.–7 p.m. daily, (540) 554-2054, short-term resupply, pizza by the slice, sandwiches, ice cream, pies (0.9 mile to VA-734, turn right, 0.7 mile to store).

⌖ **East** 1.7 miles to **Bluemont, VA [P.O. ZIP 20135: M-F 10-1 & 2-5, Sa 8:30-12; (540) 554-4537].** Follow VA-7 **East** 0.9 mile over Snickers Gap to the Snickersville Turnpike (VA-734) sign, turn right, and continue 0.8 mile to the post office on VA-760. *Lodging:* Nestled Inn, 18099 Raven's Rock Rd. Bluemont, (540-554-1200), 0.25 mile east from large parking lot on VA-7 to VA-601, then north to second driveway on the left. Boutique B&B featuring cottages, heated pool, hot tub, and breakfast for $250/night. Ask about camping options and thru-hiker specials. *Food:* 0.3 miles further on Raven Rocks Rd. Twin Oaks Tavern Winery, 18035 Raven Rocks Rd, (540) 554-4547 wine, sandwiches, cheese/bread, charcuterie Fri 12-7, Sa–Su 12-6pm.

West off VA-7 on VA-679 (Pine Grove Rd.) 0.9 mile to *Restaurant:* Horseshoe Curve Restaurant, 1162 Pine Grove Rd., (540) 554-8291, Tu–W 5–9, Th–Su 12–9. Excellent portions. Live music F–Sa 8 p.m. 0.6 more miles on Pine Grove Rd. to Pine Grove Restaurant, 574 Pine Grove Rd, (540) 554-5009, breakfast lunch, and dinner M–Th 6:30–2:30, Fri 6:30–8, Sa 7–8, Su 7–2:30. *Groceries:* 0.1 more miles west on Pine Grove Rd. to The Village Market 445 Pine Grove Rd, (540) 955-8742, convenience store, prepared pizzas, vegan options, breakfasts, appetizers, sandwiches, T 9–4, W–F 10–7, Sa 8–7, Su 8–3.

⌖ **West** 8.9 miles to **Berryville, VA [P.O. ZIP 22611: M-F 9-5, Sa 9-12:30; (540) 955-2667],**a small town with most services. *Groceries:* Martin's, Circle K, Dollar General, Family Dollar, Market Basket. *Lodging:* The Waypoint House B&B, 211 Church St., (540) 955-8218, pets permitted, call for details and availability, rooms about $150/night; Smithfield Farm, 568 Smithfield Ln., (540) 955-4389, shuttle provided, no pets; AirBnB, (540) 336-9631, shuttle provided, no pets, rooms about $250/night. *Other services:* Bee'Ville Wash-N-Go; Wild Hare Cidery; Tobacco, Convenience and Beer; Clarke County Library (540) 955-5144

Blackburn Trail Center—East 0.2 mile via either of two blue-blazed trails, (540) 338-9028. Owned, operated by PATC, houses trail crews, offers facilities for training, meetings, and seminars, and provides trailhead parking, information, and general services to hikers. A hiker cabin with 4 double bunks and a picnic pavilion. Eight tent pads and a tent platform are below the cabin. A group campground with tentsites, picnic tables, and a privy is on the north blue-blaze. Water from an outside spigot. A solar shower is located on the lower lawn. Donations appreciated.

David Lesser Shelter (1994)—Sleeps 6. Privy. Bear pole. A lean-to shelter with wooden deck and bench swing, picnic shelter, and 5 tent pads with stone fire rings and picnic tables. Water source is a spring located 0.25 mile downhill.

West Virginia

Miles from Springer	Miles to Next Point	Features	Services	Elev	Miles from Katahdin	M A P
1,020.1	1.5	Keys Gap, WV-9 East-0.3m to Sweet Springs Country Store East-5.5m to Stoney Brook Organic Farm & Hostel West-0.3m to Mountaineer Mini Mart and restaurant	R, P, w G, g, w H g, M, w	935'	1,177.3	
1,021.6	0.4	Powerline		920'	1,175.8	
1,022.0	2.3	Four Mile Campsite	C	1,120'	1,175.4	
1,024.3	0.2	Virginia–West Virginia State Line		1,200'	1,173.1	
1,024.5	0.5	Loudoun Heights Trail to Split Rock			1,172.9	
1,025.0	0.7	Chestnut Hill Road, WV-32	R	820'	1,172.4	
1,025.7	0.3	US-340, Shenandoah River Bridge (north end) East-20m to Frederick, MD West-0.1m to Quality Inn West-1.2m to Harpers Ferry KOA; 1.3m to Clarion Inn West-5.6m to **Charles Town, WV 25414** West-20m to Martinsburg, WV	R O, all L C, L, M all all	312'	1,171.7	PATC: Map 7
1,026.0	0.5	Appalachian Trail Conservancy side trail West-0.2m to **Harpers Ferry, WV, P.O. 25425**	 P, B, g, L, w, f	394'	1,171.4	
1,026.5	0.1	Jefferson Rock		425'	1,170.9	
1,026.6	0.1	Shenandoah Street; Harpers Ferry National Historical Park West-0.1m to The Outfitter at Harpers Ferry	R, P g, M, O, f	315'	1,170.8	
1,026.7	0.2	Potomac River, Goodloe E. Bryon Memorial Footbridge, West Virginia–Maryland State Line		250'	1,170.7	

Note: Camping and fires are prohibited 1.5 miles south of Keys Gap (WV-9) to the powerline 1.5 miles north of the gap. An established campsite (no water) is 0.4 mile north of the powerline. Camping also is prohibited in Harpers Ferry National Historical Park, which begins on the ridgetop about 0.5 mile south of the state line and extends north 3 miles to the Potomac River.

⚑ WV-9/Keys Gap—East 0.3 mile to *Groceries:* Sweet Springs Country Store, 34357 Charles Town Pike, Purcellville, VA 20132, (540) 668-7200, open M–F 4 a.m.–11 p.m., Sa 5 a.m.–11 p.m., Su 7 a.m.–11 p.m.; large grocery selection, deli, camp fuel, canisters, recharge devices, restrooms, ATM, accepts packages. Hikers are welcome to rest outside by the pond.

⌂ East 5.5 miles to Stoney Brook Organic Farm & Hostel, 37091 Charles Town Pike, Hillsboro, VA 20132, operated by the Twelve Tribes Spiritual Community, (540) 668-9067 or (571) 400-1586. Bunks in cabin, tent camping, meals, shower, laundry, dogs must be on leash, mail drops, designated smoking area. Call for details and request pick-up and drop-off from Keys Gap and Harpers Ferry.

West 0.2 mile and south 0.1 mile on WV-115 to *Groceries:* Torlone's Mini-Mart, (304) 725-0916, 20605 Charles Town Rd., Harpers Ferry, WV 25425 (short-term resupply), M 8–8, T–Th 8–9, Fri/Sa 8–10, closed Sun. Shirts and shoes required. *Restaurant:* Torlone's Pizza, wings, salads, burgers, Subs, (304) 725-0916, 20605 Charles Town Rd., Harpers Ferry, WV 25425, open M 2–8, T–Th 2–9, F 2–10 p.m., Sa noon–10, closed Sun. Very hiker-friendly restaurant attached to Mini-Mart. ATM, recharge devices, refill water containers. Be sure to read and sign the Hiker's Log Book.

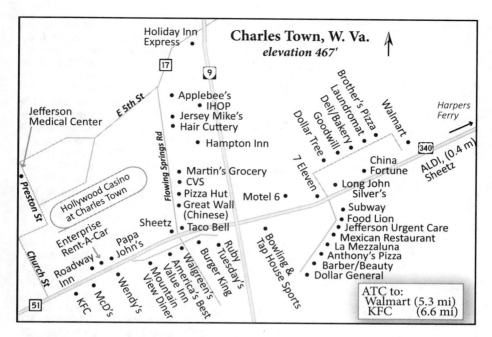

Charles Town, W. Va.
elevation 467'

Holiday Inn Express

Jefferson Medical Center

Applebee's
IHOP
Jersey Mike's
Hair Cuttery
Hampton Inn

Brother's Pizza
Laundromat
Deli/Bakery
Goodwill
Dollar Tree
Walmart

Harpers Ferry

Martin's Grocery
CVS
Pizza Hut
Great Wall (Chinese)
Taco Bell
Motel 6

7 Eleven

China Fortune
Long John Silver's
Subway
Food Lion
Jefferson Urgent Care
Mexican Restaurant
La Mezzaluna
Anthony's Pizza
Barber/Beauty
Dollar General

ALDI (0.4 m)
Sheetz

Hollywood Casino at Charles Town

Enterprise Rent-A-Car
Sheetz
Papa John's
Roadway Inn
Wendy's
McD's
KFC
Walgreen's
America's Best Value Inn
Mountain View Diner
Ruby Tuesday's
Burger King
Bowling & Tap House Sports

ATC to:
Walmart (5.3 mi)
KFC (6.6 mi)

Harpers Ferry National Historical Park—On June 30, 1944, President Franklin D. Roosevelt signed legislation designating part of the town a national monument. Gradual land acquisition in the town and surrounding ridges led to designation as a national historical park in 1963. It saw extensive Civil War action, especially before the bloody battle at nearby Antietam, MD, but is probably best known for the raid of John Brown, an abolitionist from Kansas who attempted to capture the federal arsenal here in 1859. The arsenal was to be the staging point for a slave uprising. A U.S. colonel named Robert E. Lee crushed the raid in less than 36 hours, and historians point to the event as a steppingstone to the war, which began 16 months after Brown was hanged for treason in nearby Charles Town. But, the history of Harpers Ferry is more than one event, one date, or one individual. It is multilayered, involving a diverse number of people and events that influenced the course of American history. Harpers Ferry also witnessed the first successful application of interchangeable manufacture, the arrival of the first successful American railroad, the largest surrender of federal troops during the Civil War, the education of former slaves in one of the earliest integrated schools in the United States, and the first organized civil rights movement in the country. The park's visitor center (west of town along US-340) offers plenty of parking and a free shuttle to the historic district. *Note: Hikers parking in visitors lot must register (fill out a form) at the visitor center, open every day, 9 a.m.–5 p.m.* Once parked, you can retrieve your car at any time. Entrance fee (which includes parking fees) is $20 per vehicle for parking up to 2 weeks. Today, the Park Service runs many interpretive exhibits in renovated buildings dating back to the mid-19th century. More information on the historic town, parking and free bus are available at the park's visitor center or nps.gov/hafe or by calling 304-535-6029.

US-340/Shenandoah River—*Traffic can be extremely heavy at this Trailhead, and it is neither safe nor legal to hitchhike here; local police often are nearby, watching for speeders.*

West 0.1 mile to **Lodging:** Quality Inn, 25 Union St., Bolivar, WV, (304) 535-6391, ask front desk for current rates and thru-hiker discount, usually full during holiday weekends, Wi-Fi, no pets, hot B, laundry, vending machines, hiker box; refrigerator, microwave, and coffee and tea in rooms.

West 1.2 miles to **Camping:** Harpers Ferry KOA, 343 Campground Rd, Harpers Ferry, WV 25425, (304) 535-6895, (800) 562-9497 hfinfo@racpac.com, koaharpersferry.com (short-term resupply), cabins, tent sites, and lodges; call for rates. Café, camp store with canister fuel, pool, laundry $6; leashed pets welcome $2, except Rottweilers, pit bulls, Dobermans, or any mix of those breeds.

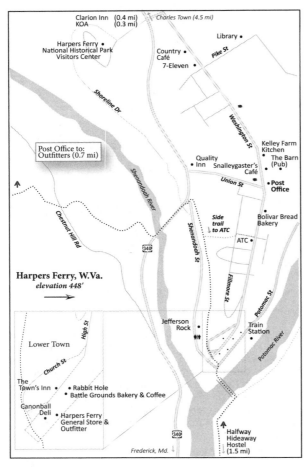

Harpers Ferry, W.Va.
elevation 448'

Overnight stay not required for $5 shower and $6 laundry. *Lodging and Restaurant:* Clarion Inn Conference Center, 4328 William L. Wilson Freeway (US-340), Harpers Ferry, WV 25425, (304) 535-6302, call for rates (20% hiker discount), microwave and refrigerator in rooms, free B, Wi-Fi with computer access, pets allowed (call for rates and conditions), laundry $2/load, indoor pool, fitness center, holds and mails guest packages, free long-term parking for guests. White Horse Tavern (attached) is an adventure-sports-themed restaurant known for its burgers, sandwiches, wings, steaks, crab cakes, bourbons, and microbrews, 10% discount for hotel guests, Open Su-Th 12–8, Fri/Sa 12–9.

West 5.6 miles to **Charles Town, WV [P.O. ZIP 25414: M–F 8:30-5, Sa 9-12:30; (304) 725-6726].** *Lodging* (see map for relative locations): Motel 6, (304) 725-1403, call for rates, smoking and nonsmoking rooms, up to 2 pets (under 50 lbs. each) can stay for free; West Ridge Inn, (304) 725-2041, prices vary, call for rates, smoking and nonsmoking rooms, coin laundry; Hampton Inn, (304) 725-2200, call for rates, nonsmoking rooms only, laundry, hot B, pets are $50/stay (or $75/stay if staying over 3 nights), indoor pool/hot tub, fitness center, business center; Holiday Inn Express, (304) 725-1330, call for rates, nonsmoking rooms only, hot B 6-9:30 M–F, 6–10 Sa/Su, laundry, fitness center, business center, outdoor pool, free shuttle service within 2 miles; Rodeway Inn and Suites, (304) 725-2081, call for rates, smoking and nonsmoking rooms available, some rooms with Jacuzzi tubs, hot B 7-10 a.m., dogs okay at $50/stay (in some rooms). *Groceries:* Super Walmart, 6 a.m.-11 p.m.; Food Lion Food Market, 7–11; several 7-Elevens, 24/7; Several Sheetz, 24/7; Aldi Supermarket, 8:30 a.m.–8 p.m. daily; Martin's, 6–11pm daily. *Other services:* Jefferson Memorial Hospital, 24/7, (304)-728-1600; Jefferson Urgent Care, M 8–7, Tu–F 8–6, Sa 8–1, Su 8–5, (304) 728-8533; WVU Medicine University Urgent Care, (304) 725-2273, M–F 8–8, Sat 8–6, Su noon–8; Charles Town Taxi (304) 901-8989; CVS Pharmacy (304) 725-3974.

West 22 miles (US-340 to WV-9) to Martinsburg, WV, with all services, including theaters, malls, as well as many restaurants.

East 22 miles to Frederick, MD, with all services, including The Trail House, an outfitter and specialty shop, 17 South Market St., (301) 694-8448, 10% thru-hiker discount. For bus service to those towns, see Area Transportation Options entry below.

Note: Hitchhiking is illegal on state-maintained roads in West Virginia. That includes US-340 and the main street through Harpers Ferry and adjacent Bolivar.

⚠️🏕 Harpers Ferry, WV [P.O. ZIP 25425: M–F 8–4, Sa 9–12; (304) 535-2479]. The post office and most services are available above the old town via the 0.2-mile blue-blazed trail to ATC headquarters (see below). The A.T. itself leads through the historic district at the bottom of the hill along the riverfronts, with museums, stores, and restaurants. In winter, many businesses in the historic district are closed or open only on weekends. The national historical park is open 7 days a week year-round (park trails close sunset to sunrise), but its visitor center closes Thanksgiving, Christmas, and New Year's Day. *Hostel & Lodging:* The Town's Inn, 175 & 179 High St., (304) 932-0677, karantownsend@gmail.com, nonsmoking property, located in historic lower town a 5-minute walk from AT, 3 minute walk from Train Station, private rooms (with reservation, pets allowed in 3 rooms, $50/night/pet fee), hostel $40 (walk-ins only, no advance reservations), microwave, fridge, Wi-Fi, and coffee/tea in all rooms, Marketplace Country Store & Self-Serve Café, hiker resupply (snacks and trail food), laundry $5, shuttles $1.50/mile roundtrip (email to check availability), A.T. Community supporter; Halfway Hideaway Hostel, 1312 Washington St., (276) 201-5739, $35 and $45 bunks, access to refrigerator, microwave, toaster oven, shower, and laundry on premises; LightHorse Inn (B&B) and Harpers Ferry Vacation Rentals (dog-friendly), (877) 468-4236, 10% hiker discount, call for availability and rates. Good Town-Trail Info available at historicharpersferry.com. *Groceries:* Harpers Ferry General Store & Outfitter 161 Potomac Street (short-term resupply, including freeze-dried food and hiker favorites), (304) 535-2087; 7-Eleven 1655 W. Washington (snacks, short-term resupply), 1 mile **west** of ATC; supermarkets and Walmart (long-term resupply) in Charles Town, 5 miles **west**. *Restaurants:* **West** of ATC: 0.1 mile, Bolivar Bread Bakery, 914 Washington St., (304) 535-8108, artisan breads, coffee, local snacks, W–F 8–4, Sa–Su 8–5; 0.3 mile, Kelley Farm Kitchen, 100% vegan, 1112 Washington St., (304) 535-9976, W 4-8, Th–Sa 11–4 & 5-8, Su 12–4; Snalleygaster's Café, 1102 Washington St., (304) 707-6129, selection of coffee, wine, beer, and snacks, F–M 9–9, Th–4–9; 1 mile, Country Café, 1723 W. Washington St. (304) 535-2327, B/L, W–F 8:30–3, Sa/Su 7:30–3. **East** of ATC 0.5 mile in lower town: Cannonball Deli, 125-129 Potomac St. (304) 535-1762, 10% hiker discounts, 11–5 daily (winter, weather dependent), A.T. Community supporter; Battle Grounds Bakery & Coffee, 180 High St., (304) 535-8583 M-F 8-5, Sa/Su 7:30-5; Plus many others *Outfitter:* Harpers Ferry General Store & Outfitter 161 Potomac Street (short-term resupply, including freeze-dried food and hiker favorites), (304) 535-2087, open M-Th 10-5, F-Su 10-6 full-service outfitter (gear, first aid, footwear), shuttle referrals, A.T. Community supporter. *Internet access:* Bolivar-Harpers Ferry Public Library, (304) 535-2301, 151 Polk St., M–W 9:30–5:30, Th 8:30–7, F 9:30–5:30, Sa 9:30–3:30; ATC headquarters (see details below). *Other services:* Banks with ATMs; dental care; Chiropractic and therapeutic massage near Harpers Ferry and Turners Gap, Dr. Jenny Foster, (also a hiker) call/text (240) 344-0066 ahead to schedule trailside treatment or possible pick-up from Harpers Ferry, Turners Gap, Rte. 40 or Rte. 17; bicycle rental and supplies at The Outfitter at Harpers Ferry, (304) 535-2087 (see additional info above; River Riders Family Adventure Resort, (304) 535-2663, call for current rates for camping, rafting, tubing, ziplining, and e-biking, or contact riverriders.com, ask about shuttle service. Harpers Ferry Outfitters, for information and reservations, contact outfitter1996@yahoo.com

Appalachian Trail Conservancy (ATC)—Reached via 0.2-mile blue-blazed trail 0.3 mile north of the junction of US-340 and Shenandoah Street, before northbounders reach the historic section of Harpers Ferry; at the corner of Washington Street and Storer College Place. Th–M 9–5, T/W 10–4; closed on some major holidays. The Visitor Center is manned only by volunteers on Tuesday and Wednesdays. Depending on volunteer availability, there may be a slight chance that the center could be closed on one of those days. Call (304) 535-6331, or check appalachiantrail.org/our-work/about-us/contact-us.

The ATC was formed in 1925 by private citizens to make the dream of an Appalachian Trail a reality. After the initial Trail route was pieced together in 1937 (much of it on roads and across private land), ATC continued to work to identify better routes for the Trail and worked with Congress, the National Park Service, the U.S. Forest Service, states, and others to ensure a continuously protected corridor. Today, ATC is the primary organization responsible for the stewardship of the footpath and 250,000 acres of public land surrounding it. Working with more than 6,000 volunteers in four ATC-run Trail crews and 31 affiliated local clubs and multiple public agencies, ATC leads the efforts to maintain and improve the footpath and protect the natural and cultural resources of the Trail corridor, engage communities along the A.T. to support it, and guard against encroachments.

Much of the behind-the-scenes headquarters work that continues to make the A.T. experience possible takes place out of sight in offices upstairs and the connected annex, although most of the staff is working remotely from homes throughout the East. The single largest source of ATC's funding is individual membership dues and small contributions. If you're not already an ATC member, consider joining here to help support continued protection of the Trail.

A.T. exhibits include a 10-foot-long raised-relief map of the A.T. Volunteers or staffer Dave Tarasevich (Pop Tart of '02) can answer your Trail questions. All hikers are encouraged to stop at ATC headquarters to sign the register. Those hiking the entire Trail, whether in sections or at once, are photographed for an official registry that allows ATC to partially track the number and demographics of 2,000-miler hopefuls year to year.

Visit appalachiantrail.org for more details. Frost-free faucet is on west (Storer College Place) side of building. Benches and picnic tables are in the side-yard tribute garden. Phone, Wi-Fi, and Internet access for hikers. Ask for ATC's often-updated "Guide to Harpers Ferry Hiker Services," with more details on area services. Driving directions are available at appalachiantrail.org.

Jefferson Rock—White blazes take you past this Harpers Ferry viewpoint that overlooks the confluence of the Potomac and Shenandoah rivers. It was named in honor of Thomas Jefferson, who was inspired by the beautiful view in 1783. Several large shale slabs originally rested naturally but not securely atop each other. "Jefferson Rock" now rests securely on a set of short pillars erected in the 1850s.

Area Transportation Options—*Vehicle rental:* Enterprise, (304) 724-6605 (be sure to key through to directly access the branch), will pick up at ATC headquarters and take you to Charles Town branch next to Rodeway Inn; allow 1-hour advance notice; enter code: W15509 to get ATC discount. *Bus service:* EPTA bus to Charles Town (Walmart) and Martinsburg operates M–F; flag the bus from the ATC or anywhere along the main Washington/High St. (stand at least 200 feet from the crest of the hill). The maximum fare is $3.50 one-way, $5 all-day pass, exact change required. Tickets and additional information at eptawv.com. No dogs; packs OK unless driver believes one may be suspicious. Times subject to change. *Shuttles:* Trailboss A.T. Shuttles, (703) 967-2226, ask about lodging options; Nina's Shuttle Service, (540) 398-9164, ninashuttles@yahoo.com, Waynesboro, PA, to Waynesboro, VA, all major airports and train stations; Mark "Strings" Cusic, (304) 433-0028, pet-friendly, Waynesboro, VA, to Duncannon, PA; Rachel Ringer (304) 283-7246, rachelringer6@gmail.com, $25 to airports, $30 Front Royal to Harpers Ferry, otherwise tips/donations; Dan Perkins, (304) 283-5174, shuttles@hykeroo.com, hykeroo.com, pet-friendly, Front Royal, VA, to Pen-Mar Park, MD/PA; Bill (240) 500-0700 out of Hagerstown, MD, covers Duncannon, PA to Front Royal, VA; River and Trail Outfitters, (301) 834-9950, 75 miles north and south of Harpers Ferry; Scott & Marie Wheaton, (540) 514-9385, based in Bluemont, VA, pet-friendly. *Trains to Washington*—Amtrak, (800) USA-RAIL, amtrak.com: Train No. 30 (Capitol Limited) departs Harpers Ferry at 11:31 a.m., 7 days a week and arrives at DC's Union Station at 1:05 p.m. Note that this train frequently runs late coming from Chicago; check status online. Train No. 29 is scheduled to leave DC daily at 4:05 p.m., arriving in Harpers Ferry at 5:16 p.m. Coach fares average $21 one way. Book early for best prices. Fares and schedules are subject to change. *The Harpers Ferry station is not staffed.* Tickets **must** be purchased in advance at amtrak.com. Backpacks allowed. A roll-on service for bicycles is available on this route for $20. Maryland Rail Commuter Service (MARC), (301) 834-8360; mtamaryland.com. Three scheduled commuter trains on the Brunswick line leave Harpers Ferry for DC on weekdays, departing at 5:27 a.m., 5:54, and 6:53, arriving at Union Station at 7:09, 7:35, and 8:32 a.m. Three trains leave DC Union Station for Harpers Ferry on weekdays, departing at 4:25, 5:40, and 6:20 p.m., and arrive at 5:49, 7:09, and 7:40 p.m. One-way fares are $13 (kiosk) and $18 purchased on board (cash only, no bills larger than $20); seats are not reserved. More trains are available at the Brunswick, MD, station (8 miles east).

Maryland

Miles from Springer	Miles to Next Point	Features	Services	Elev	Miles from Katahdin	M A P
1,026.7	0.2	Potomac River, Goodloe E. Bryon Memorial Footbridge, West Virginia–Maryland State Line		250'	1,170.7	
1,026.9	1.1	C&O Canal Towpath mp 60.2 (A.T. west jct.) *West–2.7m to C&O Huckleberry Hill Campsite*	C, w	290'	1,170.5	
1,028.0	1.5	US-340, Sandy Hook Bridge (overhead)	R	290'	1,169.4	
1,029.5	0.1	C&O Canal Towpath mp 58 (A.T. east jct.), Lockhouse 38		290'	1,167.9	
1,029.6	0.2	Keep Tryst Road; railroad tracks *West 1.1m to Cross Trails Hostel & CG* *East–2.5m to* **Brunswick, MD, P.O. 21716**	R, P H, C g, M, L	320'	1,167.8	
1,029.8	0.2	US-340: *underpass*	R	400'	1,167.6	
1,030.0	0.9	Weverton Road	R, P	420'	1,167.4	
1,030.9	2.1	Trail to Weverton Cliffs: *Potomac River view, Congressman Goodloe E. Bryon plaque*		780'	1,166.5	
1,033.0	2.0	**Ed Garvey Shelter** *(E–0.1m S; 0.5m spring), 16.1mS; 4.5mN*	S, C, w	1,100'	1,164.4	
1,035.0	0.3	Brownsville Gap: *dirt road*		1,140'	1,162.4	
1,035.3	1.4	Glenn R. Caveney Memorial Plaque		1,150'	1,162.1	
1,036.7	0.4	Crampton Gap, Gathland State Park, Gapland Road, MD-572: *frost-free faucet* *West–0.4m to Maple Tree Campground*	R, P, w C, g, f	950'	1,160.7	
1,037.1	2.6	**Crampton Gap Shelter** *(E–0.3m), 4.5mS; 5.5mN*	S, C, w	1,000'	1,160.3	
1,039.7	0.6	Trail to Bear Spring Cabin *(locked) (W–0.5m spring)*	w	1,480'	1,157.7	
1,040.3	0.2	White Rocks Cliff: *view*		1,500'	1,157.1	
1,040.5	1.1	Lamb's Knoll: *antenna tower*		1,600'	1,156.9	
1,041.6	0.5	Tower Road	R	1,300'	1,155.8	
1,042.1	0.5	**Rocky Run Shelters** *(W–0.2m), 5.5mS; 7.8mN*	S, C, w	970'	1,155.3	
1,042.6	0.5	High-tension powerline clearing		950'	1,154.8	
1,043.1	0.5	Reno Monument Road, Fox Gap *East–2m to* South Mountain Creamery	R, P M	910'	1,154.3	
1,043.6	0.3	Powerline		940'	1,153.8	
1,043.9	0.2	Dahlgren Backpacker Campground	C, sh, w	980'	1,153.5	
1,044.1	1.4	Turners Gap, US Alt. 40 *West–2.4m to* **Boonsboro, MD, P.O. 21713** *West–3.8m to Weis Supermarket*	R, P g, M, D, V, cl G	1,000'	1,153.3	
1,045.5	0.2	Monument Road	R	1,350'	1,151.9	
1,045.7	0.4	Washington Monument Road: *frost-free faucet*	R, P, w	1,400'	1,151.7	
1,046.1	2.1	Washington Monument: *view*	R, P	1,500'	1,151.3	
1,048.2	0.3	Boonsboro Mountain Road	R, P	1,300'	1,149.2	
1,048.5	0.5	Bartman Hill Trail to Greenbrier State Park (W–0.6m)	C, sh, w	1,380'	1,148.9	
1,049.0	0.6	I-70 footbridge *(north end)*, US-40, *blue-blaze to Greenbrier State Park (W–1.4m)*	R, P, C, sh, w	1,200'	1,148.4	
1,049.6	1.6	**Pine Knob Shelter** *(W–0.1m), 7.8mS; 8.3mN*	S, C, w	1,360'	1,147.8	

PATC: Map 5-6

Miles from Springer	Miles to Next Point	Features	Services	Elev	Miles from Katahdin	M A P
1,051.2	1.0	Trail to Annapolis Rock *(W–0.2m C, 0.4m spring)*	C, w	1,820'	1,146.2	
1,052.2	0.6	Black Rock Cliffs		1,800'	1,145.2	
1,052.8	4.8	Pogo Memorial Campsite *(east)*, spring *(W–30 yds.)* on Thurston Griggs Trail *(W–0.9m parking)*	C, w	1,500'	1,144.6	
1,057.6	0.2	MD-17, Wolfsville Road *West–1.8m to* shopping center *West–2m to* **Smithsburg, MD, P.O. 21783** *West–2.7m to* **Cavetown, MD, P.O. 22509;** supermarket and restaurants	R, P G, D, V G, M, D, cl G, M, f	1,400'	1,139.8	
1,057.8	0.2	**Ensign Cowall Shelter**, 8.3mS; 5.1mN	S, C, w	1,430'	1,139.6	
1,058.0	1.1	Powerline		1,440"	1,139.4	
1,059.1	1.2	MD-77, Foxville Road	R	1,450'	1,138.3	
1,060.3	0.6	Spring	w	1,300'	1,137.1	
1,060.9	0.8	Warner Gap Road: *two board bridges across stream*	R, P, w	1,150'	1,136.5	
1,061.7	1.0	Raven Rock Hollow, MD-491: *rock-hop stream*	R, w	1,190'	1,135.7	
1,062.7	1.8	**Raven Rock Shelter** *(E–0.1m spring) (W–0.2m S)*, 5.1mS; 9.8mN	S, C, w	1,480'	1,134.7	
1,064.5	2.9	Trail to High Rock: *view*	R, P	1,950'	1,132.9	
1,067.4	0.2	Pen Mar County Park: *picnic area* *East 1 block to* Zero Day Stay Hostel *East–1.4m to* **Cascade, MD, P.O. 21719** *West–1.8m to* **Rouzerville, PA, P.O. 17250**	R, P, w H G, M, sh, f G, L, M, D, cl, f	1,300'	1,130.0	
1,067.6	0.1	Mason–Dixon Line; Maryland–Pennsylvania State Line	R	1,250'	1,129.8	

PATC: Map 5-6

This section boasts easy terrain, the C & O Canal towpath along the Potomac River, a free on-trail hot-water shower, Civil War history, the War Correspondents Monument, the first monument to George Washington, and the Mason-Dixon line.

Potomac Appalachian Trail Club—The PATC maintains the 40.9 miles of A.T. in Maryland. Correspondence should be sent to PATC, 118 Park St. SE, Vienna, VA 22180; (703) 242-0315; patc.net.

Note: Overnight camping in Maryland is allowed only at designated campsites: Ed Garvey Shelter, Crampton Gap Shelter, Rocky Run Shelters, Dahlgren Back Pack Campground, Pine Knob Shelter, Annapolis Rocks, Pogo Memorial Campsite, Ensign Cowall Shelter, and Raven Rocks Shelter. All shelters in Maryland have bear boxes, and all of the campsites will have bear boxes in 2025. Dogs must be leashed. Please obey camping regulations in this heavily used section. Alcoholic beverages are prohibited on all Appalachian Trail lands in Maryland. Emergency Assistance dial 911. For 24 hr. assistance, or to report emergencies, violations and illegalities to Park Watch, call (800) 825-7275, or Natural Resources Police: (410) 260-8888.

C&O Canal Towpath—The southernmost 2.8 miles of the Trail in Maryland follow this path from which until 1924 mules towed barges, between what's left of the canal on one side and the Potomac River on the other. Stretching 185 miles from Washington, D.C., to Cumberland, MD, it was rescued from highway development by a 1954 protest hike led by Supreme Court Justice William O. Douglas, an A.T. 2,000-miler. Now, it is part of a national historical park, accessible to both hikers and bicyclists. Blazes are scarce, but the points at which the Trail enters and leaves it are hard to miss. The Maryland state line is the southern shore of the Potomac.

Keep Tryst Road—**West** 1.1 mile (left on Sandy Hook Road) to **Hostel:** Cross Trails Hostel & Campground, 19123 Sandy Hook Rd., Knoxville, MD 21758; info@xtrailshostel.org, call or text Peak Freak (443) 221-8382, bunks, separate men's & women's dorms, private rooms. Amenities include Wi-Fi, large fully equipped kitchen, comfortable indoor and outdoor lounge areas, great

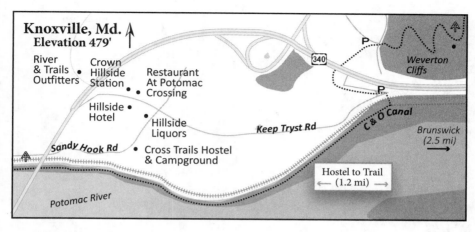

Knoxville, Md.
Elevation 479'

River & Trails Outfitters
Crown Hillside Station
Restaurant At Potomac Crossing
Hillside Hotel
Hillside Liquors
Sandy Hook Rd
Cross Trails Hostel & Campground
Keep Tryst Rd
C&O Canal
Weverton Cliffs
340
Brunswick (2.5 mi) →
Hostel to Trail ← (1.2 mi) →
Potomac River

views of the Potomac River, good times, and great vibes. Laundry a la carte, detergent included. Hammock & tent spots with picnic tables, fire pits, outdoor showers, toilet, charging stations, and enclosed pavilion. Pets are welcome, but only outside. Cash & credit cards accepted. Within walking distance of the Hillside Crown Station. Small resupply available. Free shuttle may be available upon request from mile 1029.3, right after diverging from the C & O Canal, where the trail crosses Keep Tryst Road. *Lodging:* Hillside Hotel, 19105 Keep Tryst Rd., Knoxville, MD 21758, (301) 660-3580, call for rates, continental B (6–9 a.m.), refrigerator, microwave, no pets or smoking, credit cards only. Minimum age for check-in is 21, with photo ID and credit card. *Groceries:* Crown Hillside Station, (301) 969-5013, deli hot food, pizza, ice cream, hot wings, ATM, M–F 6 a.m.–9 p.m., Sa 7–9, Su 8–8; Hillside Liquors, (301) 834-7971; both short-term resupply. *Restaurant*: The Restaurant at Potomac Crossing. *Other services:* River and Trails Outfitters, 604 Valley Rd., Knoxville, MD 21758, (301) 834-9950, rivertrail.com; zipline; canoe, kayak, tube, and bike rentals, shuttles for C&O Canal, A.T., Potomac and Shenandoah rivers. Brunswick Family Campground; cabins, tent and RV sites.

⚑ **East** 2.5 mile to **Brunswick, MD [P.O. ZIP 21716: M–F 8–4:30, Sa 9–12; (301) 434-9944]**via US-340 and MD-478 at Knoxville exit or stay on the C&O towpath to milepoint 55. *Lodging:* Holiday Inn Express, (301) 969-8020; Travel Lodge, (240) 772-9099. *Groceries:* Dollar General, (301) 969-2630; Family Dollar, (301) 969-7008; Dollar Tree, (301) 969-7006; Walgreens Pharmacy, (301) 834-8100; Weis Supermart & Pharmacy, (301) 834-4800, on MD-17 just east of US-340 junction (long-term resupply); Sheetz, (301) 834-5456; Corner Store, (301) 969-4593. *Restaurants:* McDonald's, (301) 834-5201; Papa John's, (301) 679-7272; Asia Star, (301) 676-1362; Smoketown Brewing Station, (301) 834-4828; Beans in the Belfry, (301) 834-7178; Potomac Street Grill, (301) 969-0548; Penny's Diner (24-hour), (240) 772-9099; The Hive Bakeshop, (301) 969-6506; King's Pizza, (301) 834-9999; Roy Rogers, (301) 834-8022 (Soulder Rd.); Subway, (301) 834-7940; Domino's, (301) 834-3000; Wing N Pizza Shack, (301) 834-5555; New China, (301) 834-8888; Burger King, (301) 394-2493; Dunkin'/Baskin Robbins; Adeles Tex Mex, (301) 834-3404; Boxcar Burgers, beer and ice cream, (301) 834-2612. *Internet access:* library, 915 N. Maple Ave., (301) 600-7250, open M–Th 10-8, F–Sa 10–5, closed Su. *Other services:* MARC Station,(866) 743-3682; Brunswick Sports & Apparel, (301) 834-9207; Ace Hardware, (301) 969-0107; 84 Lumber, (301) 834-8422; PNC bank with 24-hour ATM; Dr. Benjamin Weiser, DDS, (301) 834-6700; Brunswick Heritage Museum, (301) 834-7100 (local history, model railroad); Missing Sock (laundromat), (304) 876-0088; Brunswick Crossing Animal Hospital, (301) 810-3456; American Legion, (301) 834-8121; barber shop, (301) 834-5420; and municipal swimming pool, (301) 834-7567.

Ed Garvey Shelter (2001)—Sleeps 12. Composting privy. Bear pole, bear box. Active bear activity has been reported here. Two tentsites north and three tentsites south of shelter. An intermittent spring is 0.1 mile down the trail to the existing spring. The main water source is found at the end of a 0.5-mile, steep side trail in front of the shelter.

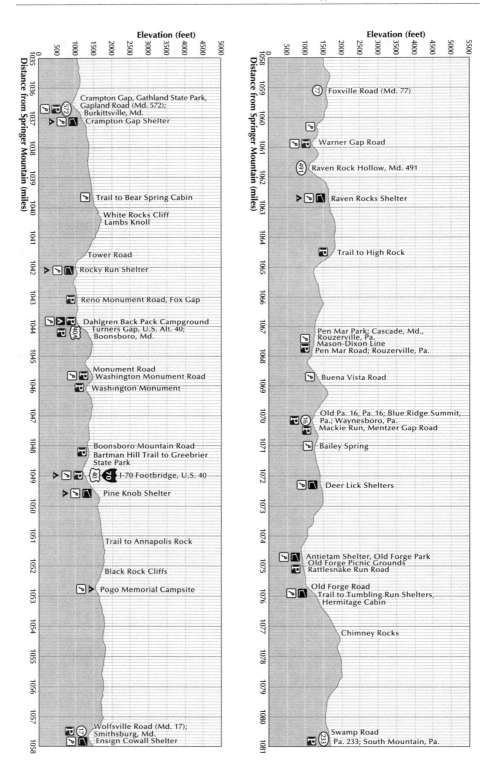

Left Panel

Elevation (feet)

Distance from Springer Mountain (miles)

- Crampton Gap, Gathland State Park, Gapland Road (Md. 572); Burkittsville, Md.
- Crampton Gap Shelter
- Trail to Bear Spring Cabin
- White Rocks Cliff Lambs Knoll
- Tower Road
- Rocky Run Shelter
- Reno Monument Road, Fox Gap
- Dahlgren Back Pack Campground
- Turners Gap, U.S. Alt. 40; Boonsboro, Md.
- Monument Road
- Washington Monument Road
- Washington Monument
- Boonsboro Mountain Road
- Bartman Hill Trail to Greebrier State Park
- I-70 Footbridge, U.S. 40
- Pine Knob Shelter
- Trail to Annapolis Rock
- Black Rock Cliffs
- Pogo Memorial Campsite
- Wolfsville Road (Md. 17); Smithsburg, Md.
- Ensign Cowall Shelter

Right Panel

Elevation (feet)

Distance from Springer Mountain (miles)

- Foxville Road (Md. 77)
- Warner Gap Road
- Raven Rock Hollow, Md. 491
- Raven Rocks Shelter
- Trail to High Rock
- Pen Mar Park; Cascade, Md., Rouzerville, Pa.
- Mason-Dixon Line
- Pen Mar Road; Rouzerville, Pa.
- Buena Vista Road
- Old Pa. 16, Pa. 16; Blue Ridge Summit, Pa.; Waynesboro, Pa.
- Mackie Run, Mentzer Gap Road
- Bailey Spring
- Deer Lick Shelters
- Antietam Shelter, Old Forge Park
- Old Forge Picnic Grounds
- Rattlesnake Run Road
- Old Forge Road
- Trail to Tumbling Run Shelters, Hermitage Cabin
- Chimney Rocks
- Swamp Road
- Pa. 233; South Mountain, Pa.

Gathland State Park—Located in Crampton Gap, the state-run facility has water (frost-free faucet), restroom (with electrical outlet and flush toilets), covered picnic pavilion, parking. No camping. Two museums—Civil War and War Correspondents, along with Gath's Tomb—are open 9–5 weekends May–Sep. The War Correspondents Monument is the only one of its kind. Constructed in 1896, it stands 50 feet high, 40 feet broad, with plaques about Battle of South Mountain history. Southbounders may want to pick up water here before heading to Ed Garvey Shelter. Northbounders might want to pick up water here, as the spring to Crampton Gap Shelter may be dry in the summer.

⚠ Gapland Road—**West** 0.4 mile on Gapland Rd., right on Townsend Rd. to *Camping:* Maple Tree Campground, 20716 Townsend Rd., Gapland, MD 21779, (301) 432-5585, thetreehousecamp.com; tentsites, treehouses, cottages; Hobbit House, ask for rates. All with picnic table, fire ring, grill. Short-term resupply; white gas, canisters; mail drops accepted; dogs on leashes okay, no extra fee.

Crampton Gap Shelter (built by CCC, 1941)—Sleeps 6. Pit privy, bear box, bear pole, deck with cooking table. Water source is an intermittent spring 0.1 mile south on the A.T. that may go dry in June. Northbounders may want to get water from faucet at Gathland State Park, 0.25 mile south on the A.T.

Rocky Run Shelters (CCC-1941, sleeps 6; PATC-2008. Sleeps 16)—Older shelter with new 2024 metal roof is on blue-blaze to piped spring just south of the new shelter. Composting privy at new shelter; pit privy at old. Bear Box and Bear pole. Newly renovated tent platforms by the Maryland Conservation Corp. and benches on the ridgeline. Hammock sites.

Reno Monument in Fox Gap marks the spot where Union Maj. Gen. Jesse Lee Reno and Confederate Gen. Samuel Garland, Jr., were wounded mortally in the Battle of South Mountain, antecedent to the bloody Battle at Antietam a few miles to the west. (General Robert E. Lee issued Special Order 191 in nearby Frederick before Antietam, a copy of which was subsequently lost and recovered by Union forces, providing valuable information.) Near the monument is the Gen. Garland Trail that leads to the stunning NC South Mountain monument; across the road is the Stonewall Regiments Monument, erected by the 17th Michigan Volunteer Infantry Regiment. **East** 2 miles to South Mountain Creamery, 8305 Bolivar Rd., (301) 371-8665, ice cream, fresh all-natural dairy products.

Dahlgren Backpack Campground—Completely renovated in 2020, with new sinks, toilets, showers, and a new roof. Bathhouse has hot showers and flush toilets. Operated by the state at no charge, the bathhouse with electrical outlets (open Apr–Oct) faces campsites with gravel tentpads, fire rings, bear box and two bear poles, hammock sites, and a utility sink (behind building). A frost-free faucet is about 100 yards up the gravel road toward the inn.

⚠ US-40-A/Turners Gap. The South Mountain Inn is closed. The state of Maryland purchased the property in 2023 and plans to convert it to a visitor center. Across the highway is the Gothic, stone Dahlgren Chapel (yes, related to the Dahlgren cannon of Civil War fame). *Other services:* chiropractic and therapeutic massage, Dr. Jenny Foster, (240) 344-0066, can pick up along the Maryland A.T., schedule permitting.

⌂ West 2.4 miles to **Boonsboro, MD [P.O. ZIP 21713: M-F 9-1 & 2-5, Sa 9-12; (301) 432-6861].** *Groceries:* Cronise Market Place (short-term resupply), (301) 432-7377, M–Sa 9–6, Su 10–6; My MiniMart & Diner, (301) 432-4646, short-term resupply, M–Tu 8–7, W 8–6, Th 8–8, F 8 a.m.–9 p.m., Sa 9 a.m.–10 p.m., Su 8–8. *Restaurants:* Subway, (301) 432-0100; Mountainside Deli, (301) 432-4646; Jeovanni's Pizza, (240) 769-0021; Potomac Street Creamery, (301) 432-5242, ice-cream shop; Stone Werks Coffee & Sweets, (678) 749-2158; Rasco N.Y. Pizza, (301) 799-5080, delivers to Trail. The Admiral (240) 998-6068. *Internet access:* library, (301) 432-5723, 401 Potomac St., has computers and Wi-Fi, M 10:30–7, Tu 12:30–9, W–Th 10:30–7, F 10:30–6, Sa 10:15–2; Turn the Page Bookstore Café, (301) 432-4588, with A.T. books and maps and espresso coffee bar. *Other services:* South Mountain Family Practice, (301) 432-0623; Marcy's Laundry, (301) 491-5849, 5:30 a.m–10 p.m. daily; H&H Truist Bank, (301) 432-5504; Middletown Valley Bank, (301) 432-3925; Pete's barber shop, (301) 432-6834; veterinary hospital, (301) 432-7120; Pleasant Valley Primary Care, (301) 799-1098; Spring Ridge Chiropractic, (301) 620-8566. Ace Hardware(799) 7070.

West 3.8 miles to **Groceries:** Weis Supermarket & Pharmacy (long-term resupply), (301) 432-3950; ACT Minmart, (301) 432-6434; Dollar General, (240) 816-0405, short-term resupply. **Restaurants:** Domino's(301) 349-3300; China Ocean, (301) 432-8588, W–Su 11–9. **Other services:** M&T Bank, (301) 432-2273; Dr. Malik Zafar, MD, (301) 432-8470; South Mountain Dental, (301) 432-4322; Boonsboro Family Dentistry & Ortho, (301) 432-6201; Body Sense Physical Therapy, (301) 432-8585; American Legion, (301) 432-5695.

East 6.8 miles to **Middletown, MD [P.O. ZIP 21769: M–F 9-1 & 2-5, Sa 9-12; (301) 371-6880].** **Groceries:** Safeway, (301) 371-3126; Fountaindale Exxon, (301) 371-9961, short-term resupply; High's, (301) 371-9961, short-term resupply. **Restaurants:** Dempsey's Grill, (301) 371-7400; The Main Cup, (301) 371-4433; Subway, (301) 371-4455; Dunkin'/Baskin-Robbins, (240) 490-8681; Cinco De Mayo Mexican, (240) 870-2131; Fratelli's Italian & Seafood, (301) 371-4000; Black Hog BBQ, (240) 490-8147; Aleko's Village Café, (301) 371-3500; Domino's Pizza, (301) 371-5801; Verona Pizza, (301) 371-7777; Tapia's on Main, (240) 490-8461; Deb's Artisan Bakehouse, (240) 409-9171, W–Sa 9:30–2; Starbucks, (301) 371-3126. **Internet access:** Library, 101 Prospect St., (301) 600-7560, M–Th 10–8, F–Sa 10–5. **Other services:** Mid-Town Laundromat, 117 Washington St, (301) 788-7585, M–Su 6–9; (2) Middle Valley Banks, (301) 371-6700, (301) 371-6060; Truist Bank, (301) 371-8860; SunTrust ATM, (800) 786-8787; PNC Bank ATM, (888) 762-2265; Middletown Valley Family Medicine, (301) 371-9000; Middletown Valley Dentistry, (301) 293-6828; CVS, (301) 371-4100; Valley Veterinarian, (301) 371-7700; Robinwood Dental Ctr., (240) 313-9660; Kane Paul, DDS, (301) 293-6828; Weeden Brett, DDS, (301) 293-6828; Goodwill, (240) 490-8019.

Washington Monument State Park—A state park built around the first monument to George Washington. The bottle-shaped structure is more modest than the one in Washington, but impressive for small-town Marylanders in 1827. When open, the observation deck on top provides views of the surrounding countryside. South of the monument, on the A.T., are picnic shelters and restroom (with electrical outlets) near the museum. Air-conditioned museum is usually open Sa–Su Jun–Aug. No camping permitted in the park. Frost-free faucet on trail above main parking lot. Overnight parking permitted in parking lot after registration at kiosk.

US-40/Greenbrier State Park—North of the I-70 footbridge, the A.T. crosses US-40. **West** 0.4 mile to the park entrance. **Note:** Park only in marked spots; citations will be issued for violations. If US-40 road spots are full, park inside Greenbrier State Park.

West 1.4 miles to **Camping:** Greenbrier State Park, (301) 791-4767, open Apr–Oct, pets on leash allowed on some sites. Visitor center, restroom with showers, concession stand, paddle-boat rental and swimming in Greenbrier Lake. Tentsites with hot showers $27.75. Reservations recommended on the weekends; two-night minimum until Labor Day. Walk-in hikers may be allowed a one-night stay if a site is available; day-use-only fee may apply; access via Bartman Hill Trail. **Other services:** Cow's Cones, 21614 National Pike, Boonsboro, MD 21713, (240) 285-2846, 1 mile west of park entrance on US-40 (1.4 mile from US-40 A.T. parking lot), soft-serve, RB floats, etc.

East 3.4 miles to **Myersville, MD [P.O. ZIP 21773: M–F 8:30-1 & 2-5, Sa 8:30-12; (301) 293-1180.]** **Groceries:** Short-term resupply: Martin's Farm Market, (301) 293-8454, M–F 8–6, Sa 8–5; Exxon, (301) 293-2178; Sunoco, (301) 293-2818; Crown, (301) 293-1622. **Restaurants:** JB Seafood, (301) 293-2722; McDonald's, (301) 293-3535, Burger King, (301) 293-3460; Subway, (301) 508-7097. **Internet access outside:** Library, 8 Harp Pl., (301) 600-7560, M–W 10–6, Tu–Th 10–8, Sa 10–5, closed F & Su. **Other services:** First United Bank, (301) 293-2390; Middletown Valley Bank, (301) 293-3400; Frederick Health Medical Primary Care, (240) 215-6310.

Pine Knob Shelter (1939)—Sleeps 5. Pit privy. Bear box & Bear pole. Shelter is located on a blue-blazed trail. Tent and hammock sites. Water source is a piped spring on north side of the shelter.

Annapolis Rock Campsite—13 tentsites and two composting privies at this popular area; caretaker on site. Tentsites are near an outstanding overlook popular with climbers. Bear box & Bear pole. No fires. Spring location is marked.

Pogo Memorial Campsite—The campsite is immediately east of the Trail; 5 individual tentsites (continuing improvements by the Maryland Conservation Corps), 2 group sites, composting privy new in 2022, Bear box & bear pole, and two nearby springs: one on the A.T., the other 30 yards on the blue-blazed Thurston Griggs Trail to the west.

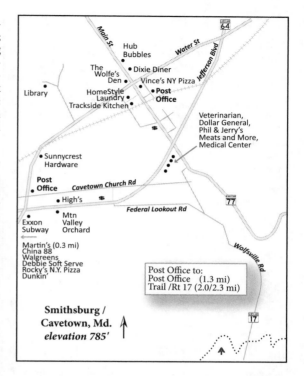

Smithsburg / Cavetown, Md.
elevation 785'

MD-17/Wolfsville Road—West 1.7 miles on Wolfsville Road and then left 0.1 mile on MD-64 to a small shopping center. *Groceries:* Phil & Jerry's Meats & More (short-term resupply), (301) 824-3750, M–Th 8–6, F–Sa 8–8; Dollar General Store, (240) 734-0530. *Other services:* veterinary clinic, (301) 416-0888; Meritus Pediatric & Adult Medicine, (301) 824-3343; pharmacy, (301) 824-3900; First United Bank & Trust, (301) 824-3838.

West 2.0 miles via Wolfsville Road and MD-77 to **Smithsburg, MD [P.O. ZIP 21783: M–F 8:30-1 & 2-4:30, Sa 8:30-12; (301) 824-2828].** *Restaurants:* Vince's New York Pizza, (301) 824-3939; Dixie Diner, (301) 824-5224, Tu–F 7–8, Sa–Su 7–2, closed M; The Wolfe's Den Bar & Grill, (301) 824-3911, L/D, Wi-Fi; Trackside Kitchen, (240) 469-9611. *Internet access:* library, (301) 824-7722, 66 W. Water St., computers and Wi-Fi, Tu 12:30–9, M, W, Th–F 10:30–7, Sa 10–2. *Other services:* Hub Bubbles Laundry, 10 Main St., open daily 6–11; Home Style Laundry, 5 W. Moose Ln., (301) 824-3533; Dr. Brian Bonham, MD, (301) 824-3343; Dr. Thomas Mussear, DDS, (301) 824-2080.

West 1.7 miles via Wolfsville Road and south on MD-64 1.0 mile to **Cavetown, MD [P.O. ZIP 21720: M–F 12:30-4:30, Sa 8:15-11:15; (301) 824-5230].** *Groceries:* Martin's, (301) 824-5160; short-term resupply: Mountain Valley Orchard, (301) 824-2089; High's, (3010 824-3930; and Exxon/AC&T, (301) 824-2646. *Restaurants:* China 88, (301) 824-7300; Subway, (301) 824-3826; Debbie's Soft Serve, (301) 824-4051; Rocky's New York Pizza, (301) 824-2065, will deliver to Trail; Domino's, (240) 734-1030; Dunkin', (301) 836-5418. *Other services:* Walgreens Pharmacy, (301) 824-2211; Smithsburg Pharmacy, (301) 824-1111; Sunnycrest Farm Store (hardware), (240) 734-1102, M–F 7–6, Sa 7–3, fuel, camping supplies; Bulldog Federal Credit Union, (301) 797-6318; Smithsburg Family Dentistry, (301) 824-5111; Lewis Orchard and Farm Market.

Ensign Cowall Shelter (1999; deck added 2021)—Sleeps 8. New composting privy (2023). Five tent pads, hammock sites, picnic table, fire ring with grill, bear box & bear pole. Water source is a boxed spring south of the shelter 0.2 mile on the A.T.; two more nice springs downhill from privy.

MD-77/Foxville Road–West 2.4 miles to Smithsburg, MD (see above).

Raven Rock Shelter (2010)—Sleeps 16. Composting privy. Bear box & Bear cables. Tent and hammock sites, picnic table. Water is a spring 200 feet east of the A.T. (on trail to former Devils Racecourse Shelter).

High Rock—"A Rock with View" and lots of graffiti was the site of a hang-gliding platform destroyed years ago. Be watchful and notice where the blue blazes are located. Both sets will get you back

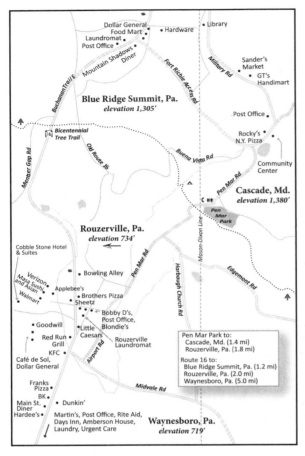

Blue Ridge Summit, Pa.
elevation 1,305'

Rouzerville, Pa.
elevation 734'

Cascade, Md.
elevation 1,380'

Waynesboro, Pa.
elevation 719'

Pen Mar Park to:
Cascade, Md. (1.4 mi)
Rouzerville, Pa. (1.8 mi)

Route 16 to:
Blue Ridge Summit, Pa. (1.2 mi)
Rouzerville, Pa. (2.0 mi)
Waynesboro, Pa. (5.0 mi)

to the Trail but can be confusing. Shoulderless Pen Mar High Rock Road leads 1.7 miles to Pen Mar Park. State police are usually on site, and the road is closed from dusk to dawn. There are video cameras on site.

Pen Mar County Park—Open from first Su in May to last Su in Oct. No camping in the park (campsite at Falls Creek 0.9 mile north). Dogs must be leashed (pack out poop). The pavilion provides views of the countryside to the west. Museum (electrical outlet). Restroom locked in the evening. Outlet behind old concession stand is left on for charging. No alcohol, smoking, or vaping is permitted in the park. Parking pass available for lot across the street from the gate; visit washco-md.net for form or call (240) 313-2700. **Hostel:** 1 block from the park is Zero Day Stay Hostel, 14530 Maryland Ave., Cascade, MD, (540) 999-6280, text first, ZeroDayStay@gmail.com, private rooms, laundry and showers for guests, Wi-Fi, Roku TV, resupply items, DIY waffles, DIY eggs, hot coffee waiting by 5:30.

East 1.4 miles to the small community of **Cascade, MD [P.O. ZIP 21719: M–F 10-1 & 2-5, Sa 8-12; (301) 241-3403]**. To reach town from the park entrance, turn left on High Rock Road to Pen-Mar Road, go straight at intersection, pass under a railroad trestle, turn right at the stop sign onto MD-550. To reach the post office, continue 0.1 mile, and turn left on Ft. Ritchie Road across from entrance to former Ft. Ritchie. **Restaurants:** Rocky's New York Pizza, (301) 241-3470; will deliver to the park; Chocolate Park Tavern, (301) 241-3352; Greenhouse Café(301) 781-7408, M-F 7-3, S,S 8-3. Taproom (301) 245-5750, Th 2-9,F,Sa 2-10, Su 2-9. **Groceries:** GT's Handimart (short-term resupply), (301) 241-3434, 4 a.m.–11 p.m. daily, ice cream, sandwiches, hot bar, ATM; Sanders Market (long-term resupply), (301) 241-3612, open M, W, Th, F 8:30–9, Tu, Sa 8:30–8. **Other services:** Ft. Ritchie Community Center, (301) 241-5085, thefrcc.org, showers and Wi-Fi (donations accepted), M–Th 5:30–8:30, F 5:30–6, Sa 9–2, Sun noon-3. **Shuttles:** Linda Ott, (240) 344-3687, from Harpers Ferry to Pine Grove Furnace; Dennis Sewell, (301) 241-3176, or Uber, (240) 529-5415, or others, (717) 977-6648, (717) 762-1217; American Legion, (301) 241-3117.

Mason-Dixon Line—This site—with a stone monument, register, and mailbox constructed by Boy Scouts—signifies the historical survey line, important again in the Civil War, that separates Maryland from Pennsylvania. When Mason and Dixon surveyed this line in 1763–67, they placed at one-mile intervals limestone blocks 3 to 5 feet long, weighing between 300 and 600 pounds, from an English quarry. Every fifth mile, a "Crown" stone was laid with the Penn coat of arms on the Pennsylvania side and the Calvert coat of arms on the Maryland side.

Pennsylvania

Miles from Springer	Miles to Next Point	Features	Services	Elev	Miles from Katahdin	M A P
1,067.6	0.1	Mason–Dixon Line; Maryland–Pennsylvania State Line	R	1,250'	1,129.8	
1,067.7	0.6	Pen Mar Road *West-1.5m to* **Rouzerville, PA, P.O. 17250** *West-2.3m to* Shop and Save	R, P G, L, M, D, cl, f G	1,240'	1,129.7	
1,068.3	0.4	Falls Creek footbridge	C, w (treat)	1,100'	1,129.1	
1,068.7	1.2	Buena Vista Road	R	1,290'	1,128.7	
1,069.9	0.3	Old PA-16	R	1,350'	1,127.5	
1,070.2	0.2	PA-16 *East-1.2m to* **Blue Ridge Summit, PA, P.O. 17214** *West-2m to* **Rouzerville, PA, P.O. 17250** *West-5m to* **Waynesboro, PA, P.O. 17268**	R, P M, D, cl, f G, L, M G, L, M, D, V, cl, f	1,200'	1,127.2	
1,070.4	0.4	Mentzer Gap Road, Mackie Run	R, P	1,250'	1,127.0	
1,070.8	0.2	Rattlesnake Run Road	R, P	1,370	1,126.6	
1,071.0	1.3	Bailey Spring: *box spring*	w	1,300'	1,126.4	
1,072.3	2.4	**Deer Lick Shelters** *(E-0.2m spring)*, 9.8mS; 3.6mN	S, w	1,420'	1,125.1	
1,074.7	0.2	Old Forge Park	R	890'	1,122.7	
1,074.9	0.2	Old Forge Picnic Grounds: *frost-free water tap*	P, w	900'	1,122.5	
1,075.1	0.6	Rattlesnake Run Road	R, P	900'	1,122.3	
1,075.7	0.2	Old Forge Road	R, P	1,000'	1,121.7	
1,075.9	1.3	**Tumbling Run Shelters**, 3.6mS; 6.8mN	S, w	1,120'	1,121.5	
1,077.2	2.6	Buzzard Peak; Trail Chimney Rocks; trail to PATC Hermitage Cabin *(locked)*		1,900'	1,120.2	
1,079.8	0.7	Snowy Mountain Road	R, P	1,680'	1,117.6	
1,080.5	0.3	Swamp Road	R	1,560'	1,116.9	
1,080.8	1.7	PA-233 *East-1.2m to* **South Mountain, PA, P.O. 17261**	R, P M, sh	1,600'	1,116.6	
1,082.5	3.0	**Rocky Mountain Shelters** *(E-0.2m S; 0.5m spring)*, 6.8mS; 5.8mN	S, w	1,520'	1,114.9	
1,085.5	1.9	US-30, Caledonia State Park, Thaddeus Stevens Museum *East-14m to* Gettysburg, PA *West-0.3m to* Bonfire Rest. & Ice Cream *West-0.8m to* Thru-It All Ministries Church Hostel *West-3.5m to* **Fayetteville, PA, P.O. 17222**	R, P, C, M, sh, w all M H G, L, M, D, cl	960'	1,111.9	
1,087.4	0.7	Quarry Gap Road	R	1,250'	1,110.0	
1,088.1	1.5	**Quarry Gap Shelters**, 5.8mS; 7.4mN	S, w	1,455'	1,109.3	
1,089.6	2.6	Stillhouse Road, Sandy Sod Junction	R	1,980'	1,107.8	
1,092.2	0.5	Middle Ridge Road	R	2,050'	1,105.2	
1,092.7	0.4	Ridge Road, Means Hollow Road	R	1,800'	1,104.7	
1,093.1	2.4	Milesburn Road, Milesburn Cabin *(locked)*	R, w	1,600'	1,104.3	
1,095.5	1.3	**Birch Run Shelter**, 7.4mS; 6.2mN	S, C, w	1,795'	1,101.9	

PATC: Map 4

PATC: Map 2-3

Miles from Springer	Miles to Next Point	Features	Services	Elev	Miles from Katahdin	M A P
1,096.8	0.6	Shippensburg Road	R, P	2,040'	1,100.6	
1,097.4	1.3	2018 A.T. Midpoint		2,000'	1,100.0	
1,098.7	1.9	PATC Michener Cabin *(locked) (E–0.2m spring)*; **2025 A.T. Midpoint**	w	1,850'	1,098.7	
1,100.6	1.1	Woodrow Road	R	1,850'	1,096.8	
1,101.7	0.3	**Toms Run Shelter**, *6.2mS; 11.1mN*	S, C, w	1,300'	1,095.7	
1,102.0	1.1	2011 A.T. Midpoint Sign		1,300'	1,095.4	
1,103.1	0.4	Michaux Road	R, P	1,320'	1,094.3	
1,103.5	1.6	Halfway Spring: *signed*	w	1,100'	1,093.9	
1,105.1	0.3	PA-233	R, P	900'	1,092.3	
1,105.4	0.2	Pine Grove Furnace State Park, Ironmasters Mansion, **Appalachian Trail Museum**	R, P, H, C, g, w, sh	850'	1,092.0	PATC: Map 2-3
1,105.6	2.3	Fuller Lake: *beach, swimming*		850'	1,091.8	
1,107.9	3.3	Side trail to Pole Steeple		850'	1,089.5	
1,111.2	1.0	Lime Kiln Road	R	1,080'	1,086.2	
1,112.2	0.4	Spring *(signed) (W–0.1m)*	w	750'	1,085.2	
1,112.6	0.5	**James Fry at Tagg Run Shelter** *(E–0.2m), 11.1mS; 8.5mN*	S, w	805'	1,084.8	
1,113.1	0.9	Pine Grove Road *(W–0.4m to Cherokee CG)*	R, C, M	750'	1,084.3	
1,114.0	1.8	PA-34, Hunters Run Road, Gardners, PA *(E–0.2m to Green Mountain Store and Deli)*	R, P, G, f	670'	1,083.4	
1,115.8	0.4	PA-94 *West–2.5m to* **Mt. Holly Springs, PA, P.O. 17065**	R, P G, L, M, D, cl	880'	1,081.6	
1,116.2	2.4	Sheet Iron Roof Road *West–0.4m to* Deer Run Camping Resort	R, P C, M, L, g, sh, cl, f	680'	1,081.2	
1,118.6	2.1	Whiskey Spring Road, Whiskey Spring	R, P, w	830'	1,078.8	
1,120.7	0.9	**Alec Kennedy Shelter** *(E–0.2m), 8.5mS; 18.4mN*	S, C, w	850'	1,076.7	
1,121.6	1.9	Center Point Knob, White Rocks Trail		1,060'	1,075.8	
1,123.5	0.6	Leidigh Drive	R, P	560'	1,073.9	
1,124.1	0.2	Backpackers' Campsite: *railroad tracks nearby*	C, w	500'	1,073.3	
1,124.3	0.1	Mountain Road, Yellow Breeches Creek *West–1.5m to* Lisa's Hostel	R H	500'	1,073.1	
1,124.4	0.2	Bucher Hill Road	R, P	500'	1,073.0	
1,124.6	2.0	PA-174, **Boiling Springs, PA, P.O. 17007** *East–0.8m to* Allenberry Inn & Playhouse *West–0.1m to* restaurants, Gelinas B&B, Food Mart *West–1m to* Karn's Store *West–2.5m to* Red Cardinal B&B	R, P, O, sh, w L, M G, L, M G, D, V L	500'	1,072.8	PATC: Map 1
1,126.6	1.1	PA-74, York Road	R, P	580'	1,070.8	
1,127.7	0.6	Lisburn Road	R, P	550'	1,069.7	
1,128.3	0.4	Boyer Road	R	550'	1,069.1	
1,128.7	1.1	PA-641, Trindle Road	R, P	540'	1,068.7	
1,129.8	0.6	Ridge Drive	R	460'	1,067.6	
1,130.4	0.7	Old Stonehouse Road	R	470'	1,067.0	
1,131.1	0.3	Appalachian Drive	R	510'	1,066.3	
1,131.4	0.6	I-76 Pennsylvania Turnpike: *overpass*	R	495'	1,066.0	

Miles from Springer	Miles to Next Point	Features	Services	Elev	Miles from Katahdin	M A P
1,132.0	0.6	Norfolk Southern Railway tracks		470'	1,065.4	
1,132.6	0.9	US-11: pedestrian footbridge West–0.5m to motels, restaurants, Travel Plaza West–5m to Carlisle, PA	R G, L, M, sh all	490'	1,064.8	
1,133.5	1.4	I-81: overpass on Bernhisel Bridge Road	R, P	480'	1,063.9	
1,134.9	1.1	Conodoguinet Creek Bridge	R, P, g	480'	1,062.5	
1,136.0	0.9	Sherwood Drive	R, P	420'	1,061.4	
1,136.9	1.0	PA-944, Donnellytown, PA: pedestrian tunnel	R	480'	1,060.5	
1,137.9	0.9	Spring at Wolf Trail junction	w	650'	1,059.5	
1,138.8	0.1	Tuscarora Trail (northern terminus), Darlington Trail		1,390'	1,058.6	PATC: Map 1
1,138.9	2.0	**Darlington Shelter**, 18.4mS; 7.3mN	S, w	1,250'	1,058.5	
1,140.9	0.3	Millers Gap Road: paved	R	700'	1,056.5	
1,141.2	5.0	PA-850, Valley Road	R, P	650'	1,056.2	
1,146.2	1.9	**Cove Mountain Shelter**, 7.3mS; 8.3mN	S, w	1,200'	1,051.2	
1,148.1	1.2	Hawk Rock: view of Duncannon		1,140'	1,049.3	
1,149.3	0.1	Inn Road	R, P	360'	1,048.1	
1,149.4	0.4	Sherman Creek Bridge	R	360'	1,048.0	
1,149.8	0.5	US-11 & 15, PA-274: underpass West–0.5m on PA-274 to Karn's Market	R, P G	385'	1,047.6	
1,150.3	1.0	Market St.; **Duncannon, PA, P.O. 17020**	R, g, C, L, M, D, O, cl, f	385'	1,047.1	
1,151.3	0.2	PA-849, Newport Road, Juniata River	R, C, O, sh	380'	1,046.1	
1,151.5	0.6	Susquehanna River, Clarks Ferry Bridge (west end) West–2m and 3.6m to motels	R, C L	380'	1,045.9	
1,152.1	0.4	US-22 & 322, Norfolk Southern Railway (E–16m to Harrisburg, PA)	R, P, all	400'	1,045.3	
1,152.5	1.7	Susquehanna Trail (1m) rejoins A.T. north		650'	1,044.9	
1,154.2	0.1	Susquehanna Trail (1m) rejoins A.T. south		1,150'	1,043.2	
1,154.3	0.2	Campsite: spring	C, w	1,160'	1,043.1	
1,154.5	3.9	**Clarks Ferry Shelter**, 8.3mS; 6.7mN	S, w	1,260'	1,042.9	
1,158.4	2.0	PA-225: footbridge	R, P	1,250'	1,039.0	
1,160.4	0.8	Table Rock: view		1,200'	1,037.0	
1,161.2	1.0	**Peters Mountain Shelter**, 6.7mS; 18.3mN	S, w	970'	1,036.2	KTA Map: Sections 7-8
1,162.2	0.6	Victoria Trail (E–1.1m to PA-325)	R, P	1,300'	1,035.2	
1,162.8	1.1	Whitetail Trail		1,310'	1,034.6	
1,163.9	1.4	Kinter View		1,320'	1,033.5	
1,165.3	2.3	Shikellimy Trail (E–0.9m to PA-325)	R, P	1,250'	1,032.1	
1,167.6	0.3	Spring: on blue-blaze	w	700'	1,029.8	
1,167.9	0.1	PA-325, Clark's Valley, Clark Creek	R, P, w	550'	1,029.5	
1,168.0	0.3	Water Tank Trail		570'	1,029.4	
1,168.3	0.1	Spring	w	620'	1,029.1	
1,168.4	2.8	Henry Knauber Trail	w	680'	1,029.0	
1,171.2	2.9	Stony Mountain; Horse-Shoe Trail		1,650'	1,026.2	
1,174.1	0.5	Yellow Springs Trail		1,380'	1,023.3	
1,174.6	2.1	Yellow Springs Village Site: trail register		1,450'	1,022.8	
1,176.7	0.2	Sand Spring Trail: The General Excavator		1,380'	1,020.7	

Miles from Springer	Miles to Next Point	Features	Services	Elev	Miles from Katahdin	M A P
1,176.9	2.3	Cold Spring Trail		1,400'	1,020.5	
1,179.2	0.5	**Rausch Gap Shelter** (E–0.3m), 18.3mS; 13.7mN	P, S, w	980'	1,018.2	
1,179.7	0.1	Rausch Creek: stone arch bridge	w	920'	1,017.7	
1,179.8	0.3	Raush Gap Village: sign		920'	1,017.6	
1,180.1	1.2	Haystack Creek: wooden bridge	w	840'	1,017.3	KTA Map: Sections 7-8
1,181.3	2.0	Second Mountain		1,350'	1,016.1	
1,183.3	0.6	Greenpoint School Road, then 150 ft. to PA-443	R	570'	1,014.1	
1,183.9	1.4	PA-443, Green Point, PA: underpass West–2.6m to Twin Grove KOA	R, P C, M, cl, sh	550'	1,013.5	
1,185.3	0.1	Swatara Gap, PA-72 East–2.4m to Lickdale, PA	R, P C, G, L, M, sh	480'	1,012.1	
1,185.4	0.3	Swatara Creek, Waterville Iron Bridge, Swatara Rail Trail		460'	1,012.0	
1,185.7	6.9	I-81: underpass	R	450'	1,011.7	
1,192.6	2.2	**William Penn Shelter** (E–0.1m); Blue Mtn. Spring (W–225 yards), 13.7mS; 4.2mN	S, w	1,300'	1,004.8	
1,194.8	1.8	PA-645: electrical outlet behind building	R, P	1,250'	1,002.6	
1,196.6	0.1	Kimmel Lookout		1,330'	1,000.8	
1,196.7	0.5	PA-501, **501 Shelter** (W–0.1m), 4.2mS; 15.3mN East–2m to **Bethel, PA, P.O. 19507** West–3.7m to **Pine Grove, PA, P.O. 17963**	R, P, S, w V G, L, M, D, V, cl	1,460'	1,000.7	
1,197.2	2.6	Pilger Ruh Spring Trail (east), Applebee Campsite (west)	C, w	1,450'	1,000.2	
1,199.8	2.0	Round Head, trail to Shower Steps	w	1,500'	997.6	
1,201.8	0.5	Shikellamy Overlook		1,390'	995.6	
1,202.3	0.1	Hertlein Campsite	C, w	1,200'	995.1	
1,202.4	3.1	Shuberts Gap		1,200'	995.0	
1,205.5	0.3	Ft. Dietrich Snyder Marker, spring (W–0.2m)	w	1,440'	991.9	
1,205.8	0.5	PA-183, Rentschler Marker	R, P	1,440'	991.6	KTA Map: Sections 1-6
1,206.3	0.8	Service road to PA-183	P	1,490'	991.1	
1,207.1	3.8	Black Swatara Spring (W–0.3m)	w	1,510'	990.3	
1,210.9	0.7	Sand Spring Trail: walled spring (E–0.2m)	w	1,510'	986.5	
1,211.6	1.9	**Eagle's Nest Shelter** (W–0.3m), 15.3mS; 15mN	S, w	1,510'	985.8	
1,213.5	2.7	Shartlesville Cross-Mountain Road; Shartlesville, PA	R	1,450'	983.9	
1,216.2	0.9	Phillip's Canyon Spring	w	1,500'	981.2	
1,217.1	0.6	Marshall's Path		1,370'	980.3	
1,217.7	2.2	Auburn Lookout		1,400'	979.7	
1,219.9	0.1	John Bartram-Schuylkill River Trail, RR tracks	R, P	420'	977.5	
1,220.0	0.2	Schuylkill River		400'	977.4	
1,220.2	0.7	Port Clinton, PA, P.O. 19549 West–0.3m to pavilion	R, P, PO, L, M, w S, C	400'	977.2	
1,220.9	2.6	PA-61, Port Clinton Avenue: underpass East–1.5m to Cabela's, motel, restaurants East–3.5m to **Hamburg, PA, P.O. 19526**	R, P B, G, L, M, O, f B, G, L, M, D, V, cl	490'	976.5	
1,223.5	2.6	Pocahontas Spring	w	1,200'	973.9	

Miles from Springer	Miles to Next Point	Features	Services	Elev	Miles from Katahdin	M A P
1,226.1	0.2	Windsor Furnace, Reservoir Road, Hamburg Reservoir (E–0.5m)	R, P, C, w	900'	971.3	
1,226.3	1.1	**Windsor Furnace Shelter**, *15mS; 9.3mN*	S, w	940'	971.1	
1,227.4	0.5	Trail to Blue Rocks Campground *(E–1.5m)*	S, C, G, cl, sh, f	1,000'	970.0	
1,227.9	1.8	Pulpit Rock: *observatory, overlook*		1,582'	969.5	
1,229.7	0.4	Trail to Blue Rocks Campground *(E–1.5m)*	S, C, G, cl, sh, f	1,150'	967.7	
1,230.1	1.7	The Pinnacle: *overlook*		1,615'	967.3	
1,231.8	0.3	Furnace Creek Trail		1,440'	965.6	
1,232.1	0.6	Gold Spring *(W–30 yds.)*	w	1,580'	965.3	
1,232.7	0.9	Blue-blazed trail to A.T. at Windsor Furnace *(W–1.5m)*		1,420'	964.7	
1,233.6	1.8	Panther Spring *(west)*	w	1,070'	963.8	
1,235.4	1.7	Hawk Mountain Road, **Eckville Shelter** *(E–0.2m)*, *9.3mS; 7.6mN*	R, P, S, w, sh	600'	962.0	
1,237.1	1.1	Hawk Mountain Sanctuary Trail *(W–2m to visitors center)*		1,330'	960.3	
1,238.2	3.3	Dans Pulpit: *trail register, view*		1,600'	959.2	
1,241.5	1.3	Tri-County Corner		1,560'	955.9	
1,242.8	1.9	**Allentown Hiking Club Shelter** *(E–0.2m spring)*, *7.6mS; 10mN*	S, w	1,350'	954.6	
1,244.7	2.2	Ft. Franklin Rd., Blue Mtn. House Road: *gravel*	R, P	1,350'	952.7	KTA Map: Sections 1–6
1,246.9	1.8	PA-309, Blue Mountain Summit B&B	R, P, w	1,360'	950.5	
1,248.7	1.0	New Tripoli Campsite *(W–0.2m): powerline*	C, w	1,400'	948.7	
1,249.7	0.7	Knife Edge "The Cliffs"		1,525'	947.7	
1,250.4	1.4	Bear Rocks		1,604'	947.0	
1,251.8	0.4	Bake Oven Knob Road: *dirt*	R, P	1,450'	945.6	
1,252.2	0.6	Bake Oven Knob		1,560'	945.2	
1,252.8	2.4	**Bake Oven Knob Shelter**, *10mS; 7.5mN*	S, w	1,380'	944.6	
1,255.2	5.1	Ashfield Road, Blue Mountain Road, Lehigh Furnace Gap: *radio tower (E–0.7m spring)* *West–2.2m to* **Ashfield, PA, P.O. 18212**	R, P, w G	1,320'	942.2	
1,260.3	0.6	**George W. Outerbridge Shelter**, *7.5mS; 17.1mN*	S, w	1,000'	937.1	
1,260.9	0.1	Lehigh Gap, PA-873 *East–2m to* **Slatington, PA, P.O. 18080**	R, P B, G, M, D, cl, f	380'	936.5	
1,261.0	0.2	Lehigh River Bridge *(east end)*, PA-873	R, P	380'	936.4	
1,261.2	0.0	PA-145 *East–2m to* **Walnutport, PA, P.O. 18088**	R B, G, M, D, V	380'	936.2	
1,261.2	0.2	PA-248: *blue-blaze to Palmerton, locked gate after 4:30 p.m. (W–2m)* *West–2m to* **Palmerton, PA, P.O. 18071**	R, P G, H, L, M, D, cl, f	380'	936.2	
1,261.4	0.8	Winter Trail *(south junction)*			936.0	
1,262.2	4.3	Winter Trail *(north junction)*			935.2	
1,266.5	4.8	Little Gap, Blue Mountain Road *East–1.5m to* **Danielsville, PA, P.O. 18038**	R, P G, L, M	1,100'	930.9	
1,271.3	2.5	Delps Trail *(E–0.25m): unreliable spring*	w	1,580'	926.1	
1,273.8	3.5	Smith Gap Road, Point Phillips Road: *paved (W–1m to water spigot, cold shower)*	R, P	1,540'	923.6	

Miles from Springer	Miles to Next Point	Features	Services	Elev	Miles from Katahdin	M A P
1,277.3	3.6	**Leroy A. Smith Shelter** *(E-0.1m S; 0.2m, 0.4m, 0.6m springs), 17.1mS; 13.8mN* *East-0.9m on* Katellen Trail to Old Grade Rd.	S, w R, P	1,410'	920.1	
1,280.9	0.3	Hahns Lookout		1,450'	916.5	
1,281.2	0.4	Lookout Rock		1,480'	916.2	
1,281.6	0.3	Powerline		1,100'	915.8	
1,281.9	2.0	PA-33 *East-1m to* **Wind Gap, PA, P.O. 18091**	R, P G, L, M, D, V, cl	980'	915.5	
1,283.9	4.4	Private road, Blue Mtn. Water Co.	R	1,580'	913.5	
1,288.3	0.5	Wolf Rocks bypass trail *(south end): signed spring*	w	1,550'	909.1	
1,288.8	0.3	Wolf Rocks		1,620'	908.6	
1,289.1	1.3	Wolf Rocks bypass trail *(north end)*		1,510'	908.3	
1,290.4	0.6	PA-191, Fox Gap	R, P	1,400'	907.0	
1,291.0	0.8	**Kirkridge Shelter**, *13.8mS; 31.5mN*	S	1,500'	906.4	
1,291.8	1.1	Lunch Rocks: *views*		1,515'	905.6	
1,292.9	2.0	Totts Gap: *gravel road, gated*	R	1,300'	904.5	
1,294.9	1.0	Mt. Minsi		1,461'	902.5	
1,295.9	0.8	Lookout Rock: *views*		800'	901.5	
1,296.7	0.5	Council Rock		600'	900.7	
1,297.2	0.2	Lake Lenape	R, P	510'	900.2	
1,297.4	0.2	PA-611 *West-0.1m to* **Delaware Water Gap, PA, P.O. 18327** *West-0.4m to* services *West-5m to* East Stroudsburg & Stroudsburg, PA	R, P H, L, M B, G, L, M, O, f B, G, L, M, O, D	400'	900.0	
1,297.6	1.0	Delaware River Bridge *(west end)*; Pennsylvania–New Jersey State Line		350'	899.8	

KTA Map: Sections 1-6

Note: Camping regulations vary depending on the type of public land. Be aware of posted notices, and check maps for boundaries. Most water sources are unreliable in summer.

🅰 **Pen Mar Rd.**—**West** 1.5 miles to **Rouzerville, PA [P.O. ZIP 17250: M–F 8:30–1 & 1–4, Sa 9–11:30; (717) 762-7050]**, with most major services, including Masa Sushi Asian Restaurant and a Verizon store (see map). *Lodging:* Cobblestone Hotel, (717) 765-0034, hiker discount, laundry, pool, free B. **West** 2.3 miles to *Groceries:* Walmart (long-term resupply) and Dollar General.

🅰 **PA-16**—**East** 1.2 miles to **Blue Ridge Summit, PA [P.O. ZIP 17214: M–F 8–12 & 1–4, Sa 9–11:30; (717) 794-2335]**. *Restaurants:* Mountain Shadows, daily, B/L/DUnique Bar and Grill; and fast-food options. *Internet access:* Blue Ridge Summit Library, M–Th 3–8, Sa 10–2. *Other services:* Blue Ridge Food Mart; bank with ATM; J.J Laundromat; barber; Dollar General.
   West 2 miles to **Rouzerville, PA** See above.
   West 2.3 miles to *Groceries:* Walmart (long-term resupply).
   🅰 **West** 5 miles to **Waynesboro, PA [P.O. ZIP 17268: M–F 8:30–5, Sa 9–12; (717) 762-1513; pick-up window only, M–F 6–5, Sa 6–12:15]**, with all major services. The Annual Mason-Dixon Appalachian Trail Outdoor Festival is Jun 10 at Red Run Park, 12143 Buchanan Trail East; waynesboroatc.org. *Lodging:* Amberson House, (717) 762-8112, phone for rates and shuttle from Trailhead, Internet access, laundry, local shuttles, and slackpacks; Days Inn, (717) 762-9113, call for current rates. *Groceries:* Martin's (long-term resupply); 7–11 (short-term resupply). *Internet access:* library, M–F 9:30–8, Sa 9–4. *Other services:* Wee Scot Book Shoppe, 4 E. Main St., Waynesboro, (717) 655-2129, weescotbookshoppe@yahoo.com; WellSpan Urgent Care, 601 E Main St Level1, (717) 765-5088,

daily 8-8; YMCA, (717) 762-6012, 810 Main St., showers; hospital; pharmacies; veterinarian; and dentist.

Deer Lick Shelters (1940s)—Two shelters, each sleeps 4. Privy. Water source is a spring 0.2 mile on a blue-blazed trail to the east of the shelter area (seasonal) or stream 50 feet north of shelter.

Tumbling Run Shelters (1940s)—Two shelters, each sleeps 4. Privy. Bear box and pole. Located on a short, blue-blazed trail. Water source is 100 yards to the west of the shelter.

A PA-233—East 1.2 miles to **South Mountain, PA [P.O. ZIP 17261: M–F 12–4, Sa 8:30–11:30; (717) 749-5833]** on South Mountain Rd. *Restaurant*: South Mountain Hotel (no indoor lodging, allows tent or hammock, $5pp), (717) 749-3845, grill-type menu, bar, M–Su 11 a.m.–11 p.m., with patio, Porta-Johns, and outside shower.

Rocky Mountain Shelters (1989)—Two shelters, each sleeps 4. Privy. Bear box. Located 0.2 mile on a steep, downhill, blue-blazed trail; for water, continue on side trail down to a road, then right 75 yards to spring.

A US-30—East 14 miles to historic Gettysburg with many motels and most major services.
　　West 0.3 mile to *Restaurant:* 65 South BBQ, (717) 401-0585, Th–Su 11–7.
　　West 0.8 mile to *Hostel:* Thru-It All Ministries Church Hostel, Pastor Beall (410) 984-0105, no drugs or alcohol, $22pp/night ($1 donated back to the Trail), bunk, shower with towel, kitchen, laundry, short-term resupply. Tenting $12/night.
　　West 3.5 miles to **Fayetteville, PA [P.O. ZIP 17222: M–F 8-4:30, Sa 8:30–12; (717) 352-2022].** *Lodging:* Rite Spot Motel/Scottish Inns & Suites, (717) 352-2144, $60s, $70d, $20eap, no pets; $10 one-way shuttle to Walmart, $5 shuttle to/from Trail, call ahead. *Restaurants:* Flamingo Family Restaurant; Giacomo's Italian Restaurant; Maria & Sal's Pizzeria. *Other services:* doctor, pharmacy, coin laundry, barber, and ATM. *Shuttles:* Robert "Junker" Freeman, (717) 491-2460, shuttles from Front Royal to DWG, slackpacks from Pen Mar to Duncannon.

Caledonia State Park—(717) 352-2161, home to the Thaddeus Stevens Blacksmith Shop Museum, but, more importantly for hot hikers, home to a swimming pool. The pool is visible as the A.T. enters a clearing in the park. Open only weekends from Memorial Day to mid-Jun, then daily to Labor Day; $4 admission. *Camping:* Campsite prices vary, open Apr through mid-Dec, electric & nonelectric, showers available. Maximum of 5 people/tents per site as long as tents don't extend beyond campsite. U.S. Sen. Thaddeus Stevens, an outspoken abolitionist, owned Caledonia Ironworks during the Civil War. Confederates burned it en route to the battle of Gettysburg. Overnight parking available at A.T. lot.

Quarry Gap Shelters (1935)—Two shelters, each sleeps 4. Privy. Bear box. Water source is 10 yards in front of the shelter.

Quarry Gap Shelters to Birch Run Shelter—Between these areas, the A.T. runs through impressive thickets of mountain laurel. Peak bloom is usually late May–early Jun.

Birch Run Shelter (2003)—Sleeps 8. Privy. Bear pole. Shelter located on the east side of the A.T. Water source is a spring 30 yards in front of the shelter.

Midpoint Marker—A new wooden sign with a register marks the 2011 midpoint of the Trail. The old one has been retired to the nearby A.T. Museum. ALDHA honorary life member Chuck Wood, a.k.a. "Woodchuck" of 1985, built and erected both markers.

Toms Run Shelter(s) (1936)—One burned in 2013; remaining shelter sleeps 4. Privy. Bear pole. Water source is a spring near old chimney.

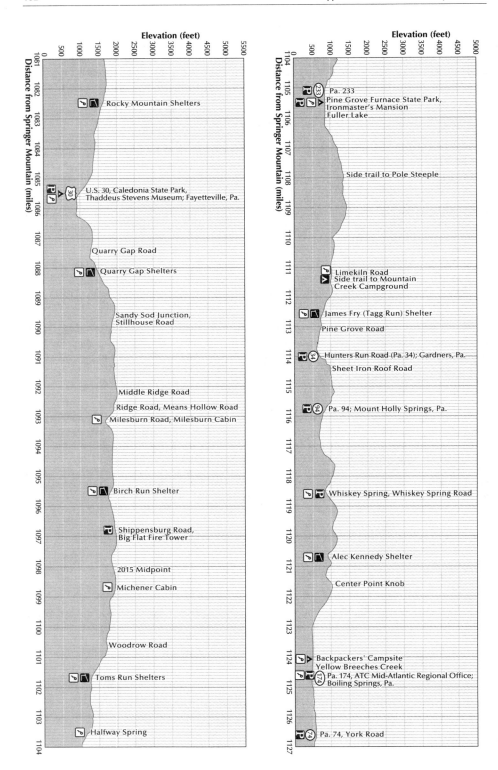

Elevation (feet)

Distance from Springer Mountain (miles)

Rocky Mountain Shelters

U.S. 30, Caledonia State Park,
Thaddeus Stevens Museum; Fayetteville, Pa.

Quarry Gap Road

Quarry Gap Shelters

Sandy Sod Junction,
Stillhouse Road

Middle Ridge Road

Ridge Road, Means Hollow Road

Milesburn Road, Milesburn Cabin

Birch Run Shelter

Shippensburg Road,
Big Flat Fire Tower

2015 Midpoint

Michener Cabin

Woodrow Road

Toms Run Shelters

Halfway Spring

Elevation (feet)

Distance from Springer Mountain (miles)

Pa. 233

Pine Grove Furnace State Park,
Ironmaster's Mansion
Fuller Lake

Side trail to Pole Steeple

Limekiln Road
Side trail to Mountain
Creek Campground

James Fry (Tagg Run) Shelter

Pine Grove Road

Hunters Run Road (Pa. 34); Gardners, Pa.

Sheet Iron Roof Road

Pa. 94; Mount Holly Springs, Pa.

Whiskey Spring, Whiskey Spring Road

Alec Kennedy Shelter

Center Point Knob

Backpackers' Campsite
Yellow Breeches Creek
Pa. 174, ATC Mid-Atlantic Regional Office;
Boiling Springs, Pa.

Pa. 74, York Road

⚠ PA-233/Pine Grove Furnace State Park—(717) 486-7174. Appalachian Trail Museum (717) 486-8126, atmuseum.org, in an old grist mill on the Trail, well worth the visit; free, see atmuseum.org for 2023 hours; parking for up to a week but register at park office. *Hostel:* Ironmasters Mansion, 1212 Pine Grove Rd., Gardners, PA 17324, (717) 486-4108, atmuseum.org/ironmasters, ironmasters@atmuseum.org, west end of Pine Grove Furnace State Park. Operated by the A.T. Museum; bunk $25, private room M–Th $60, F–Su $80; B/D $5 each; Wi-Fi, laundry. Only service dogs allowed on site. *Groceries:* Pine Grove General Store (short-term resupply), open Apr 15–mid-Nov, daily 9–7. The first opportunity for northbounders to join the traditional "half-gallon club." To belong, you have to eat a half-gallon of ice cream to mark your halfway point. *Camping:* Campground open Mar 27–Dec 12, electric & nonelectric sites, $19–$34 (resident and nonresident rates), swimming in Laurel and Fuller lakes; heated restrooms with hot showers, electric outlets, and flush toilets. Alcohol prohibited. *Shuttles:* Mike Gelinas, (717) 697-6022; Robert "Junker" Freeman, (717) 491-2460; Gary, (717) 706-2578.

Mountain Club of Maryland—MCM maintains the 16.2 miles from Pine Grove Furnace State Park to Center Point Knob and the 12.7 miles from the Darlington/Tuscarora Trail junction to the Susquehanna River. Correspondence should be sent to 7923 Galloping Circle, Baltimore, MD 21244; paulives2@aol.com.

James Fry Shelter at Tagg Run (1998)—Sleeps 9. Tentsites. Privy (composting). Bear box. Called "Tagg Run" in some sources, after the 1930s-vintage shelters it replaced. Water source is 0.4 mile east of the A.T. on a blue-blazed trail; may run dry in drought times.

⚠ Pine Grove Rd.—**West** 0.4 mile to Cherokee Family Restaurant and Campground, (717) 486-8000; tentsites with shower $20d, $10eap.
  West 1.5 miles to Mountain Creek Campground, 349 Pine Grove Rd., Gardners, PA 17324; (717) 486-7681, mtncreekcg.com; mid-Apr–Oct, tenting, cabin, hot showers, call for rates; pool, camp store, camp supplies, snack shack; pets must be kept on a leash.
  East 0.6 mile to Twirly Top, ice cream and grill, closed Su.

⚠ PA-34—**East** 0.2 mile to the Green Mountain Store and Deli (short-term resupply), (717) 486-4558, M–Sa 7–8, Su 9–6, hiking supplies, ATM, fuel canisters, Coleman by the pint. For southbounders, the first opportunity to join the Half-Gallon Club.

⚠ PA-94—**West** 2.5 miles to **Mt. Holly Springs, PA [P.O. ZIP 17065: M–F 8-1 & 2-4:30, Sa 9-12; (717) 486-3468]**. *Lodging:* Mountain Creek Tavern, 31 S. Baltimore St., Mt. Holly Springs, PA 17065, (717) 486-3823, mountaincreektavern.com, rate is $100+tax; L/D M–Th Su 11:30–9, F-Sa 11:30–10; Internet; mail drops accepted. *Restaurants:* The Italian Taxi (Pizza Shop), 225 N. Baltimore Ave., (717) 486-8513; Cassell's Grill, 5 West Pine St., (717) 486-8800, Tu–Th 3–8, F–Su 12–9; Sicilia Pizza and Subs; 3 Pines Tavern. *Internet access:* library, M–Sa. *Other services:* Dollar General and Family Dollar (short-term resupply); coin laundry; pharmacy; dentist; and bank with ATM.

⚠ Sheet Iron Roof Rd.—**West** 0.4 mile to Deer Run Camping Resort, (717) 486-8168, deerruncampingresort.com, $10 tent camping, short-term resupply, laundry, showers, Wi-Fi, pool, fishing pond, snack bar on weekends.

Alec Kennedy Shelter (1991)—Sleeps 7. Privy (composting). Bear box. Built by the MCM and Tressler Wilderness School. The shelter is 0.2 mile east on a blue-blazed trail. Water source is a spring located on a side trail behind the shelter; prone to go dry during the summer. A second source is a small stream 0.5 mile south of the shelter on the A.T.

Center Point Knob—In 2012, the Mountain Club of Maryland replaced the missing Center Point Knob bronze plaque with a replica on the original boulder.

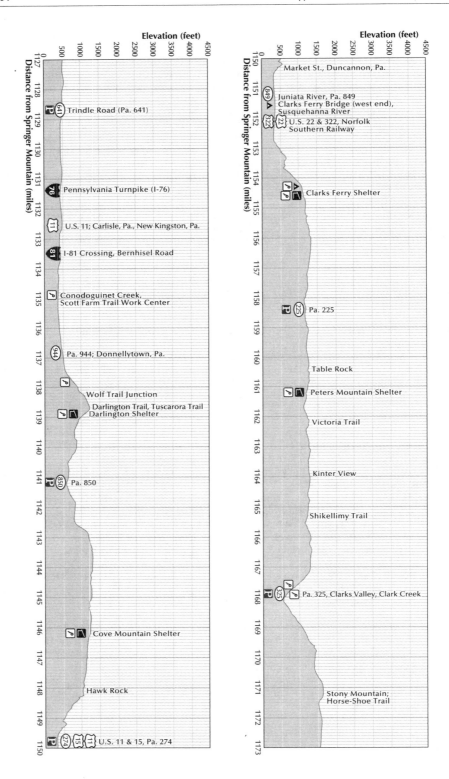

Elevation (feet)

Distance from Springer Mountain (miles)

Trindle Road (Pa. 641)

Pennsylvania Turnpike (I-76)

U.S. 11; Carlisle, Pa., New Kingston, Pa.

I-81 Crossing, Bernhisel Road

Conodoguinet Creek,
Scott Farm Trail Work Center

Pa. 944; Donnellytown, Pa.

Wolf Trail Junction

Darlington Trail, Tuscarora Trail
Darlington Shelter

Pa. 850

Cove Mountain Shelter

Hawk Rock

U.S. 11 & 15, Pa. 274

Elevation (feet)

Distance from Springer Mountain (miles)

Market St., Duncannon, Pa.

Juniata River, Pa. 849
Clarks Ferry Bridge (west end),
Susquehanna River

U.S. 22 & 322, Norfolk
Southern Railway

Clarks Ferry Shelter

Pa. 225

Table Rock

Peters Mountain Shelter

Victoria Trail

Kinter View

Shikellimy Trail

Pa. 325, Clarks Valley, Clark Creek

Stony Mountain;
Horse-Shoe Trail

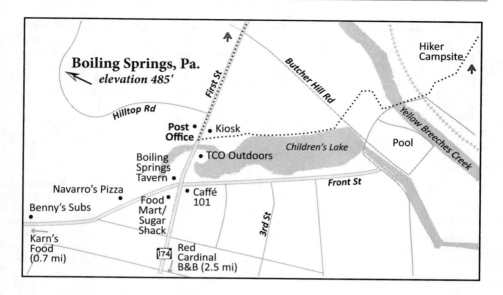

Cumberland Valley Appalachian Trail Club—CVATC maintains the 17.2 miles between Center Point Knob and the Darlington/Tuscarora Trail junction. Correspondence should be sent to P.O. Box 395, Boiling Springs, PA 17007; cvatclub.org; wbohn@paonline.com.

Note: No fires in the valley between Alec Kennedy and Darlington shelters. The Boiling Springs campsite is the only place where camping is allowed.

Mountain Rd. at Yellow Breeches Creek—West 1.5 miles to Lisa's Hostel,. (717) 226-8390, bunks and private room available (1 night), shower, laundry, light snack provided; call for prices; no walk-ins, appointment only.

Boiling Springs, PA [P.O. ZIP 17007: M–F 9–12, 1–4:30, Sa 9–12; (717) 258-6668]—Lakeside cottage, former home of the ATC's Mid-Atlantic office, now owned by town. Water pump behind building, fill here if returning/going to campsite. P.O. is across the street. *No camping at the cottage.* Limited parking at opposite end of lake in township parking lot. Lodging is limited in Boiling Springs, but a year-round campsite is south of town, before the railroad tracks. The trains do run past here all night long. Annual Appalachian Trail Music Festival on Father's Day. All these businesses are within walking distance of trail in Boiling Springs on Forge Rd. *Restaurants:* Navarro's Pizza, (717) 258-5070, L/D; Caffe 101, M–Sa 7 a.m.–9 p.m., Su 7–8; 0.5 mile to Benny's Pizza and Subs, M–Sa 10:30–10, Su 11–9; Boiling Springs Tavern. *Groceries:* Karn's Store (long-term resupply), open daily 7 a.m.–10 p.m.; Lakeside Food Mart (short-term resupply) at corner of Front and Forge. *Other services:* TCO Outdoors, (717) 609-0169, ext. 5, small outfitter with freeze-dried meals and energy snacks; bank with ATM next to post office; chiropractor; dentist, (717) 258-3858; veterinarian, 550 Park Dr.; Boiling Springs pool, (717) 258-4121, open Memorial–Labor Day, $12 admission, $7 seniors or evenings, $2 hot shower; barber; Jumpers Shoe Service, (717) 766-3422, 106 E. Main St., Mechanicsburg; Appalachian Running Co., 290 E Pomfret St., Carlisle, PA, (717) 241-5694, 4.1 miles from Trindle Rd. crossing, M–F 9–6, Sa 9–4, knowledgeable staff of experienced hikers and runners, foot scanner for proper insole fit, carries popular brands of trail-runner shoes and hiking boots and more for hikers. *Shuttles:* Mike Gelinas, (717) 697-6022; Trailangelmary, (717) 834-4706.

    West 2.5 miles on PA-174—*Lodging:* Red Cardinal B&B, (717) 245-0823, redcardinalbandb@aol.com, call for reservations and a ride; laundry available for a fee.

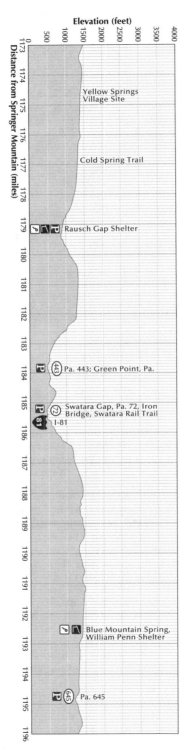

Cumberland Valley—Water is scarce between Boiling Springs and Darlington Shelter, as the A.T. winds along hedgerows and through Pennsylvania farmland. Thanks to an ambitious land-acquisition program, most of the Trail has been taken off roads through this heavily developed area, but it is still a hot walk on steamy summer days. Water can be obtained at one of the restaurants on US-11 (see below).

US-11—**West** 0.5 mile to various facilities spread along this busy highway. *Lodging:* Quality Inn, (717) 245-2242, hiker rate $60; Super 8, 1800 Harrisburg Pike, Carlisle, PA 17013, (717) 249-7000, laundry, pool, Wi-Fi; Motel 6, (717) 249-7775, continental B, pets extra and only in smoking rooms, laundry, pool, Wi-Fi; Pheasant Field B&B, (717) 258-0717, starting at $125, pet-friendly room may be available, laundry, shuttle to and from Trail with stay. Other options beyond I-81: Travel Lodge, Rodeway Inn, Howard Johnson, Quality Inn. *Restaurants:* Middlesex Diner, Dunkin', Denny's, Moonlite Diner. *Outfitter:* REI, (717) 516-6964, 6391 Carlisle Pike, Suite 100A, Mechanicsburg, PA 17050.

Other services: The Flying J Travel Plaza has a restaurant, showers, laundry, and a store (short-term resupply).
   West—5 miles to Carlisle, a large town with all major services along US-11.

Conodoguinet Creek Bridge— Trail View Market, next to Trail on Bernheisel Bridge Rd., fresh fruit, cold drinks, ice cream, snacks, ramen, chocolate milk, fresh vegetables, picnic table. An old ATC-managed farmhouse here, known as the Scott Farm, is closed permanently. Parking is available for hikers. *No camping.*

Wolf Trail—Spring water where the A.T. crosses an over-grown dirt road.

Tuscarora Trail—The northern terminus of the blue-blazed Tuscarora Trail, a 260-mile route to its southern terminus on the A.T. in Shenandoah National Park in Virginia near Matthews Arm Campground. It was blazed when maintain-ers feared that the A.T. route would be closed by private landowners.

Darlington Shelter (2005)—Sleeps 8. Privy. Bear box. Camp-sites. Water source, an intermittent spring 0.2 mile on a blue-blazed trail in front of the shelter, regularly dries up early in the hiker season. It is recommended that northbounders bring water to the shelter from the Wolf Trail spring at the base of North Mountain; southbounders, from Cove Moun-tain.

Cove Mountain Shelter (2000)—Sleeps 8. Privy. Bear box. Built with the help of the Timber Framers Guild using tim-ber salvaged from a barn, some pieces more than 100 years old. Water source is a spring 125 yards away on a steeply graded trail near the shelter.

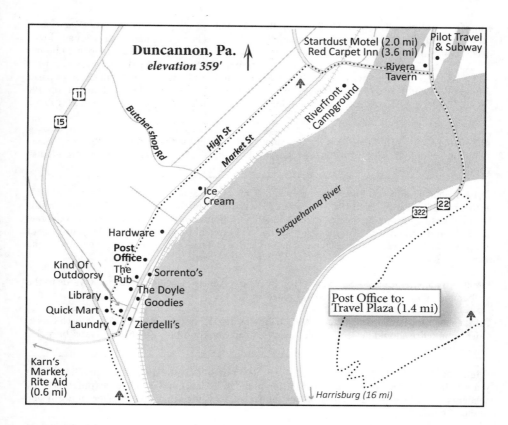

Duncannon, Pa. ↑
elevation 359'

11
15

Butcher shop Rd

High St
Market St

Riverfront Campground

Startdust Motel (2.0 mi) ↑
Red Carpet Inn (3.6 mi) ↑

Pilot Travel & Subway

Rivera Tavern

Ice Cream

Susquehanna River

322   22

Hardware •
Post Office •
Kind Of Outdoorsy
The Pub • • Sorrento's
Library •
Quick Mart •
Laundry • • Zierdelli's
• The Doyle
  • Goodies

Post Office to:
Travel Plaza (1.4 mi)

Karn's Market, Rite Aid (0.6 mi)

↓ *Harrisburg (16 mi)*

US-11/Duncannon, PA [P.O. ZIP 17020: M–F 8–11, 12–4:30, Sa 8:30–12:30; (717) 834-3332.] P.O. has a hiker box with snacks. ID required for mail drops. Duncannon is the trail town closer than any town on the A.T. to public transportation (bus, train, airport). The A.T. passes through the center of town, and all services are within a short walk. *Camping:* Riverfront Campground (south of the Clarks Ferry Bridge), (717) 834-5252, tentsites and shower (must register first), canoe and kayak rentals. *Lodging:* Doyle Hotel, 7 North Market St., Duncannon, PA 17020, (717) 596-0455, doylehotelpa.com, one of the original Anheuser-Busch hotels, more than 100 years old, newly renovated, closed M, but rooms available for arrivals on M, call to check in. Bar open Tu–Th 11–2, 4–9:30; F–Sa 11–10, Su 12–9. Kitchen closes 30 min to 1 hour before bar. Outdoor seating on balcony Sun 12–8. Room rates with own bathroom $89 + tax; with shared bathroom $59–$70 + tax. Air-conditioned rooms. To reserve room, doylehotelpa.com. Entertainment Th–Su. On US-11/15, 2 miles **north** of the truck stop, Stardust Motel, call first, (717) 834-3191, Su–Th $55S, F–Sa $65s, $5eap, laundry, no dogs, free shuttles to and from town when available. Kind of Outdoorsy Outfitter has bunk rooms, call to reserve, (717) 596-0455. Red Carpet Inn, 3.6 miles **north** on US-11, (717) 834-3320, shuttles to/from town when available, hiker-friendly. *Groceries:* On Trail, Inn Rd., Sunoco (short-term resupply). **West** of town 0.5 mile on PA-274, Karn's Market, open 7–10. (long-term resupply). *This is a dangerous walk; take safer walk at 1st right past Legion hall, through Penn Township Park, to red light at Karn's Plaza;* Rite Aid pharmacy Sa–Su 9–7, M–F 9–9; Quick Mart Convenience Store (short-term resupply), daily 6–10; Dollar General (next to Karn's). *Restaurants:* All on Market St. Momma Pat's Little Taste of Philly Grille, Th–Sa, 11–7; Wilderlove Coffee Co.(south of town), serving wide variety of coffees and other drinks, pastries, B and L sandwiches, Tu–Sa 7–2; Lindgren Craft Brewery, next to Doyle Hotel, full kitchen coming spring 2024, brewery on site, (717) 834-3448, the only brewery on the Trail; Doyle Hotel; Goodie's Café, B, closed M; The Pub, L/D; Sorrento's Pizza and Subs, L/D; Zeiderelli's Pizza, L/D, 3 B's Ice Cream Stand. North end of town: Riviera Tavern, L/D; Sheetz on Rt. 322, made-to-order. *Other services:* Mary Parry (Trailangelmary), (717) 834-4706, can shuttle from Harpers Ferry to NJ and help with any hiker needs, conveniently located on Market St. above the Pub; laundry on Market St. open 24 hours; All-American Truck Plaza on Rt. 322 (short-term resupply), $8 shower, ATM, Subway; banks with ATM; dentist; bank; veterinarian; Christ Lutheran Church, 1 block west of High St., serves pasta dinners W night 5–7 in Jun–Jul. *Outfitter:* Kind of Outdoorsy, 9 S. Market St., Duncannon, PA 17020, (717) 596-0016, accepts mail drops, include name & ETA; hiker lounge and hostel (call for reservation); showers available ($5).

York Hiking Club—YHC maintains the 6.9 miles from the Susquehanna River to PA-225. Correspondence should be sent to YHC, 2684 Forest Rd., York, PA 17402; (717) 244-6769; president@ yorkhikingclub.com.

Earl V. Shaffer—Almost all hikers recognize Earl "Crazy One" Shaffer (1918–2002) from York, PA, as the first A.T. thru-hiker. In 1948, he completed a northbound thru hike; in 1965, he did a southbound thru hike, becoming the first to record both northbound and southbound hikes. To celebrate the 50th anniversary in 1998 of his first hike, Earl did a northbound thru hike at the young age of 79. ATC's first "corresponding secretary", he was active in Trail work and promoting trails for the YHC and Susquehanna Appalachian Trail Club for many years.

Clarks Ferry Shelter (1993)—Sleeps 8. Privy. Bear box. A blue-blazed trail leads 100 yards to the shelter and 100 yards farther to a reliable piped spring.

Susquehanna Appalachian Trail Club—SATC maintains the 21.3 miles from PA-225 to Rausch Creek. Correspondence should be sent to hike-hbg@satc-hike.org or SATC Box 61001, Harrisburg, PA 17106-1001.

Peters Mountain Shelter (1994)—Sleeps 20. Privy. Bear boxes. The little shelter that Earl Shaffer built years earlier was removed in 2008 for inclusion in the A.T. Museum. Water source (unreliable) for shelter is down a steep, blue-blazed trail of almost 300 rock steps in front of shelter on north side of the mountain.

Blue Mountain Eagle Climbing Club—BMECC maintains the 61.8 miles from Rausch Creek to Tri-County Corner and the 3 miles from Bake Oven Knob to Lehigh Furnace Gap. Correspondence can be sent to P.O. Box 14982, Reading, PA 19612; (610) 326-1656; bmecc.org; info@bmecc.org.

Rausch Gap Shelter (1972, rebuilt in 2012)—Sleeps 6. Privy. Tenting along side trail. Water source is a reliable spring next to the shelter.

 PA-443—West 2.6 miles to *Camping:* Twin Grove KOA, (800) 562-5471, twingrove.com, $45 tentsite, laundry, restaurant, ice-cream parlor, Internet, pool, non-guest shower $5.

 PA-72/Swatara Gap—East 2.4 miles to Lickdale, adjacent to I-81 Exit 90. *Restaurants:* Wendy's; McDonald's & Chester Chicken in Love's Truck Plaza; Subway; Burger King; Wendy's; and 0.9 mile from PA-72, Pizza Town II, (717) 865-7970. *Lodging:* Best Western, (717) 865-4234, $109D, continental B, laundry, pool, Internet; Holiday Inn Express, (717) 865-4064, $150–$180, Free B, Internet access; SureStay Plus, (717) 865-8080, $75–$119, continental B, Internet access, laundry, pool; Fairfield Inn & Suites, (717) 865-4234, free B, Internet/Wi-Fi, laundry, pool, ask for hiker rate. *Camping:* Lickdale Campground and General Store (short-term resupply), (800) 562-2609, $39–$46/tentsite, laundry, ATM, store with rotisserie chicken, pizza, ice cream. *Other services:* Love's (showers $9, ATM), BP, and Exxon all have stores (short-term resupply).

William Penn Shelter (1993)—Sleeps 16. Privy. With second-floor loft and windows, 0.1 mile east of the A.T., often visited by summer camping groups. Water source is 200 yards on a blue-blazed trail to the west of the A.T.

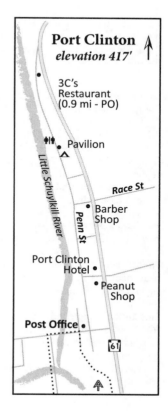

Port Clinton ↑
elevation 417'

3C's Restaurant (0.9 mi - PO)

Pavilion

Race St

Barber Shop

Little Schuylkill River

Penn St

Port Clinton Hotel

Peanut Shop

Post Office

61

▲ PA-501—East 2 miles to **Bethel, PA [P.O. ZIP 19507: M–F 8–12 & 1:15–4:30, Sa 8:30–10:30; (717) 933-8305].** *Other services:* Bethel Animal Clinic, (717) 933-4916. *Internet access:* Bethel Library, M–Th 10–8, F 10–5, Sa 9–4. *Shuttle:* Blue Sky A.T. Shuttles: Steve, (717) 649-4475; Amy, (717) 364-9665.

West 3.7 miles to **Pine Grove, PA [P.O. ZIP 17963: M–F 8:30–4:30, Sa 9–12; (570) 345-4955].** Most major services but spread out over three miles. *Lodging:* Hampton Inn, (570) 345-4505, indoor pool, laundry, Wi-Fi, hot continental B, 10% hiker discount; Baymont by Wyndham, (570) 221-6067, call for rates and services; Comfort Inn, (570) 345-8031, $80–$129d, nonsmoking rooms, pets $10, includes continental B, pool, Internet access, laundry. *Groceries:* Turkey Hill Market with ATM (short-term resupply); BG's Market (long-term resupply), daily 7–9 (both are downtown). *Restaurants:* In downtown Pine Grove 2.6 miles from hotel area are O'Neals Pub, L/D closed Su–M; Dominic's Pizza, L/D, closed Su–M; Burke's Dairy Bar plus others. *Other services:* in hotel area, Dollar General, Arby's, Sunoco, veterinarian.

501 Shelter (1980s)—Immediately north of paved PA-501, go west on the blue-blaze 0.1 mile; always open, no fee. Shelter is fully enclosed, with 12 bunks, table, chairs, skylight (a potter once had her wheel underneath), privy, and solar shower. Tentsites off woods road uphill, beyond fire ring. Water from faucet at adjacent house of BMECC caretaker. No smoking inside shelter; no alcoholic beverages allowed. Pets allowed (on leash only) if other shelter guests are willing to share and owner takes care of sanitary needs. Shuttles and motoring visitors park in public lot on paved 501 and walk in via blue-blaze. Some Pine Grove restaurants might deliver (see above).

Eagles Nest Shelter (1988)—Sleeps 8. Privy. Shelter is 0.3 mile from A.T. on a blue-blazed trail. Intermittent Yeich Spring is crossed en route to the shelter.

▲ Port Clinton, PA [P.O. ZIP 19549: M–F 12:30–4:30, Sa 8–11; (610) 562-3787]—Port Clinton allows hikers to camp free under the roof of St. John's Church pavilion; donate at stjohnspcpa.org. The pavilion, with outhouse, located 0.3 mile west of the A.T. on Penn Street, is a drug- and alcohol-free area. Permission is required for a stay of more than two nights (call LaVerne Sterner, (570) 366-0489). No car camping. Water can be obtained from a spigot outside the Port Clinton Hotel. *Lodging:* Port Clinton Hotel, (610) 562-3354, portclintonhotel.net, $65pp, $10 deposit for room key and towel, shower only $5, closed M–Tu, limited rooms available, laundry, no reservations, Wi-Fi. *Restaurants:* Port Clinton Hotel, L/D, closed M–Tu; 3-C's Restaurant, B/L, M–F 5–3, Sa–Su 6–2. *Other services:* The Port Clinton Peanut Shop, open M–Th 10–7, F–Sa 10–8, Su 10–6, with home-made goodies and snacks, cold drinks, ATM; Port Clinton Barber Shop, hiker-friendly, has music jams, may be able to provide local shuttles.

East on PA-61 1.5 miles to *Lodging:* Microtel Inn, microtelinn.com, (610) 562-4234, $84–$159d, continental B, pet-friendly ($10 nonrefundable fee), free long-distance phone, laundry, Wi-Fi. *Restaurants:* Cabela's Restaurant, B/L/D, provides shuttles from pavilion 10:15 a.m., 1:15 p.m., 5:15 p.m.; Wendy's; Burger King; Cracker Barrel; Starbucks; Cigars International; Pappy T's in Microtel Inn, L/D; Dunkin'/Baskin-Robbins; Shell with food mart (short-term resupply); Subway; Taco Bell/Long John Silver's; McDonald's; Pizza Hut/Wings Street, (610) 562-3619. *Outfitter:* Cabela's Superstore, cabelas.com, (610) 929-7000, M–Sa 8–9, Su 9–8, shuttles available from pavilion to Cabela's, leaving at 10:15 a.m. and 1:15 p.m., returning at 1 p.m. and 5 p.m., camping department, fuel (Esbit, propane/butane, Coleman Powermax), A.T. maps, ATM.

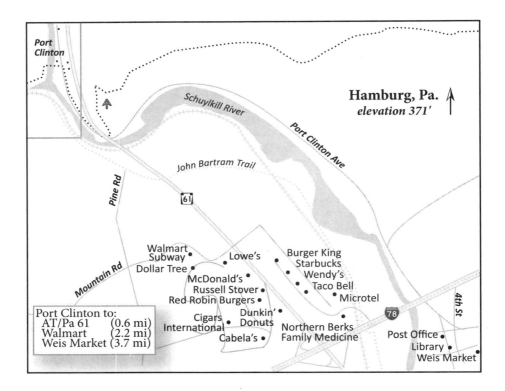

Groceries: Walmart, Aldi. *Bus service:* M–Sa from Cabela's to Hamburg to Reading with connections to Philadelphia; (610) 921-0601, bartabus.com.

East on PA-61 3 miles, then left (0.5 mile) on State Street to **Hamburg, PA [P.O. ZIP 19526; M-F 9-5, Sa 9-12; (610) 562-7812]**. Many services are located on 61 north of I-78. *Groceries:* Weis Supermarket, open daily 6–11, one block east of the town center. *Other services:* St, Luke's Health Center Care Now, (610) 628-7200; coin laundry; pharmacy; movie theater; doctor; dentist; bakery; medical center; veterinarian; banks with ATM. Near PA-61 are Redner's Market Warehouse (open 24 hrs., long-term resupply), Dollar General, Family Dollar, Rite Aid, Arby's, Xiang Shan (Chinese food), Loue's Pizza, Subway.

Hamburg Reservoir—A parking area 0.3 mile **East** of the A.T. requires free permits for overnight parking. Call the Borough of Hamburg, (610) 562-7821, for permission.

Windsor Furnace Shelter (1970s)—Sleeps 8. Privy. Tentsites. Shelter is located on a blue-blazed trail near the reservoir. Water source is the creek south of the shelter. *No campfires except at shelter. No swimming in streams or reservoir.*

Blue Rocks Campground— **East** 1.5 miles to campground, 341 Sousley Rd., Lenhartsville, PA 19534; (610) 756-6366, bluerockscampground.com; via a blue-blazed trail from Pulpit Rock and a yellow-blazed trail from The Pinnacle. Tentsites $32 M–F, 50% discount for thru-hikers M–Th, showers, swimming (non-guest) $4, laundry, Wi-Fi. Camp store (short-term resupply), M–Th 9–7, F 9–11, Sa 8–11, Su 8–7, with Coleman fuel and limited hiker supplies. Mail drops accepted. Hiker-friendly.

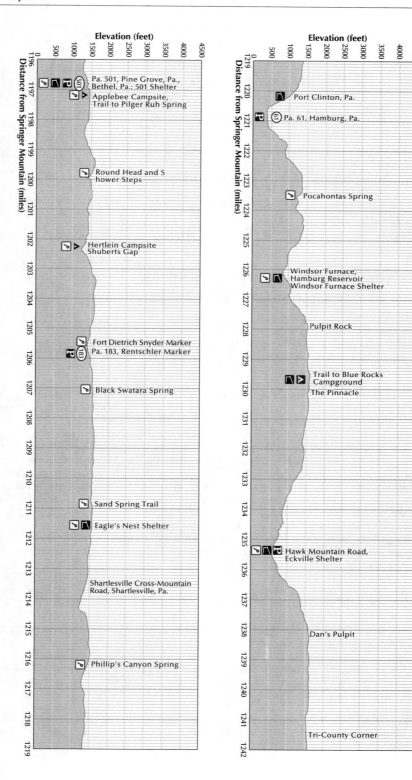

Elevation (feet)

Distance from Springer Mountain (miles)

Pa. 501, Pine Grove, Pa., Bethel, Pa.; 501 Shelter
Applebee Campsite, Trail to Pilger Ruh Spring

Round Head and Shower-Steps

Hertlein Campsite Shuberts Gap

Fort Dietrich Snyder Marker
Pa. 183, Rentschler Marker

Black Swatara Spring

Sand Spring Trail

Eagle's Nest Shelter

Shartlesville Cross-Mountain Road, Shartlesville, Pa.

Phillip's Canyon Spring

Port Clinton, Pa.

Pa. 61, Hamburg, Pa.

Pocahontas Spring

Windsor Furnace, Hamburg Reservoir
Windsor Furnace Shelter

Pulpit Rock

Trail to Blue Rocks Campground
The Pinnacle

Hawk Mountain Road, Eckville Shelter

Dan's Pulpit

Tri-County Corner

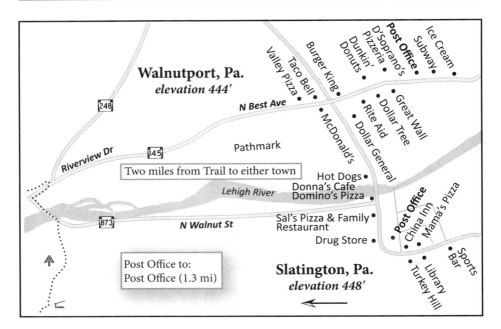

Walnutport, Pa.
elevation 444'

248

Valley Pizza
Taco Bell
Burger King
Dunkin' Donuts
D'Soprano's Pizzeria
Post Office
Subway
Ice Cream

N Best Ave

Great Wall
Dollar Tree
Rite Aid
Dollar General
McDonald's

Riverview Dr 145 Pathmark

Two miles from Trail to either town

Lehigh River

873 N Walnut St

Hot Dogs
Donna's Cafe
Domino's Pizza
Sal's Pizza & Family Restaurant
Drug Store

Post Office
China Inn
Mama's Pizza

Post Office to:
Post Office (1.3 mi)

Slatington, Pa.
elevation 448'

Sports Bar
Library
Turkey Hill

The Pinnacle—A panoramic view of Pennsylvania farmland from an elevation of 1,635 feet, said to be the best view on the A.T. in the state. Below the viewpoint lies a sheer cliff and a few caves. *No camping or fires are permitted.*

Hawk Mountain Rd.—**East** 0.2 mile to Eckville Shelter, an enclosed bunkroom that offers space for 6. No fee. Water from a spigot at the back of the caretaker's house. Solar shower, flush toilet, tent platforms, picnic table. Open year-round; privy and shower are winterized.

Hawk Mountain Sanctuary—Atop the Kittatinny Ridge sits the Hawk Mountain Visitor Center, hawkmountain.org, accessible via a 2.5-mile blue-blazed trail from the A.T. Located within the visitor center are a bookstore, gift shop, and interpretive exhibits on raptors that fly by the mountain during the migratory seasons. Several species other than raptors can be seen; 16 species of hawks, falcons, and eagles have been spotted over the mountain. Daily fee $10 adults, $7 seniors, $5 children 6–12. Open 8–5 Sep–Nov, 9–5 Dec–Aug.

Allentown Hiking Club—AHC maintains the 10.7 miles from Tri-County Corner to Bake Oven Knob. Correspondence should be sent to P.O. Box 1542, Allentown, PA 18105; allentownhikingclub.org; info@allentownhikingclub.org.

Allentown Hiking Club Shelter (1997)—Sleeps 8. Privy. Tentsites. First water source is a spring 0.2 mile downhill in front of shelter; if dry, continue downhill 0.1 mile to second spring.

PA-309—Thunderhead Lodge, (610) 248-0524, W–Th 4–9, F–Sa 12–9, Su 11–7; has water for hikers at the back of the building; no camping.

Bake Oven Knob Shelter (1937)—Sleeps 6. No privy. One of the original Pennsylvania shelters. The first water source on the blue-blazed trail is often dry; continue 200 yards to the second, more dependable spring, although both may be intermittent.

Keystone Trails Association—KTA maintains the 11.3 miles from Lehigh Furnace Gap to Little Gap. Correspondence should be sent to 46 E. Main St., Mechanicsburg, PA 17055, or call (717) 766-9690; kta-hike.org.

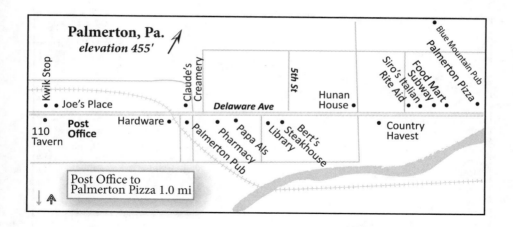

Palmerton, Pa.
elevation 455'

Kwik Stop
• • Joe's Place
Claude's Creamery
5th St
Delaware Ave
Hunan House •
Siro's Italian
Rite Aid
Subway
Food Mart
Palmerton Pizza
Blue Mountain Pub

•
110
Tavern
Post
Office
Hardware •
Palmerton Pub
Pharmacy
Papa Als
Library
Bert's Steakhouse
• Country Havest

Post Office to
Palmerton Pizza 1.0 mi

George W. Outerbridge Shelter (1965)—Sleeps 6. No privy. The surrounding area suffers from heavy-metal contamination from the zinc plant at Palmerton (see Superfund entry on next page). Water source is a piped spring north 150 yards on the A.T.

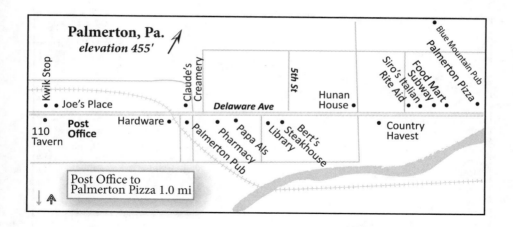 **PA-873/Lehigh Gap—East** 2 miles on PA-873 to **Slatington, PA [P.O. ZIP 18080: M–F 8:30–5, Sa 8:30–12; (610) 767-2182].** *Grocery:* Hucksters. *Restaurants:* Mama's Pizza; Sal's Pizza; China Inn; Donna's Cafe. *Internet access:* Slatington Library, M, W 9–7, Tu 9–3, F 9–5, Sa 8–2. *Other services:* coin laundry, ATM, convenience stores, A.F. Boyer Hardware store, doctor, dentist, pharmacy, bowling alley, and bus service to Walnutport and Allentown.

East 2 miles on PA-145 to **Walnutport, PA [P.O. ZIP 18088: M–F 8:30–5, Sa 8:30–12; (610) 767-5191].** *Groceries:* Dollar General and Dollar Tree (short-term resupply). *Restaurants:* Great Wall Chinese; D'Sopranos Pizza; fast-food options. *Other services:* ATM, doctor, dentist, pharmacy,.

West 2 miles on PA-248 or 2-mile blue-blaze to **Palmerton, PA [P.O. ZIP 18071: M–F 8:30–5, Sa 8:30–12; (610) 826-2286].** *Blue-blaze directions:* West 1.5 miles from the gravel lot on the northwest side of the Lehigh River over the Aquashicola Creek Bridge to the back road leading to Delaware Ave. in Palmerton. *Hostel:* Squeak's Yard, Lehigh Gap/Palmerton, PA, text (732) 228-2495. Free showers, laundry, and camping in yard, fire bowl and grill available, no hard drugs. Donations accepted in behalf of Warrior Expeditions, warriorexpeditions.org, resupply and meals within 1 block. *Lodging:* Garage Bunkroom near Bert's Steakhouse, pets allowed in the garage, call Tracy, (610) 597-2020; Sunny Rest Resort, 425 Sunny Rest Rd., (866) SUN-NY50, clothing optional, tenting available. *Groceries:* Country Harvest (both long-term resupply). *Restaurants:* Bert's Steakhouse, B/L/D; One Ten Tavern, L/D; Tony's Pizzeria; Joe's Place, deli sandwiches; Palmerton Pizza and Restaurant; Subway; Hunan House Chinese. *Internet access:* library M 10–8, Tu–F 10–5, Sa 9–4 (Sa Jul–Aug 9–1). *Other services:* coin laundry; ATM; shuttle back to the Trail, Duane Masonheimer, (610) 767-7969; Shea's Hardware and Sporting Goods, Heet, Coleman fuel, and denatured alcohol; bowling alley; Rite Aid pharmacy; doctor; dentist; and hospital.

Palmerton EPA Superfund Site—The devastation along Blue Mountain near Lehigh Gap is the result of nearly a century of zinc smelting in Palmerton. In 1980, the Environmental Protection Agency shut down the furnaces and, in 1982, put the affected area on the Superfund clean-up list. Revegetation and relocation efforts are underway, and the mountain is slowly coming back to life.

Appalachian Mountain Club-Delaware Valley Chapter—AMC-Delaware Valley maintains the 15.4 miles from Little Gap to Wind Gap and the 7.2 miles from Fox Gap to the Delaware River Bridge. Correspondence should be sent to 1180 Greenleaf Dr., Bethlehem, PA 18017; amcdv.org.

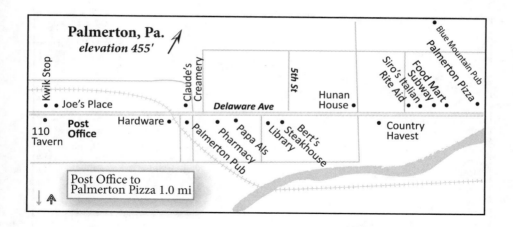 **Little Gap, Blue Mountain Drive—West** 2.5 miles to Little Gap and *Restaurant:* Covered Bridge Inn. **East** 1.1 miles to Blue Mountain Drive-in & Family Restaurant, (610) 767-6379, W 9–2, Th–Su 9–7.

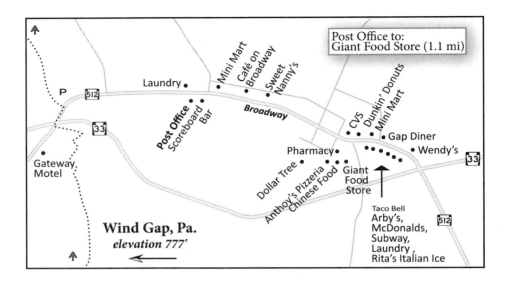

East 1.5 miles to **Danielsville, PA [P.O. 18038: M–F 9:30–1 & 2–4:30, Sa 8–12; (610) 767-6822]**. *Lodging:* Filbert B&B, (610) 428-3300, filbertbnb.com, starting at $100D (cash only), reservations required; full, hearty, country B; pay laundry; will pick up and drop off hikers and possibly shuttle; mail drops accepted only for guests, but call first; use of dining room. *Groceries:* Millers Market & Deli, (610) 767-6671.

Smith Gap Rd., Point Phillips Rd.—West 3.4 miles to **Kunkletown, PA [P.O. ZIP 18058: M–F 8–11:30, 12:30–5, Sa 8–12; (610) 381-3062.]** *Restaurant:* Kunkletown Pub, (610) 895-4255, Tu–Su 12–9.

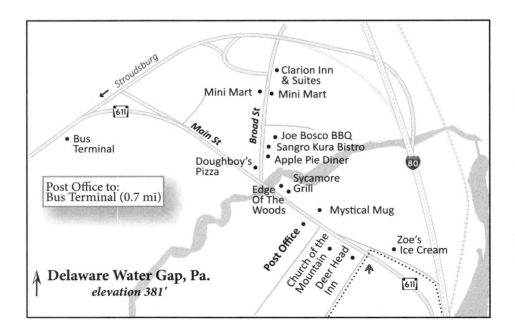

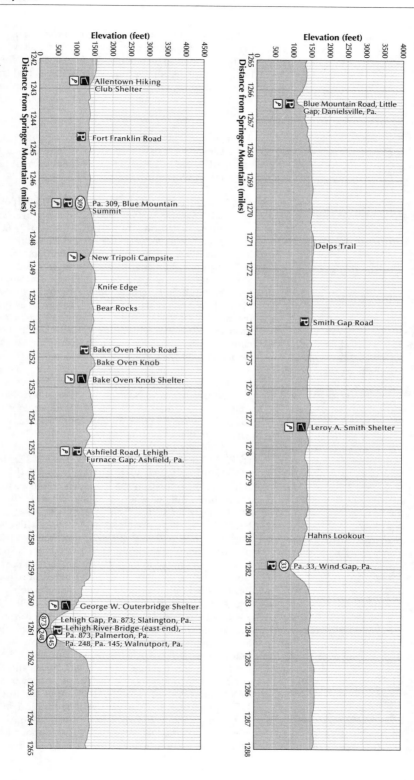

Elevation (feet)

Distance from Springer Mountain (miles)

Allentown Hiking Club Shelter

Fort Franklin Road

Pa. 309, Blue Mountain Summit

New Tripoli Campsite

Knife Edge

Bear Rocks

Bake Oven Knob Road

Bake Oven Knob

Bake Oven Knob Shelter

Ashfield Road, Lehigh Furnace Gap; Ashfield, Pa.

George W. Outerbridge Shelter

Lehigh Gap, Pa. 873; Slatington, Pa.
Lehigh River Bridge (east-end),
Pa. 873, Palmerton, Pa.
Pa. 248, Pa. 145; Walnutport, Pa.

Elevation (feet)

Distance from Springer Mountain (miles)

Blue Mountain Road, Little Gap; Danielsville, Pa.

Delps Trail

Smith Gap Road

Leroy A. Smith Shelter

Hahns Lookout

Pa. 33, Wind Gap, Pa.

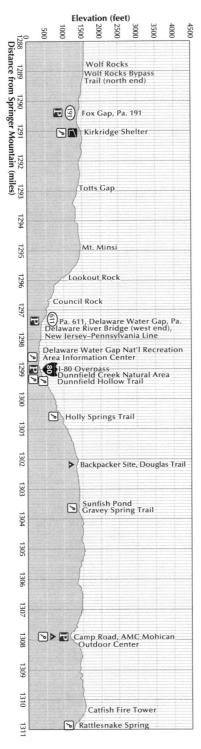

Elevation (feet)

Distance from Springer Mountain (miles)

Wolf Rocks
Wolf Rocks Bypass
Trail (north end)

Fox Gap, Pa. 191

Kirkridge Shelter

Totts Gap

Mt. Minsi

Lookout Rock

Council Rock

Pa. 611, Delaware Water Gap, Pa.
Delaware River Bridge (west end),
New Jersey–Pennsylvania Line

Delaware Water Gap Nat'l Recreation
Area Information Center
I-80 Overpass
Dunnfield Creek Natural Area
Dunnfield Hollow Trail

Holly Springs Trail

Backpacker Site, Douglas Trail

Sunfish Pond
Gravey Spring Trail

Camp Road, AMC Mohican
Outdoor Center

Catfish Fire Tower

Rattlesnake Spring

Leroy A. Smith Shelter (1972)—Sleeps 8. Privy (composting). Shelter is 0.2 mile down a blue-blazed trail. Water sources are said to be reliable; the first, 0.2 mile down the blue-blazed trail; a second, on a yellow-blazed trail 0.2 mile farther; a third, even farther, may be running when the first two are not. *Note: Water pump might be out at Kirkridge Shelter.*

Batona Hiking Club—BHC maintains the 8.5 miles from Wind Gap to Fox Gap (PA-191). Correspondence can be sent to BHC, 6651 Eastwood St., Philadelphia, PA 19149; batonahikingclub.org.

PA-33—East 1 mile to **Wind Gap, PA [P.O. ZIP 18091: M–F 8:30–5, Sa 8:30–12; (610) 863-6206]**. *Lodging:* Gateway Motel, 10 seconds from Trail, Satish, (610) 881-6045, hiker rate $90 weekends, dogs OK ($20), very hiker-friendly, free tenting with use of bathroom, shower $10, free water, shuttles available. *Groceries:* Giant Food Store (long-term resupply, 24 hrs.); Dollar TreeSunoco Mini Mart (all short-term resupply). *Restaurants:* Sal's Pizza; Hong Kong Restaurant; Jaid's Lounge; diners serving B/L/D; Rita's Ices; other fast-food options. **Other services:** coin laundry; hardware store; doctor (24-hour clinic); dentist; pharmacy; veterinarian (northeast of town on PA-512); bank with ATM.

Kirkridge Shelter (1948)—Sleeps 8. Privy. Shelter is on a blue-blazed trail with excellent views south. Water source, an outside tap to rear of shelter before the Kirkridge Retreat facility parking lot, is turned off in winter months.

PA-611/Delaware Water Gap, PA [P.O. ZIP 18327: M–F 8:30–12 & 1–4:45, Sa 8:30–11:30; (570) 476-0304]—The A.T. doesn't go through the town center, but services are within a mile of where it crosses PA-611. *Hostel:* The Presbyterian Church of the Mountain Hiker Center, (570) 992-3924, director David Childs, with overflow lean-to in backyard; please respect the good-will of Pastor Sherry Blackman and parishioners. Space with shower limited to long-distance hikers—no car or van parking or support vehicles permitted in parking lot. Two-night limit, donation suggested, absolutely no drugs or alcohol. *Lodging:* Deer Head Inn, (570) 424-2000, restaurant and finely appointed rooms; Fairmont Inn & Suites, 101 Broad St., coin laundry. *Restaurants:* Sango Kura Brewery, Th–Su 12–9; Joe Bosco Authentic Smokehouse BBQ; Apple Pie Diner; Doughboy Pizza; Deer Head Inn for fine dining F–Su, pizza, and live entertainment, oldest continuously operating jazz club in the U.S.; Sycamore Grille Restaurant & Tap Room, L/D, closed Su–M, D by reservation; Mystical Mug; Castle Inn & Shops, 20 Delaware Ave., old-fashioned ice cream. *Groceries:* Fuel Mart with ATM, Sunoco Mini Mart (short-term resupply). **Other services:** hair salon, run by Paulette, (570) 421-8218, Tu–F 10–7, Sa 10–3. ***Bus service:*** Martz Trailways, (570) 421-4451 or (570) 421-3040, to New York, Philadelphia, and Scranton, and local service on "Pocono Pony" to Stroudsburg and Delaware Water Gap National Recreation Area.

West 5 miles to East Stroudsburg and Stroudsburg, PA, full-service towns. ***Lodging:*** Super 8, (570) 420-7267, call for rates. ***Outfitters:*** Dunkelberger's Sports Outfitter, (570) 421-7950, with backpacking equipment, supplies, and clothing, is located at 6th and Main streets; Ready Set run, (570) 424-6431, after hours (570) 242-8931 (leave message), 431 Main St., Stroudsburg, PA 18360, trail running and hiking footwear, inserts, socks, nutrition, etc., mail drops accepted, open M–Sa. ***Other services:*** 7-day walk-in clinic at hospital. ***Shuttles:*** Ryan Rickley, (570) 801-0348, PA-NY.

New Jersey

Miles from Springer	Miles to Next Point	Features	Services	Elev	Miles from Katahdin	M A P
1,297.6	1.0	Delaware River Bridge (west end); Pennsylvania–New Jersey State Line		350'	899.8	
1,298.6	0.4	Delaware Water Gap National Recreation Area Kittatinny Point Visitors Center	R, P, w	350'	898.8	
1,299.0	0.1	I-80: underpass	R	350'	898.4	
1,299.1	0.1	Dunnfield Creek Natural Area: water pump at northern end of parking area	R, P, w	350'	898.3	
1,299.2	1.4	Dunnfield Creek Trail to Dunnfield Creek Falls (E-0.25m)	w	350'	898.2	
1,300.6	1.6	Holly Springs Trail (E-0.2m)	w	950'	896.8	
1,302.2	1.3	Backpacker Campsite, blue-blazed Douglas Trail West-1.8m to Worthington State Forest CG	C C, w, sh	1,300'	895.2	
1,303.5	0.1	Sunfish Pond: glacial pond, no camping		1,382'	893.9	
1,303.6	4.4	Garvey Springs Trail (W-600 ft.): orange-blazed	w	1,400'	893.8	ATC: NY-NJ Map 4
1,308.0	2.4	Camp Mohican Road: dirt road West-0.3m to AMC Mohican Outdoor Center	R, P, w C, L, M, g, sh, f	1,150'	889.4	
1,310.4	0.6	Catfish Firetower	C	1,565'	887.0	
1,311.0	0.4	Rattlesnake Spring (W-50ft.): on dirt road	w	1,260'	886.4	
1,311.4	3.9	Millbrook–Blairstown Road–County Road 602 West-1.1m to Millbrook Village Picnic Area	R, P w	1,260'	886.0	
1,315.3	1.8	Blue Mountain Lakes Road (Flatbrookville Stillwater Road) (E-0.1m piped spring)	R, P, w	1,350'	882.1	
1,317.1	1.2	Crater Lake Trail (E-0.3m): view 150 ft. east	R, P, w	1,560'	880.3	
1,318.3	1.8	Buttermilk Falls Trail West-1.5m to waterfall	C R, P	1,560'	879.1	
1,320.1	2.2	Rattlesnake Mountain: open ledges	C	1,492'	877.3	
1,322.3	3.6	**Brink Road Shelter** (W-0.2m), 31.5mS; 7mN	S, w	1,110'	875.1	
1,325.9	0.3	Culvers Gap, US-206 East-0.8m; 1m; 1.6m; 2.5m to services East-3.4m to **Branchville, NJ, P.O. 07826** West-1.8m to Forest Motel	M C, G, L, M M L	935'	871.5	
1,326.2	1.7	Sunrise Mountain Road	R	970'	871.2	
1,327.9	1.1	Culver Firetower		1,550'	869.5	
1,329.0	2.4	**Gren Anderson Shelter** (W-0.1m), 7mS; 5.9mN	S, w	1,320'	868.4	
1,331.4	0.8	Sunrise Mountain: picnic pavilion	R, P	1,653'	866.0	ATC: NY-NJ Map 3
1,332.2	2.6	Crigger Road: dirt	R	1,400'	865.2	
1,334.8	0.2	**Mashipacong Shelter**, 5.9mS; 3mN	S	1,425'	862.6	
1,335.0	2.4	Deckertown Turnpike: paved	R, P	1,320'	862.4	
1,337.4	1.8	**Rutherford Shelter** (E-0.4m), 3mS; 5.1mN	S, w	1,345'	860.0	
1,339.2	1.1	Blue Dot Trail (W-0.4m to Sawmill Lake CG)	C, w	1,600'	858.2	

Miles from Springer	Miles to Next Point	Features	Services	Elev	Miles from Katahdin	M A P
1,340.3	1.0	NJ-23; High Point State Park HQ _East–1.5m to_ High Point Mountain Motel _East–2.9m to_ Elias Cole Restaurant _West–0.7m to_ state park day-use area _West–4.4m to_ Shop Rite _West–5.6m to_ Mosey's Place _West–7.1m to_ **Port Jervis, NY, P.O. 12771**	R, P, w L, M M M, sh G, M H G, L, M, D, T	1,500'	857.1	
1,341.3	0.2	Observation platform		1,680'	856.1	
1,341.5	0.5	Side trail to High Point Monument		1,600'	855.9	
1,342.0	1.3	**High Point Shelter** (E–0.1m), 5.1mS; 12.5mN	S, w	1,280'	855.4	
1,343.3	0.8	County Road 519: _paved (E–2.5m to_ High Point Mountain Motel)	R, P, L	1,100'	854.1	
1,344.1	1.2	Courtwright Road: _gravel_	R	1,000'	853.3	
1,345.3	0.6	Ferguson Road	R	900'	852.1	
1,345.9	0.7	Gemmer Road: _paved_	R	740'	851.5	
1,346.6	0.3	Stream	w	710'	850.8	
1,346.9	0.2	Goodrich Road: _paved_	R	610'	850.5	
1,347.1	0.2	Concrete dam _(outlet of pond)_		700'	850.3	
1,347.3	0.1	Road to Jim Murray Property (W–0.2m)	S, C, w, sh	660'	850.1	
1,347.4	0.2	Goldsmith Road: _gravel_	R	600'	850.0	
1,347.6	0.6	Vernie Swamp _(northern end)_: _puncheons_		590'	849.8	
1,348.2	0.3	Unionville Road, County Road 651	R, P	610'	849.2	
1,348.5	0.6	Quarry Road	R, P	605'	848.9	
1,349.1	1.0	Lott Road, Jersey Avenue _West–0.4m to_ **Unionville, NY, P.O. 10988**	R C, G, M	590'	848.3	
1,350.1	0.5	NJ-284	R, P	420'	847.3	
1,350.6	1.0	Oil City Road	R	400'	846.8	
1,351.6	0.3	Wallkill River	R	410'	845.8	
1,351.9	2.0	Wallkill National Wildlife Preserve		410'	845.5	
1,353.9	0.5	Lake Wallkill Road (Liberty Corners Road)	R, w	440'	843.5	
1,354.4	1.5	**Pochuck Mountain Shelter,** 12.5mS; 11.6mN	S	840'	843.0	
1,355.9	1.2	Pochuck Mountain		1,200'	841.5	
1,357.1	1.5	County Road 565 _West–1.1m to_ **Glenwood, NJ, P.O. 07418**	R, P C, G, L, w	720'	840.3	
1,358.6	0.7	County Road 517 _West–1.1m to_ **Glenwood, NJ, P.O. 07418**	R, P C, G, L, w	440'	838.8	
1,359.3	0.7	Pochuck Creek: _boardwalk, bridge_		410'	838.1	
1,360.0	0.9	Canal Road	R, P	410'	837.4	
1,360.9	1.4	NJ-94 _East–1.4m to_ Appalachian Motel _East–2.4m to_ **Vernon, NJ, P.O. 07462** _West–0.1m to_ Heaven Hill Farm and Deli _West–2.5m to_ Mom's Homestyle Deli _West–6.1m to_ **Warwick, NY, P.O. 10990** _West–7.4m to_ Meadowlark Farm B&B	R, P L G, M, D, V, f G, M, w M B, G, M, D, cl C, L	450'	836.5	
1,362.3	1.7	Wawayanda Mountain: _Pinwheel's Vista_		1,340'	835.1	
1,364.0	1.1	Barrett Road, New Milford, NY	R, P	1,140'	833.4	
1,365.1	0.6	Iron Mountain Road: _bridge_ _East–1.6m to_ Wawayanda Lake	R M, w	1,060'	832.3	

ATC: NY-NJ Map 3

Miles from Springer	Miles to Next Point	Features	Services	Elev	Miles from Katahdin	M A P
1,365.7	0.2	Wawayanda Road	R	1,150'	831.7	
1,365.9	0.1	**Wawayanda Shelter** *(W-0.1m)*, *11.6mS; 12.3mN*	S	1,200'	831.5	
1,366.0	0.4	Hoeferlin Trail: *water for Wawayanda Shelter (E-0.2m)*	w	1,200'	831.4	
1,366.4	1.4	Warwick Turnpike *West-2.7m to Shop Rite, Grill, Brew Pub*	R, P G, M	1,140'	831.0	
1,367.8	1.1	Long House Road (Brady Road)	R, P	1,080'	829.6	
1,368.9	1.1	Long House Creek		1,085'	828.5	
1,370.0	0.4	New Jersey–New York State Line; State Line Trail; Hewitt, NJ *(E-1m to Lakeside Road, P)*		1,385'	827.4	

Table map column (right edge, vertical): ATC: NY-NJ Map 3

New Jersey has the highest population of bears per square mile. Southbounders are at the end of their deli-to-deli hike, whereas northbounders hungrily look forward to theirs. Thru-hiker legs are pumping at machine level now, which is good, because you may have to walk farther to find water.

Note: Bear boxes are provided at several New Jersey shelters; please use them! Bears are extremely active in this area. One bear destroyed a hiker's tent. Never feed bears or leave food unattended. Do not bury or scatter excess food; avoid eating or preparing food in your tent. It's best to eat your meals away from your camp.

Campfires are prohibited in New Jersey. Camping in areas other than those designated by signs also is prohibited in New Jersey. Hitchhiking is illegal in New Jersey.

Venomous snakes are active throughout the area during warmer months. Be cautious when hiking at night and pay attention near rocky ledges.

New York-New Jersey Trail Conference—The NY-NJ TC maintains the 163.7 miles from the Delaware River to the New York-Connecticut state line. Correspondence should be sent to NY-NJ TC, 600 Ramapo Valley Rd., Mahwah, NJ 07430; (201) 512-9348; nynjtc.org; info@nynjtc.org.

Delaware Water Gap National Recreation Area—The Kittatinny Point Visitor Center, (908) 496-4458, visible from the Trail, has restrooms and a picnic area. Open daily Memorial Day weekend–Labor Day and 3 days a week in early Sep. Water is available from a spigot to the left of the building. The Trail on Kittatinny Ridge runs through the NRA and state parks and forests, where regulations are different. The history of the recreation area is linked to a controversial 1960s plan to dam the Delaware, defeated by local opponents and the Trail community. Thru-hikers (defined by DWG as those hiking for two or more consecutive days) are permitted to camp along the Trail in the NRA with the following restrictions: one night per campsite, no more than ten persons per site, hiker camping allowed only within 100 feet of the A.T., no camping within 0.5 mile of an established roadway, no camping within 200 feet of another party, no camping from 0.5 mile south of Blue Mountain Lakes Rd. to the junction with the Buttermilk Falls Trail, no camping within 100 feet of any water source. Ground fires and charcoal stoves and grills are prohibited. Pets must be on a 6-foot leash at all times.

Holly Spring Trail—Holly Spring is 0.2 mile east of the A.T.; may fail during dry weather.

Worthington State Forest—Camping in Worthington State Forest is only permitted at **Backpacker Campsite 2** at the junction with the Douglas Trail 4.6 miles north of I-80 on the A.T. and at the state-forest campground on Old Mine Rd. (see below). Rangers patrol the area and issue fines for those violating camping restrictions. Worthington State Forest Campground, (908) 841-9575, offers riverside camping and showers. From the A.T., take the blue Douglas Trail west 1.1 mile, then turn left onto the green Rock Cores Trail for another 0.7 mile to forest office; $25/site + $5 walk-in fee, max. 6 people; no pets or alcohol. Bear boxes.

Sunfish Pond—The southernmost glacial pond on the A.T. and one of seven protected natural areas in New Jersey. *No camping or swimming is allowed at the pond.*

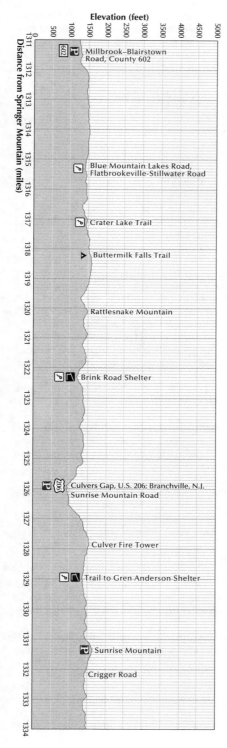

Elevation (feet)

Distance from Springer Mountain (miles)

Millbrook–Blairstown Road, County 602

Blue Mountain Lakes Road, Flatbrookeville-Stillwater Road

Crater Lake Trail

Buttermilk Falls Trail

Rattlesnake Mountain

Brink Road Shelter

Culvers Gap, U.S. 206; Branchville, N.J. Sunrise Mountain Road

Culver Fire Tower

Trail to Gren Anderson Shelter

Sunrise Mountain

Crigger Road

Garvey Spring Trail—A seasonal spring is located 600 feet west of the A.T. May fail in dry weather.

AMC Mohican Outdoor Center—West, on a dirt road, 0.3 mile; 50 Camp Mohican Rd., Blairstown, NJ 07825; (908) 362-5670, operated by the Appalachian Mountain Club (AMC). Thru-hikers, ask for rates in a shared cabin with bunk, stove, or tent camping with shower. Shower only, $5. Meal service available, ask for rates. Camp store with deli (mid-Apr to mid-Oct), sodas, ice cream, candy, and limited hiker supplies, including Coleman fuel and denatured alcohol by the ounce. The center accepts packages marked "Hold for A.T. Hiker" (with name) and sent via USPS, UPS, or FedEx; it cannot send packages. Check in at the visitor center, entrance on the left. Water available there or from a seasonal spigot near the garage across the road.

Catfish Fire Tower—Several campsites are located just north of the tower, along east side of the A.T. with good views across the valley. Get water at Mohican Outdoor Center or Rattlesnake Spring (below).

Rattlesnake Spring—Located 0.6 mile north of the Catfish Fire Tower on a dirt road about 50 feet west of the A.T. Spring may fail during drought times.

Millbrook-Blairstown Rd., CR 602—West 1.1 miles to Millbrook Village, a historical park with flush toilets and picnic area. From Oct to May, the water supply in the picnic area is cut off, and the restrooms are closed except for a unisex, handicap-accessible bathroom.

Blue Mountain Lakes Rd./Flatbrookville Stillwater Rd.—No camping from 0.5 mile south of this road to the junction with the Buttermilk Falls Trail. Several grassy areas for tenting are available 0.5–0.7 mile south of the road. The water pump no longer works, but water is available at a piped spring 100 yards east of the A.T. crossing: Follow the road downhill and 20 yards past the gate; spring is on the right side of the road.

Crater Lake—The A.T. crosses the orange Crater Lake Trail twice. From the second junction (0.4 mile north of the first), the orange trail leads east 0.3 mile to a parking area and beach; west, 0.5 mile to Hemlock Pond, which offers good swimming.

Buttermilk Falls Trail—Several campsites here, but water source is 1.5 miles west down the steep blue-blazed trail to New Jersey's highest waterfall. No camping allowed south of this point to 0.5 mile south of Blue Mountain Lakes Rd.

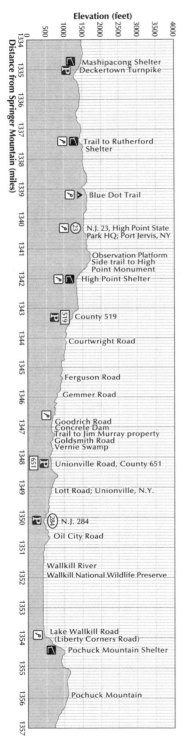

Elevation (feet)

Distance from Springer Mountain (miles)

Mashipacong Shelter
Deckertown Turnpike

Trail to Rutherford Shelter

Blue Dot Trail

N.J. 23, High Point State Park HQ; Port Jervis, NY

Observation Platform
Side trail to High Point Monument
High Point Shelter

County 519

Courtwright Road

Ferguson Road

Gemmer Road

Goodrich Road
Concrete Dam
Trail to Jim Murray property
Goldsmith Road
Vernie Swamp
Unionville Road, County 651

Lott Road; Unionville, N.Y.

N.J. 284

Oil City Road

Wallkill River
Wallkill National Wildlife Preserve

Lake Wallkill Road
(Liberty Corners Road)
Pochuck Mountain Shelter

Pochuck Mountain

Brink Shelter (2013)—Sleeps 8. Composting privy. Bear box. Built by NY-NJ TC volunteers and Stokes State Forest staff members using trees downed by Hurricane Irene. Bears and rattlesnakes are especially active here. Water source is across the road at a spring 100 yards northeast of the shelter.

US-206/Culvers Gap—*Restaurants:* Gyp's Tavern, (973) 948-5013, located on nearby Kittatinny Lake, open Su-Th 11 a.m.–11p.m., F-Sa 11 a.m.–1a.m., serves L/D (cash only); Mountain House Tavern & Grille, (973) 250-3300, open daily Su-Th 11:30–8, F-Sa 11:30–9.

East 0.8 mile to Culver Lake FLea Market with fresh baked goods, fruit, and vegetables.

East 1 mile to *Restaurant:* Jumboland Diner, B/L/D, daily 6 a.m.–9 p.m.

East 1.6 miles to *Groceries:* Dale's Market with ATM (long-term resupply). *Restaurants:* Dairy Queen. *Lodging:* Cobmin Ridge Motel, (862) 220-3137.

East 2.5 miles to *Groceries:* Yellow Cottage Deli & Bakery (short-term resupply), closed M. *Restaurants:* Riviera Maya Mexican, open daily, L/D; Firehouse Bagel Co. Temporary closure due to fire. *Camping:* Harmony Ridge Campground, (973) 948-4941, $18pp for thru-hikers. Showers and small camp store with limited supplies, including canister fuel. Call from US-206 for a ride to/from the campground.

East 3.4 miles to **Branchville, NJ [P.O. ZIP 07826: M-F 8:30-5, Sa 8:30–1; (973) 948-3580].** *Restaurants:* Most within 1 block of P.O.: A&G Pizza; Victoria Diner; China One (take-out), (973) 948-8882, The Barnyard, on US-206. *Shuttle:* George Lightcap, (201) 906-3556, beatnikhiker@gmail.com. *Other services:* bank, ATM, drugstore.

Gren Anderson Shelter (1958)—Sleeps 8. Privy. Bear box. Rooms for a few tents. Built by the now-disbanded New York section of the Green Mountain Club. Water source is a spring downhill to left of the shelter.

Sunrise Mountain—*No camping allowed at pavilion.* Nearby parking lot for day-use visitors. No water.

Mashipacong Shelter (1936)—Sleeps 8. Privy. Bear box. High bear activity in this area. A stone shelter with wooden floor. Camping, but no water available.

Rutherford Shelter (1967)—Sleeps 6. Bear box; privy. High bear activity in this area. Water source is a small stream 25 yards behind the shelter that may fail during drought times.

Blue Dot Trail—West 0.4 mile to *Camping.* Steep descent from the A.T. to Sawmill Lake Campground, (973) 875-4800, open Apr 1–Oct 31, flush toilets and potable water, no showers, $25/night + $5 walk-in fee, 6/site, no pets or alcohol.

NJ-23—High Point State Park Headquarters, 1480 State Route 23, Sussex, NJ 07461; (973) 875-4800. On the A.T., has indoor restrooms and a seasonal outdoor water spigot.

Offices are open year-round; mail drops accepted. Day-use area 0.7 mile west of the A.T. on Kuser Rd. has swimming at spring-fed Lake Marcia, a concession stand, grill, and no charge to walk-ins for hot showers; open Memorial Day–Labor Day, 10–6. High Point Monument, on a short side trail from the A.T., marks the highest point in the state, 1,803 feet. *Hostel:* See Mosey's Place below. *Camping:* See Blue Dot Trail above.

East 1 mile to *Lodging:* High Point Mountain Motel, 1328 Route 23, Wantage, NJ 07461, (973) 702-1860, highpointmountainmotel.com, $99d, $10eap, pets $10 (call ahead), includes shuttle to/from Trail, laundry service $7, soda machine, free Wi-Fi. *Restaurants:* Annabel's Pizza, (973) 875-1886; Grand Eastern Chinese, (973) 702-1138; both deliver to inn.

East 2.6 miles to *Restaurant:* Elias Cole Restaurant, (973) 875-3550, B/L/D, 7 a.m.–8 p.m. daily, cash only, home-made pie, bread, country food.

West 4.4 miles to *Groceries:* Shop-Rite supermarket (long-term resupply). *Restaurants:* Village Pizza, Dairy Queen, and McDonald's. *Other services:* bank with ATM.

Map text:
- Annabel's Pizza
- Village Office
- Post Office
- Horler's General Store
- Post Office to: Trail (0.5 mi) *via Lott Rd*
- Free camping permits at the Village Office (M-F 8 a.m. - 3 p.m.) or Horler's General Store.
- Wits End Tavern
- 284
- Lott Rd (Jersey Ave)
- **Unionville, N.Y.** *elevation 525'*
- N.Y. / N.J.
- (0.4 mi)

West 5.6 miles to *Hostel:* Mosey's Place, (845-239-3028), littlelo59@yahoo.com, reservations required, open May 1–Oct 31, call in advance; $40 includes bunk, shower, laundry, free shuttles to Port Jervis for resupply, post office, etc., and pick-up and drop-off at High Point Park HQ. Small hostel with 6 bunks owned by Mosey (AT '15). Near Metro-North train (see below).

West 7.1 miles to **Port Jervis, NY [P.O. ZIP 12771: M-F 9-5, Sa 9-1; (845) 858-8173].** *Lodging:* Erie Hotel and Restaurant, (845) 858-4100, $99. Call before sending packages; accepts them marked "Hold for Hiker" (with name). *Groceries:* MG Food Mart (both short-term resupply), Price Chopper, Sav A Lot (both long-term resupply). *Restaurants:* All within two blocks of P.O.: Front Street Café, Burger King, Brother Bruno's Pizza, Ming Moon. *Other services:* pharmacy; hospital, (845) 858-7000; bank; laundromat. *Train service:* Metro-North Railroad/NJ Transit (across from Burger King), (973) 275-5555, service to Harriman, New York City, and Secaucus, NJ Ticket machine accepts cash and credit/debit cards.

High Point Shelter (1936)—Sleeps 8. Privy. Bear box. CCC-built stone shelter with wooden floor. Water sources are two streams on the trail to the shelter; both may fail in dry years. Potable water may be found 1.5 miles south at High Point State Park headquarters.

County Rd. 519—**East** 2.5 miles to *Lodging:* High Point Mountain Motel (see above).

Road to Jim Murray Property (0.4 mile north of Goodrich Rd.)—**West** 0.2 mile. For the past 3 decades, Jim Murray (AT '89), (845) 986-0942, backpack@warwick.net, has cordially allowed long-distance

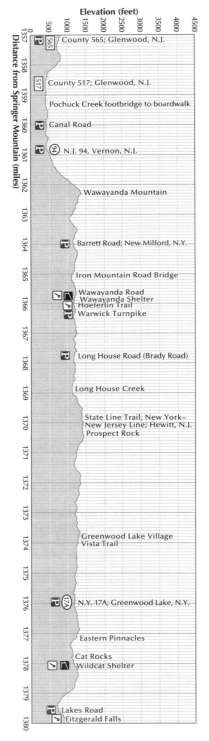

Elevation (feet)

Distance from Springer Mountain (miles)

County 565; Glenwood, N.J.

County 517; Glenwood, N.J.

Pochuck Creek footbridge to boardwalk

Canal Road

N.J. 94, Vernon, N.J.

Wawayanda Mountain

Barrett Road; New Milford, N.Y.

Iron Mountain Road Bridge

Wawayanda Road
Wawayanda Shelter
Hoeferlin Trail
Warwick Turnpike

Long House Road (Brady Road)

Long House Creek

State Line Trail, New York–
New Jersey Line; Hewitt, N.J.
Prospect Rock

Greenwood Lake Village
Vista Trail

N.Y. 17A; Greenwood Lake, N.Y.

Eastern Pinnacles

Cat Rocks
Wildcat Shelter

Lakes Road
Fitzgerald Falls

hikers year-round use of the small hiker cabin (sleeps 5), with outdoor shower and privy, on his property adjacent to the Trail. Tenting allowed; no groups. Follow the "well water" sign. This is a privately owned cabin. Be responsible, and please do not abuse this privilege.

Lott Rd.—West 0.4 mile to the town of **Unionville, NY [P.O. ZIP 10988: M–F 8–11:30 & 1–5, Sa 9–12; (845)726-6143]**. Lott Rd. is also known as Jersey Avenue. *Camping:* Hikers can use Unionville Memorial Park for tenting, with water and toilet facility; fill out permit at Horler's General Store. *Groceries:* Horler's Store with ATM (short-term resupply), (845) 726-3210, M–Sa 6–9, Su 7–7. *Restaurants:* Wit's End Tavern, (845) 726-3956, Su–Th 12–12, F–Sa noon2 a.m., hiker box, charging station, water; Annabel's Pizza & Italian Restaurant, (845) 726-9992, open daily 10–10.

Pochuck Mountain Shelter (1989)—Sleeps 6. Privy. Bear box. Water might be available 0.6 mile (steeply downhill) south of the shelter from a spigot (off late Oct–early Apr) on the north side of a vacant white house at the foot of Pochuck Mountain—a leak last summer caused it to be shut off. No camping is allowed at the house (owned by the NJ Department of Environmental Protection). A side trail 150 feet north of the Liberty Corners Rd. crossing leads 200 feet to that source. Southbounders can find water at a stream south of Sussex County Route 565.

County Roads 517 or 565—West 1.1 miles to **Glenwood, NJ [P.O. ZIP 07418: M–F 7:30–5, Sa 10–2; (973) 764-2616].** *Lodging:* Apple Valley Inn and B&B, (973) 764-3735, $150–$160, $25eap, includes full B. *Groceries:* Pochuck Valley Farm Market & Deli (short-term resupply), (973) 764-4732, with outside water spigot, ATM, and restroom. Open M–F 6–6, Sa–Su 6–5. No smoking. *Camping:* Pochuck Valley market allows limited camping for customers only; ask permission, be responsible, and please respect this privilege.

NJ-94—East 1.4 miles to *Lodging:* Appalachian Motel, 367 NJ-94, Vernon, NJ 07462; (973) 764-6070, Su–Th $85d, F–Sa $110–$140d, $10eap, no pets, laundry $10, call for possible pick-up from Route 94. Accepts packages for customers only. No smoking.

East 2.4 miles to **Vernon, NJ [P.O. ZIP 07462: M–F 8:30–5, Sa 9:30-12:30; (973) 764-9056].** See map. *Groceries:* ACME Market and Green Life Market (both long-term resupply). *Restaurants:* Crystal Cafe; Paesano Pizza; Tomato Garden Pizza; see map for other options. *Shuttle:* Ron Meyer, Vernon Taxi, (973) 632-2005. *Other services:* bank with ATM, dentist, veterinarian, and CVS.

West 0.1 mile to *Groceries:* Heaven Hill Farm, baked goods, fresh fruit and ice cream (short-term resupply), water spigot, (973) 764-5144, M–Sa 9–7 Su 9–6, Mar–

Dec. Hikers are requested to keep packs outside on left side of building.

West 2.5 miles to *Restaurants:* The Grange.

West 4.7 miles to Warwick, NY *Camping:* Warwick Drive-In, 1.9 miles south of town on Warwick Turnpike (see below).

West 6.1 miles to Warwick Laundry Center, (845) 987-5000, 7–10.

West 7.4 miles to *Lodging:* MeadowLark Farm B&B, 180 Union Corners Rd., Warwick, NY 10990, (845) 651-4286, meadowlarkfarm.com, rooms $95–$120 +tax, tent camping on lawn, $15pp includes shower and laundry. Dogs welcome. Accepts packages. Shuttles $1/mile round-trip. Car can be left here.

Wawayanda Mountain—Near summit, a blue-blazed side trail leads 0.1 mile to Pinwheel's Vista, with views to the west of Pochuck Mountain and High Point Monument.

Iron Mountain Rd.—East 1.6 miles on blue trail to Wawayanda Lake. From Memorial Weekend to Labor Day, visitors can swim 10–6. Restrooms, first-aid station, food concession (ice cream, burgers, soda), and boat rental.

Wawayanda Shelter (1990)—Sleeps 6. Privy. Bear box. Room for several tents. Water is available at the park office, reached by going north on the A.T. 0.1 mile, then east on the blue-blazed Hoeferlin Trail 0.2 mile; pay phone outside. Southbounders should get water at the office before the shelter. Water source is the restroom faucet or a seasonal spigot on the maintenance building near entrance to the fenced-in work yard.

Warwick Turnpike—West 2.7 miles to *Camping:* Warwick Drive-In, (845) 986-4440, family-owned, multiscreen drive-in theater allows tenting for hikers, with access to cold running water, restrooms, cell-phone charging station, and snack bar. Hikers may watch movies for free. No alcohol or marijuana smoking. *Groceries:* Shop-Rite (long-term resupply); Pennings Farm Market (short-term resupply), (845) 986-1059, with fresh fruit, vegetables, ice cream, bakery; grill and brew pub.

Map:

↖ ⛺ (1.4 mi)

Appalachian Motel

515

Vernon, N.J.
elevation 648'

Glenwood (4.5mi)
← Church St
644

• Paesano Pizza
• Burger King

Tomato Garden
Crystal Cafe •   • Mini   • Pizza
Dunkin' •   Mart   • Sushi Ya
   • CVS   • Lox ofBagels
Taco Bell •   • **Post Office**
     • ACME Market
China Star •
Pizza Station •
Wings
Asian Bistro •

McAfee Vernon Rd

515

Green Life Market •   • Dairy Queen
Sunrise Market •

Post Office to:
Appalachian Motel (1.2 mi)

94

New York

Miles from Springer	Miles to Next Point	Features	Services	Elev	Miles from Katahdin	M A P
1,370.0	0.4	New Jersey–New York State Line; State Line Trail; Hewitt, NJ *(E–1m to Lakeside Road, P)*		1,385'	827.4	ATC: NY-NJ: Map 3
1,370.4	3.5	Prospect Rock		1,433'	827.0	
1,373.9	2.1	Greenwood Lake (Village) Vista Trail *East–0.9m to* **Greenwood Lake, NY, P.O. 10925**	B, G, L, M, f	1,180'	823.5	
1,376.0	1.2	NY-17A *East–2m to* **Greenwood Lake, NY, P.O.10925** *East 2.3m to* Lost and Found Hostel *West–0.1m to* Bellvale Creamery *West –1.6m to* Bellvale Market and Deli *West–4.6m to* **Warwick, NY, P.O. 10990** *West–10m to* Meadow Lark Farm B&B	R, P B, G, L, M, f H M, w G, M B, G, C, M, D, cl C, L	1,180'	821.4	
1,377.2	0.6	Eastern Pinnacles		1,294'	820.2	
1,377.8	0.3	Cat Rocks		1,080'	819.6	
1,378.1	1.5	**Wildcat Shelter**, *12.3mN; 14.5mS*	S, w	1,180'	819.3	
1,379.6	0.3	Lakes Road	R, P	680'	817.8	
1,379.9	2.0	Fitzgerald Falls	w	800'	817.5	
1,381.9	1.2	Mombasha High Point		1,280'	815.5	
1,383.1	0.6	West Mombasha Road	R, P	980'	814.3	
1,383.7	0.3	Kloibers Pond outlet	w	980'	813.7	
1,384.0	0.8	Buchanan Mountain		1,142'	813.4	ATC: NY-NJ: Map 2
1,384.8	0.7	East Mombasha Road	R, P	840'	812.6	
1,385.5	0.7	Little Dam Lake		720'	811.9	
1,386.2	0.6	Orange Turnpike	R	780'	811.2	
1,386.8	0.5	Arden Mountain Sapphire Trail *(West–2.2m to NY-17, train, P)*		1,180'	810.6	
1,387.3	0.7	Agony Grind		900'	810.1	
1,388.0	0.2	NY-17, Arden Valley Road *East–2.1m to* **Southfields, NY, P.O. 10975** *West–3.7m to* Harriman, NY	R, B B, G, L, M B, G, L, M, cl, T	550'	809.4	
1,388.2	0.1	I-87 NY State Thruway: *overpass*		560'	809.2	
1,388.3	1.5	Arden Valley Road	R, P	680'	809.1	
1,389.8	0.5	Island Pond Outlet	w	1,350'	807.6	
1,390.3	0.6	Lemon Squeezer		1,150'	807.1	
1,390.9	0.6	Long Path Trail Junction		1,160'	806.5	
1,391.5	1.1	Surebridge Mountain		1,200'	805.9	
1,392.6	1.1	**Fingerboard Shelter** *(E–0.5 m on Hurst Trail to water spigot),* 14.5mS: 5.3mN	S	1,300'	804.8	
1,393.7	2.2	Arden Valley Road: *to Lake Tiorati Circle (E–0.3m)*	R, P, w, sh	1,196'	803.7	
1,395.9	0.8	Seven Lakes Drive	R, P	850'	801.5	

Miles from Springer	Miles to Next Point	Features	Services	Elev	Miles from Katahdin	M A P
1,396.7	1.2	Goshen Mountain		1,180'	800.7	
1,397.9	1.3	**William Brien Memorial Shelter** (W-0.4m spring), 5.3mS; 5.9mN	S, w	1,070'	799.5	
1,399.2	2.6	Black Mountain		1,160'	798.2	
1,401.8	0.2	Palisades Interstate Parkway: divided highway (W-0.4m to visitors center)	R, w	500'	795.6	
1,402.0	1.2	Anthony Wayne Recreation Area	w		795.4	
1,403.2	1.0	**West Mountain Shelter** (E-0.6m on Timp-Torne Trail), 5.9mS; 24.9mN	S	1,240'	794.2	
1,404.2	0.5	Seven Lakes Drive	R	610'	793.2	
1,404.7	2.0	Perkins Drive	R	950'	792.7	
1,406.7	1.6	Bear Mountain, Perkins Tower	R, P	1,305'	790.7	
1,408.3	0.7	Bear Mountain Inn, Hessian Lake East-0.3m to **Bear Mountain, NY, P.O. 10911**	R, P, B, L, M, w	155'	789.1	
1,409.0	0.1	Bear Mountain Museum and Zoo		124'	788.4	
1,409.1	0.7	US-9W, Bear Mountain Circle Bear Mountain Bridge, Hudson River West-0.9m to **Ft. Montgomery, NY, P.O. 10922**	R B, G, L, M	150'	788.3	ATC: NY-NJ: Map 2
1,409.8	0.7	NY-9D	R, P	230'	787.6	
1,410.5	1.0	Camp Smith Trail to Anthony's Nose (E-0.6m)		700'	786.9	
1,411.5	0.2	Hemlock Springs Campsite	C, w	550'	785.9	
1,411.7	3.4	Manitou Road, South Mountain Pass	R, P	460'	785.7	
1,415.1	0.2	US-9, NY-403 East-4.5m to **Peekskill, NY, P.O. 10566** West-6.3m to **Cold Spring, NY, P.O. 10516**	R, G, M G, L, M, D, V, T, cl G, L, M, O, T	400'	782.3	
1,415.3	0.3	Old Highland Turnpike: paved		440'	782.1	
1,415.6	0.1	Graymoor Spiritual Life Center-Franciscan Way: blue-blazes to ball-field	R, C, sh, w	520'	781.8	
1,415.7	1.9	Old West Point Road	R	550'	781.7	
1,417.6	0.8	Denning Hill		900'	779.8	
1,418.4	1.7	Old Albany Post Road-Chapman Road	R	607'	779.0	
1,420.1	1.0	Canopus Hill Road (E-1.6m Putnam Valley Mkt.)	R, G, M	420'	777.3	
1,421.1	2.7	South Highland Road	R, P	570'	776.3	
1,423.8	1.6	Dennytown Road: water faucet on building	R, P, C, w	860'	773.6	
1,425.4	2.1	Sunk Mine Road	R	800'	772.0	
1,427.5	2.2	NY-301 East-1m to Clarence Fahnestock State Park West-7.2m to **Cold Spring, NY, P.O. 10516**	R, P C, sh, w G, L, M, O, T	920'	769.9	
1,429.7	2.0	A.T. Connector (south end) East-0.3m to Canopus Lake Beach East-0.5m to **Raymond Torrey Memorial Shelter**, 24.9S; 3.5mN	M, sh, nw S, C	935'	767.7	ATC: NY-NJ Map 1
1,431.7	0.4	Shenandoah Mountain		1,282'	765.7	
1,432.1	1.1	Long Hill Road	R, P	1,100'	765.3	
1,433.2	1.3	Shenandoah Tenting Area (W-0.1m)	C	900'	764.2	
1,434.5	0.3	**RPH Shelter**, Hortontown Road, 4mS; 9mN	R, S, nw	350'	762.9	
1,434.8	3.2	Taconic State Parkway: underpass	R	650'	762.6	

Miles from Springer	Miles to Next Point	Features	Services	Elev	Miles from Katahdin	M A P
1,438.0	1.6	Hosner Mountain Road *West–2.5m* to S & J Deli, Dunkin', Hopewell Animal Hospital *West–3.1m* to Inn at Arbor Ridge, Smoke Haus, Dave's Kitchen & Deli	R, P G, M, V G, L. M	500'	759.4	
1,439.6	1.4	NY-52 *East–0.3m to* Stormville Market & Deli, Corrado's Pizzeria *West–1.8m to* **Stormville, NY, P.O. 12582** *West–2.5m to* Shell Food Mart & Stormville Pizza	R, P G, M, C, w G, M G, M	800'	757.8	
1,441.0	2.4	Stormville Mountain Road; I-84 overpass	R, P	950'	756.4	
1,443.4	0.1	Mt. Egbert		1,329'	754.0	
1,443.5	1.1	**Morgan Stewart Shelter**, *9mS; 7.8mN*	S, w	1,285'	753.9	
1,444.6	1.9	Depot Hill Road	R, P	1,230'	752.8	
1,446.5	0.3	Old Route 55	R, P	750'	750.9	
1,446.8	1.2	NY-55 *West–1.5m to* Pleasant Ridge Pizza & A&A Deli *West–3.1m to* **Poughquag, NY, P.O. 12570** *West–3.6m to* Stop & Shop	R, P B, M B, G, M, V G, M	720'	750.6	
1,448.0	3.0	Nuclear Lake: *outlet*		750'	749.4	
1,451.0	0.3	West Mountain		1,200'	746.4	
1,451.3	0.7	**Telephone Pioneers Shelter**, *7.8mS; 8.8mN*	S, w	910'	746.1	
1,452.0	2.4	County Road 20, W. Dover Road, Dover Oak *East–3.1m to* **Pawling, NY, P.O. 12564** *East–5m to* Hannaford	R, P B, C, G, M, D, T, cl G, M	650'	745.4	
1,454.4	0.2	NY-22, Metro-North Railroad, A.T. Train Platform; Native Landscapes & Garden Ctr. *East–0.6m to* Tony's Deli East–2.6m to **Pawling, NY, P.O. 12564** East–4.1m to Hannaford *West–2.6m* to Ben's Deli, La Guadalupana, Stupid Delicious Pizza *West–4m to* **Wingdale, NY, P.O. 12594**	R, P, M, T, sh, w, f C, G, M B, C, G, M, D, T, cl G, M B, G, M B, G, M, T, f	480'	743.0	
1,454.6	0.6	Hurds Corners Road	R	480'	742.8	
1,455.2	1.9	Pawling Nature Preserve: *trail register*		675'	742.2	
1,457.1	2.6	P.N.R. Green Trail *(W– 0.9m to* Ben's Deli, La Guadalupana, Stupid Delicious Pizza)*	G, M, B	960'	740.3	
1,459.7	0.4	Leather Hill Road: *dirt*	R	750'	737.7	
1,460.1	0.2	**Wiley Shelter**, *8.8mS; 4mN*	S, C	740'	737.3	
1,460.3	1.0	Duell Hollow Road	R, P	620'	737.1	
1,461.3	0.7	New York–Connecticut State Line; Hoyt Road *West–3.3m to* **Wingdale, NY, P.O. 12594** *West–4.7m* to Dutchess Motor Lodge and restaurants	R, P B, G, M, T, f B, G, M	400'	736.1	

ATC: NY-NJ Map 1

The first miles specifically intended for the A.T. were built in New York through Harriman-Bear Mountain state parks in 1922–23. With many parks, roads, and a railroad station right on the Trail, you may find this stretch to be a uniquely multicultural experience. The Trail drops to its lowest elevation point—124 feet—after, or just before, you pass through the Trailside Museum and Zoo at Bear Mountain. Hydration becomes an issue in this area. Don't pass up an opportunity for water.

Note: In New York, campfires are prohibited except in designated fire rings and fireplaces at established campsites and shelters. And please keep in mind when going to and from the Trail at road crossings, hitchhiking is illegal. Hikers have been cited in the past.

Prospect Rock—At 1,433 feet, this is the highest point on the A.T. in New York (Bear Mountain is 1,305 feet). This and other rock faces along this ridge provide views of Greenwood Lake to the east.

⚑ Greenwood Lake Vista Trail—This blue-blazed trail leads **East** 0.9 mile to Greenwood Lake without the fast traffic of NY-17A; from the vista, you can see Lion's Field below, the terminus of the trail. A small, green building next to the softball field has public restrooms and an outside seasonal water spigot hikers can use. **Greenwood Lake, NY [P.O. ZIP 10925: M-F 8-5, Sa 9-12; (845) 477-7328].** *Lodging:* Linden Motel, (845) 477-0851, hiker-rate $80 room with kitchenette, Wi-Fi, pool, no laundry, no pets; Lake Lodging, 1145 NY-17A, (845) 401-1016, or (845)-705-2005; newly renovated, hiker rate $85 for double room with Wi-Fi, no smoking, laundry $5, call for possible pickup/drop

Greenwood Lake, N.Y. ⬆
elevation 625'

⬆ ☗ (1.5 mi)

N.J.
N.Y.

Greenwood Lake Coffee

Linden Motel 17A

Greenwood Lake Vista Trail to ☗ (0.9 mi)

Post Office •

Kwik Mart

CVS •

Lion's Field

Planet Pizza

Lake → Lodging

The Grill •

Cumberland Farms

The Local •

Elm St

Village Buzz Café •

Mexican Zingo

Sing Loong Kitchen

Breezy Point Inn (0.7 mi)

Murphy's Tavern •

4 Brothers Pizza

Library •

Hardware •

Country Grocery

Waterstone Rd

Windermere Ave

Waterstone Inn

Post Office to:
Country Grocery (0.4 mi)

Emerald Point Restaurant

off from Trail, accepts packages marked "Hold for Hiker (with name)"; The Breezy Inn & Restaurant (1 mile south of town), 620 Jersey Ave., Greenwood Lake, NY 10925, (845) 477-8100, new owners, renovated rooms, $200d+tax for 1 night of $157d+tax for 2+ nights, no smoking or pets, ATM, Wi-Fi, call for possible pick-up from Trail, accepts packages marked "Hold for Hiker (with name)", lodging open year-round but restaurant closed off-season (approx. Nov–Mar), call in advance; Lake Lodging Motel, 1145 NY-17A, (845)705-2005, Located on the east side of the lake, hiker friendly, call for rates and reservation. *Groceries:* Country Grocery; Kwik Mart; and Cumberland Farms (open 24 hrs.), with deli sandwiches (all short-term resupply). *Restaurants:* Planet Pizza; Murphy's Tavern, L/D weekdays; Village Buzz Café, B/L; Mexican Zingo; The Grill, B/L; Sing Loong KitchenThe Local. *Other services:* True Value, fuel; CVS; Chase Bank; Greenwood Lake Taxi, (845) 477-0341 (call ahead); NJ Transit buses to New York City (njtransit.com, Routes 196, 197).

⚑ **NY-17A**—Top Dogs, L F–Su 11–3, cash only. **East** 2 miles to **Greenwood Lake**.
   West 0.1 mile to Bellvale Creamery, daily Apr–Oct 12–9 (closes earlier in spring/fall), ice cream, outside water spigot, and device charging station.
   West 1.6 miles to Bellvale Market & Deli, (845) 544-7700, T–F 8–5:30, Sa 8–5, Su 8–3.
   ⛰ **West** 4.6 miles to the larger town of **Warwick, NY [P.O. ZIP 10990: M-F 8:30-5, Sa 9-4; (845) 986-0271].** Hitchhikers have been cited leaving Warwick on NY-17A. *Groceries:* Kwik Mart, CVS (both short-term resupply); Price Chopper, open 6–11, is 1.8 miles south of town on NY-94; ShopRite is 1.9 miles south of town on NY-94 across from Pennings Farm Market (both long-term resupply). *Camping:* Warwick Drive-in Theater (near ShopRite and Pennings) allows hikers to camp overnight; restrooms, water, picnic tables, no alcohol or drugs allowed, open mid-Mar to early Nov.

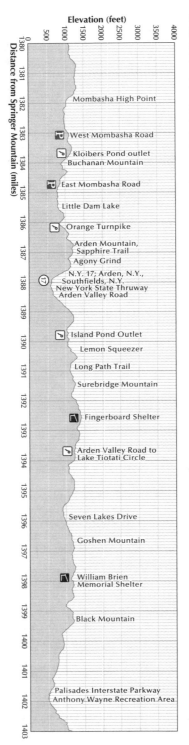

Elevation (feet) / Distance from Springer Mountain (miles)

- Mombasha High Point
- West Mombasha Road
- Kloibers Pond outlet
- Buchanan Mountain
- East Mombasha Road
- Little Dam Lake
- Orange Turnpike
- Arden Mountain, Sapphire Trail
- Agony Grind
- N.Y. 17; Arden, N.Y., Southfields, N.Y. New York State Thruway Arden Valley Road
- Island Pond Outlet
- Lemon Squeezer
- Long Path Trail
- Surebridge Mountain
- Fingerboard Shelter
- Arden Valley Road to Lake Tiotati Circle
- Seven Lakes Drive
- Goshen Mountain
- William Brien Memorial Shelter
- Black Mountain
- Palisades Interstate Parkway
- Anthony Wayne Recreation Area

Other services: NJ Transit buses run frequently in the area from Warwick to New York City; hospital; restaurants; drug store; coin laundry; bank/ATM; and hardware store. *Shuttle:* Josie's Taxi, (845) 986-8073; Warwick Taxi, (845) 544-8877.

West 10 miles to *Lodging:* MeadowLark Farm B&B (see NJ-94).

Mount Peter Hawk Watch Trailway—The third-oldest hawk watch in the country. An 800-foot spur trail leads to a small scenic-overlook platform for raptor viewing and other bird-watching. Public-access trail passes through private lands. Please stay on the trail and do not trespass.

Wildcat Shelter (1992)—Sleeps 8. Privy. Bear box. Water source is a spring 75 yards downhill and left from the shelter that might fail in dry periods.

Mombasha High Point—On a clear day, you can see the New York City skyline, including the Empire State Building.

Kloibers Pond Outlet. Located 0.1 mile north of West Momba-sha Road. Pond may be unreliable water source in prolonged dry periods.

Sterling Forest State Park—Between Greenwood Lake and Arden, 6 miles of the A.T. cross the northern portion of a 21,935-acre tract called Sterling Forest. It was the center of a decade-long struggle between a corporate private landowner and a coalition of conservation groups, state agencies in New York and New Jersey, and such organizations as the NY-NJ TC and ATC. All told, more than 30 environmental groups, along with foundations, individuals, states, and Congress, combined to contribute more than $55 million toward the purchase and protection of 14,500 acres. *Note: Hunting is allowed in season outside of the A.T. corridor.*

Sapphire Trail—Leads 2.2 miles to end across the road from the Harriman, NY, Metro-North railroad station, which is also a stop for the ShortLine (Coach USA) bus. See mta.info for train service to New York City. A safer spot than NY-17 (below) for a hiker shuttle pick up or taxi/Uber/Lyft into the town of Harriman.

NY-17—**East** 2.1 miles to **Southfields, NY [P.O. ZIP 10975: M-F 10-12 & 1-5, Sa 8:30-11:30; (845) 351-2628]**. Use caution crossing this four-lane highway. *Lodging:* Tuxedo Motel, (845) 351-4747, 985 NY-17S, Southfields, NY 10975, $60s, $65d, $10eap, hiker-friendly, Wi-Fi, laundry available, no pets, food deliveries, mail drops accepted. *Groceries:* Valero (short-term resupply), deli and snack bar closes at 3 p.m., ATM. *Other services:* ShortLine (Coach USA) buses from New York City/Tuxedo/Southfields to Harriman with a flag stop at the A.T. crossing of NY-17 and from New York City to Fort Montgomery with a regular stop at Bear Mountain Inn.

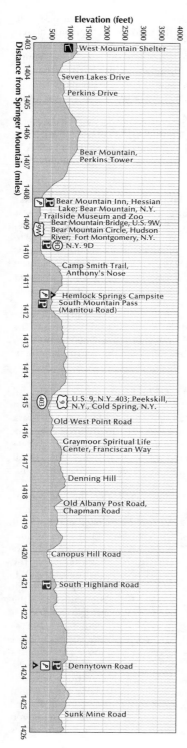

Elevation (feet)

Distance from Springer Mountain (miles)

West Mountain Shelter

Seven Lakes Drive

Perkins Drive

Bear Mountain, Perkins Tower

Bear Mountain Inn, Hessian Lake; Bear Mountain, N.Y. Trailside Museum and Zoo Bear Mountain Bridge, U.S. 9W; Bear Mountain Circle, Hudson River; Fort Montgomery, N.Y. N.Y. 9D

Camp Smith Trail, Anthony's Nose

Hemlock Springs Campsite South Mountain Pass (Manitou Road)

U.S. 9, N.Y. 403; Peekskill, N.Y., Cold Spring, N.Y.

Old West Point Road

Graymoor Spiritual Life Center, Franciscan Way

Denning Hill

Old Albany Post Road, Chapman Road

Canopus Hill Road

South Highland Road

Dennytown Road

Sunk Mine Road

West 3.7 miles to the town of **Harriman,** for lodgings, groceries, restaurants, outlet mall, and coin laundry.

Bear Mountain/Harriman State Parks—Home to the first completed section of the A.T. Dry conditions and forest fires have forced the closure of the A.T. in the park for days or even weeks in the summer. In 1994, Harriman State Park instituted a policy under which, even if other trails in the park are closed, the A.T. remains open to thru-hikers.

Note: Bear activity in the area has increased recently. Be sure to store your food carefully when camping in the park. Never feed bears or leave food unattended. Do not bury or scatter excess food; avoid eating or preparing food in your tent.

Fingerboard Shelter (1928)—Sleeps 8. No privy. A stone structure with internal fireplace. *Due to aggressive bears stealing hikers' food near the shelter, bear cables installed.*The closest dependable water is at Lake Tiorati, 0.5 mile downhill from the shelter going east on the blue-blazed Hurst Trail. Southbounders can get water at Tiorati Circle, 1.1 miles north of the shelter.

Arden Valley Rd.—East 0.3 mile to Tiorati Circle at the intersection of Seven Lakes Drive. Near the traffic circle are a picnic area and public beach on Lake Tiorati. Restrooms and water station open early Apr to mid-Oct; free showers in bath house for walk-ins when beach is open; open Memorial Day to Labor Day (weekends only through third weekend in Jun), M–F 10–5:45, Sa–Su 11–6:45; vending machines, ice-cream sandwiches, candy.

William Brien Memorial Shelter (1933)—Sleeps 8. No privy. Bear cables (increased bear activity in the area). A stone shelter built by the CCC. Water source is a spring-fed well that is prone to go dry, 80 yards downhill from the right of the shelter marked by very faded blue blazes. Water might be available from a stream 0.4 mile west of the A.T. on the yellow-blazed Menomine Trail, although it's unreliable in dry seasons. An alternative for northbounders is to stop at Tiorati Circle, get water, cook at one of the picnic tables, and hike to the shelter for the evening. Southbounders usually can get water 2.1 mile north at Beechy Bottom Brook.

Palisades Interstate Pkwy—A temporary detour (reflected in the mileage tables but subject to change over the winter) is in place to avoid this road crossing, with no pedestrian marking across a highway that sees more than 30,000 vehicles a day. Hikers are strongly encouraged to follow the detour as shown on the maps posted 0.2 mile before the highway where the Trail crosses the 1779 Trail (northbound) and 1 mile south of Seven Lakes Drive where the Trail crosses the Timp-Torne Trail (southbound). Directions for detour northbound: turn west (left) onto 1779 Trail and go 1.45 mile to the white-blazed Anthony Wayne trail. Turn right onto the Anthony Wayne trail and go 0.5 mile to cross over the highway. Continue 0.35 mile to the red-blazed Fawn Trail. Turn right onto the Fawn and go 0.3 mile to meet the blue-blazed Timp-Torne Trail. Turn right onto T-T and go 0.65 mile to the junction with the A.T. Turn left onto the Trail and continue northbound. Southbounders should turn right onto the blue-blazed Timp-Torne trail and follow the above directions in reverse to the A.T. From there, turn left onto the Trail and continue southbound. Use extreme caution if you decide to short-cut and cross; a day hiker was killed in November 2021 when crossing. From here, it is a mere 34 miles to NYC on the parkway.

West Mountain Shelter (1928)—Sleeps 8. No privy. Bear cables (increased bear activity in the area). While the detour is in place, it is 1.3 miles east on the blue Timp-Torne Trail. Water might be available at a stream 0.7 mile south of the junction to the shelter on the closed section of the A.T. or sometimes at an unreliable seasonal stream 0.2 mile before the shelter. Views of the surrounding countryside and the NYC skyline.

Bear Mountain—At 1,305 feet, this is one of the highest points on the Trail in New York and offers views of the Hudson River Valley and the New York City skyline. In the early 1900s, the state was considering a site near the base for a prison, but Mary Averell Harriman, widow of railroad magnate Edward Harriman and primary landholder in the area, had other plans. In 1910, she agreed to donate 10,000 acres for the development of a park with the condition that the state discontinue its plans for a prison. What was then known as Sing Sing Prison was eventually built on the Hudson River 20 miles south of the A.T., its location giving birth to the phrase, "sent up the river." No water available at the summit. Do not rely on the seasonally stocked soda vending machine.

More than 2 million people visit Bear Mountain each year, making this original section of the A.T. the most heavily used along the entire Trail. In September 2018, the NY-NJ Trail Conference and ATC completed a 14-year project to reroute and rebuild the A.T. near Bear Mountain. The finished Trail, almost all of which was built by volunteers, features more than 1,000 hand-hewn granite steps and more than 2 miles of treadway supported by stone cribbing. Storm damage in 2023 made a 2-mile-shorter temporary relocation necessary.

⚠ Bear Mountain, NY [P.O. ZIP 10911: M–F 9–11, closed Sa; (845) 786-3747]. P.O. may close early; call ahead. Located 0.3 mile east of the A.T. across the street from the park administration building on Seven Lakes Drive. Fort Montgomery (see below) may be a better option. Bear Mountain State Park offers seasonal concession stands, vending machines, restrooms, and water fountains. *Lodging & Restaurant:* Bear Mountain Inn (visible where the A.T. meets Hessian Lake), (845) 786-2731, $169–$269, no laundry, accepts mail drops; Hiker's Café, 7–5; Restaurant 1915, W–Th 2–8, F–Sa 2–10, Su 2–9. *Other services:* Coach USA runs buses daily from the inn to New York City; coachusa.com.

Trailside Museums and Zoo—North of the inn and south of Bear Mountain Bridge, the Bear Mountain Zoo contains many native species, including black bears, and offers a unique, and sometimes emotional, experience for thru-hikers. Within the park is also a much-photographed statue of Walt Whitman. Admission $1; A.T. hikers admitted free. The portion of the A.T. leading through the zoo to the bridge—an original section from 1923—descends to 124 feet above sea level; it's the Trail's lowest elevation between Maine and Georgia. *Dogs are not allowed in the museum/zoo section.* The gates

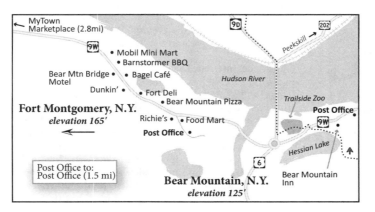

Fort Montgomery, N.Y.
elevation 165'

MyTown Marketplace (2.8mi)
Mobil Mini Mart
Barnstormer BBQ
Bear Mtn Bridge Motel
Bagel Café
Dunkin'
Fort Deli
Bear Mountain Pizza
Richie's
Food Mart
Post Office
Post Office to:
Post Office (1.5 mi)

Hudson River
Peekskill
Trailside Zoo
Post Office
Hessian Lake
Bear Mountain Inn

Bear Mountain, N.Y.
elevation 125'

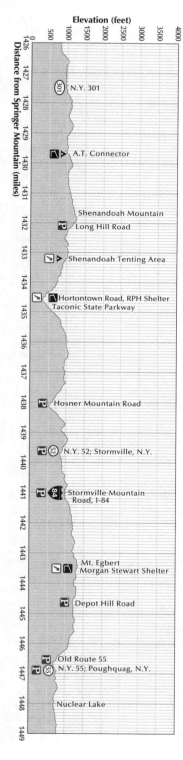

Elevation (feet)

Distance from Springer Mountain (miles)

- N.Y. 301
- A.T. Connector
- Shenandoah Mountain
- Long Hill Road
- Shenandoah Tenting Area
- Hortontown Road, RPH Shelter
- Taconic State Parkway
- Hosner Mountain Road
- N.Y. 52; Stormville, N.Y.
- Stormville Mountain Road, I-84
- Mt. Egbert
- Morgan Stewart Shelter
- Depot Hill Road
- Old Route 55
- N.Y. 55; Poughquag, N.Y.
- Nuclear Lake

open at 10 a.m.; at 4:30 p.m., the gate is closed. If you arrive when the gate is closed or are hiking with a dog, take the blue-blazed bypass trail, which becomes the official route for the period/circumstances.

Bear Mountain Circle—West 0.9 mile to **Ft. Montgomery, NY [P.O. ZIP 10922: M–F 8–1 & 2:30–5, Sa 9–12; (845) 446-8459].** *Lodging:* Bear Mountain Bridge Motel, 1041 Route 9W, (845) 446-2472, $100+tax for standard rooms (higher during special events), 4 rooms have 1 double bed, 1 room has a double and 2 twins ($140+), laundry ($10), Wi-Fi, no pets, shuttle to/from the Trail, accepts mail drops for guests only; Holiday Inn Express & Suites, (845) 446-4277, call for rates and availability. *Groceries:* Chestnut Mini Mart (short-term resupply), open 24 hours, free Wi-Fi. MyTown Marketplace (long-term resupply) is 2.8 miles farther north in Highland Falls. *Restaurants:* Fort Deli M–F 6 a.m.–9 p.m., Sa 7–9, Su 8–0; Bear Mountain Pizza, cash only, pizza, pasta, and Desserts, daily 10:30–9; Barnstormer BBQ & Pub, M W Th 4–8, F–Su L/D; Richie's Little Place, Tu–Sa D; American Burrito, 11–9 daily; Dunkin' M–F 4 a.m.–8 p.m., Sa–Su 5–8.

Bear Mountain Bridge—Built at a cost of $5 million in 1923–24 by a private company run by the Harriman family. When Earl Shaffer arrived at the bridge in 1948, he had to pay a nickel to cross. Today, only vehicles must pay.

Anthony's Nose—A half-mile **north** of NY-9D, the A.T. turns west on a dirt road, at the junction with the blue-blazed Camp Smith Trail. Going east on this trail leads 0.6 mile to the top of the mountain known as Anthony's Nose. This rock outcropping, 900 feet above the river, offers outstanding views of the Hudson River Valley. The state Office of Parks, Recreation, and Historic Preservation now owns the property; please stay on the trail. Originally, the A.T. climbed steeply to the summit but was rerouted when World War II broke out. The Nose remained closed until 1993, when the New York State Division of Military and Naval Affairs, managers of the adjacent National Guard camp, gave permission for hikers to once again walk to the summit.

Hemlock Springs Campsite—No privy. Tenting areas just east of the trail. Water source is a small spring that may fail in dry periods. *Note: Do not get water from Copper Mine Brook, which is 0.2 mi. north of campsite next to Manitou Rd., due to possible heavy-metal contamination.*

US-9—*Groceries:* Appalachian Market Deli, (845) 424-6241, Shell station/convenience store just to west at US-9/NY-403 junction, full-service, deli, grill, pizza, open 24 hours, accepts mail drops.

East 4.5 miles to **Peekskill, NY [P.O. ZIP 10566: M–F 9–5, Sa 9–4; (914) 737-6437].** If you plan to go into Peekskill, take Highland Ave. into town, rather than US-9, where the two roads fork about 3 miles from the A.T. Highland Ave. leads directly to downtown. Services are spread out over a large, bustling area, with several motels and restaurants, supermarkets, pharmacy, laundry, banks with ATM, hospital, doctor, dentist, and veterinarian. The post office is on South St., 4.5 miles from the A.T. *Internet access* Free Wi-Fi at the Field Library, 4 Nelson Ave., M, Tu, Th 9–9, W 11–9, F 9–5, Sa 10–2. *Train service:* Metro–North train to New York City, mta.info/mnr.

West 6.3 miles via Route 403 to NY-9D to **Cold Spring, NY [P.O. ZIP 10516: M-F 8:30-5, Sa 9-12; (845) 265-2193]**. *Lodging:* Countryside Motel (5.4 miles **north** of town), 3577 Route 9, Cold Spring, NY 10516, (845) 265-2090, $95+ weekdays, $160-$210 weekends, Wi-Fi; Pig Hill Inn, (845) 265-9247, $195-$295+tax, includes full B, no pets, no smoking; Cold Spring Hotel and Café, (845) 264-0824, room with queen bed and private bath, Wi-Fi, $180-$225+tax, pets $40 fee. *Restaurants:* Cold Spring Pizza, Foundry Rose Café, Rincon Argentino, J. Murphy's Pub. *Groceries:* FoodTown Supermarket (long-term resupply), open daily 7–9. *Outfitter:* Old Souls Outfitter, (845) 809-5886, oldsouls.com, daily 10–6, small outfitter with very limited camping supplies including boots, packs, canister fuel, clothing, socks, etc. *Shuttle:* Highland Transit Taxi, (845) 265-8294; Village Taxi, (845) 265-2200. *Train service:* Metro-North service to New York City, mta.info/mnr.

Graymoor Spiritual Life Center—Hikers are permitted to sleep at the monastery's ball-field picnic shelter, with water, power outlets, a cold-water shower Apr 1–Nov 1, and a privy. The shelter is open all season. Directions: North of US-9, the A.T. climbs uphill and crosses a second paved road leading to the center. Here, NoBos should follow the blue blazes: Turn east on Franciscan Way, left on St. Anthony Way, and left on St. Joseph Drive to the ballfield. SoBos will cross unpaved Old West Point Rd. onto the Graymoor driveway; continue straight, then north where the driveway forks. Local deli may deliver to the picnic shelter. El Coyote restaurant is 0.5 mile south on US-9.

Canopus Hill Rd.—East 1.6 miles to the Putnam Valley Market (short-term resupply), (845) 528-8626, with pizza, hot food from the grill, ATM. Open M–Sa 6–9. *Directions:* east on Canopus Hill Rd. 0.3 mile to intersection with Canopus Hollow Road. Continue 0.1 mile south on Canopus Hollow Rd., turn west on Sunset Hill Rd. 1.2 miles to store. Sunset Hill Rd., a steep, winding road, climbs 400 feet from Canopus Hill Rd.

Dennytown Rd.—Water available 50 feet west of A.T. from spigot on the side of the pump building. Opens third F of Apr, closes last Su of Oct. Thru-hikers are allowed to camp for free in the grassy area beyond the parking lot, just east of the trail; be careful to camp away from where cars might park. A group camping area is across the paved road directly opposite the pump building; go uphill on dirt road 200 yards to group sites with picnic tables, trash cans, and portable toilet. Reservations required; fee is $2 per person at the group sites; call park office, (845) 225-7207.

NY-301/Clarence Fahnestock State Park—East 1 mile to the park's office and paid campground near Pelton Pond, (845) 225-7207, $15/night for a site with picnic table, fire ring, and grill; bathrooms and showers nearby. Rowboats and kayaks available to rent. Same-day reservations allowed until 3 p.m. It's another mile north to the free hikers' tenting area and Raymond Torrey Memorial Shelter. Northbounders might want to hike 2 miles farther on the A.T. to the blue A.T. Connector (aka Appalachian Way) to access the shelter and free tenting area (see below). Southbounders going to the paid campground should follow the directions to the Raymond Torrey Shelter (see below), then take the access road south to the campground entrance. Camping mid-May to mid-Nov at the paid campground, or free designated hiker camping area and shelter are open year-round and a short walk from Canopus Lake Beach. To reach the beach from the park office on NY-301, continue north 0.5 mile to reach the access road across from the campground entrance, turn left onto the access road, and go 0.4 mile to the beach. See details under Raymond Torrey Memorial Shelter for list of services available at the beach. Garrison Pizzeria & Restaurant, (845) 265-3344, will deliver to campground.

West 7.2 miles to Cold Spring (see US-9 above).

Raymond Torrey Memorial Shelter (2021)—Sleeps 8. Tenting is available in the field next to the shelter. To reach the shelter, leave the A.T. 2 miles north of NY-301, and go east on the blue-blazed Appalachian Trail Connector trail (also called Appalachian Way), 0.3 mile to the beach and another 0.2 mile to the shelter. Southbounders reach the north end of the blue connector trail 0.25 mile south of the viewpoint on the A.T., at the northern end of Canopus Lake. The beach area is visible from the overlook. Southbounders should take the blue trail 0.65 mile to the shelter and 0.2 mile farther to the beach. No privy, but flush toilets, free showers, and potable water are available just uphill from the beach. The beach has a concession stand (open Su–F 9–5, Sa 9–6 Memorial Day–late Jun, then daily through Labor Day) and grill (closes one hour earlier); grilled sandwiches, soda, ice cream, first-aid supplies, and toiletries. The beach area and showers close after Labor Day, but the park keeps a bathroom open year-round with access to water and power outlets for hikers; call the park office in advance to confirm off-season, (845) 225-7207.

Water System Closures in New York: After conducting an in-depth assessment, the National Park Service closed four wells along the Appalachian Trail in New York, as it was not possible to maintain them to safe standards under the Clean Water Act. Wells at the following sites are closed: Shenandoah Tenting Area, RPH Shelter, Morgan Stewart Shelter, Wiley Shelter.

Shenandoah Tenting Area—0.1 mile west. Group camping is permitted.

RPH Shelter (1982)—Sleeps 6. Privy. Formerly a closed cabin, it was renovated as a three-sided shelter with a covered front porch, picnic table. Water source is a nearby stream 0.1 mile south of the shelter. Pump closed by the NPS.

Hosner Mountain Rd.—West 2.5 miles to *Groceries:* S & J Deli Superette, (845) 227-4697, short-term resupply, M–F 8–5, Sa 7:30–6, Su 8–3. *Restaurants:* Dunkin', daily 5 a.m.–10 p.m. *Other services:* Hopewell Animal Hospital, (845) 221-PETS (7387).
    West 2.8 miles via NY-52 to *Restaurants:* Fratello's Pizza, Su–Th 10–10, F–Sa 11–10, Sun 11:30–8.
    West 3.1 miles via NY-52 to *Lodging:* Inn at Arbor Ridge, 17 Route 376 & Route 52, Hopewell Junction, NY 12533, (866) 767-0285, $150–$180; smoke-free hotel, spa tub, Wi-Fi, pet-friendly. *Restaurants:* Smoke Haus & Deli, (845) 221-9195, all-day B, specialty sandwiches, burgers, BBQ, M–Sa 6–6, Su 7–3.; Dave's Kitchen and Deli, M–F 6–5, Sa 8–3.

⋔ NY-52—East 0.4 mile to *Groceries and Camping:* Stormville Market & Deli (at Leetown Rd.), (845) 592-0419, short-term resupply, M–Sa 6 a.m.–7 p.m., Su 7–2. Allows camping behind building. *Restaurant:* Corrado's Pizzeria & Gelateria (next to Stormville Market), M–Sa 11–9.
    West 1.8 miles to **Stormville, NY [P.O. ZIP 12582: M-F 8:30-5, Sa 9-12; (845) 226-2627]**.
    West 2.5 miles via Old NY-52 to *Groceries:* Shell Food Mart (short-term resupply). *Restaurant:* Stormville Pizza, Tu–Sa 11–8, Su 12–8.

Morgan Stewart Shelter (1984)—Sleeps 6. Privy. Water pump closed by the NPS.

⋔ NY-55—West 1.5 miles to *Restaurants:* Pleasant Ridge Pizza, L/D, F–Sa 11–10, Su–Th 11–9; A&A Deli, M–F 7–7, Sa 7–6, Su 8–3. *Other services:* Total Care pharmacy; Dutchess Dental Care; Dutchess County Bus, (845) 473-8424, Route E runs M–Sa from Poughkeepsie to Pawling along NY-55, stopping at A&J Deli (junction of Route 216) and Stop & Shop (see Poughquag), with possible flag stop at the A.T. crossing of NY-55 near the Nuclear Lake parking area (fare $1.75 one-way; see schedule and route map at dutchessny.gov).
    West 3.1 miles to **Poughquag, NY [P.O. ZIP 12570: M-F 8:30-1 & 2-5, Sa 8:30-12:30; (845) 724-4763]**. *Groceries:* Stop & Shop, M–Sa 7:30–12, Su 7 (long-term resupply); Dollar General; Cumberland Farms; Shell Mini-Mart. *Restaurants:* Beekman Square Diner, Brothers Trattoria, Great Wall Chinese,Dunkin'. *Other services:* Key Bank.

Nuclear Lake—The site of a nuclear fuels-processing research facility until 1972. After the Park Service acquired the lands, the buildings were razed, and the area was tested and given a clean bill of health, allowing the Trail to be rerouted along the shore. No camping allowed.

Telephone Pioneers Shelter (1988)—Sleeps 6. Privy. Built with the assistance of the White Plains Council of the Telephone Pioneers of America. Water source is the stream crossed by the side trail leading to the shelter.

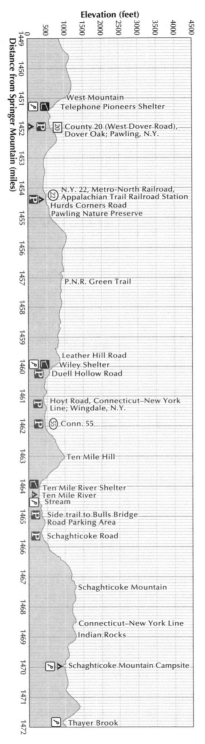

Elevation (feet)

Distance from Springer Mountain (miles)

West Mountain
Telephone Pioneers Shelter

County 20 (West Dover Road),
Dover Oak; Pawling, N.Y.

N.Y. 22, Metro-North Railroad,
Appalachian Trail Railroad Station
Hurds Corners Road
Pawling Nature Preserve

P.N.R. Green Trail

Leather Hill Road
Wiley Shelter
Duell Hollow Road

Hoyt Road, Connecticut–New York
Line; Wingdale, N.Y.

Conn. 55

Ten Mile Hill

Ten Mile River Shelter
Ten Mile River
Stream

Side trail to Bulls Bridge
Road Parking Area

Schaghticoke Road

Schaghticoke Mountain

Connecticut–New York Line

Indian Rocks

Schaghticoke Mountain Campsite

Thayer Brook

⚠ ⌂ County 20/West Dover Rd.—East 3.1 miles to **Pawling, NY [P.O. ZIP 12564: M–F 8:30–5, Sa 9–12; (845) 855-2669]**. Northbounders might want to hike 2.4 miles more to NY-22 for easier access. *Camping:* The town allows hikers to camp in its Edward R. Murrow Memorial Park, 1 mile from the town center on West Main (142 Lakeside Dr.). The park offers a pavilion, lake swimming, restroom. No dogs permitted. Two-night maximum. *Groceries:* Hannaford, 7–10 daily, 2 miles south from town center on Rt. 22 (long-term resupply); La Guadalupana Mini-Mart and CVS (both short-term resupply). *Restaurants:* Vinny's Deli & Pasta, Village Pizza, Gaudino's Pizzeria, Great Wall Chinese, McKinney & Doyle, Tacos & Cones. *Other services:* Seguondo Taxi, (845) 264-3020; doctor; dentist; coin laundry; banks with ATM; pharmacy; Metro-North train service to NYC, mta.info/mnr or call (877) 690-5114 for fare and schedule; Dutchess County Bus, (845) 473-8424, Route E runs M–Sa from Poughkeepsie to Pawling and Wingdale along NY-55, stopping at Pawling Chamber of Commerce and Hannaford, $1.75 one way (see schedule and route map at dutchessny.gov). *Internet access:* Pawling Free Library, 11 Broad St., Tu–Th 12–8, F 12–5, Sa 10–4, Su 12-4 (except Jul–Aug). *Please leave packs and poles outside or in the hallway.*

Dover Oak—On the north side of West Dover Rd., reportedly the largest oak tree on the A.T. Its girth 4 feet from the ground is more than 20 feet, 4 inches; estimated by some to be more than 300 years old, although state authorities suggest it might be half that.

⚠ NY-22/Appalachian Trail Railroad Station. *Other services:* Native Landscapes & Garden Center; 991 Route 22, Pawling, NY 12564, (845) 855-7050; owner Pete Muroski, a hiker and hiker-friendly offers water, free outdoor shower (clothes on), use of restrooms; power outlets. No camping but mail drops accepted. Snacks, cold drinks, and limited hiker supplies, including canister fuel. Open Apr 1–Dec 24 9–5; limited access other months.

East 0.6 mile to *Camping & Groceries:* Tony's Deli (short-term resupply), open M–Th 6–4, F– Sa 6 a.m.–11 p.m., Su 5–3, offers camping ($2pp), water, and 24-hour bathroom.

West 0.1 mile to *Restaurants:* Roseann's Kitchen Food Truck, M–F 11–3 (seasonal), but check Facebook as location may vary; DC Malaysia Food Truck, W–Su 11–4 (seasonal) but check Facebook as location may vary.

East 2.6 miles to Pawling (see County 20/West Dover Rd. above). Take NY-22 to Coulter Ave., and follow to Main St. in town.

West 2.6 miles to *Groceries & Restaurant:* La Guadalupana Mini-Market (short-term resupply), M–Sa 6 a.m.–9 p.m., Su 7 a.m.–9 p.m.; Stupid Delicious Pizza,

Su–Th 11–9, F–Sa 11–10. *Other services:* Dutchess County Bus, (845) 473-8424, Route E runs M–Sa from Poughkeepsie to Pawling and Wingdale along NY-55/NY-22, stopping at La Guadalupana and Cousin's Café (see Hoyt Rd. below). Fare is $1.75 one-way; see dutchessny.gov.

West 4 miles to Wingdale (see Hoyt Rd. below).

Commuter Train: On the south side of NY-22, the Trail passes the A.T. station of Metro-North, a New York City commuter train, (877) 690-5116, mta.info/mnr. Trains leave the platform on Sa and Su at 2:35 p.m., 4:35 p.m., and 6:35 p.m. and arrive at Grand Central Terminal 2¼ hours later. Trains leave Grand Central at 7:05 a.m. and 9:05 a.m. on Sa and Su and arrive at the A.T. platform 2¼ hours later. Fares vary, peak/off-peak, one-way/round-trip, and range from $18 one way to $36 round-trip. Weekday, additional weekend services available to New York City from stations in nearby Pawling and Harlem Valley–Wingdale.

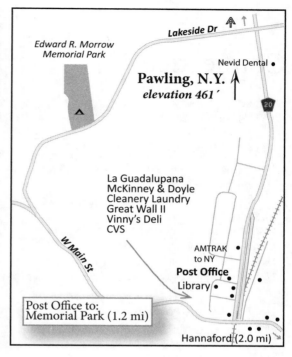

La Guadalupana
McKinney & Doyle
Cleanery Laundry
Great Wall II
Vinny's Deli
CVS

Pawling Nature Reserve Trails—West 0.9 mile to *Groceries & Restaurant:* Ben's Deli; La Guadalupana Mini-Market; Stupid Delicious Pizza (see above). The A.T. meets the Green Trail of the Pawling Nature Reserve 2.5 miles north of Hurds Corners Rd. Follow the Green Trail 0.9 mile to its end (with the final 0.1 mile blazed orange) at Furlong Road. Go 1 block west to reach NY-22; turn right for deli and restaurants. Continue north 0.8 mile to reach the Harlem Valley-Wingdale train station and 1.7 miles to reach Wingdale (below).

Wiley Shelter (1940; renovated 2014)—Sleeps 6. Privy. Renovated as part of an Eagle Scout project. Tent platforms. Water pump closed by the NPS.

⋔ Hoyt Rd.—West 3.3 miles via Hoyt Rd. and NY-55 to **Wingdale, NY [P.O. ZIP 12594: M–F 8–12:30 & 1:30–5, Sa 8–12:30; (845) 832-6147]**. To reach Harlem Valley–Wingdale Metro-North Train Station, continue south on NY-22 for about one mile. *Groceries:* Wingdale Super Market with ATM and deli (short-term resupply), open 7 a.m.–8 p.m. daily. *Restaurants:* Cousin's Pizza; Peking Kitchen; Cousin's Café; Dunkin'. *Other services:* Dover Plains Library, M–F 10–8, Sa 10–4, Internet access, printing, copying; Wingdale Orlando Family Hardware, (845) 832-0501, orlandofamilyhardware.com, limited fuel and camping supplies; Dutchess County Bus, (845) 473-8424, Route E runs M–Sa from Poughkeepsie to Pawling and Wingdale along NY-55/NY-22, stopping at Cousin's Café; $1.75 one way (see dutchessny.gov).

West 4.7 miles to *Groceries & Restaurant:* Ben's Deli; La Guadalupana Mini-Market; Stupid Delicious Pizza; see above.

Connecticut

Miles from Springer	Miles to Next Point	Features	Services	Elev	Miles from Katahdin	M A P
1,461.3	0.7	New York–Connecticut State Line; Hoyt Road *West-3.3m to* **Wingdale, NY, P.O. 12594** *West-4.7m to* Dutchess Motor Lodge and restaurants	R, P G, M, T, f L, M	400'	736.1	
1,462.0	1.1	CT-55 *East-2.5m to* **Gaylordsville, CT, P.O. 06755**	R, P G, M	580'	735.4	
1,463.1	1.0	Ten Mile Hill		1,000'	734.3	
1,464.1	0.2	**Ten Mile River Shelter**, *4mS; 8.8mN*	S	290'	733.3	
1,464.3	0.1	Ten Mile River: *footbridge*	C	280'	733.1	
1,464.4	0.6	Stream	w		733.0	
1,465.0	0.7	Bulls Bridge Road; side trail to Bulls Bridge parking area *(E-0.2m)* *East-0.5m to* Country Market	R, P G	450'	732.4	
1,465.7	1.7	Schaghticoke Road	R, P	320'	731.7	
1,467.4	1.2	Schaghticoke Mountain		1,331'	730.0	
1,468.6	1.4	Connecticut–New York State Line		1,250'	728.8	ATC: MA-CT Map 4
1,470.0	1.9	Schaghticoke Mountain Campsite	C, w	950'	727.4	
1,471.9	1.0	Thayer Brook	w	900'	725.5	
1,472.9	0.3	**Mt. Algo Shelter**, *8.4mS; 7.5mN*	S, C, w	655'	724.5	
1,473.2	3.0	CT-341, Schaghticoke Road *(new road walk)* *East-0.8m to* **Kent, CT, P.O. 06757** *East-3.3m to* Cooper Creek B&B	R, P G, L, M, D, f, sh L	350'	724.2	
1,476.2	0.7	Skiff Mountain Road	R	850'	721.2	
1,476.9	0.7	Caleb's Peak		1,160'	720.5	
1,477.6	0.5	St. Johns Ledges		900'	719.8	
1,478.1	2.3	River Road: *southern jct.*	R, P	480'	719.3	
1,480.4	0.4	**Stewart Hollow Brook Shelter**, *7.5mS; 10mN*	S, C, w	400'	717.0	
1,480.8	2.0	Stony Brook Campsite	C, w	440'	716.6	
1,482.8	0.8	River Road: *spring*	R, P, w	460'	714.6	
1,483.6	0.9	Silver Hill Campsite: *swing*	C	1,000'	713.8	
1,484.5	0.1	CT-4 *East-0.9m to* **Cornwall Bridge, CT, P.O. 06754** *East-1.9m to* Housatonic Meadows State Park	R G, L, M, O, V, f C, sh	700'	712.9	
1,484.6	0.1	Guinea Brook: *road bypass in high-water*		650'	712.8	
1,484.7	1.1	Old Sharon Road	R	750'	712.7	ATC: MA-CT Map 3
1,485.8	0.1	Hatch Brook		880'	711.6	
1,485.9	1.1	Pine Knob Loop Trail: *Housatonic Meadows SP (E-0.9m)*	C, sh	1,150'	711.5	
1,487.0	2.2	Cesar Road, Cesar Brook Campsite	R, C, w	760'	710.4	
1,489.2	0.1	Carse Brook	w	810'	708.2	

Miles from Springer	Miles to Next Point	Features	Services	Elev	Miles from Katahdin	M A P
1,489.3	1.1	West Cornwall Road *East–2.2m to* **West Cornwall, CT, P.O. 06796** *West–4.7m to* **Sharon, CT, P.O. 06069**	R, P G, L, O G, L, M, D, cl	800'	708.1	
1,490.4	0.9	**Pine Swamp Brook Shelter**, *10mS; 13.2mN*	S, C, w	1,075'	707.0	
1,491.3	0.3	Mt. Easter Road	R	1,150'	706.1	
1,491.6	1.2	Mt. Easter		1,350'	705.8	
1,492.8	0.8	Sharon Mountain Campsite	C, w	1,200'	704.6	
1,493.6	2.2	Hang Glider View		1,150'	703.8	
1,495.8	0.4	Belter's Campsite	C, w	770'	701.6	
1,496.2	0.6	US-7, CT-112	R, P	520'	701.2	
1,496.8	0.1	US-7, Warren Turnpike, Housatonic River Bridge *East–0.2m to Mountainside Cafe*	R, P M	500'	700.6	
1,496.9	1.8	Mohawk Trail Junction *(E–0.2m to Mountainside Cafe)*	M	500'	700.5	
1,498.7	0.1	Water Street, hydroelectric plant *East–0.5m to* **Falls Village, CT, P.O. 06031**	R, P, C, w, sh C, M	530'	698.7	
1,498.8	0.3	Iron Bridge: *Housatonic River, picnic area*	R, P	510'	698.6	
1,499.1	1.1	Housatonic River Road: *Great Falls*	R, P	650'	698.3	
1,500.2	2.2	Spring	w	750'	697.2	
1,502.4	0.7	Prospect Mountain		1,475'	695.0	
1,503.1	0.1	**Limestone Spring Shelter** *(W–0.5m), 13.2mS; 7.9mN*	S, C, w	980'	694.3	
1,503.2	0.5	Rand's View		1,250'	694.2	
1,503.7	0.3	Giant's Thumb: *rock formation*		1,220'	693.7	
1,504.0	2.8	Billy's View		1,150'	693.4	
1,506.8	0.7	US-44 *West–0.4m to* **Salisbury, CT, P.O. 06088** *West–2.4m to* Lakeville, CT	R, H G, L, M, f L, M, cl, f	700'	690.6	
1,507.5	2.2	CT-41, Under Mountain Road *West–0.4m to* **Salisbury, CT, P.O. 06088** *West–2.4m to* Lakeville, CT	R, P, H G, L, M, f L, M, cl, f	720'	689.9	
1,509.7	0.8	Lions Head		1,738'	687.7	
1,510.5	0.6	**Riga Shelter**, *7.9mS; 1.2mN*	S, C, w	1,610'	686.9	
1,511.1	0.6	Ball Brook Group Campsite	C, w	1,650'	686.3	
1,511.7	0.5	**Brassie Brook Shelter**, Brassie Brook *(south branch), 1.2mS; 8.8mN*	S, C, w	1,705'	685.7	
1,512.2	0.2	Undermountain Trail, Riga Junction *East–1.9m to* CT-41	R, P	1,820'	685.2	
1,512.4	0.6	Bear Mountain Road	R	1,920'	685.0	
1,513.0	0.5	Bear Mountain: *rock observation tower*		2,316'	684.4	
1,513.5	0.4	Connecticut–Massachusetts State Line		1,800'	683.9	

(vertical text at right: ATC: MA-CT Map 3)

Note: Southbounders and northbounders pass each other regularly now. Southbounders should consider the hunting seasons and the need to wear bright "blaze" orange. If hiking with a four-footed friend, keep its safety in mind, too. Campfires are prohibited on the Trail in Connecticut, and camping is permitted only at designated sites. Ridgerunners patrol the state's 53 A.T. miles and serve as caretakers at Sages Ravine campsite.

AMC–Connecticut Chapter—The Trails Committee of the AMC–Connecticut Chapter maintains the 53.2 miles from the New York–Connecticut state line to Sages Ravine, just across the Massachusetts line. The club can be reached at (413) 528-6333; ct-amc.org.

 **CT-55—East** 2.5 miles to **Gaylordsville, CT [P.O. ZIP 06755: M–F 8-1 & 2-5, Sa 8-12; (860) 354-9727].** *Groceries:* New Country Store, (860) 799-5858 (short-term resupply), M–F 6–8, Sa 6–6, Su 6–3, with deli, ATM. *Restaurants:* Salinas Restaurant and Pizza, (860) 355-2448; Gaylordsville Diner, (860) 210-1622; The Old Oak Tavern, (860) 355-1100.

Ten Mile River Shelter (1996)—Sleeps 6. Privy. Bear box. Tentsites at nearby campsite. Water pump shut off.

 **Bulls Bridge Rd.**—**East** 0.5 mile to Country Market (short-term resupply) with ATM and Internet access.

Mt. Algo Shelter (1986)—Sleeps 6. Privy. Bear box. Water source is on blue-blaze leading to shelter, 15 yards in front of shelter.

 **CT-341—East** 0.8 mile to **Kent, CT [P.O. ZIP 06757: M–F 8-1 & 2-5, Sa 8:30-12:30; (860) 927-3435].** *Lodging:* Fife 'n Drum Inn & Restaurant, (860) 927-3509, fifendrum.com, restaurant M–Th (closed Tu) 11:30–9:30, F–Sa 11:30–10, Su 11:30–8:30, $200d plus tax weekdays, $215d plus tax weekends, $25+eap, call for reservations. *Groceries:* Davis IGA (long-term resupply). *Restaurants:* Kent Pizza Garden, L/D, 11–10; Villager Restaurant, open daily 6 a.m.–11 p.m. *Outfitter:* Sundog Shoe and Leather, sundogshoe@aol.com, (860) 927-0009, 10% thru-hiker discount, boots, socks, insoles, Tu–Sa 10–5, Su 12–5. *Internet access:* Kent Memorial Library, M–F 10–5:30, Sa 12–4. *Other services:* showers (coin-op) and restrooms at the Welcome Center; banks with ATM; doctor; dentist; pharmacy; House of Books, open daily, with guides, maps, fax,UPS/FedEx services.
 North 3.3 miles via US-7 to *Lodging:* Cooper Creek B&B, (860) 927-4334. Hiker rate Su–Th $95, includes shuttle to Kent and B. No mail drops, no pets; check in at 3 p.m.; shuttle to and from Kent; slackpacking for guests; out-of-area shuttles (Wassaic, NY, train station, airports) with advance notice.

Kent, Conn.
elevation 392'

Quality • Thrift
Cornwall Bridge (8.6 mi)
Main St
7
• Bank
Fife 'n Drum Restaurant & Inn •
Welcome Center
Kent Pharmacy
Housatonic River
Ace • Hardware
• IGA
• Laundry
• **Post Office**
Sundog Shoe •
• Library
• The Villager
• Books
Kent Pizza Garden
Shanghai Chinese
Macedonia Rd
Animal Clinic •
Mobile Mart
Post Office to: General Store (0.4 mi)

Stewart Hollow Brook Shelter (1980s)—Sleeps 6. Privy. Bear box. Water source is reliable Stony Brook, 0.4 mile north of the shelter on the A.T.

Silver Hill Campsite—Campsite, privy, swing, and pavilion sheltering two picnic tables. Bear box. Water pump off.

Mohawk Trail—The former A.T. route starts north of Guinea Brook on the A.T., passes through Cornwall Bridge, and returns near Falls Village.

 **CT-4—East** 0.9 mile to **Cornwall Bridge, CT [P.O. ZIP 06754: M–F 8:30-1 & 2-5, Sa 9-12; (860) 672-6710].** *Lodging:* Hitching Post Motel, (860) 672-6219,

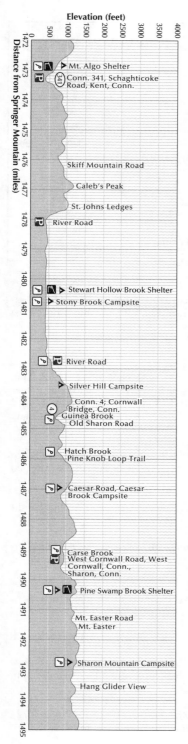

Elevation (feet)

Distance from Springer Mountain (miles)

Mt. Algo Shelter
Conn. 341, Schaghticoke Road, Kent, Conn.

Skiff Mountain Road

Caleb's Peak

St. Johns Ledges

River Road

Stewart Hollow Brook Shelter
Stony Brook Campsite

River Road

Silver Hill Campsite
Conn. 4; Cornwall Bridge, Conn.
Guinea Brook
Old Sharon Road

Hatch Brook
Pine Knob Loop Trail

Caesar Road, Caesar Brook Campsite

Carse Brook
West Cornwall Road, West Cornwall, Conn.; Sharon, Conn.

Pine Swamp Brook Shelter

Mt. Easter Road
Mt. Easter

Sharon Mountain Campsite

Hang Glider View

$130d and up weekdays, $150d and up weekends, $15eap, laundry service $5 and up, shuttle available depending on staffing; Housatonic Meadows Lodge B&B, (860) 672-6067, $110; Cornwall Inn & Restaurant, open year-round, (800) 786-6884, cornwallinn.com, hiker rate $125D, $150 for 4 in room with 2 queen beds, includes continental B, pool, hot tub, Internet access, restaurant and lounge open Th–Su, L/D $8–$30. *Groceries:* Cornwall Market (short-term resupply), (860) 619-8199, deli, bakery, coffee, B, and more; M–F 6–5, Sa–Su 7–5. *Outfitter:* Housatonic River Outfitters, 24 Kent Rd., (860) 672-1010, hflyshop@aol.com, open 7 days 9–5, limited hiker gear, canister fuel and fuel by ounce, will accept UPS and FedEx but not responsible for packages. *Other services:* hardware store; Housatonic Veterinary Care, (860) 672-4948. *Camping:* Housatonic Meadows State Park, (860) 672-6772, 1 mile north of town on US-7. Campsite $36 per night, up to 6 per site; open mid-Apr to Jan 1, water shut off Oct 15. The park may be self-service midweek; registration information at the main cabin by the gate. Showers free but check with registration desk; no pets, no alcoholic beverages allowed. Accessible from the A.T. via Pine Knob Loop Trail (see below).

Guinea Brook—The AMC Connecticut Chapter installed stepping stones in the brook. In heavy rain, you may want to take the bypass: Northbounders should turn east on CT-4 and go downhill to unpaved Old Sharon Rd. on the north, which rejoins the A.T. on the other side of the stream. Southbounders should turn east on the dirt road that the Trail crosses before the brook, then follow it to CT-4, and turn south.

Pine Knob Loop Trail—Housatonic Meadows State Park (see above) can be reached from the A.T. by taking the blue-blazed Pine Knob Loop Trail 0.5 mile to US-7, then following the highway north for 0.4 mile. You can return to the A.T. via the Pine Knob Loop Trail.

West Cornwall Rd.—**East** 2.2 miles to **West Cornwall, CT [P.O. ZIP 06796: M–F 9:30-1 & 2–4:30, Sa 9–12; (860) 672-6791]**, site of a historical covered bridge over a whitewater section of the Housatonic River. *Lodging:* Private groups only: Bearded Woods 'One-of-a-Kind' Bunk & Dine, (860) 480-2966, beardedwoods.com. Shuttles to/from the Trail and the local P.O. Call or text Hudson for reservations (no walk-ins); 1–6 p.m. Will pick up from West Cornwall, Falls Village, or Salisbury; ID required. Free slackpacking between those locations with second-night stay; longer shuttles of any distance for a fee. Not a party place, no pets, no mail drops.

West 4.7 miles to **Sharon, CT [P.O. ZIP 06069: M–F 9:30-4:30, Sa 9:30-12:30; (860) 364-5306]**, with a supermarket, restaurant serving B/L/D, laundry, motel, bank with ATM, pharmacy, and hospital.

Pine Swamp Brook Shelter (1989)—Sleeps 6. Privy. Bear box. Water is available on the blue-blazed trail.

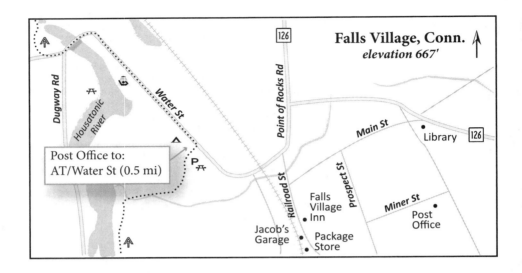

US-7/Warren Turnpike—*Restaurant:* Mountainside Café, (860) 824-7876, Tu–Su 7–3. After crossing Housatonic River and before Trail turns left on Warren Turnpike at high school, cross bridge over railroad tracks, then continue 0.2 mile.

Mohawk Trail—**East** 0.2 mile to Mountainside Café (above).

Water St.—**East** 0.5 mile to **Falls Village, CT [P.O. ZIP 06031: M–F 8:30–1 & 2–5, Sa 8:30–12; (860) 824-7781]**. *Restaurants:* Falls Village Inn, upscale but hiker-friendly, L/D but no lodging. *Other services:* Falls Village Package Store, (860) 824-7971, open M–Sa 9–8, Su noon–5; has sodas and hiker snacks, allows hikers to charge phones, get water, and use phone to call area restaurants; bank with ATM at corner of Rtes. 7 & 126.

Hydroelectric Plant—Cold shower and water are available outside the small, vine-covered building past the transformer. Look for silver shower head poking through ivy, with a small concrete pad below. Water faucet is below shower head.

Wheelchair-accessible trail—The A.T. hooks up with the River Trail, converted to create a handicap-accessible loop trail using part of the A.T. and an old racetrack.

Iron Bridge over Housatonic—The original bridge, recently renovated, was built by the Berlin Construction Co. of Connecticut in 1903. The same company built the iron bridge that now takes hikers over Swatara Creek in Pennsylvania.

Picnic Area—North of bridge along the river, opposite the power plant, are picnic tables (no water), fire pits, a privy, trash cans, and parking area.

Limestone Spring Shelter (1986)—Sleeps 6. Privy is uphill to the right. Bear box. Follow the stream to where a spring comes out of a small limestone cave.

Rand's View—The A.T. passes this vista, with views of the Taconic Range from Lion's Head to Mt. Everett and Jug End. *No camping allowed.*

US-44—**West** 0.4 mile to **Salisbury, CT [P.O. ZIP 06068: M–F 8:30–1 & 2–5, Sa 9–12; (860) 435-5072]**. For northbounders, turn west on US-44 to town. For southbounders, it is best to follow CT-41,

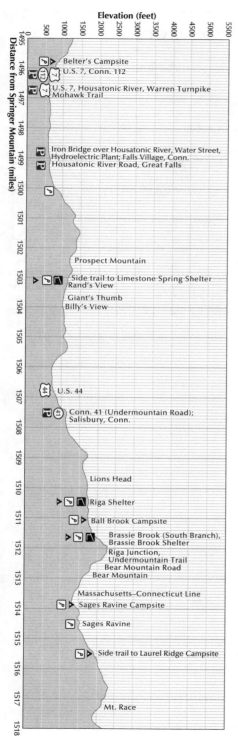

Elevation (feet)

Belter's Campsite
U.S. 7, Conn. 112
U.S. 7, Housatonic River, Warren Turnpike
Mohawk Trail

Iron Bridge over Housatonic River, Water Street,
Hydroelectric Plant; Falls Village, Conn.
Housatonic River Road, Great Falls

Prospect Mountain

Side trail to Limestone Spring Shelter
Rand's View
Giant's Thumb
Billy's View

U.S. 44

Conn. 41 (Undermountain Road);
Salisbury, Conn.

Lions Head

Riga Shelter

Ball Brook Campsite

Brassie Brook (South Branch),
Brassie Brook Shelter
Riga Junction,
Undermountain Trail
Bear Mountain Road
Bear Mountain

Massachusetts–Connecticut Line
Sages Ravine Campsite

Sages Ravine

Side trail to Laurel Ridge Campsite

Mt. Race

Under Mountain Rd., 0.8 mile into town. Water is available from a fountain at town hall and also from a spigot in the cemetery on Cobble Rd. (located behind a large cement cross about 200 feet right of the maintenance shed). *Lodging:* Maria McCabe offers rooms to hikers in her home, 4 Grove St., (860) 435-0593, $35pp, includes shower, use of living room, cooking outside, pets outside (no fee), no visitors in home, cash only, shuttle to laundry, mail drops accepted for guests; Vanessa Breton, 7 The Lockup Rd., (860) 435-9577, offers 3 rooms in her home for up to 5 hikers, $40pp, includes shower, laundry $5, use of living room, cooking outside, pets outside (no fee), no visitors in home, cash only, mail drops accepted for guests. Several inns and B&Bs in the area. *Groceries:* LaBonne's Epicure Market, (860) 435-2559 (long-term resupply), M–Sa, open 8–7, Su until 6. *Restaurants:* Sweet William's Bakery, (860) 435-8889, baked goods, coffee, 7–5. *Internet access* Scoville Memorial Library, M–F 9–5. *Other services:* Salisbury General Store and Pharmacy (short-term resupply, including fuel), (860) 435-9388, M–F 8–6, Sa 8–5, Su 8–4 (pharmacy closed Su); bank with ATM; The Auto Shop, Coleman fuel and denatured alcohol. When open, town hall offers restroom and phone inside.

West 2.4 miles to **Lakeville.** *Restaurants:* Mizza's Restaurant and Pizza, (860) 435-6266, free delivery; On the Run Coffee Shop, (860) 435-2007, open every day 5:30 a.m.–2 p.m. *Other services:* hardware store, laundry open 24 hrs., bank with ATM.

CT-41 (Under Mountain Rd.)—**West** 0.8 mile to Salisbury (see previous entry).

Riga Shelter (2023)—Newly reconstructed by AMC–CT Chapter volunteers. Sleeps 6. Privy, tentsites, platform. Bear box. The only shelter in Connecticut with a view. It opens to the east, providing sunrise views. Water is a spring on a blue-blazed trail to the left of the clearing at the A.T. A second source is where the trail to the shelter crosses a small stream. Spring may not run in dry years.

Brassie Brook Shelter (2023)—Newly reconstructed by AMC–CT Chapter volunteers. Sleeps 6. Privy. Bear box. Tentsites. Water is available from a stream on the A.T. 50 feet north of the side trail to the shelter.

Bear Mountain—At 2,316 feet, this is the highest peak in Connecticut but not the highest ground,

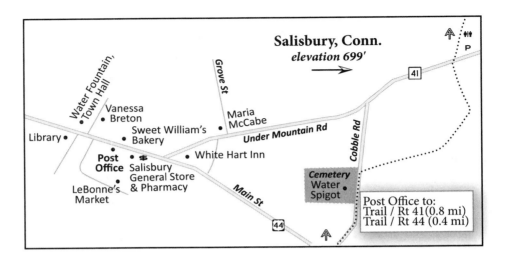

which instead falls on the flank of nearby Mt. Frissel, the peak of which is in Massachusetts. The northbound descent into Sages Ravine is rocky and steep. In foul weather, an alternative route for northbounders is east on the Undermountain Trail for 0.8 mile, then north on the Paradise Lane Trail for 2.1 miles, reconnecting with the A.T. near Sages Ravine, a net 1.7-mile detour. No camping on summit.

Massachusetts

Miles from Springer	Miles to Next Point	Features	Services	Elev	Miles from Katahdin	M A P
1,513.5	0.4	Connecticut–Massachusetts State Line		1,800'	683.9	
1,513.9	0.6	Sages Ravine Brook Campsite	C, w	1,360'	683.5	
1,514.5	1.0	Sages Ravine	w	1,340'	682.9	
1,515.5	1.8	Side trail to Laurel Ridge Campsite	C, w	1,750'	681.9	
1,517.3	0.9	Mt. Race: *open ledges*		2,365'	680.1	
1,518.2	0.7	Race Brook Trail, campsite *(E–0.2m)*, stream *(E–0.4m)* *East–2.5m to MA-41*	C, w R, P	1,950'	679.2	ATC: MA-CT Map 3
1,518.9	0.7	Mt. Everett		2,602'	678.5	
1,519.6	0.4	Guilder Pond Picnic Area	R, P	2,042'	677.8	
1,520.0	0.1	**The Hemlocks Shelter**, *8.8mS; 0.1mN*	S, w	1,880'	677.4	
1,520.1	0.6	**Glen Brook Shelter**, *0.1mS; 14.3mN*	S, C, w	1,885'	677.3	
1,520.7	1.7	Elbow Trail		1,750'	676.7	
1,522.4	1.1	Jug End		1,750'	675.0	
1,523.5	0.9	Jug End Road (Curtiss Road) *(E–0.25m spring)*	R, P, w	890'	673.9	
1,524.4	1.8	MA-41; Undermountain Road *West–0.1m to* April Hill (Greenagers) *West–1.2m to* **South Egremont, MA, P.O. 01258**	R w M	810'	673.0	
1,526.2	1.8	Sheffield–Egremont Road; Shay's Rebellion Monument	R, P	700'	671.2	
1,528.0	0.9	US-7 *East–3.2m to* **Sheffield, MA, P.O. 01257** *West–1.5m to* Guido's Fresh Marketplace; Big Y *West–1.8m to* **Great Barrington, MA, P.O. 01230** *West–2.8 to* shopping center	R B, g, L, M G, M all G, cl, f	700'	669.4	
1,528.9	2.0	Kellogg Road, Housatonic River Bridge	R, P	720'	668.5	
1,530.9	1.4	Home Road	R, P	1,150'	666.5	
1,532.3	2.1	East Mountain	w	1,800'	665.1	
1,534.4	1.1	Ice Gulch; **Tom Leonard Shelter** *(E–0.2m stream)*, *14.3mS; 5.4mN*	S, w	1,540'	663.0	
1,535.5	0.9	Lake Buel Road	R, P	1,150'	661.9	
1,536.4	1.2	MA-23 *East–4.3m to* **Monterey, MA, P.O. 01245** *West–1.6m to* East Mountain Retreat Center *West–4m to* **Great Barrington, MA, P.O. 01230**	R, P H all	1,050'	661.0	ATC: MA-CT Map 2
1,537.6	0.8	Blue Hill Road (Stony Brook Road)	R, P	1,550'	659.8	
1,538.4	0.6	Benedict Pond *(W–0.5m)*, Beartown State Forest	C, w	1,620'	659.0	
1,539.0	0.8	The Ledges		1,820'	658.4	
1,539.8	1.7	**Mt. Wilcox South Shelter**, *5.4mS; 2mN*	S, w	1,720'	657.6	
1,541.5	0.6	**Mt. Wilcox North Shelter** *(E–0.3m)*, *2mS; 15mN*	S, w	2,100'	655.9	
1,542.1	3.2	Beartown Mountain Road	R, w	1,800'	655.3	
1,545.3	0.3	Fernside Road/Jerusalem Road	R, P, w	1,200'	652.1	
1,545.6	1.5	Shaker Campsite	C, w	1,000'	651.8	

Miles from Springer	Miles to Next Point	Features	Services	Elev	Miles from Katahdin	MAP
1,547.1	0.5	Tyringham Cobble		1,240'	650.3	
1,547.6	1.1	Jerusalem Road: *spring* *West–0.6m to* **Tyringham, MA, P.O. 01264**	R, P, w, g L, w	930'	649.8	
1,548.7	1.9	Tyringham Main Road (*W–1.1m to town*)	R, P, L, w	930'	648.7	
1,550.6	0.4	Webster Road	R, P, w	1,800'	646.8	
1,551.0	2.0	Brook	w		646.4	
1,553.0	1.9	Goose Pond Road	R, P	1,650'	644.4	
1,554.9	0.5	Upper Goose Pond	w	1,500'	642.5	
1,555.4	0.3	Old chimney and plaque		1,520'	642.0	
1,555.7	1.2	**Upper Goose Pond Cabin** (*W–0.5m*), 15mS; 9.3mN	S, C, w	1,480'	641.7	
1,556.9	0.1	I-90 Massachusetts Turnpike: *overpass*	R	1,400'	640.5	
1,557.0	0.3	Greenwater Brook	w	1,400'	640.4	
1,557.3	0.8	US-20 *East–0.1m to* Berkshire Lakeside Lodge *West–5m to* **Lee, MA, P.O. 01238**	R, P L all	1,400'	640.1	
1,558.1	0.5	Tyne Road	R, P	1,750'	639.3	
1,558.6	1.8	Becket Mountain		2,180'	638.8	
1,560.4	2.3	Finerty Pond	w	1,900'	637.0	
1,562.7	0.2	County Road	R, P	1,850'	634.7	
1,562.9	1.6	Bald Top		2,040'	634.5	
1,564.5	0.7	**October Mountain Shelter**, 9.3mS; 9mN	S, C, w	1,950'	632.9	
1,565.2	1.5	West Branch Road	R, P	1,960'	632.2	
1,566.7	2.0	Washington Mountain Road, Pittsfield Road *East–0.1m to* the Cookie Lady *East–5m to* **Becket, MA, P.O. 01223**	R, P g, L, D, V	2,000'	630.7	
1,568.7	1.2	Stream	w	1,950'	628.7	
1,569.9	0.7	Blotz Road	R, P	1,850'	627.5	
1,570.6	2.7	Warner Hill		2,050'	626.8	
1,573.3	0.3	**Kay Wood Shelter** (*E–0.2m*), 9mS; 17.1mN	S, w	1,860'	624.1	
1,573.6	2.1	Grange Hall Road	R, P	1,650'	623.8	
1,575.7	0.1	CSX Railroad crossing		1,250'	621.7	
1,575.8	0.5	Depot Street: *water spigot at 83 Depot St.*	R, H, w	1,240'	621.6	
1,576.3	1.0	Mass. 8, Mass. 9; **Dalton, MA, P.O. 01226**	R, B, C, G, L, M, D, cl, f	1,200'	621.1	
1,577.3	3.7	Gulf Road	R, P	1,180'	620.1	
1,581.0	0.4	Crystal Mountain Campsite (*E–0.2m*)	C, w	2,100'	616.4	
1,581.4	2.5	Gore Pond		2,050'	616.0	
1,583.9	0.7	Cheshire Cobbles: *views*		1,850'	613.5	
1,584.6	0.4	Furnace Hill Road	R	960'	612.8	
1,585.0	0.1	Main St., Hoosic River, Ashuwillticook Rail Trail	R, P, M	950'	612.4	
1,585.1	0.5	Church St., School St., hiker kiosk, **Cheshire, MA, P.O. 01225** *West–75 yds. to* Father Tom Campsite	R, B, G, M C, w	970'	612.3	
1,585.6	0.8	MA-8 *East–0.8m to* Harbour House Inn *East–2.4m to* Berkshire Outfitters *East–4m to* **Adams, MA, P.O. 01220** *West–0.2m to* O'Connell's Convenience Store	R L, G O, f B, G, L, M, D, V, cl g, M	1,000'	611.8	

ATC: MA-CT Map 2

ATC: MA-CT Map 1

Miles from Springer	Miles to Next Point	Features	Services	Elev	Miles from Katahdin	M A P
1,586.4	2.7	Outlook Avenue	R	1,350'	611.0	
1,589.1	0.9	Old Adams Road	R	2,350'	608.3	
1,590.0	0.6	**Mark Noepel Shelter** *(E–0.2m), 17.1mS; 7.1mN*	S, C, w	2,750'	607.4	
1,590.6	2.2	Jones Nose Trail, Saddle Ball Mountain		3,238'	606.8	
1,592.8	0.5	Notch Road; Rockwell Road: *pond*	R, P	3,290'	604.6	
1,593.3	2.4	Mt. Greylock, Summit Road; Bascom Lodge, War Memorial	R, P, L, M, sh, w	3,491'	604.1	
1,595.7	0.8	Mt. Williams: *view*		2,951'	601.7	
1,596.5	0.1	Notch Road	R, P	2,400'	600.9	
1,596.6	2.1	Money Brook Trail to **Wilbur Clearing Shelter** *(W–0.3m), 7.1mS; 12.8mN*	S, C, w	2,310'	600.8	
1,598.7	0.5	Pattison Road	R, P, w	900'	598.7	
1,599.2	0.4	Catherine Street-Phelps Road	R	670'	598.2	
1,599.6	0.1	MA-2: *Hoosic River, railroad tracks overpass* *East–100 yards to overnight parking* *East–0.6m to West's Variety, Chinese Buffet* *East–1m to YMCA* *East–2.5m to* **North Adams, MA, P.O. 01247** *West–0.4m to Stop & Shop, motel* *West–0.6m to veterinarian* *West–1.4m to motels, restaurants, groceries* *West–2.6m to* **Williamstown, MA, P.O. 01267**	R, P, B P g, M, cl sh B, G, L, M, D, V, cl G, L V G, L, M, cl, f B, G, L, M, D, sh	650'	597.8	ATC: MA-CT Map 1
1,599.7	1.7	Massachusetts Avenue *East–0.6m to Renee's Diner*	M	675'	597.7	
1,601.4	1.0	Pete's Spring *(SE)*; Sherman Brook primitive campsite *(W–0.1m)*	C, w	1,300'	596.0	
1,602.4	1.3	Pine Cobble Trail		2,010'	595.0	
1,603.7	0.4	Massachusetts-Vermont State Line; Long Trail *(southern terminus): sign*		2,330'	593.7	

From the peak of Mt. Everett to the summit of 3,491-foot Mt. Greylock, the Trail crosses the hills and valleys of The Berkshires, known as a cultural mecca of theater, music, art, and dance and frequented by famous writers and artists since the mid-1800s. The Berkshires have retained much of its rural character, as the Trail winds through agricultural lands and small towns and traverses wilderness forested ridgelines. Juicy, sweet blueberries abound in season.

Note: The state line is south of Sages Ravine, near the junction with Paradise Lane Trail. Camping is allowed only at shelters and the following designated campsites: Sages Ravine, Laurel Ridge, Race Brook Falls, Shaker, Crystal Mountain, and Sherman Brook. Ridgerunners employed by the state Department of Conservation and Recreation and the Appalachian Mountain Club (AMC) patrol the trail during the summer months.

Sages Ravine—Two tent platforms and campsites with group site, privy. Spring is uphill of site or get water from stream. The bridge across Sawmill Brook to campsite is out, but the brook is easily crossed under normal conditions. Staffed by Appalachian Mountain Club ridgerunners who take turns as caretakers. No fires permitted. No fees charged.

Western Massachusetts Chapter of the Appalachian Mountain Club—The Massachusetts A.T. Management Committee of the AMC–Western Massachusetts Chapter maintains 89.2 miles from the Sages Ravine area to the Massachusetts–Vermont state line. Correspondence should be sent to the Western Massachusetts Chapter–AMC, BOX 2281, Pittsfield, MA 02102, or at@amc-wma.org; amc-wma.org/at.

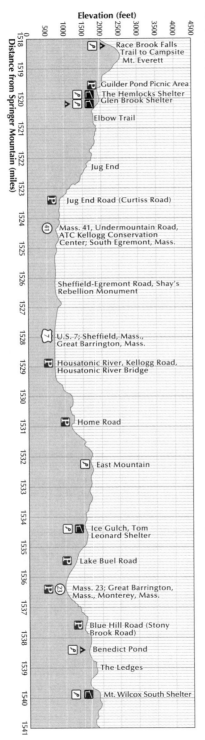

Berkshire Bus Service—The Berkshire Regional Transit Authority, (413) 499-2782 or (800) 292-2782, berkshirerta.com, serves the Trail towns of Great Barrington, Lee, Dalton, Cheshire, Adams, North Adams, and Williamstown. The buses run M–F 5:45 a.m.–7:20 p.m. and Sa 7:15 a.m.–7 p.m.; no service Su or holidays. Call for accurate, up-to-date information. The buses can be flagged down anywhere along MA-2 or 8 or US-7, but there are designated bus stops. Popular trips for hikers include rides from Dalton west into Pittsfield, the region's hub with all major services, and from Cheshire south to the Berkshire Mall, with a limited number of stores and a 10-screen cinema. Maximum fare one way is $4.50 ($1.75 two adjacent towns; cash; drivers cannot make change); ask for free transfers. Senior rates available.

Peter Pan Bus Lines—(800) 343-9999, peterpanbus.com. Buses run daily each way between NYC and Williamstown, MA, stopping at towns near the A.T., including Canaan and Danbury in Connecticut and Sheffield, Great Barrington, Lee, Pittsfield, and Williamstown in Massachusetts. Call for schedules and rates.

Laurel Ridge Campsite—0.1 mile south of Bear Rock Falls, 5 campsites and one group site with 3-tent platform. Privy. Bear box. Water source is a spring off a short side trail south of campsites. *No fires permitted in this area.*

Race Mountain—A spectacular walk on a clear day; spooky when foggy. It's a steep drop-off to the east.

Race Brook Falls Campsite—0.2 mile east on the Race Brook Trail. Group camping area, 4 tent platforms, 4 tent pads, privy, bear box. Water source is stream north of the campsite.

Mt. Everett—This range is the second-highest on the A.T. in Massachusetts.

Guilder Pond—The short side trail to the west leads to this pond in Mt. Everett State Reservation. Picnic table and privy. For conservation reasons, please, no camping or swimming.

The Hemlocks Shelter (1999)—Sleeps 10. Privy. Bear box. Nestled in a hemlock grove, the shelter offers a sleeping loft with overhang. Water source is on the blue-blazed access trail. If you cannot find water here, Glen Brook crosses the A.T. 50 yards north of the access trail to the shelter.

Glen Brook Shelter (1987)—Sleeps 6. Privy. Bear box. Two tent platforms and large tenting area. Water source is a reliable stream in front of, and downhill from, the shelter.

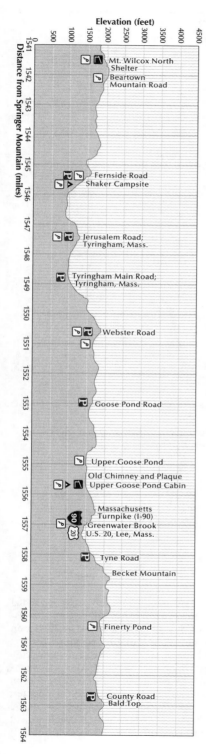

Elevation (feet)

Distance from Springer Mountain (miles)

Mt. Wilcox North Shelter

Beartown Mountain Road

Fernside Road
Shaker Campsite

Jerusalem Road;
Tyringham, Mass.

Tyringham Main Road;
Tyringham, Mass.

Webster Road

Goose Pond Road

Upper Goose Pond

Old Chimney and Plaque
Upper Goose Pond Cabin

Massachusetts
Turnpike (I-90)
Greenwater Brook
U.S. 20, Lee, Mass.

Tyne Road

Becket Mountain

Finerty Pond

County Road
Bald Top

⚠ MA-41 (Undermountain Rd.)—West 0.1 mile to the April Hill Conservation and Education Center (formerly the Kellogg Conservation Center), now owned by Greenagers, a nonprofit organization that employs teen-agers and young adults in the fields of conservation, sustainable farming, and environmental leadership. No camping or parking, but water from a hose and charging outlets are available. Trailhead parking is available on Sheffield–Egremont Rd., 1.8 Trail miles north. For more information, visit greenagers.org.

West 1.2 miles to **South Egremont, MA [P.O. ZIP 01258: M-F 8:15-12 & 12:30-4, Sa 9-11:30; (413) 528-1571].** *Restaurant:* Mom's Country Café, B/L, M–Su 7–3, water available from outdoor spigot; Harmony Market (short-term resupply). *Internet access:* library, M, Tu & Th 10–6, Sa 9–noon. *Other services:* bank with ATM; Harmony Market (short-term resupply).

East 4.6 miles to *Lodging:* Race Brook Lodge, 864 South Undermountain Rd. (see Sheffield listing).

Shays' Rebellion Monument—A recently refurbished stone marker at the Trail crossing of Sheffield–Egremont Rd. commemorates the last skirmish of a bloody farmers' revolt led by Revolutionary War veteran Daniel Shays against government taxes and tactics in 1787. The incident assisted Federalists in making their case for a strong central government with powers to tax and maintain a standing army.

⚠ US-7—East 2.8 miles to **Sheffield, MA [P.O. ZIP 01257: M-F 9-4:30, Sa 9-12; (413) 229-8772].** *Shuttles:* Jess Treat, call or text (860) 248-5710, jesstrea@gmail.com. *Lodging:* Race Brook Lodge, 864 South Undermountain Rd. (MA-41), (413) 229-2916, rblodge.com, a restored 1790s barn, A.T.-hiker special $95 for 2 people weeknights includes B, $20 additional for 3rd or 4th person, $10 ride to town, pick-up and drop-off at Jug End Rd. or Salisbury, Conn., regular summer rates Su–Th $120–$260, F–Sa $155–$335, $20eap, pets allowed in same room $15, mail drops for guests only. Stagecoach Tavern open for D Th–Su. *Restaurants:* Robert's Pizza W-Th,Sa 4-8, Sa 4-9; The Marketplace Kitchen and Café, M-F 7-3, Sa 8-3, Su 9-2;. *Other services:* The Pass cannabis dispensary, (413) 644-6892, thepass.com, 9–8 daily, cash and debit cards only; bank; ATM; and bus service.

West 1.0 mile to Fiddleheads Grille, (413) 644-2999, Th 12–8, F–Sa 12–9, Su 12–3.

West 1.7 miles to The Bistro Box, (413) 717-5958, burgers and dogs, sandwiches, ice cream; Th–Tu 11–4, closed W.

West 2.3 miles to Guido's, with organic produce and deli; Big Y Foods, M–Th & Sa–Su 9–7, F 10–6; Great Barrington Bagel Co., bagels and sandwiches, M-F 6:30-3, Sa-Su 7-3.

⚠ West 3.4 miles to **Great Barrington, MA [P.O. ZIP 01230: M-F 8:30-4:30, Sa 8:30-12:30; (413) 528-3670].**

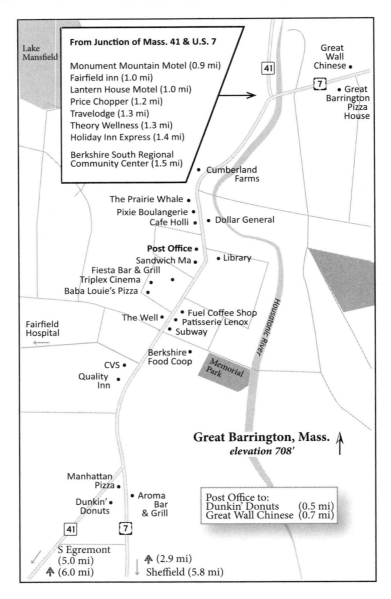

From Junction of Mass. 41 & U.S. 7

Monument Mountain Motel (0.9 mi)
Fairfield inn (1.0 mi)
Lantern House Motel (1.0 mi)
Price Chopper (1.2 mi)
Travelodge (1.3 mi)
Theory Wellness (1.3 mi)
Holiday Inn Express (1.4 mi)

Berkshire South Regional
Community Center (1.5 mi)

Lake Mansfield

Great Wall Chinese •

7

• Great Barrington Pizza House

• Cumberland Farms

The Prairie Whale •
Pixie Boulangerie •
Cafe Holli •   • Dollar General

Post Office •
Sandwich Ma •   • Library
Fiesta Bar & Grill
Triplex Cinema •
Baba Louie's Pizza •

The Well •   • Fuel Coffee Shop
• Patisserie Lenox
• Subway

Fairfield Hospital
←

Berkshire • Food Coop
CVS •
Quality Inn •

Memorial Park

Housatonic River

Great Barrington, Mass. ↑
elevation 708'

Manhattan Pizza •
Dunkin' • Donuts   • Aroma Bar & Grill

41   7

Post Office to:
Dunkin' Donuts   (0.5 mi)
Great Wall Chinese (0.7 mi)

S Egremont
(5.0 mi)
↙
⚚ (6.0 mi)

⚚ (2.9 mi)
↓ Sheffield (5.8 mi)

Lodging: Quality Inn, (413) 528-3150, rates $104–$269, $10eap, max 4/room, no pets, continental B, Wi-Fi; Lantern House Motel, (413) 528-2350, outdoor saltwater pool, call for pricing and reservations, Wi-Fi, continental B, no pets; Travelodge, (413) 528-2340, $99s, $109 and up, higher on weekends and during special events, $10eap, max 2/room, pets allowed in some rooms for $10 fee, laundry, Wi-Fi, continental B, outdoor pool; Holiday Inn Express, (413) 528-1810, minimum 20% hiker discount, call for current rates, extended continental B, no pets, Wi-Fi, indoor pool, computer available for guests; Berkshire Marriott Fairfield Inn, (413) 644-3200, berkshiremarriott.com, call for rates, full hot B, laundry, no pets, indoor and outdoor pools, Wi-Fi and guest's computer; The Briarcliff Motel, (413) 528-3000, thebriarcliffmotel.com, $175 and up in summer, continental B, Wi-Fi; Monument Mountain Motel, US-7, 247 Stockbridge Rd., (413) 528-3272, monument mountainmotel.com, $105 and up, higher on weekends and during special events, no pets, laundry, pool, coffee and tea when office is open, mail drops accepted for guests. *Groceries:* Price Chopper, M–Sa 6–midnight, Su 7–midnight (long-term resupply). *Restaurants:* Numerous, in town center and north along US-7. *Other services:* Berkshire South Regional Community Center, 15 Crissey Rd., (413) 528-2810, 1 mile north of the town center on US-7, sells day passes for section- and thru-hikers for $8/person. Day pass entitles guests to the use of the entire facility—showers, saunas, aquatic center, fitness room, and classes. Berkshire South has a limited number of tent platforms available at no charge on a first-come/ first-served basis; 1 to 2 tents/platform only. No tenting elsewhere on grounds. For more information, please call or visit berkshiresouth.org. All hikers must check in at the front desk upon arrival. Free community supper served every M 5–6. Smoking, drugs, alcohol, and dogs are prohibited on the center grounds. On Berkshire Regional Transit Bus Route #21, let the driver know, and she/he will take you to Berkshire South; fee 85¢–$1.75 cash; berkshireta.com. Shopping center 2.8 miles **west** of Trail (1 mile north of town center on US-7) has groceries, pharmacy, coin laundry, hardware store. Theory Wellness cannabis dispensary, 394 Stockbridge Rd., (413) 650-5527, daily 8–10, cash or debit cards only. Taxi, (413) 528-0911. Laundry Land now open for coin laundry, 9–9, 11 School St. downtown. *Shuttles:* Joe at Great Barrington Shuttle, (413) 717-0751. *Bus service:* In front of chamber of commerce in town (buy tickets from driver) and at Fairgrounds Plaza, Barrington Plaza, and Rite Aid.

Tom Leonard Shelter (1988)—Sleeps 10. Two tent platforms, 5 tentsites. Privy. Bear box. Located just south of Ice Gulch, a deep cleft in the landscape. Water source is a very cold stream 0.2 mile down a ravine on a blue-blazed trail to the left of the shelter.

⚠ MA-23—East 4.3 miles to **Monterey, MA [P.O. ZIP 01245: M-F 8:30-1 & 2-4:30, Sa 9-11:30; (413) 528-4670]**.
    West 4 miles to Great Barrington.

Benedict Pond, Beartown State Forest—West 0.5 mile on a blue-blazed side trail to a beach with picnic tables, tentsites $14.

Mt. Wilcox South Shelter (1930/2007)—Old shelter sleeps 6. Privy. Bear box. Built as a CCC project; approach trail was part of the original A.T. in Massachusetts. Shelter completed in 2007 is just beyond old one; 5 tentsites behind old shelter. Water source is the spring crossed en route to the shelter.

Mt. Wilcox North Shelter (1930s)—Sleeps 10. Four tentsites. Privy. Bear box. Shelter is on a 0.3-mile blue-blazed trail. Water source, in front of the shelter, may go dry in late summer.

Shaker Campsite—Two tent platforms, privy, bear box, space for 4-5 tents. Water is north on the A.T. at stream crossing. Bear sightings have been frequent here.

Tyringham Cobble—Formed by a geological event that separated this hill from the mountain behind it, the cobble rises 400 feet above the village below. The hill and nearly 200 acres around it are owned by the Trustees of Reservations, a Massachusetts conservation trust.

⚠ Jerusalem Rd.—West 0.6 mile to **Tyringham, MA [P.O. ZIP 01264: M-F 9-12:30 & 4-5:30, Sa 8:30-12:30; (413) 243-1225]**. May also be reached from Tyringham Main Rd. 1.1 mile north on A.T. Water fountain outside post office. Library open T 3–5, Sa 10–12; Wi-Fi and computer available Santarella Gardens is located 0.8mi north of the post office on the main road leading out of town, The gardens along with the eclectic house is worth the walk to see it.

Jerusalem Rd. Spring—West several yards to short path on left that leads to a piped spring (if you pass the first house on the right, you've gone too far). Opposite spring is the Running Spring Farm stand, with cold beverages, snacks, and eggs for sale. Device-charging outlet, recycling and trash receptacles, and book exchange available.

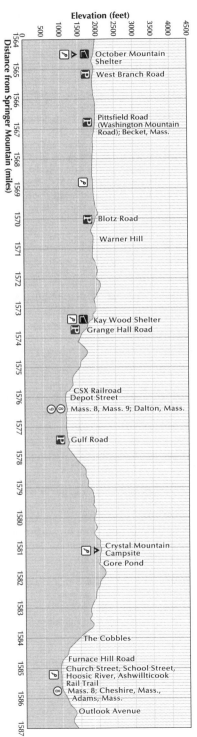

Elevation (feet)

Distance from Springer Mountain (miles)

October Mountain Shelter

West Branch Road

Pittsfield Road (Washington Mountain Road); Becket, Mass.

Blotz Road

Warner Hill

Kay Wood Shelter
Grange Hall Road

CSX Railroad
Depot Street
Mass. 8, Mass. 9; Dalton, Mass.

Gulf Road

Crystal Mountain Campsite
Gore Pond

The Cobbles

Furnace Hill Road
Church Street; School Street;
Hoosic River, Ashwillticook
Rail Trail
Mass. 8; Cheshire, Mass.,
Adams, Mass.

Outlook Avenue

Upper Goose Pond Cabin—AMC–Western Massachusetts Chapter A.T. Management Committee maintains this cabin on a 0.5-mile side trail north of the pond. The cabin offers bunks, fireplace, covered porch, privy, bear boxes, swimming, tentsites, and platforms. Open daily mid-May to mid-Oct. During the summer, the resident volunteer caretaker brings water by canoe from a spring across the pond; otherwise, the pond is the water source. When the caretaker is not in residence or the cabin is closed for the season, hikers may camp on the porch or tent platforms. Two privies behind the cabin and near tentsites. No fee is charged for staying at this site; donations appreciated.

US-20—**East** 0.1 mile to *Lodging:* Berkshire Lakeside Lodge, 3949 Jacob's Ladder Rd., Becket, MA 01223; (413) 243-9907, berkshirelakesidelodge.com, $60–$165 (call for reservations), use of outside grill, canoes, and kayaks; continental B, Wi-Fi, minifridge and coffee pot in each room; food delivery available; mail drops accepted for non-guests, no fee but call ahead.

West 5 miles to **Lee, MA [P.O. ZIP 01238: M-F 8:30–4:30, Sa 9-12; (413) 243-1392]**. A full-service town with a mile-long downtown area and entrance/exit to the Massachusetts Turnpike (I-90). Nearby Lenox is home to the famous Tanglewood Performing Arts Center and the summer residence of the Boston Symphony Orchestra. Tanglewood also offers other types of concerts in an outdoors setting and spectacular July Fourth fireworks. *Lodging:* Pilgrim Inn, (413) 243-1328, Su–Th $89–$119, F–Sa $105–$205, $10eap, continental B, coffee in room, pool, Wi-Fi, microwave, fridge, laundry; EconoLodge, (413) 243-0501, $118–$139s/d weekdays, $150-175 weekends, Wi-Fi, microwave, fridge, continental B; Sunset Inn, 150 Housatonic St., (413) 243-0302, $98–$118, fridge, microwave, Wi-Fi; Quality Inn, 170 Housatonic St, Lee, MA 01238, (413)243-0143, $102-112 Su-Th, F-Sa $205-297, Wi-Fi, Breakfast. *Groceries:* Price Chopper and Big Y supermarkets (long-term resupply). *Restaurants:* Starving Artist Creperie and Café (7:30–4), Rose's Restaurant (B/L 7–2), and numerous other restaurants and fast-food chains. *Outfitter:* Arcadian Shop, (413) 637-3010, 91 Pittsfield Rd., Lenox, MA 01230, arcadian.com, full-service outfitter, accepts mail drops, about 6 miles west on US-20 from downtown Lee. *Other services:* Canna Provisions cannabis dispensary, 220 Housatonic St., (413) 394-5055, cannaprovisions.com, 8 a.m.–10 p.m. daily, cash or debit cards only.

October Mountain Shelter (1990)—Sleeps 10. Five tentsites. Privy. Bear box. Loft overhangs picnic table. Water from a stream just south of the shelter on the A.T.—blue-blazed trail to water source closed for rerouting/construction around dangerous erosion, but water source still available.

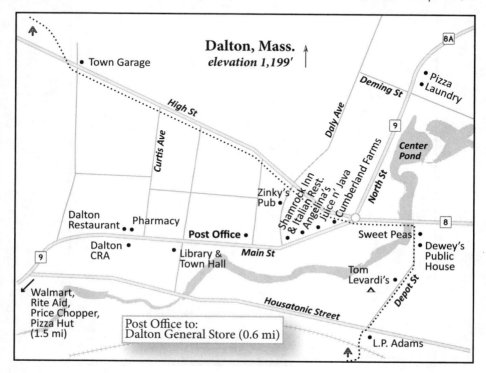 **Washington Mountain Rd.**—**East** 0.1 mile to the new "Cookie Lady" family taking the place of Roy and Marilyn Wiley at Blueberry Hill, 47 Washington Mountain Rd., Washington, MA 01223; pick-your-own blueberry farm, water, cookies, take-a-break area, electricity, and tenting with permission. Phone, text, or e-mail: (860) 942-1038, atblueberryhill@gmail.com.

East 5 miles to **Becket, MA [P.O. ZIP 01223: M–F 8-4, Sa 9–11:30; (413) 623-8845]**, where the A.T. ironically is listed as a historical site in a town settled more than 300 years ago and home to the renowned Jacob's Pillow Dance festival and school. *Lodging:* Becket Motel, 29 Chester Rd., Becket, MA 01223, (413) 623-2244, the becketmotel@gmail.com, thebecketmotel.com, $100 and up, coin laundry, free shuttles to/from Trail, Wi-Fi, mail drops accepted for guests only. *Restaurants:* Papa Bob's, 71 Chester Rd., (413) 623-8777, papabobsbecket.com, open Tu–F 3–midnight, Sa 1–midnight, Su 1–11; Becket Liquor Store and Route 8 Pub, route8pub.com, (413) 623-6026, liquor store open 11–8, pub 11–9, both closed M. *Other services:* Canna Corner cannabis dispensary, (413) 770-4823, open 10–7 daily, cash or debit card only; doctor, veterinarian.

Kay Wood Shelter (1980s)—Sleeps 10. Privy, bear boxes, and tent pads. Shelter is named for Kay Wood, an early Trail angel, long-time Trail maintainer, and 1988–89 thru-hiker who died in 2010 at age 91. Water source is on a blue-blazed trail to the left of the shelter.

Dalton, MA [P.O. ZIP 01226: M–F 8:30-4:30, Sa 9–12; (413) 684-0364]—The A.T. goes through the eastern side of town, where most services are available. Depot St., which the A.T. follows into town from the south, offers Dewey's Public House and Restaurant, and Sweet Pea's ice cream. Other services are within 0.5 mile of the A.T. *Lodging:* Thomas Levardi, 83 Depot St., (413) 684-3359, cell (413) 212-9691, allows hikers to use a water spigot outside his home and provides the hospitality of his front porch and back yard for tenting (limited space, get permission first; no dogs); Shamrock Village Inn, (413) 684-0860, S–Th 2 doubles, queen, or a king $80, F–Sa $85, pets $75 deposit, hiker box, Wi-Fi, laundry ($5 non-guests), ask about 10% hiker discount; hiker-friendly Econo Lodge, 2.1 miles **west**, 16 Cheshire Rd., Pittsfield, MA, $99 weekday, $149 weekend, no laundry, across from resupply and restaurants. *Groceries:* Cumberland Farms with ATM. *Restaurants:* Zinky's Pub, 51

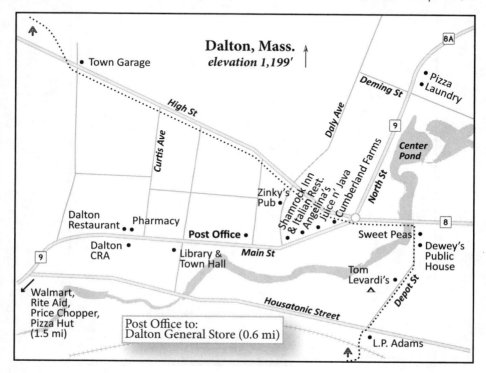

Dalton, Mass.
elevation 1,199'

- Town Garage
- Pizza
- Laundry
- High St
- Deming St
- Daly Ave
- Curtis Ave
- Cumberland Farms
- 9
- Center Pond
- North St
- Zinky's Pub
- Shamrock Inn & Italian Rest.
- Angelina's
- Juice n' Java
- Dalton Restaurant
- Pharmacy
- Post Office
- Sweet Peas
- 8
- Dalton CRA
- Library & Town Hall
- Main St
- Dewey's Public House
- 9
- Tom Levardi's
- Depot St
- Walmart, Rite Aid, Price Chopper, Pizza Hut (1.5 mi)
- Housatonic Street
- Post Office to: Dalton General Store (0.6 mi)
- L.P. Adams
- 8A

Daly Ave., (413) 684-9766, L/D closed Tu, call for hours; Angelina's Subs with veggie burgers; Juice 'n' Java, 661 Main St., specialty coffee and sandwiches, M–F 6:30–3, Sa–Su 7–3; Dalton Restaurant, serves B/L/D daily, T–F 5:30–7, Sa 6am-7pm, Su 6–12; Hot Harry's Fresh Burritos; Union Block Bakery; PortaVia. *Internet access:* Library, 1-hour limit. *Other services:* Dalton CRA, 400 Main St., free showers with towel and soap to hikers; Dalton Laundry, closed M Tu–F 9–5, Sa 9–4, Su 10–3; banks; L.P. Adams, 484 W. Housatonic St. (near Trail south of town), provides free denatured alcohol and Coleman fuel outside front entrance 24/7; doctor; dentist; pharmacy. *Bus service:* BRTA connects to shopping centers 2 miles west of Dalton and to the center of Pittsfield, with all major services.

Crystal Mountain Campsite—0.2 mile east. Privy. Bear box. Space for 6-8 tents. Water is north on Trail or on side trail off access trail to campsite; may go dry in summer.

The Cobbles—These outcroppings of marble overlook the Hoosic River Valley and offer views of Cheshire and Mt. Greylock. The Hoosic River, which is crossed in Cheshire, flows north and empties into the Hudson River in New York.

Cheshire, MA [P.O. ZIP 01225: M-F 7:30-1 & 2-4:30, Sa 8:30-11:30; (413) 743-3184]—The Trail skirts the town center to the east and crosses MA-8, 0.4 mile east of the main stoplight at Church

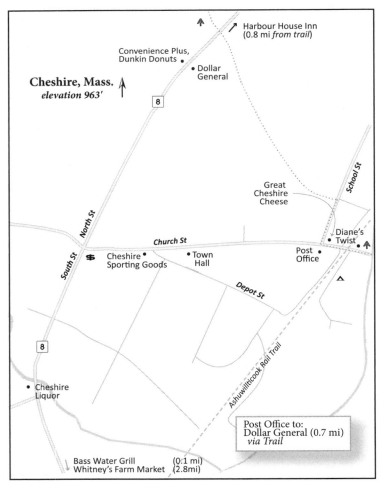

Cheshire, Mass.
elevation 963'

Harbour House Inn
(0.8 mi *from trail*)

Convenience Plus,
Dunkin Donuts

Dollar General

Great Cheshire Cheese

School St

North St

Church St

South St

Cheshire Sporting Goods

Town Hall

Diane's Twist

Post Office

Depot St

Ashuwillticook Rail Trail

Cheshire Liquor

Post Office to:
Dollar General (0.7 mi)
via Trail

Bass Water Grill   (0.1 mi)
Whitney's Farm Market   (2.8mi)

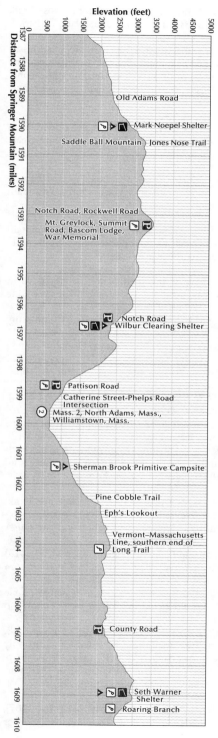

St. Camping is available at The Father Tom Campsite, named after the late Father Tom Begley, former longtime pastor at St. Mary's Church in Cheshire who hosted hikers at the church and completed the A.T. himself. The town-owned site is sponsored by the Cheshire Community Association. Go 75 yards south (across Church St.) from Diane's Twist, past the snowplow. Tentsites, a porta-potty, hammock poles, a picnic table, water spigot, bicycles to borrow, and electrical outlets are available. For individual hikers only, no vehicle staging inside campsite fence; no organized groups; 10 tents and maximum two-night stay. No smoking/alcohol/drugs of any kind. No fires. Open May 1–Oct 31. *Restaurants:* Diane's Twist, opens at 11, mid-May–mid-Sep, deli sandwiches, soda, and ice cream (cash only). *Other services:* Cheshire Sporting Goods, 50 Church St., T–F 4 p.m.–7, Sa 10–3:30, dehydrated food and limited hiker supplies, accepts mail drops; public library in town hall, M 8–4, Tu–W–F 9–4, Th 9–5; bank with ATM. *Bus service:* BRTA stop across from post office, connections to Berkshire Mall and Adams, MA

MA-8—East 0.8 mile to *Lodging:* Harbour House Inn, (413) 553-3128, harbourhouseinn.com, harbourhouseinn@gmail.com, call for thru-hiker rate, B included, mail for guests only, Wi-Fi.

East 2.4 miles to *Outfitter:* Berkshire Outfitters, (413) 743-5900, berkshireoutfitters@gmail.com, berkshireoutfitters.com, Tu–Sa 10–5; hiker-friendly outfitter has hiker supplies and handles minor equipment repairs.

East 4 miles to **Adams, MA [P.O. ZIP 01220: M–F 8:30–4:30, Sa 10–12; (413) 743-5177]**, an alternative to the smaller town of Cheshire. Adams is accessible by the BRTA bus service. *Lodging:* The Trail in Adams, 10 Pleasant St, (413)743-9600, $175-199; Mount Royal Inn, (413) 776-7329, north 2 miles from downtown Adams on MA-8, rooms $100. *Groceries:* Adams Hometown Market (long-term resupply). *Restaurants:* AJ's Trailside Pub; Daily Grind, B/L; Coffee Liberation Front, B/L; McDonald's; and Domino's. *Other services:* Thrifty Bundle coin laundry, banks, hardware store, doctor, dentist, Walgreens, veterinarian, and Western Union.

West 0.1 mile to *Groceries:* Dollar General.

West 0.2 mile to *Groceries:* Convenience store (short-term resupply), Dunkin'.

Mark Noepel Shelter (1985)—Sleeps 10. Two tentsites and 2 tent platforms, group site, privy, and bear box. Water source is a stream on a blue-blazed trail to the right of the shelter.

Saddle Ball Mountain—At 3,238 feet and located at the A.T. junction with the Jones Nose Trail, Saddle Ball is the A.T.'s first 3,000-footer north of North Marshall in Shenandoah National Park.

Mt. Greylock—Topped by a war memorial, paved road, and Bascom Lodge, Greylock is Massachusetts' highest peak (3,491 feet). A stone tower, crowned by a night-lit globe, is a tribute to the state's war dead. You can climb the 89 steps to the top for views of the Green, Catskill, and Taconic mountains and surrounding towns. *Note: Thunderbolt Shelter on Mt. Greylock is an emergency-only warming hut. No camping or fires on the summit.*

Bascom Lodge—Operated by Bascom Lodge Group, (413) 743-1591, bascomlodge.net, open daily, B (8–10), L (11–4:30), D (7, $30), showers & towel $5, bunk $36, private rooms $125–$190d, $20eap, open Jun–Oct. Closed M–Tu; water available from spigot behind lodge.

Wilbur Clearing Shelter (1970)—Sleeps 8. Tentsites and platforms. Privy. Bear box. Located 0.3 mile down the Money Brook Trail; very popular during the summer months. Water source is a stream to the right of the shelter that might go dry in late summer.

⚠ Catherine St./Phelps Rd.—Joshua Moran of 138 Catherine St., North Adams, provides 3 mountain bicycles for hikers to use to ride to nearby services. Hikers can leave their packs at Moran's property while using the bikes (west on Catherine St., third house on the left; see map).

⚠ MA-2/North Adams—BRTA hourly bus service is available on this road. Note: The city of North Adams extends more than one mile west and several miles east of the Trail; the Williamstown line is 1.4 miles west of the Trail. See map.

East 100 yards to overnight parking on north side of MA-2, opposite the Greylock Community Club.

East 0.6 mile to *Groceries:* West's Variety (short-term resupply). *Restaurants:* Oriental Chinese Buffet, AYCE L/D. *Other services:* Thrifty Bundle Coin laundry; Clear Sky cannabis dispensary, 221 State Rd., (888) 540-2343, shopclearsky.com, M–Th 10–8, Sa 10–9, Su 10–7, cash or debit cards only.

East 1.0 mile to YMCA, free showers, hiker-friendly.

⛑ East 2.5 miles to **North Adams, MA [P.O. ZIP 01247: M-F 8:30-4:30, Sa 10-12; (413) 664-4554]**. *Lodging:* Holiday Inn Berkshires, 40 Main St., (413) 663-6500, $129–$220, pool, fitness center. *Groceries:* Big Y Foods (long-term resupply); Cumberland Farms (short-term resupply). *Restaurants:* Boston Seafood Restaurant, Freight Yard Pub, Ramunto's Pizza, Desperado's Fresh Mexican Grill, Brewhaha coffee shop, many other restaurants and fast-food chains. *Other services:* banks with ATM, hardware store, doctor, dentist, veterinarian, and movie theater. *Shuttles:* Dave Ackerson, 82 Cherry St., North Adams, MA 01247, (413) 346-1033, daveackerson@yahoo.com; Bill Beattie, (413) 281-9330, text preferred.

West 0.4 mile to *Groceries:* Super Stop & Shop, ATM, pharmacy, Western Union, and bank. *Lodging:* Tourists, (413) 346-4933, rooms starting at $199, also serves B/L/D. A trail and suspension footbridge on the property connects to the A.T. *Restaurant:* Trail House Kitchen and Bar. *Other services:* veterinarian, 0.6 mile.

West 1.4 miles to municipal border with **Williamstown** and *Lodging:* Williamstown Motel, (413) 458-5202, $59–89s, $10eap, continental B, Wi-Fi, Internet, fridge, microwave, call for pick-up from MA-2 and Phelps Rd.; Howard Johnson, (413) 458-8158, hojowt.com, $59–$149 rate based on season and day of week, no pets, continental B, pool, pick-up/drop-off at Trail when available; Maple Terrace Motel, (413) 458-9677, mapleterrace.com, $100–$200 includes B, Wi-Fi, heated pool, two rooms for pets, all rooms nonsmoking; The Willows Motel, 480 Main St., Williamstown, MA 01267, (413) 458-5768, willowsmotel.com, Su–Th $89–$139, F–Sa $109–$149, includes continental B, microwave, Internet, free laundry, and shuttles to/from Trail, mail drops accepted for guests only (call first); Fairfield Inn and Suites, (413) 458-7333, rooms starting at $126. *Restaurants:* See map. *Groceries:* Wild Oats Whole Foods Market (long-term resupply). *Other services:* Silver Therapeutics cannabis dispensary, 238 Main St., (413) 458-6244, silver-therapeutics.com, daily 10–8, cash or debit cards only.

West 2.6 miles to **Williamstown, MA [P.O. ZIP 01267: M-F 8:30-4:30, Sa 9-12; (413) 458-3707]**, home of Williams College, the venue for a number of ALDHA Gatherings. *Lodging:* Cozy Corner

Motel, (413)458-3707, cozycornermotel.com, $69–$109, $10eap, continental B, microwave/fridge, Wi-Fi, pet-friendly, will pick up and drop off; Williams Inn, (413) 458-9371, $180–$295 and up. ***Restaurants:*** See map. ***Other services:*** banks with ATM; doctor; dentist; pharmacy; movie theater; bookstore; Nature's Closet, (413) 458-7909, naturescloset.net, M–Sa 10–6, Su 11–5, includes the Gear Den of used outdoor clothing and gear on consignment; Bonanza Peter Pan bus line, (800) 343-9999, peterpanbus.com; Green Mountain Express bus, M–F, (802) 447-0477.

Massachusetts Ave.—East 0.6 mile to Renee's Diner, B/L, M–Sa 7–2, Su 7–1.

Sherman Brook Campsite—Two tent platforms, tentsites. Privy. Bear box. Water at Pete's Spring just east of the Trail and south of the 0.1-mile loop blue-blazed trail to the campsite. A blue-blaze west of the Trail, north of the campsite, lets you bypass a boulder field in bad weather.

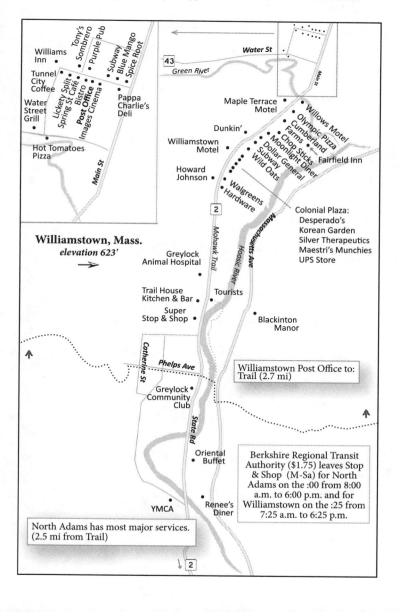

Williamstown, Mass.
elevation 623'

Williamstown Post Office to:
Trail (2.7 mi)

Berkshire Regional Transit Authority ($1.75) leaves Stop & Shop (M–Sa) for North Adams on the :00 from 8:00 a.m. to 6:00 p.m. and for Williamstown on the :25 from 7:25 a.m. to 6:25 p.m.

North Adams has most major services. (2.5 mi from Trail)

Vermont

Miles from Springer	Miles to Next Point	Features	Services	Elev	Miles from Katahdin	M A P
1,603.7	0.4	Massachusetts-Vermont State Line Long Trail *(southern terminus): sign, congruent with the A.T. for the next 105.5 miles northbound to Maine Junction at Willard Gap*		2,330'	593.7	
1,604.1	2.7	Brook	w	2,300'	593.3	
1,606.8	2.1	County Road	R, P	2,290'	590.6	
1,608.9	0.6	**Seth Warner Shelter** *(W–250ft), 12.8mS; 4.8mN*	S, C, w	2,203'	588.5	
1,609.5	3.7	Roaring Branch	w	2,470'	587.9	
1,613.2	0.5	Stamford Stream	w	2,040'	584.2	
1,613.7	2.5	**Congdon Shelter**, *4.8mS; 5.9mN*	S, C, w	2,060'	583.7	
1,616.2	1.8	Harmon Hill: *views of Bennington, VT*		2,325'	581.2	
1,618.0	1.6	VT-9, City Stream *East–2.5m to* Woodford Mtn. General Store *West–5.1m to* **Bennington, VT, P.O. 05201** *West–7m to* North Bennington, VT	R, P, w C, G, L B, G, L, M, D, cl, f G, L, M	1,360'	579.4	ATC: NH-VT Map 8
1,619.6	1.6	**Melville Nauheim Shelter** *(E–250 ft.), 5.9mS; 8.5mN*	S, C, w	2,330'	577.8	
1,621.2	2.6	Hell Hollow Brook	w	2,350'	576.2	
1,623.8	1.8	Little Pond Lookout		3,060'	573.6	
1,625.6	2.5	Glastenbury Lookout		2,920'	571.8	
1,628.1	0.3	**Goddard Shelter**, *8.5mS; 4.3mN*	S, w	3,540'	569.3	
1,628.4	4.0	Glastenbury Mountain		3,748'	569.0	
1,632.4	3.7	**Kid Gore Shelter** *(E–300ft),* Caughnawaga Tentsites *(W–50ft), 4.3mS; 4.6mN*	S, C, w	2,795'	565.0	
1,636.1	0.9	South Alder Brook	w	2,600'	561.3	
1,637.0	1.5	**Story Spring Shelter**, *4.6mS; 10.4mN*	S, C, w	2,810'	560.4	
1,638.5	2.1	USFS-71	R	2,500'	558.9	
1,640.6	3.8	Stratton-Arlington Road (Kelley Stand Road)	R, P, w	2,230'	556.8	
1,644.4	3.0	Stratton Mountain: *firetower, caretaker cabin* *East–0.8m to* Gondola to Stratton Village		3,936'	553.0	
1,647.4	0.2	Stratton Pond Trail to +**Stratton Pond Shelter** & **Campsites** *(W–1,000ft.), 10.4mS; 5.4mN*	S, C, w	2,565'	550.0	ATC: NH-VT Map 7
1,647.6	1.9	Stratton Pond, Lye Brook Trail to +Stratton View Tenting Area *(W–0.7m)* and **Shelter**	C, w	2,555'	549.8	
1,649.5	2.8	Winhall River: *bridge*	w	2,175'	547.9	
1,652.3	0.9	Branch Pond Trail to **William B. Douglas Shelter** *(W–0.5m), 5.4mS; 3.6mN*	S, w	2,210'	545.1	
1,653.2	2.1	Prospect Rock, side trail to Old Rootville Road *West–150 ft. to stream; 2m to VT-11 & 30*	R, P, w	2,079'	544.2	
1,655.3	0.4	**Spruce Peak Shelter** *(W–0.1m), 3.6mS; 4.9mN*	S, C, w	2,180'	542.1	
1,655.7	1.9	Spruce Peak *(W–300 ft.)*		2,040'	541.7	
1,657.6	0.5	Stream: *footbridge*	w		539.8	

Miles from Springer	Miles to Next Point	Features	Services	Elev	Miles from Katahdin	M A P
1,658.1	2.0	VT-11 & 30 *East-0.5m to* Pinnacle Lodge *East-2.1m to* Lodge at Bromley *East-2.5m to* Bromley Market and Deli *East-3.0m on VT-30 to* Bromley View Inn *East-4.2m to* Hapgood General Store *West-3.6m to* motels and diner; *3.8m to* motel *West-5.5m to* **Manchester Center, VT, P.O. 05255**	R, P, w L, cl L G, M L g, M L, M B, H, G, L, M, O, D, V, cl, f	1,840'	539.3	
1,660.1	1.0	**Bromley Shelter** *(E-110 yards), 4.9mS; 8.1mN*	S, C, w	2,560'	537.3	
1,661.1	2.5	Bromley Mountain: *ski-patrol hut*		3,260'	536.3	
1,663.6	1.6	Mad Tom Notch, USFS-21; Peru, VT	R, P	2,446'	533.8	
1,665.2	1.7	Styles Peak		3,394'	532.2	
1,666.9	1.3	Peru Peak		3,429'	530.5	
1,668.2	0.5	**+Peru Peak Shelter**, *8.1mS; 4.7mN*	S, C, w	2,605'	529.2	
1,668.7	0.2	Griffith Lake, +Griffith Lake Tenting Area	C, w	2,600'	528.7	ATC: NH-VT Map 7
1,668.9	2.0	Griffith Lake *(north end)*	w	2,600'	528.5	
1,670.9	2.0	Baker Peak		2,850'	526.5	
1,672.9	1.5	**Lost Pond Shelter** *(W-100 ft.), 4.7mS; 2.8mN*	S, C, w	2,150'	524.5	
1,674.4	0.1	Old Job Trail to **Old Job Shelter** *(E-1.3m), 2.8mS; 1.5mN*	S, C, w	1,525'	523.0	
1,674.5	0.1	Big Branch suspension bridge		1470'	522.9	
1,674.6	1.3	**Big Branch Shelter**, *1.5mS; 3.3mN*	S, C, w	1,460'	522.8	
1,675.9	2.0	Danby–Landgrove Road, USFS-10, Black Branch *West-3.5m to* **Danby, VT, P.O. 05739**	R, P, w B, G	1,500'	521.5	
1,677.9	0.1	**+Little Rock Pond Shelter** and Tenting Area, *3.3mS; 5mN*	S, C, w	1,920'	519.5	
1,678.0	0.2	Spring: *water for LRP Shelter*	w	1,854'	519.4	
1,678.2	4.0	Green Mountain Trail to Homer Stone Brook Trail		1,854'	519.2	
1,682.2	0.5	Trail to White Rocks Cliffs: *vista (W-0.2m)*		2,400'	515.2	
1,682.7	0.6	**Greenwall Shelter** *(E-0.2m), 5mS; 5.3mN*	S, C, w	2,025'	514.7	
1,683.3	0.8	Bully Brook: *cascades*	w	1,760'	514.1	
1,684.1	0.1	Sugar Hill Road	R	1,260'	513.3	
1,684.2	2.1	VT-140, Roaring Brook *West-2.8m to* **Wallingford, VT, P.O. 05773**	R, P, w B, g, L, M	1,160'	513.2	
1,686.3	1.5	Bear Mountain		2,240'	511.1	
1,687.8	2.6	**Minerva Hinchey Shelter** *(E-200 ft.), 5.3mS; 3.7mN*	S, C, w	1,605'	509.6	
1,690.4	0.1	Clarendon Gorge Wildlife Management Area; Mill River Suspension Bridge	w	800'	507.0	
1,690.5	1.0	VT-103: *railroad tracks*	R, P, B	860'	506.9	ATC: NH-VT Map 6
1,691.5	0.5	**Clarendon Shelter** *(E-400 ft.), 3.7mS; 6.1mN*	S, C, w	1,190'	505.9	
1,692.0	0.4	Beacon Hill		1,740'	505.4	
1,692.4	2.0	Lottery Road	R	1,720'	505.0	
1,694.4	0.8	Cold River Road: *paved* *East-2.7m to* Pierce's Store	R, P g, M	1,400'	503.0	
1,695.2	0.8	Gould Brook: *ford*	w	1,480'	502.2	
1,696.0	0.7	Upper Cold River Road: *gravel road* *East-2.5m to* Pierce's Store	R, w g, M	1,630'	501.4	
1,696.7	0.9	Sargent Brook Bridge: *gravel road*	R, w	1,730'	500.7	

Miles from Springer	Miles to Next Point	Features	Services	Elev	Miles from Katahdin	M A P
1,697.6	4.3	**Governor Clement Shelter**, 6.1mS; 4.3mN	S, C, w	1,900'	499.8	
1,701.9	2.5	**Cooper Lodge**, 4.3mS; 3mN Blue-blazed trail to Killington Peak (4,241') (E–0.2m): summit and gondola	S, C, w M	3,900'	495.5	
1,704.4	1.9	Jungle Jct.; Sherburne Pass Trail to **Pico Camp** (E–0.5m), 3mS; 2.5mN	S, w	3,480'	493.0	
1,706.3	1.9	**Churchill Scott Shelter** (W–0.1m), 2.5mS; 3.2mN	S, C, w	2,560'	491.1	
1,708.2	1.0	US-4 (west of Sherburne Pass) East–0.9m to Inn at Long Trail West–1.4m to Mendon Mountain View Lodge West–8.6m to **Rutland, VT, P.O. 05701**	R, P, w B, C, L, M B, L all	1,880'	489.2	
1,709.2	0.9	Maine Junction at Willard Gap, Long Trail to **Tucker-Johnson Shelter** (W–0.2m), 3.2mS; 9.2mN	S, C, w	2,250'	488.2	
		Caution-Make sure you're on the A.T. and not the Long Trail at this junction				
1,710.1	1.1	Sherburne Pass Trail: to Inn at Long Trail (E–0.5m)	C, L, M	2,440'	487.3	
1,711.2	0.3	Kent Brook Trail junction (E–0.4m to US-4)	PO, B, G, L, M, O	1,700'	486.2	ATC: NH-VT Map 6
1,711.5	0.7	VT-100, Gifford Woods State Park East–0.6m to **Killington, VT, P.O. 05751**	R, P, S, C, w, sh B, G, L, M, O	1,660'	485.9	
1,712.2	1.2	Kent Pond, Mountain Meadows Lodge, trail to Base Camp Outfitters (E–0.3m to US-4) Thundering Brook Road (southern jct.)	L, M, O R	1,450'	485.2	
1,713.4	0.2	Thundering Brook Road (northern jct.)	R, P	1,280'	484.0	
1,713.6	0.3	Thundering Falls: 900 ft. boardwalk		1,226'	483.8	
1,713.9	0.5	River Road (E–0.5m to Killington pool)	R, P	1,214'	483.5	
1,714.4	3.8	Quimby Mountain		2,550'	483.0	
1,718.2	0.8	**Stony Brook Shelter** (E–250 ft.), 9.2mS; 10.1mN	S, C, w	1,760'	479.2	
1,719.0	3.9	Stony Brook Road, Stony Brook	R, w	1,360'	478.4	
1,722.9	0.7	Chateauguay Road	R	2,000'	474.5	
1,723.6	2.1	Lakota Lake Lookout		2,640'	473.8	
1,725.7	2.4	Side trail to the Lookout: private cabin (W–0.2m)		2,320'	471.7	
1,728.1	3.8	**Winturri Shelter** (W–0.2m), 10.1mS; 12.6mN	S, w	1,910'	469.3	
1,731.9	0.9	VT-12, Gulf Stream Bridge East–3.8m to **Woodstock, VT, P.O. 05091** West–0.2m to On The Edge Farm Store	R, P, w G, L, M, D, V G	882'	465.5	
1,732.8	1.3	Dana Hill		1,530'	464.6	
1,734.1	1.5	Woodstock Stage Road, Barnard Brook East–0.9m to **South Pomfret, VT, P.O. 05067**	R, P, w G, M	820'	463.3	
1,735.6	0.7	Bartlett Brook Road (1,050'): gravel, footbridge, brook	R, w	1,050'	461.8	AMC: NH-VT Map 5
1,736.3	1.8	Pomfret-South Pomfret Road, Pomfret Brook (980') (E–1.3m to South Pomfret)	R, P, w	980'	461.1	
1,738.1	2.0	Cloudland Road (W–0.2m to Cloudland Farm)	R, P, g	1,370'	459.3	
1,740.1	0.3	Thistle Hill		1,800'	457.3	
1,740.4	1.5	**Thistle Hill Shelter** (E–0.1m), 12.6mS; 9mN	S, w	1,480'	457.0	
1,741.9	3.3	Joe Ranger Road	R, P	1,280'	455.5	
1,745.2	0.6	VT-14, White River; West Hartford, VT East–7m to **Hartford, VT, P.O. 05047** East–8m to White River Jct., VT	R, P, C, w B, G H, all	390'	452.2	

Miles from Springer	Miles to Next Point	Features	Services	Elev	Miles from Katahdin	M A P
1,745.8	0.8	Tigertown Road, Podunk Road	R, P	540'	451.6	
1,746.6	2.1	Podunk Road, Podunk Brook	R, w	860'	450.8	
1,748.7	0.5	Griggs Mountain		1,570'	448.7	
1,749.2	3.5	**Happy Hill Shelter** (E-0.1m), 9mS; 7.6mN	S, C, w	1,460'	448.2	
1,752.7	0.8	Elm St. Trailhead	R, P	750'	444.7	
1,753.5	0.6	US-5, Main St. West-0.25m to **Norwich, VT, P.O. 05055**	R B, H, G, L, M	537'	443.9	
1,754.1	0.4	I-91; VT-10A: A.T. on sidewalk	R	450'	443.3	
1,754.5	0.5	Connecticut River; Vermont–New Hampshire State Line	R	380'	442.9	

AMC: NH-VT Map 5

+ Fee charged

Notes: Avoid Vermont trails in "mud season," mid-Apr to Memorial Day. Hiking there in wet, sloppy conditions leads to serious Trail erosion. To prevent future problems and costly interventions with bears, please follow the latest recommendation from the ATC to carry your food in a bear resistant storage container. appalachiantrail.org/news/atc-recommends-a-t-visitors-carry-bear-resistant-food-storage-containers.

Green Mountain Club—GMC maintains the 150.8 miles from the Massachusetts–Vermont border to the Connecticut River on the Vermont–New Hampshire border. Correspondence should be sent to GMC at 4711 Waterbury–Stowe Rd., Waterbury Center, VT 05677; (802) 244-7037; fax, (802) 244-5867; gmc@greenmountainclub.org, greenmountainclub.org.

GMC Shelter Fees— GMC Shelter Fees - Effective with the 2023 hiking season, fees were no longer collected at the shelters and campsites listed below. Voluntary donations and contributions are accepted.

- Griffith Lake
- Griffith Lake Tenting Area
- Little Rock Pond
- Little Rock Pond Shelter & Tenting Area
- Peru Peak Shelter
- Stratton Pond
- Stratton Pond Shelter
- Stratton View Tenting Area

Caretakers are present throughout the season, May–Oct, at several locations. Through conversation and example, caretakers educate hikers about Leave No Trace practices and perform Trail and shelter maintenance. Most importantly, caretakers compost sewage at high-use fee sites and a few no-fee shelter sites in southern Vermont.

Long Trail—At the Vermont–Massachusetts state line, the A.T. joins the Long Trail (L.T.) for 105.2 miles, to "Maine Junction" at Willard Gap. At Maine Junction, the A.T. leads toward Maine, and the L.T. continues north, reaching the Canadian border in another 166.5 miles. Completed in 1930, the L.T. served as one inspiration for the A.T. The L.T. and A.T. are seeing increased traffic in Vermont. Please use only designated shelters and campsites and make use of privies and wash pits to protect water quality and reduce the visible and permanent impact of greater use of the Trail.

Seth Warner Shelter (2022)—Sleeps 8. Privy. Currently one primitive tentsite behind the shelter and one in front. Water available 0.4 mile north; no water at shelter.

Congdon Shelter (1967)—Sleeps 8. Privy. Tentsites north and south of the shelter. Small brook east of the shelter. If the brook is dry, follow downstream to larger Stamford Stream.

⚠ VT-9—East 2.5 miles to *Groceries:* Woodford Mountain General Store (short-term resupply), (802) 681-7580, M–Sa 6–6, Su 10–5, deli, Heet. *Camping and Lodging:* Greenwood Lodge and Campsites, Prospect Access Rd., 311 Greenwood Drive, Woodford, VT 05201, (802) 442-2547, campvermont.com/greenwood, open mid-May to late Oct, HI lodging, 20 beds and campsites, call for rates.

⛺ **West** 5.1 miles to **Bennington, VT [P.O. ZIP 05201: M–F 8-5, Sa 9-2; (802) 442-2421].** *Lodging:* Catamount Motel, 500 South St., (802) 442-5977, $75s, $85d, $5eap, $10 dog, hiker-friendly; Bennington Motor Inn, 143 Main St., (802) 442-5479, $89–$200;The Hotel Vervana, 141 West Main St., (802) 442-8351, $129–$220; Autumn Inn, 924 Main St., (802) 447-7625, $89; Starlight Inn, 357 US-7, (802) 442-9200, $99. *Groceries:* Henry's Market; Spice'n Nice Natural Foods; Yott's Market. *Restaurants:* Madison Brewing Company; Blue Benn Diner, B/L/D; The Local, B/L; Lucky Dragon, L/D; Your Belly's Deli, L. *Internet access* Library has Wi-Fi. *Other services:* Dollar General; coin laundry; banks with ATM; Express Care, (802) 447-0477, walk-in clinic open daily 8–6 near hospital; doctor; dentist; pharmacy; veterinarian; hardware store; and $2 showers available at Town Recreation Center on Gage Street. Community bikes for hiker use available at the Bike Hub, (802) 445-4000, info@ourbikehub.com. *Shuttles:* Walt's Taxi, (802) 442-9052, $12 Trail to town. *Public transportation:* Bus station at 215 Pleasant St. Green Mountain Express, (802) 447-0477, greenmtncn.org, use free Emerald Line, M–F to VT-9 trail head, with connection on the The Moover, (802) 464-8487, M–F, in Wilmington to Greyhound, (802) 231-2222, and Amtrak, (800) 872-7245, in Brattleboro. Use Purple line M–F to Williams Inn, Williamstown, MA, to connect to both Peter Pan Bus Lines, (800) 343-9999, to NYC and Boston; or Berkshire Transit, (413) 499-2782 to North Adams and Pittsfield, MA Use Orange Line daily service to Manchester. Vermont Translines, (844)

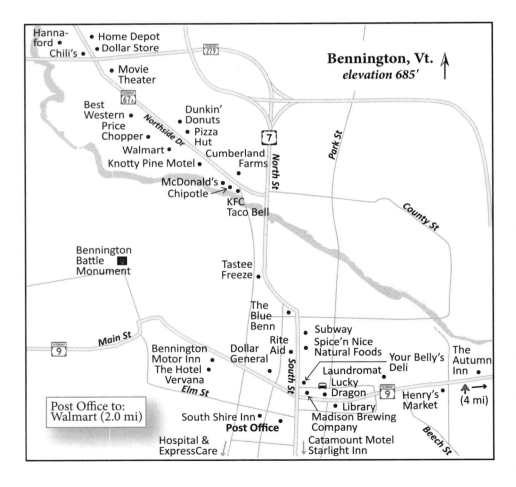

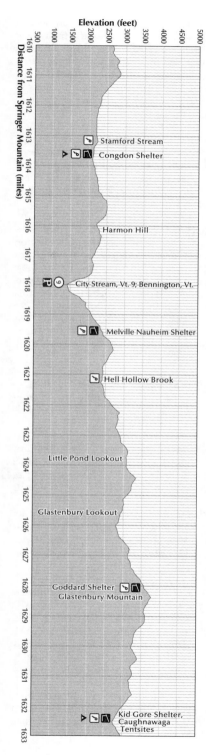

Elevation (feet)

Distance from Springer Mountain (miles)

888-7267; morning bus service to Greyhound, Albany, NY, and Albany International Airport; afternoon bus service to Burlington, VT, and Burlington International Airport, with stops in Manchester, Wallingford, Rutland, Brandon and Middlebury. Yankee Trails, (800) 822-2400, yankeetrails.com, to Greyhound in Albany.

West 7 miles to **North Bennington, VT**, Routes 67 and 7A, and *Lodging:* Knotty Pine Motel, 130 Northside Dr., (802) 442-5487, knottypinemotel.com, starting at $160, pets accepted on limited basis, continental B, Wi-Fi, pool, holds packages only for guests; Best Western, 200 Northside Dr., (802) 442-6311; Hampton Inn, 51 Hannaford Square, (802) 440-9862. *Groceries:* Price Chopper, Walmart, Hannaford, ALDI supermarkets (long-term resupply). *Restaurants:* See map. *Other services:* movie theater.

Melville Nauheim Shelter (1977)—Sleeps 8. Privy. Tentsites. Water source is a stream on A.T. just north of the shelter side trail.

VT-9 to Kelley Stand Rd.—*Note: This section of the Trail is receiving heavy use and experiencing resource damage as a result. GMC encourages hikers to use the designated shelters and campsites. If you must camp between shelters, please follow Leave No Trace practices, and camp 200 feet away from the Trail and all water sources.*

Goddard Shelter (2005)—Sleeps 12. Privy. Bear box. The shelter has a front porch with a view to the south. Tent only north of the shelter and west of the A.T. Water source is a spring 50 yards south on the A.T. *To preserve the pristine nature of the spring, no tenting is allowed south of the shelter and east of the trail.*

Glastenbury Mountain (3,748 ft.). The original firetower was built in 1927 and renovated in 2005 but is **now closed** (stairs removed). Remains of the old firewarden's cabin and woodstove can be seen to the west of the Trail, south of the summit. Porcupines are active in this area; take precautions with your gear.

Kid Gore Shelter (1971)—Sleeps 8. Privy. Bear boxes. Fifty yards east of the Trail. Ecologically fragile area. Tentsites located 50 yards north on A.T. at the former Caughnawaga Shelter site. Water source is a reliable brook near Caughnawaga tentsites. An unreliable spring is 30 yards north of the shelter.

Caughnawaga Tentsites— No sign; west side of Trail 50 yards south of Kid Gore Shelter. Tenting only. A 1930s shelter was torn down in July 2008.

Story Spring Shelter (1963)—Sleeps 8. Privy. Bear boxes. Limited tenting (few, if any, level sites). Water source is a spring north on the A.T. 50 yards.

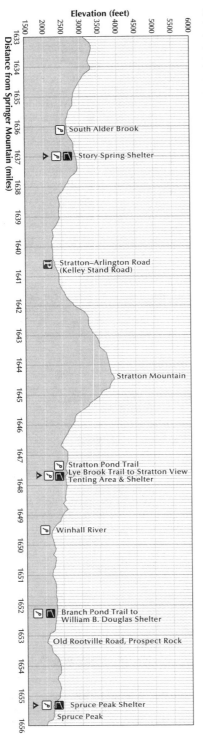

Elevation (feet)

Distance from Springer Mountain (miles)

South Alder Brook

Story Spring Shelter

Stratton–Arlington Road (Kelley Stand Road)

Stratton Mountain

Stratton Pond Trail
Lye Brook Trail to Stratton View Tenting Area & Shelter

Winhall River

Branch Pond Trail to William B. Douglas Shelter

Old Rootville Road, Prospect Rock

Spruce Peak Shelter
Spruce Peak

Stratton Mountain—Although he offered several variations on the story about how he first thought of the A.T., many believe it was on the slopes of Stratton Mountain that Benton MacKaye first imagined a long-distance trail that would link the high peaks of the Appalachian Mountains. A firetower tops the summit and is open to hikers. *No camping or fires on the summit.* A side trail at the summit leads east 0.8 mile to a ski gondola at the top of Stratton Ski Area; this hut is not available for hiker use. The gondola ($20 round-trip, usually free for thru-hikers) has operated in past years, allowing hikers to ride down to Stratton Village, which has an outfitter, grocery store, and restaurants. Please check with Stratton Mountain staff, (802) 297-4000, to see if the gondola is available for hiker use.

Stratton Pond Shelter (1999)—Sleeps 20. Privy. Bear box. Overnight fee. Go 1,000 feet west via Stratton Pond Trail. No tenting at this shelter, but you may tent on platforms at the nearby Stratton View Tenting Area; otherwise, within 0.5 mile of the pond, camping is permitted only at designated sites. Shelter has an open first floor, table, bunks, and an enclosed loft. Water source is an intermittent spring to the right of the Willis Ross clearing at Stratton Pond or the piped Bigelow Spring at Stratton Pond about 0.1 mile down the Lye Brook Trail. *No fires at this shelter.*

William B. Douglas Shelter (1956, renovated 2004)—Sleeps 10. Privy. Go 0.5 mile west via the Branch Pond Trail. Water source is a spring located south of the shelter.

Prospect Rock—Views of Manchester and Mt. Equinox. The gravel Old Rootville Rd. leads steeply downhill 2 miles to VT-11 & 30 and another 1.6 miles to the Price Chopper grocery store in Manchester Center.

Spruce Peak Shelter (1983)—Sleeps 12. Privy. This shelter with a covered front porch is 0.1 mile west on a spur trail and includes a wood stove and door. Water source is a boxed spring 35 yards to the right (compass south) of the shelter.

VT-11 & 30—East 0.5 miles to *Lodging:* Pinnacle Lodge, 311 VT-11, Winhall, VT 05340, (802) 558-5370, $135 (sleeps 4), coin laundry, Wi-Fi, pet friendly.
    East 2.1 miles to *Lodging:* Sun Lodge, 4216 VT-11, Peru, VT 05152; (802) 824-6941, $129s/d (includes B; laundry extra), weekends higher, Wi-Fi, Rt. 11 & 30 Trailhead shuttle, and mail drops accepted (non-guest mail-drop fee, $10).
    East 2.5 miles via VT-11 to *Groceries:* Bromley Market, 3776 VT-11, Peru, VT 05152; (802) 824-4444, fresh foods, deli open 7–7, 7 days, some hiker supplies, mail drops accepted.

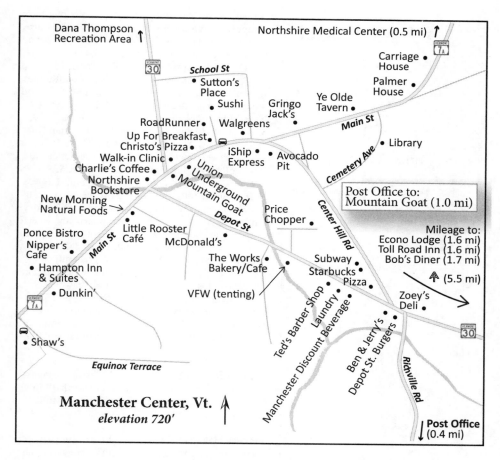

Map: Manchester Center, Vt., elevation 720'

Labels on map:
Dana Thompson Recreation Area ↑
Northshire Medical Center (0.5 mi) ↑
VERMONT 30
School St
Sutton's Place
Sushi
Gringo Jack's
Ye Olde Tavern
Carriage House
Palmer House
Main St
RoadRunner
Walgreens
Up For Breakfast
Christo's Pizza
Walk-in Clinic
Charlie's Coffee
Northshire Bookstore
New Morning Natural Foods →
iShip Express
Avocado Pit
Library
Cemetery Ave
Union Underground
Mountain Goat
Price Chopper
Post Office to: Mountain Goat (1.0 mi)
Ponce Bistro
Nipper's Cafe
Little Rooster Café
McDonald's
Main St
Depot St
Center Hill Rd
Mileage to: Econo Lodge (1.6 mi) Toll Road Inn (1.6 mi) Bob's Diner (1.7 mi)
The Works Bakery/Cafe
Subway
Starbucks
Pizza
Hampton Inn & Suites
Dunkin'
VFW (tenting)
Ted's Barber Shop
Laundry
Manchester Discount Beverage
Ben & Jerry's
Depot St. Burgers
Zoey's Deli
⚑ (5.5 mi)
VERMONT 7A
Shaw's
Equinox Terrace
Manchester Center, Vt. ↑ elevation 720'
VERMONT 30
Richville Rd
Post Office (0.4 mi) ↓

East 2.6 miles to Seesaw's Lodge, 3574 VT-11, Peru, VT 05152, (802) 824-5533; call for room rates; restaurant M 5–11.

East 4.2 miles to Hapgood General Store, (802) 824-4800, next to Peru P.O., open 7–5, pizza, beer.

West 3.6 miles to *Lodging:* EconoLodge Motel, (802) 362-3333, $100d, $10eap, higher on weekends; Toll Road Inn, (802) 362-1711, $137d, $20eap; The Chalet Motel, A Travelodge by Wyndham, (802) 362-1622, $98. *Restaurants:* Bob's Diner, B/L; Pearl's Place and Pantry, D; Raven's Den Steakhouse and Taproom, D; Zoey's Double Hex, L/D.

🅐 **West** 5.5 miles to **Manchester Center, VT [P.O. ZIP 05255: M-F 8:30–4:30, Sa 9-12; (802) 362-3070]**. Pick up mail at the post office on the way into town to avoid an extra walk. The Mountain Goat is a good resource for hiker services in town. The Dana Thompson Recreation Area is a short walk from the center and offers showers for long-distance hikers during regular business hours; (802) 362-1439. *Note:* During the Vermont Summer Festival Horse shows, Jul–mid-Aug, affordable lodging will be difficult to find in the area. *Lodging:* Sutton's Place, 50 School St., (802) 362-1165, suttonsplacevermont.com, owner Frank Sutton has hosted hikers more than 15 years, $80S, $95d, $115t plus tax, a/c, Wi-Fi, accepts mail drops and is within walking distance of all services; Palmer House Resort Motel, 5383 Main St., (800) 917-6245, palmerhouse.com, midweek rate $125s/d, $2eap, based on availability, weekends higher, light continental B $2.50, no pets, heated outdoor pool with Jacuzzi, accepts mail drops; Carriage House Motel, (802) 362-1706, carriagehousemotel.com, Jun rate $135d (higher rest of season), $25eap, no pets, opens end of May, 1 mile east of town on VT-7; Hampton Inn, $159 and up, $229 weekends. *Groceries:* Price Chop-

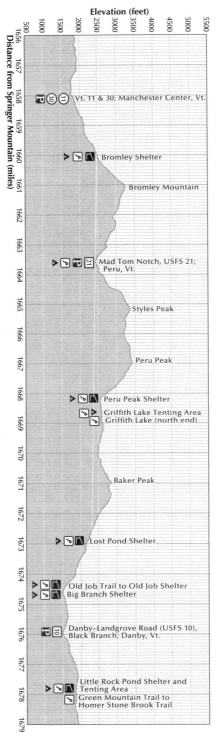

per with ATM, Shaw's supermarkets (both long-term resupply). *Restaurants:* Manchester Pizza House, Firefly Bar & Grill, Mrs. Murphy's Doughnuts and Coffee Shop, Avocado Pit (closed Su), Up For Breakfast (7–12:30), Christo's Pizza, Ben & Jerry's Scoop Shop, Zoey's Deli, Starbucks, Subway, RoadRunner, Union Underground (grill) and several fast-food outlets. *Internet access:* library, M–F 10–6, Sa 10–4; Northshire Bookstore, M–Th 10–7, F–Sa 10–9; I Ship Express (below). *Outfitter:* The Mountain Goat, 4886 Main St., (802) 362-5159, open M–Sa 10–6, Su 10–5, full-service outfitter, fuel by the ounce, custom footbeds and orthotics, mail drops (USPS, UPS & FedEx) accepted. *Other services:* I Ship Express, 5018 Main St., (802) 362-1652, M–F 9:30–5, Sa 9:30–noon, packing and shipping services; coin laundry; bank with ATM; doctor; dentist; pharmacy; veterinarian; Manchester Taxi, (802) 362-4118 and (802) 688-6426; Leonard's Taxi, (802) 362-2620; Green Mountain Express, (802) 447-0477, greenmtncn.org, $2 bus service between Manchester and Bennington, flag stop across from Walgreens and Shaw's; Marble Valley Regional Transportation, thebus.com, $2 bus service between Manchester and Rutland/Killington, stops along the US-7 corridor (Danby, Wallingford, North Clarendon); Vermont Translines, see Bennington.

Bromley Shelter (2003)—Sleeps 12. Privy (composting). Tent platforms and campsite are north 0.1 mile. Unreliable spring at the terminus of the spur trail. *No water for next 8 miles.*

Bromley Mountain—An observation tower that was torn down in 2012 will be rebuilt, thanks to donations from many, including ALDHA; GMC hoped to have it done by the 2023 hiking season. Ski trails lead to Bromley Base Lodge area. The ski patrol warming hut is open for use; privy on summit; no water.

Peru Peak Shelter/Griffith Lake Tenting Area (1935/1979/2000)—Sleeps 10. Privy. Bear boxes. Overnight fee. Camping permitted only at designated tent platforms within 0.5 mile of Griffith Lake. Water source is the pond or a brook near the shelter.

Lost Pond Shelter (2009)—Sleeps 8. Privy. Tentsites. Water source is nearby stream.

Old Job Shelter (1935/2009)—1.3 miles on Old Job Trail. Sleeps 8. Privy. Tentsites. Water source is in front of the shelter at Lake Brook.

Big Branch Shelter (1963)—Sleeps 8. Privy. Tent-sites north of shelter. Close to USFS 10 and receives heavy

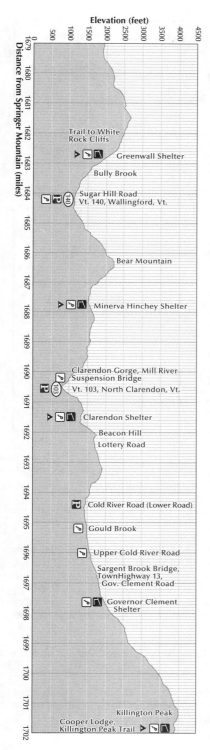

Elevation (feet)

Trail to White
Rock Cliffs

Greenwall Shelter

Bully Brook

Sugar Hill Road
Vt. 140, Wallingford, Vt.

Bear Mountain

Minerva Hinchey Shelter

Clarendon Gorge, Mill River
Suspension Bridge
Vt. 103, North Clarendon, Vt.

Clarendon Shelter

Beacon Hill
Lottery Road

Cold River Road (Lower Road)

Gould Brook

Upper Cold River Road

Sargent Brook Bridge,
TownHighway 13,
Gov. Clement Road

Governor Clement
Shelter

Killington Peak
Cooper Lodge,
Killington Peak Trail

weekend use. Good soaking pools. Water source is Big Branch, located in front of the shelter.

⚠ **USFS 10, Danby–Landgrove Rd.**—Light traffic, may be a difficult hitch on weekdays. **West** 3.5 miles to **Danby, VT [P.O. ZIP 05739: M–F 7:15-10:15 & 11:15-2:15, Sa 7:30-10:30; (802) 293-5105].** *Groceries:* Mt. Tabor Country Store, 1072 US-7, (802) 293-5641, M–Sa 5–8, Su 6–7, short-term resupply. *Other services:* Silas Griffith Library, open W 2–7, Sa 9–12; MVRT, (802) 773-3244, thebus.com, Manchester-to-Rutland commuter, M–Sa $2, departs for Manchester from the Mt. Tabor Country Store, for Rutland, from Brooklyn Rd.

Little Rock Pond Shelter and Tenting Area (2010)—Sleeps 12. Tent platforms. Privy. Bear box. Overnight fee. Spring located north on Trail.

Greenwall Shelter (1962/2009)—**East** on side trail 0.2 mile. Sleeps 8. Privy. Tentsites. Water source is a spring, prone to fail in dry seasons, 200 yards along a trail behind the shelter.

⚠ **VT-140**—*Note: Camping is only permitted at designated campsites and shelter areas between Rt. 140 and Hanover.*
 West 2.8 miles to **Wallingford, VT [P.O. ZIP 05773: M–F 8-4:30, Sa 9-12; (802) 446-2140].** *Lodging:* Several AirBnBs, $125 and up. *Restaurants:* The Main Street Café, 5 N. Main St., (802) 446-6169, serves B/L Th-Su 8–2 p.m. closed M-W; Sweet Birch Café, 15 S. Main St., M–Su 7–2; Hotty's Restaurant scheduled to open in 2025, 137 N. Main St., open W-Th 11-8, F-Su 10-8, closed M, Tu, send email for status at hottoddysvt@ gmail.com. *Groceries:* Village Market, 15 S. Main St, open M-Sa, closed Su, short-term supply, deli counter, fresh fruits & vegetables, beer, wine, bulk foods. Call 802-446-3771; Cumberland Farms, Tennybrook, Family Dollar (all short-term resupply). *Internet access:* Gilbert Hart Library, M, W–Sa. *Other services:* ATM; dentist; Biana Hair Studio; MVRT, (802) 773-3244, thebus.com, Manchester-to-Rutland commuter, M–Sa $2, departures and arrivals near Cumberland Farms; Vermont Translines (see Bennington, page 194).
 Minerva Hinchey Shelter (1969/2006)—Sleeps 8. Privy. Tenting area. Shelter relocated in 2024 from east side of A.T. to west side. Spring on east side 100 ft south of shelter -look for "water" sign.
 Clarendon Gorge Wildlife Management Area—A suspension bridge 0.1 mile south of VT-103 overlooks a favorite swimming hole for residents. Built in 1974, this bridge is dedicated to the memory of Robert Brugmann, who drowned while trying to cross the swollen Mill River. Swimming in the gorge is hazardous during high water. Watch for broken glass. *No camping or fires permitted in the Gorge.*

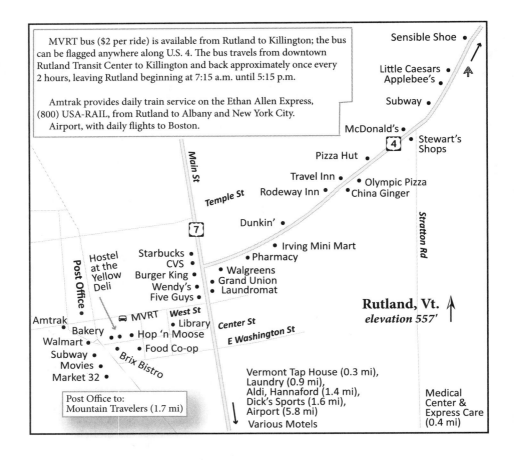

MVRT bus ($2 per ride) is available from Rutland to Killington; the bus can be flagged anywhere along U.S. 4. The bus travels from downtown Rutland Transit Center to Killington and back approximately once every 2 hours, leaving Rutland beginning at 7:15 a.m. until 5:15 p.m.

Amtrak provides daily train service on the Ethan Allen Express, (800) USA-RAIL, from Rutland to Albany and New York City. Airport, with daily flights to Boston.

Sensible Shoe •

Little Caesars •
Applebee's •

Subway •

McDonald's •
[4] • Stewart's Shops
Pizza Hut •
Travel Inn • • Olympic Pizza
Rodeway Inn • • China Ginger

Main St
Temple St

Dunkin' •
[7]

• Irving Mini Mart
• Pharmacy

Hostel   Starbucks •
at the   CVS •
Yellow   Burger King • • Walgreens
Deli   Wendy's • • Grand Union
                  Five Guys • • Laundromat

Post Office

Amtrak •
• Bakery   MVRT   West St
Walmart •   • Library   Center St
Subway •   • Hop 'n Moose   E Washington St
Movies •   • Food Co-op
Market 32 •   Brix Bistro

Post Office to:
Mountain Travelers (1.7 mi)

Vermont Tap House (0.3 mi),
Laundry (0.9 mi),
Aldi, Hannaford (1.4 mi),
Dick's Sports (1.6 mi),
Airport (5.8 mi)
Various Motels

Rutland, Vt.
elevation 557'

Stratton Rd

Medical Center & Express Care (0.4 mi)

Note: A ridgerunner may be found along the Coolidge Range at the these locations, although a fee is not charged: Clarendon Shelter, Governor Clement Shelter, Cooper Lodge, Pico Camp, and Churchill Scott Shelter.

Clarendon Shelter (1952)—Sleeps 10. Moldering privy. Bear box. Tentsites. Water source is a stream 15 yards east of the shelter.

Cold River Rd.—East 2.7 miles to Shrewsbury Co-op at Pierces' Store, (802) 492-3326, short-term resupply, sandwiches and daily specials, M–Sa 7–7, Su 8–5. (Distance from Upper Cold River Rd. is 2.5 miles.)
    West 0.7 mile to Wilmouth Hill Rd to Stone's Throw Farm, 120 Wilmouth Hill Rd., Shrewsbury, Vt 05738, open daily 7-7 June-October, fresh local produce, home-baked sourdough bread, dairy products, dehydrated foods, fuel canisters, insect repellant, free WI-FI, charging ports, water, portajohn, accepts mail drops.

Governor Clement Shelter (1929/ 2009)—Sleeps 10. Moldering privy. Tentsites. Water source is a brook 63 yards east of the shelter.

Cooper Lodge (1939)—Sleeps 12. Cooper Pooper Privy. Tent platforms. This enclosed stone cabin was built by the Vermont Forest Service and the CCC. Behind the shelter is a 0.2-mile side trail to Killington Peak. Water source is a spring 100 ft. north on the A.T.

Killington Peak—Reached by a steep 0.2-mile side trail from Cooper Lodge. At 4,241 feet, this is the highest point near the Trail in Vermont and the second-highest peak in the state. The open, rocky summit offers panoramic views, and, on a clear day, you can see the White Mountains of New Hampshire and the Adirondacks of New York. At the summit, a short side trail leads to the Summit Peak Lodge, dining and bar service 11–4:30, operated by the Killington ski resort, may be closed for special events, call (800) 621-6867; shops are located below at the village reached by the gondola. K-1 Gondola ($30) operates from late Jun to fall-foliage season, 10–5. K-1 Base Lodge on the Killington Access Rd. is on the MVRT Diamond Express bus route to Rutland. A GMC ridgerunner patrols the Coolidge Range (including Killington and Pico) and might be available to answer natural-history and Trail questions.

Jungle Junction-Sherburne Pass Trail—Named after a 1938 hurricane left behind a "jungle" of blow-downs (and essentially broke the A.T. as a continuous footpath a year after it opened as such). The blue-blazed Sherburne Pass Trail (former A.T.) leads 3.1 miles north to Sherburne Pass on US-4, directly to the Inn at Long Trail (opened in 1938, ironically), and continues north of the inn 0.5 mile to reconnect with the A.T. east of Deer Leap.

Pico Camp (1959)—Sleeps 12. Privy. An enclosed shelter located 0.5 mile east on the Sherburne Pass Trail, the former A.T. Water source is 45 yards north on the Sherburne Pass Trail.

Rutland city watershed: The western flanks of the Coolidge Range comprise a major portion of Rutland's watershed. Please camp only at designated sites and use facilities provided. Fires are not permitted.

Churchill Scott Shelter (2002)—Sleeps 8. Privy (composting). Tent platform. Water on spur trail downhill behind shelter.

⋔ US-4—East 0.9 mile uphill along a busy thoroughfare to *Lodging:* The Inn at Long Trail, 709 Route 4, Sherburne Pass, Killington, VT 05751; (802) 775-7181, innatlongtrail.com; closed mid-Apr, reopens Memorial Day weekend. The inn offers discounted rooms for hikers with full B; one room designated for hikers with pets, no dogs in the lodge. McGrath's Irish Pub serves L/D 11:30 a.m.–9 p.m. Live Irish music on weekends. Coin laundry, hiker box, outside water spigot, Wi-Fi. Mail drops by UPS or Fed Ex only. Parking, tent camping across the street. Inn opens at 7 a.m., B 7:30–9:30, all meals open to the public. MVRT Diamond Express bus service daily from inn to Rutland. *Shuttles:* Killington Taxi, (802) 442-9718 (seasonal); Gramps Shuttle, (802) 236-6600; Uber. *Note: A safer alternative to the roadwalk in heavy traffic is to cross Route 4 and continue on the A.T. north 1.9 miles to the northern terminus of the Sherburne Pass Trail, which will lead you 0.5 mile south directly to the inn.*

West 8.6 miles to the city of **Rutland, VT [P.O. ZIP 05701: M-F 8-5, Sa 8-12; (802)773-0301]**, with all major services and chain motels; See map. *Hostel:* Hikers Hostel at the Yellow Deli (Twelve Tribes), 23 Center St., (802) 683-9378 or (802) 775-9800, hikershostel.org, located downtown next to the transit center, open year-round, monetary donation or work-trade appreciated but not required, includes B, common room, laundry, separate bunk rooms for men and women, possible shuttles, limited resupply, mail drops accepted. *Groceries:* Rutland Food Coop on Wales St., Grand Union, Hannaford and ALDI on US-7, Market 32 (formerly Price Chopper) and Walmart on Merchant's Row (all long-term resupply). *Restaurants:* Hop'n Moose (a.k.a. Rutland Beer Works), 41 Center St., W–F 4–9, Sa 12–9, Su 12–8, closed M-Tu, pizza, locally brewed beer; Brix Bistro, 118 Merchants Row, W–Sa 4–9; The Bakery, 122 West St., Tu–S 8–1; Yellow Deli, L/D, 15% discount to hikers, closed Sa; farmers market (Sa), plus others. *Outfitters:* Dick's Sporting Goods at Green Mountain Shopping Plaza can be reached via local MVRT bus. *Internet access:* Rutland Free Library. *Other services:* Rutland Regional Medical Center Hospital; Express Care, (802) 773-3386, 215 Stratton Rd., daily 8–8; Clear Choice MD Urgent Care, (802) 772-4165, 173 S. Main St., daily 8–8; veterinarians; Rutland Taxi, (802) 236-3133; Roy's Taxi, (802) 236-1966; All Occasion Transportation, (802) 683-0018. *Public transportation:* Bus station located at Marble Valley Transit Center, 80 West St. Marble Valley Regional Transit, (802) 773-3244, thebus.com, Diamond Express $2 daily service in the Rutland–Killington area, M–Sa to Manchester; M–Sa to Middlebury. Vermont Translines

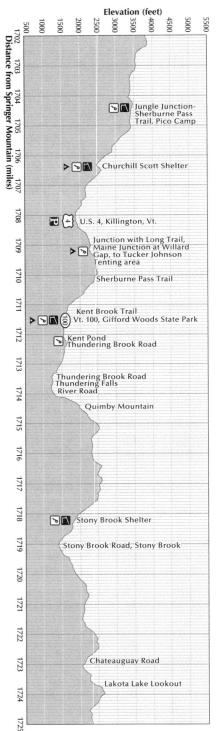

Elevation (feet)

Jungle Junction-Sherburne Pass Trail, Pico Camp

Churchill Scott Shelter

U.S. 4, Killington, Vt.

Junction with Long Trail, Maine Junction at Willard Gap, to Tucker Johnson Tenting area

Sherburne Pass Trail

Kent Brook Trail
Vt. 100, Gifford Woods State Park

Kent Pond
Thundering Brook Road

Thundering Brook Road
Thundering Falls
River Road

Quimby Mountain

Stony Brook Shelter

Stony Brook Road, Stony Brook

Chateauguay Road

Lakota Lake Lookout

(see Bennington above). Daily flights to Boston from Rutland Airport. Amtrak, from downtown Rutland on Ethan Allen Express to NYC's Penn Station.

Maine Junction-Willard Gap. The L.T. continues north 166.5 miles to Canada, while the A.T. diverges to the east toward New Hampshire and Maine.

Tucker-Johnson Shelter (2018)—Located on the L.T. 0.4 mile north of Maine Junction. Shelter burned down in 2011; new one sleeps 8. Tenting area. Moldering privy. Bear box. Water source is Eagle Square Brook, 100 ft. north.

⚠**VT-100**—The A.T. passes through Gifford Woods State Park, (802) 775-5354, shelters, tentsites, and bathhouse visible from the Trail. **Camping:** 4 primitive sites $6, shelters $30–$40; tent-sites $20–$30 up to 4 people, cabin $60 for 4 people, two-night minimum cabin reservation in Jul–Aug, $1/pet/night, coin-operated showers 50¢ (5 mins.), water spigot. Space fills up quickly during the fall "leaf season." **Shuttles:** See US-4 above.

East 0.6 mile to US-4 and **Killington, VT [P.O. ZIP 05751: M-F 8:30-11 & 12-4:30, Sa 8:30-12; (802) 775-4247].** *Lodging:* Greenbrier Inn, (802) 775-1575, greenbriervt.com, call for rates, continental B, pool *Groceries:* Killington Deli & Market Place, (802) 775-1599, killingtondeli.com, (short-term resupply), M–Sa 6:30 a.m.–7 p.m., Su 6:30–6, sandwiches, hot-meal specials, liquor store, and ATM. *Outfitter:* See below. *Other services:* MVRT bus stop nearby at Welcome Center.

⚠**Kent Pond, Thundering Brook Rd.**—on A.T. *Lodging:* Mountain Meadows Lodge, 285 Thundering Brook Rd., Killington, VT 05751; (802) 775-1010, mountainmeadowslodge.com, ask for hiker rates. Hikers not staying at the lodge may have a reasonably priced B/D; kayaking on Kent Pond. Hiker box inside; outdoor water spigot; mail drops accepted. This is not a hostel, but a country inn and wedding venue; please be respectful of nonhiker guests.

East 0.3 mile on side cross-country ski trail (sign marked B.C.O.) to *Outfitter:* Base Camp, 2363 US-4, Killington, VT 05751; (802) 775-0166, basecampvt. com; on bus route to Rutland, open daily 10–5; backpacking equipment, clothing, and supplies, freeze-dried food, fuel canisters, disc golf, outside deck area with recharging outlets; mail drops accepted. MVRT bus stop to Rutland at Welcome Center.

East 0.6 mile to all the Killington services on US-4 above: A safer alternative to walking on VT-100.

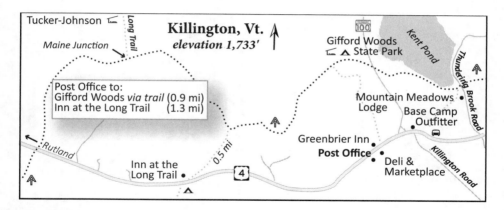

Thundering Falls—A 2007-8 relocation, which took 30 years from conception to completion, eliminated a road walk and added views of Thundering Falls and the Ottauquechee River. The new path descends through northern-hardwood forest to the base of high Thundering Falls and then through the open Ottauquechee River floodplain. A wheelchair-accessible boardwalk built by the Green Mountain Club and financed by ATC and the National Park Service crosses the river and floodplain.

River Rd.—East 0.5 mile to Johnson Recreation Center pool ($4 nonresident fee), call (800) 422-2711 for hours. **East** 0.7 mile to Sherburne Memorial Library, M–F open until 5:30, Sa open until 1, closed Su.

Stony Brook Shelter (1997)—Sleeps 6. Privy. Bear box. Tentsites. Brook 100 yards north of shelter on A.T.

Side Trail to the Lookout—One of the few views between Killington Peak and New Hampshire. Follow side trail 0.2 mile west to a private cabin. Use care on ladder that leads up to an observation deck. No water. The owners permit its use by hikers; please be responsible to ensure that this privilege continues.

Wintturi Shelter (1994)—Sleeps 6. Privy. Tentsites. Spring 300 ft. to the north of the shelter.

VT-12—*Please respect landowners at this road crossing by not camping in woods or fields near VT-12.*
    East 3.8 miles to **Woodstock, VT [P.O. ZIP 05091: M-F 8:30-5, Sa 9-12; (802) 457-1323]**. Home of the Marsh-Billings-Rockefeller National Historical Park. Services include several expensive motels and inns, grocery (long-term resupply), restaurants, bank with ATM, doctor, dentist, pharmacy, and movie theater open F–Su. *Groceries:* Gillingham and Sons, 16 Elm St., M-Sa 8:30-5, Su 10-4. *Internet access:* library, M–Sa.
    West 0.1 mile to *Groceries:* On the Edge farm stand, owners Dana and Bill, open Th-Su 10–5:00, M-W by chance, delicious home-made pies, seasonal veggies, fruit, cold drinks, ice cream, cheese, smoked meat, bread rolls, breakfast burritos, jerky, and water, Wi-Fi, portajohn.
    West 0.2 miles *Coffee Shop:* Abracadabra Coffee Co., large variety of hot and cold drinks, pastries. M-F 8-2, Sa-Su 8-3.
    West 6.4 miles to **Barnard, VT [P.O. ZIP 05031: M-F 9:30-12:30 & 1:30-4:30, Sa 8:30-11; (802) 234-5404]** *Groceries:* Barnard General Store (short-term resupply), 6134 VT-R.12 (802) 234-9688, M-Sa 7-7 Su 8-6, B, L from deli counter, B menu on weekends, free Wi-Fi, ATM. *Camping:* Silver Lake State Park (802)-234-9451, across road from general store, open Memorial Day to Labor Day, campsites $28-30, lean-tos $38-40, 4 campers allowed per site, park admission $5, coin showers, canoe/kayak rentals on lake. Call beforehand to determine availability.
    Woodstock Stage Rd.—East 0.9 mile to **South Pomfret, VT [P.O. ZIP 05067: M-F 12:30-4:30, Sa 8:30-11:30; (802) 457-1147]**. *Groceries:* Teago General Store (short-term resupply), M-Sa 7-6,

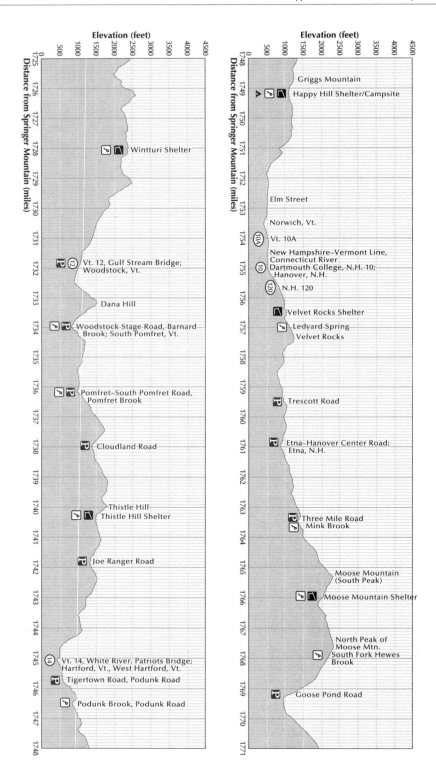

Elevation (feet)

Distance from Springer Mountain (miles)

Wintturi Shelter

Vt. 12, Gulf Stream Bridge; Woodstock, Vt.

Dana Hill

Woodstock-Stage Road, Barnard Brook; South Pomfret, Vt.

Pomfret–South Pomfret Road, Pomfret Brook

Cloudland Road

Thistle Hill
Thistle Hill Shelter

Joe Ranger Road

Vt. 14, White River, Patriots Bridge; Hartford, Vt., West Hartford, Vt.
Tigertown Road, Podunk Road

Podunk Brook, Podunk Road

Elevation (feet)

Distance from Springer Mountain (miles)

Griggs Mountain

Happy Hill Shelter/Campsite

Elm Street

Norwich, Vt.

Vt. 10A

New Hampshire–Vermont Line, Connecticut River
Dartmouth College, N.H. 10; Hanover, N.H.

N.H. 120

Velvet Rocks Shelter

Ledyard Spring
Velvet Rocks

Trescott Road

Etna–Hanover Center Road; Etna, N.H.

Three Mile Road
Mink Brook

Moose Mountain (South Peak)

Moose Mountain Shelter

North Peak of Moose Mtn.
South Fork Hewes Brook

Goose Pond Road

Su 8–4, deli sandwiches and P.O. inside store. *Internet access:* library, Wi-Fi, Tu, Th, Sa.

Thistle Hill Shelter (1995)—Sleeps 8. Privy. Tentsites. The Cloudland privy was moved to Thistle Hill, partly with ALDHA's help. Two nearby streams for water.

⚡ VT-14—On the A.T., **West Hartford, VT [P.O. closed]**. *Camping:* "The Hart Family," Randy and Lynda, long-time Trail angels with a home with a big "AT" on the blue barn, are around to offer offer tenting, water, portajohn, WI-FI including charging outlets, call 802-295-1948; Steve "Capt. Stash" at Hartford Sign Co., 5255 VT-14, West Hartford, VT 05084 ("1722" on A.T. sign), (802) 295-6631, allows tenting and mail drops via UPS. *Internet access:* library, M–Th, Sa, Wi-Fi.

　East 7 miles to **Hartford, VT [P.O. ZIP 05047: M-F 8-12 & 2-5, Sa 9-11:30; (802) 295-5511]**. Free bus service from Hartford, VT, to West Lebanon or Hanover, NH, on Advance Transit Green Route.

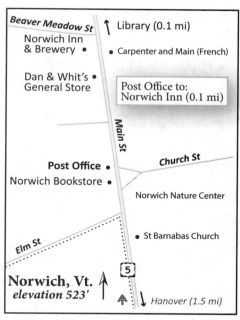

Norwich, Vt.
elevation 523'

Beaver Meadow St ｜ ↑ Library (0.1 mi)

Norwich Inn
& Brewery ●　● Carpenter and Main (French)

Dan & Whit's ●
General Store　Post Office to:
　　　　　　　Norwich Inn (0.1 mi)

Main St

Post Office ●　**Church St**
Norwich Bookstore ●

　　　Norwich Nature Center

Elm St　● St Barnabas Church

5

⬆ ↓ Hanover (1.5 mi)

　East 8 miles to **White River Junction**, a large town with all services and free Advance Transit bus service on the orange route. Near the Greyhound bus station on 44 Sykes Mountain Ave. is a super 8 motel, Comfort Inn, several other major chains, a Chinese Buffet, McDonald's, and The Station Market. Amtrak provides daily train service on the Vermonter, (800) USA-RAIL. *Hostel:* Hotel Coolidge (Hosteling International), 39 South Main St., White River Junction, VT 05001; (802) 295-3118, (800) 622-1124, hotelcoolidge.com; often full, call for rates and availability, kitchen, laundry, Wi-Fi; walk to restaurants, banks, and stores. *Restaurant:* entrance from Hotel Coolidge, B, L M-Sa, closed Su.

Happy Hill Shelter (1998)—Sleeps 8. Privy. Tentsites. The oldest A.T. shelter (built in 1918, before the A.T.) was torn down, then burned; the debris was carried out. In 1998, a new shelter was built about 0.2 mile north of the original. ALDHA members worked on this project after the 1997 Gathering. Water source is an unreliable brook near the shelter.

⚡🏠 US-5/Norwich, VT [P.O. ZIP 05055: M-F 8:30-5, Sa 9-12; (802) 649-1608]—**West** 0.25 mile to the Norwich Historical Society at the corner of Elm and Main streets; has benches for hikers to rest on and outside charging ports on the side of their building facing Elm St. St Barnabas Episcopal Church, 262 Main St, has been allowing hikers to camp. *Lodging:* Norwich Inn & Jasper Murdock Alehouse & Microbrewery, 325 Main St., (802) 649-1143, norwichinn.com; call for possible hiker discount rate. Built in 1791 as a stagecoach inn. *Restaurants:* Norwich Inn, W–F B 7:30–10, Sa–Su brunch 9–2, pub serves at 3, D daily. *Groceries:* Dan & Whits (long-term resupply), 319 Main St., (802) 649-1602, open daily 7–9, a sprawling, eclectic general store, the motto of which is, "If we don't have it, you don't need it." *Internet access:* library, M–Sa. *Other services:* Norwich Bookstore; library closed Su; bank with ATM; free bus service to Hanover on Advance Transit Brown or Green routes.

New Hampshire

Miles from Springer	Miles to Next Point	Features	Services	Elev	Miles from Katahdin	M A P
1,754.5	0.5	Connecticut River; Vermont–New Hampshire State Line	R	380'	442.9	
1,755.0	0.7	NH-10, Dartmouth College On A.T.-**Hanover, NH, P.O. 03755** East-2m to Sunset Motor Inn	R, C, G, L, M, O, D, V, B, sh, cl, f L, cl	520'	442.4	
1,755.7	0.8	NH-120	R	490'	441.7	
1,756.5	0.5	**Velvet Rocks Shelter** (W–0.2m) (N–0.2m w), 7.6mS; 9.7mN	S	1,040'	440.9	
1,757.0	0.8	Ledyard Spring (W–0.4m): water for Velvet Rocks Shelter	w	1,200'	440.4	
1,757.8	1.7	Velvet Rocks		1,243'	439.6	
1,759.5	1.4	Trescott Road	R, P	915'	437.9	
1,760.9	2.5	Etna–Hanover Center Road East-0.9m to Etna, NH	R, P, H G, f, sh	845'	436.5	ATC: NH-VT Map 5
1,763.4	0.2	Three Mile Road	R, P	1,350'	434.0	
1,763.6	1.6	Mink Brook	w	1,320'	433.8	
1,765.2	0.8	Moose Mountain (South Peak)		2,290'	432.2	
1,766.0	1.2	**Moose Mountain Shelter**, 9.7mS; 5.9mN	S, C, w	1,850'	431.4	
1,767.2	0.7	Moose Mountain (North Peak)		2,300'	430.2	
1,767.9	1.3	South Fork, Hewes Brook	w	1,100'	429.5	
1,769.2	2.0	Goose Pond Road	R, P	952'	428.2	
1,771.2	0.5	Holts Ledge: peregrine falcon rookery		1,930'	426.2	
1,771.7	0.9	**Trapper John Shelter** (W–0.2m), 5.9mS; 6.9mN	S, C, w	1,345'	425.7	
1,772.6	1.9	Dartmouth Skiway, Lyme-Dorchester Rd. West-3.2m to **Lyme, NH, P.O. 03768**	R, P G, L, M, V	880'	424.8	
1,774.5	0.1	Grant Brook	w	1,090'	422.9	
1,774.6	3.7	Lyme–Dorchester Road, Smarts Mountain Trailhead	R, P, w	1,100'	422.8	
1,778.3	0.1	Smarts Mountain Tentsite	C, w	3,200'	419.1	
1,778.4	3.9	**Fire Warden's Cabin**, firetower, 6.9mS; 5.6mN	S, w	3,230'	419.0	
1,782.3	0.4	South Jacob's Brook	w	1,450'	415.1	
1,782.7	0.7	Eastman Ledges		2,010'	414.7	
1,783.4	0.3	North Jacobs Brook: water for Hexacuba Shelter	w	1,900'	414.0	
1,783.7	1.4	**Hexacuba Shelter** (E–0.3m), 5.6mS; 16mN	S, w	1,980'	413.7	ATC: NH-VT Map 4
1,785.1	0.2	Mt. Cube (south summit); Cross Rivendell Trail Junction		2,909'	412.3	
1,785.3	1.5	Mt. Cube, side trail to north summit		2,911'	412.1	
1,786.8	1.8	Brackett Brook: ford	w	1,400'	410.6	
1,788.6	1.6	NH-25A: beach on lake (E–0.1m) East-4.8m to **Wentworth, NH, P.O. 03282**	R, P G	900'	408.8	
1,790.2	0.6	Cape Moonshine Road	R	1,400'	407.2	
1,790.8	2.3	Ore Hill Campsite (E–0.1m)	C, w	1,720'	406.6	

Miles from Springer	Miles to Next Point	Features	Services	Elev	Miles from Katahdin	M A P
1,793.1	0.3	Ore Hill		1,850'	404.3	
1,793.4	2.5	NH-25C, Ore Hill Brook *East–4m to* **Warren, NH, P.O. 03279**	R, P G, M, D, cl	1,550'	404.0	
1,795.9	0.4	Mt. Mist		2,200'	401.5	
1,796.3	0.1	Hairy Root Spring, Webster Slide Trail	w	1,600'	401.1	
1,796.4	1.9	Wachipauka Pond	w	1,493'	401.0	
1,798.3	1.1	NH-25, Oliverian Brook: *ford, road bypass if high water* *East–0.4m to* **Glencliff, NH, P.O. 03238**	R, P, w H, sh, cl, f	1,000'	399.1	
1,799.4	0.4	**Jeffers Brook Shelter**, *16mS; 6.9mN*	S, C, w	1,350'	398.0	
1,799.8	0.3	Long Pond Road, USFS-19	R	1,330'	397.6	
1,800.1	0.4	High Street, Glencliff Trailhead	R, P	1,480'	397.3	
1,800.5	2.6	Hurricane Trail		1,680'	396.9	
1,803.1	0.9	Mt. Moosilauke *(south peak)*, Carriage Rd.		4,460'	394.3	
1,804.0	0.4	Mt. Moosilauke *(north peak)* *East–3.7m on* Gorge Brook Trail to DOC Ravine Lodge	R	4,802'	393.4	
1,804.4	1.5	Benton Trail		4,550'	393.0	
1,805.9	0.4	Asquam Ridge Trail *(E–4m to DOC Ravine Lodge)*		4,050'	391.5	
1,806.3	0.4	**Beaver Brook Shelter** and **Campsite**, *6.9mS; 9mN*	S, C, w	3,750'	391.1	
1,806.7	1.1	Beaver Brook Cascades	w	3,000'	390.7	
1,807.8	0.6	Kinsman Notch; NH-112 *(E–0.3m to Lost River Gorge)* *East–4-5m to* **North Woodstock, NH, P.O. 03262** *East–6m to* **Lincoln, NH, P.O. 03251**	R, P, w H, G, L, M, cl, f all	1,870'	389.6	
1,808.4	2.7	Dilly Trail		2,650'	389.0	
1,811.1	1.3	Gordon Pond Trail		2,700'	386.3	
1,812.4	1.9	Mt. Wolf *(east peak)*		3,478'	385.0	
1,814.3	0.5	Reel Brook Trail		2,600'	383.1	
1,814.8	0.5	Powerline		2,625'	382.6	
1,815.3	1.4	**Eliza Brook Shelter** and **Campsite**, *9mS; 4.1mN*	S, C, w	2,400'	382.1	
1,816.7	1.1	Harrington Pond		3,400'	380.7	
1,817.8	0.9	South Kinsman Mountain		4,358'	379.6	
1,818.7	0.4	North Kinsman Mountain		4,293'	378.7	
1,819.1	0.2	Mt. Kinsman Trail		3,900'	378.3	
1,819.3	1.9	Kinsman Pond Trail *(south)* to +AMC **Kinsman Pond Shelter** and **Campsite** *(E–0.1m)*, *4.1mS; 15.3mN*	S, C, w	3,750'	378.1	
1,821.2	0.9	+AMC Lonesome Lake Hut; Lonesome Lake Trail *West–1.7m to* Lafayette Pl W on I-93	L, M, w R, P, B, C	2,760'	376.2	
1,822.1	0.5	Kinsman Pond Trail *(north)*		2,294'	375.3	
1,822.6	1.1	Basin–Cascade Trail; Cascade Brook: *ford*	w	2,084'	374.8	
1,823.7	0.2	Whitehouse Brook	w	1,610'	373.7	
1,823.9	0.2	Pemi Trail		1,520'	373.5	
1,824.1	0.1	Franconia Notch, I-93, US-3: *underpass, Pemiga-wasset River* *East–5.8m to* **North Woodstock, NH, P.O. 03262** *East–7.3m to* **Lincoln, NH, P.O. 03251** *West–8m to* Franconia, NH	R H, G, L, M, cl, f all B, G, L, M	1,450'	373.3	

ATC: NH-VT Map 4

ATC: NC-VT Map 3

Miles from Springer	Miles to Next Point	Features	Services	Elev	Miles from Katahdin	M A P

1,824.2	0.5	Franconia Notch Bike Path
		    East–0.2m to Whitehouse Trail (follow east 0.8m to hiker parking)
		    East–1m to Flume Visitors Center
		    West–2.1m to Lafayette Campground
			R, P, B
			
			M
			C, B, P
				1,450'	373.2	

1,824.7	2.0	Flume side trail		1,800'	372.7	
1,826.7	0.3	+AMC Liberty Springs Tentsite	C, w	3,870'	370.7	
1,827.0	1.8	Franconia Ridge Trail, Mt. Liberty (E–0.3m)		4,260'	370.4	
1,828.8	0.7	Little Haystack Mountain; Falling Waters Trail (W–3.2m to Lafayette Place East on I-93): above treeline for next 2.5 miles north on Franconia Ridge	R, P, B, C	4,800'	368.6	
1,829.5	1.0	Mt. Lincoln		5,089'	367.9	

1,830.5	0.8	Mt. Lafayette; Greenleaf Trail (W–0.2m spring)
		    West–1.1m to +AMC Greenleaf Hut
		    West–4m to Lafayette Pl East on I-93
			w
			L, M, w
			R, P, B, C
				5,260'	366.9	

1,831.3	2.0	Skookumchuck Trail Jct.: above treeline for the next 2.5 miles south on Franconia Ridge		4,680'	366.1	
1,833.3	0.7	Garfield Pond	w	3,860'	364.1	
1,834.0	0.2	Mt. Garfield		4,500'	363.4	
1,834.2	0.2	Garfield Trail (W–4.8m to Gale River Loop Road)	P, R, B	4,180'	363.2	
1,834.4	0.5	+AMC **Garfield Ridge Shelter** and **Campsite** (W–0.1m), 15.3mS; 6.4mN	S, C, w	3,900'	363.0	
1,834.9	1.6	Franconia Brook Trail		3,420'	362.5	
1,836.5	0.6	Gale River Trail (W–4m to Gale River Loop Road)	P, R, B	3,390'	360.9	
1,837.1	0.8	+AMC Galehead Hut, Twin Brook Trail	L, M, w	3,780'	360.3	
1,837.9	2.0	South Twin Mtn., North Twin Spur		4,902'	359.5	
1,839.9	1.3	Mt. Guyot; Bondcliff Trail to +AMC **Guyot Shelter** and **Campsite** (E–0.8m), 6.4mS; 9.8mN	S, C, w	4,580'	357.5	
1,841.2	1.2	Zealand Mountain		4,250'	356.2	
1,842.4	0.4	Zeacliff Pond Trail (E–0.1m)	w	3,800'	355.0	
1,842.8	0.1	Zeacliff Trail (1.4m): rejoins A.T. north		3,700'	354.6	
1,842.9	1.1	Zeacliff: overlook to the east		3,700'	354.5	
1,844.0	0.1	Lend-a-Hand Trail, Whitewall Brook	w	2,750'	353.4	
1,844.1	0.2	+AMC Zealand Falls Hut	L, M, w	2,630'	353.3	
1,844.3	1.3	Zealand Trail Jct. (W–2.3m to Zealand Road): join former railroad bed	P, R, B	2,460'	353.1	
1,845.6	0.8	Zeacliff Trail (1.4m): rejoins A.T. south		2,448'	351.8	
1,846.4	0.5	Thoreau Falls Trail		2,460'	351.0	
1,846.9	2.0	Shoal Pond Trail (E–0.8m)	w	2,500'	350.5	
1,848.9	1.0	+AMC **Ethan Pond Shelter** and **Campsite**, 9.8mS; 17.4mN	S, C, w	2,860'	348.5	
1,849.9	0.3	Willey Range Trail		2,680'	347.5	
1,850.2	1.1	Kedron Flume Trail		2,450'	347.2	
1,851.3	0.2	Arethusa–Ripley Falls Trail		1,600'	346.1	
1,851.5	0.3	Railroad Tracks, Willey House Station Road, Ethan Pond Trailhead	R, P	1,440'	345.9	

1,851.8	0.1	Crawford Notch, US-302, Presidential Range
		    East–1.8m to Dry River Cmpground
		    East–3m to Crawford Notch CG
		    East–10m to **Bartlett, NH, P.O. 03812**
		    West–1m to Willey House
		    West–3.7m to +AMC Highland Ctr.
			R, P, B
			C, cl, sh
			C, sh
			M, L
			M
			B, L, M, sh
				1,275'	345.6	

ATC: NC-VT Map 3

Miles from Springer	Miles to Next Point	Features	Services	Elev	Miles from Katahdin	M A P
1,851.9	0.1	Saco River: *footbridge*		1,350'	345.5	
1,852.0	0.1	Saco River Trail *(south) (W–1.2m to Willey House)*	M	1,350'	345.4	
1,852.1	1.6	Saco River Trail *(north) (E–2m to Dry River Campground)*	C, cl, sh	1,400'	345.3	
1,853.7	1.4	Webster Cliffs		3,025'	343.7	
1,855.1	1.4	Mt. Webster		3,910'	342.3	
1,856.5	1.7	Mt. Jackson		4,052'	340.9	
1,858.2	0.8	+AMC Mizpah Spring Hut, +AMC Nauman Tentsite	C, L, M, w	3,800'	339.2	
1,859.0	0.9	Mt. Pierce *(Mt. Clinton): above treeline for the next 12.7 miles north*		4,312'	338.4	
1,859.9	0.8	Spring	w	4,350'	337.5	
1,860.7	0.5	Mt. Eisenhower Loop Trail *(north)*; Edmands Path		4,475'	336.7	
1,861.2	0.6	Spring	w	4,480'	336.2	
1,861.8	1.0	Mt. Franklin		5,004'	335.6	
1,862.8	0.1	Mt. Monroe Loop Trail *(north)*		5,075'	334.6	
1,862.9	0.8	+AMC Lakes of the Clouds Hut: *"The Dungeon"*	L, M, w	5,125'	334.5	
1,863.7	0.4	Davis Path; Westside Trail *(south)*		5,625'	333.7	
1,864.1	0.2	Gulfside Trail		6,150'	333.3	

1,864.3	0.2	Mt. Washington, summit building, observatory
		    Mt. Washington, NH, P.O. 03589 *(not recommended)*
		       East–8m on Auto Road to NH-16
		Tuckerman Ravine Trail to + AMC **Hermit Lake Shelters** *(E–2m), 17.4S; 7.1mN;* Pinkham Notch at NH-16 *(E–4.2m)*
			R, P, M
			
			R, P
			S, C, w
			R, P, B, G, L, M, sh, f
				6,288'	333.1	

1,864.5	0.1	Trinity Heights Connector		6,100'	332.9	
1,864.6	0.1	Cog Railroad tracks		6,090'	332.8	
1,864.7	0.5	Great Gulf Trail		5,925'	332.7	
1,865.2	0.1	Westside Trail		5,500'	332.2	
1,865.3	0.3	Mt. Clay Loop Trail *(south)*		5,400'	332.1	
1,865.6	0.5	Jewell Trail		5,400'	331.8	
1,866.1	0.1	Greenough Spring *(west)*	w	5,100'	331.3	
1,866.2	0.1	Sphinx Col; Mt. Clay Loop Trail *(north)*		5,025'	331.2	
1,866.3	0.5	Sphinx Trail		4,975'	331.1	
1,866.8	0.5	Cornice Trail; Monticello Lawn		5,325'	330.6	
1,867.3	0.3	Six Husbands Trail		5,325'	330.1	
1,867.6	0.2	Mt. Jefferson Loop *(north)*		5,125'	329.8	
1,867.8	0.7	Edmands Col; Gulfside Spring *(E–50 yds.)*; Spaulding Spring *(W–0.2m)*	w	4,938'	329.6	
1,868.5	0.6	Israel Ridge Path to +RMC **The Perch Shelter** and **Campsite** *(W–0.9m), 7.1mS; 2.7mN*	S, C, w	5,475'	328.9	

1,869.1	0.5	Thunderstorm Junction
		   West–1.1m to +**RMC Crag Camp Cabin**
		   West–1.2m on Lowe's Path to Mt. Adams and
		   +**RMC Gray Knob Cabin**, *2.7mS; 23.2mN*
			S, w
			S, w
				5,490'	328.3	

1,869.6	0.4	Air Line Trail *(south)*		5,125'	327.8	

1,870.0	0.5	+AMC Madison Spring Hut
		   Valley Way Trail to USFS Valley Way Tentsite
		   (3,900') (W–0.6m)
			L, M, w
			C, w
				4,825'	327.4	

ATC: NH-VT Map 2

Miles from Springer	Miles to Next Point	Features	Services	Elev	Miles from Katahdin	M A P
1,870.5	0.2	Mt. Madison		5,366'	326.9	
1,870.7	0.3	Howker Ridge Trail		5,100'	326.7	
1,871.0	0.7	Osgood Junction; Parapet Trail; Daniel Webster Scout Trail		4,822'	326.4	
1,871.7	1.3	Osgood Ridge: *above treeline for the next 12.7 miles south*		4,300'	325.7	
1,873.0	0.6	USFS Osgood Campsite; Osgood Cutoff	C, w	2,540'	324.4	
1,873.6	0.2	The Bluff at Parapet Brook; Great Gulf Trail *(south)*	w	2,450'	323.8	
1,873.8	0.1	Madison Gulf Trail; West Branch of the Peabody River	w	2,300'	323.6	
1,873.9	1.8	Great Gulf Trail *(north)*		2,290'	323.5	
1,875.7	0.2	Lowe's Bald Spot: *rock dome*		2,875'	321.7	
1,875.9	0.1	Mt. Washington Auto Road	R, P	2,675'	321.5	
1,876.0	0.8	Raymond Path		2,625'	321.4	
1,876.8	0.5	George's Gorge Trail		2,525'	320.6	
1,877.3	0.5	Crew Cutoff Trail		2,075'	320.1	
1,877.8	0.1	Pinkham Notch, NH-16, Pinkham Notch Visitors Center, +AMC Joe Dodge Lodge *East–16m to* Intervale, NH *East–18m to* North Conway, NH *West–2m to* Wildcat Mtn. Gondola *West–11m to* **Gorham, NH, P.O. 03581**	R, P, B, G, L, M, sh, f M, L, O G, L, M, O, D all	2,050'	319.6	
1,877.9	0.8	Square Ledge Trail		2,020'	319.5	ATC: NH-VT Map 2
1,878.7	0.8	Wildcat Ridge Trail to Glen Ellis Falls		1,990'	318.7	
1,879.5	0.3	Open Ledge, Sarge's Crag		3,000'	317.9	
1,879.8	1.0	Spring *(west)*		3,250'	317.6	
1,880.8	1.1	Wildcat Mountain, Peak D: *gondola*		4,020'	316.6	
1,881.9	0.4	Wildcat Mountain, Peak C		4,298'	315.5	
1,882.3	0.5	Wildcat Mountain, Peak B		4,330'	315.1	
1,882.8	0.9	Wildcat Mountain, Peak A		4,442'	314.6	
1,883.7	0.7	Carter Notch, +AMC Carter Notch Hut *(E–0.2m)* Nineteen Mile Brook Trail *(W–3.6m to NH-16)*	L, M, w R, B	3,350'	313.7	
1,884.4	0.5	Spring *(W–60 yards)*	w	4,300'	313.0	
1,884.9	0.4	Carter Dome, Rainbow Trail		4,832'	312.5	
1,885.3	0.4	Black Angel Trail		4,600'	312.1	
1,885.7	0.6	Mt. Hight: *views*		4,675'	311.7	
1,886.3	0.8	Zeta Pass, Carter Dome Trail *(W–0.8m reliable spring)*	w	3,890'	311.1	
1,887.1	1.3	South Carter Mountain		4,458'	310.3	
1,888.4	0.3	Middle Carter Mountain		4,610'	309.0	
1,888.7	0.3	Mt. Lethe		4,584'	308.7	
1,889.0	1.9	North Carter Mountain		4,539'	308.4	
1,890.9	0.7	+AMC **Imp Shelter** and **Campsite** *(W–0.2m)*, 23.2mS; 6.3mN	S, C, w	3,250'	306.5	
1,891.6	1.4	Stony Brook Trail *(W–3.6m to NH-16)*; Moriah Brook Trail *(E)*	R, P	3,127'	305.8	
1,893.0	1.2	Carter Moriah Trail to Mt. Moriah (4,049') *(W–0.2m)*		4,000'	304.4	
1,894.2	0.2	Middle Moriah		3,640'	303.2	
1,894.4	1.1	Kenduskeag Trail		3,300'	303.0	

Miles from Springer	Miles to Next Point	Features	Services	Elev	Miles from Katahdin	M A P
1,895.5	1.1	Rattle River	w	1,700'	301.9	
1,896.6	0.4	East Rattle River: *difficult in high water*	w	1,500'	300.8	
1,897.0	1.9	**Rattle River Shelter** and **Campsite**, *6.3mS; 13.9mN*	S, C, w	1,260'	300.4	ATC: NH-VT Map 2

1,898.9	0.3	US-2, Shelburne, NH
		    West–1.8m to White Birches Camping Park
		
		    West–3.6m to **Gorham, NH, P.O. 03581**
		
		    West–5.6 to Walmart
		    West–8m to Berlin, NH
			R, P
			H, C, G, cl, sh
			H, B, G, L, M, O, cl, f
			G
			all, D
				780'	298.5	

1,899.2	0.2	North Road, Androscoggin River	R	750'	298.2	
1,899.4	1.0	Hogan Road: *unpaved*	R, P	760'	298.0	
1,900.4	2.1	Brook	w	1,350'	297.0	
1,902.5	2.2	Mt. Hayes, Mahoosuc Trail		2,555'	294.9	
1,904.7	1.1	Cascade Mountain		2,631'	292.7	
1,905.8	1.0	Trident Col Tentsite *(W–0.1m)*	C, w	2,020'	291.6	ATC: NH-VT Map 1
1,906.8	0.6	Trident Pass, Page Pond	w	2,240'	290.6	
1,907.4	1.1	Wockett Ledge		2,780'	290.0	
1,908.5	1.5	Dream Lake Inlet, Peabody Brook Trail	w	2,610'	288.9	
1,910.0	0.7	Moss Pond	w	2,630'	287.4	
1,910.7	2.8	Austin Brook Trail Jct. to **Gentian Pond Shelter** and **Campsite** *(E–0.2m), 13.9mS; 5.8mN*	S, C, w	2,166'	286.7	
1,913.5	0.6	Mt. Success		3,565'	283.9	
1,914.1	1.3	Success Trail *(W–3m to Success Pond Road)*	R, P	3,170'	283.3	
1,915.4	0.6	New Hampshire–Maine State Line		2,972'	282.0	

+ Fee charged; RMC = Randolph Mountain Club

At Hanover, southbounders will have already experienced the White Mountains. Northbounders should gear up for the conditions ahead.

Considered one of the most challenging states, it is also one of the most rewarding. As the trees get shorter and the views get longer, you've entered the krummholz zone, where trees are stunted with flag-like tops due to stress from the wind and cold. Boreal bogs are home to local carnivorous plant species, sundew and pitcher plants. Hardy, yet delicate alpine flowers—Labrador tea, bunchberry, mountain sandwort, and cloudberry—may be in bloom when you pass through. Spruce grouse, winter wren, dark-eyed junco, and the white-throated sparrow will greet you along the way.

Much of the Trail is above timberline, where the temperature may change very suddenly; snow is possible in any season. Snow falls on Mt. Washington every month of the year. High winds and dense fog are common. Most shelters and campsites charge a fee.

Note: Tenting is prohibited within 200 feet of the A.T. from the Connecticut River (Vermont state line) to the summit of Mt. Moosilauke. Many water sources in southern New Hampshire are not always reliable, including sources at, or adjacent to, shelters.

Dartmouth Outing Club—DOC maintains the 53.3 miles from the Connecticut River to Kinsman Notch in New Hampshire. Correspondence should be sent to DOC Box 9, Hanover, NH 03755; (603) 646-2428; dartmouth.edu/~doc. The DOC no longer uses orange-and-black paint for blazes, although many are still visible. The DOC does continue to use orange and black on trail signs.

⚠️ 🏠 **Hanover, NH [P.O. ZIP 03755: M–F 8:30–5, Sa 8:30–12, lobby opens at 7 a.m.; (603) 643-5201]**— See map. Home of Dartmouth College. The A.T. passes through the center of Hanover, and most

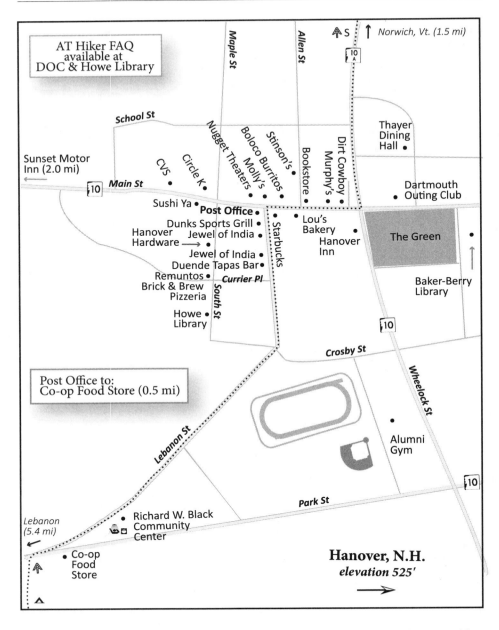

AT Hiker FAQ
available at
DOC & Howe Library

Norwich, Vt. (1.5 mi)

Maple St

Allen St

School St

Thayer
Dining
Hall

Sunset Motor
Inn (2.0 mi)

Nugget Theaters

Boloco Burritos

Stinson's

Bookstore

Dirt Cowboy

Murphy's

CVS

Circle K

Molly's

Dartmouth
Outing Club

Main St

Sushi Ya

Post Office

Lou's
Bakery

The Green

Dunks Sports Grill

Hanover
Hardware

Jewel of India

Starbucks

Hanover
Inn

Jewel of India

Duende Tapas Bar

Remuntos

Brick & Brew
Pizzeria

Currier Pl

South St

Baker-Berry
Library

Howe
Library

Crosby St

Post Office to:
Co-op Food Store (0.5 mi)

Wheelock St

Lebanon St

Alumni
Gym

Park St

Lebanon
(5.4 mi)

Richard W. Black
Community
Center

Hanover, N.H.
elevation 525'

Co-op
Food
Store

services are along the route of the Trail. At the center of town and the Dartmouth Green, a blue-blazed side trail leads (Trail-west) to Robinson Hall and the office of the Dartmouth Outing Club (DOC) in Room 113, (603) 646-2428, dartmouth.edu/~doc/. DOC has student volunteers (DOC tours), Su–Th 2–6, phone, and Internet access. This is a good place to begin in town. The college does not allow nonstudents to stay in student housing. Dartmouth College security has reported problems with improper use of college facilities and buildings by hikers; hikers must not enter dormitories, offices, laundry rooms, etc., without permission or try to sleep overnight in those locations, including the DOC building. Public (on-street) consumption of alcohol is illegal downtown. *Camping:* Tenting is permitted in the woods, past the soccer fields, if you are 200 feet from the

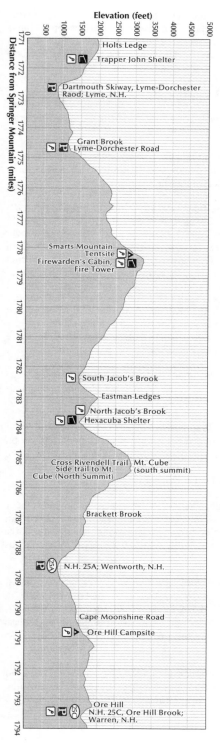

Elevation (feet)

Holts Ledge
Trapper John Shelter
Dartmouth Skiway, Lyme-Dorchester Raod; Lyme, N.H.
Grant Brook
Lyme-Dorchester Road
Smarts Mountain Tentsite
Firewarden's Cabin,
Fire Tower
South Jacob's Brook
Eastman Ledges
North Jacob's Brook
Hexacuba Shelter
Cross Rivendell Trail \ Mt. Cube
Side trail to Mt.   (south summit)
Cube (North Summit)
Brackett Brook
N.H. 25A; Wentworth, N.H.
Cape Moonshine Road
Ore Hill Campsite
Ore Hill
N.H. 25C, Ore Hill Brook;
Warren, N.H.

Distance from Springer Mountain (miles)

Trail and on Forest Service land. *Lodging:* Hanover Inn, (603) 643-4300, hanoverinn.com, rooms start at $369; 23 Six South St. Hotel; under $200 rooms found in Lebanon, 5 miles south of Hanover. *Groceries:* Hanover Food Co-op (long-term resupply), bulk and natural foods; Circle K, CVS Pharmacy, and Stinson's Village Store (all short-term resupply). *Restaurants:* Molly's Restaurant and Bar; Basecamp Café; Ramunto's Pizza; Lou's Bakery & Restaurant, B/L; Thayer Hall, the Dartmouth dining hall, B/L/D; Duende Tapas Bat; Boloco Burritos; Jewel of India; Dirt Cowboy Café; Dunks sports Grill; Murphy's. *Internet access:* Howe Public Library and DOC. *Outfitters:* In West Lebanon: EMS, (603) 298-7716; and L.L.Bean Outlet, (603) 298-6975—take "Orange" bus route, switch to "Red," and ask the driver to let you off at the Powerhouse Mall. In Lebanon Omer and Bob's Sport Shop; *Other services:* True Value Hardware, Coleman fuel, denatured alcohol; Richard Black Recreation Center, Lebanon and Park streets, shower and laundry for hikers M–F during summer; bookstores; dentist; doctor; hospital; movie theater; optician; banks with ATM; pharmacy; barber shop; Hanover Veterinary Clinic, (603) 643-3313, (603) 643-4829 after hours; Hanover Hot Tubs. *Bus service:* Advance Trans-it, advancetransit.com, is a local bus service, 6–6, M–F only. All routes are free; can be picked up outside the Hanover Inn (going north) or in front of Dartmouth Bookstore on Main St. (going south); offers transportation throughout Hanover and to White River Junction, VT (where there is an Amtrak station), Lebanon, and West Lebanon, with all major services. Bus schedules available in the bookstore. Bus service to Boston by Dartmouth Coach, (800) 637-0123, and Greyhound, (800) 231-2222. *Long-term parking:* Available for hikers in "A" lot, east of campus. Call parking operations, (603) 646-2204, for directions and to make arrangements. *Shuttles:* Stray Kat's A.T. Hiker Shuttle, (603) 252-8295, 24-hour notice please, commercially insured; Big Yellow Taxi, (603) 643-8294.

East (south)—2.0 miles to *Lodging:* Sunset Motor Inn, (603) 298-8721, on NH-10, on the "Orange" bus route, $99–$129 through May, $104–$123 Jun–Sep, no pets, no smoking, CATV, continental B, shuttle and laundry may be available if you ask the owners; Super 8 Motel in White River Junction, VT, (802) 295-7577, $110, on the "Orange" bus route; Days Inn in Lebanon, NH, (603) 448-5070, on the "Blue" bus route.

Velvet Rocks Shelter (1980s/2006)—Sleeps 6. Privy. On blue-blazed loop trail with access from the north and south. Water source is Ledyard Spring along the northern access trail. During dry periods, hikers may want to bring water from town.

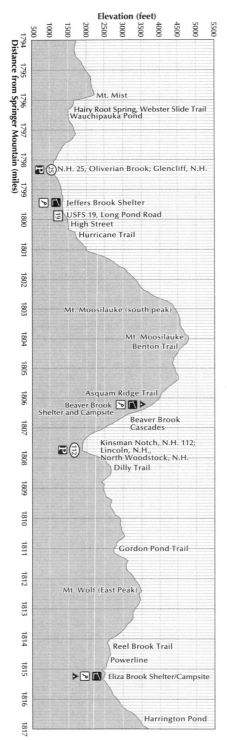

Elevation (feet)

Distance from Springer Mountain (miles)

Mt. Mist

Hairy Root Spring, Webster Slide Trail
Wauchipauka Pond

N.H. 25, Oliverian Brook; Glencliff, N.H.

Jeffers Brook Shelter
USFS 19, Long Pond Road
High Street
Hurricane Trail

Mt. Moosilauke (south peak)

Mt. Moosilauke
Benton Trail

Asquam Ridge Trail
Beaver Brook
Shelter and Campsite
Beaver Brook
Cascades

Kinsman Notch, N.H. 112;
Lincoln, N.H.,
North Woodstock, N.H.
Dilly Trail

Gordon Pond Trail

Mt. Wolf (East Peak)

Reel Brook Trail
Powerline
Eliza Brook Shelter/Campsite

Harrington Pond

Etna-Hanover Center Rd.—East 0.9 mile to *Groceries:* Etna General Store (limited resupply), (603) 643-1655, M–F 6 a.m.–7 p.m., Sa 8–7, Su 8–6, deli, snacks, sandwiches, cold drinks, fuels, beer, hot food weekdays, showers, restroom.

Moose Mountain Shelter (2004)—Sleeps 8. Privy. Log shelter built entirely with hand tools by DOC. Water is on the A.T. north of the shelter—follow loop trail to end.

Trapper John Shelter (1990s)—Sleeps 6. Privy uses an old chair. Tentsites. Water source is a brook 15 yards to the left of the shelter.

Lyme-Dorchester Rd.—West 3.2 miles to **Lyme, NH [P.O. ZIP 03768: M–F 7:45-12 & 1:30-5:15, Sa 7:45-12; (603) 795-4421].** *Lodging:*Dowd's Country Inn B&B, 9 Main St., (603) 795-4712, dowdscountryinn.com; $160D. One or two rooms are pet-friendly. Internet access and Wi-Fi. Weekend prices may vary depending on availability. Includes full country B and all NH taxes. Call from Trail for shuttle. *Restaurant:* Stella's Italian Kitchen & Market, L/D M–Sa, closed Su. *Other services:* Country store and deli (short-term resupply), open daily; banks with ATM; Lyme Home and Hardware store; veterinarian.

Smarts Mountain Tentsites—Cleared area for three tents. Privy. Water from Mike Murphy Spring (see next entry).

Smarts Mountain Firewarden's Cabin—Sleeps 8. Privy. Panoramic views from the abandoned firetower on Smarts Mountain summit. Water source is Mike Murphy Spring 0.2 mile north of cabin on blue-blazed Daniel Doan Trail.

Hexacuba Shelter (1989)—Sleeps 8. Tentsites. Privy (penta-style). Water source is an unreliable stream at the blue-blaze junction to the shelter. Alternative source is 0.3 mile south on the A.T. at North Jacobs Brook.

NH-25A—East 0.1 mile to lake with beach for swimming; 4.8 miles to **Wentworth, NH [P.O. ZIP 03282: M–F 9:30-12:30 &1:30-4:30, Sa 7:15-12; (603) 764-9444].** *Groceries:* Shawnee's General Store (long-term resupply), (603) 764-5553, M–Th 5 a.m.–7 p.m., F 5–9, Sa 6–7; Dollar General.

Cape Moonshine Rd.—East 1 mile to *Work for stay:* Dancing Bones Village, hipcamp.com, an independent community.

Ore Hill Campsite (2000)—Shelter burned down in late 2011; camping with privy (medieval-style). Water source is a spring on the path 100 yards in front of the former shelter foundation.

⚠ **NH-25C**—East 4 miles to **Warren, NH [P.O. ZIP 03279: M–F 7:30–9:30 & 3–5, Sa 7:30–12; (603) 764-5733]**. *Groceries:* Appleknockers General Store and Hardware, (603) 764-9496, open 5:30 a.m.–8 p.m. M–F, 7 a.m.–8 p.m. Sa–Su, deli, pizza, groceries, fuels, and camping supplies. *Restaurants:* Calamity Jane's, B/L/D, (603) 764-5288, closed W–Tu, M Th 8 a.m.–1:30 p.m., F 8 a.m.–7:30 p.m., Sa 8–3, Su 8–1; Ore Mill Bar & Grill, (603) 764-6069, call for hours; Moose Scoops ice cream, Wi-Fi, water for hikers. *Other services:* hardware store, doctor. See Warren's "Mystery Missile"—according to the *Boston Globe*, it is one of New England's eight most bizarre roadside attractions.

⚠ **NH-25**—East 0.4 mile to **Glencliff, NH [P.O. ZIP 03238: M–F 12–2, Sa 7–1; (603) 989-5154]**. This is a prudent mail drop for northbounders to pick up cold-weather gear before entering the high country of the White Mountains. *Hostel:* The Hikers Welcome Hostel, 1396 NH-25, (603) 989-0040 or (203) 605-9430, hikerswelcome.com; owned by John "Pack Rat" Robblee (AT '94, PCT '99, CDT '06) and Alyson Robblee; walk-ins only; no reservations needed; call for rates and services.

Oliverian Brook—The brook can be a difficult ford after rain. Be careful.

Jeffers Brook Shelter (1970s)—Sleeps 10. Privy. Located on a spur trail. Water source is Jeffers Brook, located in front of the shelter.

The White Mountains—One of the most impressive sections of the A.T., the Whites offer magnificent views with miles of above-treeline travel. Extra caution should be exercised while above treeline, due to rapidly changing weather and the lack of protection from it. Carry cold-weather gear, even in the middle of summer. Winter weather, including sleet, snow, and ice, is possible on these high ridges year-round. Each year, carelessness ends in death for a few visitors to the Whites. Pay close attention at Trail intersections. The Appalachian Mountain Club (AMC) maintains many trails that cross the A.T., and the A.T. route is commonly referred to on signs and in guidebooks by the name of the local trail it follows, such as "Franconia Ridge Trail." The tables beginning on page 207 show those names in the far right column. (And, to add to the confusion, sections above treeline from Mizpah Hut to Madison Hut are often marked with yellow blazes on rock cairns, to stand out in the snow.) When above treeline, stay on the Trail. This alpine zone is home to very fragile plants. One misplaced bootstep can destroy them.

Backcountry regulations—Each summer, AMC serves tens of thousands of backpackers and campers at its backcountry shelters and campsites in the White Mountain National Forest. To prevent the Whites from being "loved to death," the USFS, in conjunction with AMC and the New Hampshire state parks agency, established a strict set of backcountry rules for the White Mountains. Please follow the rules. Hikers should be aware of all pertinent rules and regulations pertaining to camping in these areas and should not be surprised if they are rigorously enforced by ridgerunners and rangers. This especially applies to those who choose to camp immediately adjacent to huts, shelters, caretaker campsites, and road crossings. Hikers who ignore posted warnings may well receive hefty tickets. You will encounter forest protection areas (FPAs), where camping and fires are prohibited. The following regulations apply in those areas: no camping above treeline (where trees are less than eight feet high); no camping within 0.25 mile of huts, shelters, or tentsites except at the facility itself; no camping within 200 feet of the Trail. Groups of 6 or more should contact AMC Group Notification System, outdoors.org, (603) 466-2721 x8150, so it can effectively manage all large groups that stay at AMC sites. AMC-managed sites can accommodate groups of up to 10. USFS parking fees are established throughout the Whites; be prepared to pay if you park at Forest Service trailheads.

Mt. Moosilauke—The north side of Mt. Moosilauke is slick, particularly in rain. Be careful! Sections use rebar, rock steps, and wooden blocks for footing. For northbounders, it is the first mountain above treeline. For southbounders, the meadow at the base of the southern side is the first pastureland they encounter on the A.T. From the summit, Franconia Ridge, as well as the rest of the Whites, can be seen to the northeast; the Green Mountains are visible to the west. Remnants of

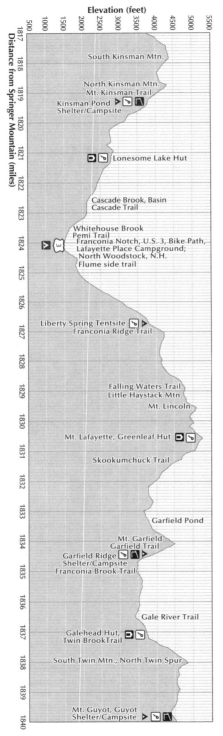

the 1860 Prospect House, a tourist spot that burned down in 1942, can still be seen at the summit. The Gorge Brook Trail leads 3.7 miles to the privately owned DOC Moosilauke Ravine Lodge.

Beaver Brook Shelter and Campsite (1980s)—Sleeps 10. Privy (composting). Completed by DOC and ALDHA members, site includes 2 small tent pads and a nice view of Franconia Ridge. Water source is Beaver Brook on the spur trail to the shelter.

Appalachian Mountain Club—AMC maintains 120 miles of the A.T. and many of the surrounding trails between Kinsman Notch and Grafton Notch in Maine; (603) 466-2721; outdoors.org.

AMC Tentsites, Shelters, and Campsites—"Tentsites" have designated tenting areas and platforms or pads. "Shelters" are three- or four-sided structures. "Campsites" have designated tenting areas and a shelter. See below for description of "huts," where reservations are required. Tentsites, shelters, and campsites are on a first-come, first-served basis. Caretakers are in residence at the following tentsites, shelters, and campsites, where an $15 overnight fee is charged: Kinsman Pond Campsite, Liberty Spring Tentsite, Garfield Ridge Campsite, 13 Falls Tentsite, Guyot Campsite, Ethan Pond Campsite, Nauman Tentsite, Imp Campsite, and Speck Pond Campsite (Maine). A caretaker works at those sites due to the locations' popularity and the fragility of their resources. The remaining tentsites, shelters, and campsites, except those operated by the Randolph Mountain Club, are available to backcountry travelers at no charge. *All AMC campsites now have metal bear boxes available while a caretaker is on site.*

The AMC Appalachian Trail Thru-Hiker Pass program is geared toward any northbounder, southbounder, flip-flopper, or section-hiker. This pass offers a discount through the AMC campsites in the White Mountains. After you spend your first night at one of their sites, every site after that is 50% off at $5 a night. With the purchase of the pass, you will receive a punch card for two free baked goods and a free bowl of soup redeemable at any AMC Hut, as well as 10% off any gear. This pass also is good for discounts at the Pinkham Notch Visitor Center and the Highland Center, as well as 30% off lodging and camping at the Mohican Outdoors Center in New Jersey.

A *work-for-stay option* is possible for thru-hikers at the tentsites and shelter sites that have caretakers. This is at the discretion of the caretaker and may not always be available. A maximum of two thru-hikers per night can be accommodated in that way at each site, and each will be expected to contribute an hour of work.

AMC Huts—These large, enclosed lodges sleep from 36 to 90 people. Rates range from $174 to 375 per person, depending on the day, AMC membership, and the hut. A crew ("croo") staffs these facilities during the full-service season. An overnight stay includes bunk space, pillow, blanket, bathroom privileges (no showers), and potable water. If you plan to stay three consecutive nights, a discounted package rate is available all summer. Rates for self-service seasons are significantly less ($60) than full-service seasons. Each hut has trained wilderness first-aid staff, and the facilities' crews give natural- and cultural-history evening programs. The huts also contain excellent libraries and displays on cultural and natural history.

If you plan to pay for a stay in one of the huts, make reservations, (603) 466-2727, especially for the weekends when bunk spaces fill quickly. Call AMC or check outdoors.org to verify the huts' opening and closing dates as well as perhaps-revised 2024 rates and make reservations. You may also be able to make a reservation by having a caretaker at one of the other huts or campsites radio ahead for you. The huts cater mainly to families and weekend hikers. AMC had wells drilled at all the huts, so you can look forward to water that meets state health standards. During the self-service season, a caretaker is at Lonesome Lake, Zealand, and Carter huts. Schedules vary from hut to hut; check individual listings for specific dates. Thru-hikers are given member rates as long as they mention that they are thru-hikers.

Work exchange at the huts—Thru-hikers can sometimes arrange with the croo to work off stays at the full- or self-service huts. Most huts can accommodate one or two working thru-hikers each night—except for Lakes of the Clouds Hut, which takes up to four thru-hikers—but availability of work is never guaranteed. Work-for-stay is at the discretion of the hut croo. When work is available, thru-hikers are asked to put in two hours either at night or in the morning; when work is not available, the full fee may be charged. Please give other thru-hikers a chance to work off their stay, and limit your use of the work-for-stay option to no more than three huts.

AMC Books and Maps: amcstore.outdoors.org/collections/books-maps

⋔ NH-112/Kinsman Notch—**East** 0.3 mile to Lost River Gorge and Boulder Caves, a series of streams, caves, and waterfalls owned by the Society for the Protection of New Hampshire Forests, lostrivergorge.com. Self-guided tour of gorge, ecology trail, and nature garden, $26 ($23 with reservation), Th–M.

East 4 miles to *Hostel:* The Notch Hostel, 324 Lost River Rd. (NH-112), North Woodstock, NH 03262 ; (603) 348-1483, notchhostel.com. Lodging in large farmhouse $45pp includes bunk, fresh linens, towel, shower, laundry, tentsite $30; Internet/Wi-Fi. Beer and wine OK in moderation; no liquor. Dogs $20 only in private rooms, by reservation. Call or text for reservations and shuttles.

East 5 miles to **North Woodstock, NH [P.O. ZIP 03262: M-F 9:30-12:30 & 1:30-4:30, Sa 9-12; (603) 745-8134]**, which also is accessible from Franconia Notch (below). See map. *Hostel:* Old Colony Ski Club, 12 Paradise Rd., North Woodstock, NH 03262, (603)-745-7753, oldcolonyskiclub.com. Recently opened to hikers, $25 one-year membership plus $25 per night includes shuttle to/from trailhead. Stay includes linens, towel, Wi-Fi, and kitchen privileges, mail drops accepted. Must be 21+, no tenting. *Lodging:* Woodstock Inn, (603) 745-3951 or (800) 321-3985, $167 weekdays, $214 weekends, includes B, nonsmoking rooms, 10 pet-friendly rooms, pool at Alpine Village, brew pub, restaurant B/L/D; Inn, (603) 745-2416, $109, game room, gas grills, picnic tables, deli, ATM, laundry. *Groceries:* Wayne's Market (long-term resupply), deli, craft-beer selection, and subs (grinders). *Restaurants:* See map. *Shuttles:* The Hiker Shuttle Connection, (603) 348-7422, 6:30 a.m.–midnight year-round.

East—6 miles to **Lincoln, NH** (see below).

Eliza Brook Shelter and Campsite (2010)—Shelter sleeps 8. Privy (composting). Bear box. Four hardened tent pads. Water source is Eliza Brook.

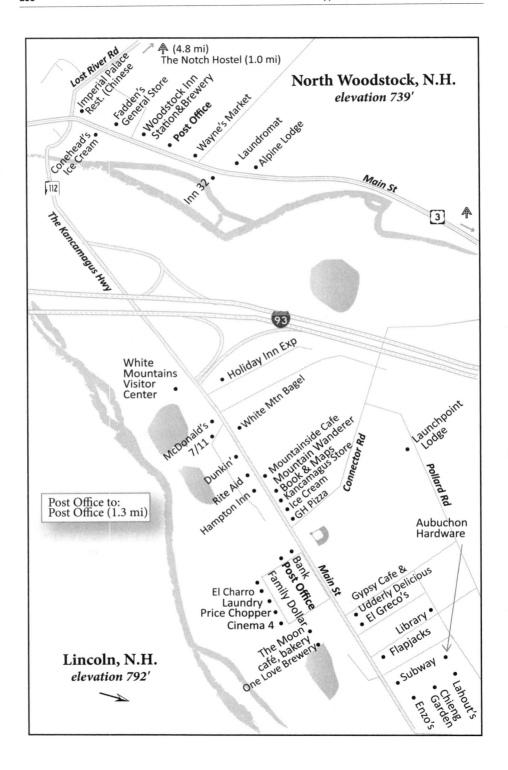

North Woodstock, N.H.
elevation 739'

⚑ (4.8 mi)
The Notch Hostel (1.0 mi)

Lost River Rd

Imperial Palace Rest. (Chinese

Fadden's General Store

Woodstock Inn Station&Brewery

Post Office

Wayne's Market

Laundromat

Alpine Lodge

Conehead's Ice Cream

112

Inn 32

Main St

3 ⚑

The Kancamagus Hwy

93

White Mountains Visitor Center

Holiday Inn Exp

White Mtn Bagel

McDonald's
7/11

Dunkin'

Rite Aid

Hampton Inn

Mountainside Cafe
Mountain Wanderer
Book & Maps
Kancamagus Store
Ice Cream
GH Pizza

Connector Rd

Launchpoint Lodge

Pollard Rd

Post Office to:
Post Office (1.3 mi)

Aubuchon Hardware

Bank
Post Office
Family Dollar

El Charro
Laundry
Price Chopper
Cinema 4

Main St

Gypsy Cafe &
Udderly Delicious
El Greco's

Library

The Moon
café, bakery
One Love Brewery

Flapjacks

Subway

Lincoln, N.H.
elevation 792'

Lahout's
Chieng Garden
Enzo's

Kinsman Pond Shelter and Campsite (2007)—Shelter sleeps 15. Privy (composting). Two single and two double tent platforms. Bear box. Overnight fee $15pp, caretaker on site. Water source is Kinsman Pond; treat your water.

Lonesome Lake Hut—This southernmost hut offers swimming in Lonesome Lake. Full-service May 30–Oct 19. Self-service Jan 1–May 26 and after Oct 23.

⚠ **I-93/US-3/Franconia Notch**—*Shuttle:* The Hiker Shuttle Connection, (603) 348-7422, 6 a.m.–2 a.m. year-round; from A.T. in Franconia Notch, follow Rt. 3 south to Exit 34A for shuttle pick-up on Rt. 3.

East on Franconia Bike Path: East 0.2 mile to Whitehouse Trail then 0.8 mile to AMC shuttle stop and hiker parking on US-3.

East—On Franconia Bike Path: East 1 mile to Flume Visitor Center, with snack bar/restaurant, and ice cream. Open daily early May to late Oct, 9–5. Call about mail drops; (603) 745-8391. Admission to see The Flume itself is $18.

East 5.8 miles to North Woodstock (see above).

East 7.3 miles to **Lincoln, NH [P.O. ZIP 03251: M–F 8-5, Sa 8-12; (603) 745-8133]**. See map. *Lodging:* Mt. Liberty Lodging, owners Mike and Susan Izard (A.T. '95), (603) 745-3600, mtlibertylodging. com, $75–$85d (seasonal), includes shuttle to/from Trail and to town, laundry $5, pool, and river. *Groceries:* Price Chopper (full-service grocery). *Outfitters:* Lahout's Summit Shop, (603) 745-2882, full-service outfitter, Coleman and alcohol by the ounce; Art's Outdoor Outfitter.

West 2.1 miles to *Camping:* Lafayette Campground, (603) 823-9513, with tentsites. Call for rates, coin-operated hot showers $1, store (short-term resupply), Coleman fuel by the quart, outside soda vending machine. Park rangers hold packages mailed to Franconia Notch State Park, Lafayette Place Campground, Franconia, NH 03580. Write the date you expect to arrive on the package. Open mid-May to Columbus Day. Campground is usually filled by noon on weekends. AMC shuttle stop.

West 8 miles to Franconia; I-93 North at NH-18. *Lodging:* Gale River Motel, 1 Main St., Franconia, NH 03580, (603) 823-5655 or (800) 255-7989, galerivermotel.com, info@galerivermotel .com, $125–$155 Jun–Sep, $135–$250 foliage season, $125–$1 in between and ski season, shuttle to and from Trail when available, seasonal pool, hot tub, Internet access, laundry, call ahead for mail drops; White Mountain Best Western, $145–$170, indoor pool, hot tub, Internet access. *Groceries:* Mac's Market (long-term supply). *Internet access:* library. *Other services:* pizza, restaurant, bank, ATM, Concord Coach bus service.

Liberty Springs Tentsite—Privy (composting). Bear box. Seven single and three double tent platforms. Overnight fee $15pp, caretaker on site. Water source is the spring on the A.T.

Franconia Ridge—In any kind of weather, this ridge walk will leave you awestruck. Beautiful views from the summit of Mt. Liberty can be reached from the A.T. south 0.3 mile on Franconia Ridge Trail.

Greenleaf Hut—Visible from the summit of Mt. Lafayette, it is 1.1 miles on the Greenleaf Trail to the hut. Self-service May 16–26. Full service May 30–Oct 19.

Garfield Ridge Shelter and Campsite (2011)—Shelter sleeps 12. Privy (composting). Two single and five double tent platforms. Bear box. Overnight fee $15pp, caretaker on site. Water source is a spring at the junction to the campsite.

Galehead Hut—Rebuilt 1999–2000, with wheelchair-accessible design. Full service May 30–Oct 19.

Guyot Shelter and Campsite (1977)—Shelter sleeps 12. Privy (composting). Bear box. Four single and two double tent platforms. Bear box. Located 0.8 mile east on Bondcliff Trail. Overnight fee $15pp, caretaker on site. Water source is a spring at the campsite.

Zealand Falls Hut—Next to beautiful falls. Full service May 30–Oct 19. Self-service Jan 1–May 26 and after Oct 23.

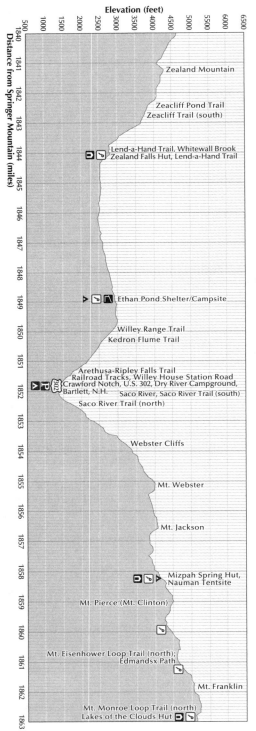

Ethan Pond Shelter and Campsite (1957)— Shelter sleeps 10. Privy (composting). Three single and two double tent platforms. Bear box. Overnight fee $15pp, caretaker on site. Water source is the inlet brook to the pond.

US-302/Crawford Notch—East 1.8 miles to *Camping:* Dry River Campground, (603) 374-2272, $35d, tent-sites and 3 shelters available ($40/shelter); dogs welcome, coin laundry, and showers 25¢. Trail access to A.T. Mail drops accepted at P.O. Box 177, Twin Mountain, NH 03595 (Crawford Notch State Park). *Shuttle:* AMC shuttle stop at Webster Cliff/A.T. Trailhead.

East 3 miles to *Camping:* Crawford Notch Campground, crawfordnotch.com, (603) 374-2779; coin-operated shower for guests; dogs; campsites $48–$52 (2-night minimum), additional fee for up to 4; cabins $110 for up to 4 people; yurt $100; laundry for overnight guests only; limited supplies.

East 10 miles to the small town of **Bartlett, NH [P.O. ZIP 03812: M–F 8:30–10:30 & 11:30–3:30, Sa 8:30–12; (603) 374-2351]**.

West 1 mile to the Willey House (Crawford Notch State Park).

West 3.7 miles to *Lodging:* AMC's Highland Center, Route 302, Bretton Woods, NH 03575; (603) 278-4453, outdoors.org, limited hiker supplies, AYCE B $15, 6:30–10; trail L $15, 10–4; 4-course D $30, reserve seat by 6; bunk room in lodge $193/289/308 2/4/6 bunk room, cost per room, includes B/D; private room in lodge from $322-380pp, includes B/D; Shapleigh Bunkhouse, from $63pp includes bunk, shower, towel, and B. Facilities generally are for overnight guests only. Mail drops accepted, UPS only. *Shuttle:* AMC shuttle stop. *Other services:* Showers at the Crawford Notch Depot, 9–4 Memorial Day–Columbus Day.

Presidential Range—The highest part of the Trail in New Hampshire, with 25 miles of ridge-walking between Crawford Notch and Pinkham Notch, most of which is above treeline (about 4,400 feet). The A.T. skirts many peaks, which can be reached by short side trails leading to, and often over, the summits.

Saco River Trail—connects the Willey House site to Dry River Campground.

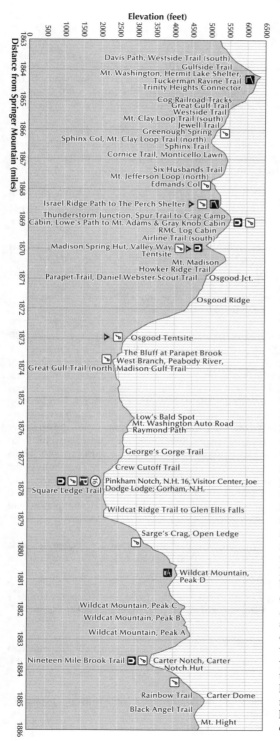

Elevation (feet)

Distance from Springer Mountain (miles)

Davis Path, Westside Trail (south)
Gulfside Trail
Mt. Washington, Hermit Lake Shelter,
Tuckerman Ravine Trail
Trinity Heights Connector
Cog Railroad Tracks
Great Gulf Trail
Westside Trail
Mt. Clay Loop Trail (south)
Jewell Trail
Greenough Spring
Sphinx Col, Mt. Clay Loop Trail (north)
Sphinx Trail
Cornice Trail, Monticello Lawn
Six Husbands Trail
Mt. Jefferson Loop (north)
Edmands Col
Israel Ridge Path to The Perch Shelter
Thunderstorm Junction, Spur Trail to Crag Camp
Cabin, Lowe's Path to Mt. Adams & Gray Knob Cabin
RMC Log Cabin
Airline Trail (south)
Madison Spring Hut, Valley Way
Tentsite
Mt. Madison
Howker Ridge Trail
Parapet Trail, Daniel Webster Scout Trail   Osgood Jct.

Osgood Ridge

Osgood Tentsite

The Bluff at Parapet Brook
West Branch, Peabody River,
Great Gulf Trail (north) Madison Gulf Trail

Low's Bald Spot
Mt. Washington Auto Road
Raymond Path

George's Gorge Trail

Crew Cutoff Trail
Pinkham Notch, N.H. 16, Visitor Center, Joe
Square Ledge Trail Dodge Lodge; Gorham, N.H.

Wildcat Ridge Trail to Glen Ellis Falls

Sarge's Crag, Open Ledge

Wildcat Mountain,
Peak D

Wildcat Mountain, Peak C
Wildcat Mountain, Peak B
Wildcat Mountain, Peak A

Nineteen Mile Brook Trail   Carter Notch, Carter
Notch Hut

Rainbow Trail   Carter Dome
Black Angel Trail
Mt. Hight

Mizpah Spring Hut and Nauman Tentsite—Self-service May 16–26; full-service May 30–Oct 19. Tentsite, five single and three double tent platforms. Composting privy. Bear box. Overnight fee $15pp. Water source for tentsite is a stream or potable water from hut (if open).

Lakes of the Clouds Hut—Constructed in 1915 at an elevation of 5,050 feet, the highest, largest, and most popular hut. Full-service May 30–Sep 22, with no self-service operation. "The Dungeon," a small basement shelter, is available to thru-hikers for $15, with access to hut restroom and the common area; it sleeps only 6, first-come/first-served, no reservations. "The Dungeon" is an emergency-only shelter when the hut is closed; must not be used as a destination.

Mt. Washington Auto Road/Mt. Washington—The highest peak in the Northeast (6,288 feet). Since it is also accessible by the Auto Road and a cog railroad, there are many tourist services. (Note: In 2007, 8 hikers were arrested for mooning said cog railroad; take heed.) The cog railroad can provide one-way rides down, if space is available, for $86pp. The summit building is operated by the New Hampshire Division of Parks and Recreation and houses Mt. Washington Observatory, mountwashington.org; "Extreme Mt. Washington" ($2 admission); a snack bar; a post office. The state park is open daily 8–8 early May–early Oct, weather permitting. A hiker room is downstairs, with a table, restroom, and a space to rest. (Absolutely no overnight stays are allowed.) Over the years, many buildings have come and gone on the summit, including a 94-bedroom hotel completed in 1873 and destroyed by fire in 1908. The summit is under cloud cover about 55 percent of the time. Average summertime high is 52 degrees, and the average wintertime high is 15 degrees. On April 12, 1934, an on-land wind speed of 231 mph was recorded. If you see a staff meteorologist, ask about the "Century Club." The upper plateau is home to large grassy areas, strewn with rocks but known as "lawns." These lawns hold many species of plants and animals otherwise found only on high mountain peaks and in tundra areas hundreds of miles to the north. Mt. Washington Stage offers a one-way shuttle between the summit and Pinkham Notch Visitor Center for $55 hikers, $30 dogs ($75 after 4 p.m.); make arrangements on the summit or at Pinkham Notch.

Mt. Washington, NH [P.O. ZIP 03589: M–Sa 10–4; (603) 846-5570]—The post office in the summit building is *not* recommended as a mail drop. Its hours are limited, and it caters to those who visit the summit and desire to have the distinguished Mt. Washington postmark; since there is little space for storing mail drops, they may be redirected to other New Hampshire post offices, well off the Trail.
   East 8 miles via Auto Road to NH-16.

Tuckerman Ravine Trail—A steep, 4.2-mile route from Mt. Washington to Pinkham Notch. In bad weather, you may wish to use this trail to get below treeline and bypass the exposed northern loop of the Presidential Range, but this precarious route is no picnic in icy conditions.

Hermit Lake Shelters—At the base of the Tuckerman Ravine bowl, 2 miles downhill, with steep rock- and boulder-scrambling from the summit; 8 lean-tos, 3 tent platforms, $15pp; pets are not permitted overnight in the shelters; caretaker year-round.

Edmands Col—Just down to the east in the col is a reliable spring and the site of the former Edmands Col emergency shelter. Also, look for a bronze tablet in memory of J. Rayner Edmands, who was instrumental in the construction of most of the graded paths through the northern Presidentials.

Randolph Mountain Club—RMC maintains the 2.2 miles from Edmands Col north of Mt. Washington to Madison Spring Hut; randolphmountainclub.org.

Randolph Mountain Club (RMC) Cabins and Shelters—Randolph Mountain Club was named an A.T. maintaining club by ATC in 2010. In addition to the 2.2 miles of the A.T. north of Edmands Col, RMC maintains a network of 100 miles of hiking trails, principally on the northern slopes of Mounts Madison, Adams, and Jefferson in the Presidential Range of the White Mountain National Forest and on the Crescent Range in the town of Randolph. The RMC maintains several cabins and shelters below treeline in the Presidential Range that are often used by A.T. hikers seeking shelter from the exposed ridgeline. Crag Camp and Gray Knob are cabins. The Perch is a lean-to. All camps are available to the public on a first-come, first-served basis. If a site is full, the caretaker may ask visitors to move to another RMC facility, if space is available. Groups are limited to 10. To maintain serenity, cellular phones may not be used at any of the camps. Gas stoves at both cabins are available to the public; at all other times, users must bring their own stoves. Year-round, the weather is far harsher and colder here than "below the notches." RMC relies on visitors to carry out their trash and help keep the cabin and woods clean. To support the caretakers' wages and maintain the camps, fees are charged on a per-night basis. If the caretaker is absent, please mail fees to: Treasurer, RMC, Randolph, NH 03570.

RMC The Perch (1948)—Shelter sleeps 8. Privy. Four tent platforms, $15pp fee. Water source is crossed en route to the shelter. Accessible via Israel Ridge Trail from Mt. Jefferson at Edmands Col, 0.9 mile and a 600-foot descent from the A.T.

RMC Crag Camp Cabin (1909/1993)— Sleeps 20. Water is available from a spring, approximately 0.25 mile west on the Gray Knob Trail. Located 1.1 miles and 1,200-foot descent from the A.T. Caretaker in Jul–Aug; $50pp.

RMC Gray Knob Cabin (1905/1989)—Sleeps 15. Water from a spring, approximately 0.25 mile east on Gray Knob Trail. Resident caretaker year-round; $50pp. Heated in winter; 1.2 miles and 1,200-foot descent from A.T.

Madison Spring Hut—Located in a col 0.5 mile south of the summit of Mt. Madison. Full service May 30–Sep 29, with no self-service operation.

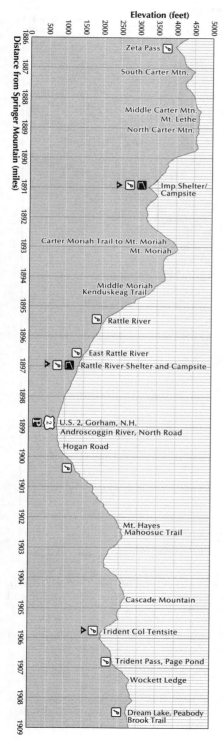

Elevation (feet)

Distance from Springer Mountain (miles)

Zeta Pass

South Carter Mtn.

Middle Carter Mtn.
Mt. Lethe
North Carter Mtn.

Imp Shelter/
Campsite

Carter Moriah Trail to Mt. Moriah
Mt. Moriah

Middle Moriah
Kenduskeag Trail

Rattle River

East Rattle River
Rattle River Shelter and Campsite

U.S. 2, Gorham, N.H.
Androscoggin River, North Road

Hogan Road

Mt. Hayes
Mahoosuc Trail

Cascade Mountain

Trident Col Tentsite

Trident Pass, Page Pond

Wockett Ledge

Dream Lake, Peabody
Brook Trail

Valley Way and Osgood Tentsites—These two primitive, no-fee U.S. Forest Service tentsites, below treeline on Mt. Madison, are often used by hikers starting or finishing the traverse of the Presidential Range. Valley Way Tentsite is off the A.T., 0.6 mile west of Madison Springs Hut, with two large tent platforms and a privy. Osgood Tentsite is 3 miles north of the hut, along the A.T., and has three tentsites, privy, and spring. Bear box.

NH-16/Pinkham Notch—Pinkham Notch Visitor Center; front desk, (603) 466-2721. AMC's New Hampshire headquarters, located on the A.T., offers a store with limited hiker supplies, restroom, coin-operated showers (open 24 hours), AMC shuttle stop, and Concord Coach bus service (see below). The center holds packages sent to AMC Visitor Center, c/o Front Desk, NH-16, Gorham, NH 03581. *Restaurant:* Cafeteria with AYCE $15 B, deli L (not AYCE) 9:30–4, trail L $13, $30 D (thru-hikers get member rates). *Lodging:* Joe Dodge Lodge, (603) 466-2727, $198–$238 includes B/D. Prices can change; contact AMC for the most current rates.
    East 13–16 miles to Intervale, NH *Outfitter:* Ragged Mountain Equipment, (603) 356-3042, open daily, backpacking gear and repair service. *Lodging:* Cranmore Mountain Lodge, 859 Kearsage Rd., North Conway, NH 03860; (603) 356-2044, $174d includes B, seasonal heated pool, spa, mail drops accepted. *Other services:* Peter Limmer & Sons Shop, (603) 356-5378, located on NH-16A, home of legendary hand-made hiking boots, will repair many brands of boots and hiking gear with priority to thru-hikers; closed Su–M.
    East 18 miles to North Conway, NH, a tourist town with most major services, including several outfitters, a supermarket, cobbler, coin laundry, bank, ATM, hospital, veterinarian, pharmacy, one-hour photo, movie theater, hotels, and restaurants.
    West 1 mile to the Wildcat Mountain Chairlift, daily mid-Jun to mid-Sep, 10–4:45 (fall hours, Sa–Su 10–5), offers rides to and from the A.T. on the top of Wildcat Mountain; $17 round-trip.
    West 11 miles to Gorham, NH (see below).

Concord Coach Bus Service—Service between Boston and Pinkham Notch, as well as Gorham, Berlin, and Conway, (800) 639-3317, concordcoachlines.com. Departs Pinkham Notch daily at 8:07 a.m. and arrives at Boston South Station at 12:20 p.m. The bus to Pinkham Notch departs Boston at 3:25 p.m. and arrives at Pinkham Notch at 8:10 p.m. One-way, $39; round-trip, $73.

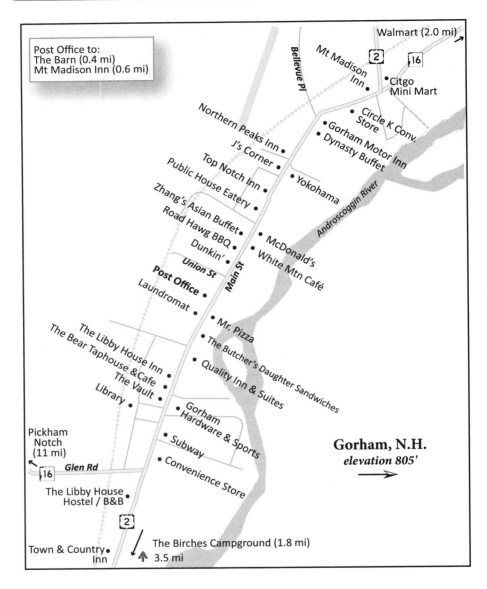

Post Office to:
The Barn (0.4 mi)
Mt Madison Inn (0.6 mi)

Walmart (2.0 mi)

Gorham, N.H.
elevation 805'

Carter Notch Hut—The northernmost hut, located on the banks of two small lakes in Carter Notch. It is the original hut, built in 1914. Full-service May 30–Oct 19; self-service Jan 1–May 26 and after Oct 23.

Imp Shelter and Campsite (1981)—Shelter sleeps 16. Privy (composting). Four single, one double tent platform. Bear box. Overnight fee $15pp, caretaker on site. Water is stream near shelter.

Rattle River Shelter (1980s)—Sleeps 8. Privy. Shelter built by USFS. Water source is Rattle River.

US-2—West 1.8 miles to *Hostel:*Located next to A.T., The Birches Loft at White Birches Camping Park, owners Bob and Janet Langlands, 218 State Rt. 2, Shelburne, NH 03581; (603) 466-2022, whitebirchescamping.com, whitebirch131@gmail.com; May 1–end of Oct, tent sites $26–$38 per

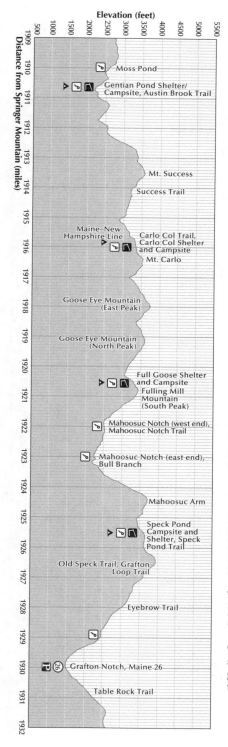

Elevation (feet)

Distance from Springer Mountain (miles)

Moss Pond

Gentian Pond Shelter/
Campsite, Austin Brook Trail

Mt. Success

Success Trail

Maine–New
Hampshire Line

Carlo Col Trail,
Carlo Col Shelter
and Campsite

Mt. Carlo

Goose Eye Mountain
(East Peak)

Goose Eye Mountain
(North Peak)

Full Goose Shelter
and Campsite

Fulling Mill
Mountain
(South Peak)

Mahoosuc Notch (west end),
Mahoosuc Notch Trail

Mahoosuc Notch (east end),
Bull Branch

Mahoosuc Arm

Speck Pond
Campsite and
Shelter, Speck
Pond Trail

Old Speck Trail, Grafton
Loop Trail

Eyebrow Trail

Grafton Notch, Maine 26

Table Rock Trail

night, cabins and RV trailers $89–$109; swimming pool.

West 3.6 miles to **Gorham, NH [P.O. ZIP 03581: M–F 8:30–5, Sa 8:30–12; (603) 466-2182]**. The postmaster requests that all packages include your legal name and ETA; use bold letters/colors and have ID; can knock on door inside lobby to pick up mail drops after hours. *Hostel:* The Barn Hostel, 55 Main St., (603) 466-2271, thelibbyhouse@gmail.com. Libby House B&B offers rooms in the barn hostel $35pp, tent and hammock $25; Wi-Fi, full kitchen, TV, shower, shuttles, no pets, $5 laundry; free mail drops for guests ($15 non-guests). *Lodging:* Libby House B&B, (603) 466-2271 or (603) 723-6129, $109–$135, includes continental B, Wi-Fi; Rodeway Inn, (603) 466-3312, starts at $119; Northern Peaks, (603) 466-2288, $81/room (single queen/microwave/minifridge), dogs welcome ($15), a/c, hot tub, hiker box, mail drops for guests; Town & Country Inn, US-2, (603) 466-3315, $151, pets welcome ($25), mail drops accepted; Quality Inn, 130 Main St., $139. *Groceries:* Super Walmart (long-term resupply) located 2 miles north of town on NH-16. *Restaurants:* Mr. Pizza, J's Corner, and various fast-food options. *Outfitter:* Gorham Hardware/Sports Center, (603) 466-2312, boots and hiker gear, Coleman fuel and alcohol by the ounce. *Internet access:* public library, M, W, F, 10–7, Tu, Th 10–8, closed weekends, located near railroad, nominal fee. *Other services:* Trail Angels Hiker Services, (978) 855-9227, trailangelshikerservices.com, shuttles, mail drops, guide service, etc.; coin laundry; bank with ATM; dentist; free concerts on the common Tu evenings; TriCounty CAP Transit, local Berlin–Gorham shuttle bus, (888) 997-2020, tccap.org, no Su service, stops at Walmart.

West 8 miles to small city of Berlin, NH, and the Androscoggin Valley Hospital.

⚠ North Rd/Hogan Rd Junction—East 1.8 miles to *Hostel:* The Mahoosic, 130 North Rd, Shelburne, NH 03581, (603) 466-2190. Bunkbeds $45, B, Wi-Fi, Lockers, grill, fridge, picnic tables, accepts packages for guests, bicycles, showers $5 for non-guests.

Trident Col Tentsite—Four tent pads. Privy (composting). Bear box. Water source is an intermittent spring on a side trail.

Gentian Pond Shelter and Campsite (1974)—Shelter sleeps 14. Privy (composting). Bear box. Three single and one double tent platform. Water source is the inlet brook of Gentian Pond.

Maine

Miles from Springer	Miles to Next Point	Features	Services	Elev	Miles from Katahdin	MAP
1,915.4	0.6	New Hampshire–Maine State Line		2,972'	282.0	
1,916.0	0.4	Carlo Col Trail Jct. to **Carlo Col Shelter** and **Campsite** (W–0.3m), 5.8mS; 4.8mN West–2.6m to Success Pond Road	S, C, w R, P	2,945'	281.4	
1,916.4	1.4	Mt. Carlo		3,565'	281.0	
1,917.8	0.4	Goose Eye Trail to Goose Eye Mountain (West Peak) (W–0.1m) West–3.2m to Success Pond Road	 R, P	3,854'	279.6	
1,918.2	1.3	Goose Eye Mountain (East Peak)		3,794'	279.2	
1,919.5	1.0	Goose Eye Mountain (North Peak)		3,675'	277.9	
1,920.5	0.3	**Full Goose Shelter** and **Campsite**, 4.8mS; 5.0mN	S, C, w	3,030'	276.9	
1,920.8	1.2	Fulling Mill Mountain (South Peak)		3,395'	276.6	
1,922.0	1.0	Mahoosuc Notch Trail; Mahoosuc Notch (west end) West–2.5m to Success Pond Road	w R, P	2,400'	275.4	
1,923.0	1.5	Mahoosuc Notch (east end), Bull Branch	C, w	2,150'	274.4	
1,924.5	0.6	Mahoosuc Arm Summit, Joe May Cut-off Trail Jct.		3,765'	272.9	
1,925.1	0.3	Speck Pond Brook: outlet of Speck Pond		3,430'	272.3	
1,925.4	1.1	Speck Pond Trail, +AMC **Speck Pond Shelter** and **Campsite** (W–0.1m): last water for the next 3.5 miles north, 5.0mS; 6.9mN West–3.6m to Success Pond Road	S, C, w R, P	3,500'	272.0	
1,926.5	1.5	Old Speck Trail and Grafton Loop Trail Junction East–0.3m to summit and observation tower		3,985'	270.9	
1,928.0	0.9	Eyebrow Trail: upper junction		2,480'	269.4	
1,928.9	1.0	Brook: last water for the next 3.5 miles south	w	2,500'	268.5	
1,929.9	0.1	Eyebrow Trail: lower junction		1,530'	267.5	
1,930.0	0.8	Grafton Notch, ME-26 East–5m to Grafton Notch Campground East–13m to Stony Brook Recreation & Camping	R, P C C, g, M, sh, f	1,495'	267.4	
1,930.8	1.5	Table Rock Trail: upper junction		2,125'	266.6	
1,932.3	0.8	**Baldpate Lean-to**, 6.9mS; 3.5mN	S, w	2,645'	265.1	
1,933.1	0.9	Baldpate Mountain (West Peak)		3,662'	264.3	
1,934.0	0.5	Baldpate Mountain (East Peak); Grafton Loop Trail Junction		3,812'	263.4	
1,934.5	1.3	Little Baldpate Mountain		3,442'	262.9	
1,935.8	0.5	**Frye Notch Lean-to**, Frye Brook: 3.5mS; 10.5mN	S, w	2,280'	261.6	
1,936.3	3.2	Surplus Mountain: highpoint on NE ridge		2,875'	261.1	
1,939.5	0.8	Dunn Notch and Falls: ford West Branch Ellis River	w	1,350'	257.9	
1,940.3	1.8	East B Hill Road East–8m to **Andover, ME, P.O. 04216** East–11m to East Andover, ME; "The Cabin"	R, P, C G, L, M, f H	1,485'	257.1	
1,942.1	0.1	Burroughs Brook: ford, outlet of Surplus Pond	w	2,050'	255.3	
1,942.2	2.8	Gravel logging road	R	2,050'	255.2	

MATC: Maine Map 7

Miles from Springer	Miles to Next Point	Features	Services	Elev	Miles from Katahdin	M A P
1,945.0	1.3	Wyman Mountain *(North Peak)*		2,945'	252.4	
1,946.3	1.4	**Hall Mountain Lean-to**, *10.5mS; 12.8mN*	S, w	2,635'	251.1	
1,947.7	0.9	Sawyer Notch, Sawyer Brook: *ford*	w	1,095'	249.7	
1,948.6	1.8	Moody Mountain		2,440'	248.8	
1,950.4	2.8	South Arm Road, Black Brook, *ford, privy* *East-9m to* **Andover, ME, P.O. 04216** *East-12m to* East Andover, ME; "The Cabin" *West-4.5m to* South Arm Campground	R, P, C, w H, G, L, M, f H C, G, cl, sh	1,410'	247.0	MATC: Maine Map 7
1,953.2	3.2	Old Blue Mountain		3,600'	244.2	
1,956.4	1.0	Bemis Stream Trail		3,350'	241.0	
1,957.4	1.7	Bemis Mountain *(West Peak)*		3,592'	240.0	
1,959.1	1.5	**Bemis Mountain Lean-to**, *12.8mS; 8.3mN*	S, w	2,790'	238.3	
1,960.6	2.1	Bemis Range *(Second Peak): open ledges*		2,915'	236.8	
1,962.7	0.2	Gravel road: *former rail bed*	R	1,550'	234.7	
1,962.9	0.8	Bemis Stream: *ford*	w	1,495'	234.5	
1,963.7	0.8	ME-17: *view of Mooselookmeguntic Lake* *West-11m to* **Oquossoc, ME, P.O. 04964**	R, P G, M, f	2,200'	233.7	
1,964.5	0.8	Spruce Mountain		2,530'	232.9	
1,965.3	1.8	Moxie Pond	w	2,400'	232.1	
1,967.1	0.3	Long Pond: *sandy beach*	w	2,330'	230.3	
1,967.4	0.5	**Sabbath Day Pond Lean-to**, *8.3mS; 11.2mN*	S, w	2,390'	230.0	
1,967.9	4.1	Houghton Fire Road		2,300'	229.5	
1,972.0	1.2	Little Swift River Pond Campsite: *piped spring*	C, w	2,460'	225.4	
1,973.2	1.5	Chandler Mill Stream: *outlet of boreal bog*	w	2,150'	224.2	
1,974.7	2.1	South Pond	w	2,174'	222.7	
1,976.8	0.1	ME-4 *West-9m to* **Rangeley, ME, P.O. 04970**	R, P H, G, L, M, O, D, cl, f	1,700'	220.6	
1,976.9	0.6	Sandy River: *footbridge*	w	1,595'	220.5	
1,977.5	1.1	Gravel road		1,750'	219.9	MATC: Maine Map 6
1,978.6	0.9	**Piazza Rock Lean-to**, *11.2mS; 8.9mN*	S, C, w	2,080'	218.8	
1,979.5	0.4	Ethel Pond	w	2,200'	217.9	
1,979.9	0.6	Saddleback Stream	w	2,350'	217.5	
1,980.5	0.2	Moose and Deer Pond outlet near Eddy Pond: *last water for the next 6 miles north*	w	2,616'	216.9	
1,980.7	0.8	Gravel logging road		2,625'	216.7	
1,981.5	1.0	Treeline: *above treeline for the next 2.9 miles north*		3,700'	215.9	
1,982.5	0.6	Saddleback Mountain		4,120'	214.9	
1,983.1	1.0	Berry Pickers Trail			214.3	
1,984.1	0.3	The Horn		4,041'	213.3	
1,984.4	0.4	Treeline: *above treeline for the next 2.9 miles south*		3,620'	213.0	
1,984.8	1.3	Redington Stream Campsite *(W-0.2m spring)*	C, w	3,170'	212.6	
1,986.1	0.4	Saddleback Junior: *open summit*		3,655'	211.3	
1,986.5	1.0	Brook: *last water for the next 6 miles south*	w	3,200'	210.9	
1,987.5	2.7	**Poplar Ridge Lean-to**, *8.9mS; 8mN*	S, w	2,920'	209.9	
1,990.2	0.1	Orbeton Stream: *ford*	w	1,550'	207.2	

Miles from Springer	Miles to Next Point	Features	Services	Elev	Miles from Katahdin	M A P
1,990.3	0.7	Gravel road: *old rail bed; northbound turn Trail E–100 ft. to reenter woods*		1,650'	207.1	
1,991.0	0.7	Sluice Brook	w	2,145'	206.4	
1,991.7	0.5	Logging road		2,300'	205.7	
1,992.2	1.1	Logging road: *Perham Stream nearby*	w	2,300'	205.2	
1,993.3	1.1	Lone Mountain		3,280'	204.1	
1,994.4	1.1	Mt. Abraham Trail *(E–1.7m to summit; 4,050')*		3,184'	203.0	
1,995.5	0.8	**Spaulding Mountain Lean-to**, *8mS; 18.6mN*	S, w	3,140'	201.9	
1,996.3	0.7	Trail to Spaulding Mountain *(E–0.1m to summit)*		4,010'	201.1	
1,997.0	1.4	Bronze plaque *1937 completion of the final two miles of the original A.T.*		3,500'	200.4	MATC: Maine Map 6
1,998.4	2.2	Sugarloaf Mountain Trail *(E–0.3m spring; 0.6m to summit)*	w	3,540'	199.0	
2,000.6	0.1	South Branch Carrabassett River: *ford*	w	2,100'	196.8	
2,000.7	1.0	Caribou Valley Road: *gravel (E–4.3m ME-27)*	R, P	2,220'	196.7	
2,001.7	1.1	Crocker Cirque Campsite *(E–0.2m): spring*	C, w	2,710'	195.7	
2,002.8	1.0	South Crocker Mountain *(W–150 ft. to summit)*		4,040'	194.6	
2,003.8	1.0	North Crocker Mountain		4,228'	193.6	
2,004.8	2.1	Stream	w	3,300'	192.6	
2,006.9	2.1	Stream: *in stand of large white birch trees*	w	2,500'	190.5	
2,009.0	0.8	ME-27 *East–2m to Mountainside Grocers* *East–18m to Kingfield, ME* *West–5m to **Stratton, ME, P.O. 04982***	R, P G H, G, L, M, D H, G, L, M, cl, f	1,450'	188.4	
2,009.8	0.2	Stratton Brook Pond Road	R, P	1,250'	187.6	
2,010.0	0.9	Stratton Brook: *footbridge*	w	1,230'	187.4	
2,010.9	1.3	Cranberry Stream Campsite	C, w	1,350'	186.5	
2,012.2	1.7	Bigelow Range Trail, Cranberry Pond *(W–0.2m stream)*	w	2,400'	185.2	
2,013.9	0.2	Horns Pond Trail		3,200'	183.5	
2,014.1	0.3	**Horns Pond Lean-tos**, *18.6mS; 10.2mN*	S, C, w	3,160'	183.3	
2,014.4	0.1	Spring	w	3,400'	183.0	
2,014.5	0.1	Side trail to North Horn *(W–0.2m summit)*		3,792'	182.9	
2,014.6	2.1	South Horn		3,831'	182.8	MATC: Maine Map 5
2,016.7	0.3	Bigelow Mountain *(West Peak)*		4,145'	180.7	
2,017.0	0.2	Bigelow Col, Fire Warden's Trail, Avery Memorial Campsite	C, w	3,850'	180.4	
2,017.2	0.2	Spring	w	3,900'	180.2	
2,017.4	1.9	Bigelow Mountain; Avery Peak		4,090'	180.0	
2,019.3	0.1	Safford Brook Trail		2,260'	178.1	
2,019.4	1.8	Safford Notch and campsite *(E–0.3m)*	C, w	2,230'	178.0	
2,021.2	1.4	Little Bigelow Mountain *(west end)*		3,035'	176.2	
2,022.6	1.7	Little Bigelow Mountain *(east end)*		3,010'	174.8	
2,024.3	1.5	**Little Bigelow Lean-to**, *10.2mS; 7.7mN*	S, C, w	1,760'	173.1	
2,025.8	0.1	East Flagstaff Road	R	1,200'	171.6	
2,025.9	1.3	Bog Brook Road, Flagstaff Lake *(W–0.2m): inlet*	R, P, w	1,150'	171.5	

Miles from Springer	Miles to Next Point	Features	Services	Elev	Miles from Katahdin	MAP
2,027.2	1.3	Flagstaff Lake: *privy*	C, w	1,210'	170.2	
2,028.5	0.1	Long Falls Dam Road	R, P	1,225'	168.9	
2,028.6	0.3	Jerome Brook	w	1,300'	168.8	
2,028.9	1.3	Logging road: *gravel*		1,400'	168.5	
2,030.2	0.8	Roundtop Mountain		1,760'	167.2	
2,031.0	0.3	Stream	w	1,360'	166.4	
2,031.3	0.7	West Carry Pond *(west side)*	w	1,320'	166.1	
2,032.0	0.7	**West Carry Pond Lean-to**, *7.7mS; 10mN*	S, w	1,340'	165.4	MATC: Maine Map 5
2,032.7	1.5	West Carry Pond *(east side)*: side trail west to Arnold Point Beach on Arnold Trail	w	1,320'	164.7	
2,034.2	0.2	Arnold Swamp: *many bog bridges*		1,255'	163.2	
2,034.4	0.2	Long Pond Road	R	1,250'	163.0	
2,034.6	0.8	Sandy Stream, Middle Carry Pond Road: *bridge*	R, w	1,229'	162.8	
2,035.4	0.7	East Carry Pond logging road: *gravel*	R	1,250'	162.0	
2,036.1	1.7	East Carry Pond *(north end)*	w	1,237'	161.3	
2,037.8	0.7	Scott Road: *main logging road*	R	1,300'	159.6	
2,038.5	3.5	North Branch of Carrying Place Stream: *ford*	w	1,200'	158.9	
2,042.0	0.2	**Pierce Pond Lean-to**, *10mS: 9.7mN*	S, w	1,150'	155.4	
2,042.2	0.2	Wooden Dam: *outlet of Pierce Pond*		1,120'	155.2	
2,042.4	0.3	Trail to Harrison's Pierce Pond Camps *(E-0.1m)*	R, L, M, w	1,100'	155.0	
2,042.7	0.7	Otter Pond Road: *gravel*		1,080'	154.7	
2,043.4	0.4	Trail to pool at base of waterfalls *(E-0.1m)*: Pierce Pond Stream	w	850'	154.0	
2,043.8	1.9	Otter Pond Stream: *bridge*	w	900'	153.6	
2,045.7	0.3	Kennebec River: *ferry*	w	490'	151.7	
2,046.0	2.7	US-201 *East-150 yards to* Caratunk House Hiker B&B *East-0.3m to* **Caratunk, ME, P.O. 04925** *East-1m to* Sterling Inn *East-16.5m to* Bingham, ME *West-2m to* Northern Outdoors *West-3.5m to* Three Rivers Trading Post *West-7m to* The Forks, ME	R, P L, g H, L, g, sh, cl G, L, M, cl C, L, M, sh, cl C, L, M, g C, G, f	520'	151.4	
2,048.7	1.4	Holly Brook	w	900'	148.7	
2,050.1	1.2	Hangtown Road: *gravel logging road*	R	1,240'	147.3	MATC: Maine Map 4
2,051.3	0.4	Boise–Cascade logging road	R, P	1,400'	146.1	
2,051.7	0.2	**Pleasant Pond Lean-to**, *9.7mS; 9mN*	S, w	1,320'	145.7	
2,051.9	1.1	Trail to Pleasant Pond Beach *(E-0.2m)*		1,360'	145.5	
2,053.0	4.9	Pleasant Pond Mountain		2,477'	144.4	
2,057.9	0.1	Moxie Pond *(south end)*, Joe's Hole, Troutdale Rd.	R, P	970'	139.5	
2,058.0	1.1	Baker Stream: *ford*	w	1,010'	139.4	
2,059.1	1.4	Joe's Hole Brook	w	1,240'	138.3	
2,060.5	0.2	Bald Mountain Brook Campsite	C, w	1,200'	136.9	
2,060.7	1.4	**Bald Mountain Brook Lean-to**, *9mS; 4.1mN*	S, w	1,280'	136.7	
2,062.1	0.6	Summit bypass trail		2,250'	135.3	
2,062.7	0.3	Moxie Bald Mountain		2,629'	134.7	

Miles from Springer	Miles to Next Point	Features	Services	Elev	Miles from Katahdin	M A P
2,063.0	0.7	Summit bypass trail		2,490'	134.4	
2,063.7	1.1	Trail to Moxie Bald Mtn. (north peak) (W–0.7m)		2,320'	133.7	
2,064.8	0.5	**Moxie Bald Lean-to**, 4.1mS; 8.9mN	S, w	1,220'	132.6	
2,065.3	1.6	Gravel road		1,290'	132.1	
2,066.9	1.9	Bald Mountain Stream: outlet of Bald Mtn. Pond, ford	w	1,213'	130.5	
2,068.8	1.5	Bald Mountain Stream Road: gravel	R	1,100'	128.6	
2,070.3	0.3	Marble Brook and "Jeep Road"		990'	127.1	
2,070.6	3.1	West Branch Piscataquis River: ford	w	900'	126.8	MATC: Maine Map 4
2,073.7	2.3	**Horseshoe Canyon Lean-to**, 8.9mS; 12mN	S, w	880'	123.7	
2,076.0	0.3	East Branch Piscataquis River: ford	w	650'	121.4	
2,076.3	0.1	Old Bangor and Aroostook Railroad bed		800'	121.1	
2,076.4	3.0	Shirley–Blanchard Road: paved	R, P	880'	121.0	
2,079.4	1.1	Blue-blaze to Pleasant St., Lake Hebron East–0.3m to road, then 1.7m to Monson, ME	C R, P	900'	118.0	
2,080.5	0.8	Buck Hill		1,390'	116.9	
2,081.3	1.4	Trail to Doughty Ponds		1,240'	116.1	
2,082.7	0.1	ME-15 East–4m to **Monson, ME, P.O. 04464**; ATC Visitors Center West–10m to Greenville, ME	R, P H, G, L, M, O, cl, sh, f G, L, M, O, D, V, f	1,215'	114.7	
		Enter the "100 Mile Wilderness"				
2,082.8	1.1	Goodell Brook, Spectacle Pond Outlet	w	1,163'	114.6	
2,083.9	0.7	Bell Pond	w	1,278'	113.5	
2,084.6	1.1	Lily Pond	w	1,130'	112.8	
2,085.7	0.8	**Leeman Brook Lean-to**, 12mS; 7.4mN	S, w	1,060'	111.7	
2,086.5	0.4	North Pond: outlet	w	1,000'	110.9	
2,086.9	1.3	North Pond Tote Road	R	1,100'	110.5	
2,088.2	0.8	Rim of Bear Pond Ledges		1,200'	109.2	
2,089.0	0.2	James Brook	w	950'	108.4	
2,089.2	0.1	Gravel haul road	R	1,000'	108.2	MATC: Maine Map 3
2,089.3	0.2	Little Wilson Falls: 60 ft. high		850'	108.1	
2,089.5	0.4	Little Wilson Falls Trail, Little Wilson Stream: ford	w	750'	107.9	
2,089.9	1.9	Gravel road: follow for 100 yds.	R	900'	107.5	
2,091.8	0.1	Big Wilson Tote Road	R	620'	105.6	
2,091.9	0.5	Thompson Brook	w	620'	105.5	
2,092.4	0.3	Big Wilson Stream: ford	w	600'	105.0	
2,092.7	0.4	CPKC Railway tracks		850'	104.7	
2,093.1	0.6	**Wilson Valley Lean-to**, 7.4mS; 4.7mN	S, w	1,000'	104.3	
2,093.7	2.6	Old winter logging road		1,190'	103.7	
2,096.3	0.1	Wilber Brook	w	660'	101.1	
2,096.4	0.5	Vaughn Stream: top of 20 ft. waterfall		670'	101.0	
2,096.9	0.1	Bodfish Farm–Long Pond Tote Road	R	650'	100.5	
2,097.0	0.7	Long Pond Stream: ford	w	620'	100.4	
2,097.7	0.1	Side trail to Slugundy Gorge and Falls		870'	99.7	
2,097.8	3.1	**Long Pond Stream Lean-to**, 4.7mS; 4.4mN	S, w	930'	99.6	

Miles from Springer	Miles to Next Point	Features	Services	Elev	Miles from Katahdin	M A P
2,100.9	0.9	Barren Mountain: *abandoned firetower*		2,670'	96.5	
2,101.8	2.1	**Cloud Pond Lean-to** *(E–0.4m), 4.4mS; 7.5mN*	S, w	2,420'	95.6	
2,103.9	2.2	Fourth Mountain *(plane crash site 0.3m N)*		2,383'	93.5	
2,106.1	0.5	Third Mountain Trail			91.3	
2,106.6	0.6	Third Mountain, Monument Cliff		2,061'	90.8	
2,107.2	1.3	West Chairback Pond side trail *(E–0.2m pond)*	w	1,770'	90.2	MATC: Maine Map 3
2,108.5	0.4	Columbus Mountain: *open ledge*		2,325'	88.9	
2,108.9	0.5	**Chairback Gap Lean-to**, *7.5mS; 9.9mN*	S, w	2,000'	88.5	
2,109.4	0.4	Chairback Mountain		2,219'	88.0	
2,109.8	1.8	Semiopen ledges, *views*		2,000'	87.6	
2,111.6	0.5	East Chairback Pond side trail *(W–0.2m)*	w	1,630'	85.8	
2,112.1	0.7	Small stream and spring	w	1,250'	85.3	
2,112.8	0.5	Katahdin Iron Works Road *(E–0.5m P)* *East–20m to Brownville Junction on ME-11* *West–1.5m to +AMC Gorman Chairback Lodge* *West–6.1m to +AMC Little Lyford Pond Cabins*	R, P C, G L L	750'	84.6	
2,113.3	0.2	West Branch Pleasant River: *ford (E–0.2m P)*	P, w	680'	84.1	
2,113.5	0.1	Trail to Pugwash Pond, Pleasant River Campsites, Hay Brook Parking Area *(E–0.7m)*	P, C, w	680'	83.9	
2,113.6	1.0	The Hermitage		695'	83.8	
2,114.6	0.7	Gulf Hagas Trail: *5.2m loop, rejoins A.T. north*	w	950'	82.8	
2,115.3	3.5	Gulf Hagas Cut-off Trail: *5.2m loop, rejoins A.T. south*	w	1,050'	82.1	
2,118.8	0.9	Gulf Hagas Brook; **Carl A. Newhall Lean-to**, *9.9mS; 7.2mN*	S, w	1,860'	78.6	
2,119.7	0.9	Gulf Hagas Mountain		2,683'	77.7	
2,120.6	0.7	Sidney Tappan Campsite: *spring (E–0.2m)*	C, w	2,425'	76.8	
2,121.3	1.6	West Peak		3,178'	76.1	
2,122.9	0.6	Hay Mountain		3,244'	74.5	
2,123.5	1.1	White Brook Trail		3,125'	73.9	
2,124.6	1.4	White Cap Mountain: *view of Katahdin*		3,654'	72.8	MATC: Maine Map 2
2,126.0	2.0	**Logan Brook Lean-to**, *7.2mS; 3.6mN*	S, w	2,480'	71.4	
2,128.0	1.6	Logan Brook Road	L, M	1,650'	69.4	
2,129.6	0.3	**East Branch Lean-to**, *3.6mS; 8.1mN*	S, w	1,225'	67.8	
2,129.9	1.6	East Branch Pleasant River: *ford*	w	1,200'	67.5	
2,131.5	0.3	Mountain View Pond: *outlet*	w	1,597'	65.9	
2,131.8	1.3	Spring *(east)*	w	1,580'	65.6	
2,133.1	1.4	Little Boardman Mountain *(300 ft. to summit)*		2,017'	64.3	
2,134.5	0.9	Johnston Pond Road: *gravel*	R, P	1,380'	62.9	
2,135.4	2.3	Crawford Pond: *outlet, no camping*	w	1,240'	62.0	
2,137.7	3.7	**Cooper Brook Falls Lean-to**, *8.1mS; 11.4mN*	S, C, w	880'	59.7	
2,141.4	1.3	Jo-Mary Road *East–6m to Jo-Mary Lake Campground* *East–17m to ME-11 and Brownville Junction*	R, P, C, w C, G, cl, sh R	625'	56.0	
2,142.7	1.3	Side trail to Cooper Pond *(E–0.2m)*		600'	54.7	
2,144.0	0.3	Gravel logging road: *snowsled bridge*	R	520'	53.4	
2,144.3	1.3	Mud Brook, Mud Pond Outlet: *bridge*	w	508'	53.1	
2,145.6	1.7	Antlers Campsite	C, w	500'	51.8	

Miles from Springer	Miles to Next Point	Features	Services	Elev	Miles from Katahdin	M A P
2,147.3	1.8	Lower Jo-Mary Lake: *sand beach*	w	580'	50.1	
2,149.1	0.5	**Potaywadjo Spring Lean-to**, *11.4mS; 4.5mN*	S, w	710'	48.3	
2,149.6	0.1	Twitchell Brook: *bridge*	w	590'	47.8	
2,149.7	1.2	Pemadumcook Lake: *Katahdin view*	w	580'	47.7	
2,150.9	0.7	Deer Brook		588'	46.5	
2,151.6	0.1	Gravel logging road		580'	45.8	MATC: Maine Map 2
2,151.7	0.1	Mahar Trail/Mahar Tote Road		580'	45.7	
2,151.8	1.1	Branch of Nahmakanta Stream: *ford*		580'	45.6	
2,152.9	0.7	Tumbledown Dick Stream: *ford*		590'	44.5	
2,153.6	1.5	**Nahmakanta Stream Lean-to**, *4.5mS; 5.6mN*	S, C, w	600'	43.8	
2,155.1	0.9	Tumbledown Dick Trail		625'	42.3	
2,156.0	0.3	Wood Rat's Spring	w	740'	41.4	
2,156.3	0.3	Gravel road	R	749'	41.1	
2,156.6	0.9	Nahmakanta Lake *(south end)*: gravel beach	R, P, C, w	650'	40.8	
2,157.5	1.3	Prentiss Brook	w	590'	39.9	
2,158.8	0.3	Sand Beach 50 ft. east: *spring*	w	595'	38.6	
2,159.1	0.1	Wadleigh Stream	w	680'	38.3	
2,159.2	1.9	**Wadleigh Stream Lean-to**, *5.6mS; 8.1mN*	S, w	685'	38.2	
2,161.1	1.2	Nesuntabunt Mountain: *views*		1,520'	36.3	
2,162.3	1.2	Logging road: *gravel*	R	1,010'	35.1	
2,163.5	0.4	Crescent Pond *(west end)*	w	980'	33.9	
2,163.9	1.0	Pollywog Gorge: *views*		1,050'	33.5	
2,164.9	0.7	Pollywog Stream: *logging road, bridge*	R, P, w	682'	32.5	
2,165.6	1.3	Flume in gorge: *remains of old logging dam*		1,000'	31.8	
2,166.9	0.4	Murphy Pond outlet stream	w	1,020'	30.5	
2,167.3	2.0	**Rainbow Stream Lean-to**, *8.1mS; 11.5mN*	S, C, w	1,020'	30.1	
2,169.3	1.8	Rainbow Lake *(west end)*: dam on side trail with *Katahdin view*	w	1,080'	28.1	
2,171.1	1.7	Rainbow Spring Campsite	C, w	1,100'	26.3	MATC: Maine Map 1
2,172.8	1.7	Trail to Rainbow Mountain *(E-.75m to summit)*		1,100'	24.6	
2,174.5	0.1	Rainbow Lake *(east end)*	w	980'	22.9	
2,174.6	1.7	Trail to Little Beaver and Big Beaver ponds		1,100'	22.8	
2,176.3	2.5	Rainbow Ledges		1,517'	21.1	
2,178.8	0.7	**Hurd Brook Lean-to**, *11.5mS; 13.7mN*	S, w	710'	18.6	
2,179.5	2.7	Spring	w	740'	17.9	
2,182.2	0.1	Golden Road (Greenville-Millinocket Road)	R	600'	15.2	
2,182.3	0.2	Abol Bridge over West Branch of Penobscot River *On A.T.–Abol Bridge Campground and Store* *On A.T.–DOC Abol Pines* *East-20m to* **Millinocket, ME, P.O. 04462** *East-27m to Medway, ME* *East-88m to Bangor, ME*	R, P C, G, M, sh C, S H, G, L, M, D, O, cl B, L, O all	588'	15.1	
2,182.5	0.3	Junction of Golden Road and Old State Road	R	600'	14.9	
2,182.8	0.2	Gravel pit	R	600'	14.6	
2,183.0	0.1	Abol Stream Trail, Abol Stream, Baxter Park Boundary: *bridge, ski trail (E-1m to Abol Beach)*	w	620'	14.4	

Miles from Springer	Miles to Next Point	Features	Services	Elev	Miles from Katahdin	M A P
2,183.1	0.3	BSP hiker kiosk, registration for "The Birches Campsite"; Abol Pond Trail, Blueberry Ledges Trail		620'	14.3	
2,183.4	0.1	Katahdin Stream: *bridge*	w	620'	14.0	
2,183.5	0.7	Foss and Knowlton Ponds Trail		630'	13.9	
2,184.2	2.2	Foss and Knowlton Brook: *footbridge*	w	625'	13.2	
2,186.4	0.5	Pine Point	w	640'	11.0	
2,186.9	0.9	Lower Fork Nesowadnehunk Stream: *ford*	w	630'	10.5	
2,187.8	0.4	Upper Fork Nesowadnehunk Stream: *ford*	w	800'	9.6	
2,188.2	0.4	Rocky Rips: *below ledge*	w	850'	9.2	
2,188.6	0.2	Big Niagara Falls	w	900'	8.8	
2,188.8	0.1	Spring *(E–150 ft.)*	w	990'	8.6	
2,188.9	0.9	Toll Dam and Little Niagara Falls		1,030'	8.5	
2,189.8	0.1	Daicey Pond Nature Trail		1,090'	7.6	
2,189.9	0.5	+Daicey Pond Campground Road; ranger station *(E–0.1m)*	R, P, L, w	1,100'	7.5	
2,190.4	0.8	Tracy and Elbow Ponds Trail		1,100'	7.0	MATC: Maine Map 1
2,191.2	0.9	Outlet of Grassy Pond	w	800'	6.2	
2,192.1	0.1	Cross Perimeter Road (Tote Road) *East–8.7m to* BSP Togue Pond Visitors Center *East–10.7m to* Kathadin Forest Cabins *East–11.3 to* Penobscot Outdoor Center *East–15.7m to* Golden Road *East–17m to* Northwoods Trading Post, Big Moose Inns *East–23.3m to* Hidden Springs Campground *East–25.7 m to* **Millinockett, ME, P.O. 04462**	R L C G, L, M C, sh H, G, L, M, D, O, cl	1,070'	5.3	
2,192.2	1.0	+Katahdin Stream Campground, ranger station; +**The Birches Campsite** *(E–0.25m), 13.7mS*	R, P, S, C, w	1,070'	5.2	
2,193.2	0.1	The Owl Trail *(W–2.2m to summit)*		1,570'	4.2	
2,193.3	0.1	Katahdin Stream: *footbridge*	w	1,500'	4.1	
2,193.4	1.5	Katahdin Stream Falls: *privy*	w	1,550'	4.0	
2,194.9	0.1	"The Cave": *small slab cave*		4,500'	2.5	
2,195.0	0.8	Hunt Spur, *treeline at base of "The Boulders"*		3,400'	2.4	
2,195.8	0.6	Gateway to Tablelands		4,600'	1.6	
2,196.4	1.0	Abol Trail, Thoreau Spring	w	4,627'	1.0	
2,197.4		Katahdin *(K'taadn)*, Baxter Peak: *sign, plaque, cairn,* **Northern terminus**		5,268'	0.0	

+ Fee charged; ~ Northbound long-distance hikers only at The Birches

Hikers in Maine encounter approximately 282 miles of lakes, bogs, moose, loons, hand-over-hand climbs, and a 100-mile wilderness that is neither 100 miles nor truly a wilderness. It is a mystical, magical place to begin or end your A.T. journey.

Note: No camping is allowed above treeline on the A.T. in Maine.

Carlo Col Shelter and Campsite (1976)—Off Trail 0.3 mile **west** on Carlo Col Trail. Shelter sleeps 8. Privy (composting). Two single and one double tent platforms. Bear box. Water source is a spring left of the lean-to.

Full Goose Shelter and Campsite (1978)—Shelter sleeps 8. Privy (composting). Many hikers choose to stay here before or after Mahoosuc Notch. Three single and one double tent platforms. Bear box. Water source is stream behind shelter.

Mahoosuc Notch—Famous for ice in deep crevices throughout the year. Many call this scramble under, around, over, and between boulders the most difficult mile on the Trail.

Speck Pond Shelter and Campsite (1968)—Off Trail 0.1 mile **west** on Speck Pond Trail. Shelter sleeps 8. Privy (composting). Three single and three double tent platforms. Cookstoves only. Bear box. Overnight fee $10pp. Speck Pond is the highest body of water in Maine. Water source is a spring on the blue-blazed trail behind the caretaker's yurt.

⚠ **ME-26/Grafton Notch**—Difficult hitch, very light traffic. **East** 5 miles to *Camping:* Grafton Notch Campground, 1472 Bear River Rd., Newry, ME 04261, (207) 824-2292, campgrafton.com, private campground, 15 wooded sites $30s/d ($8eap up to 6), with fire pit and picnic table, hot showers and flush toilets, showers only $8, leashed dogs, open mid-May through Columbus Day.

East 13 miles to Stony Brook Recreation, 3036 Main St., Hanover, ME 04237, (207) 824-2836, convenience store & restaurant (summer hours F–Sa 6 a.m.–9 p.m., Su–Th 6 a.m.–8 p.m.); tentsites $37, riverside campsite $39, lean-tos $40, showers, laundry, mini-golf, shuffleboard, pool (in season), shuttles with reservation.

East 19 miles to *Lodging:* Bethel Village Motel, (207) 824-2989, 88 Main St., Bethel, ME 04217, call for rates and reservations, no mail drops; Bethel Outdoor Adventures and Campground, 121 Mayville Rd., Bethel, ME 04217, (207) 824-4224, bethelout dooradventures.com. Open May 15–Oct 15, tenting $40 for 4 adults includes electric and water, near Bethel stores, includes showers, laundry, Wi-Fi. Must call and check in by 5 p.m. No same day check ins after 5 p.m.

Post Office to:
Andover General Store (0.2mi)
← East B Hill Rd (8.2 mi)
South Arm Rd (9.2 mi) →

120

The Cabin (11.mi)
E. Andover

Newton St

Pine Ellis •
Hiking Lodge

Akers Ski •

• Mills
Market

Pine St

Kate's Kones •

Main St

Lone Mountain Campground (1.2mi)

Post Office •

Library •

Andover, Maine ⚡
elevation 703'

East 19 miles to *Outfitter:* True North Adventurewear, (207) 824-2201, 196 Walkers Mills Rd., Bethel, ME 04217, full outfitter and resupply. Warranties, swap, repair, boots, gear, food.

East 22 miles to *Lodging:* West Bethel Motel, (207) 836 3575, 764 West Bethel Rd., Bethel, ME 04286, Rooms $50d, $25eap. cont breakfast, Wi-Fi, grill, picnic table, lounge with fridge, range, table to prep food, corn hole. Accepts packages for guests. Pet friendly. Call for shuttle availability.

Maine Appalachian Trail Club—MATC maintains the 267.4 miles from Grafton Notch to Katahdin. Correspondence should be sent to MATC, P.O. Box 7564, Portland, ME 04112; matc.org.

Baldpate Lean-to (1995)—Sleeps 8. Privy. Water source is a spring behind the lean-to.

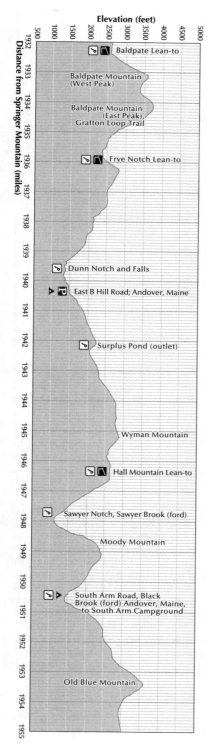

Elevation (feet)

Baldpate Lean-to

Baldpate Mountain
(West Peak)

Baldpate Mountain
(East Peak),
Grafton Loop Trail

Frye Notch Lean-to

Dunn Notch and Falls

East B Hill Road; Andover, Maine

Surplus Pond (outlet)

Wyman Mountain

Hall Mountain Lean-to

Sawyer Notch, Sawyer Brook (ford)

Moody Mountain

South Arm Road, Black
Brook (ford) Andover, Maine,
to South Arm Campground

Old Blue Mountain

Distance from Springer Mountain (miles)

Frye Notch Lean-to (1983)—Sleeps 6. Privy. Water from Frye Brook in front of the lean-to.

⚠ East B Hill Rd./Andover—East 8 miles to **Andover, ME [P.O. ZIP 04216: M–F 9:15–12 & 1–4:15, Sa 9–12; (207) 392-4571].** Andover also can be reached via South Arm Rd., 9.5 miles north on the A.T. Neither road has much traffic. *Lodging:* Pine Ellis Hiking Lodge, 20 Pine St. (P.O. Box 12), (207) 392-4161, pineellislodging.com; hiker-friendly hosts Ilene Trainor and friends; located near P.O. and stores; large, shared room in house or bunkhouse in backyard $30pp, private rooms $50s, $75d, $85t, all stays include shower, laundry (loaner clothes), morning coffee/muffins, Wi-Fi, CATV. For a fee: long-distance shuttles to/from Trailhead, slackpacking from Grafton Notch to Rangeley. Credit cards accepted; mail drops accepted for guests; no dogs. *Camping:* 1.2 miles south on South Main St. to Lone Mountain Campground, (207) 392-0019, lone mountaincampground.com. *Groceries:* Mills Market, 7 days, 5 a.m.–9 p.m., resupply, deli, pizza; free tenting. *Internet access:* Andover Public Library, 8 computers and Wi-Fi, Tu–Th & Sa 1–4:30, Th also 6–8.

East 11 miles to East Andover and *Lodging:* The Cabin, (207) 392-1333, owned by Margie Towne (Honey); log cabin with bunkroom and private room. Reservations only; alumni always welcome. A friend of hikers for more than two decades, does shuttles, takes cash/checks.

Hall Mountain Lean-to (1978)—Sleeps 6. Privy. Water source is a spring south of the lean-to on the A.T.; might have to walk downstream.

⚠ South Arm Rd.—East 9 miles to Andover, ME (see above).

West 3.5 miles to *Camping:* South Arm Campground, (207) 364-5155, open mid-May to mid-Sep; $18+tax per site, up to 2. Camp store (short-term resupply); showers 25¢; coin laundry; canoe, kayak, and boat rentals. No credit cards. Packages accepted at P.O. Box 310, Andover, ME 04216.

Bemis Mountain Lean-to (1988)—Sleeps 8. Privy. Water source is small spring to left of lean-to.

⚠ ME-17—West 11 miles to **Oquossoc, ME [P.O. ZIP 04964: M–F 11:30–3:30, Sa 9–12; (207) 864-3685].** *Groceries:* Oquossoc Grocery, (207) 864-3662 (short-term resupply), open daily 5 a.m.–7 p.m., with pizza and subs. *Restaurants:* Portage Tap House, local beers on tap, wood-fired oven pizza; Gingerbread House, B/L/D with daily specials, hardy servings, ice cream, desserts.

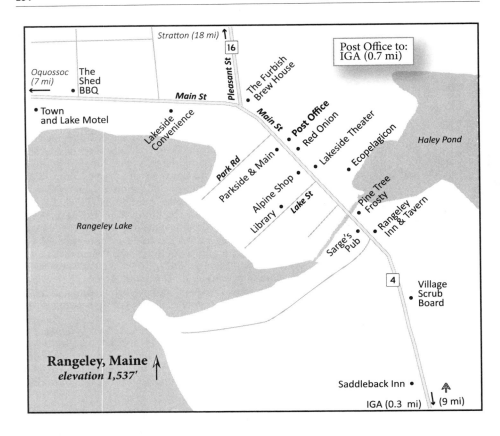

Sabbath Day Pond Lean-to (1993)—Sleeps 8. Privy. A sandy beach, 0.3 mile south on the A.T., provides an excellent swimming opportunity. Water source is Sabbath Day Pond in front of the lean-to.

Little Swift River Pond Campsite (1975)—Privy. Water from piped spring near pond. Sometimes a canoe is available; be sure to leave it upside-down after use.

ME-4—West 9 miles to **Rangeley, ME [P.O. ZIP 04970: M-F8:30–12:30 & 1:30–4:15, Sa 9:30–12; (207) 864-2233]**, where services are spread along ME-4. **Lodging:** Rangeley Inn & Tavern, (207) 864-3341, $125–$300, ask for hiker discount, free kayaks, Wi-Fi; Rangeley Saddleback Motor Inn, (207) 864-3434, $170d 1-2 People, $15eap, Wi-Fi; Town and Lake Motel, (207) 864-3755 Call for rates. Laundry on site, walk to town, free kayak and canoe. **Groceries:** IGA Supermarket (long-term resupply). **Restaurants:** Rangeley Inn Tavern, B (7-10) and D (5–9) daily; Furbish Brew House & Eats, closed M–Tu, open W–Su 12–8, full menu and pizza; Parkside Main Café, L/D; Sarge's Pub & Grub, L/D; Red Onion, L/D; The Shed BBQ, L/D; Keeps Corner, café and bakery. **Outfitter:** Alpine Shop, (207) 864-3741, Coleman fuel and alcohol by the ounce; Ecopelagicon, 7 Pond St., (207) 864-2771, freeze-dried meals, backpacker supplies, Leki warranty service; fuel, slackpacking/shuttles, Wi-Fi, mail drops accepted. **Internet access:** Rangeley Public Library. **Other services:** banks with ATM; Village Scrub Board coin laundry; doctor; Rangeley Region Health Center, (207) 864-4397; dentist; bookstore; Rangeley Adventure Co., 7 Pond St., has a town-wide hiker fest Labor Day weekend.

　　　West 15 miles to Oquossoc (see entry above).

Piazza Rock Lean-to (1993)—Sleeps 8. Privy; two-seater with cribbage board. Tent platforms. Water source is the stream that passes through the campsite. MATC caretaker in residence.

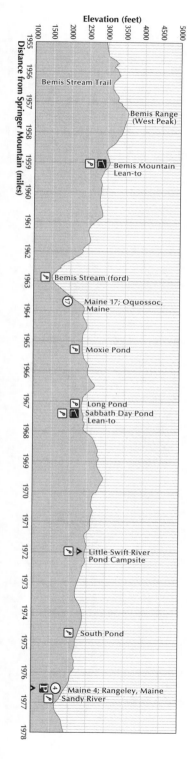

Elevation (feet)

Distance from Springer Mountain (miles)

Bemis Stream Trail

Bemis Range (West Peak)

Bemis Mountain Lean-to

Bemis Stream (ford)

Maine 17; Oquossoc, Maine

Moxie Pond

Long Pond
Sabbath Day Pond Lean-to

Little Swift River Pond Campsite

South Pond

Maine 4; Rangeley, Maine
Sandy River

Saddleback Mountain—One of the most spectacular above-treeline stretches of the Trail in Maine; you may not notice the ski resort on one side. For many years, Saddleback was the controversial "missing link" in Maine during federal attempts to buy lands along the Trail to protect it from encroaching development. In late 2000, a deal was struck to sell a Trail corridor across Saddleback to the government, but it does permit future development of the resort, which has been sold three times since then and is growing.

Redington Stream Campsite—0.7 mile north of Saddleback's Horn, at the east base of the Horn (middle peak of the Saddleback mountain range), right where the descent from the Horn levels off and the Trail heads for Saddleback Junior. The blue-blazed side trail leads 1,100 feet to water that might not be reliable. It is about 400 feet along this side trail from the A.T. to the privy. Before you reach the privy, side trails branch off to tent pads, with a current capacity of about two tents each. Open fires are *absolutely prohibited* at this campsite as it is in a very vulnerable softwood stand. Stoves are allowed, as usual.

Poplar Ridge Lean-to (1961)—Sleeps 6. Privy. This shelter uses the increasingly rare "baseball bat" design for its sleeping platform. Water source is the brook in front of lean-to.

Spaulding Mountain Lean-to (1989)—Sleeps 8. Privy. Water source is a small spring to right of lean-to.

Sugarloaf Mountain—A 0.6-mile side trail east leads to the summit of Sugarloaf, where, on clear days, panoramic views include glimpses of Katahdin and Mt. Washington. Cool spring water can be found at 0.3 mile. This side trail was the last section of the original A.T. to open, in August 1937.

Crocker Cirque Campsite (1975)—Privy. Numerous campsites; east on a 0.2-mile side trail, one large group platform, 2 small platforms. Water source is the spring.

ME-27—East 2 miles to *Groceries:* Mountainside Grocers (long-term resupply), (207) 237-2248, at the base of Sugarloaf access road; open 7–7. *Hostel:* Hostel of Maine, 3004 Town Line Rd., Carrabassett Valley, ME 04947, (207) 237-0088 hostelofmaine.com. Clean and cozy lodge, bunks $45, private room $109, includes pick-up and drop-off on demand, linens, continental B, shower w/ towel, Wi-Fi. Also available: laundry, resupply, pizza, beer, wine, ice cream, board games, books, slackpacking, and shipping. Well-behaved pets OK in private rooms; mail drops accepted.
    East 18 miles to *Hostel:* Terrapin Hostel, 65 High St., Kingfield, ME 04947, (207) 491-7786, owned by Lauran Dwyer, terrapinhostel@yahoo.com, terrapinhostel.com, dorm-style rooms $40 per bed, private rooms $80–$100 (double and suite). Free Wi-Fi, continental B, fully equipped kitchen, foosball, pool table, darts, instruments, wrap-

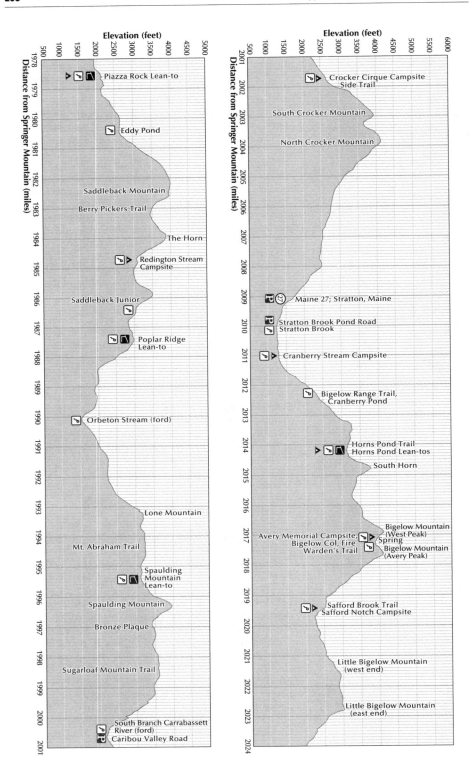

Elevation (feet)

Distance from Springer Mountain (miles)

Piazza Rock Lean-to

Eddy Pond

Saddleback Mountain

Berry Pickers Trail

The Horn

Redington Stream Campsite

Saddleback Junior

Poplar Ridge Lean-to

Orbeton Stream (ford)

Lone Mountain

Mt. Abraham Trail

Spaulding Mountain Lean-to

Spaulding Mountain

Bronze Plaque

Sugarloaf Mountain Trail

South Branch Carrabassett River (ford)
Caribou Valley Road

Elevation (feet)

Distance from Springer Mountain (miles)

Crocker Cirque Campsite Side Trail

South Crocker Mountain

North Crocker Mountain

Maine 27; Stratton, Maine

Stratton Brook Pond Road
Stratton Brook

Cranberry Stream Campsite

Bigelow Range Trail, Cranberry Pond

Horns Pond Trail
Horns Pond Lean-tos

South Horn

Bigelow Mountain (West Peak)

Avery Memorial Campsite,
Bigelow Col, Fire Warden's Trail
Spring
Bigelow Mountain (Avery Peak)

Safford Brook Trail
Safford Notch Campsite

Little Bigelow Mountain (west end)

Little Bigelow Mountain (east end)

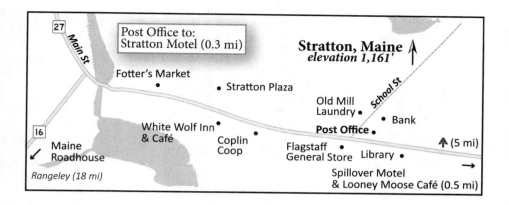

around porch, backyard; resupply options nearby. Shuttles available; fees vary depending on location.

West 5 miles to **Stratton, ME [P.O. ZIP 04982: M–F 8:30–1 & 1:30–4, Sa 8:30–11:00; (207) 246-6461].** *Hostel:* The Maine Roadhouse, (207) 670-4159, 901 Rangeley Rd. (Route 16), Coplin Plantation, ME 04970 (4.3 miles west of Stratton village), owned by Jenn Kent and Jenn Mastracchio, themaineroadhouse@gmail.com; bunks $50–$70 (twin-sized memory-foam mattress, two built-in personal outlets, fan, privacy curtain); private room $55–$60, includes shuttles to and from Stratton Trailhead, town runs (additional fee for shuttle to other destinations), showers, laundry, loaner clothes, full kitchen, BBQ grill, picnic tables, outdoor fire pit, Wi-Fi, full resupply on site; mail drops accepted. B $12. No tenting. *Lodging:* Spillover Motel, (207) 246-6571, $115–$124 (standard double room), $124–$134 for studio suite, pets okay ($20), continental B, community kitchen, Wi-Fi, showers for non-guests $15, located south of town; White Wolf Inn, 146 Main St. (P.O. Box 590), (207) 246-2922, L/D, closed Tu–W (call for room), weekdays $98s/d, weekends $108s/d, dogs $15, accepts packages for guests. *Groceries:* Fotter's Market (long-term resupply), with deli, Coleman fuel and denatured alcohol by the ounce, M–Th 8–7 F–Sa 8–8 Su 9–5; The Coplin Co-op, organic groceries. *Restaurants:* White Wolf Café, L/D, F fish fry (closed Tu & Wed); Stratton Plaza, Tu–Sa 11–9, Su 12–8, pizza, L/D; Flagstaff General Store, M–F 5–9, Sa 7–9, Su 6–7 full menu; The Looney Moose Café, B/L, W–Su; Back Strap Bar & Grill, F–M 12–8, Tu 4–8. *Internet access:* library. *Other services:* Old Mill Coin laundry; bank; ATM; Mt. Abram Regional Health Center, (207) 265-4555, located in Kingfield, an A.T. Community.

Cranberry Stream Campsite (1995)—Privy. Stream is the water source.

Horns Pond Lean-tos (1997)—Two lean-tos; each sleeps 8. Privy. Located on a clear pond at which fishing is permitted. A MATC caretaker is in residence in this heavily used area. Water source is an often-dry spring on the A.T., north of the lean-tos, or Horns Pond.

Bigelow Mountain—Known as Maine's "Second Mountain," the Bigelow Range might look very different today had it not been for the efforts of many conservation groups, including MATC. During the 1960s and '70s, land developers had plans to turn the Bigelow Range into the "Aspen of the East," but opponents forced a state referendum on the issue. In 1976, the citizens of Maine decided to have the state purchase the land and create a 33,000-acre wilderness preserve.

Bigelow Col and Avery Memorial Campsite—Tent platforms. Privy. Spring located in the col. This deep cleft between West Peak and Avery Peak is a beautiful (although often cold) place to spend the night. You can catch the sunset or sunrise views from either peak. The spring is unreliable in dry years; one maintained water site is behind the red maintenance shack, to left down unblazed trail.

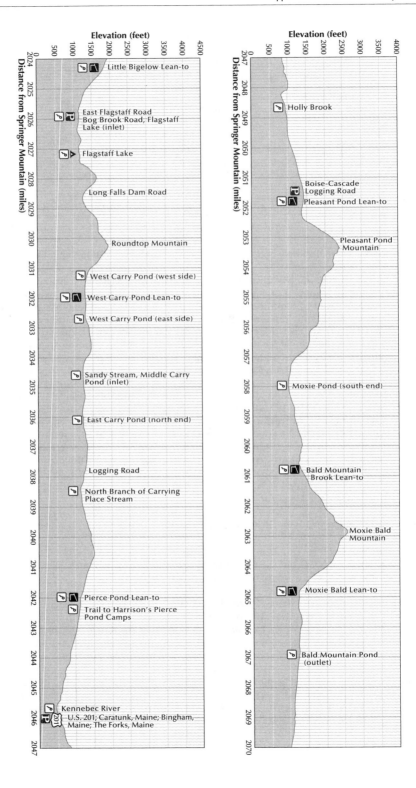

Elevation (feet)

Distance from Springer Mountain (miles)

Little Bigelow Lean-to

East Flagstaff Road
Bog Brook Road; Flagstaff
Lake (inlet)

Flagstaff Lake

Long Falls Dam Road

Roundtop Mountain

West Carry Pond (west side)

West Carry Pond Lean-to

West Carry Pond (east side)

Sandy Stream, Middle Carry
Pond (inlet)

East Carry Pond (north end)

Logging Road

North Branch of Carrying
Place Stream

Pierce Pond Lean-to

Trail to Harrison's Pierce
Pond Camps

Kennebec River

U.S. 201; Caratunk, Maine; Bingham,
Maine; The Forks, Maine

Elevation (feet)

Distance from Springer Mountain (miles)

Holly Brook

Boise-Cascade
Logging Road

Pleasant Pond Lean-to

Pleasant Pond
Mountain

Moxie Pond (south end)

Bald Mountain
Brook Lean-to

Moxie Bald
Mountain

Moxie Bald Lean-to

Bald Mountain Pond
(outlet)

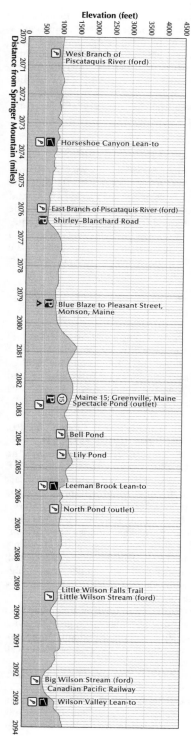

Elevation (feet) — Distance from Springer Mountain (miles)

- West Branch of Piscataquis River (ford)
- Horseshoe Canyon Lean-to
- East Branch of Piscataquis River (ford)
- Shirley–Blanchard Road
- Blue Blaze to Pleasant Street, Monson, Maine
- Maine 15; Greenville, Maine
- Spectacle Pond (outlet)
- Bell Pond
- Lily Pond
- Leeman Brook Lean-to
- North Pond (outlet)
- Little Wilson Falls Trail
- Little Wilson Stream (ford)
- Big Wilson Stream (ford)
- Canadian Pacific Railway
- Wilson Valley Lean-to

Safford Notch Campsite—Privy. Located 0.3 mile east. Tent pads and platforms. Water source is Safford Brook, downhill from the campsite.

Little Bigelow Lean-to (1986)—Sleeps 8. Privy. Plenty of tentsites at this lean-to. Swimming in "the Tubs" along the side trail. Water source is a spring 50 yards in front of the lean-to.

West Carry Pond Lean-to (1989)—Sleeps 8. Privy. Swimming in pond. Water source is a spring house to the left of the lean-to or West Carry Pond.

Arnold Trail—From West Carry to Middle Carry Pond, the A.T. follows the route of the historic Arnold Trail. In 1775, Benedict Arnold and an army of 1,150 Revolutionaries used this trail en route to Quebec, where they hoped to mount a surprise winter attack on the British. Like so many hikers, the army literally bogged down in the streams and swamps of the area, and, as a result, the remaining 650 men were so weakened by the passage that the attack was unsuccessful. Prior to Arnold's transit, the Abenaki Indians used the route as a portage around rapids on the Dead River, the waters of which now fill artificial Flagstaff Lake.

Pierce Pond Lean-to (1970)—Sleeps 6. Privy (moldering). Located on the east bank of Pierce Pond, with swimming, sunsets, and wildlife. Water source is the pond or stream on a side trail to Harrison's Pierce Pond Camps (see below). If deciding to take a swim, buddy-up and be conscious of the fact that these Maine ponds often have underwater "cells" of 40-degree water. A young 2012 thru-hiker drowned here after diving in to swim off a 20-mile day.

Harrison's Pierce Pond Camps (1934)—Traditional Maine camp on blue-blazed trail across Pierce Pond Stream. Tim Harrison caters primarily to vacationers and anglers. Breakfast with juice, $9–$12; cabin, shower, towel, $40pp with B. If staying at Pierce Pond Lean-to, make reservations for B the night before. Water spigot; no credit cards; pets must be on leash.

Kennebec River—The most formidable unbridged water-crossing on the A.T. Ironically, the Indian word "Kennebec" means "long, quiet water." A thru-hiker drowned in 1985 trying to ford the river, and another hiker drowned as recently as May 2018. Many other hikers have had close calls. Dangers include rocks, strong currents, and unpredictable water levels due to releases from the dams upstream. ATC and MATC strenuously urge hikers not to attempt to ford the river. *Purists also should note that a ferry is the official "white-blaze" route*, as well as the original, historical route of the A.T. across the Kennebec. This is a free service funded by ATC, MATC, and ALDHA. Hikers need to arrive a half-hour before the

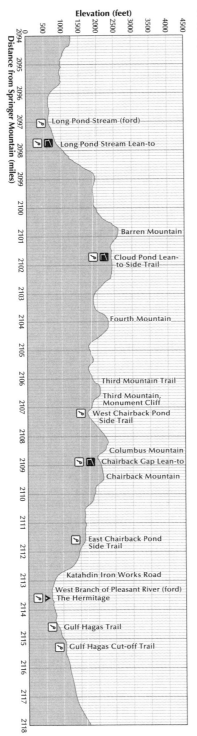

ferry ceases operation. If late, be prepared to wait, and note that camping and fires are prohibited on both banks of the river. You will be required to sign a release form before crossing, wear a life jacket during the crossing, and follow the instructions of the ferry operator; please cooperate in these matters. If river conditions or weather make the crossing dangerous, the service will be discontinued until conditions improve. The ferry is for hiker and pack—the operator will not carry your pack so you can attempt to ford.

Kennebec River Ferry—Over the last 30 years, canoes have ferried more than 22,000 hikers across the Kennebec River. For the 2024 hiker season, with the financial support of the ATC, HydroFlask, ALDHA, MATC, and the upstream dam operator, Greg Caruso of Maine Guide Service LLC will handle this monumental task. Shuttles possible after the ferry service ends; contact Greg at (207) 858-3627 or gcaruso@myfairpoint.net for details. The ferry will operate daily, at no cost to hikers, *tentatively* (contact MATC) from:

> May 21–Jun 30 9–11 a.m.
> Jul 1–Sep 30   9–2 p.m.
> Oct 1–Oct 12   9–11 a.m.

In off-hours, hikers can schedule a $50 crossing. In early May and late Oct, the ferry also will be available when time and weather allow. Exact hours and dates will be posted at Pierce Pond and Pleasant Pond lean-tos and online at matc.org. After the regular season, ferry service is available for a fee of $50 for 1–2 hikers.

US-201—East 0.3 mile on Main St. to **Caratunk, ME [P.O. ZIP 04925: M–F 2–4, Sa 7:30–11:15; (207) 672-3416]**.

East 1 mile on US-201 to *Lodging and resupply:* The Sterling Inn, 1041 US-201 (P.O. Box 129), Caratunk, ME 04925 (207) 672-3333, mainesterlinginn.com, reservations recommended. Bunk room $50; private rooms $70s/$100d (shared bed), $100d (2 beds), and $160 (4), includes B, shower, laundry, and sales tax. Free local shuttle to/from Trailhead, post office, and area restaurants. Free Wi-Fi, laundry, shower, recharge, and LD calling. Package shipping available. Debit/credit cards accepted, multiple-night discounts, well-behaved pets okay. Long-term resupply (Caratunk Country Store), shower, laundry, and mail drops free for non-guests.

East 16.5 miles to the small town of Bingham, with restaurants, coin laundry, pharmacy, and grocery stores (all long-term resupply). *Lodging:* Bingham Motor Inn, (866) 806-6120, binghammotorinn.com, new owner, call for rates and reservations.

West 2 miles to *Lodging:* Northern Outdoors Resort, 1771 US-201, The Forks, ME 04985, (800) 765-7238; Call for rates and hiker discount; lodge rooms (max 4), cabin tents and tentsites; serves B/L/D; coin laundry, hot tub, pool, ATM, no pets, accepts mail drops; Kennebec River rafting trips (class IV); Kennebec River Pub and Brewery on site; free shuttle to/from Trail coincides with ferry schedule; all hikers welcome to the free shuttle, free shower, and free Internet.

West 3.5 miles to **Services:** Three Rivers Trading Post, grocery store open May-Oct F & Sat, Jul & Aug Tues-Sat; restaurant, 4–Closing; Three Rivers Whitewater, (207) 663-2104, threeriverswhitewater.com, campsites $20–25pp /night, bunk house $32–37pp /night, showers available.

West 7 miles to **Lodging:** The Inn by the River, 2777 US-201, The Forks, ME 04985, (207) 663-2181, innbytheriver.com; rooms with whirlpools and private porches start at $121, $79eap, B/L/D, tubing, accepts packages for guests. **Groceries:** Berry's General Store and Hardware, (207) 663-4461, open daily 5 a.m.–7 p.m., accepts credit and debit cards; Heet, food, pizza, sandwiches, short-term resupply; summer hours 5–8; in same building as West Forks P.O.

Pleasant Pond Lean-to (1958, renovated 1991)—Sleeps 6. Privy. Sandy beach on Pleasant Pond is 0.2 mile from the lean-to. Water source is a small brook crossed on the path to the lean-to or pond.

Bald Mountain Brook Lean-to (1994)—Sleeps 8. Privy. Water source is Bald Mountain Brook, in front of the lean-to.

Moxie Bald Lean-to (1958)—Sleeps 6. Privy. Many moose in the area. Water source is nearby stream.

West Branch of Piscataquis River—Normally knee-deep, this ford can be dangerous during periods of heavy rain. Do not attempt to cross in high water.

Horseshoe Canyon Lean-to (1991)—Sleeps 8. Privy. Lean-to is located on a blue-blaze. Water source is a spring at the A.T. junction or the river in front of, and below, the lean-to.

East Branch of the Piscataquis River—Like its West Branch, the 50-foot-wide East Branch of the Piscataquis can be tricky fording during periods of heavy rain.

Blue-blaze to Monson—Northbounders have an alternative route to Monson, 3.3 miles south of ME-15, near Lake Hebron; signs will point you in the right direction. This route leads a short distance to Pleasant St., where you will go left 2 miles into town.

⚠ ⌂ **ME-15—East** 4 miles to **Monson, ME** [P.O. ZIP 04464: M-F 9:15-12:15 & 1:15-4:15, Sa 7:30-11; (207) 997-3975]. Post office accepts debit cards with limited cash back. **Lodging:** Shaw's Hiker Hostel, 40+ years serving hikers, 17 Pleasant St. (P.O. Box 72) USPS Packages must go to PO Box 72, Monson, ME, 04464. FedEx and UPS packages must go to 17 Peasant St., Monson ME, 04464, (207) 997-3597, shawshiker hostel.com; owned by thru-hikers Kimberly and Jarrod Hester

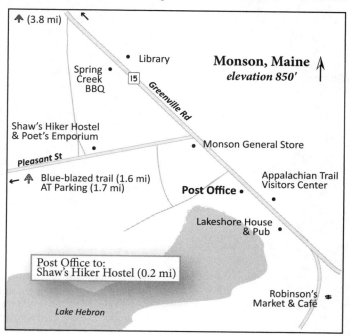

(3.8 mi)

Library

Spring
Creek
BBQ

15 Greenville Rd

Monson, Maine
elevation 850'

Shaw's Hiker Hostel
& Poet's Emporium

Monson General Store

Pleasant St

Blue-blazed trail (1.6 mi)
AT Parking (1.7 mi)

Post Office •

Appalachian Trail
Visitors Center

Lakeshore House
& Pub

Post Office to:
Shaw's Hiker Hostel (0.2 mi)

Robinson's
Market & Café

Lake Hebron

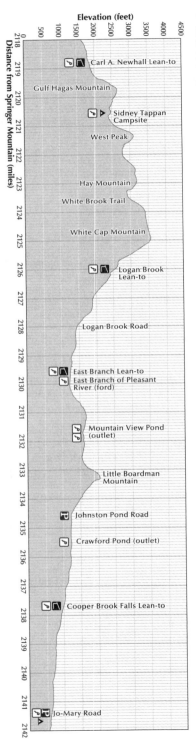

Elevation (feet)

Distance from Springer Mountain (miles)

Carl A. Newhall Lean-to
Gulf Hagas Mountain
Sidney Tappan Campsite
West Peak
Hay Mountain
White Brook Trail
White Cap Mountain
Logan Brook Lean-to
Logan Brook Road
East Branch Lean-to
East Branch of Pleasant River (ford)
Mountain View Pond (outlet)
Little Boardman Mountain
Johnston Pond Road
Crawford Pond (outlet)
Cooper Brook Falls Lean-to
Jo-Mary Road

("Hippie Chick and Poet"); open May–Oct, bunks $30pp, private guest rooms $70s/d, tenting $15pp; credit cards and advance reservations accepted; B $11 daily with regular, gluten-free, and vegan pancakes (outside guests welcome); Wi-Fi, shuttles, slackpacking, and food drops available. Long-term resupply and Poet's Emporium carries extensive ultralight gear; guest use of kayak and canoe; dogs welcome. Mail drops free for guests; non-guest mail drops, laundry, and showers are $5 each. **Lakeshore House Lodging & Pub**, 9 Tenney Hill Rd., Box 307, Monson, ME 04464, (207) 997-7069, lshmonson@yahoo.com, owner Nick Fusco. On Lake Hebron, open year-round, credit cards accepted. Bunks start at $30pp, private rooms $100; dog-friendly; laundry; Wi-Fi; free Trailhead pick-up and drop-off; mail drops accepted ($5 non-guests). Pub with full bar, draft beer, home-made food, open mic Th 5–8 p.m., live music Su 3–6 p.m., open Wed–Su 12–9, closed M ($5 non-guest services include shuttle to or from Trail, shower, laundry). *Groceries:* Monson General Store, (207) 997-3800, long-term resupply, open daily 6:30 a.m.–7 p.m., deli, fresh-baked bread and pastries; A.E. Robinson Market, M–Su 4a.m.–9 p.m., pizzas, calzones, hot sandwiches, ATM; Shaw's Hiker Hostel. *Restaurants:* Lakeshore House Pub, L/D, Wed–Su 12–9, live music Su 3–6 p.m., open mic Th 5–8 p.m.; Spring Creek BBQ, Th–Sa 11–8, Su 11–4. *Outfitter:* Poet's Emporium gear shop at Shaw's Hiker Hostel, open daily 8–11 a.m. and 2–6 p.m. *Internet access:* Monson Public Library, Tu 12–4:30, Th 2:30–6:30, Sa 10–2. *Shuttles:* Shaw's and Lakeshore House. *Other services:* Appalachian Trail Conservancy Visitor Center, (207) 573-0163, next to town hall in the Historical Society building, open 8-11, 1-5 daily, Jun–Oct; Wi-Fi. Long-distance hikers can obtain information about the 2024 Baxter State Park hiker permits, which are free. Staff are available to help plan logistics for the 100-Mile Wilderness and Katahdin. Trail conditions posted daily. Community and day-hike information available.

West 10.3 miles to Greenville, Moose-head Lake's main tourist town and gateway to Maine's North Woods.

Groceries: Indian Hill Trading Post (long-term resupply), indianhill.com (207)695-2104, Mo-Sa 8-8, Su 8-6. *Restaurants:* Kelly's Landing, AYCE B on Su; The Stress-Free Moose Pub; Dockside. *Outfitter:* Northwoods Outfitters, (207) 695-3288, maineoutfitter.com, daily 8–5, Internet (fee), and coffee at the Hard Drive Café inside store. *Other services:* Indian Hill Trading Post, 8-7 daily, indianhill.com, (207) 695-2104; banks with ATM; Harris Drug Store, (207) 695-2921; Charles A. Dean Memorial Hospital, 24-hour ER, (207) 695-5200; Greenville Veterinary Clinic, (207) 695-4408.

"100-Mile Wilderness"—Signs at each end of this section proclaim this area's remoteness and warn the unprepared hiker to stay away, but don't be intimidated. Hikers should remember to bring cash for Baxter State Park.

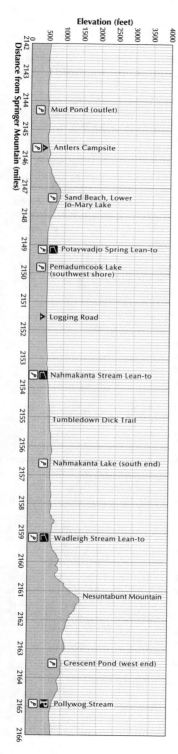

Elevation (feet)

Distance from Springer Mountain (miles)

Mud Pond (outlet)

Antlers Campsite

Sand Beach, Lower Jo-Mary Lake

Potawadjo Spring Lean-to

Pemadumcook Lake (southwest shore)

Logging Road

Nahmakanta Stream Lean-to

Tumbledown Dick Trail

Nahmakanta Lake (south end)

Wadleigh Stream Lean-to

Nesuntabunt Mountain

Crescent Pond (west end)

Pollywog Stream

Leeman Brook Lean-to (1987)—Sleeps 6. Privy. Water source is stream in front of the lean-to.

Wilson Valley Lean-to (1993)—Sleeps 6. Privy. Located north of Big Wilson Stream. Water source is a small spring in front of the lean-to, on the opposite side of the A.T.

Long Pond Stream Lean-to (1991)—Sleeps 8. Privy. Swimming in the scenic Slugundy Gorge and falls located 0.1 mile south, on a side trail 150 yards off the A.T. Water source, a small stream to the left of the lean-to, has been unreliable in recent years.

Cloud Pond Lean-to (1992)—Sleeps 6. Privy 0.4 mile east. Water source is Cloud Pond, in front of the lean-to, or a spring to the north of the side trail to the lean-to.

Chairback Gap Lean-to (1954)—Sleeps 6. Privy. Water source, a small spring downhill and north of the lean-to 25 yards, is prone to go dry and is unreliable in drier years.

⚠ Katahdin Iron Works (KIW) Rd. and West Branch of Pleasant River—Look for signs of a fresh relocation and follow the new route.

West on KIW Rd. to *Lodging:* AMC Gorman Chairback Lodge (0.3 mile to left on Gorman Chairback Camp Rd., 1.2 mile to lodge), $100-124 and Little Lyford Pond Cabins (4.9 mile to left on Frenchtown Rd., 1.2 mile to lodge), (603) 466-2727; outdoors.org; $87-108 for bunkroom space, possible two-night minimum, B/L/D included; accepts mail drops at P.O. Box 310, Greenville, ME 04441.

East 20 miles to ME-11 and Brownville Junction. *Groceries:* The General Store and More (short-term resupply), (207) 965-8100, deli.

The Hermitage—Camping is not allowed inside this protected area, a national landmark owned by The Nature Conservancy. Look for the plaque to learn the meaning of its name. Home to magnificent old-growth white pines. *Camping:* Maine North Woods, $12 tent-sites at Pleasant River Campsites 0.7 mile **east** of the Hermitage area. Maine North Woods, Box 425, Ashland, ME 04732, (207) 435-6213, northmainewoods. org; contact it at the gatehouse; reservations strongly recommended.

Gulf Hagas—If you've got the food and the time, you may want to take this side trail. The gulf was formed by water eroding the slate walls of a narrow canyon. The result of this sculpting is a stretch of many spectacular waterfalls nestled in a chasm about 500 feet deep. If you want a taste of the gulf's scenery, Screw Auger Falls is only 0.2 mile from the A.T. on Gulf Hagas Brook. A 5.2-mile loop hike is possible using the Rim and Gulf Hagas trails. MATC stations a ridgerunner in the area, which receives a tremendous amount of day use. *No camping allowed.*

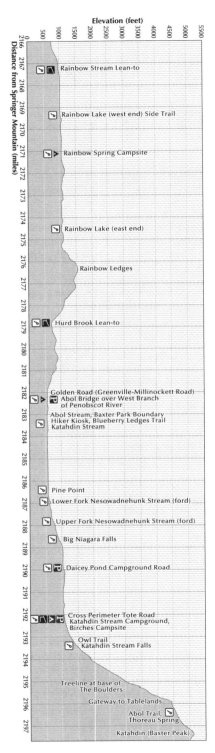

Elevation (feet)

Distance from Springer Mountain (miles)

Rainbow Stream Lean-to

Rainbow Lake (west end) Side Trail

Rainbow Spring Campsite

Rainbow Lake (east end)

Rainbow Ledges

Hurd Brook Lean-to

Golden Road (Greenville-Millinockett Road)
Abol Bridge over West Branch
of Penobscot River
Abol Stream, Baxter Park Boundary
Hiker Kiosk, Blueberry Ledges Trail
Katahdin Stream

Pine Point
Lower Fork Nesowadnehunk Stream (ford)

Upper Fork Nesowadnehunk Stream (ford)

Big Niagara Falls

Daicey Pond Campground Road

Cross Perimeter Tote Road
Katahdin Stream Campground,
Birches Campsite
Owl Trail
Katahdin Stream Falls

Treeline at base of
The Boulders
Gateway to Tablelands
Abol Trail,
Thoreau Spring
Katahdin (Baxter Peak)

Carl A. Newhall Lean-to (1986)—Sleeps 6. Privy. Lean-to is north of Gulf Hagas Brook, the water source.

Sidney Tappan Campsite—Privy. Follow the blue-blaze 0.2 mile east to water; trail begins just north of the campsite.

Logan Brook Lean-to (1983)—Sleeps 6. Privy. Water source is Logan Brook behind the lean-to; cascades are farther upstream.

East Branch Lean-to (1996)—Sleeps 8. Privy. Water source is the East Branch of the Pleasant River, in front.

Cooper Brook Falls Lean-to (1956)—Sleeps 6. Full-moon privy. Tentsite on trail to lean-to. A waterfront lean-to with numerous pools and falls. Water source is Cooper Brook in front of lean-to.

Antlers Campsite—Campsites are on the edge of Lower Jo-Mary. Fort Relief privy to the west of the Trail. Water source is Jo-Mary Lake.

Potaywadjo Spring Lean-to (1995)—Sleeps 8. Privy. Water source is the 15-foot-wide Potaywadjo Spring, to the right of the lean-to.

Nahmakanta Stream Lean-to (2017)—Sleeps 8. Privy. Water is the stream in front of shelter.

Wadleigh Stream Lean-to (1981)—Sleeps 6. Privy. Located 0.5 mile north of Nahmakanta Lake, which has a sandy beach. Water source is a spring on the beach.

Rainbow Stream Lean-to (1971)—Sleeps 6. Privy. Home of the A.T.'s best totem pole; often crowded with hiker groups. Good tenting and hammocking above and behind the lean-to. Water source is Rainbow Stream, in front.

Rainbow Spring Campsite—Privy. Water source is a flowing spring at the shore of Rainbow Lake.

Hurd Brook Lean-to (1959)—Sleeps 6. Privy. During high water, Hurd Brook, 50 feet south of the lean-to, can be deep and swift, and the ford dangerous. Area is frequented by hunters. Water source is Hurd Brook. Southbounders might want to tank up at the spring 0.7 mile north of the lean-to.

"Golden Road" and Abol Bridge. *Camping:* Abol Bridge Campground and Store, (207) 447-5803, abol-campground.com, open May 15–Oct 1, located along the road on the West Branch of the Penobscot River and Abol Stream, phone and website out at time of publication; Department of Conservation's Abol Pines, seasonal, tentsite or space in one of two six-person lean-tos, $15pp plus tax for out-of-state residents, reached by following a dirt road 75 yards east in front of the camp store. *Groceries:* Abol Bridge Store (short-term resupply), credit cards accepted. *Restaurant:* The Northern Restaurant, daily 11–6, warm food, cold beer.

East 20 miles to Millinocket, ME (near end of chapter).

Baxter State Park—The northern terminus of the Appalachian Trail, hosted by Baxter State Park, is Baxter Peak on Katahdin, Maine's highest mountain. Katahdin, along with the surrounding landscape, is part of a 209,644-acre wilderness sanctuary and forest preserve, Baxter State Park; baxterstateparkauthority.com. The lands were donated in perpetual trust to the people of Maine by former Governor Percival Proctor Baxter, who served from 1921 to 1924. BSP is self-supporting, in large part due to Baxter's endowment funds and by his design and is administered separately from any other agency or state park in Maine. Baxter's goal was to place preservation of natural resources as a priority over their recreational use, so some of BSP's regulations and policies are markedly different from what may be encountered elsewhere along the A.T.

Unlike the surrounding landscape south, Katahdin is exposed to extreme weather, including high winds, and has gotten snow during every month of the year. No shelters are located above treeline (north of Katahdin Stream Campground), and all trails to the summit are completely exposed. On humid, unsettled, late-summer days, for example, it is wise to start down by 1 p.m. to avoid electrical storms.

Katahdin—The translation of the Abenaki word, *K'taadn,* is "greatest mountain." Maine's Penobscots considered the mountain a holy place and believed in Pamola, the deity of Katahdin, who purportedly would destroy any man who ventured too close to the mountain. The first recorded ascent of Katahdin by Euro Americans came on Aug 13, 1804, when a party led by Charles Turner, Jr., reached the summit by the same rocks-and-roots route used by the A.T.—the Hunt Trail (named after Irving Hunt, a sporting-camp owner who cut the trail). Since then, the mountain has captured the imagination of many, including Henry David Thoreau, who explored the area in 1846. Thoreau Spring on the Tableland bears his name, although he likely never made it there. From Katahdin Stream Campground, it is a 10.4-mile trip to the summit and back. The ascent packs an elevation gain of 4,000 feet into 5 miles. Backpacks may be left at the ranger station at the campground, where you can borrow a daypack and obtain information on weather conditions. The park posts recommended "cut-off" times for beginning your climb: In Aug, hikers are advised to start by 11 a.m.; in Sep, by 10 a.m.; in Oct, by 9 a.m. Park rules require that you sign in at the campground before your climb and sign out on your return. Don't forget to make your final, or first, register entry on the ranger station's front porch.

Permits—Every A.T. long-distance hiker must register with a ranger upon entering BSP. An information kiosk is located on the A.T. 1 mile north of Abol Bridge. The 12 hikers using The Birches (see below) must sign up at the Abol Stream kiosk and also with the ranger at Katahdin Stream Campground. A Baxter Park "A.T. Steward" patrols the area to help hikers with information on the A.T. and the park.

Camping—Camping is allowed only in designated campsites in the park. Long distance hikers can either stay at the first-come, first-serve Birches campsite or reserve another campsite in the park.

The Birches—Two 4-person lean-tos and tenting space for 4 additional people are available at this site not far from Katahdin Stream Campground. Advance reservations are not required; the fee to stay there is $10pp. Cash only inside park.

The Birches is 9.9 miles from Abol Bridge via the A.T. or 4.4 miles from Abol Bridge via the Blueberry Ledges Trail. Use of The Birches is limited strictly to 12 long-distance or thru-hikers who have hiked at least 100 contiguous miles up to and including entering the BSP. Stays at The Birches are limited to one night. Park authorities have posted a sign-up sheet for long-distance hikers at the information kiosk just north of Abol Bridge. If all 12 spaces are claimed for the night that you planned to stay at The Birches, you need to stay elsewhere. Your choices include the Abol Bridge private campground; the nearby state-owned Abol Pines site on the West Branch of the Penobscot (both are fee sites); standard-reservation campsites in the park at Katahdin Stream Campground, Foster Field Group Campsite, or any other available site of your choice in the park, if they are not already full; or staying in a campground or motel near Millinocket, if available. In Jul and Aug, and on fall weekends, it is difficult to get a site at Katahdin Stream or anywhere in the park, because sites are often reserved months in advance. However, Labor Day–Oct 22, it is possible (although not certain) that you will find vacant sites at Katahdin Stream during the week.

Reservation Campgrounds—The fee is $32 for either lean-to or tentsite (4- to 6-person capacity). A "rolling reservations" policy is available four months in advance of the day you wish to stay within the park. If you want Jun 3, you need to know your reservation will not be processed before Feb 3. The traditional opening day to make walk-in reservations is the closest business day to Jan 15. Please call the park at (207) 723-5140 or check the website for updates. More information, and a chart outlining when reservations can be made, is at baxterstateparkauthority.com. The site provides the many different ways reservations may be secured; you are strongly advised to review those options.

The overnight camping season is May 15–Oct 22 each year. After Oct 22, overnight camping is prohibited anywhere within the park. You may camp at the private Abol Bridge campground or the state-owned Abol Pines Campground downriver and across the road from Abol Bridge. Both charge fees. Your hike to the summit is then 15 miles one way from this area outside the park. Another option when BSP is closed for camping is to stay in Millinocket and hire one of the local shuttle services to transport you in and out of Baxter on the day of your hike. Southbounders should note that the A.T. from Katahdin Stream Campground to Baxter Peak might not be open until early Jun. Northbounders should note that they can check reservation availability by either going on-line or calling. With other mail requests coming in daily, that may not guarantee a spot. Between Jun 16 and Oct 22, campsite reservations may be made with a credit card via phone or Internet for any unreserved site in the park for any date.

Northbounders who plan to have family and friends meet them at the park should reserve campsites in advance. Labor Day weekend is especially busy, with a traditional native-American event reserving the entire Katahdin Stream Campground. If driving into the park, there is a $15 fee at the gate for out-of-state residents.

Southbound thru-hikers beginning their trek at Katahdin should make reservations for campsites well in advance of their starting dates. During July and Aug, campsites normally are booked to maximum levels. We suggest you reserve a site for the nights before and after climbing Katahdin. For reservations and other information, contact Baxter State Park.

Parking—A day-use parking reservation system is in place at all Katahdin trailheads for users driving into the park. You can make a reservation online (baxterstateparkauthority.com) for the Trailhead of your choice for a $5 fee. Out-of-state residents can reserve a spot no earlier than two weeks before arrival; Maine residents can reserve any time after Apr 1. When parking lots fill, visitors will be directed to open lots and alternate trailheads by the rangers at the gatehouse. Families or friends who are picking up hikers are allowed to drive to the Katahdin Stream trailhead, even if it is full, if they arrive in the afternoon and do not plan to hike the mountain.

Weather—Baxter State Park posts daily weather reports and trail-status alerts during the hiking season at 7 a.m. Before Memorial Day and any time after late Sep, it is not uncommon for some trails to be closed for public-safety reasons or to protect the alpine-plant communities. The "class day" system has been discarded. Going forward, the mountain either will be open for hiking or it won't. Hikers who choose to hike on closed trails are subject to a court summons, fine, and revocation of park-visitation privileges.

Trail Closings on Katahdin—It is advised to plan to hike Katahdin before Oct 15. In this northerly climate, chances are high that you will be unable to successfully finish your hike at Katahdin's summit after this date. Winter hiking season is Dec 1–Mar 31; during that period, you must obtain a permit from the park to climb Katahdin.

In some years, access to the park road and trails up Katahdin can be closed by snowstorms in September and October. On those days, the A.T. up to Baxter Peak is open only when conditions permit (see above). Each day at 7 a.m., park rangers post the weather forecast and trail alerts. Trail closures are not uncommon in late Sep–Oct. When the trails are closed, anyone hiking beyond the designated Trailhead is subject to a court summons and fine and revocation of park privileges. If you must be rescued, assistance will be delayed until the rescuers can proceed safely; you could be found negligent and liable for all costs of search and rescue.

After Oct 22, Baxter State park is open for day use only (sunrise to sunset), conditions permitting. Vehicular access to the park after Oct 22 is at the discretion of the park director and should not be planned on after Nov 1. Call park headquarters if you have questions about road access before May 15 or after Oct 22.

Dogs—Dogs are **not** allowed in the park. See Millinocket and Medway entries for kennels.

Pamphlet—*Long-Distance Hiking in Baxter State Park*, a pamphlet, is available on request from BSP. It has a map of the A.T. and the Blueberry Ledges Trail, information about the park, and a message from park management.

Mail and Messages—BSP does not accept mail or packages. Mail drops should be arranged through the Millinocket post office.

> IMPORTANT NOTE: Park regulations limit hiking groups to no more than 12 individuals; larger groups will be required to separate themselves into separate groups of 12 with at least a mile of trail between them. This regulation is designed to prevent large groups from dominating the experience at Baxter Peak. Public consumption of alcohol is prohibited on the summit. The park asks, "Please assist us in respecting the spectacular natural setting Percival Baxter generously preserved by complying with this regulation." Plan ahead!
> **CELEBRATE QUIETLY * SAVE ALCOHOL FOR LATER * HIKE IN SMALL GROUPS.**

2,000-Miler Certificate Applications—ATC has asked Katahdin Stream Campground rangers to hand out forms to all northbounders who are about to finish the Trail, in an effort to expedite the processing of 2,000-miler certificates. See requirements on page 16. The Appalachian Long Distance Hikers Association provides "I Hiked ALDHA Way" patches (page 271) and certificates to ALDHA members who complete all sections of the A.T. or do a thru hike, (www.aldha.org/aldhaway).

Reaching Baxter State Park—No public transportation is available to and from BSP. Unless you have someone meeting you at the park, you'll need to arrange for a shuttle or hitch 24 miles from the Trail to Millinocket. Rides are usually easy to find, since almost everyone headed out of the park must go through Millinocket.

⚠ **Baxter State Park Rd.**—BSP Togue Pond Visitor Center, M–Th 7–3, F–Su 7–6; maps, guidebooks, additional information; beach, and picnic area (no camping).
   East 2 miles from the park's south gate to *Lodging:* Acadian Timber Forest Cabins, (877) 622-2467, log cabin on Sunday Pond, spectacular view of Katahdin, $97 per night, sleeps 6, with gas heat, stove, and privy; advance reservations necessary.
   East 2.6 miles to *Camping:* Penobscot Outdoor Center on Pockwockamus Pond, (207) 723-3580, tentsites $30s/d $15eap, bunkhouse $150 up to 4, cabin tent $75s/d $30eap, showers $5 for non-guests.
   East 7 miles to Golden Road junction (8 miles from here to Abol Bridge).
   East 8.3 miles to *Groceries:* Golden Road Crossing (short-term resupply), (207) 723-4326, open 7–9, A.T. maps, books, trail guides, patches, and souvenirs. *Lodging:* Big Moose Inn, (207) 723-8391, bigmoosecabins.com, inn room with shared bath $70; camping $15pp; lean-to $18pp; cabins, call for rates; restaurant and bar open W–Su 5–9pm, no pets.
   East 15.6 miles to *Camping:* Wilderness Edge Campground, (207) 447-8485 or (207)723-6631, tentsites $12.50pp/night, shower without stay $10, wecamp.me.com

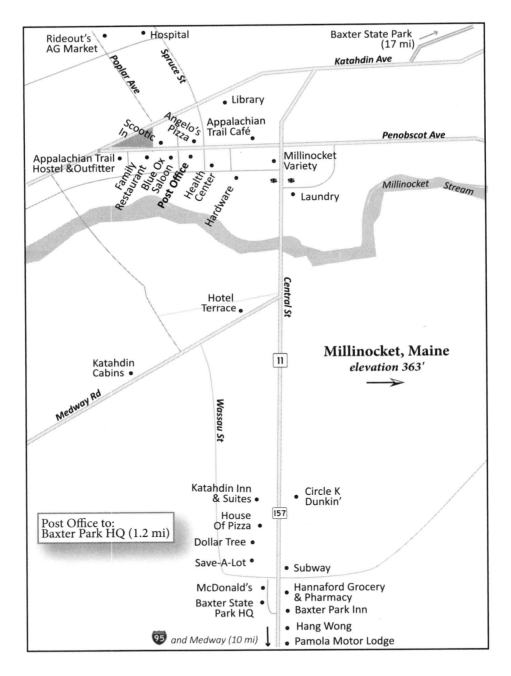

Rideout's AG Market
Hospital
Baxter State Park (17 mi)
Katahdin Ave
Poplar Ave
Spruce St
Library
Appalachian Trail Café
Scootic In
Angelo's Pizza
Penobscot Ave
Appalachian Trail Hostel &Outfitter
Family Restaurant
Blue Ox Saloon
Post Office
Health Center
Hardware
Millinocket Variety
Millinocket Stream
Laundry
Hotel Terrace
Central St
Millinocket, Maine
elevation 363'
11
Katahdin Cabins
Medway Rd
Wassau St
Katahdin Inn & Suites
Circle K
Dunkin'
157

Post Office to: Baxter Park HQ (1.2 mi)

House Of Pizza
Dollar Tree
Save-A-Lot
Subway
McDonald's
Hannaford Grocery & Pharmacy
Baxter State Park HQ
Baxter Park Inn
Hang Wong
95 *and Medway (10 mi)*
Pamola Motor Lodge

⌂ **East** 17 miles from the park's south gate to **Millinocket, ME [P.O. ZIP 04462: M–F 9–4, Sa 9–11:30; (207) 723-5921]**. BSP Headquarters, (207) 723-5140, is at 64 Balsam Dr.; park reservations, publications, maps, and general information. *Lodging:* Appalachian Trail Hostel and Outfitter, 33 Penobscot Ave., (207) 723-4321, appalachiantraillodge.com, operated by Danya "Loins of Arabia" Saadawi and Koty "Trash Panda" Sapp, open Memorial Day–Oct 22, no pets in lodge, $35 bunkroom, $50-

70 private bunk, $60–$70 private room (shared bath), family suite (private bath) $110d (sleeps 4; $10eap); showers or laundry for non-guests $5, loaner clothes; Wi-Fi. Daily shuttle service to and from Katahdin Stream ranger station, 4–4:30 p.m., $80 for 1, $40 each for 2, $20eap. Southbounders special: $90 shuttle from Medway bus stop, bunkroom lodging, shuttle to Katahdin Stream ranger station, $130pp includes extra night, B, and shakedown. Katahdin Inn & Suites, (207) 723-4555, $120d, $15eap, dogs $15/night, continental B, indoor pool and hot tub, Wi-Fi, computer access, fitness center, laundry. Baxter Park Inn, (207) 723-9777, call for rates, continental B. Pamola Motor Lodge, (800) 575-9746, (207) 723-9746, pamolalodge.com, call for best rates, continental B, Internet access, hot tub, lounge, laundry service. Hotel Terrace, (207) 723-4545, call for prices. 100-Mile Wilderness Inn, 96 Oxford St.,Millnockett, 04462, (207) 731-3537, 100milewildernessinn.com, owner Gail Wourms, bunks $35 includes showers, laundry $5, private rooms $85 and up include showers, pet friendly, grab-n-go B, snacks, coffee tea, use of kitchenette, Net-flix; shuttles and food drops to 100-Mile Wilderness, Baxter State Park, and area bus stations available; mail drops accepted. **Restaurants:** Appalachian Trail Café, B only; Scootic Inn, Tu–Sa D 3–9 p.m.; Ruthie's Hotel Terrace, B/L (10–2)/D; Hang Wong at Pamola Inn; Angelo's Pizza Grille, L/D; BBQ House; others shown on map. **Outfitter:** Outfitter at A.T. Lodge, open 8–12, 2-6, full line of gear and food resupply including packs, tents, pads, poles, stoves, fuel, cookware, water filters, maps, head lamps, rain gear, socks, dehydrated/freeze-dried foods, snacks, etc. Also, workshops, shakedowns, and shuttles. **Other services:** Most major services are available in town, including supermarkets, coin laundries, and banks with ATM; Millinocket Regional Hospital, (207) 723-5161. Millinocket has no bus service, but Cyr Bus Lines of Old Town, Maine, serves nearby Medway (see below). **Kennel services:** Katahdin Kritters Pet Resort, 20 Dirigo Dr., East Millinocket, ME 04430, (207) 746-8040, Kelly Seile will take care of your furry pet while you're hiking in BSP, call for rates and shuttle services; Connie McManus, (207) 723-6795, will pick up at Abol Bridge and house dogs for thru-hikers. **Shuttle:** Katahdin Shuttle LLC, (207) 447-0337, to/from Baxter, Bangor, and beyond. Lloyd can help organize your hike with resupply/food drops throughout the "100-mile wilderness.", Slack Packing, Pet-friendly, available May 15 to Oct 22.

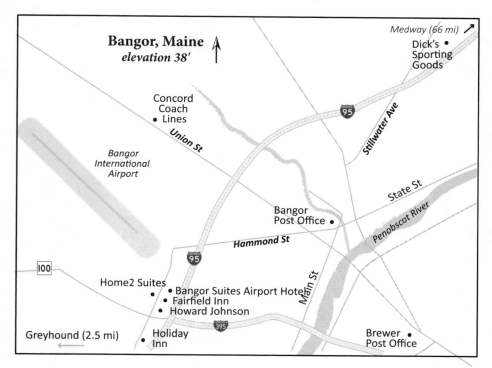

⋀ **Medway**—*Lodging:* Rivers Edge Motel, (207) 746-5162, 10 miles east on ME-157, queen $85, two double beds $95, plus tax, pets $20, restaurant on premises, pet-friendly, rooms; Gateway Inn, medwaygateway.com, (207) 746-3193, $69.95 and up, dogs welcome; Pine Grove Campground and Cottages, (207) 746-5172, pinegrovecampgroundandcottages.com, tentsites, fully equipped cottages, dogs welcome, free use of canoe and kayak for guests, will pick up at bus station. *Bus service:* Cyr Bus Lines of Old Town, Maine, serves northern Maine; 10 miles east on ME-757, (207) 927-2335, (207) 827-2010, or (800) 244-2335, cyrbustours.com. A bus departs Bangor at 6:00 p.m. and arrives at Medway at 7:40 p.m.; departs Medway at 9:30 a.m. and arrives at Bangor at 10:50 a.m.; fee $12 one way. *Shuttle:* Maine Quest Adventures, (207) 746-9615, mainequestadventures.com; Medway bus stop to Baxter SP or Abol Bridge, call for prices; will shuttle to all points in 100-mile Wilderness and to/from all Maine airports.

⋀ **Bangor**—A city with all major services, bangorinfo.com. For those traveling to or returning from BSP, Bangor has a bus station and airport. The Chamber of Commerce, (207) 947-0307, can provide information as you prepare for your hike or return. For information on local transportation in the Bangor area: BAT Commuter Connection, (207) 992-4670, bangormaine.gov. *Lodging:* Many motels and a mall are near the airport, including Days Inn, (207) 942-8272; Econo Lodge, (207) 945-0111; Fairfield Inn, (207) 990-0001; Howard Johnson's, (207) 947-3464; Holiday Inn, (207) 947-0101. *Outfitters:* Dick's Sporting Goods, (207) 990-5932, located in the Bangor Mall. *Bus service:* Concord Coach, (800) 639-3317; Cyr Bus Lines with daily transportation to Medway, (800) 244-2335 (see above).

Message to the Class of 2025

2025 THRU-HIKER & 2,000-MILER AWARD CEREMONY

At the 2025 Gathering in Abingdon, VA, ALDHA will recognize both thru-hikers and section-hikers who finish their journeys this year. You will be called up to the stage at the Friday-night meeting during the Class Years event to receive an end-to-end certificate and a "I Hiked ALDHA Way" patch from ALDHA. This year's Gathering will be held Oct. 10–12, 2025.

Special notice to 2025 thru-hikers and 2,000-Milers: Bring your Trail-worn *Appalachian Trail Thru-Hikers' Companion* (or the Maine section in its entirety) and a completed-trail form to the registration desk, and your Gathering fee is on ALDHA!

Post Offices Along the A.T.

Post offices are listed here in south-to-north order. *Note: Many post offices (perhaps all) have been shaving one hour or more off their daily hours, either in the morning, the afternoon, or at lunch time.* Changes we have verified are reflected here, but please take this development into account in your planning for picking up packages—call ahead!

Local post office telephone numbers can be verified by calling (800) 275-8777 or consulting usps.com.

Post offices printed in **bold** are located on, or within one mile of, the Trail.

Town	ZIP Code	Hours/Phone
Suches, GA	30572	M–F 12:15–4:15 p.m., closed Sa (706) 747-2611
Blairsville, GA	30512	M–F 9–4:30, Sa 9–12 (706) 896-4123
Helen, GA	30545	M–F 8:30–5, Sa 9–12 (706) 878-2422
Hiawassee, GA	30546	M–F 8:30–5, Sa 8:30–12 (706) 896-3632
Clayton, GA	30525	M–F 8:30–5, Sa 8:30–12 (706) 782-5795
Franklin, NC	28734	M–F 8:30–5, Sa 9–12 (828) 524-3219
Bryson City, NC	28713	M–F 9–4:30, Sa 10–12 (828) 488-3481
Robbinsville, NC	28771	M–F 9–4:30, closed Sa (828) 479-3397
Fontana Dam, NC	28733	M–F 11:45–3:45, closed Sa (828) 498-2315
Gatlinburg, TN	37738	M–F 9–5, Sa 9–11 (865) 436-3229
Cherokee, NC	28719	M–F 9–4:30, closed Sa (828) 497-3891
Newport, NC	37821	M-F 8:30-4:30 & Sa 9:30–12 (423) 623-6136
Hot Springs, NC	**28743**	M–F 9–11:30 & 1–4, Sa 9–10:30 (828) 622-3242
Erwin, TN	37650	M–F 8:30–4:45, Sa 10–12 (423) 743-9422
Unicoi, TN	37692	M–F 8:45–12 & 1–3:45, Sa 8:30–10:30 (423) 743-4945
Elk Park, NC	28622	M–F 9–12:30 & 1:30–4, Sa 8–11:30 (828) 733-5711
Roan Mountain, TN	37687	M–F 8–12 & 1–4, Sa 7:30–9:30 (423) 772-3014

Town	ZIP Code	Hours/Phone
Hampton, TN	37658	M–F 7:30–11:30 & 12:30–4, Sa 8–10 (423) 725-2177
Shady Valley, TN	37688	M–F 8–12, Sa 8–10 (423) 739-2173
Damascus, VA	**24236**	M–F 8:30–1 & 2–4:30, Sa 9–11 (276) 475-3411
Troutdale, VA	24378	M–F 8–12, Sa 8:30–11:30 (276) 677-3221
Sugar Grove, VA	24375	M–F 8:30–12:30 & 1:30–3:30, Sa 8:15–10:30 (276) 677-3200
Marion, VA	24354	M–F 9–5, Sa 9:30–12 (276) 783-5051
Atkins, VA	24311	M–F 8:45–12 & 12:30–3:15, Sa 9–10:45 (276) 783-5551
Bland, VA	24315	M–F 8:30–11:30 & 12–4, Sa 9–11 (276) 688-3751
Bastian, VA	24314	M–F 8–12, Sa 9:15–11:15 (276) 688-4631
Pearisburg, VA	**24134**	M–9–11 & 12:15-4:30, Sa 10–12 (540) 921-1100
Catawba, VA	**24070**	M–F 9–12 & 1–4, Sa 8–10:30 (540) 384-6011
Daleville, VA	**24083**	M–F 8:30–5, Sa 8:30–12:30 (540) 992-4422
Troutville, VA	**24175**	M–F 9–12 & 1–5, Sa 9–11 (540) 992-1472
Buchanan, VA	24066	M–F 8:**3**0–1 & 1:30–4:30, Sa 10–12 (540) 254-2178
Big Island, VA	24526	M–F 8:15–12 & 1–4, Sa 8–10 (434) 299-5072
Glasgow, VA	24555	M–F 8–11:30 & 12:30–4:30, Sa 8:30–10:30 (540) 258-2852
Buena Vista, VA	24416	M–F 8:30–4:30, closed Sa (540) 261-8959
Lexington, VA	24450	M–F 9–5, Sa 10–12 (540) 463-6449
Montebello, VA	24464	M–F 10–2, Sa 10–1 (540) 377-9218
Waynesboro, VA	22980	M–F 9–5, closed Sa (540) 942-7320
Elkton, VA	22827	M–F 8:30–4:30, Sa 9–11 (540) 298-7772
Luray, VA	22835	M–F 8:30–4:30, closed Sa (540) 743-2100
Front Royal, VA	22630	M–F 8:30–5, Sa 8:30–1 (540) 635-7983
Linden, VA	22642	M–F 8–12 & 1–5, Sa 8–12 (540) 636-9936

Town	ZIP Code	Hours/Phone
Bluemont, VA	20135	M–F 10–1 & 2–5, Sa 8:30–12 (540) 554-4537
Berryville, VA	22611	M–F 9–5, Sa 9–12:30 (540) 955-2667
Charles Town, WV	25414	M–F 8:30–5, Sa 9–12:30 (304) 725-6726
Harpers Ferry, WV	**25425**	M–F 8–4, Sa 9–12 (304) 535-2479
Brunswick, MD	21716	M–F 8–4:30, Sa 9–12 (301) 434-9944
Boonsboro, MD	21713	M–F 9–1 & 2–5, Sa 9–12 (301) 432-6861
Middletown, MD	21769	M–F 9–1 & 2–5, Sa 9–12 (301) 371-6880
Myersville, MD	21773	M–F 8:30–1 & 2–5, Sa 8:30–12 (301) 293-1180
Smithsburg, MD	21783	M–F 8:30–1 & 2–4:30, Sa 8:30–12 (301) 824-2828
Cavetown, MD	21720	M–F 12:30–4:30, Sa 8:15–11:15 (301) 824-5230
Cascade, MD	21719	M–F 10–1 & 2–5, Sa 8–12 (301) 241-3403
Blue Ridge Summit, PA	17214	M–F 8–12 & 1–4, Sa 9–11:30 (717) 794-2335
Rouzerville, PA	17250	M–F 8:30–1 & 2–4:30, Sa 8:30–11:30 (717) 762-7050
Waynesboro, PA	17268	M–F 8:30–5, Sa 9–12 (717) 762-1513
South Mountain, PA	17261	M–F 12–4, Sa 8:30–11:30 (717) 749-5833
Fayetteville, PA	17222	M–F 8–4:30, Sa 8:30–12 (717) 352-2022
Mt. Holly Springs, PA	17065	M–F 8–1 & 2–4:30, Sa 9–12 (717) 486-3468
Boiling Springs, PA	**17007**	M–F 9–12 & 1–4:30, Sa 9–12 (717) 258-6668
Duncannon, PA	**17020**	M–F 8–11, 12–4:30, Sa 8:30–12:30 (717) 834-3332
Bethel, PA	19507	M–F 8–12, 1:15–4:30, Sa 8:30–10:30 (717) 933-8305
Pine Grove, PA	17963	M–F 8:30–4:30, Sa 9–12 (570) 345-4955
Port Clinton, PA	**19549**	M–F 12:30–4:30, Sa 8–11 (610) 562-3787
Hamburg, PA	19526	M–F 9–5, Sa 9–12 (610) 562-7812
Slatington, PA	18080	M–F 8:30–5, Sa 8:30–12 (610) 767-2182

Town	ZIP Code	Hours/Phone
Walnutport, PA	18088	M–F 8:30–5, Sa 8:30–12 (610) 767-5191
Palmerton, PA	18071	M–F 8:30–5, Sa 8:30–12 (610) 826-2286
Danielsville, PA	18038	M–F 9:30–1 & 2–4:30, Sa 8–12 (610) 767-6882
Kunkletown, PA	18058	M–F 8–11:30 & 12:30–5, Sa 8–12 (610) 381-3062
Wind Gap, PA	**18091**	M–F 8:30–5, Sa 8:30–12 (610) 863-6206
Delaware Water Gap, PA	**18327**	M–F 8:30–12 & 1–4:45, Sa 8:30–11:30 (570) 476-0304
Branchville, NJ	07826	M–F 8:30–5, Sa 8:30–1 (973) 948-3580
Port Jervis, NY	12771	M–F 9–5, Sa 9–1 (845) 858-8173
Unionville, NY	**10988**	M–F 8–11:30 & 1–5, Sa 9–12 (845) 726-6143
Glenwood, NJ	07418	M–F 7:30–5, Sa 10–2 (973) 764-2616
Vernon, NJ	07462	M–F 8:30–5, Sa 9:30–12:30 (973) 764-9056
Greenwood Lake, NY	10925	M–F 8–5, Sa 9–12 (845) 477-7328
Warwick, NY	10990	M–F 8:30–5, Sa 9–4 (845) 986-0271
Southfields, NY	10975	M–F 10–12, 1–5, Sa 8:30–11:30 (845) 351-2628
Bear Mountain, NY	**10911**	M–F 9–11, closed Sa (845) 786-3747
Ft. Montgomery, NY	**10922**	M–F 8–1 & 2:30–5, Sa 9–12 (845) 446-8459
Peekskill, NY	10566	M–F 9–5, Sa 9–4 (914) 737-6437
Cold Spring, NY	10516	M–F 8:30–5, Sa 9–12 (845) 265-2193
Stormville, NY	12582	M–F 8:30–5, Sa 9–12 (845) 226-2627
Poughquag, NY	12570	M–F 8:30–1 & 2–5, Sa 8:30–12:30 (845) 724-4763
Pawling, NY	12564	M–F 8:30–5, Sa 9–12 (845) 855-2669
Wingdale, NY	12594	M–F 8–12:30 & 1:30–5, Sa 8–12:30 (845) 832-6147
Gaylordsville, CT	06755	M–F 8–1 & 2–5, Sa 8–12 (860) 354-9727
Kent, CT	**06757**	M–F 8–1 & 2–5, Sa 8:30–12:30 (860) 927-3435

Town	ZIP Code	Hours/Phone
Cornwall Bridge, CT	**06754**	M–F 8:30–1 & 2–5, Sa 9–12 (860) 672-6710
West Cornwall, CT	06796	M–F 9:30–1 & 2–4:30, Sa 9–12 (860) 672-6791
Sharon, CT	06069	M–F 9:30–4:30, Sa 9:30–12:30 (860) 364-5306
Falls Village, CT	**06031**	M–F 8:30–1 & 2–5, Sa 8:30–12 (860) 824-7781
Salisbury, CT	**06068**	M–F 8:30–1 & 2–5, Sa 9–12 (860) 435-5072
South Egremont, MA	01258	M–F 8:15–12 & 12:30–4, Sa 9–11:30 (413) 528-1571
Sheffield, MA	01257	M–F 9–4:30, Sa 9–12 (413) 229-8772
Great Barrington, MA	01230	M–F 8:30–4:30, Sa 8:30–12:30 (413) 528-3670
Monterey, MA	01245	M–F 8:30–1 & 2–4:30, Sa 9–11:30 (413) 528-4670
Tyringham, MA	**01264**	M–F 9–12:30 & 4–5:30, Sa 8:30–12:30 (413) 243-1225
Lee, MA	01238	M–F 8:30–4:30, Sa 9–12 (413) 243-1392
Becket, MA	01223	M–F 8–4, Sa 9–11:30 (413) 623-8845
Dalton, MA	**01226**	M–F 8:30–4:30, Sa 9–12 (413) 684-0364
Cheshire, MA	**01225**	M–F 7:30–1 & 2–4:30, Sa 8:30–11:30 (413) 743-3184
Adams, MA	01220	M–F 8:30–4:30, Sa 10–12 (413) 743-5177
North Adams, MA	01247	M–F 8:30–4:30, Sa 10–12 (413) 664-4554
Williamstown, MA	01267	M–F 8:30–4:30, Sa 9–12 (413) 458-3707
Bennington, VT	05201	M–F 8–5, Sa 9–2 (802) 442-2421
Manchester Center, VT	05255	M–F 8:30–4:30, Sa 9–12 (802) 362-3070
Danby, VT	05739	M–F 7:15–10:15 & 11:15–2:15, Sa 7:30–10:30 (802) 293-5105
Wallingford, VT	05773	M–F 8–4:30, Sa 9–12 (802) 446-2140
Rutland, VT	05701	M–F 8–5, Sa 8–12 (802) 773-0301
Killington, VT	**05751**	M–F 8:30–11 & 12–4:30, Sa 8:30–12 (802) 775-4247
Pittsfield, VT	05762	M–F 8–12 & 2–4:30, Sa 8:30–11:30 (802) 746-8953

Town	ZIP Code	Hours/Phone
Woodstock, VT	05091	M-F 8:30–5, Sa 9–12 (802) 457-1323
Barnard, VT	05031	M-F 9:30-12:30 & 1:30-4:30, Sa 8:30-11 (802) 234-5404
South Pomfret, VT	**05067**	M-F 12:30–4:30, Sa 8:30–11:30 (802) 457-1147
Hartford, VT	05047	M-F 8–12 & 2-5, Sa 9–11:30 (802) 295-5511
Norwich, VT	**05055**	M-F 8:30–5, Sa 9–12 (802) 649-1608
Hanover, NH	**03755**	M-F 8:30–5, Sa 8:30–12 (603) 643-5201
Lyme, NH	03768	M-F 7:45–12 & 1:30–5:15, Sa 7:45–12 (603) 795-4421
Wentworth, NH	03282	M-F 9:30–12:30 & 1:30–4:30, Sa 7:15–12 (603) 764-9444
Warren, NH	03279	M-F 7:30–9:30 & 3-5, Sa 7:30–12 (603) 764-5733
Glencliff, NH	**03238**	M-F 12–2, Sa 7–1 (603) 989-5154
North Woodstock, NH	03262	M-F 9:30–12:30 & 1:30–4:30, Sa 9–12 (603) 745-8134
Lincoln, NH	03251	M-F 8–5, Sa 8–12 (603) 745-8133
Bartlett, NH	03812	M-F 8:30–10:30 & 11:30–3:30, Sa 8:30–12 (603) 374-2351
Mt. Washington, NH	**03589**	M-Sa 10–4, not recommended for mail drop (603) 846-5570
Gorham, NH	03581	M-F 8:30–5, Sa 8:30–12 (603) 466-2182
Andover, ME	04216	M-F 9:15–12 & 1-4:15, Sa 9–12 (207) 392-4571
Oquossoc, ME	04964	M-F 11:30–3:30, Sa 9–12 (207) 864-3685
Rangeley, ME	04970	M-F 8:30–12:30 & 1:30–4:15, Sa 9:30–12 (207) 864-2233
Stratton, ME	04982	M-F 8:30–1 & 1:30–4, Sa 8:30–11 (207) 246-6461
Caratunk, ME	**04925**	M-F 2–4, Sa 7:30–11:15 (207) 672-3416
Monson, ME	04464	M-F 9:15–12:15 & 1:15–4:15, Sa 7:30–11 (207) 997-3975
Millinocket, ME	04462	M-F 9–4, Sa 9–11:30 (207) 723-5921

MAIL DROPS

Many thru-hikers use "mail drops" to send themselves supplies. The *Companion* lists US Postal Service (USPS) offices and also establishments that accept packages from shippers such as UPS and FedEx. Mail drops can be sent to both types of locations, but it is important to address them differently. Post offices accept only mail; a post office will not accept a FedEx or UPS package, generally speaking (the carriers have arrangements in some areas for this). Only post offices will accept packages addressed to a "General Delivery" address. USPS will forward unopened first-class and "priority" items at no additional fee. **UPS and FedEx packages cannot be sent to "General Delivery"**; you must provide a physical address other than a post office, such as a street number, and (for FedEx) a telephone number for those shipments. Please assist the businesses and post offices by printing legibly and practicing the following labeling instructions:

> Your Full Name (no nicknames or Trail names)
> c/o the business (or *General Delivery,* if a post office)
> City/State/ZIP Code
> *Please Hold for Thru-hiker or Section-Hiker*
> (and estimated date of arrival)

To obtain prefilled/printed labels for the most frequently used locations, try AT Mailing Labels at aldha.org/labels/at.

At the post office, be prepared to show a photo ID when you pick up your package. Postmasters are one of a thru-hiker's best friends on the Trail. Help them help you and other hikers by following the labeling instructions above for all your mail. If you leave the Trail for any reason, send a postcard to any post office that has packages for you to let them know what to do with your packages.

To ensure that your food parcels don't pick up any "unwanted visitors" before you arrive, double-bag and securely seal all parcels.

Hostels, Camping & Showers

The first thing that comes to a hiker's one–track mind when she/he hits town is FOOD and lots of it, followed by a good hot shower and affordable accommodations. In the pursuit of just food, shower, and laundry, some hikers want to minimize the town experience and return to the Trail as soon as possible, usually the same day. This list provides low–cost options and will help you to keep the grunge at bay. Campgrounds were chosen for their proximity to the Trail, and consideration was given if they allowed nonguest showers, while keeping in mind you'll likely be traveling on foot. There are many other campgrounds listed in the *Companion* that are best reached by car or require a longer walk.

The A.T. Passport program was developed by Jeff Taussig as a way for hikers to document their journeys with "stamps" from participating establishments, with net proceeds going to the ATC. Purchase passports at atctrailstore.org and find more information at atpassport.com.

Establishments printed in **bold** are located on or within one mile of the Trail.
NA=not available
n/c= no charge
S = shelter; H = hostel; C = camping; L = lodging; B = bunk

State	On-Trail Miles from Springer	Location; Establishment	Guest Fee	Non-guest Shower-only fee	A.T.Passport
GA	-8.8	**Amicalola Falls State Park**	C$30		P
GA	20.5	Suches: Hidden Pond Hostel	call		P
GA	31.3	**Mountain Crossings**	H$30		
GA	69.4	Dicks Creek Gap: Around the Bend Hostel	H$		
NC	105.9	Rock Gap: Standing Indian Campground	C$16	$2	
NC	109.6	Winding Stair Gap: Chica & Sunsets Hostel	H$55		P
NC	136.9	Wesser: **Nantahala Outdoor Center**	$30		
NC	166.6	**Fontana Dam Visitors Center**		n/c	P
TN	241.3	Discerning Hike Hostel	H$70+		
TN	241.8	Green Corner Rd: **Standing Bear Farm**	H$25, C$20	$5	P
NC	268.6	Garneflo Gap: Happy Gnomad Hiker House	H$20		
NC	275.2	Hot Springs: **The Sunnybank Inn** **The Hostel at Laughing Heart Lodge**	H$30, L$30 C$15-20, L$45	$5	P P
TN	291.5	Greeneville: **Hemlock Hollow Hostel**	C$15, L$22–$55	$4	P
TN	320.0	Sams Gap: Natures Inn Hostel	Call		
TN	344.6	Erwin: **Nolichucky Hostel and Outfitters**	H$30, C$15	$5	P
TN	368.9	Greasy Creek Gap: **Greasy Creek Friendly**	H$20	$3	P
TN	395.6	US-19E: **Mountain Harbour B&B and Hostel** The Refuge Hostel	H$30 H$20	$10 $5	P
TN	407.7	Roan Mtn: Scotty's Roan Mtn Budget Hostel	Call		P
TN	420.3	Dennis Cove: **Kincora Hostel** **Black Bear Resort**	$5 donation H$30, C$15, L$60+	$5	P P
TN	428.8	Shook Branch Rd: **Boots Off Hostel**	H$30+, C$15+	$5	

State	On-Trail Miles from Springer	Location; Establishment	Guest Fee	Non-guest Shower-only fee	A.T.Passport
TN	449.2	TN-91: The Rabbit Hole	Call	Call	
VA	471.0	Damascus: **The Place** **Broken Fiddle** **Song Peddler Rest & Woodchuck Hostel** **Crazy Larry's Hostel** **Lady Di's B&B**	H$10 H$40 donation varies L$60	$5	P P P
VA	518.9	USFS Hurricane Campground	C$20	$2	
VA	520.5	VA-650: Troutdale Baptist Church	H donation	n/c	P
VA	534.6	VA-16: Marion	H$35		
VA	556.1	VA-610: **Quarter Way Inn**	H$33, C$18		P
VA	558.6	VA-42: Bear Garden Hiker Hostel Appalachian Dreamer Hiker Hostel	H$20 H$25, donation		
VA	571.5	VA-727: Burkes Garden Hostel	H$35+ C$20		
VA	576.3	VA-623: Garden Mountain Hostel	H$15–$30		
VA	610.5	VA- 606: **Trent's Grocery Store** Weary Feet Hostel	C$6 H$25, C$10	$3 $8	P
VA	625.7	Sugar Run Rd: **Woods Hole Hostel**	H$24, C$15		P
VA	637.4	Pearisburg: Holy Family Church Hostel Angel's Rest Hiker's Haven	H$10 H$25, C$12	$7 pass	P
VA	704.9	VA-624: **Four Pines Hostel**	H donation		P
VA	706.5	VA-785: Solstice Farm Brewery	C n/c		
VA	732.1	US-11: **BeeCh Hill B&B/Hostel**	H$30 C$20		
VA	744.2	Black Horse Gap: Duck-N-Hut Hikers Hostel	H donation		
VA	752.2	VA-43: Anchorage House Hostel	B$25		
VA	758.8	VA-614: Middle Creek Campground	C$10, L$65/2	$5	P
VA	787.6	Glasgow: Glasgow Hiker Shelter Stanimals 328 Hostel	n/c H$30, C	n/c	
VA	809.4	Buena Vista: Glen Maury Campground	C$5+	n/c	
VA	828.3	Montebello: Montebello Camping & Fishing	C$17.50s, $26.50d		
VA	834.9	Tye River: Crabtree Falls Campground	C$30d	n/c	
VA	843.8	Rusty's Hard Time Hollow	donation		
VA	845.5	VA-664 *East 5.5m to* Devil's Backbone Brewery		n/c	
VA	864.6	Waynesboro: Stanimal's 328 Hostel Grace Evangelical Lutheran Church YMCA/ALDHA Hiker Pavilion	H $35 H donation C donation	n/c n/c	P P
VA	892.7 918.4 927.1	SNP: **Loft Mountain Campground** **Lewis Mountain Campground** **Big Meadows Campground**	C $30 C $30 C $30		
VA	944.7	US-211: Luray: Open Arms at Edge of Town Hostel	H $35, C $20		P
VA	972.4	US-522: **Mountain Home Cabin**	H $35	$5	P
VA	978.2	VA-638 or VA-725: Wonderland Hiker Refuge	donation		
VA	1,005.9	**Bears Den Hostel**	H $30, C $15	$3	P
VA	1,013.9	**Blackburn Trail Center**	H, C, donations		P
WV	1,025.7	Harpers Ferry: KOA	Call		
WV	1,026.0	Harpers Ferry Hostel	H$35-$45		

State	On-Trail Miles from Springer	Location; Establishment	Guest Fee	Non-guest Shower-only fee	A.T.Passport
MD	1,029.6	Keep Tryst Rd: Cross Trails Hostel & Campground Huckleberry Hill Hiker Biker Campsite	Call Call		
MD	1,036.7	Gapland Rd. West: **Maple Tree Campground**	Call		
MD	1,043.9	**Dahlgren Backpack Campground**	C n/c	n/c	
MD	1,067.4	Pen Mar County Park: **Zero Day Stay Hostel**	text		
PA	1,085.5	US-30: **Thru-It All Hostel**	H$25		P
PA	1,105.4	PA-233: **Pine Grove Furnace State Park** **Ironmasters Mansion**	C$5 H$25		P
PA	1,116.2	Sheet Iron Roof Road: Deer Run Camping Resort	C$10		
PA	1,124.3	Boiling Springs: Lisa's Hostel **Boiling Springs Pool**	must call	$1	
PA	1,132.6	US-11, Carlisle: **Flyin' J Travel Plaza**		Call	
PA	1,150.3	Duncannon: **Doyle Hotel** Kind of Outdoorsy Hostel	call call	$5	P
PA	1,151.5	Duncannon: Riverfront Campground	call	Call	
PA	1,220.2	Port Clinton Pavilion	C n/c		
PA	1,235.4	Hawk Mountain Road: **Eckville Shelter** (solar shower)	B, C n/c	n/c	
PA	1,261.2	Palmerton: Squeak's Yard	H donation	n/c	
PA	1,297.4	DWG: **Presbyterian Church of the Mountain Hostel**	H donation		P
NJ	1,308.0	**Mohican Outdoor Center**	L, C call	$5	P
NJ	1,339.2	Sawmill Lake Campground	C$25 + $5		
NJ	1,340.3	High Point State Park day-use area Mosey's Place	B$40	n/c	P
NY	1,376.0	NY-17A: Lost and Found Hostel	H$45		
NY	1,393.6	Arden Valley Rd: Tiorati Circle		n/c	
NY	1,415.5	**Graymoor Spiritual Life Center**	C	n/c	
NY	1,427.4	NY-301: **Clarence Fahnestock State Park**	C$15	n/c	
CT	1,484.4	Cornwall Bridge: Housatonic Meadows State Park	C$36	n/c	
CT	1,498.6	Falls Village: **Hydroelectric Plant**		n/c	
MA	1,527.9	US-7: Berkshire South Community Center	C n/c	$5	
MA	1,575.7	Dalton: **Tom Levardi's 83 Depot St.**	C n/c		P
MA	1,576.2	Cheshire: **Father Tom Campsite**	C n/c		
MA	1,599.5	MA-2: **North Adams YMCA**		n/c	
VT	1,708.1	Rutland: Hostel at the Yellow Deli	H donation		P
VT	1,711.4	VT-100: **Gifford Woods State Park**	S$27–$29, C$20–$22	50¢	
VT	1,753.4	Norwich: **Norwich Hiker Hostel**	H$45, C$25	$15	
NH	1,798.2	Glencliff: **Hikers Welcome Hostel**	Call		P
NH	1,807.7	NH-112/Kinsman Notch: The Notch Hostel North Woodstock: Old Colony Ski Club	H$45, C $35 H$25+$25		P
NH	1,824.0	I-93, US-3, Franconia Notch: Lafayette Place Campground	C$25d	$1	
NH	1,851.7	US-302, Crawford Notch: Dry River Campground Crawford Notch Campground AMC Highland Center, Shapleigh Bunkhouse	C$25d C$48-$52d H$46+	25¢	
NH	1,877.7	NH-16: **Pinkham Notch Visitors Center**		coin	
NH	1,898.8	US-2, Shelburne: The Birches Loft at White Birches Camping Park	C$26-$38		P

State	On-Trail Miles from Springer	Location; Establishment	Guest Fee	Non-guest Shower-only fee	A.T.Passport
NH	1,898.8	Gorham: The Barn at Libby House	H$35, C$25		P
ME	1,929.9	Grafton Notch Campground	C$30	$8	
ME	1,940.2	East Andover: The Cabin South Arm Campground	donation	n/c	P
ME	2,008.9	Stratton: Hostel of Maine The Maine Roadhouse	H$39 H$45-$50		
ME	2,045.9	US-201: **Sterling Inn**	B$40	$3	
ME	2,082.6	Monson: Lakeshore House Shaw's Hiker Hostel	B$30+ B$30, C$15	$5 $5	P P
ME	2,182.2	Golden Road: **Abol Bridge Campground, Abol Pines**	TBD C$15pp		
ME	2,192.0	Millinocket: A.T. Lodge	B$30-$40	$5	P

Additional lodging and service providers included in the A.T. Passport program include:

A.T. Kick-Off, Amicalola Falls State Park, GA
Survivor Dave's Trail Shuttles, Atlanta, GA
Len Foote Inn, Amicalola Falls State Park, GA
Blood Mountain Cabins, Blairsville, GA
Budget Inn, Hiawassee, GA
Ron's Appalachian Trail Shuttle, Hiawassee, GA
Holiday Inn Express, Blairsville, GA
Three Eagles Outfitter, Franklin, NC
Outdoor 76 Outfitter, Franklin, NC
First Baptist Hiker Breakfast, Franklin, NC
Currahee Brewery, Franklin, NC
Lazy Hiker Brewery, Franklin, NC
Nantahala General Store, Bryson City, NC
Fontana Dam Visitor Center, Fontana Dam, NC
Bluff Mountain Outfitter, Hot Springs, NC
Hiker's Ridge Ministry Center, Hot Springs, NC
Spring Creek Tavern, Hot Springs, NC
Smoky Mountain Diner, Hot Springs, NC
Hot Springs, NC, Library
Bob's Dairyland, Roan Mountain, TN
Montgomery Homestead Inn, Damascus, VA
Mt. Rogers Outfitters, Damascus, VA
MoJo's Trailside Café, Damascus, VA
Mt. Rogers Visitor Center, Marion, VA
Settlers' Museum, Atkins, VA
Trent's Grocery, Bland, VA
Holiday Lodge, Pearisburg, VA
MacArthur Inn, Pearisburg, VA

The Captain's, Stony Creek, VA
Howard Johnson Express Inn, Daleville, VA
Outdoor Trails Outfitter, Daleville, VA
Three Li'l Pigs, Daleville, VA
Devils Backbone Brewery, Roseland, VA
Appalachian Trail Conservancy Headquarters, Harpers Ferry, WV
Burgundy Lane B&B, Waynesboro, PA
Appalachian Trail Museum, Gardners, PA
Pine Grove General Store, Gardners, PA
TCO Outdoors, Boiling Springs, PA
Pheasant Field B&B, Carlisle, PA
Port Clinton Hotel, Port Clinton, PA
Port Clinton Barber Shop, Port Clinton, PA
Port Clinton Peanut Shop, Port Clinton, PA
John Stempa, Kunkletown, PA
Mohican Outdoor Center, Blairstown, NJ
High Point State Park, Sussex, NJ
Native Landscapes, Pawling, NY
Upper Goose Pond Cabin, MA
Mountain Goat Outfitter, Manchester Center, VT
The Inn at Long Trail, Killington, VT
Mountain Meadows Lodge, Killington, VT
The Hart Family, West Hartford, VT
Dancing Bones Community, Wentworth, NH
Moose Scoops Ice Cream, Warren, NH
Chet's One Step at a Time, Lincoln, NH
Annual ALDHA Gathering

Equipment
Manufacturers & Distributors

Most manufacturers and distributors stand behind their products and will often replace or repair equipment while you are on the Trail. Usually, it is best to deal directly with the manufacturer rather than going through an outfitter along the Trail (except where noted below). A few telephone calls can save lost time and prevent a lot of headaches.

AntiGravity Gear
(910) 794-3308
www.antigravitygear.com

Arc 'Teryx
(866) 458-BIRD
www.arcteryx.com

Asolo
(603) 448-8827, ext. 105
www.asolo.com

Backcountry Gear
(800) 953-5499
www.backcountrygear.com

Big Agnes
(877) 554-8975
www.bigagnes.com

Black Diamond
(800) 775-5552
www.blackdiamondequipment.com

Campmor
(800) 226-7667
www.campmor.com

Camelbak
(877) 404-7673
www.camelbak.com

Cascade Designs/MSR
(800) 531-9531
www.cascadedesigns.com

Cedar Tree Industry
(276) 780-2354
www.thepacka.com

Columbia
(800) 622-6953
www.columbia.com

Darn Tough
(877) 327-6883
www.darntough.com

Eastern Mountain Sports
(888) 463-6367
www.ems.com

Enlightened Equipment
www.enlightenedequipment.com

Etowah Outfitter/Etowah Gear
(678) 767-8051
www.shop.backpackingadventuregear.com

Eureka
(888) 6EUREKA
www.eurekacampingctr.com

Ex Officio
(800) 644-7303
www.exofficio.com

Feathered Friends
(206) 292-2210
www.featheredfriends.com

Frogg Toggs
(800) 349-1835
www.froggtoggs.com

Gossamer Gear
(512) 374-0133
www.gossamergear.com

Granite Gear
(218) 834-6157
www.granitegear.com

Gregory Mountain Products
(877) 477-4292
www.gregorypacks.com

Hi-Tec Sports, USA
(800) 521-1698
www.us.hi-tec.com

Hyperlite Mountain Gear
(800) 464-9208
www.hyperlitemountaingear.com

Jacks 'R' Better Quilts
(757) 643-8908
www.jacksrbetter.com

Katadyn
(800) 755-6701
www.katadyn.com

Kelty Pack, Inc.
(866) 349-7225, (800) 535-3589
www.kelty.com

Leki
(800) 255-9982, ext 150
www.leki.com

LiteAF
(609) 535-5389
www.liteaf.com

L.L.Bean
(800) 441-5713
www.llbean.com

Lowe Alpine Systems
(303) 926-7228
www.lowealpine.com

Marmot
(888) 357-3262
www.marmot.com

Merrell
(800) 288-3124
www.merrell.com

Mont-bell
(303) 449-5331
www.montbell.com

Montrail
(855) 698-7245
www.montrail.com

Moonbow Gear
(603) 744-2264
www.moonbowgear.com

Mountain Hardwear
(877) 927-5649
www.mountainhardwear.com

Mountain Laurel Design
(540) 588-1721
www.mountainlaureldesign.com

Mountainsmith
(800) 426-4075, ext. 2
www.mountainsmith.com

Nemo Equipment
(800) 997-9301
www.nemoequipment.com

The North Face
(855) 500-8639
www.thenorthface.com

Osprey
(866) 284-7830
cs@ospreypacks.com

Outdoor Research
(888) 467-4327
www.outdoorresearch.com

Patagonia
(800) 638-6464
www.patagonia.com

Primus
(888) 546-2267
www.primusstoves.com

Princeton Tec
(609) 298-9331
www.princetontec.com

Purple Rain Adventure Skirts
www.purplerainskirts.com

REI
(800) 426-4840
www.rei.com

Royal Robbins
(800) 587-9044
www.royalrobbins.com

Salomon
(800) 654-2668
www.salomonsports.com

Sawyer
(800) 356-7811
www.sawyer.com

Sea to Summit
www.seatosummitusa.com

Sierra Designs
(800) 736-8592
www.sierradesigns.com

Six Moon Designs
(503) 430-2303
www.sixmoondesigns.com

Snow Peak
(503) 697-3330
www.snowpeak.com

Suunto
(855) 258-0900
www.suunto.com

Tarptent by Henry Shires
(650) 587-1548
www.tarptent.com

Teva/Deckers Corporation
(800) 367-8382
www.teva.com

Thermarest
(800) 531-9531
www.thermarest.com

Thrupack
www.thrupack.com

ULA-Equipment
(435) 753-5191
www.ula-equipment.com

Vasque
(800) 224-4453
www.vasque.com

Western Mountaineering
(408) 287-8944
www.westernmountaineering.com

Zpacks
www.zpacks.com

ZZManufacturing (Zipztove)
(800) 594-9046
www.zzstove.com

Complete list of major and cottage-gear manufacturers
www.aldha.org/at/gear

Acknowledgments

ALDHA members do field research for each section of the Trail and are instrumental in gathering information. Without the hard work of the following ALDHA field editors, and other volunteers, this book would not have been possible:

- Laurie Adkins: Southwest Virginia
- Leonard "Habitual Hiker" Adkins: Central Virginia
- Bill "Cooker Hiker" Cooke: Vermont
- David "Gourmet Dave" Hennel: Shenandoah National Park
- Sue "The Real Gourmet" Hennel: Shenandoah National Park
- Deidre "Dedragon" Burroughs Howell: Georgia, North Carolina
- Lisa "Anything" Jenkins: Northern Virginia, West Virginia
- John "Dice" LaManna: Great Smoky Mountains National Park, North Carolina, Tennessee
- Robert "Sparky" Palermo: Pennsylvania, New Jersey, New York, Connecticut, Massachusetts, Vermont, New Hampshire
- Kevin "Slider" Reardon: Maine
- Mike "Wingheart" Wingeart: Maryland

Mileage figures are based on information from the 2025 edition of the Appalachian Trail Conservancy's *Appalachian Trail Data Book*, edited by volunteer Daniel Chazin since 1983.

recreation • lifestyle • conservation

MOUNTAINEERS BOOKS, including its two imprints, Skipstone and Braided River, is a leading publisher of quality outdoor recreation, sustainability, and conservation titles. As a 501(c)(3) nonprofit, we are committed to supporting the environmental and educational goals of our organization by providing expert information on human-powered adventure, sustainable practices at home and on the trail, and preservation of wilderness.

Our publications are made possible through the generosity of donors, and through sales of 700 titles on outdoor recreation, sustainable lifestyle, and conservation. To donate, purchase books, or learn more, visit us online:

MOUNTAINEERS BOOKS

1001 SW Klickitat Way, Suite 201 • Seattle, WA 98134
800-553-4453 • mbooks@mountaineersbooks.org • mountaineersbooks.org

An independent nonprofit publisher since 1960

YOU MAY ALSO ENJOY: